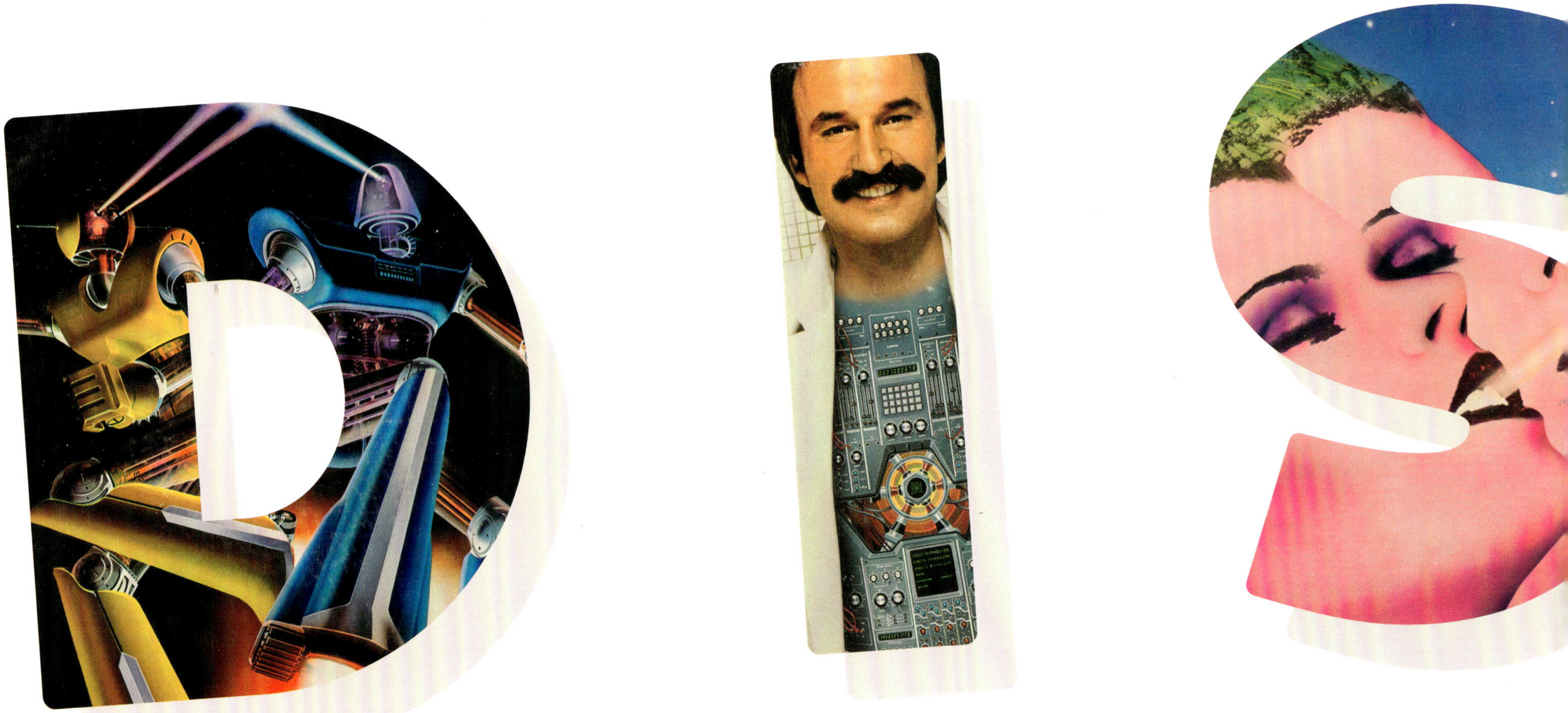

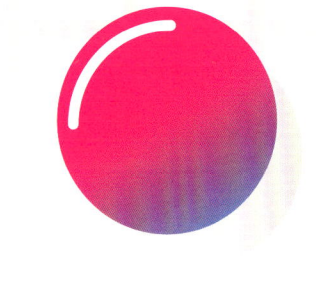

Presentented by

Disco Patrick & Patrick Vogt

FIRST PUBLISHED IN 2014 BY SOUL JAZZ BOOKS,
A DIVISION OF SOUL JAZZ RECORDS LTD.

SOUL JAZZ RECORDS
7 BROADWICK STREET
LONDON W1F 0DA
ENGLAND
WWW.SOULJAZZRECORDS.CO.UK

DESIGN & LAYOUT:
PATRICK VOGT

COMPILED BY:
PATRICK LEJEUNE

PHOTOGRAPHY:
PATRICK VOGT, AXEL BISCHOFF

TEXT AND INTERVIEWS:
CLAES AKA DISCOGUY, PATRICK LEJEUNE

FONT DESIGN (LUCIEN & FATFRANK):
JEFF SCHREIBER

© SOUL JAZZ BOOKS.
PUBLISHED BY SOUL JAZZ BOOKS.
A DIVISION OF SOUL JAZZ RECORDS LTD.
© SOUL JAZZ RECORDS LTD 2014

ALL RIGHTS RESERVED. NO PART OF THIS PUBLICATION MAY BE REPRODUCED, STORED IN A RETRIEVAL SYSTEM, OR TRANSMITTED, IN ANY FORM OR ANY MEANS, ELECTRONIC, MECHANICAL, PHOTOCOPYING, RECORDING, OR OTHERWISE, WITHOUT THE WRITTEN PERMISSION OF THE PUBLISHER AND THE COPYWRITER OWNER. ALL OPINIONS EXPRESSED WITHIN THIS PUBLICATION ARE THOSE OF THE AUTHOR AND NOT NECESSARILY OF THE PUBLISHER.

DISTRIBUTED BY THAMES & HUDSON (WORLD EXCL. N. AMERICA) AND ARTBOOK/D.A.P. (NORTH AMERICA)

ISBN: 978 0 9572600 2 3

DISCO PATRICK & PATRICK VOGT WISH TO THANK:
SOUL JAZZ BOOKS (STUART, KAREN AND STEVE) FOR BELIEVING IN US. MICHEL GENDREAU, JOHN MORALES MARC JANSSEN, CLAES 'DISCOGUY' WIDLUND (DISCO-DISCO.COM), ADVANCE COMMUNICATIONS (EVERT HOITING, AXEL BISSCHOFF, ROGER WIEKKEN, TIM BAHNEN), SARAH MOLS AND SUSAN LEJEUNE FOR THEIR SUPPORT.

SOUL JAZZ WISH TO THANK:
TOM MOULTON, NICKY SIANO, ANGELA SCOTT, PETE REILLY, KAREN TATE, MARK GARLAND, ELISA LESHOWITZ, JULIE VERMEILLE, CONNY DICKGREBER, NEAL BIRNIE, NICOLE MCKENZIE, JIM CRONSHAW, KARL SHALE, WAYNE GILBERT, ABI CLARKE, SCOTT BETHELL, DEAN ATKINS, SHELLEY LATIMER, STEVE PLATT, JEYDA BICER, THEO LEANSE, JONATHAN BURNIP, PIERCE SMITH, IMGMAR VAN WIJNSBERG, BOUDEWIJN VAN WIJK, ANDERS SJOELIN, LUTZ FALLDORF, JEFFREY STOTHERS, MAURIZIO MOROZZO, DANILO DURANTE, LUCIANO CANTONE, JEREMIAH LEWIS, MATT FISHER, ERNIE B, MARIA CALERO, JOSE SANTOS LUISA DA SILVA, MAGNUS HOGMUR, YVES LE CARPENTIER AND YLAN PHAM.

DISCLAIMER:
ALL COPYRIGHTS IN THE INDIVIDUAL RECORD COVERS ARTWORK ARE ALL HELD BY THE ORIGINAL RECORD COMPANIES AND/OR DESIGNERS. THE AUTHOR AND PUBLISHER APOLOGISE FOR ANY OMISSIONS OR ERRORS, WHICH CAN BE CORRECTED IN FUTURE EDITIONS.

THE RECORD SLEEVES AND DESIGNS REMAIN COPYRIGHT OF THE ORIGINAL COPYRIGHT HOLDERS.

THE AUTHOR OF THE TEXT ASSERTS HIS MORAL RIGHTS.
ALL RIGHTS TO ANY OTHER USE OF THE TEXT OR ARTWORK AND PHOTOGRAPHS IS HEREBY RESERVED.

Contents

Foreword
By Tom Moulton - 6
By Nicky Siano - 8

Introduction
By Claes 'Discoguy' Widlund - 10

Disco Patrick
Welcome - 12

Disco Labels & Albums
1. *AVI - 14*
2. *Ariola - 22*
3. *Black Sun - 28*
4. *Butterfly - 32*
5. *Casablanca and sub-labels - 38*
6. *Delite - 66*
7. *Emergency - 74*
8. *Fantasy and Wmot - 78*
9. *Malligator-Crocos - 94*
10. *Matra - 100*
11. *Montage - 104*
12. *OUT - 108*
13. *Philadelphia International Records - 116*
14. *Prelude - 134*
15. *Salsoul and sub-labels - 146*
16. *SAM - 168*
17. *TK and sub-labels - 172*
18. *Unidisc - 210*
19. *Uniwave - 218*
20. *Vanguard - 224*
21. *Venture - 232*
22. *West End - 236*

Other Albums
23. *Roller Disco - 242*
24. *Disco Instruction Albums - 254*
25. *Disco Samplers - 260*
26. *Atlantic, Motown and other labels - 272*

12-Inch Covers
27. *12-Inch Covers - 334*

Scrapbook
A selection of adverts - 378

Foreword by Tom Moulton

Disco! The name conjures up so many thoughts of happy, exciting times when we were all living for the weekend. A time when we went to clubs and parties and we all just wanted to have a great time. We had our own music and the excitement of the music made us all move. We were always looking for something new to excite us on the dance floor and we had our favourites that got us up onto the floor.

The music was very soulful in the beginning. The breaks and the drops in the music added to the energy and it made everything seem to go to a higher level. It's called the disco era because it made everyone notice that there was another form of music happening, and it started in the clubs and then eventually on the radio expanding into pop and rock with a club beat.

To look back on it now, it was really 'good time' music. Most of our memories of it bring back the excitement and energy of the time and in a way our personal diary of the events. The music was very creative and the covers also express that same feeling. Now with this new book of some of the great albums of the time we can relive the time, think back about who you might have fallen in love with at the time and friends you made. If this is new to you, this will give you a better understanding of what was happening music-wise and why so many look back on this era as the fun party era.

Tom Moulton

TJM-TJM / Casablanca 1979
Art Direction And Design: David Flemming, Gribbitt! / TJM Logo Illustration: Dennis Millard / TJM Logo Design: Henry Vizcarra

Foreword by Nicky Siano

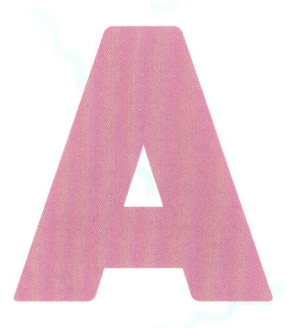

At the age of 16, in 1971, I became the DJ at one of the biggest bars in New York City, The Roundtable. For two years prior I had followed a small underground network of dance heads from bar to bar. Sanctuary, Tamburlaine, The Jungle, Ginza, The Firehouse, The Planetarium, Haven and Limelight were a few of organised crime's incarnations for the growing audience who longed to dance. Then, out of the blue, I was taken to my first REAL dance head experience, The Loft. It was on that dance floor (1200 square feet of heaven), in that crowded tiny space, that I decided I HAD TO BE A DJ.

I had already discovered my affinity for this new type of music called R&B. There was James Brown and his protégé Lyn Collins ('Think'), Diana Ross ('Surrender'), The Supremes ('Stoned Love'), The Jackson 5 ('I Wanna Be Where You Are'), Ultra High Frequency ('We're On The Right Track), The Trammps ('Zing Went The Strings Of My Heart') and First Choice ('Armed and Extremely Dangerous') — these were a few of the 45s I had begun collecting. But at the Loft I experienced how a DJ [David Mancuso] could create atmosphere, and present an experience to enhance the dance floor madness.

With my job at the Roundtable coming to an end, I begged my older brother to invest his $10,000 insurance settlement into this growing new enterprise, the club scene. Thus The Gallery was born, and for six years it set the pace for every club and DJ in New York City. The Gallery became the place where DJs and fans came to hear the newest dance records, where fashion designers came to see the latest trends, and where potential club owners gawked at the grandeur of an organic and original idea.

Frankie Knuckles and Larry Levan became employees and close friends, both in awe of the fashion industry cavalcade that graced the premises. Calvin Klein, Steven Burrows, Willi Smith, Giogio di Sant' Angelo, Billie Blair - who danced in short dresses that rode up just enough for the audience to see her skivvies' embroidered with BILLIE BLAIR in a dark lace thread - David Bowie and Mick Jagger strolling in with Donyale Luna on his arm. It was a spectacular visual and visceral circus, stimulating the senses beyond capacity, a Broadway show with you starring on centre stage.

Then Billboard magazine decided these songs, generating so much interest and so many sales, had to have a name and a convention to exploit their marketing potential. Thus the Disco Chart and the Disco Convention were born. Goodbye underground and interesting, hello cheap, exploitive and almost laughable imitation.

But some continued to get it right. When I met Steve Rubell in 1975 he was just launching a club in a restored country club on the Douglaston Golf Course in Queens. It was called Enchanted Gardens, or as we loveably donned it, the Enchanted Hell Hole. He hired me that night, I don't remember if it was before or after I bedded him. He loved my music, and became a Gallery regular, sitting under my booth at the Gallery almost every Saturday night, watching everything Robert De Silva, my very talented light man, and I did. Looking up at our super structure I designed for our lighting, which seemed to disappear into the ceiling, Steve was inspired to take the experience to a new level.

Two years later Steve asked me to join him at a space on West 54th St, an old CBS television studio, Studio 54, which he was opening as the ultimate DISCO. And that is exactly what it was. It took every idea, and every effect we had developed in the last nine years to the tenth degree. Confetti guns would cover the dance floor, leaving it three inches deep with confetti by the end of the night, when dancers would then collect the mixture as a keepsake. Each lighting effect disappeared into the ceiling, only to give way to another sparkling eye opener being lowered just above dancers' heads. It was mind boggling, and very entertaining. Unfortunately, it took a very dark turn - where David and I professed a spiritual aspect to the experience, Steve accentuated the physical aspect, where sex and drugs became an absolute prerequisite to the already stimulating atmosphere. It was the beginning of the end, and within just three years of great nights, Studio 54 closed, and disco was declared dead on a Chicago stadium's outfield.

Cry not dancers, for at the same time, Frankie Knuckles was discovering a new groove in Chicago, which still rocks the dance world, HOUSE MUSIC.

Nicky Siano

Nicky Siano at The Gallery

Introduction

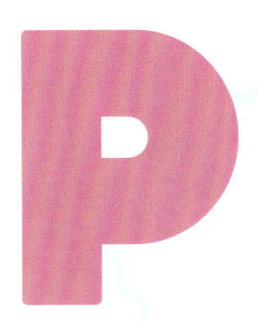

People say that you should not judge a book by its cover, but what about a book containing over 2000+ disco era record covers? The rule for all covers is that they should appeal to the buyer, and this can take many forms - sexy, futuristic, humorous or even tacky. No matter what, this book will show you all of these and more. So let's step back in time to this fantastic era when the mirror balls glittered brighter, the dancers dressed sharper and the disco music swirled you across the dancefloor.

Some people say the disco scene started in the early 1970s - '71 to '73 - but I guess that really depends on what you think is DISCO! The discotheque scene had already started back then, with clubs playing music on records to their audience. In these clubs, the disc jockey (DJ) was the guy putting the records on the turntables, often talking to the crowd in a radio DJ kind of way.

This became closer to what we first think of as disco with David Mancuso's underground invite-only Loft parties (which began in 1970) and Nicky Siano's club The Gallery (which opened in 1972), both in New York. Siano would also later DJ at the most high profile disco of all, Studio 54.

Other people say the disco days started in the mid 70s and that's also my opinion. I think that in tunes from around '74 to '76 you can start to hear more of what I call 'the disco sound' than you could just a couple of years earlier. One of the first disco hits was Gloria Gaynor's 'Never Can Say Goodbye', which topped the US dance charts back in 1974.

Most of the first disco hits from the mid 70s often had a slower tempo, around 90-110 bpm (beats per minute) but over time disco music became faster (110-140 bpm) and more importantly the songs became longer. The person initially responsible for this was Tom Moulton, who thought the 'standard' three-minute songs were too short and so he came up with an idea. "There's got to be a way to make it longer where you don't lose that feeling. Where you can take them to another level." He sat at home and recorded a tape on which he mixed together two copies of the same song - to make a longer version - and that's how he invented the disco-mix. This breakthrough made him one of the hottest and most credited remixers of all time and soon everyone wanted 'A Tom Moulton Mix' of their song. But Tom had a hard time trying to get these longer versions on vinyl.
The problem was that the seven-inch single couldn't hold more than four to five minutes of music. That's why he was often forced to make two versions of a song - an album version, which would be the full-length mix, and a shorter seven-inch single with the best parts of the long version. But Moulton really wanted people to hear the longer version, especially on the dancefloor so along with his mastering man, José Rodriguez, he decided to press a single on ten-inch vinyl instead of seven-inch. The next single they choose to cut instead on 12-inch - the same format as an album - and this was how they came to invent the 12-inch single, which quickly became the preferred format for all DJs.

Not surprisingly, many disco song lyrics are about dancing; Chic's 'Dance, Dance, Dance' and 'Everybody Dance', Saturday Night Band's 'Come On Dance, Dance', Jimmy Bo Horne's 'Dance Across the Floor' and Liquid Gold's 'Dance Yourself Dizzy' to name just a few.

The lyrics are mostly happy and about dancing, loving and having a good time, but another important ingredient in this pre-AIDS time was, of course, SEX! Just listen to probably the best-known 'sexy' hit of the era, Donna Summer's almost 17-minutes long disco orgy 'Love To Love You Baby'. This was literally like having an orgasm on the dancefloor. Sexual undertones are very common in disco tunes; ORS's 'Body To Body Boogie', Shades of Love's 'Keep In Touch (Body to Body)', Peter Brown's 'Do Ya Wanna Get Funky With Me?', James Bond-actress Britt Ekland's 'Do It To Me (Once More With Feeling)' among others. The sex appeal of disco music also found its way to the big screen, if in a different way. For example in the Dudley Moore movie '10' a disco version of the classical Ravel tune 'Bolero' by Thijs Van Leer played a central role. In fact many classical pieces were 'discofied', both off and on the screen. Tunes like 'Night On Disco Mountain' (based on 'Night On Bald Mountain') and 'A Fifth of Beethoven' (based on Beethoven's 'Fifth Symphony') were both featured in the movie that would break disco out of the clubs and into homes all over the world - Saturday Night Fever.

But it wasn't just that disco inspired movies - disco was just as much influenced by other media as vice versa. You'll find disco tunes based on different cartoon characters, like Donald Duck in Rick Dees' 'Disco Duck', or the many songs released about Superman when the movie hit the silver screen. Other movies that inspired disco tunes include the Star Wars trilogy, which scored big hits for Meco (who also made a disco version of the main theme from the Superman movie).

Legendary writer/producer Kenton Nix also wrote a song inspired by the Star Wars movies. Kenton recalls how he wrote Ednah Holt's 'Serious, Sirius Space Party'; "Larry Levan and I were Trekkies and Star Wars freaks. Larry said to me 'Why don't you write a song about a party in outer space and talk about the characters like they are at the Garage (legendary NYC club - the Paradise Garage) and the Garage is in space and everyone has a membership: you know, Darth, Kirk, Luke, OB1 and everybody. And they're just rocking, just up there dancing.' So I did it."

The Paradise Garage was predominantly a gay club, and the gay crowd have always been very open and quick to pick up on new types of music and trends. This was the case with disco - it first became popular in gay clubs, before reaching the masses through the movie

Saturday Night Fever. The gay scene got it's own icons in the Village People, who with their hit song 'YMCA', got people running to YMCAs all over the world. They followed this with a hit paying tribute to the US Navy, 'In The Navy'.

But one really has to say that the Saturday Night Fever movie was the big breakthrough for disco music. From having been the music found in the clubs and discotheques, everything exploded overnight. The Bee Gees became disco icons and almost all of the songs from the soundtrack became hits. All of a sudden EVERYONE wanted to be a part of the growing disco scene. Even the most unlikely of artists and groups wanted their part of the action, so there appeared tracks such as Kiss's 'I Was Made For Lovin' You', Cher's 'Take Me Home', Rod Stewart's 'Da Ya Think I'm Sexy?' and the Rolling Stones' 'Miss You'.

The Saturday Night Fever movie also set a standard for the look of a clubber. Most of the guys were all Tony Manero [John Travolta] look-a-likes, in polyester shirts and suits, doing the Hustle in their platform shoes. The ladies were dressed up in [preferably] designer dresses and worked the dancefloor in their high heels. Some of the most popular designers back then can be heard on Sister Sledge's classic tune 'He's The Greatest Dancer', where the group sing 'Halston, Gucci, Fiorucci'.

But if Saturday Night Fever got the disco ball rolling, it was really the record labels and the clubs that had laid the foundations. Whilst the film was released in December 1977, record labels like West End, Prelude (which both started in 1976) and Salsoul Records (which started in 1974) already ruled the dance scene, especially in New York. These were all small independent labels, quick to pick up on trends and who saw the potential of disco. Larger record companies didn't really get on the disco train until the era had already started. Other labels that released good disco music were Atlantic, Casablanca, Columbia Records, and the Miami based T.K. Disco.

The domination of New York based record companies lasted until around 1980. But just as there were so many disco records released there were almost as many different labels. Many of these released just a few records, mainly 12-inch singles, before they folded. But that's also part of the charm of disco. As a collector or fan, even now you can still find great 'new' disco records that you didn't know on labels you have never heard of. Some of the record labels that 'discoholics' like myself keep looking for include P&P, Sound of New York, RSO, BC, De-Lite, Fantasy and Red Greg. What's also fascinating about these labels is that they all had their own unique sound - so you can often hear a tune and identify what label it was released on.

It's maybe hard to understand today the impact disco music had back in the 1970s. Most hit US songs became worldwide hits - no matter where you lived people sang 'Good Times', 'Upside Down' or any of the other hits that ruled the charts either in New York or in Hong Kong.

The disco era was also (unfairly) known for 'one hit wonders'; Lipps Inc's 'Funky Town', Patrick Hernandez's 'Born To Be Alive', Penny McLean's 'Lady Bump', Alicia Bridges' 'I Love The Nightlife', Tamiko Jones' 'Can't Live Without Your Love', Melba Moore's 'This Is It', Jackie Moore's 'This Time Baby' and Anita Ward's 'Ring My Bell'. Some of these artists had long careers and recorded notable songs after (or before) their own huge hit - but these songs would always be compared to their biggest worldwide smash. Anita Ward for example released a great dance track called 'Don't Drop My Love' and Melba Moore also sang the equally great 'You Stepped Into My Life'.

But it seems like everything that's good and popular comes to an end, and some would say that so did disco - but not me! Around 1980 the Disco Sucks campaign began. People were even burning disco records on stakes, just like in the mediaeval days of the witch hunts. All of a sudden you couldn't listen or dance to disco music any longer, or as Marvin Schlachter, owner of Prelude Records said about the 'death of disco' in a 1980 Billboard interview, "The problem really started with the companies who were late getting into the disco scene. When they woke up, they cut lots of disco records and flooded the market."

So what happened was that the disco scene returned to the clubs where it had all first begun and, with new technical equipment, drum machines and synths, the music transformed - from disco - to disco! Well, actually people preferred not to call this 'new' music disco any longer. Even though I still think you could call it disco, it was called things like 'garage' - from the legendary NYC club Paradise Garage where Larry Levan ruled, or 'house' - from Chicago's Warehouse club where Frankie Knuckles was the resident DJ. The more uptempo tunes were called Hi Energy (Hi-NRG) or Euro, since this kind of music was very popular in Europe at the time.

But for me the best name for all of these genres of 'previously called disco music' would be 'dance' music. It still has the same meaning as when disco started - music designed for people to move and have fun to!

Now move on and get a glimpse of the visual history of disco music through the record covers collected and presented in this book by Disco Patrick and Patrick Vogt.

Enjoy and Disco-on!

Claes 'Discoguy' Widlund
www.disco-disco.com

Disco Patrick

WELCOME TO MY DISCO COVERS CATALOGUE.

From the start when I first began collecting records in 1979, I have always been fascinated by the cover art of disco albums and 12-inch singles. In this book there are over 2000 reproductions of these artworks.

Disco music originally came directly out of the underground clubs and dance floors. It was also new music, a break from the past. The first section of this book is dedicated to releases from the disco record companies who started and ushered in the genre. These labels were almost all (though not exclusively) independent labels run by individuals who were as passionate about disco music as the fans who bought and danced to these records. Most major record companies came on board later, with special mention to Atlantic, Motown and Columbia, the latter through its successful association with Philadelphia International Records.

As there are many major record labels that released disco music I have made an (admittedly large) selection of the ones that I personally find essential. This is a selection of the covers I have found up until now. I know there are many more but somehow I had to make certain choices, and this is what you can see in the book.

In the major disco albums section I have added the year and catalog-matrix number. I have only listed the disco-funk-jazz records issued on each label. This means that I have left out rock, comedy and any other music styles for each featured label discography, so missing catalog-matrix numbers could be either a non-disco release or one I have inadvertently missed.

A special thanks to my friend, soul/funk expert Marc Janssen; for granting me access to his endless vinyl archives and sharing his astoundingly extensive knowledge of records.

Enjoy!
Disco Patrick

African Suite - African Suite / MCA 1980
Illustration: William Rieser / Design: Vartan

LE PAMPLEMOUSSE
MY LOVE IS BURNING UP

Disco Labels & Albums

Chapter 1
AVI Records

FOUNDED BY ED COBB IN 1974. AVI RECORDS CLOSED IT'S DOORS IN 1985.

AVI - American Variety International - was a 1970s label founded on the west coast of America in 1974 by Edward Cobb and Ray Harris. Cobb had been a songwriter in the 1960s and wrote Gloria Jones' 'Tainted Love', and Brenda Holloway's 'Every Little Bit Hurts' amongst others. Rather than aimed at the pop market, AVI was often more club oriented in its sound.

Production team Laurin Rinder and W. Michael Lewis were the driving force behind the label with many releases, often experimental in their sound. Rinder had been a session musician since his teens and Lewis had been a member of the San Francisco psychedelic rock group Quicksilver Messenger Service when the pair first met in the late 1960s. After some session work for AVI in 1974, they were asked to cut some disco sides and began making music under a variety of guises including El Coco, Le Pamplemousse (which featured the vocals of The Jones Girls) and, from 1977 onwards, also recorded under their own names. The pair would be responsible for an estimated 30 albums in the label's lifetime!

The label also picked up some Chicago-based productions for national distribution including Lowrell and Captain Sky, and similarly did the same with Clarence Lawton in Philadelphia, releasing material by The Destinations and Baby Washington. AVI also signed up Gloria Jones to do remakes of some of her sixties songs, including a new version of the classic 'Tainted Love'. British producer Ian Levine also released several productions on the label including James Wells and LJ Johnson among others.

By the turn of the decade the label had lost direction and AVI Records finally closed its doors in 1985, with Rinder leaving the music business and Lewis continuing as a session musician to this day.

Left: Le Pamplemousse - My Love Is Burning Up / AVI 1981
Cover Design And Art: Bob Wynne

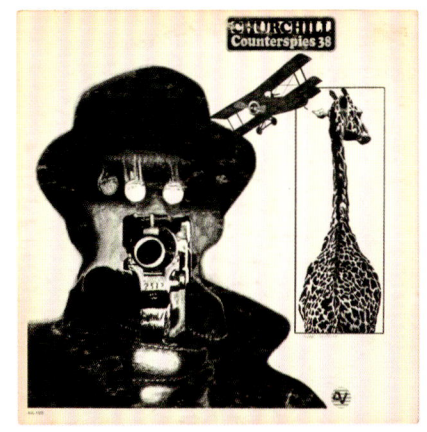

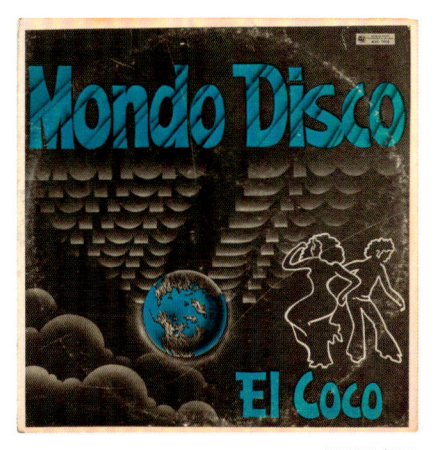

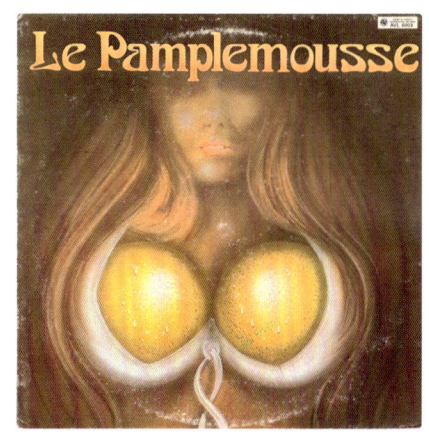

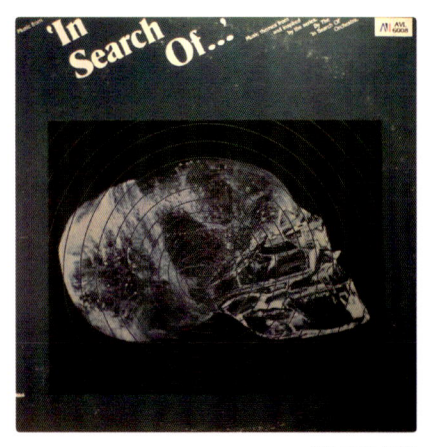

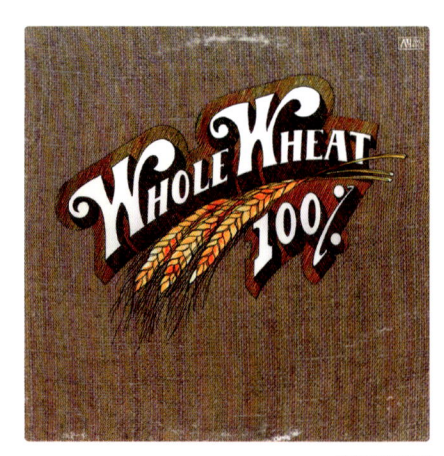

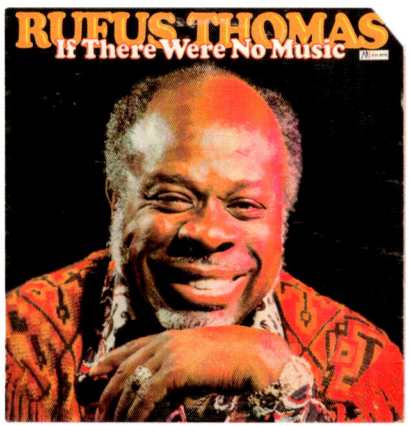

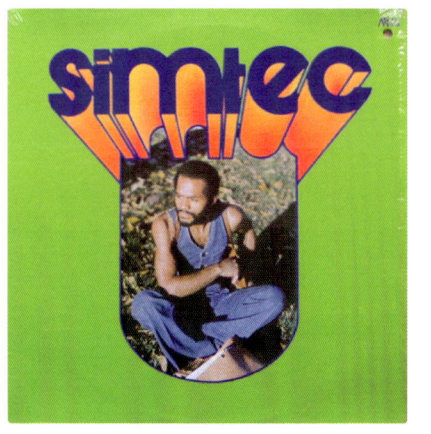

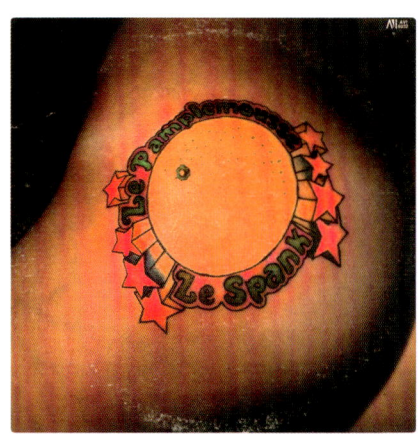

AVI 1020 / 1973	AVI 1039 / 1975	AVI 1040 / 1975	AVL 6003 / 1976
AVL 6004 / 1976	AVL 6006 / 1976	AVL 6008 / 1977	AVI 6011 / 1977
AVI 6012 / 1977	AVI 6013 / 1977	AVI 6015 / 1977	AVI 6017 / 1977
AVI 6026 / 1977	AVI 6027 / 1977	AVI 6028 / 1977	AVI 6032 / 1977

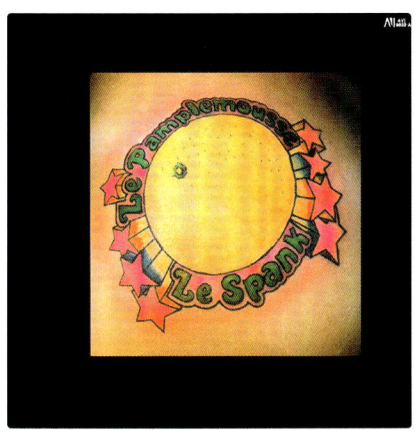

AVI 6032-A / 1977

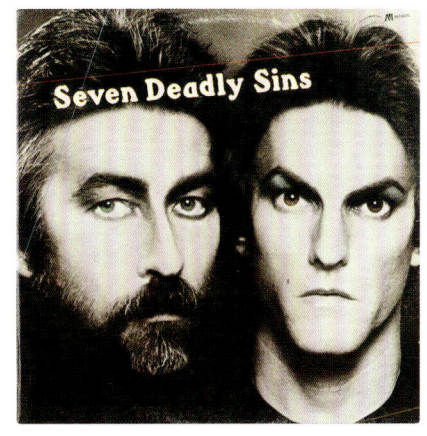

AVI 6035 / 1977

AVI 6036 / 1978

AVI 6038 / 1978

AVI 6040 / 1978

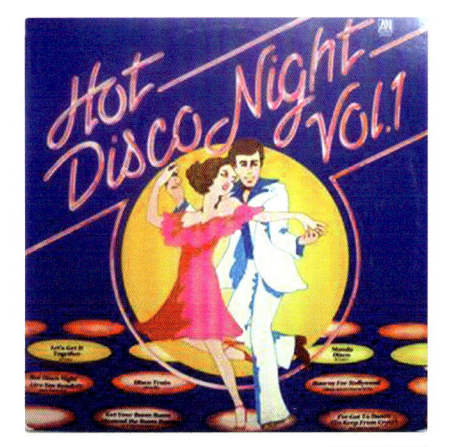

AVI 6041 / 1978

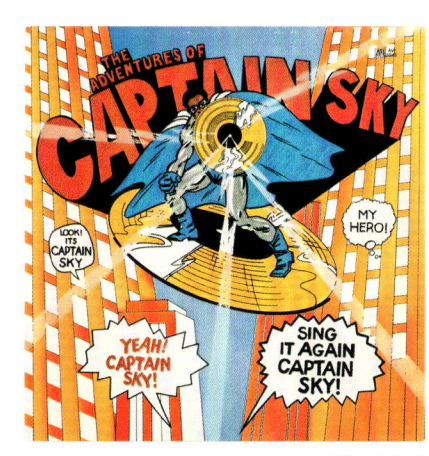

AVI 6042 / 1978

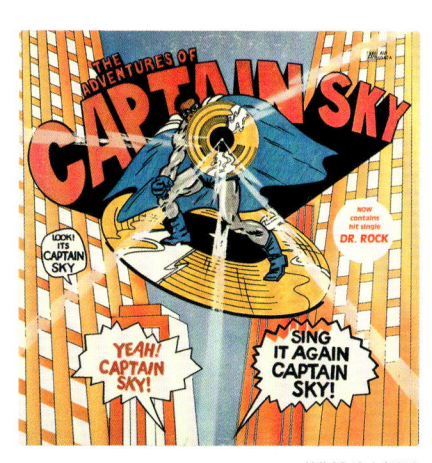

AVI 6042-A / 1978

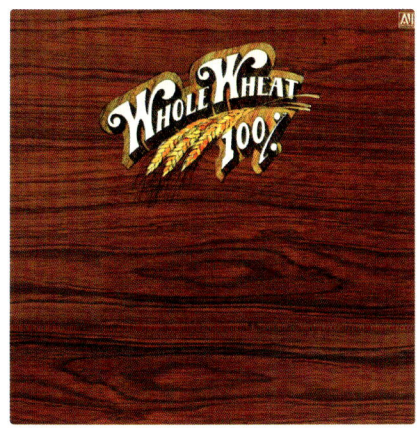

AVI 6043 / 1978

AVI 6044 / 1978

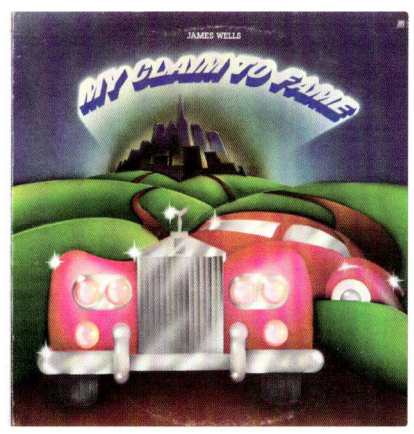

AVI 6045 / 1978

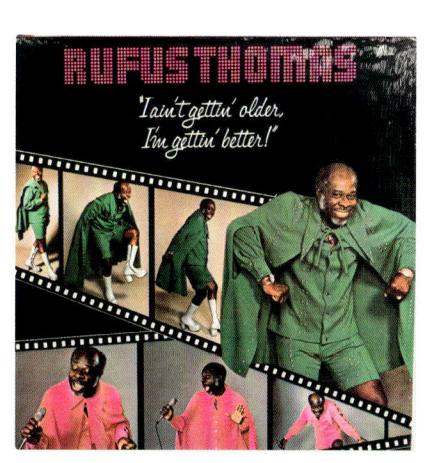

AVI 6046 / 1978

AVI 6048 / 1978

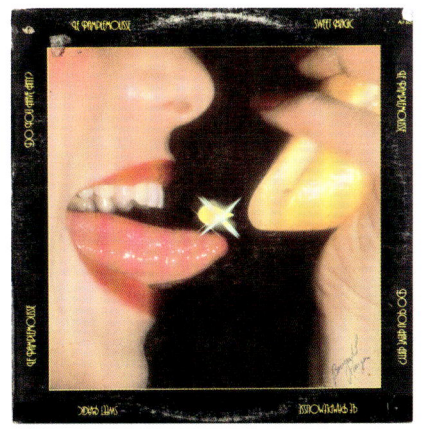

AVI 6053 / 1978

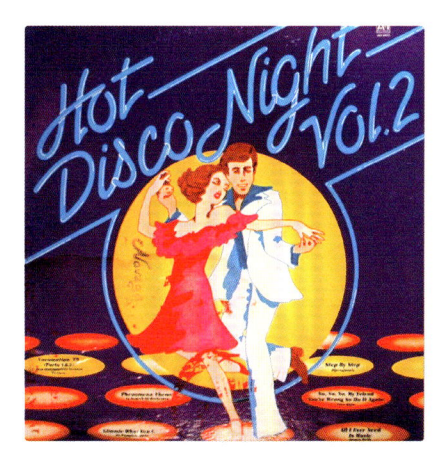

AVI 6055 / 1979

AVI 6057 / 1979

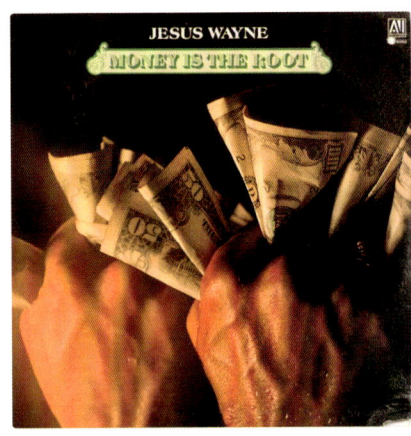

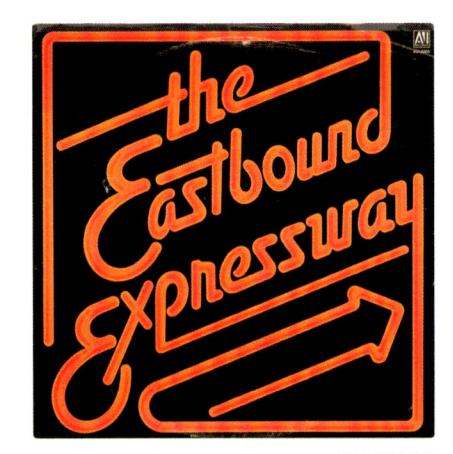

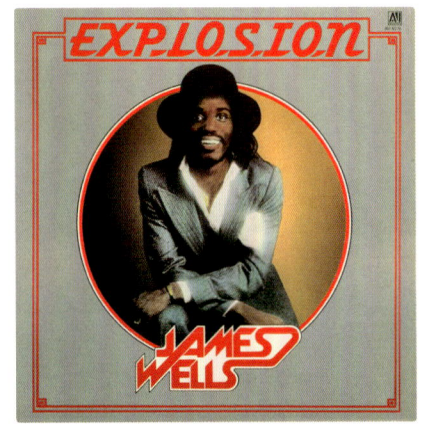

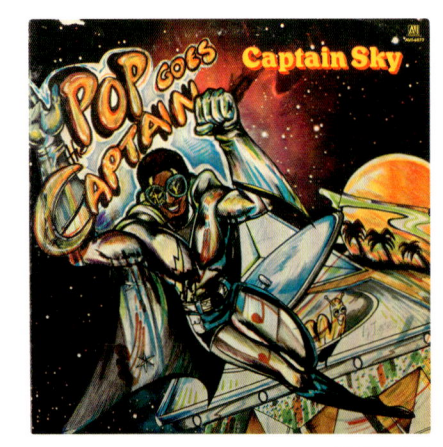

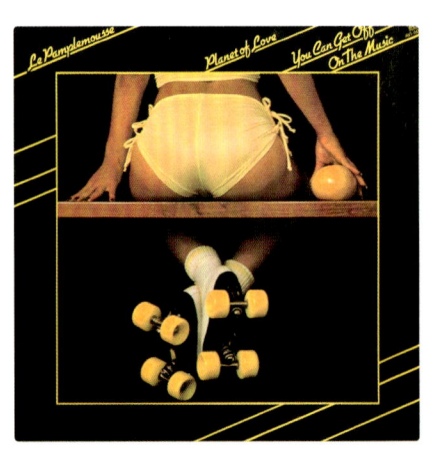

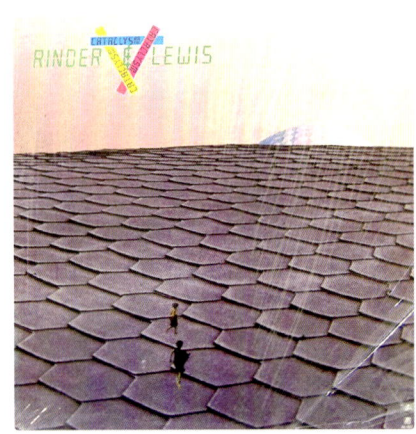

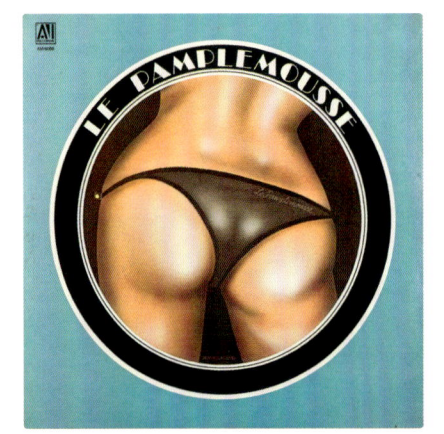

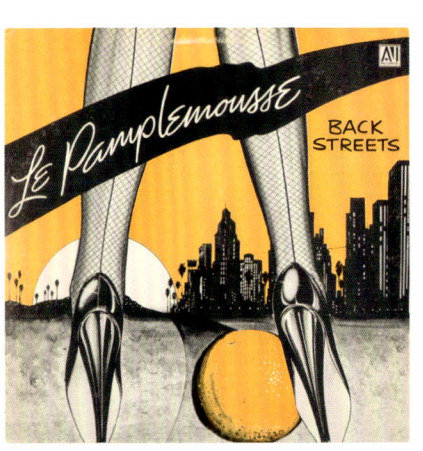

AVI 6060 / 1979	AVI 6064 / 1979	AVI 6068 / 1979	AVI 6070 / 1979
AVI 6073 / 1979	AVI 6076 / 1979	AVI 6077 / 1979	AVI 6080 / 1979
AVI 6082 / 1980	AVI 6087 / 1980	AVI 6088 / 1980	AVI 6093 / 1981
AVI 6097 / 1981	AVI 6100 / 1982	AVI 6102 / 1982	AVI 6105 / 1982

Solar Source - Now's The Time / AVI 1981
Album Design And Art Bob Wynne

AVI 6111 / 1982    AVI 6113 / 1982 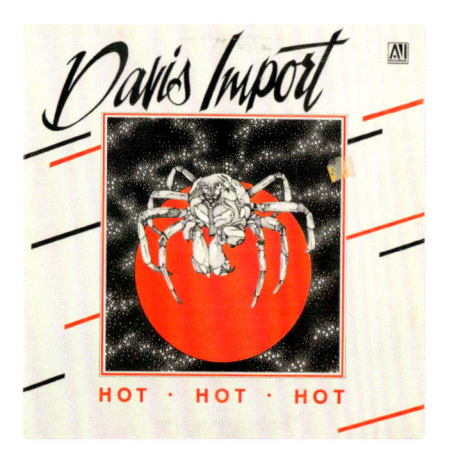   AVI 6115 / 1982 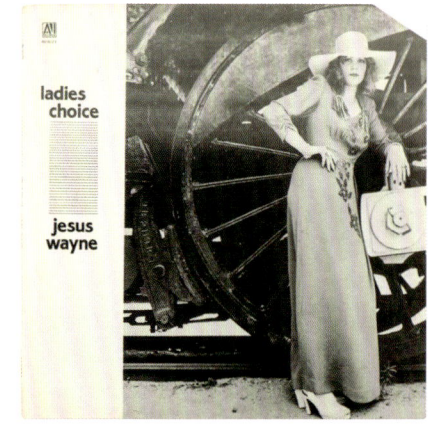   AVI 6123 / 1982

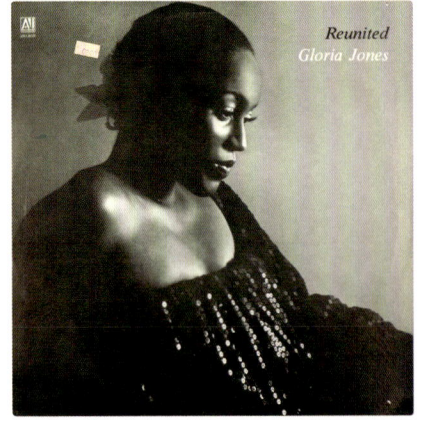

AVI 6135 / 1982    AVI 8508 / 1983 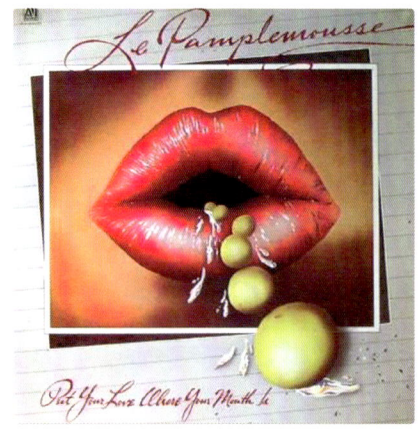   AVI 8682 / 1984 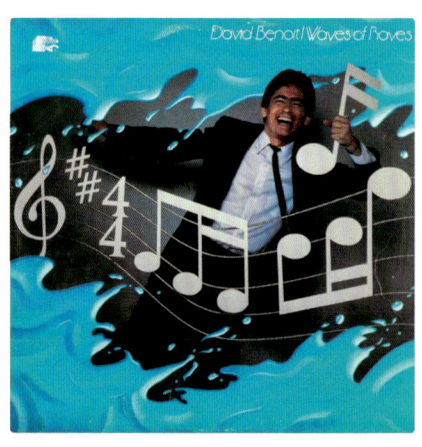   AVI 8712 / 1984

AVI 8714 / 1984 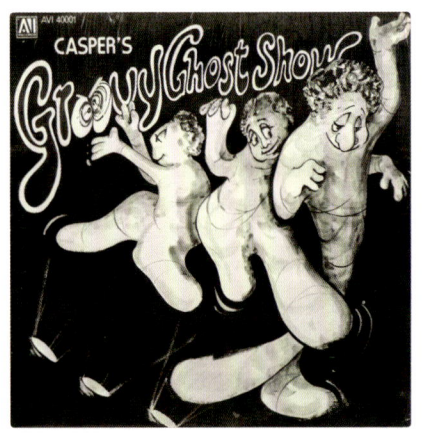   AVI 40001 / 1980    AVI 40002 / 1980    AVI 40003 / 1980

AVI 40004 / 1980    AVI 40007 / 1981 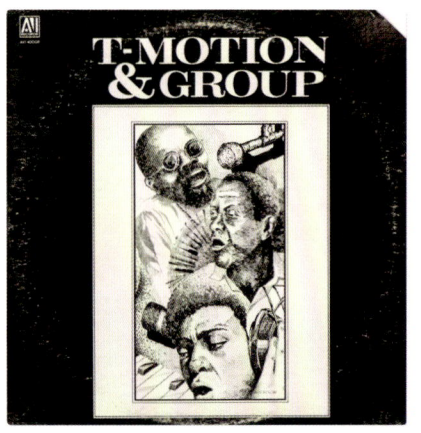   AVI 40008 / 1981 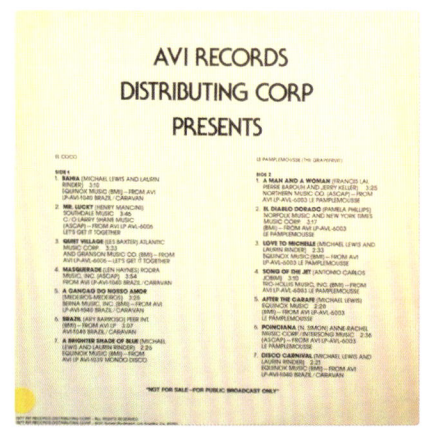   AVSM-9006 / 1977

Matrix numbers

AVI

AVL 1020	Churchill	Counterspies 38	1975
AVI 1039	El Coco	Mondo Disco	1975
AVI 1040	El Coco	Brazil	1975
AVL 6003	Le Pamplemousse	Le Pamplemousse	1976
AVL 6004	Tchou Tchou Combo	Tchou Tchou Combo	1976
AVL 6006	El Coco	Let's Get It Together	1976
AVL 6008	In Search Of Orchestra	In Search Of...	1977
AVL 6011	100% Whole Wheat	100% Whole Wheat	1977
AVL 6012	El Coco	Cocomotion	1977
AVL 6013	Doug Richardson	Night Talk	1977
AVL 6015	Rufus Thomas	If There Were No Music	1977
AVI 6016	We Five	Take Each Day As It Comes	1977
AVL 6017	Kelly Stevens	When You Wish Upon A Star	1977
AVL 6025	David Benoit	Heavier Than Yesterday	1977
AVL 6026	Discognosis	Discognosis	1977
AVL 6027	Baby Rocker	Young And Mean	1977
AVI 6028	Simtec Simmons	Simtec	1977
AVI 6032	Le Pamplemousse	Le Spank	1977
AVI 6034	Don Bennett	The Prince Teddy Album	1977
AVI 6035	Laurin Rinder & W. Michael Lewis	Seven Deadly Sins	1977
AVI 6035	Renzo Fraise	Finalemente A Jazz Experience	1978
AVI 6038	Baby Washington	I Wanna Dance	1978
AVI 6040	Dave Williams	Soul Is Free	1978
AVI 6041	Various	Hot Disco Night Vol. I	1978
AVI 6042	Captain Sky	The Adventures Of Captain Sky	1978
AVI 6042-A	Captain Sky	The Adventures Of Captain Sky	1978
AVI 6043	100% Whole Wheat	Ice, Fire & Desire	1978
AVI 6044	El Coco	Dancing In Paradise	1978
AVI 6045	James Wells	My Claim To Fame	1978
AVI 6046	Rufus Thomas	I Ain't Getting Older, I'm Getting Funkier	1978
AVI 6048	Tee Cee's, The	Disco Love Bite	1978
AVI 6053	Le Pamplemousse	Sweet Magic	1978
AVI 6056	Doris Jones	Suddenly I'm Alive	1978
AVI 6055	Various	Hot Disco Night Vol.2	1979
AVI 6057	Seventh Avenue	Midnight In Manhattan	1979
AVI 6058	Rinlew Allstars	Rinlew Allstars	1979
AVI 6059	Passion	Passion	1979
AVI 6060	Jesus Wayne	Money Is The Root	1979
AVI 6064	L.J. Johnson	L.J.'s Love Suite	1979
AVI-6066	Croisette	Keep It On Ice	1979
AVI 6068	Eastbound Expressway	Eastbound Expressway	1979
AVI 6069	Evelyn Thomas	Have A Little Faith In Me	1979
AVI 6070	Lowrell	Lowrell	1979
AVI 6073	Rinder & Lewis	Warriors	1979
AVI 6076	James Wells	Explosion	1979
AVI 6077	Captain Sky	Pop Goes The Captain	1979
AVI 6080	Le Pamplemousse	Planet Of Love	1979
AVI 6074	David Benoit	Can You Imagine	1980
AVI 6082	El Coco	Revolución	1980
AVI 6083	Samson	African Trilogy And Other Curious	1980
AVI 6087	Rinder & Lewis	Cataclysm	1980
AVI 6088	Le Pamplemousse	Le Pamplemousse	1980
AVI 6092	Cheetah	Cheetah	1981
AVI 6093	Love Twins	Temptation	1981
AVI 6097	Le Pamplemousse	My Love Is Burning Up	1981
AVI 6099	Rinder & Lewis	Full Circle	1982
AVI 6100	Captain Sky	The Return Of Captain Sky	1982
AVI 6102	El Coco	El Coco	1982
AVI 6105	Le Pamplemousse	Back Streets	1982
AVI 6110	Rinder And Lewis	Half Circle	1982
AVI 6111	Love Twins	On Fire	1982
AVI 6113	El Coco	Collectables	1982
AVI 6114	David Benoit	Stages	1982
AVI 6115	Davis Import	Hot-Hot-Hot	1982
AVI 6116	Ketty Lester	A Collection Of Her Best	1982
AVI 6123	Jesus wayne	Ladies Choice	1982
AVI 6130	Amrakus	A Space Rock Opera	1982
AVI 6135	Gloria Jones	Reunited	1982
AVI 6138	David Benoit	Digits	1983
AVI 6143	Oliver Sain	Fused Jazz - A Collection	1983
AVI 8508	Various	Jazz Fusion	1983
AVI 8524	Various	Hot Disco Fever	1983
AVI 8553	Supermax	Live - Volume One	1983
AVI 8554	Oliver Sain	Fused Jazz - A Collection	1983
AVI 8682	Le Pamplemousse	Put Your Love Where Your Mouth Is	1984
AVI 8701	Arnold McCuller	A Part Of Me That's You	1984
AVI 8712	David Benoit	Waves Of Raves	1984
AVI 8714	Air Force	Air Force	1984
AVI 40001	Casper	Casper's Groovy Ghost Show	1980
AVI 40002	Davis Import	You're The One	1980
AVI 40003	Jesus Wayne	Jesus Wayne	1980
AVI 40004	Midnight Wind	Midnight Wind	1980
AVI 40007	Solar Source	Now's The Time	1981
AVI 40008	T-Motion & Group	T-Motion & Group	1981
AVSM-9006	El Coco / Le Pamplemousse	Avi Records Distributing Corp Presents	1977

NEW BIRTH

PLATINUM CITY

Disco Labels & Albums

Chapter 2
Ariola Records

FOUNDED IN GERMANY BY BERTELSMANN IN 1958. ARIOLA AMERICA WAS FOUNDED IN 1975 IN LOS ANGELES. RELEASED DISCO BETWEEN 1975-80. CURRENTLY OWNED BY SONY MUSIC ENTERTAINMENT.

Left: New Birth - Platinum City / Ariola 1979

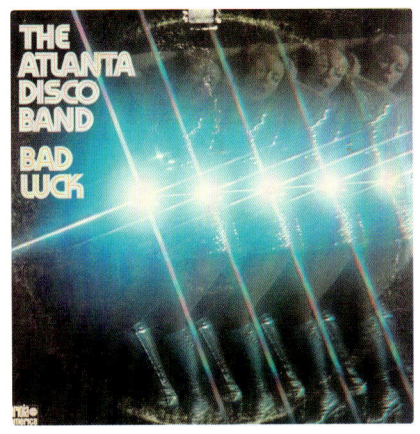

ST-50004 / 1975 
ST-50009 / 1976 
ST-50012 / 1976 
ST-50013 / 1976

ST-50021 / 1977 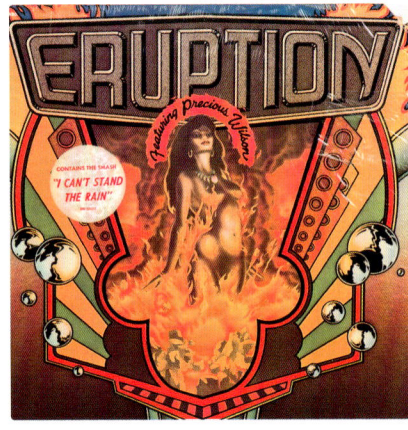
SW 50033 / 1978 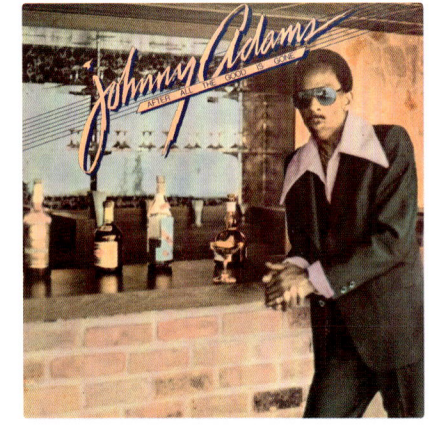
SW 50036 / 1978 
SW 50038 / 1978

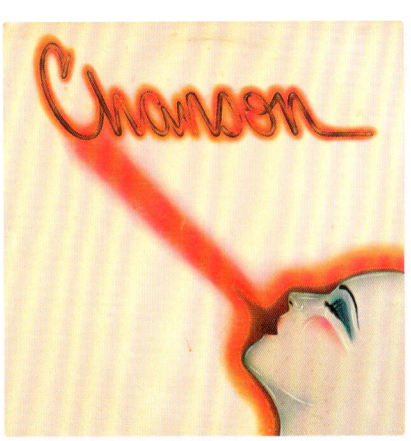

SW 50039 / 1978
SW 50040 / 1978 1978 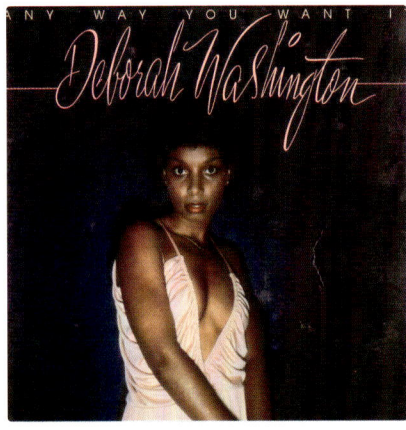
SW 50041 / 1979 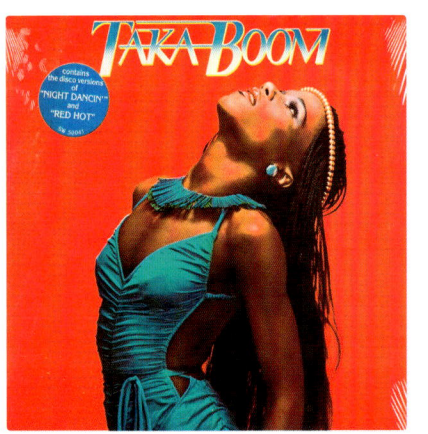
SW 50043 / 1978 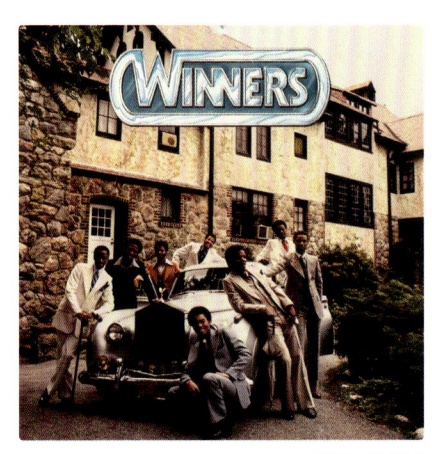

SW 50044 / 1978
SW 50045 / 1979 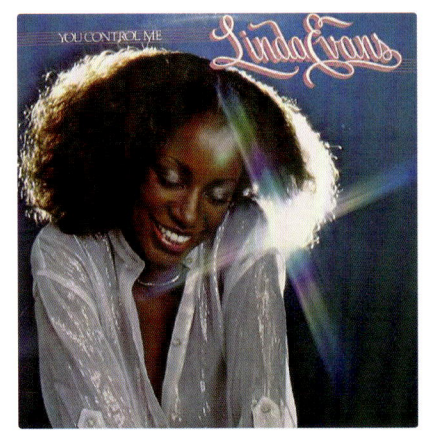
SW 50051 / 1978 
SW 50052 / 1979 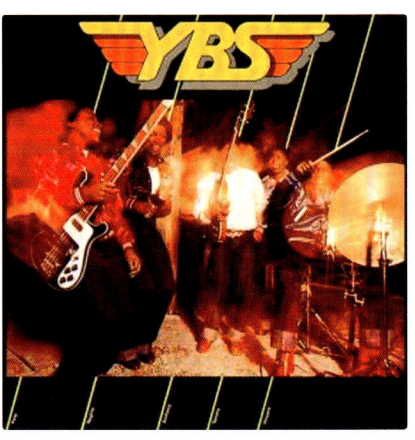

24

Sister Power · Sister Power / Ariola 1979
Art Direction & Design: John Georgopoulos / Photography: Tom Keller

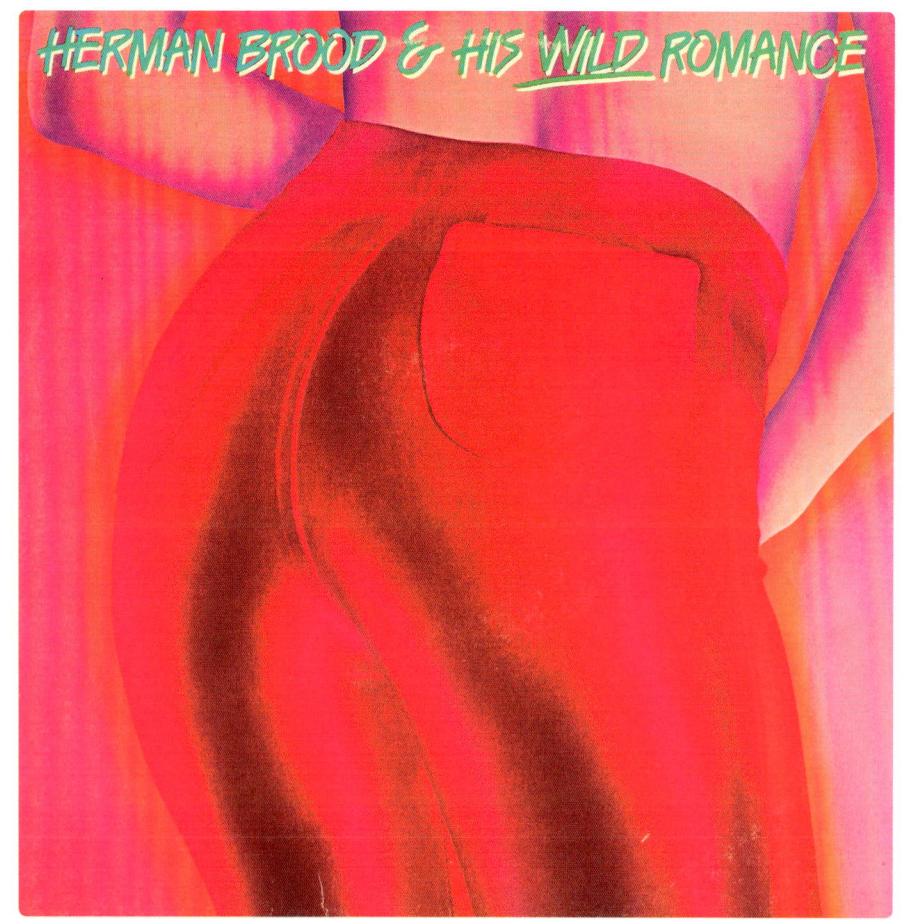

SW 50059 (front) / 1979

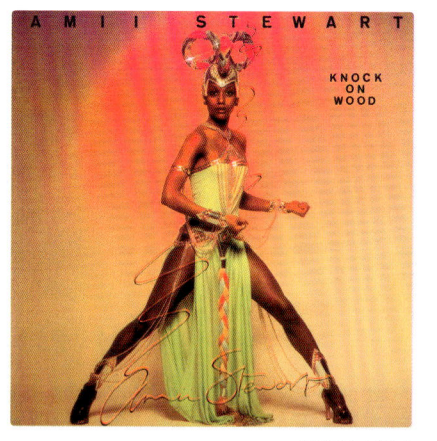

SW 50054 / 1979

SW 50056 / 1979

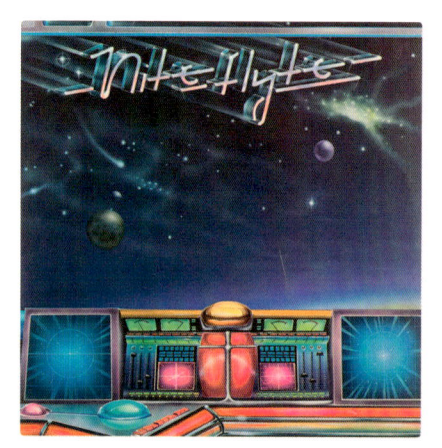

SW 50060 / 1979

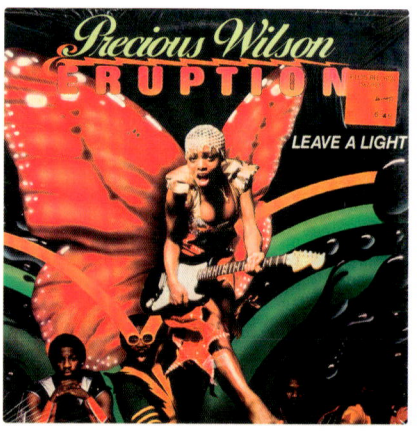

SW 50061 / 1979

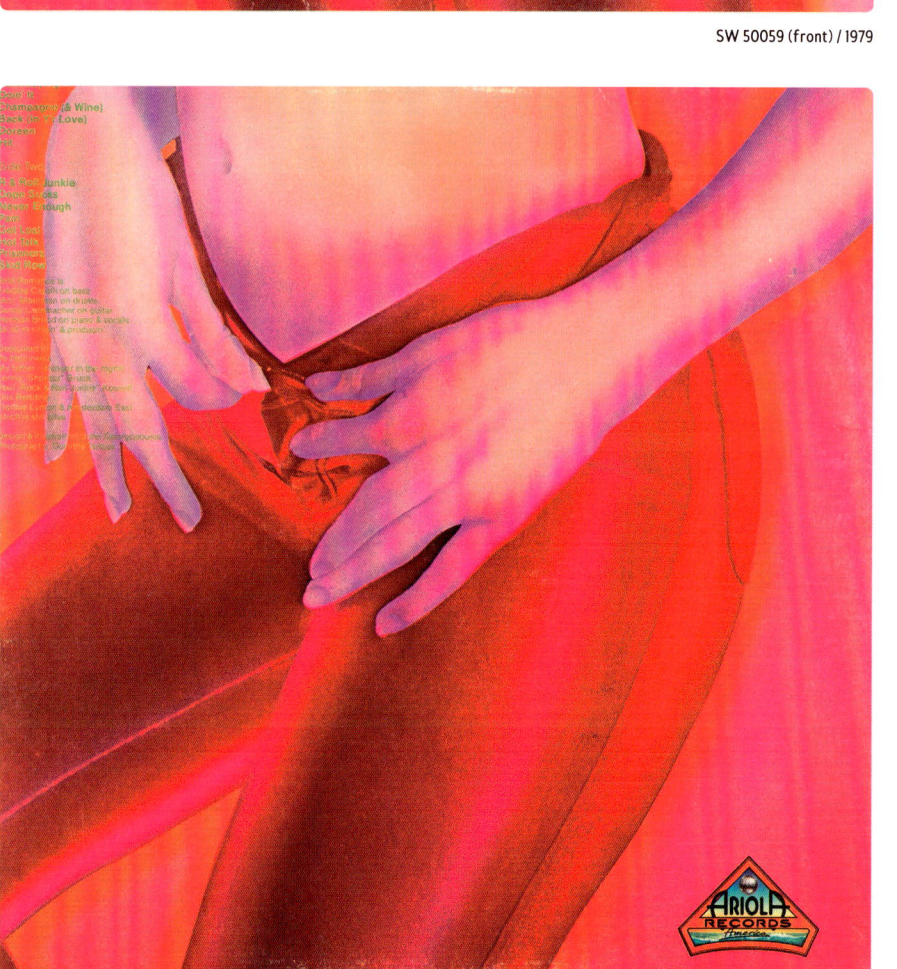

SW 50062 / 1979

SW 50065 / 1979

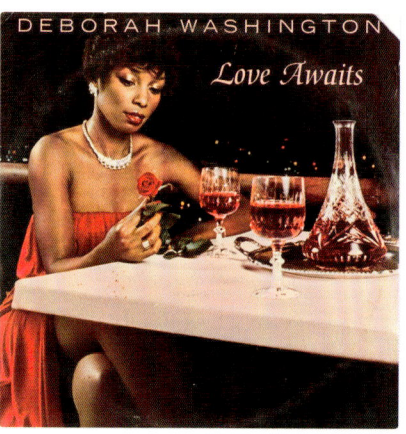

SW 50059 (back) / 1979

SW 50066 / 1979

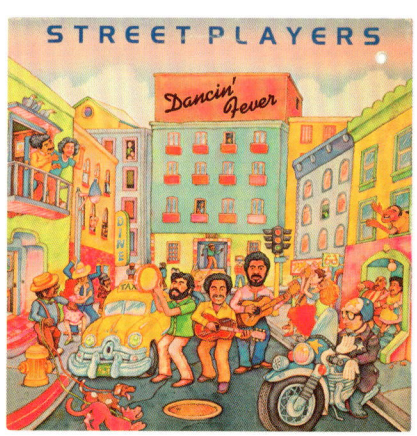

SW 50071 / 1979

Matrix numbers

SW 50072 / 1979

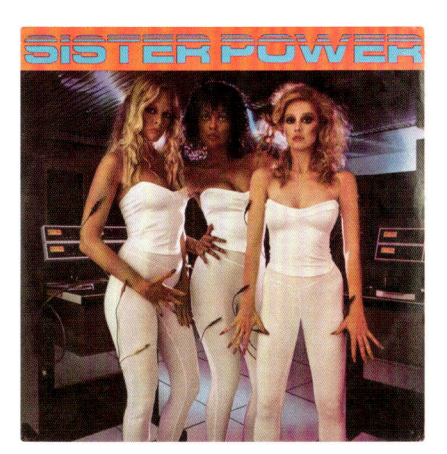

SW 49901 / 1979

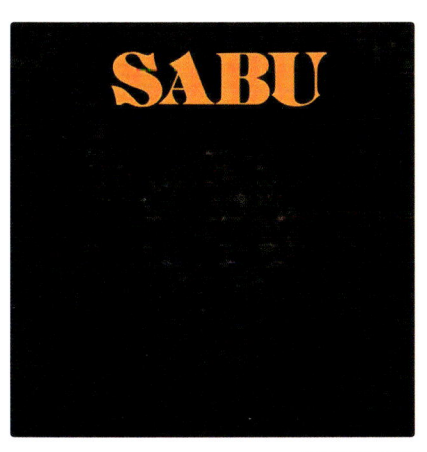

SW 49902 / 1979

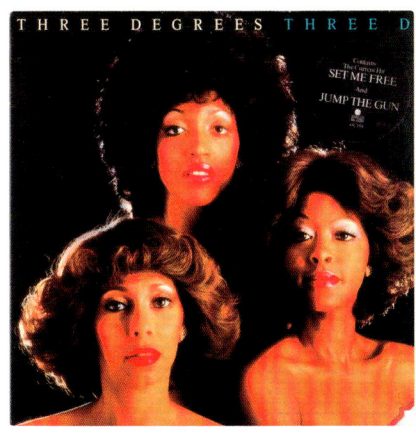

OL-1501 / 1980

ARIOLA

ST-50004	The Atlanta Disco Band	Bad Luck	1975
ST-50009	Alexander's Discotime Band	Songs That Were Mother's	1976
ST-50011	Various	The Big Dance Records In The Big Apple	1976
ST-50012	John Valenti	Anything You Want	1976
ST-50013	Spin	Spin	1976
ST-50021	Muscle Shoals Horns	Doin' It To The Bone	1977
SW-50033	Eruption Featuring Precious Wilson	Eruption	1978
SW-50036	Johnny Adams	After All The Good Is Gone	1978
SW-50038	Eon	Eon	1978
SW-50039	Chanson	Chanson	1978
SW-50040	Deborah Washington	Any Way You Want It	1978
SW-50041	Taka Boom	Taka Boom	1979
SW-50043	Winners	Winners	1978
SW-50044	The Three Degrees	New Dimensions	1978
SW-50045	Linda Evans	You Control Me	1979
SW-50051	Beverly & Duane	Beverly & Duane	1978
SW-50052	Yates Brothers & Sisters	YBS	1979
SW-50054	Amii Stewart	Knock On Wood	1979
SW-50056	Chapter 8	Chapter 8	1979
SW-50059	Herman Brood & His Wild Romance	Herman Brood & His Wild Romance	1979
SW-50060	Niteflyte	Niteflyte	1979
SW-50061	Precious Wilson & Eruption	Leave A Light	1979
SW-50062	New Birth	Platinum City	1979
SW-50065	Chanson	Together We Stand	1979
SW-50066	Deborah Washington	Love Awaits	1979
SW-50069	Saragossa Band	Saragossa Band	1979
SW-50071	Street Players	Dancin' Fever	1979
SW-50072	Amii Stewart	Paradise Bird	1979
SW-49900	Ullanda	Love Zone	1979
SW-49901	Sister Power	Sister Power	1979
SW-49902	Sabu	Sabu	1979
OL-1501	Three Degrees	3D	1980
OL-1507	Wills, Viola	If You Could Read My Mind	1980

Maruha
Disco 'Round The World

Disco Labels & Albums

Chapter 3
Black Sun Records

MONTREAL BASED LABEL, ACTIVE 1981-87, A SUBSIDIARY OF MATRA RECORDS OWNED BY UNIDISC.

Left: Martina - Martina / Black Sun 1981

SUN-3 / 1980

SUN-1 / 1981

SUN-2 / 1980

SUN-4 / 1981

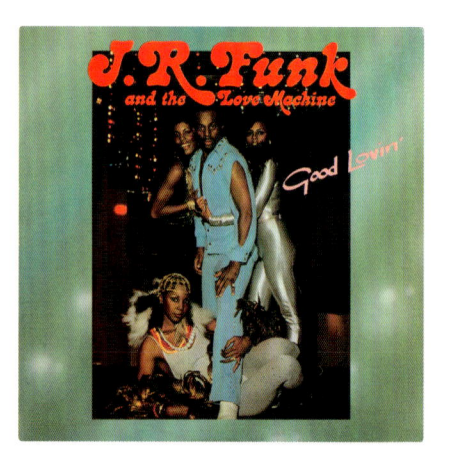

SUN-5 / 1982

SUN-3 (Back) / 1980

SUN-8 / 1983

Matrix numbers

SUN-6 / 1982

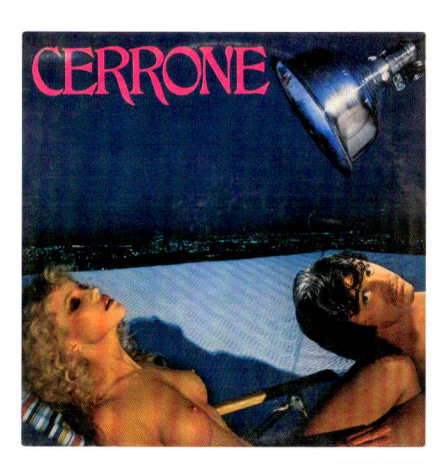

ULP-19 / 1980

ULP-20 / 1980

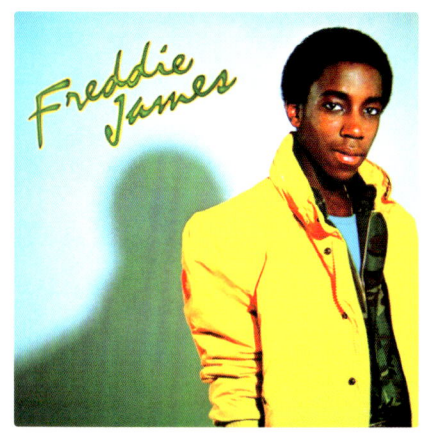

WLP-1028 / 1981

BLACK SUN

SUN-1	Martina	Martina	1981
SUN-2	Silvetti	I Love You	1980
SUN-3	Cappuccino	Cappuccino	1980
SUN-4	Imagination	Body Talk	1981
SUN-5	J.R. Funk And The Love Machine	Good Lovin'	1981
SUN-6	Imagination	In The Heat Of The Night	1982
SUN-8	Brooklyn Express	Burnin' Up	1983
ULP-19	Cerrone	Cerrone VI	1980
ULP-20	Cerrone	Cerrone VII - You Are The One	1980
WLP-1028	Freddie James	Freddie James	1981

Boogie Down!

BLACKWELL

Disco Labels & Albums

Chapter 4
Butterfly Records

US DISCO LABEL, FOUNDED BY A.J. CERVANTES IN 1977.

Left: Blackwell - Boogie Down / Butterfly 1978
Design: Glenn Ross / Photography: Buddy Rosenberg, Bob Levy

FLY 001 / 1977

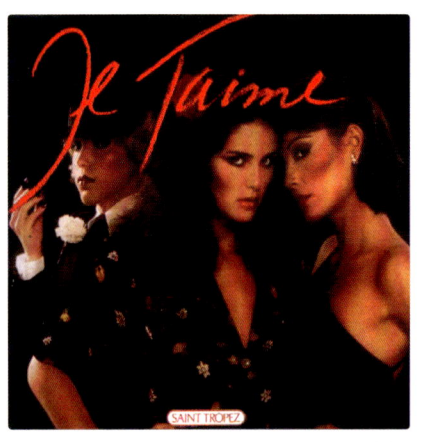

FLY 002 / 1977

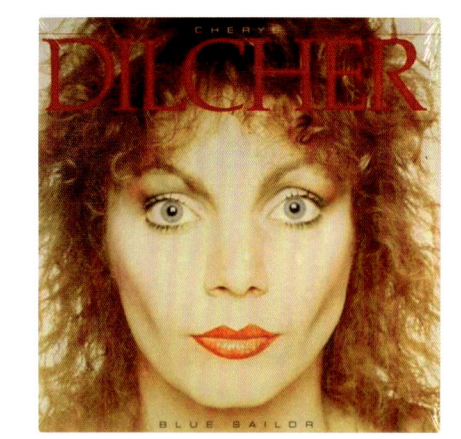

FLY 003 / 1977

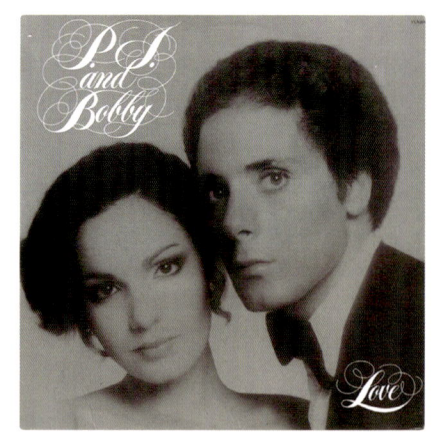

FLY 004 / 1977

FLY 005 / 1977

FLY 006 / 1977

FLY 007 / 1977

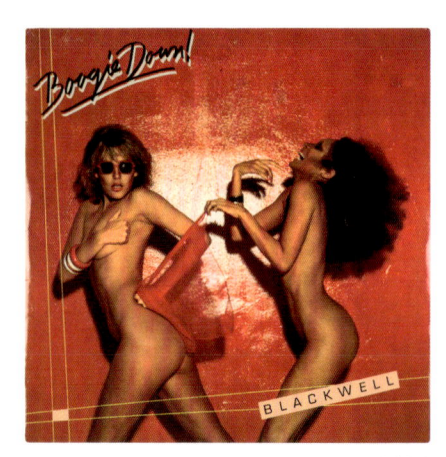

FLY 008 / 1978

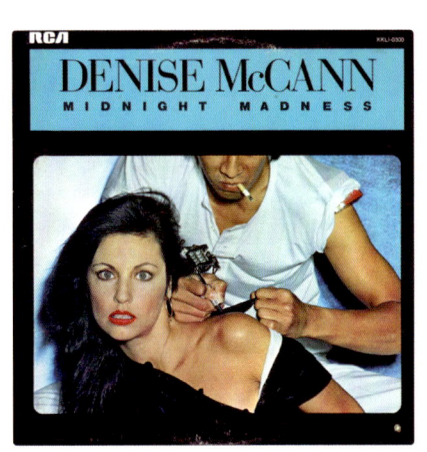

FLY 009 / 1978

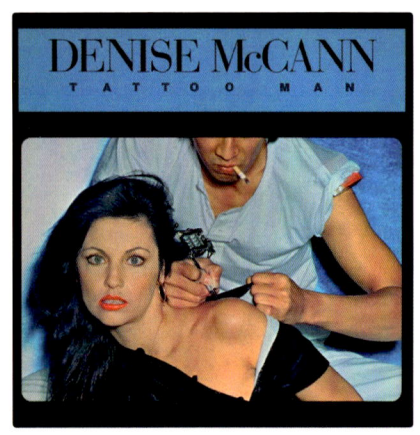

FLY 009 / 1978

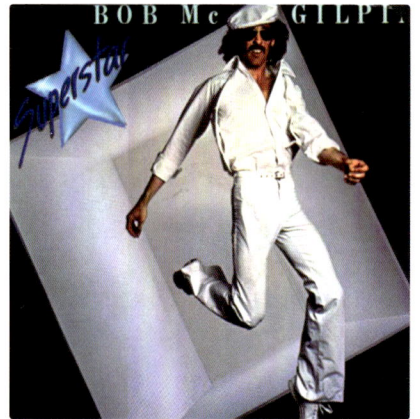

FLY 010 / 1978

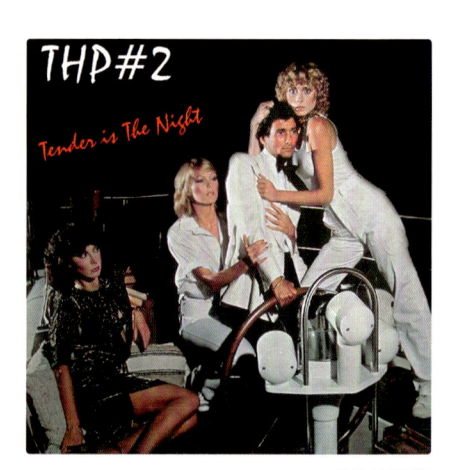

FLY 014 / 1978

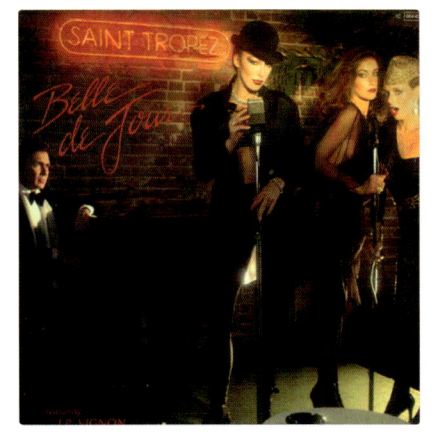

FLY-3100 / FLY 016 / 1978

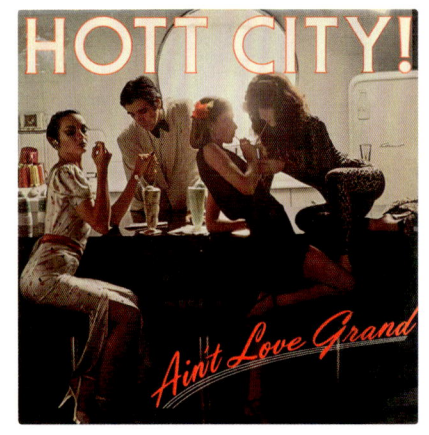

FLY-3101 / 1979

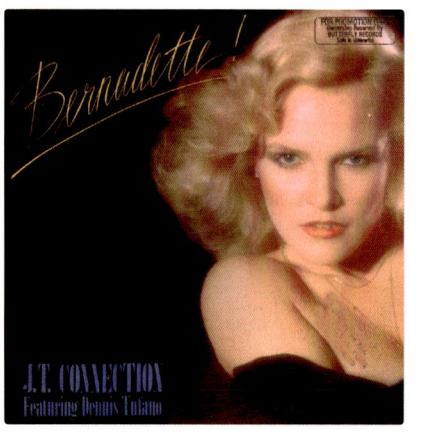

FLY-3102 / 1979

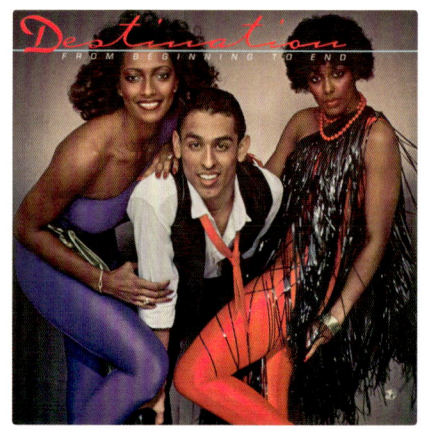

FLY-3103 / 1979

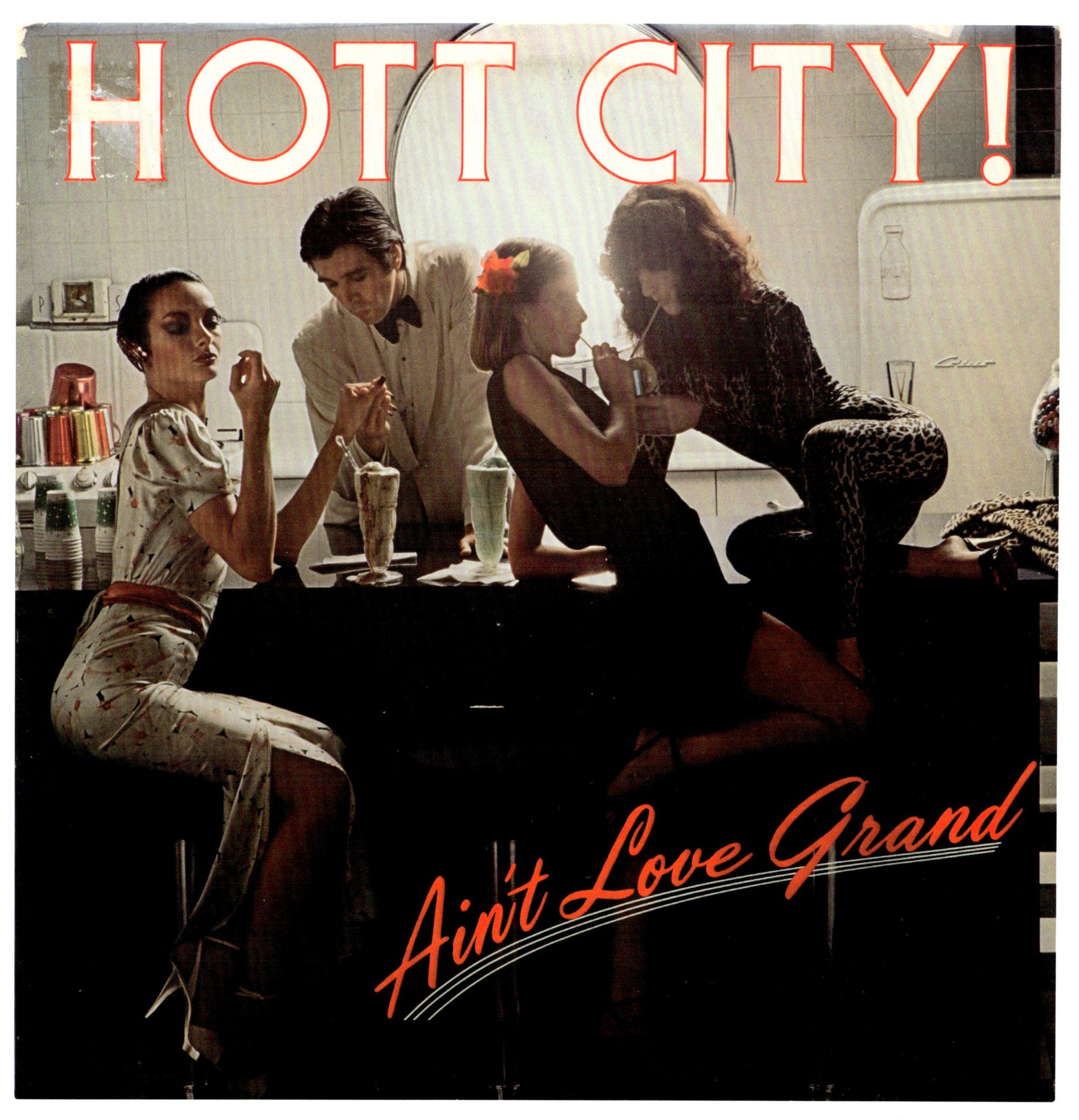

Hot City - Ain't Love Grand / Butterfly 1979
Photography: Graham Henman

FLY-3104 / 1979

FLY-3107 / 1980

FLY-31110 / 1979

Innersleeve

Matrix numbers

FLY-3105 / 1979

FLY-3106 / 1979

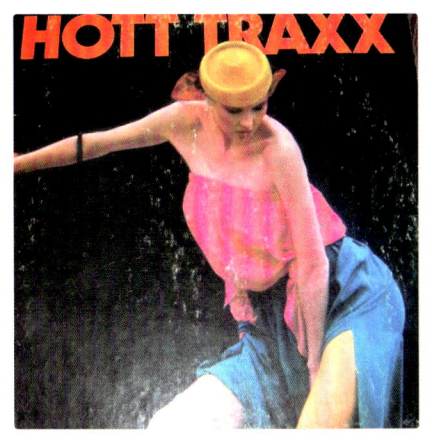

box set 5 albums

BUTTERFLY

FLY 001	The Firesign Theatre	Just Folks... A Firesign Chat	1977
FLY 002	Saint Tropez	Je T'Aime	1977
FLY 003	Cheryl Dilcher	Blue Sailor	1977
FLY 004	P.J. And Bobby	Love	1977
FLY 005	THP Orchestra	Two Hot For Love	1977
FLY 006	Grand Tour	On Such A Winter's Day	1977
FLY 007	Tuxedo Junction	Tuxedo Junction	1977
FLY 008	Blackwell	Boogie Down	1978
FLY 009	Denise McCann	Tattoo Man	1978
FLY 010	Bob Mc Gilpin	Superstar	1978
FLY 014	THP	#2 Tender Is The Night	1978
FLY 016	Saint Tropez	Belle De Jour	1978
FLY-3100	Saint Tropez	Belle De Jour	1978
FLY-3101	Hott City	Ain't Love Grand	1979
FLY-3102	J.T. Connection Feat. Dennis Tufano	Bernadette	1979
FLY-3103	Destination	From Beginning To End	1979
FLY-3104	Bob McGilpin II	Get Up	1979
FLY-3105	Tuxedo Junction	Tuxedo Junction II Take The A Train	1979
FLY-3106	Denise McCann	I Have A Destiny	1979
FLY-3107	Abbe	Rainbows	1980
FLY-3110	Fire And Ice	Fire And Ice	1979
	Hott Traxx	5 Album Set	

EDDIE DRENNON
IT DON'T MEAN A THING

Disco Labels & Albums

Chapter 5
Casablanca and sub-labels

Left: Eddie Drennon - It Don't Mean A Thing / Casablanca 1978
Art Direction And Design: Edward Becket, Gribbitt / Photography: Ron Slenzak, Scott Hensel

History of Casablanca Records

Casablanca Records was founded in 1973 by former Buddah Records executives Neil Bogart, Cecil Holmes, Larry Harris and Buck Reingold. Bogart, the driving force behind the label, was born in Brooklyn, New York in 1943. Born Bogatz, he changed his name to Bogart after his childhood movie idol Humphrey Bogart and the record label was named after the classic movie in which the actor starred.

In the mid 1960s Bogart was working in MGM Records' promotions department when he was brought into Cameo/Parkway Records. In 1967 Cameo/Parkway was sold and Bogart became the general manager of Buddah Records. In 1973 he formed Casablanca Records, initially funded by Warner Brothers. Originally he wanted to call the label Emerald City, after the film The Wizard of Oz, but Warners owned the rights to the movie Casablanca and it was therefore easier to get the permission to use this name. Unfortunately Warners and Bogart were unable to get on and soon came to an agreement that he would pay back the money on a monthly basis that Warners had put into the company - which he did.

After the split with Warners, Casablanca moved to Sunset Boulevard, Los Angeles. Here the whole of the office interior was decorated to resemble the Casablanca movie, with Bogart's office a complete replica of Rick's American Café, and the employees referred to the office as 'The Casbah'.

Neil Bogart's first big signing was the rock group Kiss but it was disco music with which Casablanca became most associated. Giorgio Moroder and partner Pete Bellotte had been working together for some years when, in 1975, Donna Summer came up with the idea of 'Love to Love You, Baby', partly inspired by the Jane Birkin & Serge Gainsbourg's 'Je T'Aime...Moi Non Plus', a song that Summer also covered in a disco style, produced by Moroder and Bellotte (released as a bonus 12-inch single with the Thank God It's Friday soundtrack on Casablanca).

Love to Love You, Baby was originally just a three-minute single produced by Moroder. The song was recorded in Germany (where Moroder and Summer were based) and released on Moroder's Oasis label, which Bogart had agreed to distribute in the USA. The seven-inch was not a commercial success - Donna Summer was actually relieved thinking it was maybe a little too raunchy. But Neil Bogart got hold of the single and loved it; playing it at a party at his house, his friends begged him to play it over and over again. Consequently he called Moroder and asked him to make it much longer, and the result was an almost 17 minute long disco orgy!

The team (Giorgio, Pete and Donna) was very productive, releasing five albums in the space of three years on Casablanca; A Love Trilogy and Four Seasons of Love were both released in 1976. I Remember Yesterday, released in the summer of 1977, was a concept album with each song representing a musical style from a different decade. For example the title song is a 1920s Charleston. But the huge hit from the album was the song that correctly represented the era of 'The Future' - 'I Feel Love'.

This groundbreaking release was the first disco track to use completely electronic backing, and featured the distinctive 'galloping bassline' (alternating the same note an octave apart), which soon become a standard in disco music. This new, fresh sound was copied immediately with varying results. It is absolutely one of the most important disco songs ever and it definitely helped Casablanca Records and the disco scene to become as huge as it was during the late 1970s and early 1980s.

Around 1977 Neil Bogart also took Casablanca into the movies with Casablanca Filmworks, scoring successes with The Deep (music composed by John Barry), the brilliant Midnight Express (music composed by Giorgio Moroder) and Thank God It's Friday.

The 'Star Wars' album from 1977 was the big break for Casablanca recording artist Meco (Domenico Monardo). The first Star Wars movie hit the silver screen that year and everything related to the movie was hot, especially Meco's disco version of the score.

The 'Star Wars And Other Galactic Funk' album sold platinum and gave Millennium Records (one of Casablanca Records' sub-labels) their first number one hit.

According to Billboard magazine the single 'Star Wars' by Meco is still the biggest selling instrumental single of the last 50 years, reaching platinum status in the United States - an official two million records sold according to the RIAA and another two million sold around the world.

Whilst Casablanca continued to have great commercial success, its near legendary 'disco party' lifestyle, expense account living and hyper marketing budgets meant that it was nearly always in financial difficulty. Or as Frederic Dannen's wrote in his book Hit Men 'If you were cruising along Sunset Boulevard in the late seventies and saw what appeared to be an enormous Mercedes dealership, chances were good that you'd just stumbled upon the parking lot of Casablanca Records.' In 1977 Bogart sold half of his company to Polygram.

In 1979 Neil Bogart helped Ian Schrager and Steve Rubell, the owners of Studio 54, to release the double album 'A Night at Studio 54', packed with classic Casablanca disco tracks; Village People's 'YMCA', Cher's 'Take Me Home', Donna Summer's 'Last Dance' and Patrick Juvet's 'America'.

Unfortunately this project was too little and too late to stop Casablanca's spiraling cash deficit and in 1980 Polygram acquired the remaining 50% of the label, but without Bogart the label soon faded. With the proceeds from the sale Bogart set up Boardwalk Records. Sadly he died just two years later from lung cancer, aged just 39.

CASABLANCA SUB-LABELS:

CHOCOLATE CITY
Founded by former fellow Buddah Records co-worker Cecil Holmes in 1975. Artists included Cameo, Brenda & The Tabulations and Randy Brown.

PARACHUTE
Situated just down the block from Casablanca, founded by Russ Regan in 1977. Artists included Liquid Gold, Morris Jefferson and David Castle.

MILLENNIUM
Founded by Russ Regan in 1976, changed distribution from Casablanca to RCA in 1979 before the Polygram sale, most famous artist Meco.

OASIS
Started by Giorgio Moroder in Munich in early 1970s, before becoming a sub-label of Casablanca in 1975. Artists included Donna Summer and producers Giorgio Moroder and Roberta Kelly who all moved over to Casablanca main label.

There were also short-lived imprints like EARMARC (founded by Marc Paul Simon) and AMERICAN INTERNATIONAL RECORDS (owned by the motion picture company of the same name).

CASABLANCA MAKES MUSIC FOR EVERY BODY
Bodies with Soul
Bodies that Steam your Senses
Bodies that Burn with Sound
Bodies for Sensuous Pleasure
GIORGIO
OCLP 5004
NBLP 7031
OCLP 5006
CCLP 2001
Bodies that Love to Love
Bodies with Built-in Funk
Bodies that Dance
ROBERTA KELLY
PARLIAMENT
Casablanca
Music for Every Body
OCLP 5003
OCLP 5005
NBLP 7022
OASIS
THE CASABLANCA FAMILY OF ARTISTS ARE MORE THAN ANY BODY COULD ASK.
Cecil Holmes' Chocolate City

It's no secret...
CONFESSIONS
by
D.C. LaRUE
Tell it like it is!
Produced by Bob Esty
on Casablanca Record and FilmWorks, Inc.
A Pyramid Recording Co., Inc. Production

A Hot Summer's Knight
GIORGIO
KNIGHTS IN WHITE SATIN
GIORGIO
includes
"I Wanna Funk With You Tonite"
The producer that brought you Donna Summer & Roberta Kelly
Donna Summer Love To Love You Baby OCLP 5003
Donna Summer A Love Trilogy OCLP 5004
Donna Summer Four Seasons Of Love NBLP 7038
Roberta Kelly Trouble Maker OCLP 5005
Giorgio Knights In White Satin OCLP 5006
on Oasis Records and Tapes
OASIS

Adverts

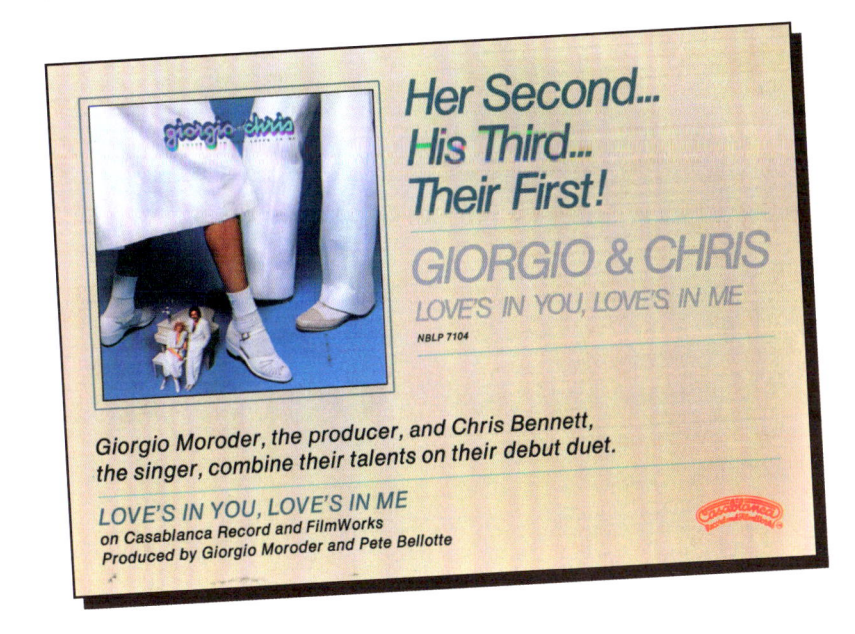

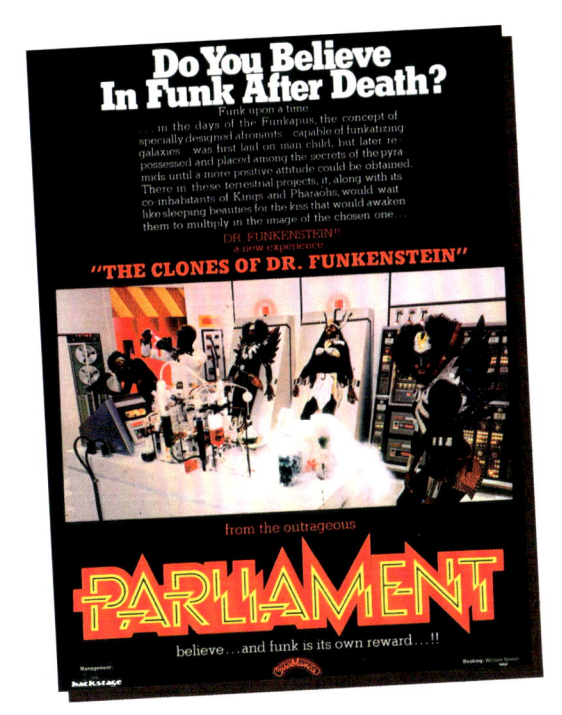

NBLP 000 / 1975

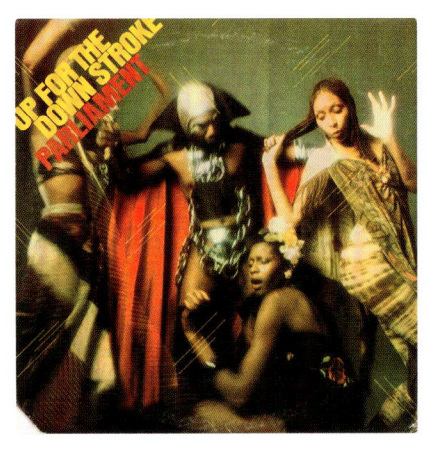

NBLP 7002 / 1974

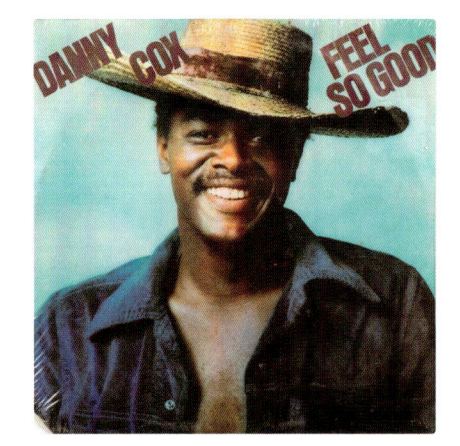

NBLP 7008 / 1974

NBLP 7009 / 1975

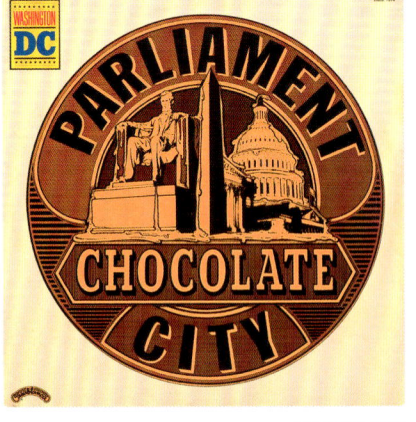

NBLP 7014 / 1975

NBLP 7017 / 1975

NBLP 7019 / 1975

NBLP 7022 / 1975

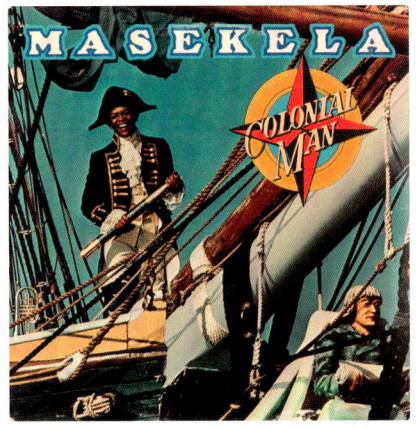

NBLP 7023 / 1976

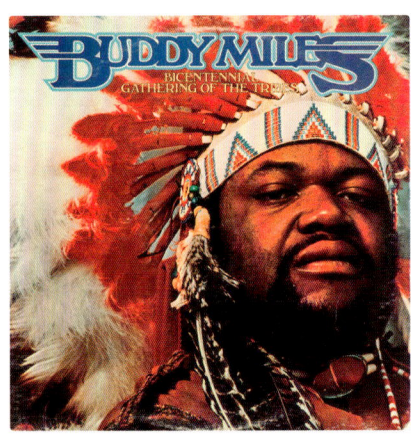

NBLP 7024 / 1976

NBLP 7029 / 1976

NBLP 7030 / 1975

NBLP 7031 / 1976

NBLP 7034 / 1976

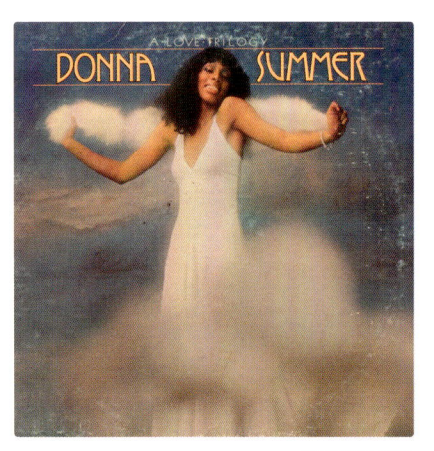

NBLP 7035 / 1976

NBLP 7038 / 1976

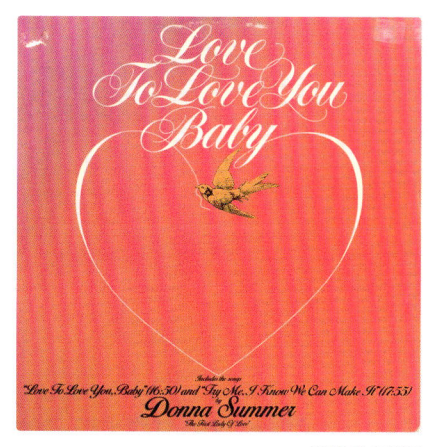

NBLP 7041 / 1976 
NBLP 7042 / 1976 
NBLP 7047 / 1977 
NBLP 7050 / 1977

NBLP 7053 / 1977 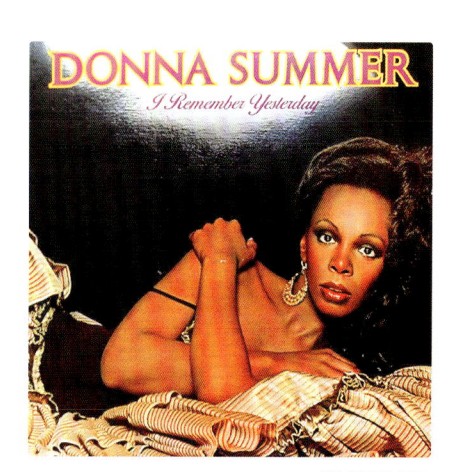
NBLP 7056 / 1977 
NBLP 7058 / 1977 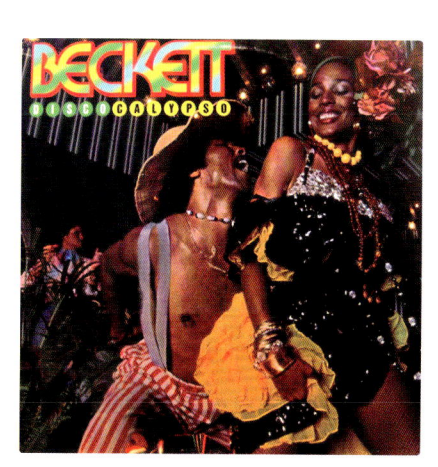
NBLP 7059 / 1977

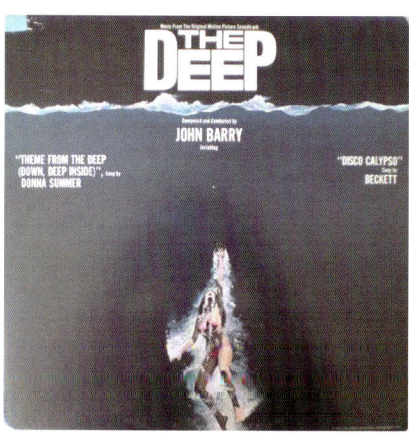

NBLP 7060 / 1977 
NBLP 7061 / 1977 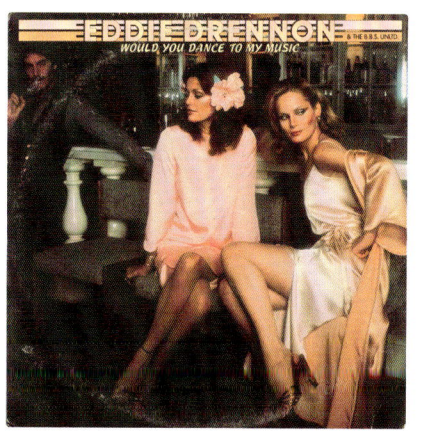
NBLP 7062 / 1977 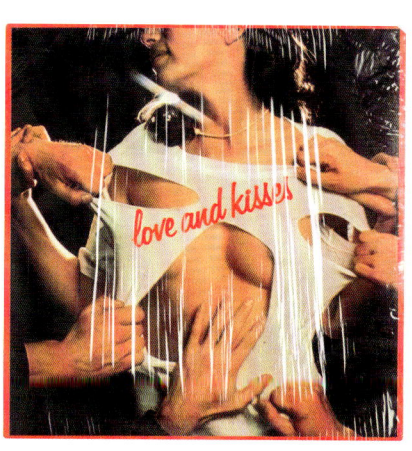
NBLP 7063 / 1977

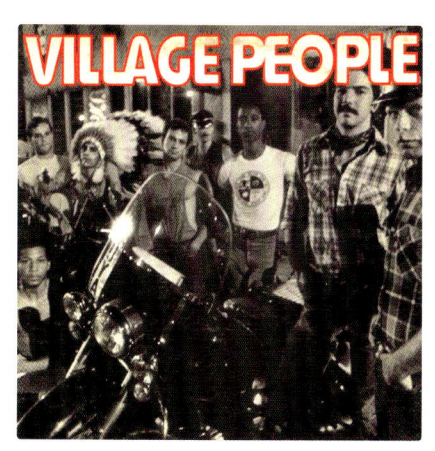

NBLP 7064 / 1977
NBLP 7065 / 1977 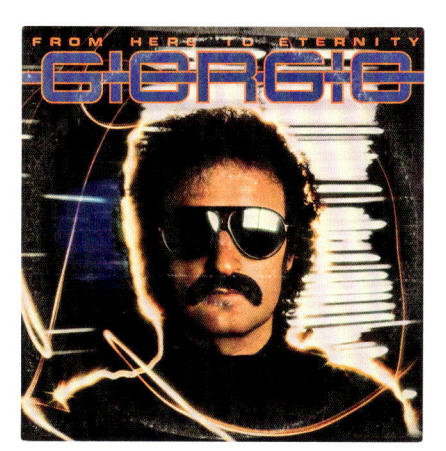
NBLP 7066 / 1977 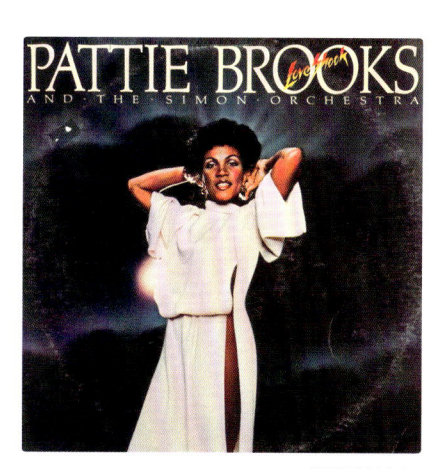
NBLP 7069 / 1977

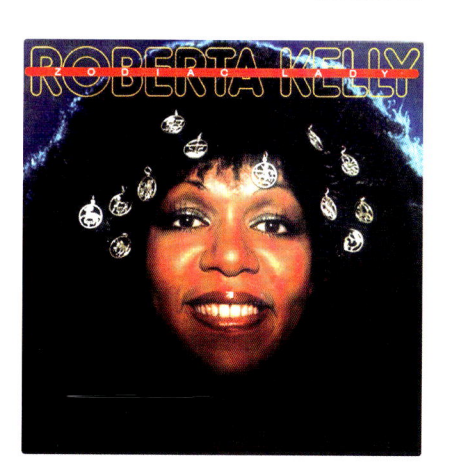

NBLP 7070 / 1977

NBLP 7072 / 1977

NBLP 7075 / 1977

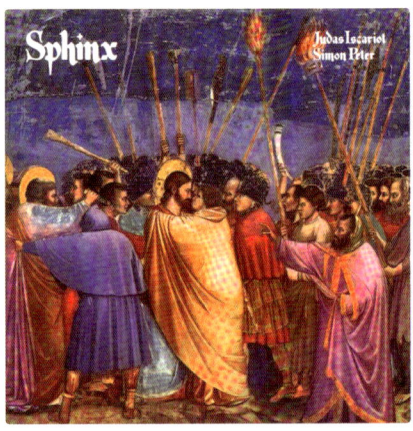

NBLP 7077 / 1977

NBLP 7078 / 1977

NBLP 7079 / 1977

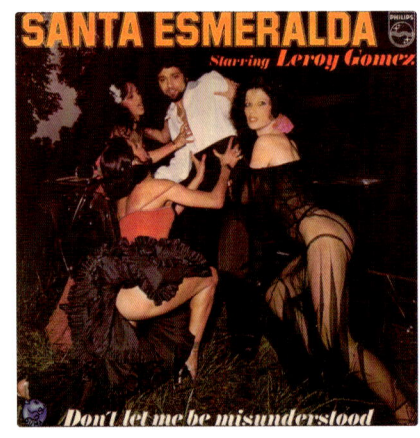

NBLP 7080 / 1977

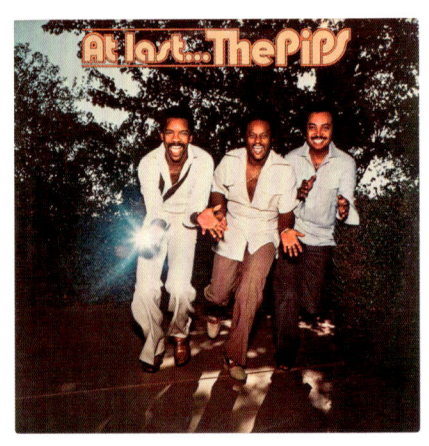

NBLP 7081 / 1977

NBLP 7084 / 1977

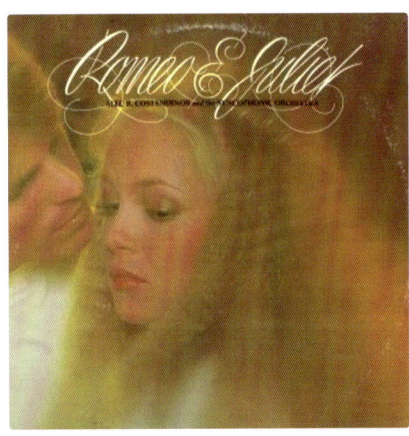

NBLP 7086 / 1978

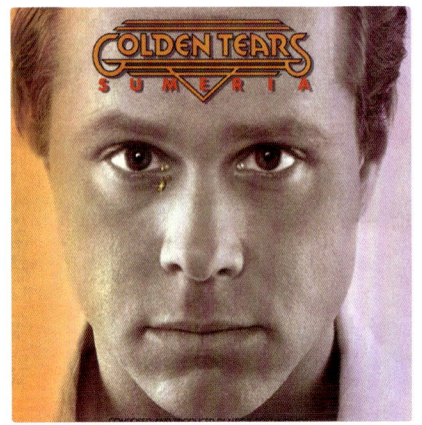

NBLP 7087 / 1978

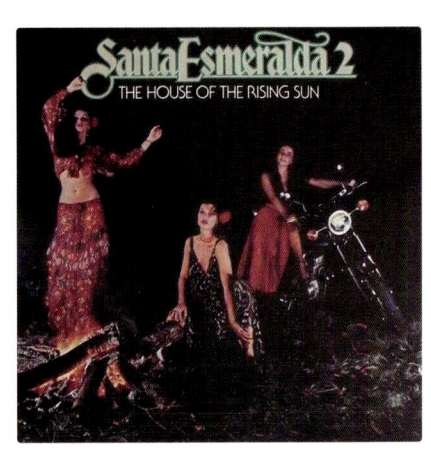

NBLP 7088 / 1978

NBLP 7089 / 1978

NBLP 7090 / 1978

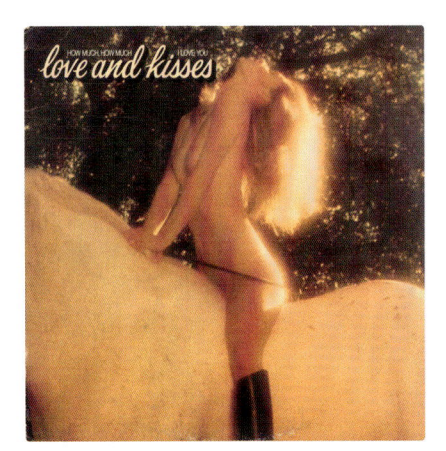

NBLP 7091 / 1978

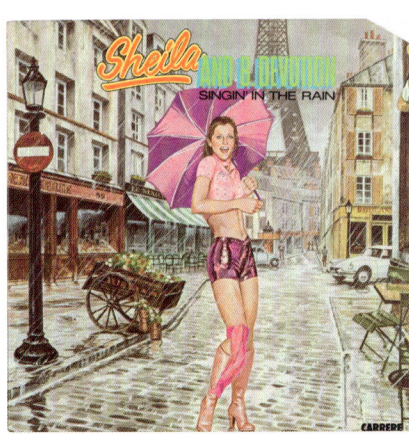

NBLP 7093 / 1978

Lipps Inc.- Pucker Up / Casablanca 1980
Art Direction: Phyllis Chotin / Design: Art Hotel / Illustration: Sketch Bruckner

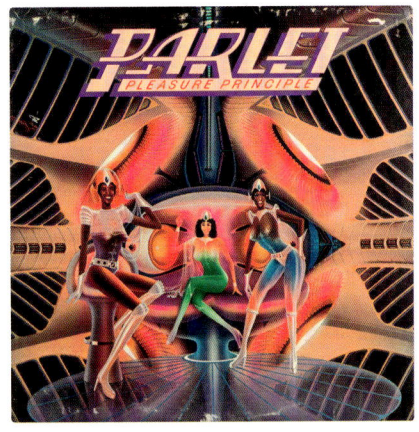

NBLP 7094 / 1978
NBLP 7095 / 1978 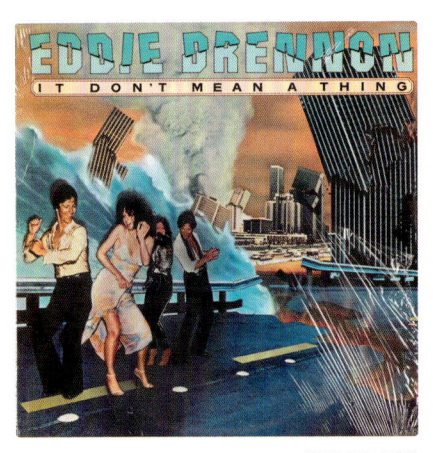
NBLP 7096 / 1978 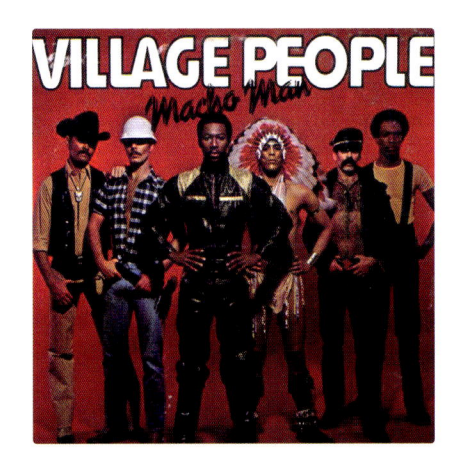
NBLP 7097 / 1977 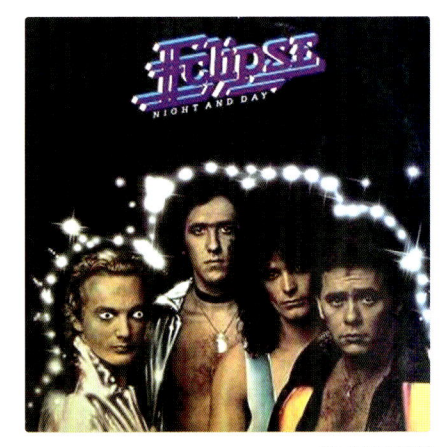
NBLP 7098 / 1978 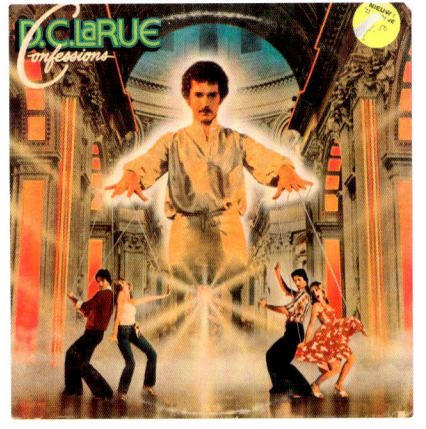
NBLP 7099 / 1978 
NBLP 7101 / 1978 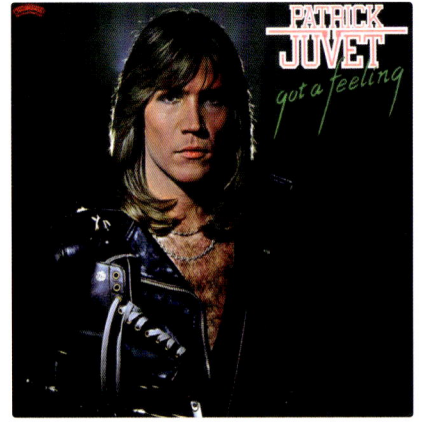
NBLP 7102 / 1978 
NBLP 7103 / 1978 
NBLP 7104 / 1978 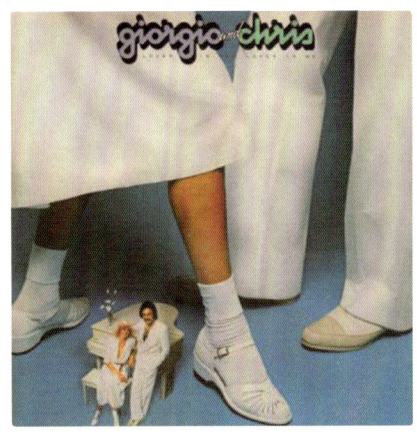
NBLP 7105 / 1978 
NBLP 7106 / 1978 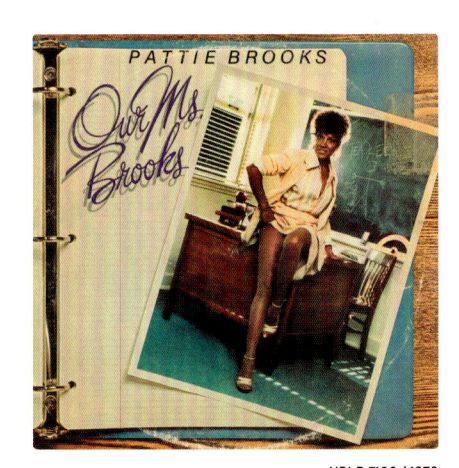
NBLP 7107 / 1978 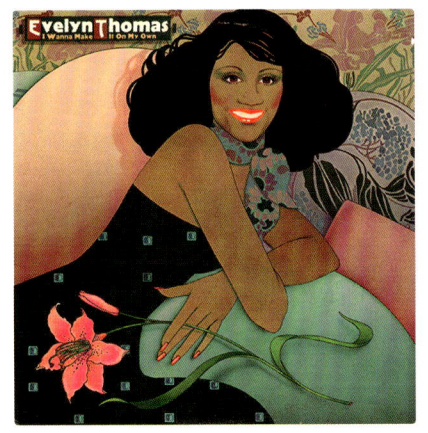
NBLP 7108 / 1978 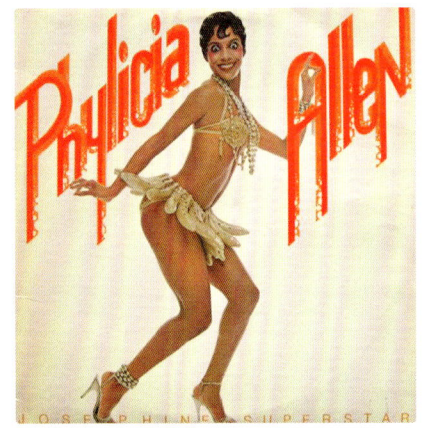
NBLP 7109 / 1978 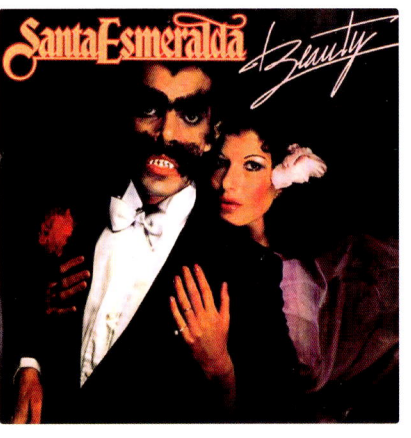
NBLP 7110 / 1978

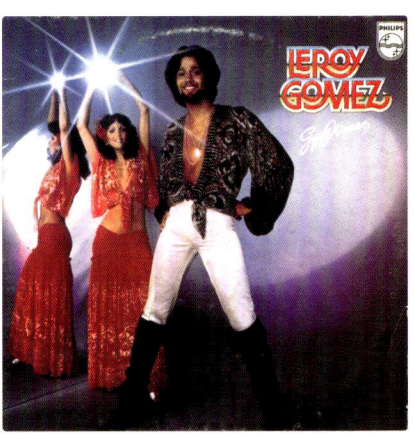

NBLP 7111 / 1978	NBLP 7112 / 1978	NBLP 7113 / 1978	NBLP 7114 / 1978
NBLP 7115 / 1978	NBLP 7116 / 1978	NBLP 7117 / 1978	NBLP 7118 / 1978
NBLP 7119 / 1978	NBLP 7124 / 1978	NBLP 7125 / 1978	NBLP 7125 / 1978
NBLP 7126 / 1978	NBLP 7128 / 1979	NBLP 7129 / 1979	NBLP 7031 / 1979

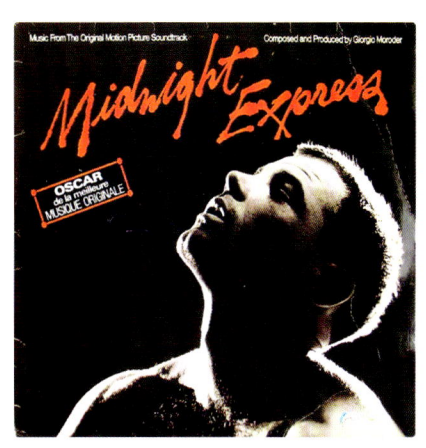

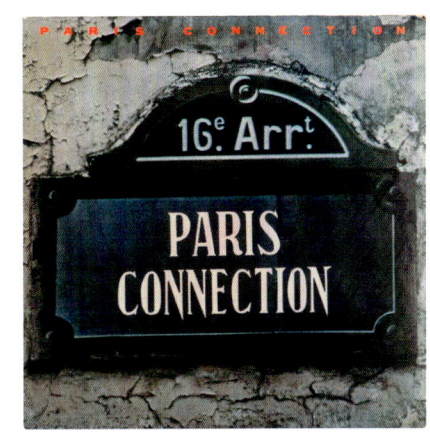

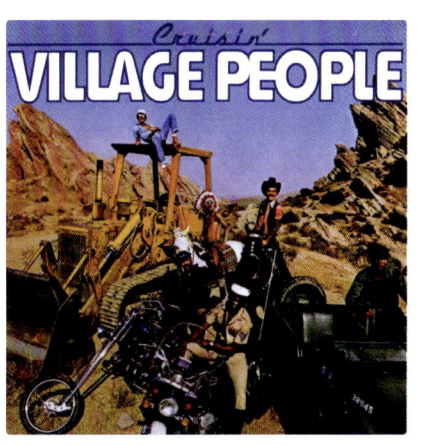

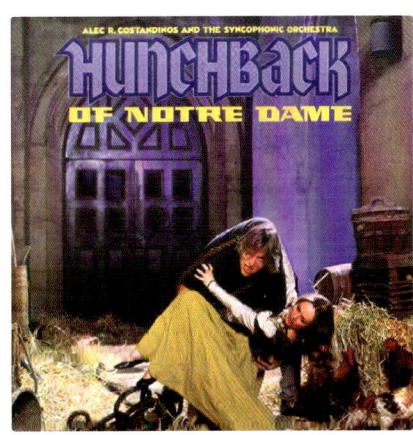

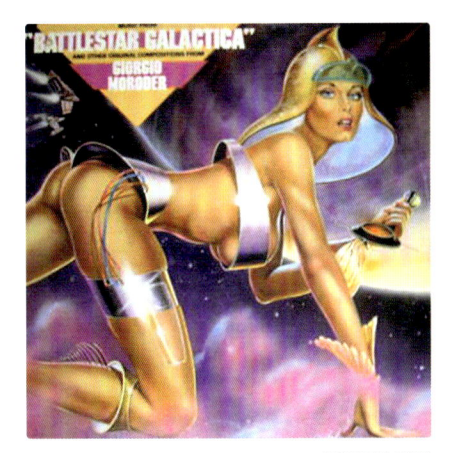

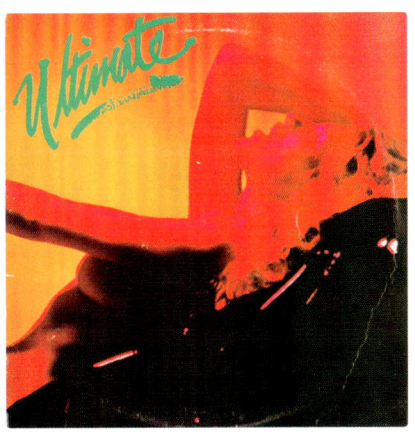

NBLP 7132 / 1979

NBLP 7133 / 1979

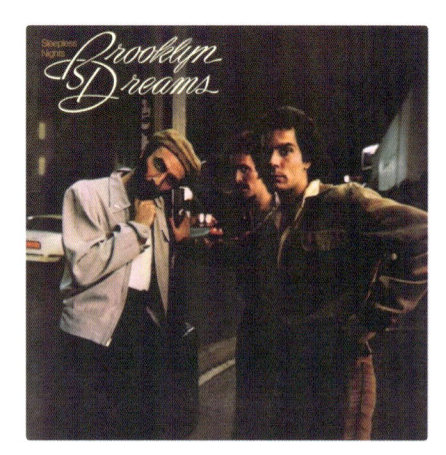

NBLP 7135 / 1979

NBLP 7136 / 1979

NBLP 7137 / 1979

NBLP 7138 / 1979

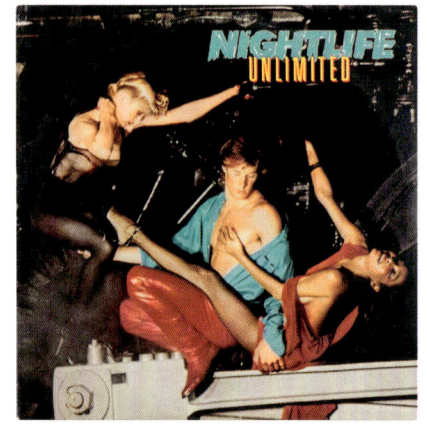

NBLP 7139 / 1979

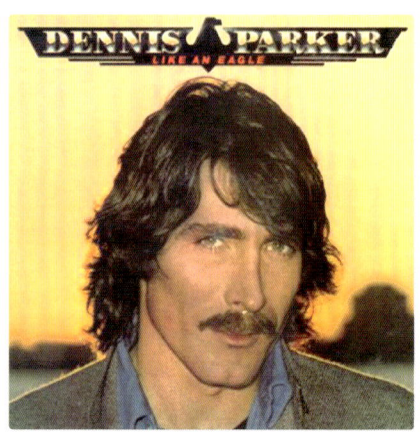

NBLP 7140 / 1979

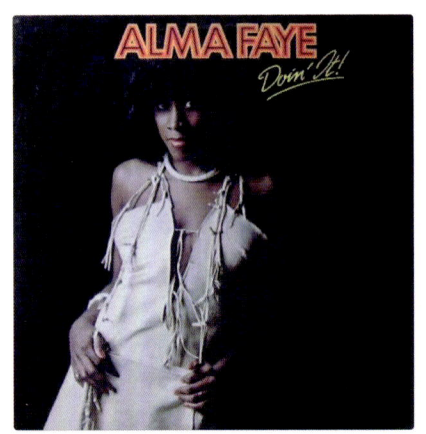

NBLP 7143 / 1979

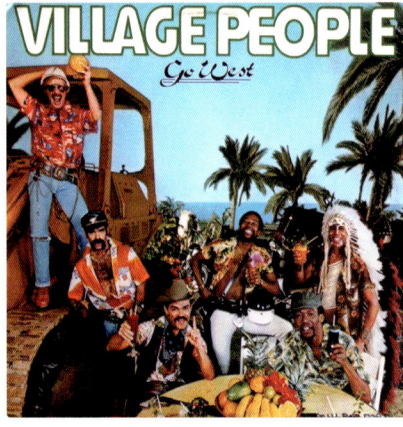

NBLP 7144 / 1979

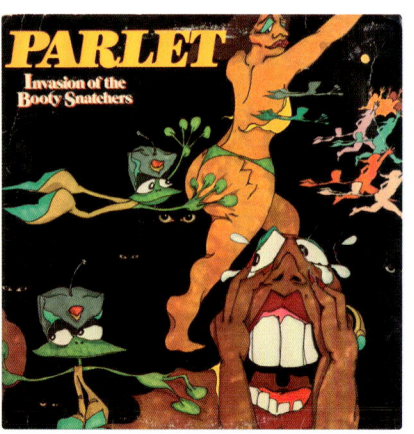

NBLP 7146 / 1979

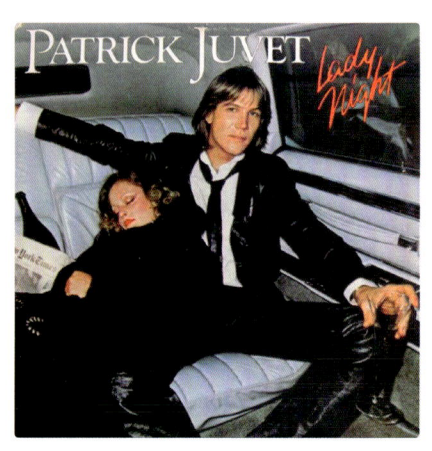

NBLP 7148 / 1979

NBLP 7150 / 1979

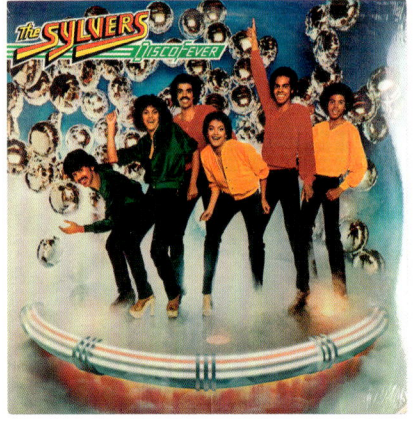

NBLP 7151 / 1979

NBLP 7154 / 1979

NBLP 7155 / 1979

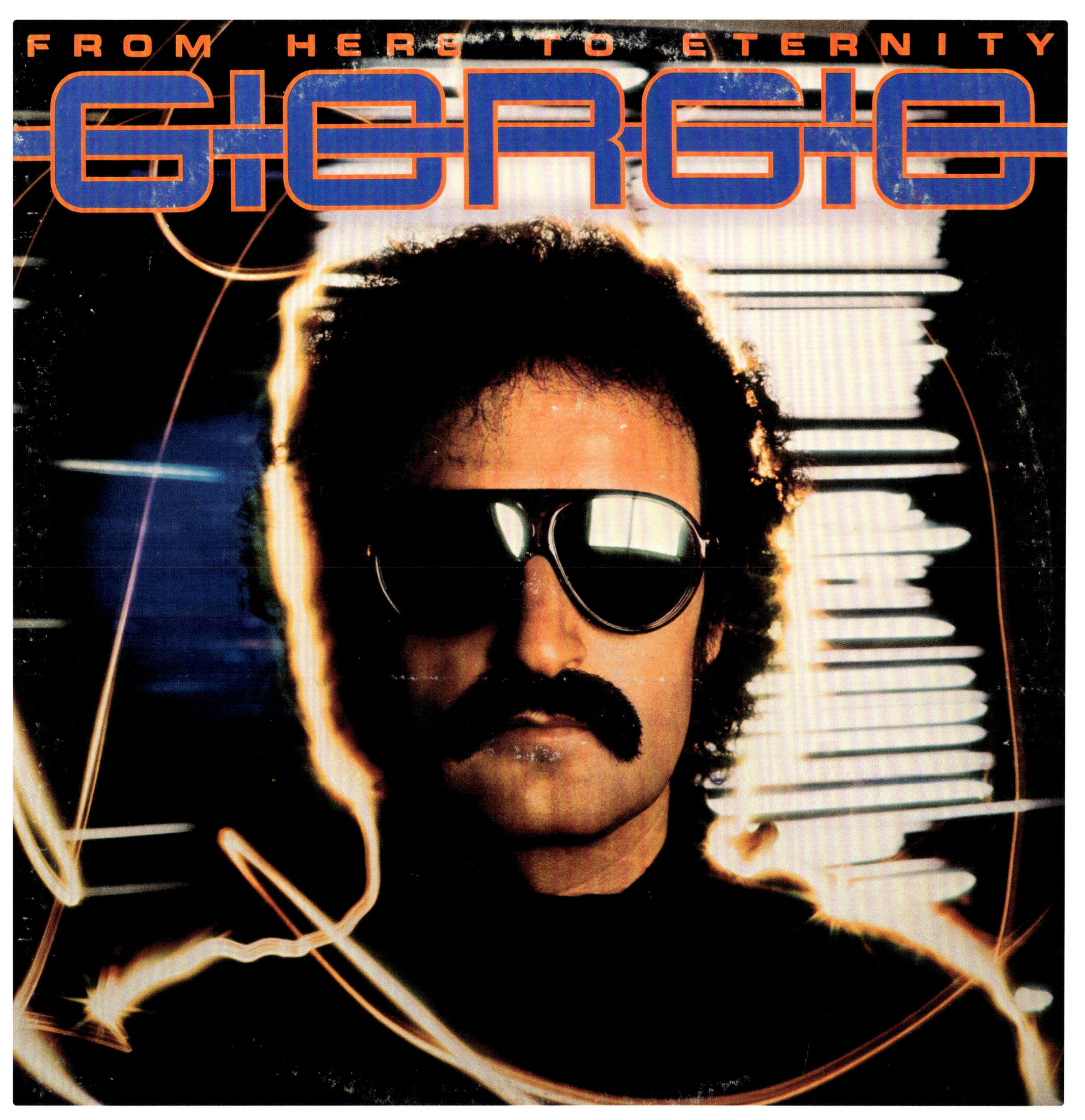

Giorgio-From Here To Eternity / Casablanca 1977
Art Direction: Phyllis Chotin And Henry Vizcarra-Gribbitt / Design: Henry Vizcarra-Gribbitt / Photography: Ronald Slenzak

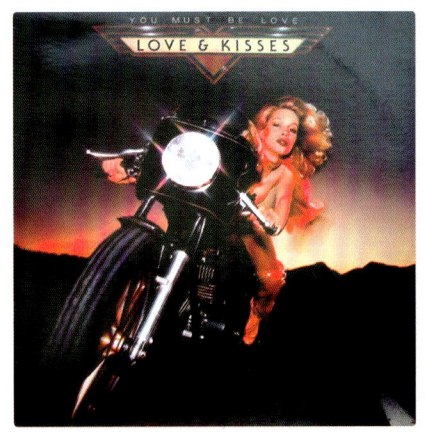

NBLP 7157 / 1979

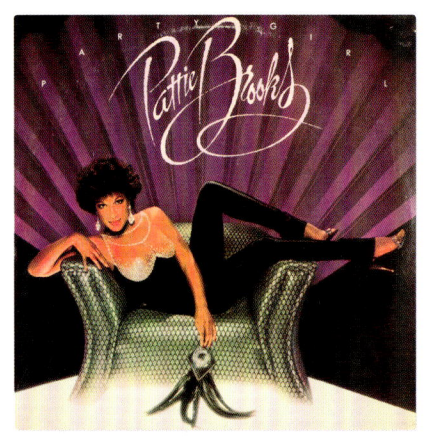

NBLP 7158 / 1979

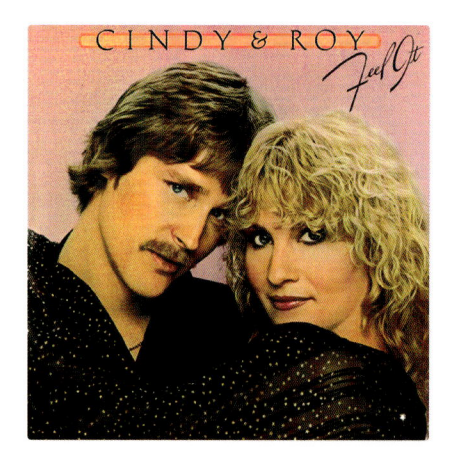

NBLP 7159 / 1979

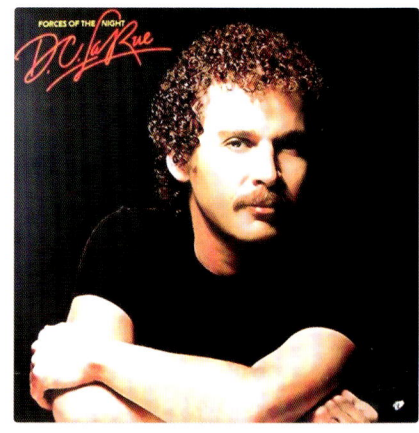

NBLP 7160 / 1979

NBLP 7161 / 1979

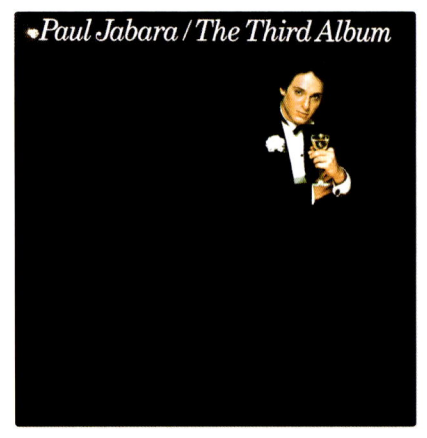

NBLP 7163 / 1979

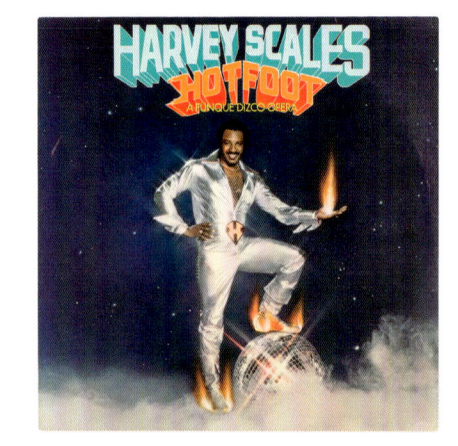

NBLP 7164 / 1979

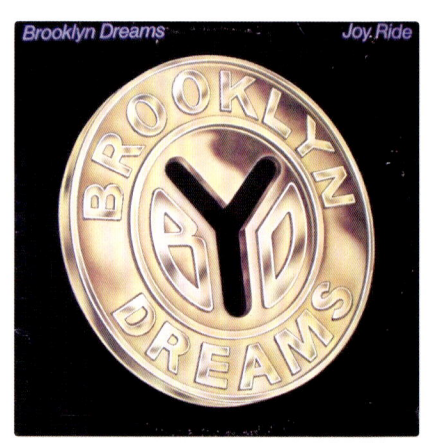

NBLP 7165 / 1979

NBLP 7166 / 1979

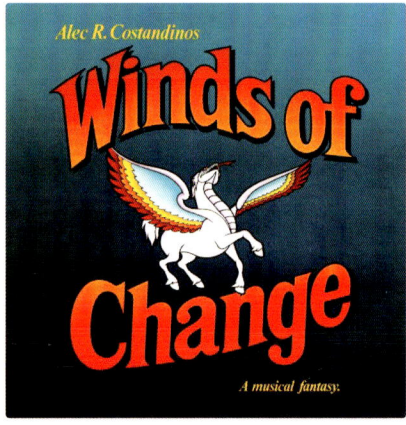

NBLP 7167 / 1979

NBLP 7168 / 1979

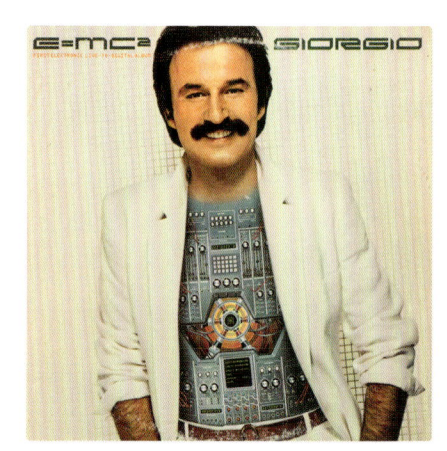

NBLP 7169 / 1979

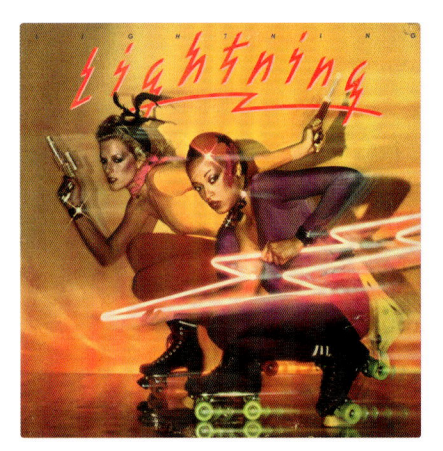

NBLP 7170 / 1979

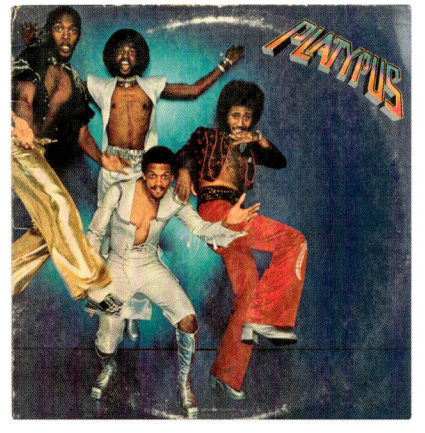

NBLP 7171 / 1979

NBLP 7172 / 1979

NBLP 7175 / 1979

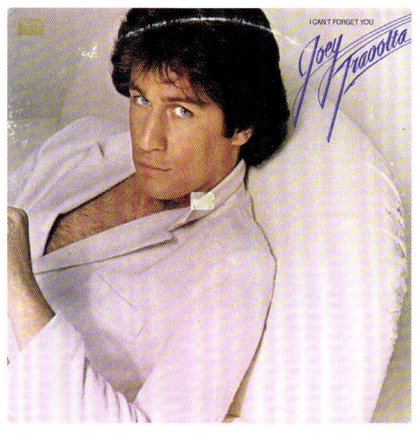

NBLP 7176 / 1979 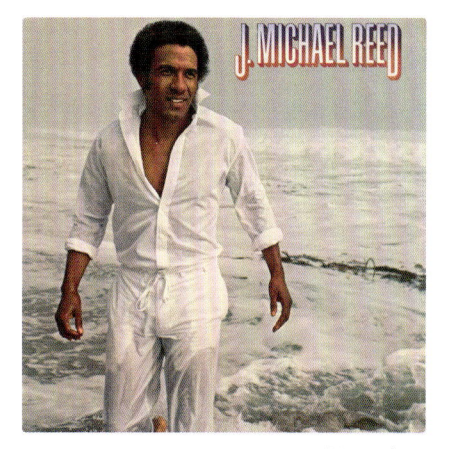
NBLP 7177 / 1979 
NBLP 7178 / 1979 
NBLP 7184 / 1979

NBLP 7187 / 1979 
NBLP 7189 / 1979 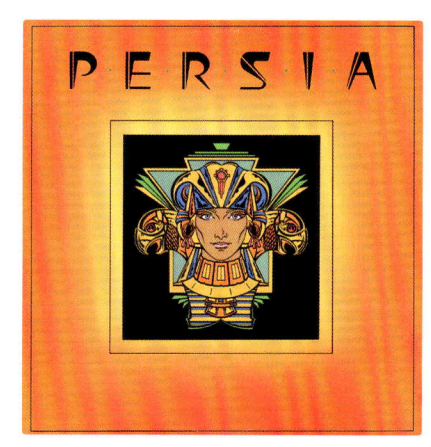
NBLP 7190 / 1979 
NBLP 7191 / 1979

NBLP 7192 / 1979 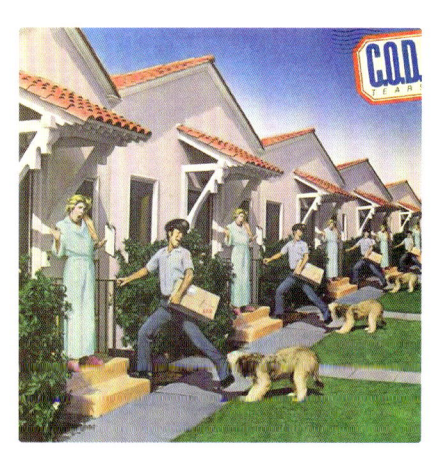
NBLP 7193 / 1979 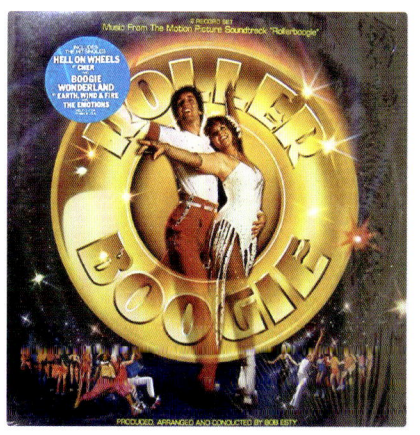
NBLP 7194 / 1979 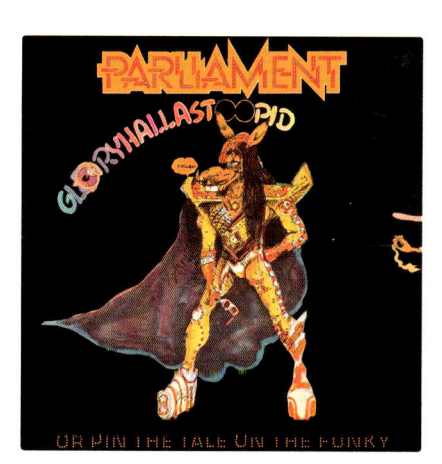
NBLP 7195 / 1979

NBLP 7197 / 1980
NBLP 7201 / 1979 
NBLP 7202 / 1979 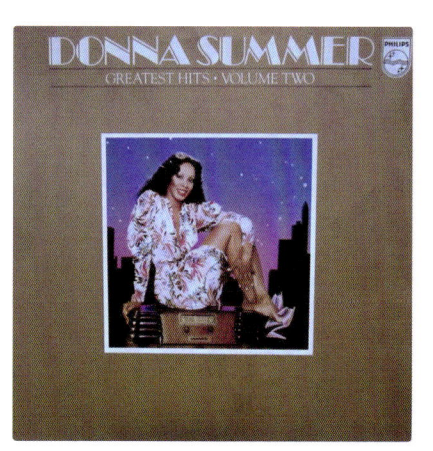
NBLP 7206 / 1980

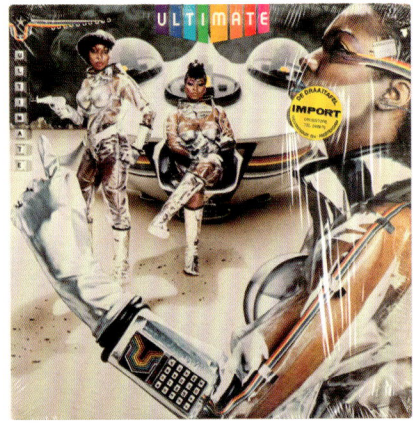

NBLP 7208 / 1980 
NBLP 7210 / 1980 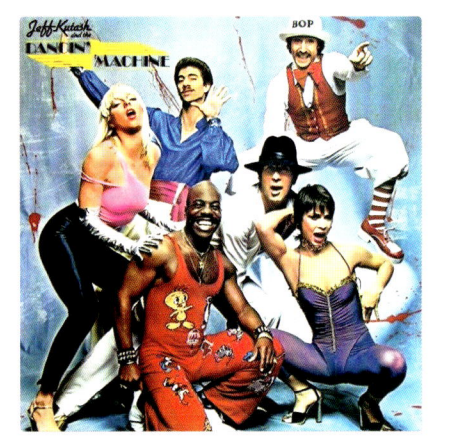
NBLP 7211 / 1980 
NBLP 7215 / 1980

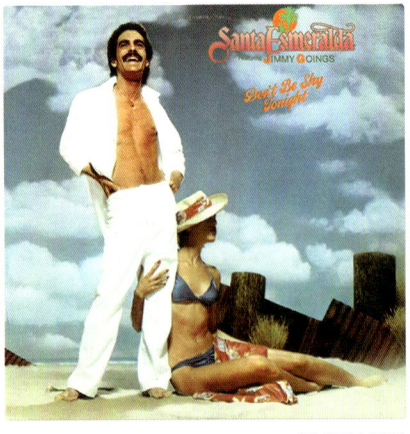

NBLP 7216 / 1980 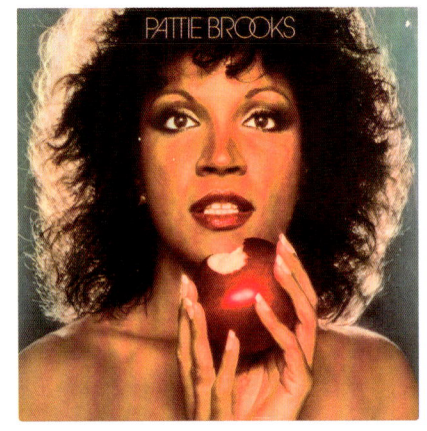
NBLP 7219 / 1980 
NBLP 7220 / 1980 
NBLP 7221 / 1980

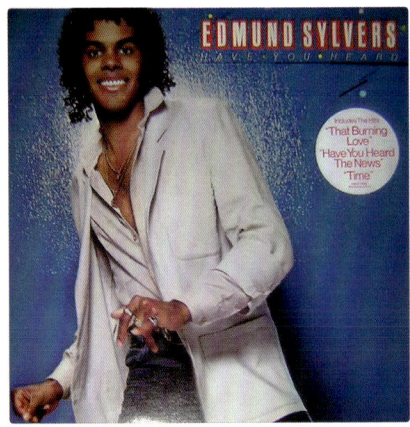

NBLP 7222 / 1980 
NBLP 7223 / 1980 
NBLP 7224 / 1980 
NBLP 7227 / 1980

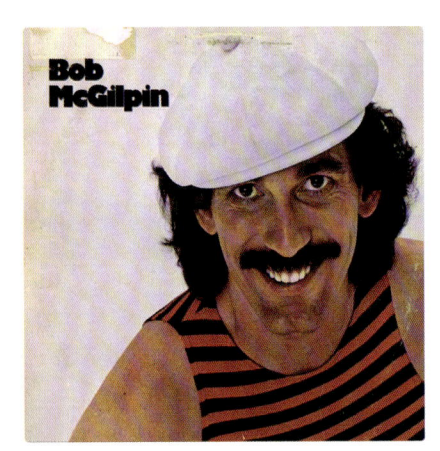

NBLP 7230 / 1980
NBLP 7231 / 1980 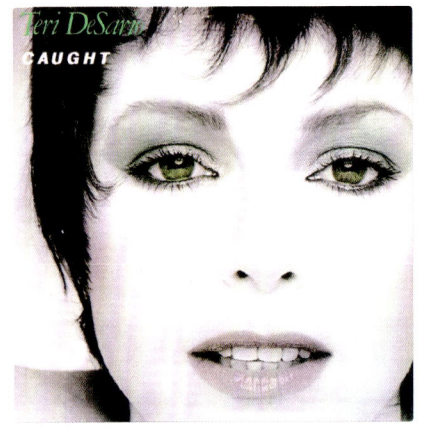
NBLP 7241 / 1980 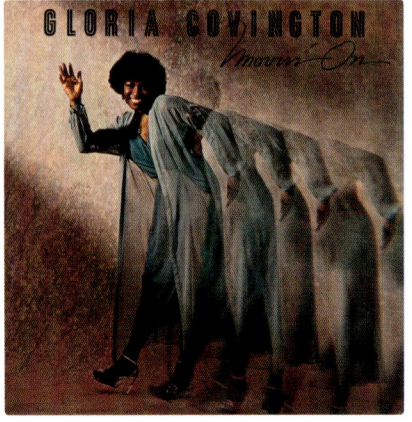
NBLP 7242 / 1980

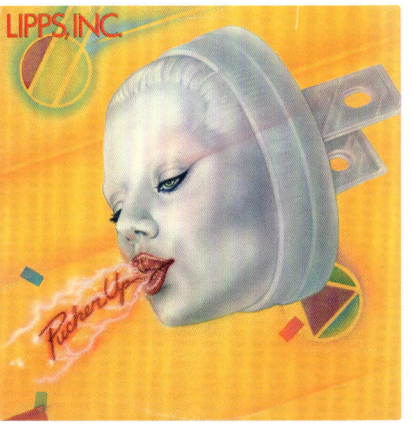

Munich Machine-Body Shine / Casablanca 1979
Design: Henry Vizcarra / Gribbitt / Photography: Gary Bernstein

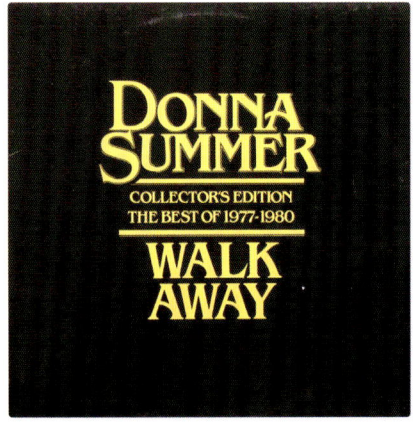

NBLP 7244 / 1980

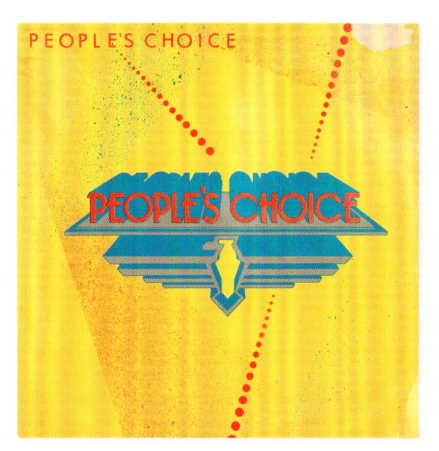

NBLP 7246 / 1980

NBLP 7249 / 1980

NBLP 7256 / 1981

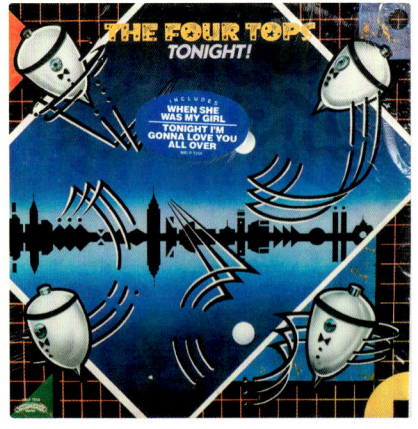

NBLP 7258 / 1981

NBLP 7260 / 1981

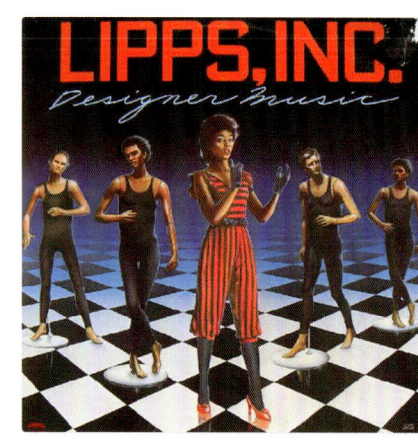

NBLP 7262 / 1981

NBLP 7265 / 1982

NBLP 7266 / 1982

NBLP 7267 / 1982

NBLP 7271 / 1982

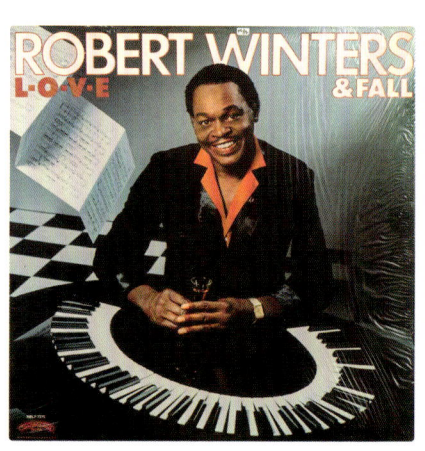

NBLP 7275 / 1982

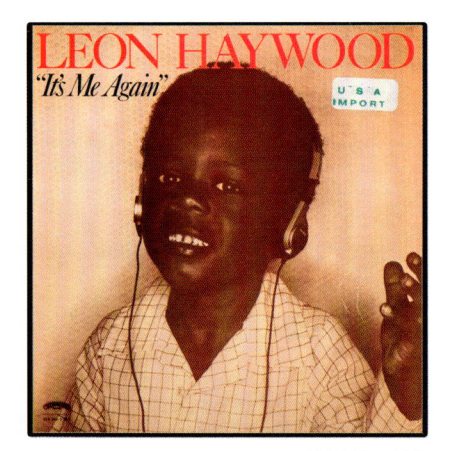

422 810 304-1 / 1983

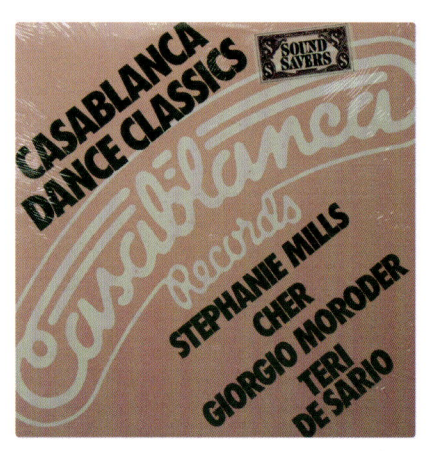

884 053-M-1 / 1985

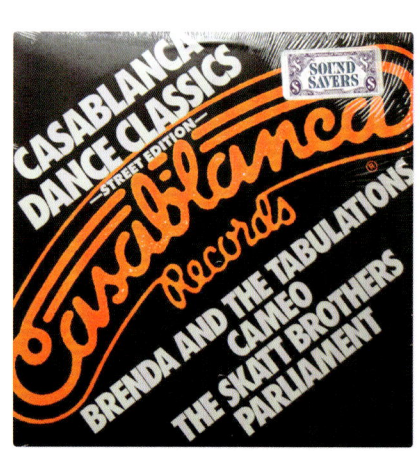

826973-M-1 / 1986

Morris Jefferson-Spank Your Blank Blank / Parachtue 1978
Design: Stephen Lumel / Gribbitt / Photography: Ron Slenzak

Parachute Records

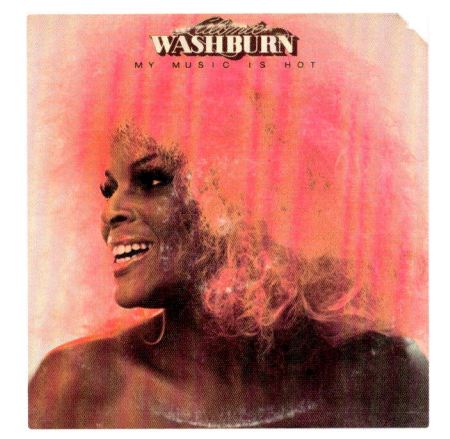

RRLP 9001 / 1977
RRLP 9003 / 1978 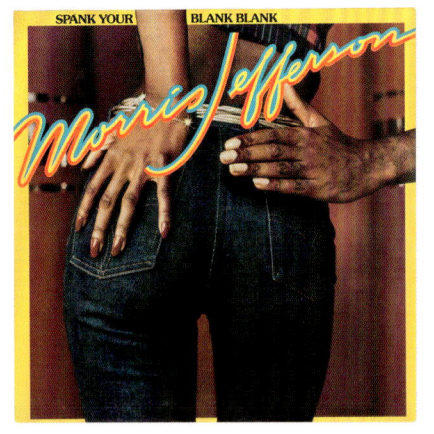
RRLP 9004 / 1978 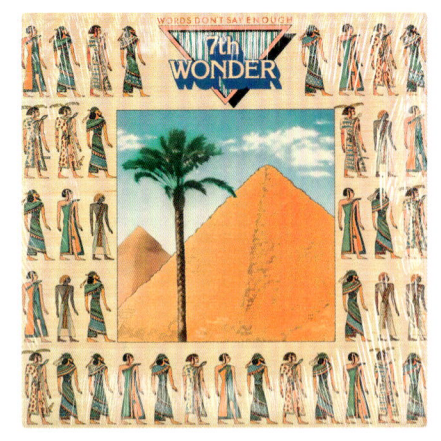
RRLP 9005 / 1978 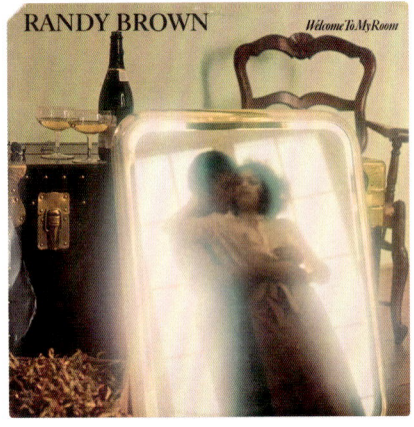
RRLP 9009 / 1978 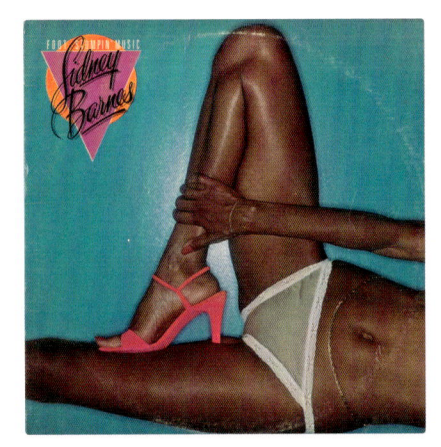
RRLP 9010 / 1979 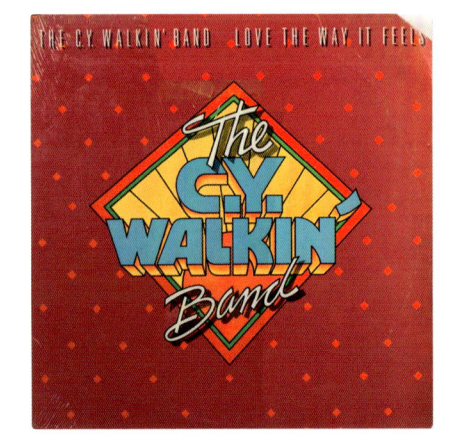
RRLP 9012 / 1979 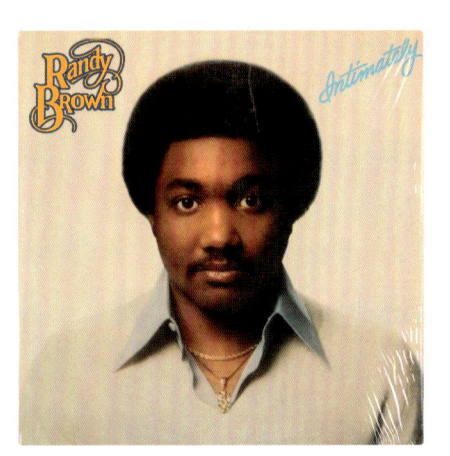
RRLP 9013 / 1979 
RRLP 9014 / 1979 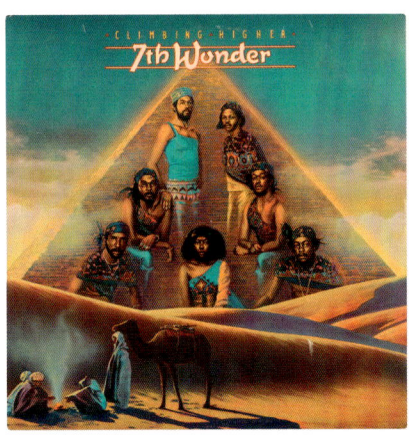
RRLP 9016 / 1979 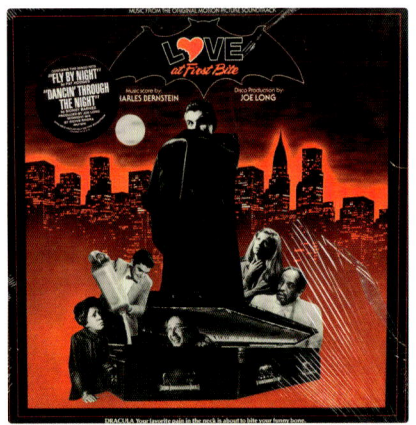
RRLP 9017 / 1979 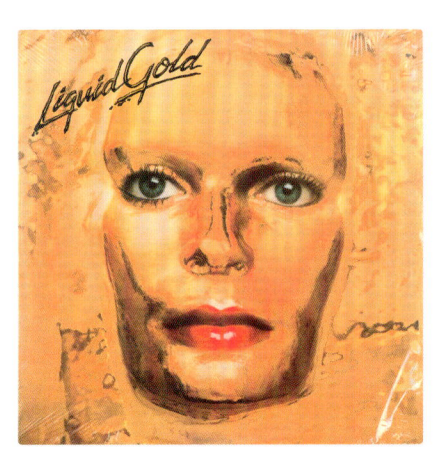

Chocolat City Records

CCLP 2001 / 1976
CCLP 2001 / 1976 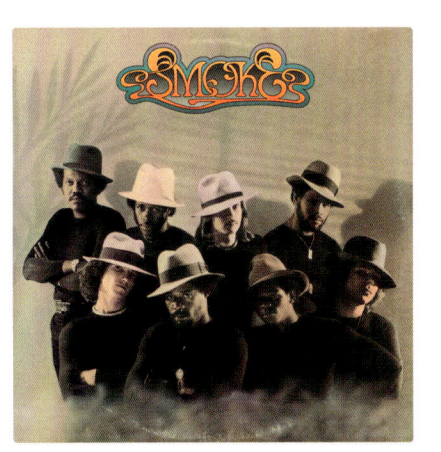
CCLP 2002 / 1977 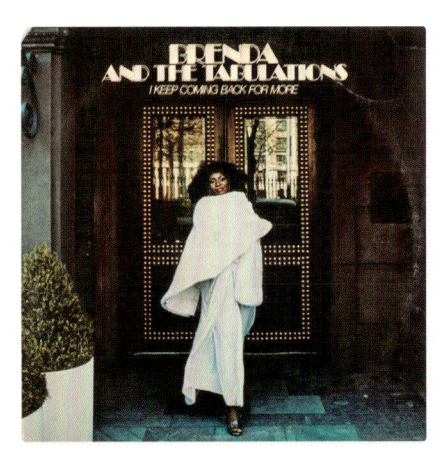

58

Cameo · Secret Omen / Casablanca 1979
Art Direction And Design: Edward Becket, Gribbitt / Illustration: Carl Ramsey

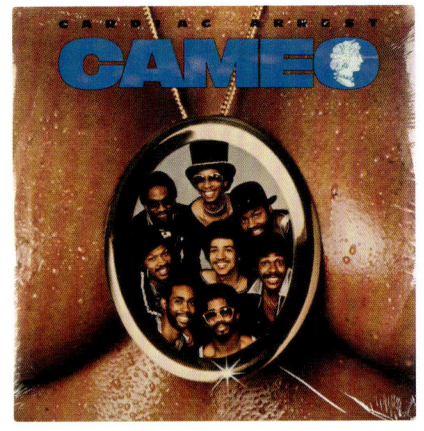

CCLP 2003 / 1977
CCLP 2004 / 1977 
CCLP 2005 / 1978 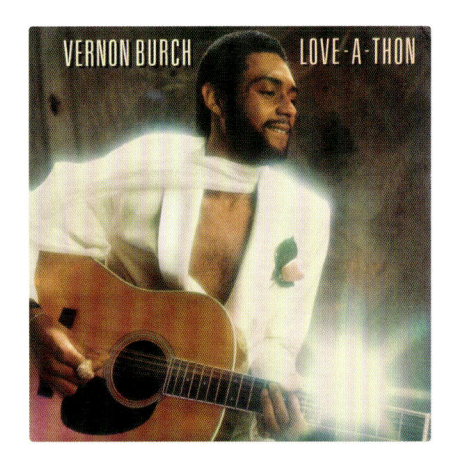
CCLP 2006 / 1978 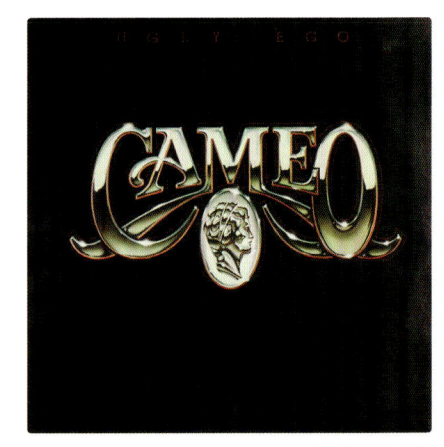
CCLP 2007 / 1979 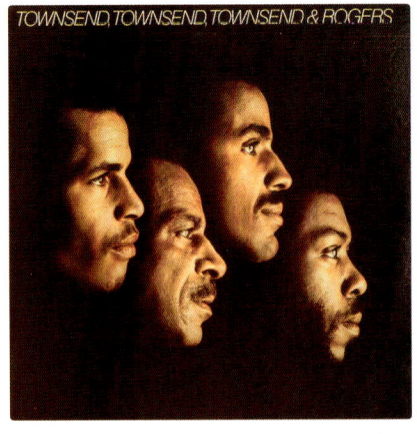
CCLP 2008 / 1979 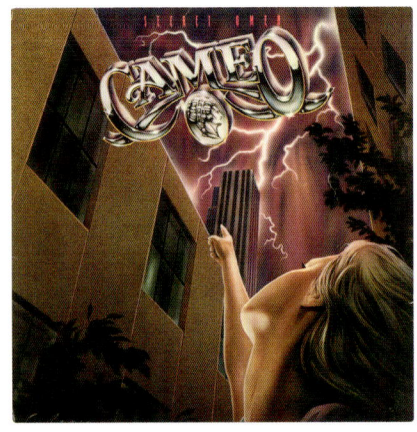
CCLP 2009 / 1979 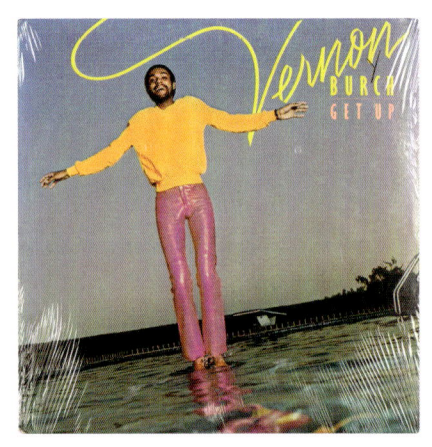
CCLP 2010 / 1980 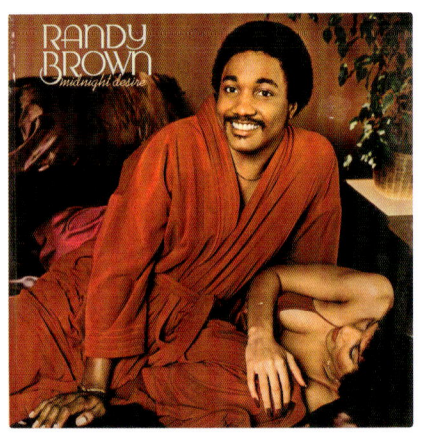
CCLP 2011 / 1980 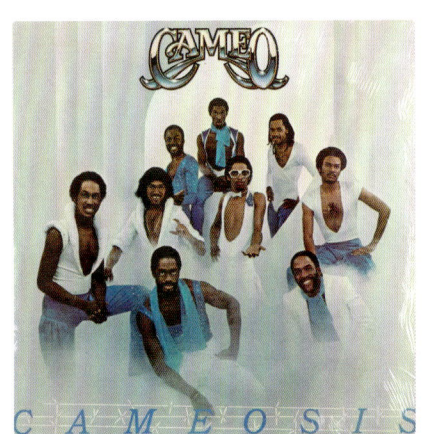
CCLP 2012 / 1980 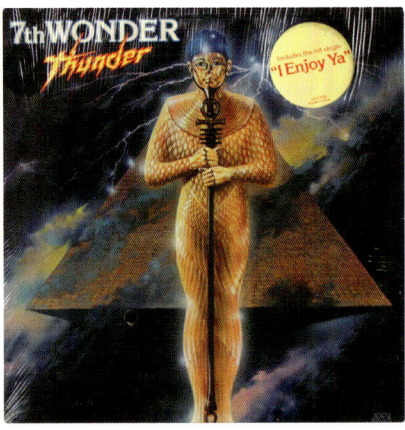
CCLP 2013 / 1980 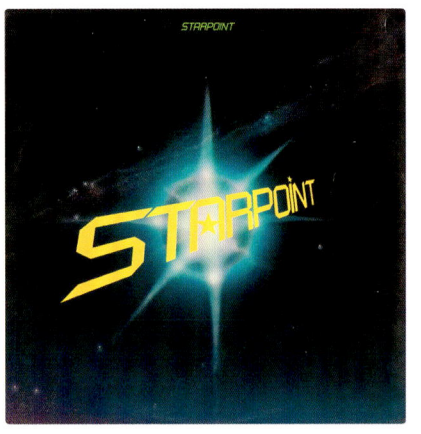
CCLP 2014 / 1980 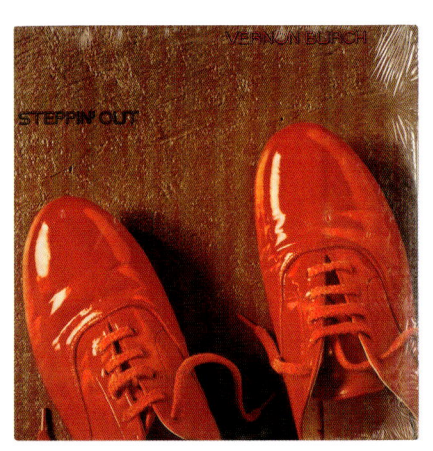
CCLP 2015 / 1980 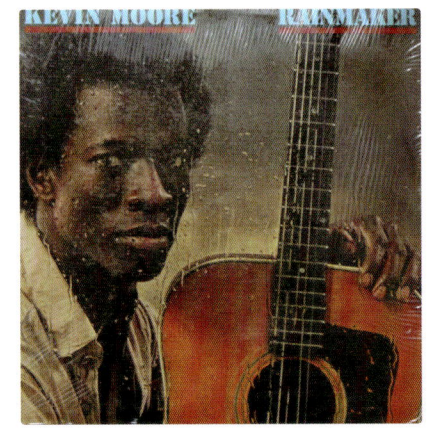
CCLP 2016 / 1980 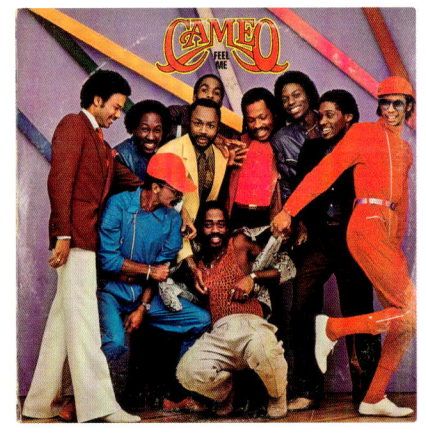
CCLP 2017 / 1981 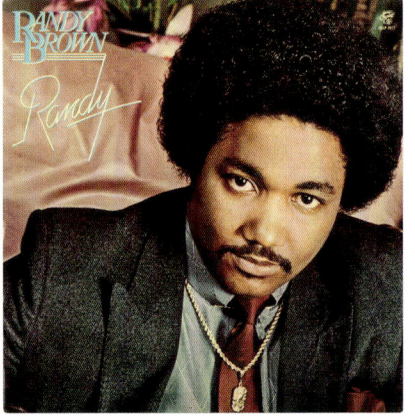
CCLP 2018 / 1981 

60

CCLP 2019 /1981  CCLP 2020 / 1981 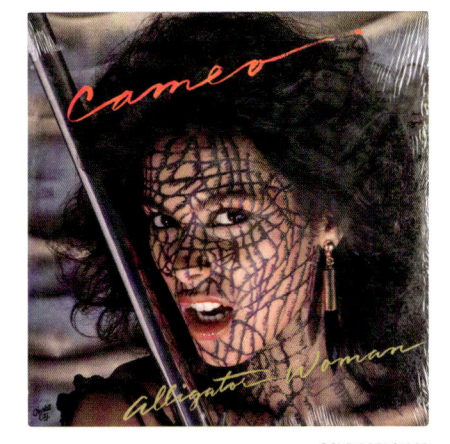 CCLP 2021 / 1982  CCLP 2022 / 1982

Millenium Records

MNLP 8001 / 1977 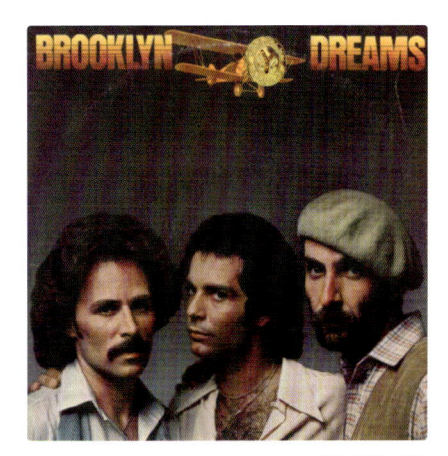 MNLP-8002 / 1977  MNLP 8004 / 1977

MNLP 8006 / 1978  MNLP 8008 / 1978 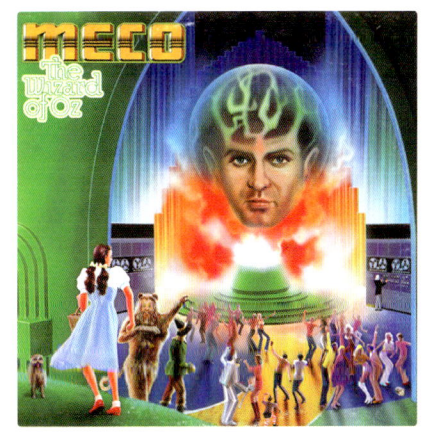 MNLP 8009 / 1979 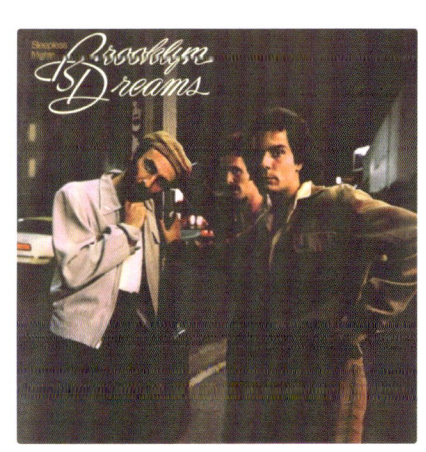 MNLP 8011 / 1979

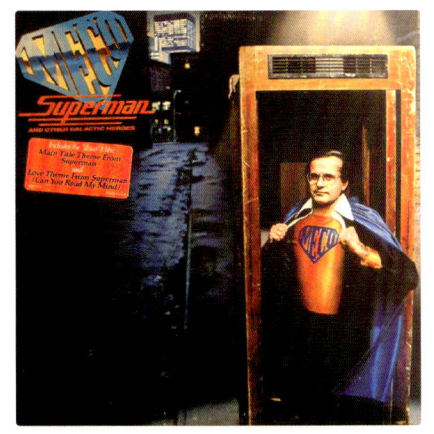

MNLP 8012 / 1979 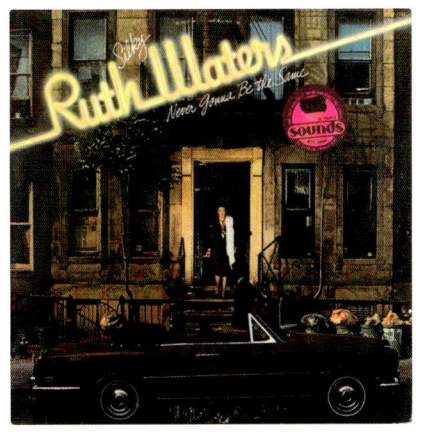 BXL1-7744 / 1979

CASABLANCA

Cat. No.	Artist	Title	Year
NBLP 000	Various	From The Casbah	1975
NBLP 7002	Parliament	Up For The Down Stroke	1975
NBLP 7008	Danny Cox	Feel So Good	1974
NBLP 7009	Greg Perry	One For The Road	1975
NBLP 7011	Bobby & James Purify	You & Me Together Forever	1975
NBLP 7012	Long John Baldry	Good To Be Alive	1975
NBLP 7014	Parliament	Chocolate City	1975
NBLP 7017	Masekela	The Boy's Doin' It	1975
NBLP 7019	Buddy Miles	More Miles Per Gallon	1975
NBLP 7022	Parliament	Mothership Connection	1975
NBLP 7023	Masekela	Colonial Man	1976
NBLP 7024	Buddy Miles	Bicentennial Gathering Of The Tribes	1976
NBLP 7026	Margaret Singana	Where Is The Love	1976
NBLP 7027	Giants	Thanks For The Music	1976
NBLP 7029	Jeannie Reynolds	Cherries, Bananas & Other Fine Things	1976
NBLP 7031	Frankie Crocker's Heart And Soul Orchestra	Presents The Disco Suite Symphony No. 1 In Rhythm And Excellence	1976
NBLP 7033	The Group With No Name	Moon Over Brooklyn	1976
NBLP 7034	Parliament	The Clones Of Dr. Funkenstein	1976
NBLP 7035	Donna Summer	A Love Trilogy	1976
NBLP 7036	Masekela	Melody Maker	1976
NBLP 7038	Donna Summer	Four Seasons Of Love	1976
NBLP 7041	Donna Summer	Love To Love You Baby	1976
NBLP 7042	Various	Get Down And Boogie	1976
NBLP 7047	Various	Wildflowers 3: The NY Loft Jazz Sessions	1977
NBLP 7050	Frankie Crocker & The Heart And Soul Orchestra	Frankie Crocker & The Heart And Soul Orchestra	1977
NBLP 7053	Parliament	Parliament Live - P.Funk Earth Tour	1977
NBLP 7054	Jimmy James & The Vagabonds	Life	1977
NBLP 7055	Paul Jabara	Shut Out	1977
NBLP 7056	Donna Summer	I Remember Yesterday	1977
NBLP 7058	Munich Machine	Munich Machine	1977
NBLP 7059	Beckett	Disco Calypso	1977
NBLP 7060	John Barry	The Deep (Music From The Original Motion Picture Soundtrack)	1977
NBLP 7061	Larry Santos	Don't Let The Music Stop	1977
NBLP 7062	Eddie Drennon & The B.B.S. Unlimited	Would You Dance To My Music	1977
NBLP 7063	Love And Kisses	Love And Kisses	1977
NBLP 7064	Village People	Village People	1977
NBLP 7065	Giorgio	From Here To Eternity	1977
NBLP 7066	The Pattie Brooks & Simon Orchestra	Love Shook	1977
NBLP 7069	Roberta Kelly	Zodiac Lady	1977
NBLP 7070	Arthur Wayne	Another Island	1977
NBLP 7071	Dave Grusin	Bobby Deerfield: Music From The Original Motion Picture Soundtrack	1977
NBLP 7072	Rare Gems Odyssey	Rare Gems Odyssey	1977
NBLP 7075	Jeannie Reynolds	One Wish	1977
NBLP 7077	Sphinx	Sphinx	1977
NBLP 7078	Donna Summer	Once Upon A Time...	1977
NBLP 7079	Masekela	You Told Your Mama Not To Worry	1977
NBLP 7080	Santa Esmeralda	Don't Let Me Be Misunderstood	1977
NBLP 7081	Pips, The	At Last...	1977
NBLP 7082	Margaret Singana	Tribal Fence	1977
NBLP 7084	Parliament	Funkentelechy Vs. The Placebo Syndrome	1977
NBLP 7086	The Alec R. Costandinos & Syncophonic Orchestra	Romeo & Juliet	1978
NBLP 7087	Sumeria	Golden Tears	1978
NBLP 7088	Santa Esmeralda 2	The House Of The Rising Sun	1978
NBLP 7089	Roberta Kelly	Gettin' The Spirit	1978
NBLP 7090	Munich Machine	A Whiter Shade Of Pale	1978
NBLP 7091	Love And Kisses	How Much, How Much I Love You	1978
NBLP 7093	Sheila & B. Devotion	Singin' In The Rain	1978
NBLP 7094	Parlet	Pleasure Principle	1978
NBLP 7095	Eddie Drennon	It Don't Mean A Thing	1978
NBLP 7096	Village People	Macho Man	1978
NBLP 7097	Eclipse	Night And Day	1977
NBLP 7098	D.C. LaRue	Confessions	1978
NBLP 7099	Various	Thank God It's Friday (The Original Motion Picture Soundtrack)	1978
NBLP 7101	Patrick Juvet	Got A Feeling	1978
NBLP 7102	Paul Jabara	Keeping Time	1978
NBLP 7103	The Sylvers	Forever Yours	1978
NBLP 7104	Giorgio And Chris	Love's In You, Love's In Me	1978

Matrix numbers

NBLP 7105	Harvey Scales	Confidential Affair	1978
NBLP 7106	Pattie Brooks	Our Ms. Brooks	1978
NBLP 7107	Evelyn Thomas	I Wanna Make It On My Own	1978
NBLP 7108	Phylicia Allen	Josephine Superstar	1978
NBLP 7109	Santa Esmeralda	Beauty	1978
NBLP 7110	Leroy Gomez	Gypsy Woman	1978
NBLP 7111	Space	Deliverance	1978
NBLP 7112	Wright Brothers Flying Machine	Wright Brothers Flying Machine	1978
NBLP 7113	The Pips	Callin'	1978
NBLP 7114	Giorgio Moroder	Midnight Express - Music From The Original Motion Picture Soundtrack	1978
NBLP 7115	Teri De Sario	Pleasure Train	1978
NBLP 7116	Paris Connection	Paris Connection	1978
NBLP 7117	Alec R. Costandinos	Trocadero Lemon Blue	1978
NBLP 7118	Village People	Crusin'	1978
NBLP 7119	Donna Summer	Live And More	1978
NBLP 7124	The Alec R. Costandinos And Syncophonic Orchestra	The Hunchback Of Notre Dame	1978
NBLP 7125	Parliament	Motor Booty Affair	1978
NBLP 7126	Giorgio Moroder	Music From "Battlestar Galactica" And Other Original Compositions	1978
NBLP 7128	Ultimate	Ultimate	1979
NBLP 7129	C.D. Band	HooDoo VooDoo	1979
NBLP 7131	Space	Just Blue	1979
NBLP 7132	Meadowlark Lemon	My Kids	1979
NBLP 7133	Cher	Take Me Home	1979
NBLP 7135	Brooklyn Dreams	Sleepless Nights	1979
NBLP 7136	Meco	Superman And Other Galactic Heroes	1979
NBLP 7137	Munich Machine	Body Shine	1979
NBLP 7138	Bad News Travels Fast	Look Out	1979
NBLP 7139	Nightlife Unlimited	Nightlife Unlimited	1979
NBLP 7140	Dennis Parker	Like An Eagle	1979
NBLP 7143	Alma Faye	Doin' It	1979
NBLP 7144	Village People	Go West	1979
NBLP 7146	Parlet	Invasion Of The Booty Snatchers	1979
NBLP 7148	Patrick Juvet	Lady Night	1979
NBLP 7150	Donna Summer	Bad Girls	1979
NBLP 7151	Sylvers, The	Disco Fever	1979
NBLP 7153	Tony Orlando	I Got Rhythm	1979
NBLP 7154	Leroy Gomez	I Got It Bad	1979
NBLP 7155	Meco	Moondancer	1979
NBLP 7157	Love & Kisses	You Must Be Love	1979
NBLP 7158	Pattie Brooks	Party Girl	1979
NBLP 7159	Cindy & Roy	Feel It	1979
NBLP 7160	D.C. LaRue	Forces Of The Night	1979
NBLP 7161	Various	A Night At Studio 54	1979
NBLP 7163	Paul Jabara	The Third Album	1979
NBLP 7164	Harvey Scales	Hot Foot (A Funque Dizco Opera)	1979
NBLP 7165	Brooklyn Dreams	Joy Ride	1979
NBLP 7166	The Ritchie Family	Bad Reputation	1979
NBLP 7167	Alec R. Costandinos	Winds Of Change - A Musical Fantasy - Music From The Original Motion Picture Soundtrack	1979
NBLP 7168	Joel Diamond Experience	Joel Diamond Experience	1979
NBLP 7169	Giorgio	$E=MC^2$	1979
NBLP 7170	Lightning	Lightning	1979
NBLP 7171	Platypus	Platypus	1979
NBLP 7172	T.J.M.	TJM	1979
NBLP 7175	Santa Esmeralda	Another Cha-Cha	1979
NBLP 7176	Joey Travolta	I Can't Forget You	1979
NBLP 7177	J. Michael Reed	J. Michael Reed	1979
NBLP 7178	Teri DeSario	Moonlight Madness	1979
NBLP 7179	Kenny Nolan	Night Miracles	1979
NBLP 7180	Four On The Floor	Four On The Floor	1979
NBLP 7181	Bad News Travels Fast	Ordinary Man	1979
NBLP 7182	The Alec R. Costandinos & Synchophonic Orchestra	Untitled	1979
NBLP 7183	Village People	Live And Sleazy	1979
NBLP 7184	Cher	Prisoner	1979
NBLP 7187	Tony Rallo & The Midnite Band	Burnin' Alive	1979
NBLP 7189	Loose Change	Loose Change	1979
NBLP 7190	Persia	Persia	1979

NBLP 7191	Donna Summer	On The Radio: Greatest Hits Vol. 1 & 2	1979
NBLP 7192	Skatt Bros.	Strange Spirits	1979
NBLP 7193	C.O.D.	Tears	1979
NBLP 7194	Various	Music From The Motion Picture Soundtrack "Roller Boogie"	1979
NBLP 7195	Parliament	GloryHallaStoopid (Pin The Tale On The Funky)	1979
NBLP 7197	Lipps, Inc.	Mouth To Mouth	1980
NBLP 7198	Various	All That Jazz - Music From The Original Motion Picture Soundtrack	1979
NBLP 7201	Donna Summer	Greatest Hits - Volume One	1979
NBLP 7202	Donna Summer	Greatest Hits - Volume Two	1979
NBLP 7206	Various	Foxes (Original Soundtrack)	1980
NBLP 7210	Danielle	Danielle	1980
NBLP 7211	The Jeff Kutash And Dancin' Machine	Jeff Kutash And The Dancin' Machine	1980
NBLP 7215	John & Arthur Simms	John & Arthur Simms	1980
NBLP 7216	Santa Esmeralda	Don't Be Shy Tonight	1980
NBLP 7218	Various	The Original Soundtrack Album / The Hollywood Knights	1980
NBLP 7219	Pattie Brooks	Pattie Brooks	1980
NBLP 7220	Village People	Can't Stop The Music / The Original Soundtrack Album	1980
NBLP 7221	Platypus	Cherry	1980
NBLP 7222	Edmund Sylvers	Have You Heard	1980
NBLP 7223	The Ritchie Family	Give Me A Break	1980
NBLP 7224	Parlet	Play Me Or Trade Me	1980
NBLP 7226	Brooklyn Dreams	Won't Let Go	1980
NBLP 7227	Bobbi Walker	Diamond In The Rough	1980
NBLP 7230	Bob McGilpin	Bob McGilpin	1980
NBLP 7231	Teri DeSario	Caught	1980
NBLP 7241	Gloria Covington	Movin' On	1980
NBLP 7242	Lipps, Inc.	Pucker Up	1980
NBLP 7244	Donna Summer	Walk Away Collector's Edition (The Best Of 1977-1980)	1980
NBLP 7246	People's Choice	People's Choice	1980
NBLP 7247	D.C. LaRue	Star Baby	1980
NBLP 7249	Parliament	Trombipulation	1980
NBLP 7256	Mantra	Mantra	1981
NBLP 7258	The Four Tops	Tonight!	1981
NBLP 7260	Meco	Impressions Of An American Werewolf In London	1981
NBLP 7262	Lipps, Inc.	Designer Music	1981
NBLP 7265	Stephanie Mills	Tantalizingly Hot	1982
NBLP 7266	Four Tops	One More Mountain	1982
NBLP 7267	Various	Funky Fitness	1982
NBLPH 7269	Stomu Yamashta	Original Music From The Motion Picture Soundtrack "Tempest"	1982
NBLP 7271	Dusty Springfield	White Heat	1982
NBLP 7275	Robert Winters And Fall	L-O-V-E	1982
422-810 304-1	Leon Haywood	It's Me Again	1983
884 053-1 M-1	Casablanca Dance Classics		1985
826 973-1 M-1	Casablanca Dance Classics	Street Edition	1986

PARACHUTE

RRLP 9001	Lalomie Washburn	My Music Is Hot	1977
RRLP 9003	Morris Jefferson	Spank Your Blank Blank	1978
RRLP 9004	7th Wonder	Words Don't Say Enough	1978
RRLP 9005	Randy Brown	Welcome To My Room	1978
RRLP 9009	Sidney Barnes	Foot Stompin' Music	1978
RRLP 9010	The C.Y. Walking Band	Love The Way It Feels	1979
RRLP 9012	Randy Brown	Intimately	1979
RRLP 9013	Westside Strutters	Gershwin '79	1979
RRLP 9014	7th Wonder	Climbing Higher	1979
RRLP 9016	Joe Long, Charles Bernstein	Music From The Original Motion Picture Soundtrack "Love At First Bite" (LP)	1979
RRLP 9017	Liquid Gold	Liquid Gold	1979

CHOCOLAT CITY

CCLP 2001	BlackSmoke	BlackSmoke	1976
CCLP 2001	Smoke	Smoke	1976
CCLP 2002	Brenda & The Tabulations	I Keep Coming Back For More	1977
CCLP 2003	Cameo	Cardiac Arrest	1977
CCLP 2004	Cameo	We All Know Who We Are	1977
CCLP 2005	Vernon Burch	Love-A-Thon	1978
CCLP 2006	Cameo	Ugly Ego	1978
CCLP 2007	Townsend, Townsend, Townsend & Rogers	Townsend, Townsend, Townsend & Rogers	1979
CCLP 2008	Cameo	Secret Omen	1979

Matrix numbers

CCLP 2009	Vernon Burch	Get Up	1979
CCLP 2010	Randy Brown	Midnight Desire	1980
CCLP 2011	Cameo	Cameosis	1980
CCLP 2012	7th Wonder	Thunder	1980
CCLP 2013	Starpoint	Starpoint	1980
CCLP 2014	Vernon Burch	Steppin' Out	1980
CCLP 2015	Kevin Moore	Rainmaker	1980
CCLP 2016	Cameo	Feel Me	1980
CCLP 2017	Randy Brown	Randy	1981
CCLP 2018	Starpoint	Keep On It	1981
CCLP 2019	Cameo	Knights Of The Sound Table	1981
CCLP 2020	Starpoint	Wanting You	1981
CCLP 2021	Cameo	Alligator Woman	1982
CCLP 2022	Starpoint	All Night Long	1982

MILLENIUM

MNLP 8001	Meco	Music Inspired By Star Wars And Galactic Funk	1977
MNLP 8002	Brooklyn Dreams	Brooklyn Dreams	1977
MNLP 8004	Meco	Encounters Of Every Kind	1977
MNLP 8006	Ruby Winters	I Will	1978
MNLP 8007	Joey Travolta	Joey Travolta	1978
MNLP 8008	The Good Vibrations	I Get Around	1978
MNLP 8009	Meco	The Wizard Of Oz	1978
MNLP 8011	Brooklyn Dreams	Sleepless Nights	1979
MNLP 8012	Meco	Superman And Other Galactic Heroes	1979
BXL1-7744	Ruth Waters	Never Gonna Be The Same	1979

OASIS

OCLP-5004	Donna Summer	A Love Trilogy	1976
OCLP-5005	Roberta Kelly	Trouble Maker	1976
OCLP-5006	Giorgio	Knights In White Satin	1976
25 218 OT	Speed Limit	Cruisin'	1977
26 172 OT	Stainless Steal	Can-Can	1978

When he gets down, you get collared.

SILVER·BLUE
including:
Tennessee Waltz
Light My Fire/Alexander's Ragtime Band
So Rare/Land Of A Thousand Dances

He calls himself Silver Blue, and he's the mastermind behind the hottest, funkiest new disco sound in America.
You already know his hit single "Tennessee Waltz"—because it's receiving more house action and radio play than just about any disco song of the year.
But what you may not know is that there's a lot more music—just as provocative as "Tennessee Waltz"—on the new Silver Blue album.
"Silver Blue." His debut album, featuring the hit single "Tennessee Waltz." On Epic Records and Tapes.

"Epic" are trademarks of CBS Inc. © 1978 CBS Inc.

DAZZLE

Disco Labels & Albums

Chapter 6
De-Lite Records

FOUNDED IN 1969 BY PRODUCER GENE REDD AS R&B LABEL. MAIN ARTIST WAS KOOL AND THE GANG BUT BRANCHED OUT INTO DISCO WITH THE SUCCESS OF CROWN HEIGHTS AFFAIR. IN 1985 DE-LITE WAS MERGED INTO POLYGRAM SUB-LABEL MERCURY RECORDS. CURRENTLY OWNED BY UNIVERSAL.

Left: Dazzle - Dazzle / De-Lite 1979
Design: Joseph Kotleba / Photography: Dazzling Dick Fegley

DE-2003 / 1969

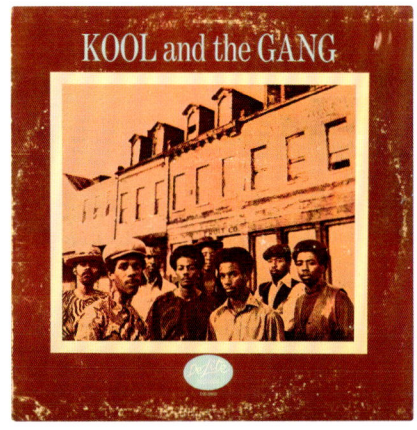

BE 899.004-H / 1969

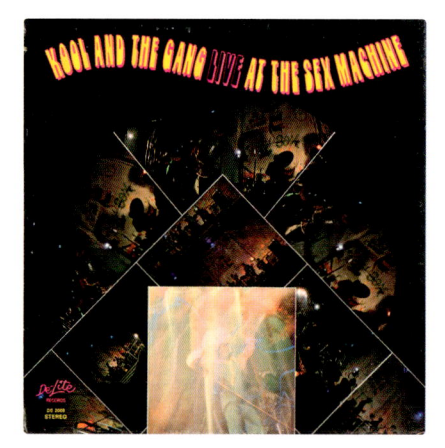

DE-2008 / 1971

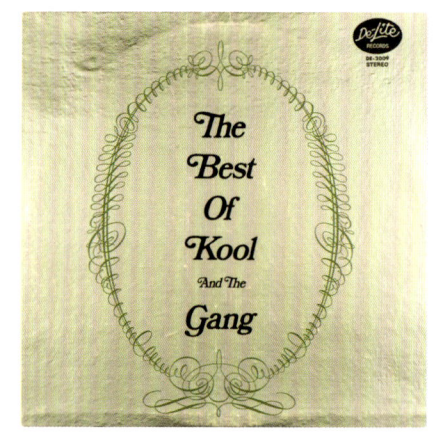

DE-2009 / 1971

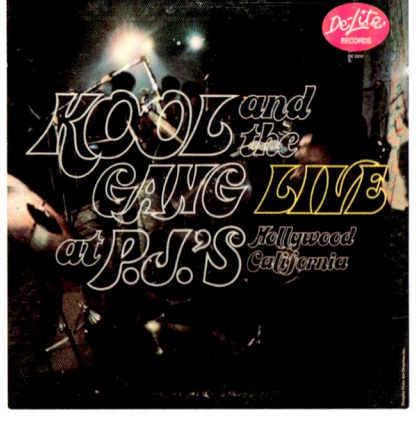

DE-2010 / 1971

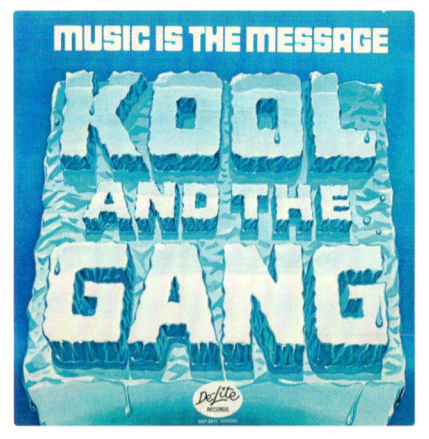

DEP-2011 / 1972

DEP-2012 / 1972

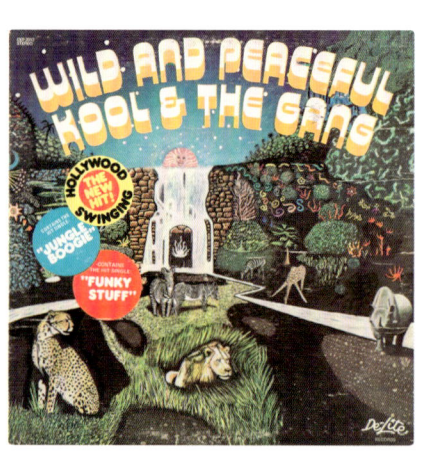

DEP-2013 / 1973

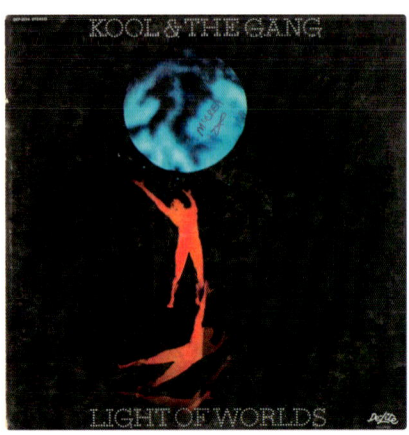

DEP-2014 / 1974

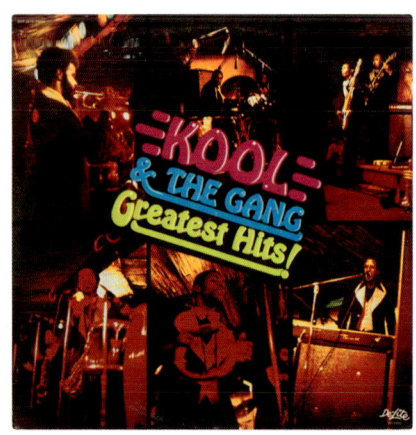

DEP-2015 / 1975

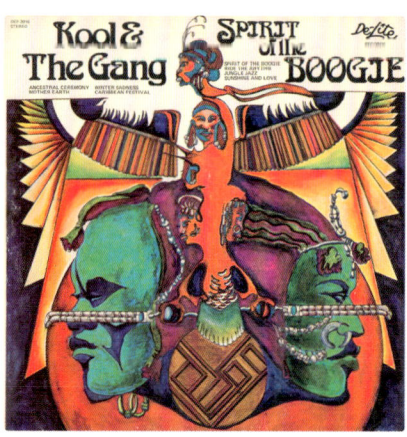

DEP-2016 / 1975

DEP-2017 / 1975

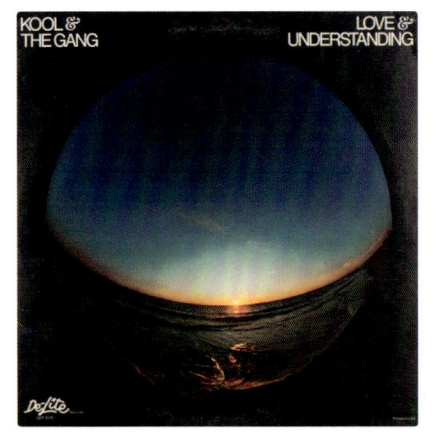

DEP-2018 / 1976

DEP-2019 / 1975

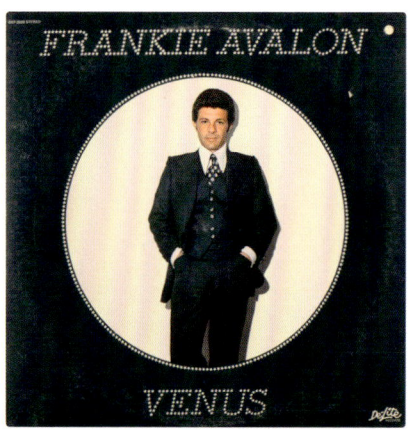

DEP-2020 / 1976

DEP-2021 / 1975

DEP-2022 / 1976

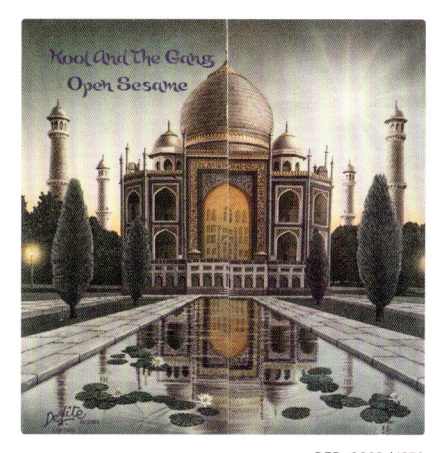

DEP-2023 / 1976

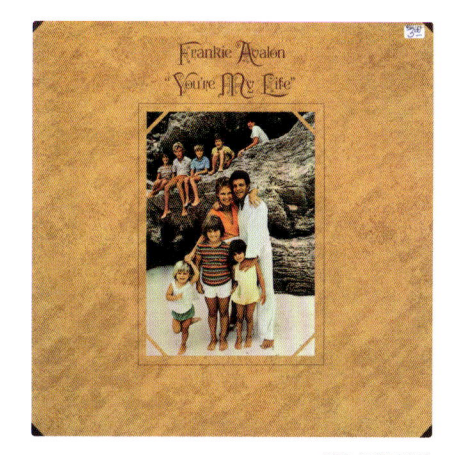

DEP-2027 / 1976

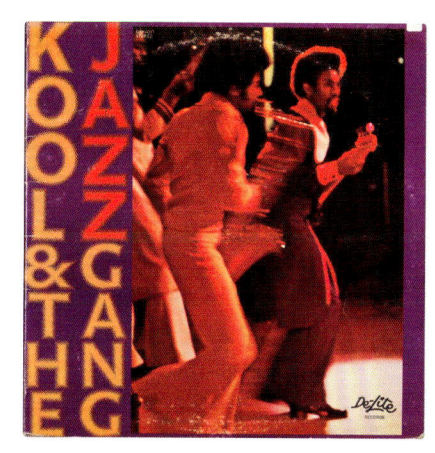

DEP-4001 / 1973

DE-4002 / 1977

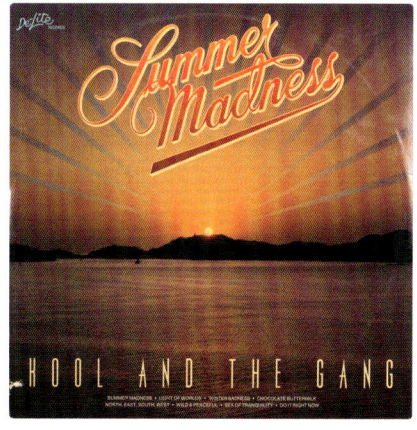

DE-4002 / 1977

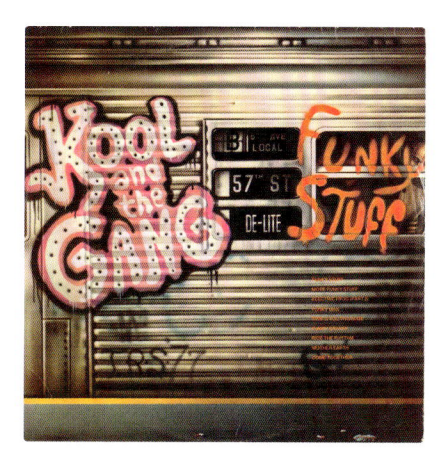

DE-4003 / 1977

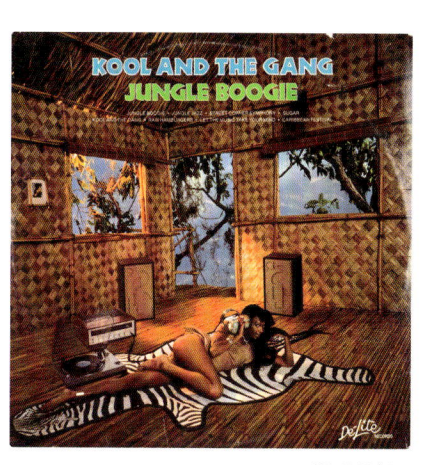

DE-4003 / 1977

DE-4004 / 1977

DSR 8501 / 1981

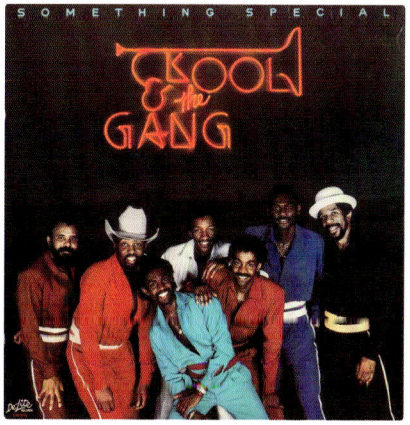

DSR 8502 / 1981

DSR 8503 / 1982

DSR 8504 / 1982

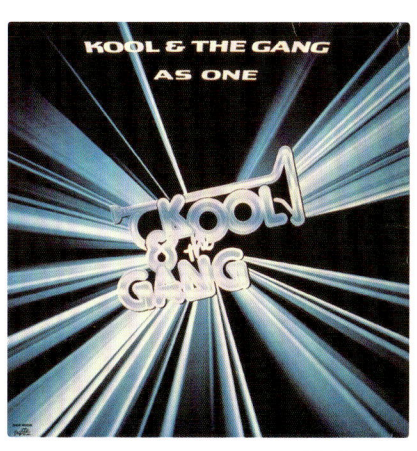

DSR 8505 / 1982

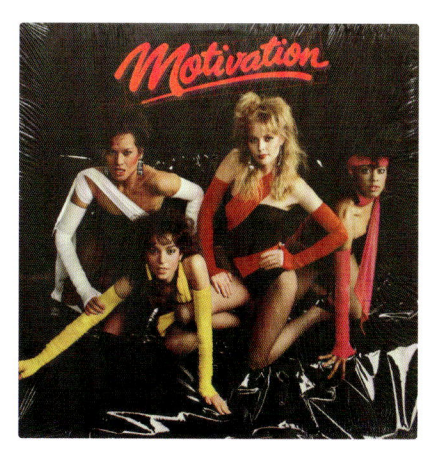

DSR 8506 / 1983

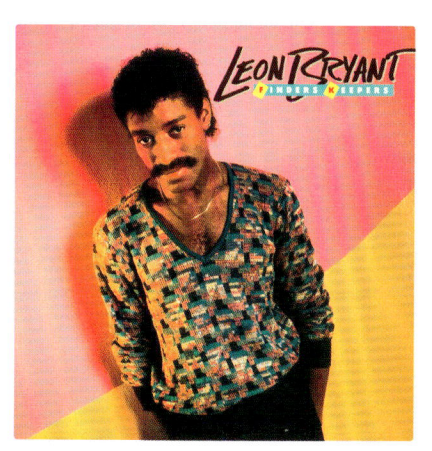

DSR 8507 / 1984

DSR 8508 / 1983

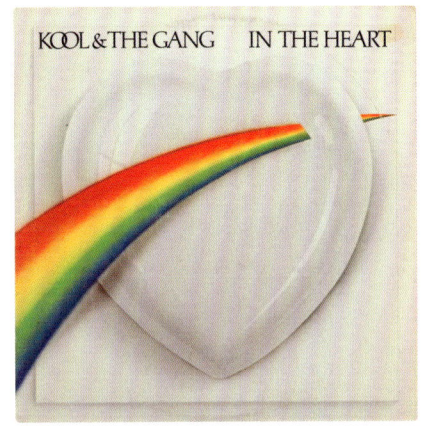

DSR 8509 / 1984

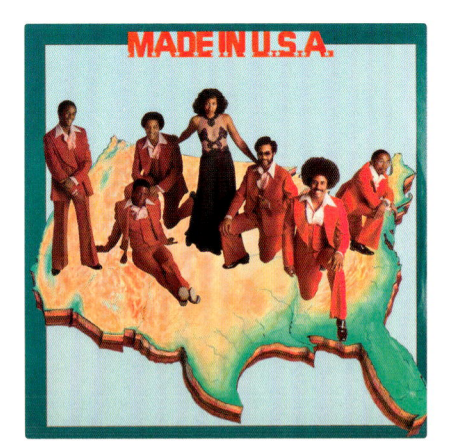

DSR 9500 / 1977

DSR 9501 / 1977

DSR-9505 / 1978

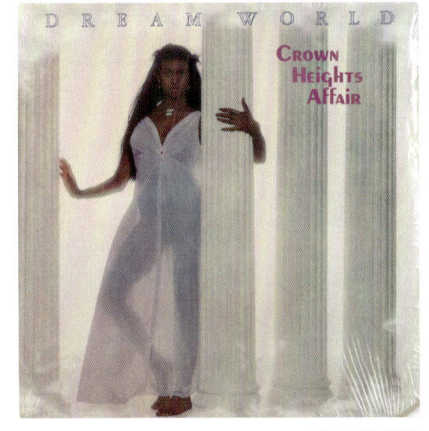

DSR-9506 / 1978

DSR-9507 / 1978

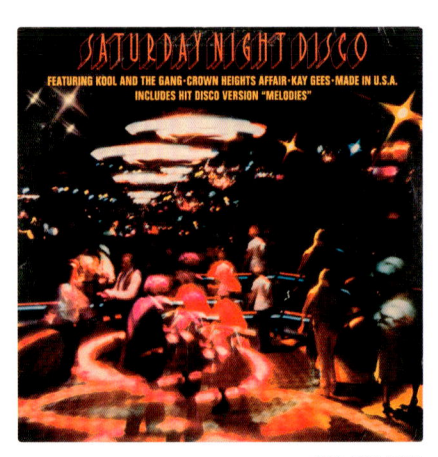

DSR-9508 / 1978

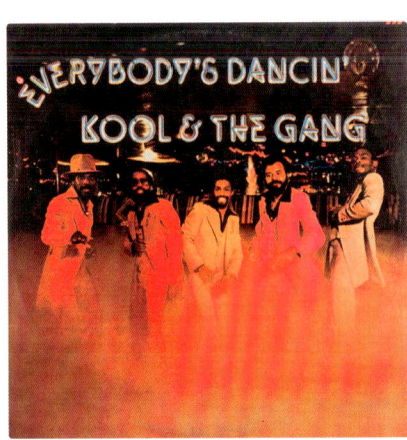

DSR-9509 / 1978

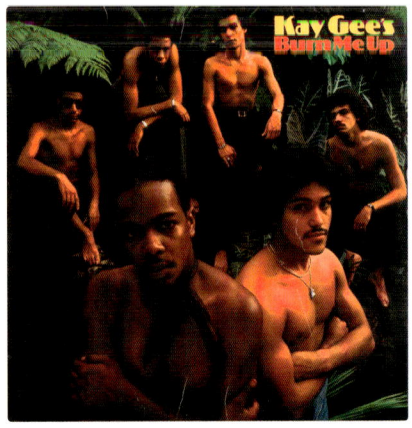

DSR-9510 / 1979

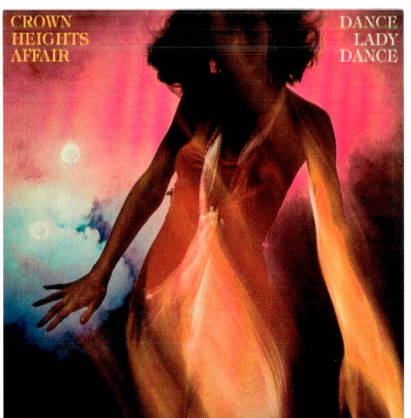

DSR-9512 / 1979

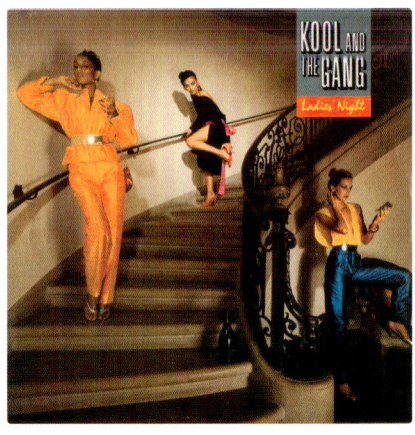

DSR-9513 / 1979

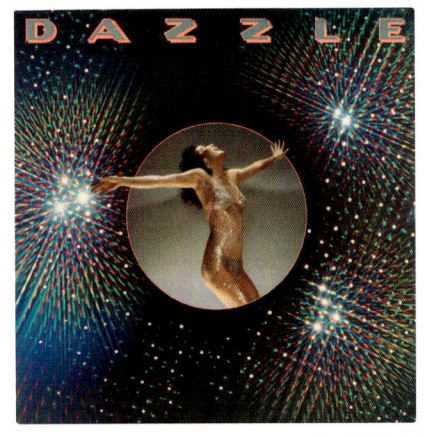

DSR-9514 / 1979

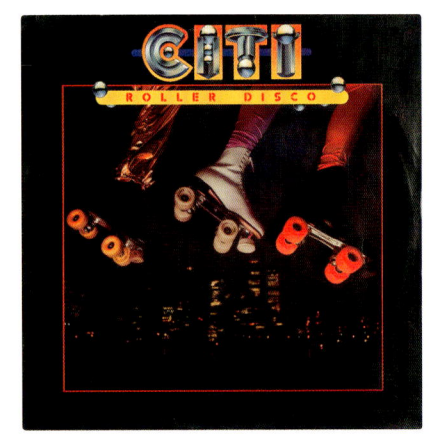

DSR-9515 / 1979

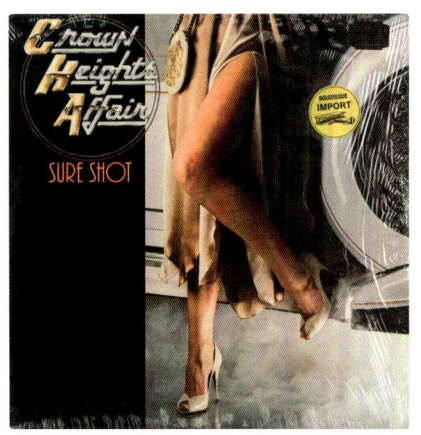

DSR-9517 / 1980

DSR-9520 / 1980

Kool And The Gang-Jungle Boogie / Delite 1977
Art Direction: Horace Fernandez / Photography: Joel Brodsky / Illustration: Todd Schorr

Crown Heights Affair - Struck Gold / Delite 1983
Design: Mo Strom for Bob Heimall Inc.

Matrix numbers

DELIGHT

DE-2003	Kool & The Gang	Kool And The Gang	1969
DE-2008	Kool & The Gang	Live At The Sex Machine	1971
DE-2009	Kool & The Gang	The Best Of Kool And The Gang	1971
DE-2010	Kool & The Gang	Live At P.J.'s	1971
DEP-2011	Kool & The Gang	Music Is The Message	1972
DEP-2012	Kool & The Gang	Good Times	1972
DEP-2013	Kool & The Gang	Wild And Peaceful	1973
DEP-2014	Kool & The Gang	Light Of Worlds	1974
DEP 2015	Kool & The Gang	Greatest Hits	1975
DEP-2016	Kool & The Gang	Spirit Of The Boogie	1975
DEP-2017	The Crown Heights Affair	Dreaming A Dream	1975
DEP-2018	Kool & The Gang	Love & Understanding	1976
DEP-2019	Various	Hustle Hits	1975
DEP-2020	Frankie Avalon	Venus	1976
DEP-2021	Crown Heights Affair	Foxy Lady	1975
DEP-2022	Crown Heights Affair	Do It Your Way	1976
DEP-2023	Kool & The Gang	Open Sesame	1976
DE-2024	Benny Troy	Tearin' Me To Pieces	1976
DEP-2025	Otherside	Rock-X-Ing	1977
DEP-2026	Made In USA	Made In USA	1977
DEP 2027	Franky Avalon	You're My Life	1978
DEP-4001	Kool & The Gang	Kool Jazz	1973
DE-4002	Kool & The Gang	Hollywood Swinging/Summer Madness	1977
DE-4003	Kool & The Gang	Funky Stuff / Jungle Boogie	1977
DE-4004	Various	Starship (The De-Lite Superstars)	1977
DSR-9500	Made In USA	Made In USA	1977
DSR-9501	Kool & The Gang	The Force	1977
DSR-9502	Crown Heights Affair	Do It Your Way	1976
DSR-9503	Otherside	Rock-X-Ing	1977
DSR-9504	Frankie Avalon	You're My Life	1977
DSR-9505	Kay-Gee's	Kilowatt	1978
DSR-9506	Crown Heights Affair	Dream World	1978
DSR-9507	Kool & The Gang	Spin Their Top Hits	1978
DSR-9508	Various	Saturday Night Disco	1978
DSR-9509	Kool & The Gang	Everybody's Dancin'	1978
DSR-9510	Kay Gee's	Burn Me Up	1979
DSR-9512	Crown Heights Affair	Dance Lady Dance	1979
DSR-9513	Kool & The Gang	Ladies' Night	1979
DSR-9514	Dazzle	Dazzle	1979
DSR-9515	Citi	Roller Disco	1979
DSR-9517	Crown Heights Affair	Sure Shot	1980
DSR-9518	Kool & The Gang	Celebrate!	1980
DSR-9520	Coffee	Slippin' And Dippin'	1980
DSR 8501	Leon Bryant	Leon Bryant	1981
DSR 8502	Kool & The Gang	Something Special	1981
DSR 8503	coffee	second cup	1982
DSR 8504	Crown Heights Affair	Think Positive!	1982
DSR 8505	Kool & The Gang	As One	1982
DSR 7000	Kool & The Gang	At Their Best	1983
DSR 8506	Motivation	Motivation	1983
DSR 8508	Kool & The Gang	In The Heart	1983
DX-1-510	Crown Heights Affair	Struck Gold	1983
DSR 8507	Leon Bryant	Finders Keepers	1984
DSR 8509	Kool & The Gang	Emergency	1984
DSRD 8510	Kool & The Gang	Best Of Kool & The Gang	1985

VICOR

VI-7001	Street People	Street People	1976
VI 7002	Rhythm Makers	The Soul On Your Side	1976
VI 7003	Jeanne Napoli	Jeanne	1976

GANG

GANG-101	Kay-Gees	The Keep On Bumpin' & Masterplan	1974
GANG-102	Kay-Gees	The Find A Friend	1976

RED COACH

RCL 6000	Everyday People	The The Everyday People	1972

CAFÉ

D.D. Sound
DISCO DELIVERY

Disco Labels & Albums

Chapter 7
Emergency Records

INDEPENDENT US LABEL FOUNDED IN 1979, SPECIALISED IN EURO AND ITALIAN DISCO. CLOSED IN 1989, SOLD TO UNIDISC.

Left: D.D.Sound-Cafe / Emergency 1979
Design: Marucelli & Marinoni / Photography: Karim

EMLP 7502 / 1979

EMLP 7506 / 1980

EMLP 7503 / 1979

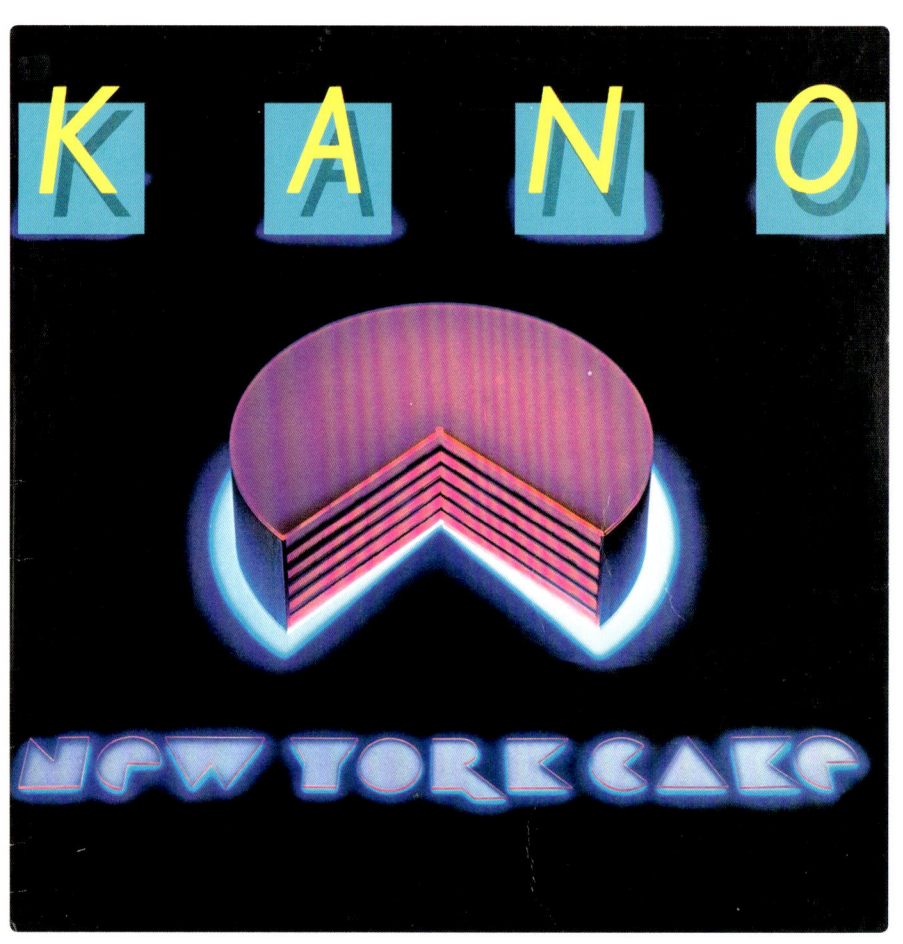

EMLP 8501 / 1981

EMLP 7503 / 1979

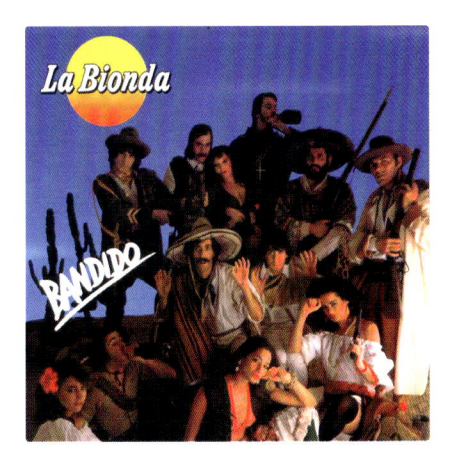

EMLP 7504 / 1979

EMLP 7505 / 1980

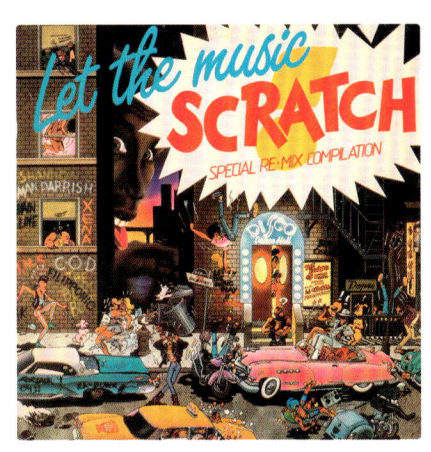

EMLP 7506 / 1984

Matrix numbers

EMERGENCY

VSD 79364	D.D. Sound	Café	1979
EMLP 7502	Max Berlins	World Wide Party	1979
EMLP 7503	Difference	High Fly	1979
EMLP 7504	La Bionda	Bandido	1979
EMLP 7505	Kano	Kano	1980
EMLP 7506	Easy Going	Casanova	1980
EMLP 7506	Various	Let The Music Scratch	1984
EMLP 7507	Various	This Is The Funk!	1986
EMLP 8501	Kano	New York Cake	1981

Fat Larry's Band
Lookin' For Love

Disco Labels & Albums

Chapter 8
Fantasy and Wmot

FOUNDED IN SAN FRANCISCO, USA, BY MAX AND SOL WEISS IN 1949. SEAMLESSLY MOVED FROM SOUL AND JAZZ REPERTOIRE INTO THE DISCO ERA IN THE MID-1970S THROUGH THE COMMERCIAL SUCCESS OF ARTISTS SUCH AS THE BLACKBYRDS AND LATER SIDE EFFECT, PLEASURE AND SYLVESTER.

Left: Fat Larry`s Band - Lookin` For Love / Fantasy 1979
Art Direction: Phil Caroll / Design: Kris Johnson / Photography: Phil Bray

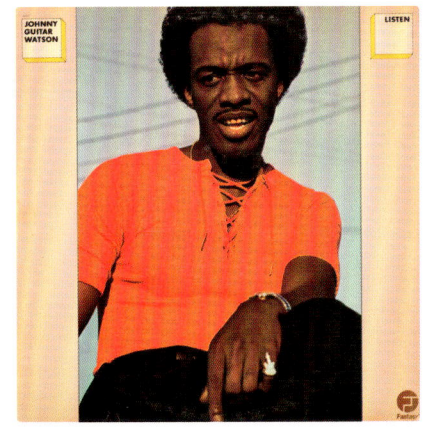

F-9437 / 1973 
F-9444 / 1974 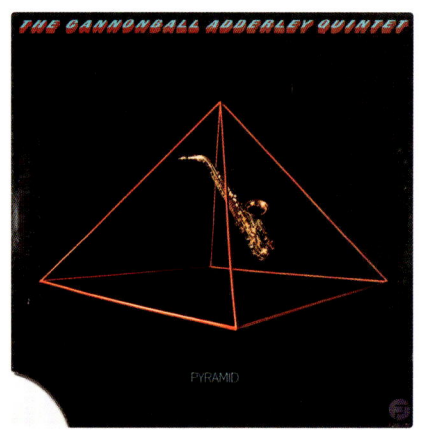
F-9455 / 1974 
F-9472 / 1974

F-9473 / 1975
F-9476 / 1975 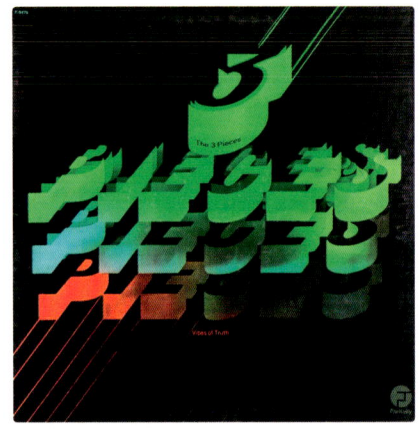 
F-9478 / 1975 
F-9479 / 1975

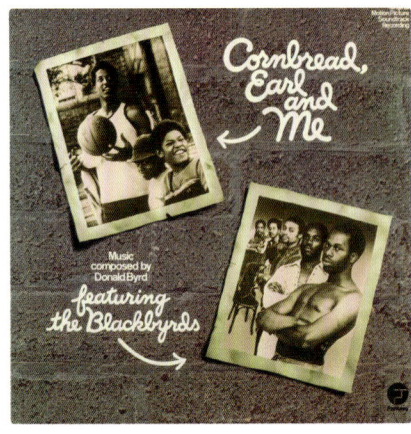

F-9483 / 1975 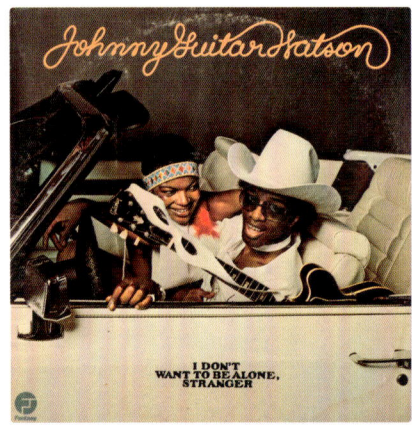
F-9484 / 1975 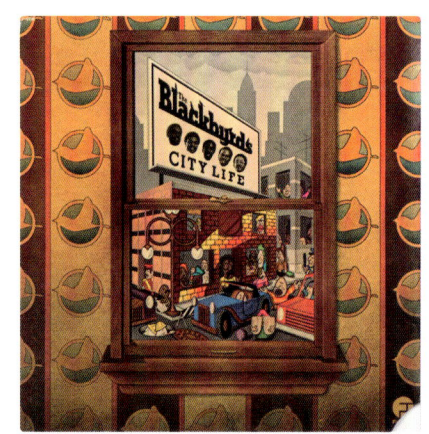
F-9490 / 1975 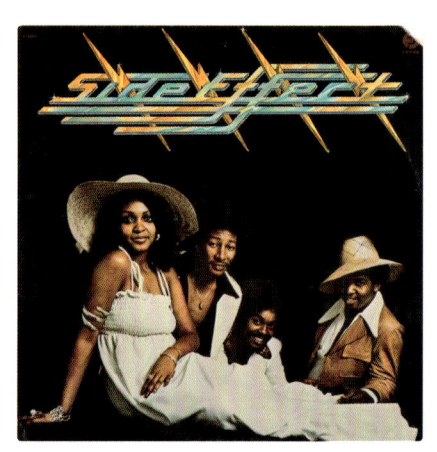
F-9491 / 1975

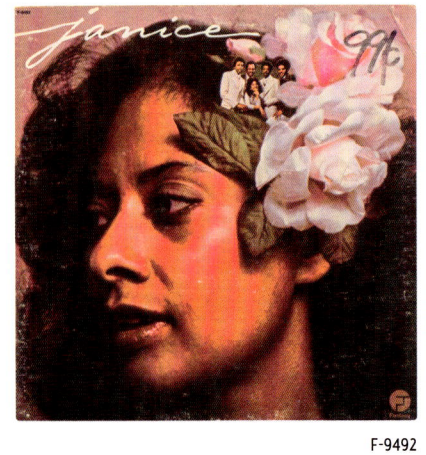

F-9492
F-9493 / 1976 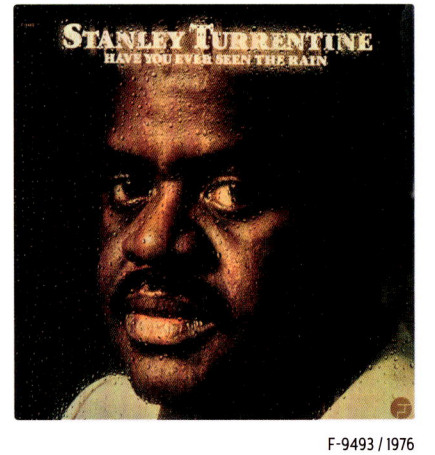
F-9506 / 1976 
F-9508 / 1976

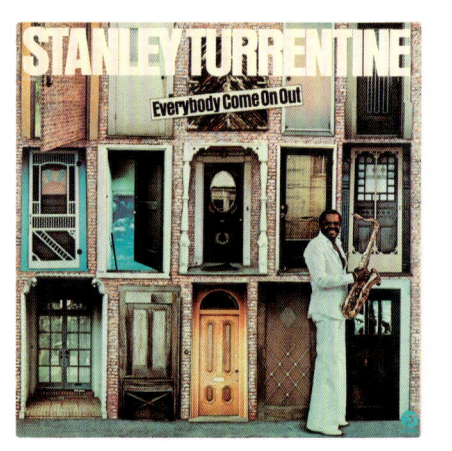

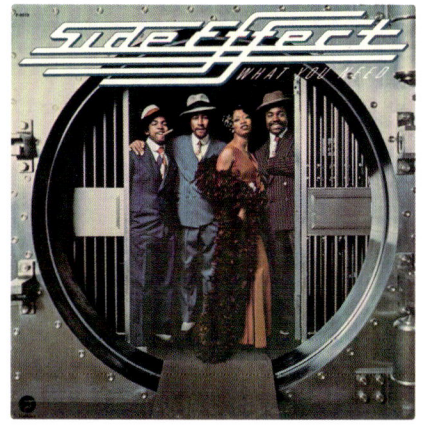

F-9513 / 1976

F-9516 / 1977

F-9517 / 1977

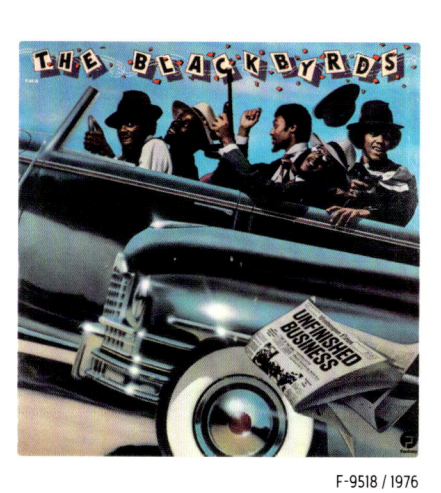

F-9518 / 1976

F-9519 / 1976

F-9523 / 1977

F-9524 / 1977

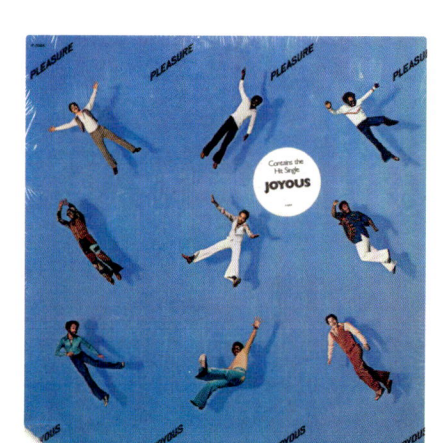

F-9526 / 1977

F-9531 / 1977

F-9531 / 1977

F-9533 / 1977

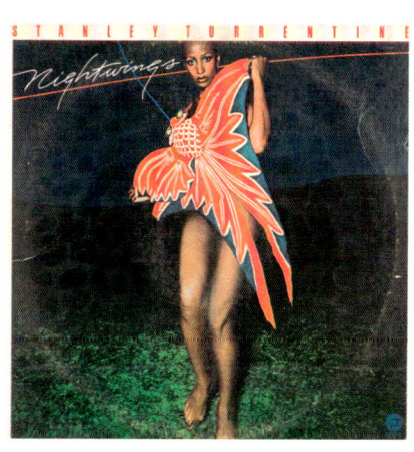

F-9534 / 1978

F-9535 / 1977

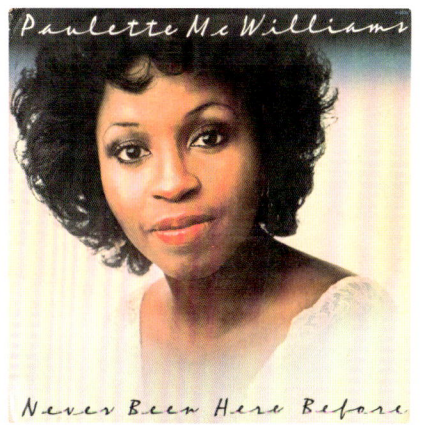

F-9536 / 1977

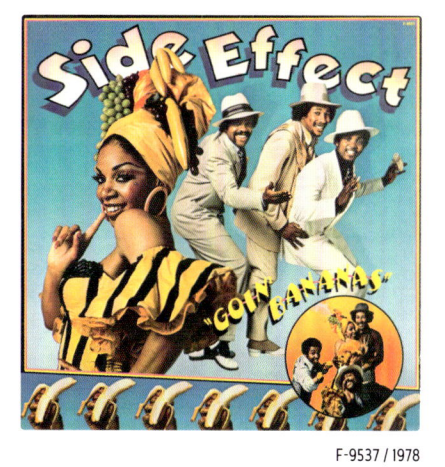

F-9537 / 1978

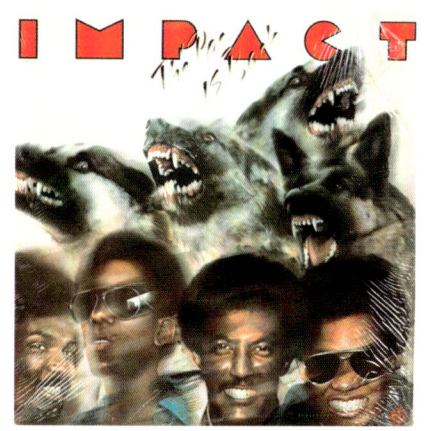

F-9539 / 1977

Time Is Movin'   In Life   Enter In   Party Land   Unfinished Business   Lady   You've Got That Something
Produced by Donald Byrd for Blackbyrd Productions, Inc.
℗ 1976, Fantasy® Records, Tenth and Parker, Berkeley, Ca. 94710

THE BLACKBYRDS

F-9518

The Blackbyrds–Unfinished Business / Fantasy 1976
Art Direction: Phil Caroll / Cover–Phil Carol, Phil Bray / Lettering: Lance Anderson

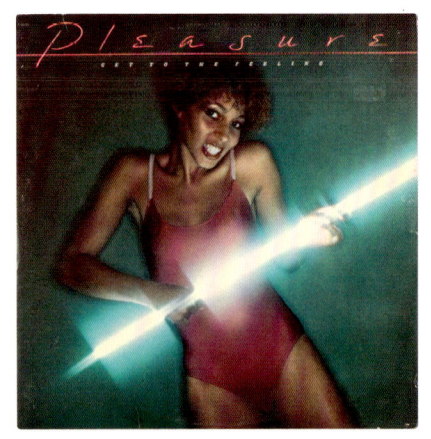

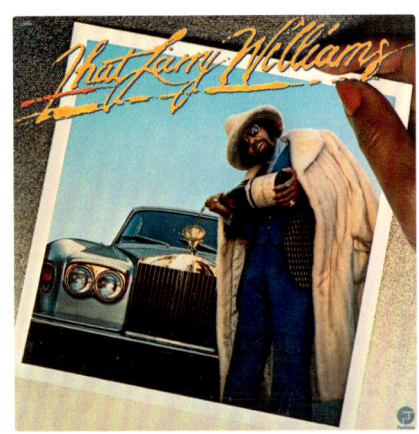

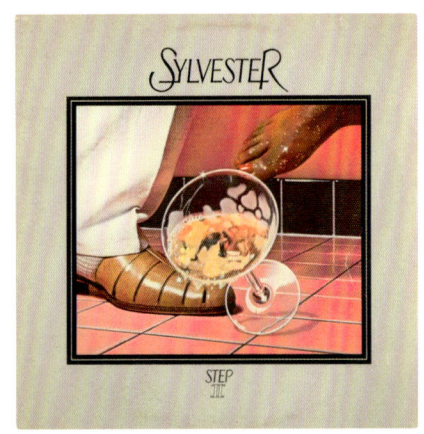

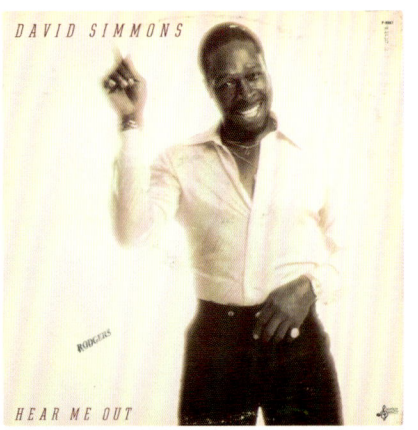

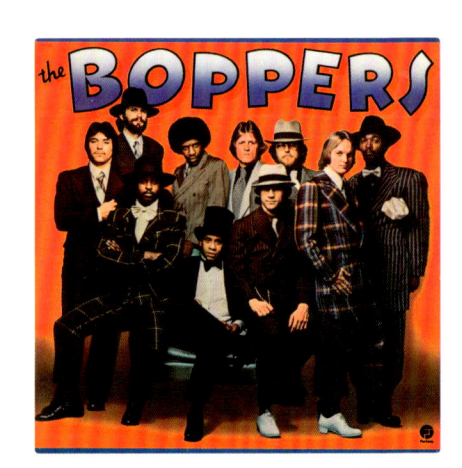

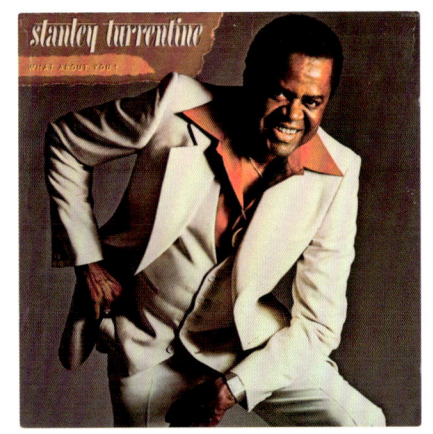

F-9541 / 1977	F-9545 / 1978	F-9546 / 1978	F-9547 / 1978
F-9548 / 1978	F-9549 / 1978	F-9550 / 1978	F-9552 / 1978
F-9553 / 1978	F-9556 / 1978	F-9561 / 1978	F-9562 / 1978
F-9563 / 1978	F-9565 / 1978	F-9566 / 1978	F-9567 / 1978

F-9569 / 1978

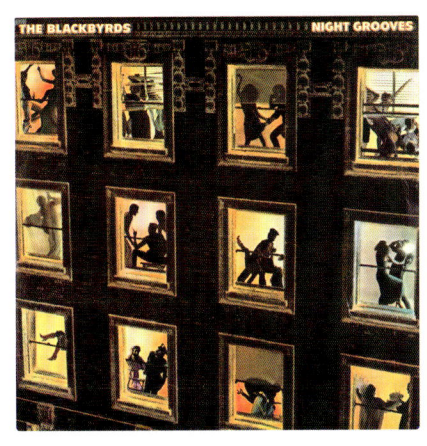

F-9570 / 1978

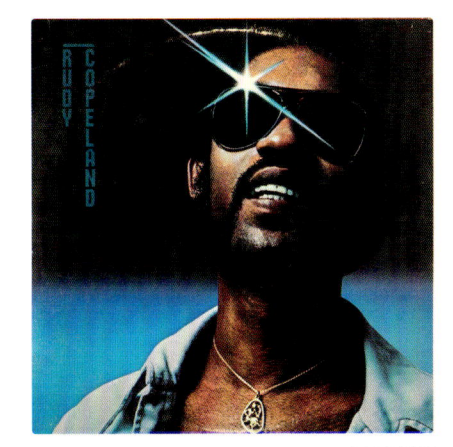

F-9573 / 1978

F-9574 / 1978

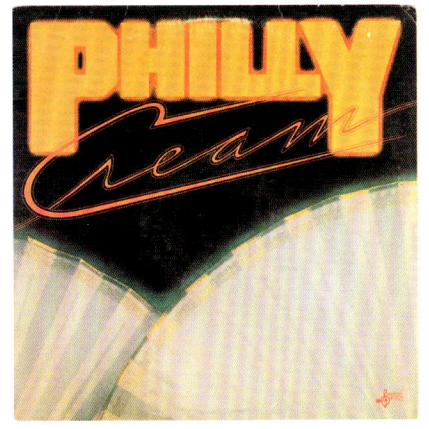

F-9575 / 1979

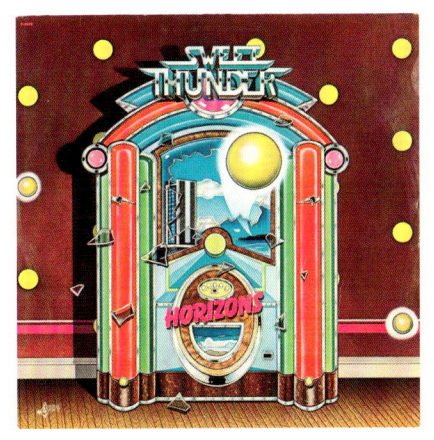

F-9576 / 1979

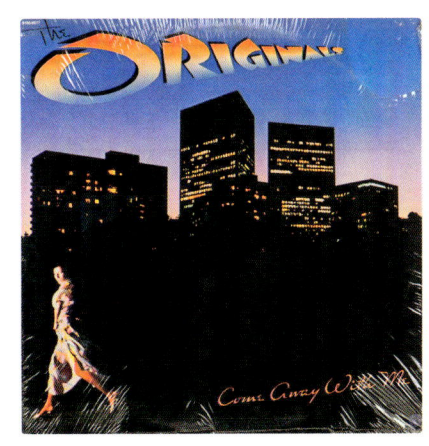

F-9577 / 1979

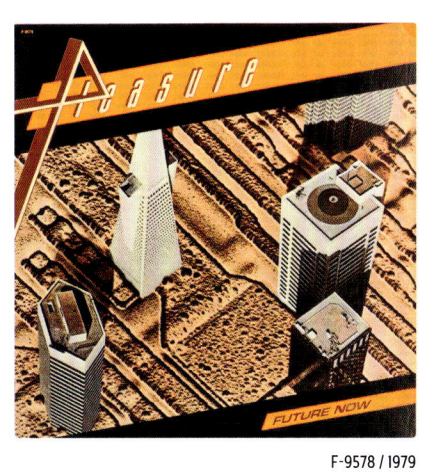

F-9578 / 1979

F-9579 / 1979

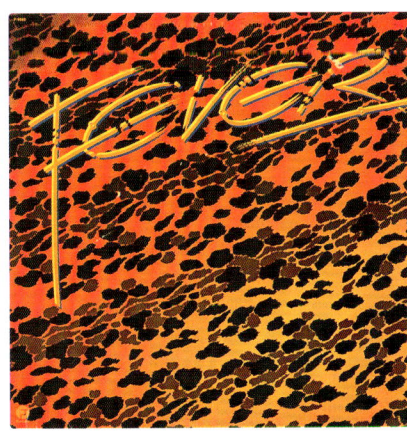

F-9580 / 1979

F-9581 / 1979

F-9582 / 1979

F-9583 / 1979

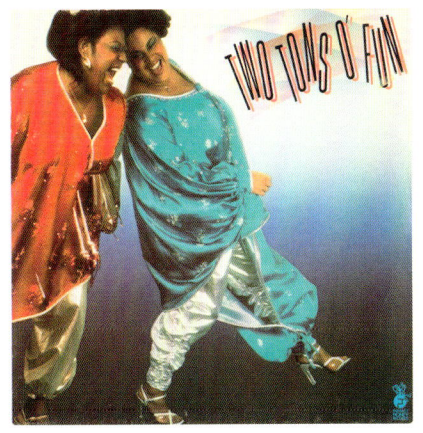

F-9584 / 1980

F-9587 / 1979

F-9588 / 1979

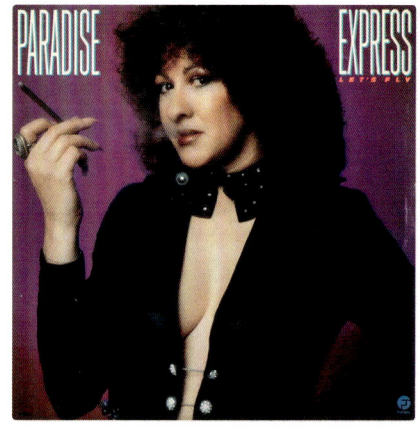

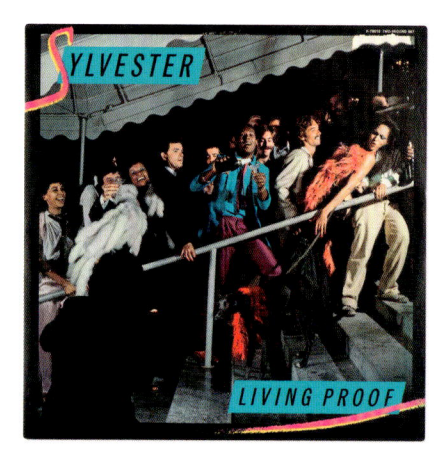

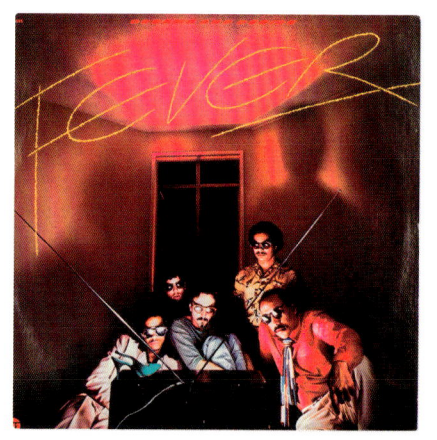

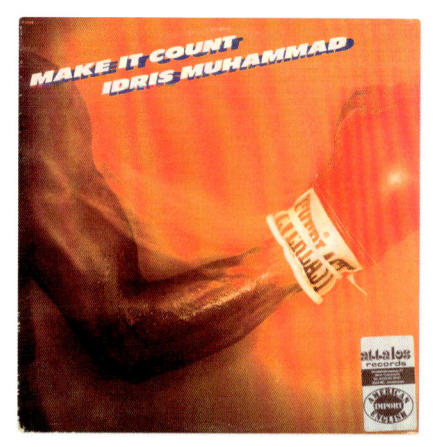

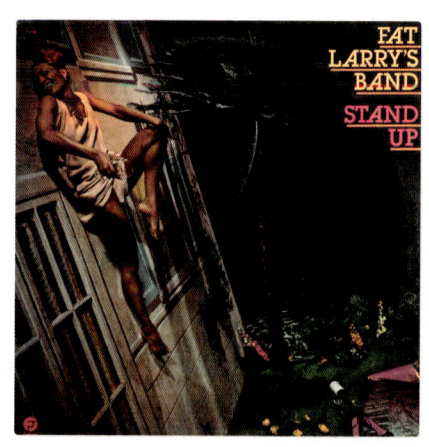

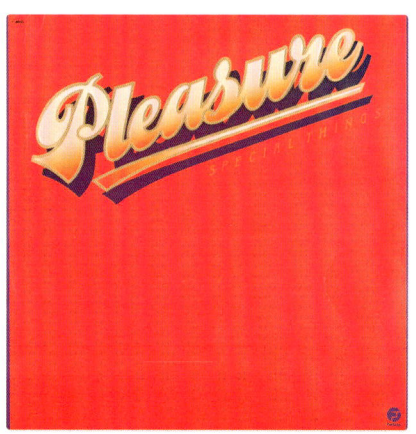

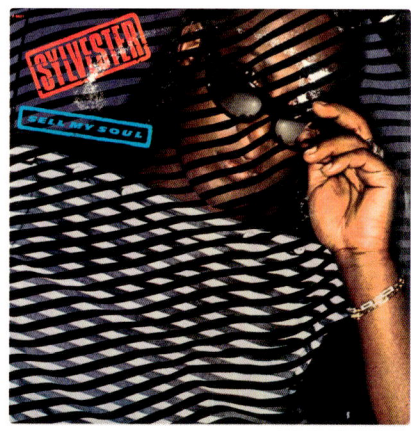

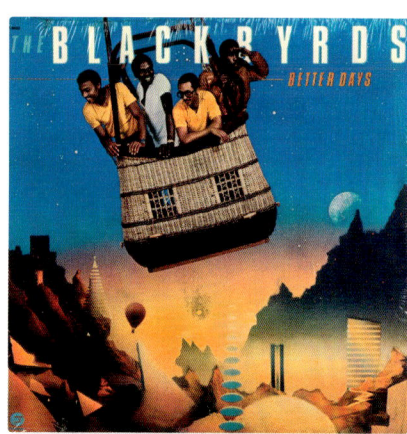

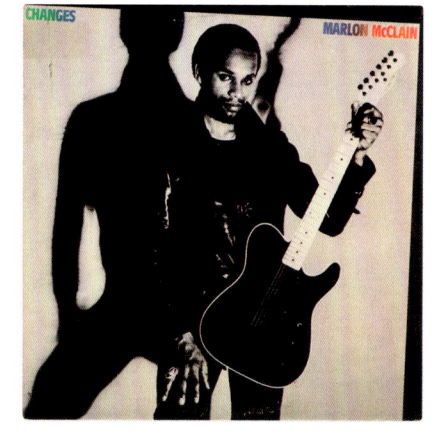

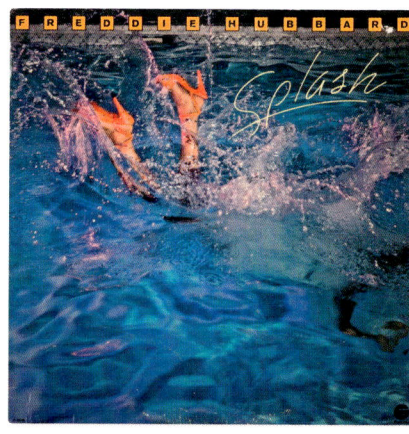

F-9589 / 1979
F-9591 / 1980
F-9594 / 1980
F-9595 / 1980
F-9596 / 1980
F-9597 / 1980
F-9598 / 1980
F-9599 / 1980
F-9600 / 1980
F-9601 / 1980
F-9602 / 1980
F-9604 / 1980
F-9605 / 1980
F-9606 / 1981
F-9607 / 1981
F-9610 / 1981

Slick · Slick / Fantasy-Wmot 1979
Design: Kris Johnson / Photography: Phil Bray

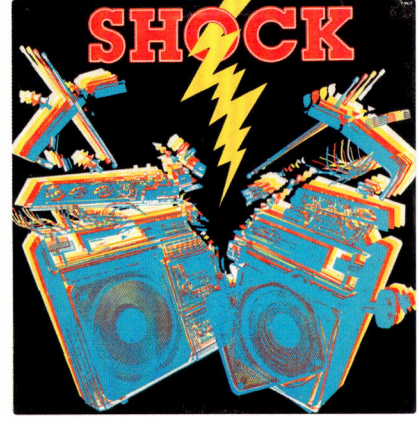

F-9613 / 1981 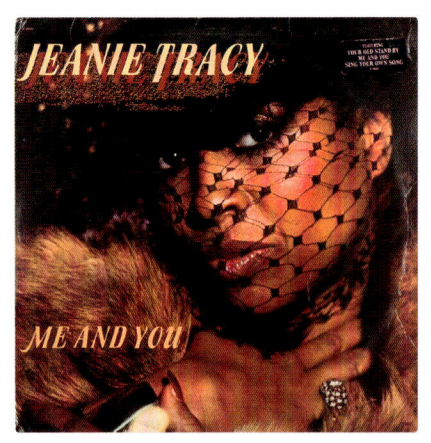
F-9614 / 1982 
F-9615 / 1982 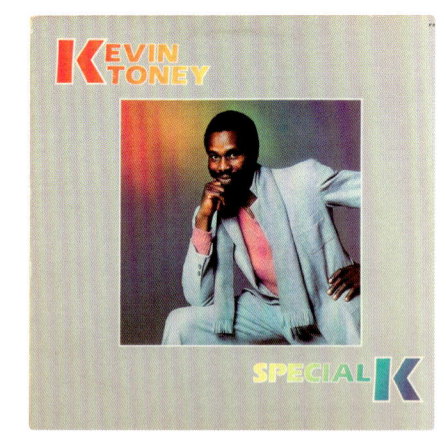
F-9616 / 1982

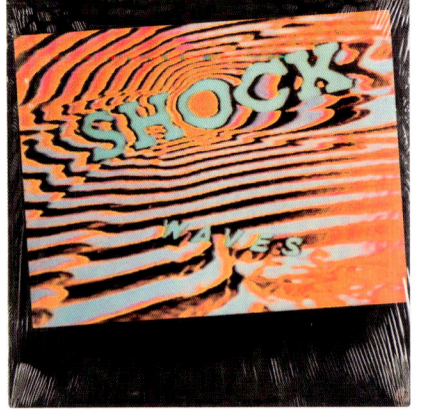

F-9619 / 19822 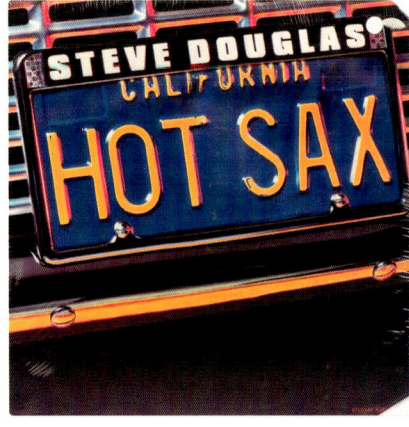
F-9620 / 1982 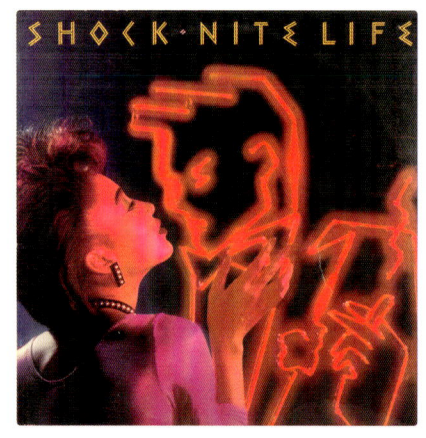
F-9622 / 1983 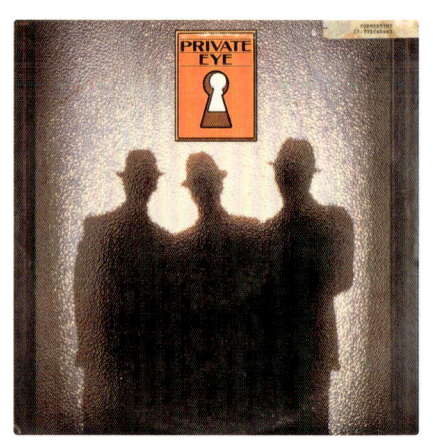
F-9624 / 1983

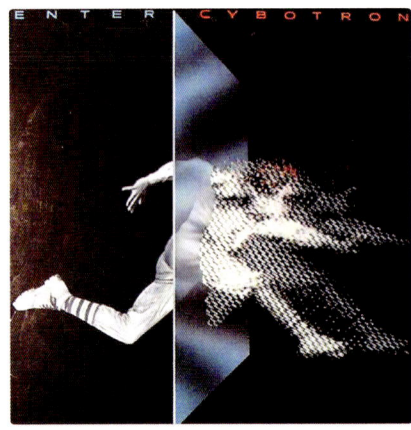

F-9625 / 1983 
F-9642 / 1986 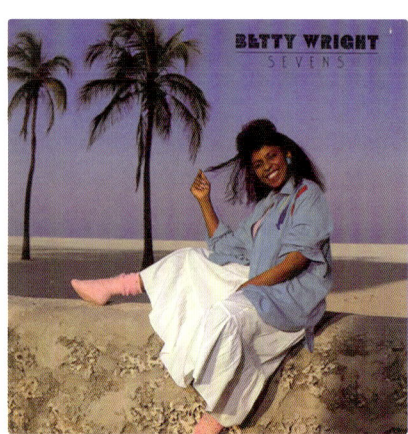
F-9644 / 1986 
F-9648 / 1986

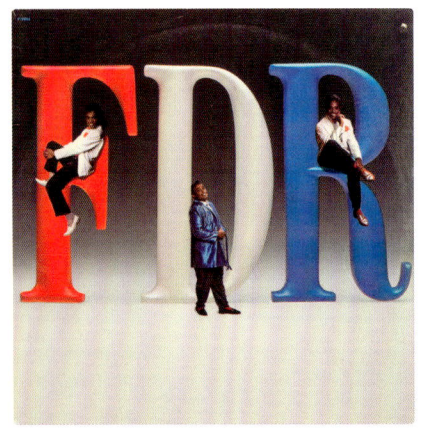

F-9652 / 1987
F-9654 / 1987 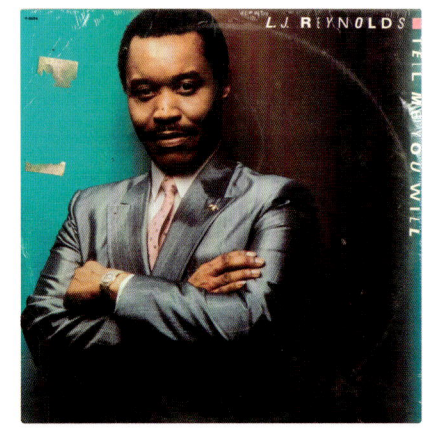
F-9659 / 1988

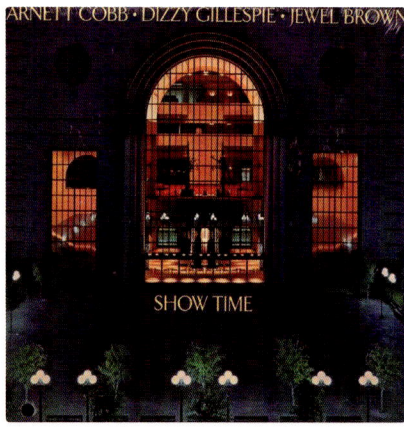

Pleasure - Get to The Feeling / Fantasy 1978
Art Direction: Phil Caroll / Design: Dennis Gassner / Photography: Phil Bray

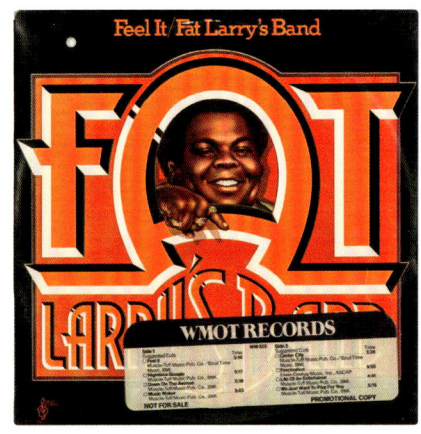

WM 625 / 1976 
WM 626 / 1976 
WM 2-5000 / 1976 
FT 564 / 1979

JW 37060 / 1980 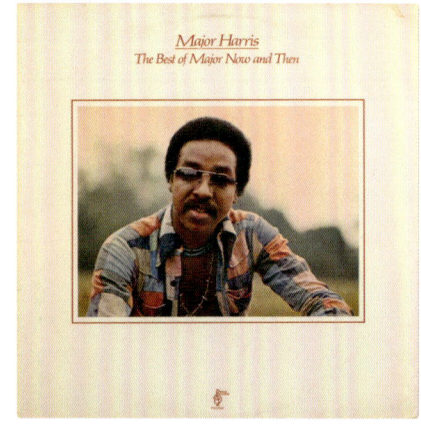
PW 37067 / 1981 
JW 37074 / 1981 
JW 37081 / 1981

WMLP 5001 / 1979 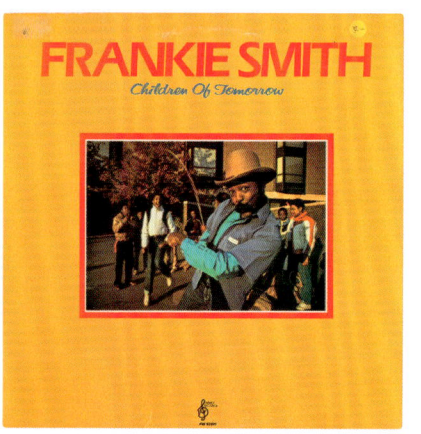
FW 37391 / 1981 
FW 37667 / 1981

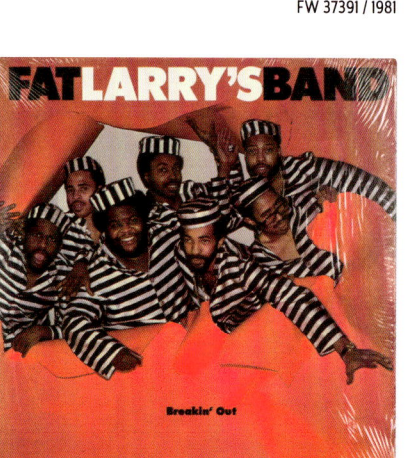

FW 37968 / 1982
540054 / 1983

Matrix numbers

FANTASY

6000	Kenny Burrell	Up The Street, 'Round The Corner, Down The Block	1974
6001	Cannonball Adderley Quintet, The	Pyramid	1974
F-9437	Johnny Guitar Watson	Listen	1973
F-9444	The Blackbyrds	The Blackbyrds	1974
F-9472	The Blackbyrds	Flying Start	1974
F-9473	Pleasure	Dust Yourself Off	1975
F-9476	Three Pieces	Vibes of Truth	1975
F-9478	Stanley Turrentine	In the Pocket	1975
F-9479	Arthur Adams	Home Brew	1975
F-9483	Blackbyrds, The	Cornbread, Earl And Me	1975
F-9484	Johnny "Guitar" Watson	I Don't Want to Be Alone Stranger	1975
F-9490	The Blackbyrds	City Life	1975
F-9491	Side Effect	Side Effect	1975
F-9492	Janice	Janice	1975
F-9493	Stanley Turrentine	Have You Ever Seen the Rain	1976
F-9506	Pleasure	Accept No Substitutes	1976
F-9508	Stanley Turrentine	Everybody Come On Out	1976
F-9513	Side Effect	What You need	1976
F-9516	Roger Glenn	Reachin'	1977
F-9517	Spiders Webb	I Don't Know What's On Your Mind	1977
F-9518	Blackbyrds, The	Unfinished Business	1976
F-9519	Stanley Turrentine	The Man With The Sad Face	1976
F-9523	Arthur Adams	Midnight Serenade	1977
F-9524	Pete and Sheila Escovedo	Solo Two	1977
F-9526	Pleasure	Joyous	1977
F-9531	Sylvester	Sylvester	1977
F-9533	Cal Tjader	Guarabe	1977
F-9534	Stanley Turrentine	Nightwings	1978
F-9535	The Blackbyrds	Action	1977
F-9536	Paulette McWilliams	Never Been Here Before	1977
F-9537	Side Effect	Going Bananas	1978
F-9539	Impact	The Pac Is Back	1977
F-9541	Checkmates Ltd.	We Got the Moves	1977
F-9545	Pete & Sheila Escovedo	Happy Together	1978
F-9546	Originals	Another Time, Another Place	1978
F-9547	Sweet Thunder	Sweet Thunder	1978
F-9549	Martha Reeves	We Meet Again	1978
F-9550	Pleasure	Get To The Feeling	1978
F-9552	Phil Hurtt	Giving It Back	1978
F-9553	Larry Williams	That Larry Williams	1978
F-9556	Sylvester	Step II	1978
F-9557	SofTouch	SofTouch	1978
F-9561	David Simmons	Hear Me Out	1978
F-9562	Boppers	The Boppers	1978
F-9563	Stanley Turrentine	What About You!	1978
F-9565	F.L.B.	Spacin' Out	1978
F-9566	Idris Muhammad	You Ain't No Friend Of Mine!	1978
F-9567	Damon Harris	Damon	1978
F-9569	Side Effect	Rainbow Visions	1978
F-9570	The Blackbyrds	Night Grooves	1978
F-9572	David Bromberg	My Own House	1978
F-9573	Rudy Copeland	Rudy Copeland	1978
F-9574	Paradise Express	Paradise Express	1978
F-9575	Philly Cream	Philly Cream	1979
F-9576	Sweet Thunder	Horizons	1979
F-9577	the Originals	Come Away With Me	1979
F-9578	Pleasure	Future Now	1979
F-9579	Sylvester	Stars	1979
F-9580	Fever	Fever	1979
F-9581	Idris Muhammad	Foxhuntin'	1979
F-9582	Phil Hurtt	PH Factor	1979
F-9583	Slick	Slick	1979
F-9584	Two Tons O'Fun	Two Tons O'Fun	1980
F-9587	Fat Larry's Band	Lookin' For Love	1979
F-9588	David Simmons	The World Belongs To Me	1979
F-9589	Paradise Express	Let's Fly	1979
F-9590	David Bromberg Band	You Should See The Rest Of The Band	1980
F-9591	Martha Reeves	Gotta Keep Moving	1980
F-9594	Sylvester	Living Proof	1980
F-9595	Fever	Dreams And Desire	1980
F-9596	Slick	Go For It	1980
F-9597	Ike Turner	The Edge	1980
F-9598	Idris Muhammad	Make It Count	1980
F-9599	Fat Larry's Band	Stand Up	1980
F-9600	Pleasure	Special Things	1980
F-9601	Sylvester	Sell My Soul	1980
F-9602	The Blackbyrds	Better Days	1980
F-9604	Stanley Turrentine	Use The Stairs	1980
F-9605	The Two Tons	Backatcha	1980
F-9606	Marlon McClain	Changes	1981
F-9607	Sylvester	Too Hot To Sleep	1981
F-9609	Woody Herman	Feelin So Blue	1981
F-9610	Freddie Hubbard	Splash	1981
F-9611	Tom Fogerty	Deal It Out	1981
F-9612	Tom Coster	T.C.	1981
F-9613	Shock	Shock	1981
F-9614	Jeanie Tracy	Me And You	1982
F-9615	Freddie Hubbard	Keystone Bop	1982
F-9616	Kevin Toney	Special K	1982
F-9618	Bill Evans	Eloquence	1982
F-9619	Shock	Waves	1982
F-9620	Steve Douglas	Hot Sax	1982
F-9622	Shock	Nite Life	1983
F-9623	Tom Coster	Ivory Expedition	1983
F-9624	Private Eye	Private Eye	1983
F-9625	Cybotron	Enter	1983
F-9626	Freddie Hubbard	A Little Night Music	1983
F-9631	The Look	Everybody's Acting	1984

FLB - Spacin' Out / WMOT Records 1978
Art Direction, Illustration: Phil Caroll / Design: Dennis Gassner, Lucinda Cowell

Matrix numbers

FANTASY

F-9632	Steve Douglas	King Cobra	1984
F-9633	Albert King	I'm In A Phone Booth Baby	1984
F-9634	Boys Town Gang	A Cast Of Thousands	1984
F-9642	The Dramatics	Somewhere In Time (A Dramatic Reunion)	1986
F-9644	Betty Wright	Sevens	1986
F-9648	Lenny Williams	New Episode	1986
F-9652	FDR	FDR	1987
F-9653	Pam Anderson	Something Special	1987
F-9654	L.J. Reynolds	Tell Me You Will	1987
F-9656	Boys On The Block	Blockbusters	1987
F-9659	Arnett Cobb, Dizzy Gillespie, Jewel Brown	Show Time	1988

WMOT

WM 625	Fat Larry's Band	Feel It	1976
WM 626	Sweet Thunder	Above The Clouds	1976
WM 2-5000	Blue Magic/Major Harris/Margie Joseph	Live!	1976
FT 564	Fat Larry's Band	Brite City Lights (UK only)	1979
WMLP 5001	Philly Cream	No Time Like Now	1980
JW-37060	Barbara Mason	A Piece Of My Life	1980
PW-37067	Major Harris	The Best Of Major Now And Then	1981
JW-37074	Heaven And Earth	That's Love	1981
JW-37081	Cecil Parker	Chirpin'	1981
FW-37391	Frankie Smith	Children Of Tomorrow	1981
FW-37443	Tom Grant	You Hardly Know Me	1981
FW-37571	Kalapana	Alive	1981
FW 37668	Brandi Wells	Watch Out	1981
FW-37968	Fat Larry's Band	Breakin' Out	1982
540054	Fat Larry's Band	Straight From The Heart (UK only)	1983

Révélacion
DON'T GIVE A DAMN

Disco Labels & Albums

Chapter 9
Malligator-Crocos Records

FRENCH DISCO LABEL FOUNDED BY CERRONE IN 1976

Malligator went by the name of Alligator for a short while before settling on its final name. Through his experiences as a musician and producer, Cerrone became one of the very first disco artist/producers to create his own independent label.
Sub-labels: Crocos Records, On The Air Music.

Left: Revelacion - Don't Give A Damn / Malligator 1979
Design: Morillon

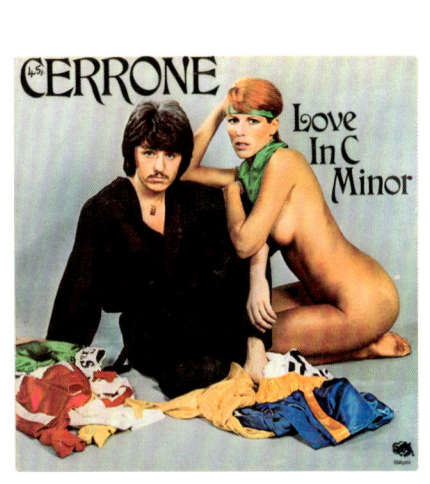

773 801 / 1976	773 802 / 1977	773 803 / 1977	773 804 / 1978
773 805 / 1978	773 806 / 1978	773 807 / 1978	773 807 / 1978
773 808 / 1978	773 809 / 1979	773 810 / 1979	773 811 / 1979
J 1611 161 / 1978	J 1611-182 / 1979	J FL 1611 / 1979	MRI 40-21000 / 1979

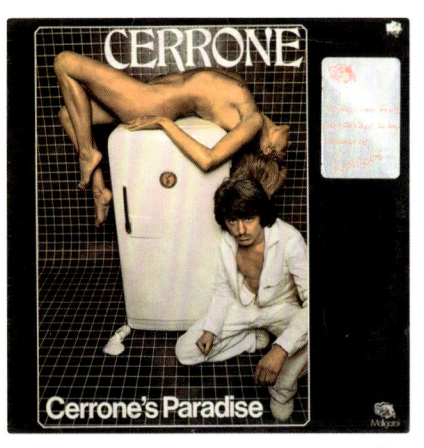

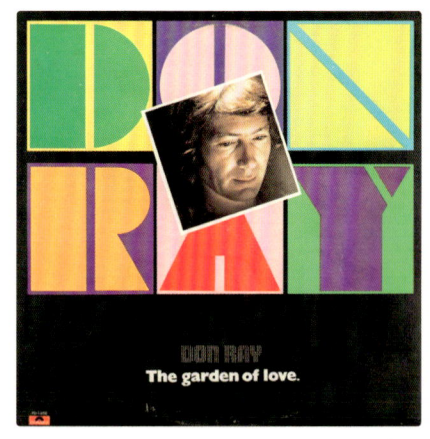

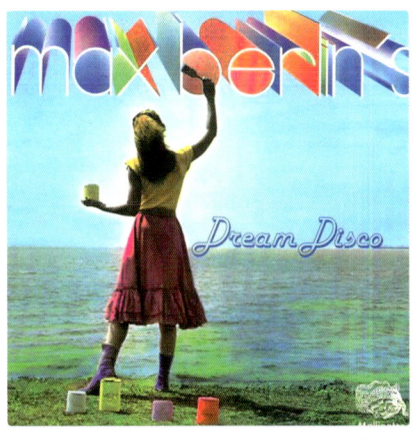

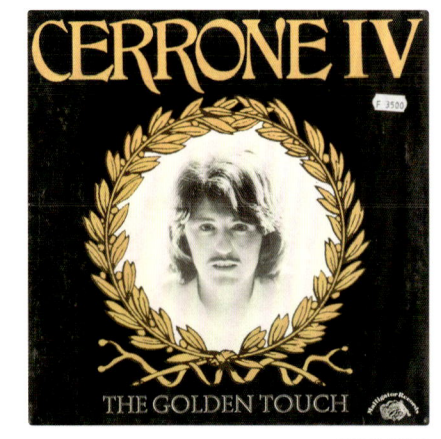

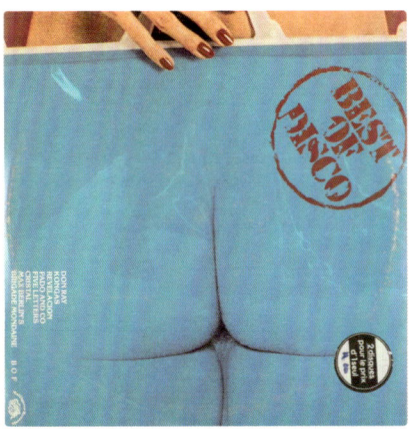

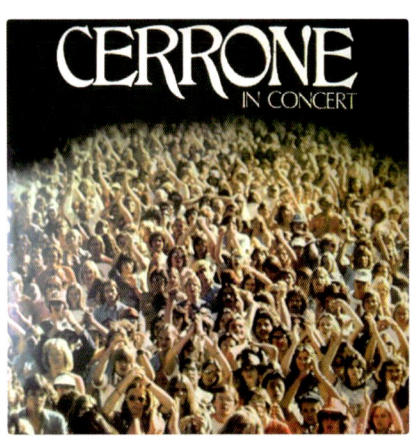

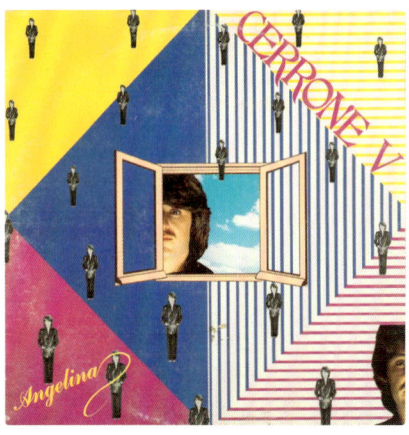

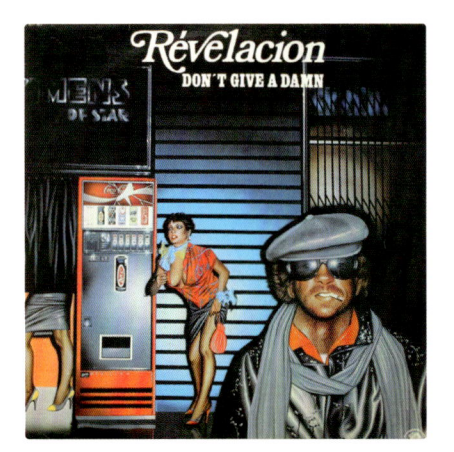

773 801 Ⓐ

SIDE I:
LOVE IN 'C' MINOR
(Alec/R. Costandinos & Cerrone)

SIDE II:
1) BLACK IS BLACK
(S. Wadey/T. Hayes & M. Grainger)
2) MIDNITE LADY
(Alec/R. Costandinos & Cerrone)

Recorded at Trident Studios
London
Sept. & Oct. '76
Sound Engineer:
Peter "Fairly" Kelsey
Tape Ops:
Steve, Geoff, Stephen,
John, Neil
Thank You:
Sarah, Sue, Peter Booth
Bernie "Clic" Spratt.
Ray Staff
Thank You: Brainiac, Psycho
and Gunpowder Green.

The Musicians were:
Mo Foster – Bass
Tony Carr – Percussion
John Dean – Percussion
Hughie Burns – Guitar
Collin Green – Guitar
Alan Hawkshaw – Keyboards
Don Ray – Keyboards
Ray Swinfield – Flute & Sax
John Watson's Brass Section
Pat Halling String Ensemble
The BV's were beautifully sung
By Joanne Willams
Stephanie De Sykes,
Madeline Bell, Jackie Sullivan,
Jean Hawker.
I played the drums.
Thank you Don Ray
and R. Costandinos
for your talent and
artistry.
Thank you Daniel
Galfo for your
moral support.

CERRONE
"A Cerrone Production"

the birds of paris
Photo by: G. Spitzer

DISTRIBUTION
wea
filipacchi music
A Warner Communications Company

Malligator

MADE IN FRANCE

Cerrone - Love In C Minor (back) / Malligator 1976
Photo: G.Spitzer

ZL 37407 / 1980

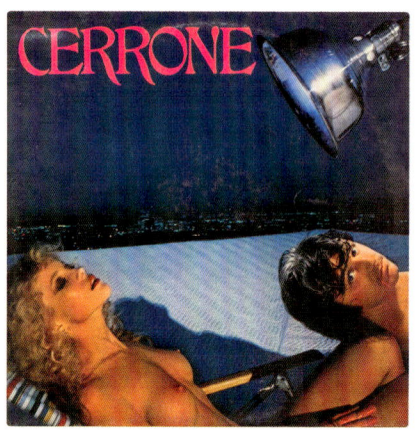

ZL 37485 / 1981

ZL 37.391 / 1980

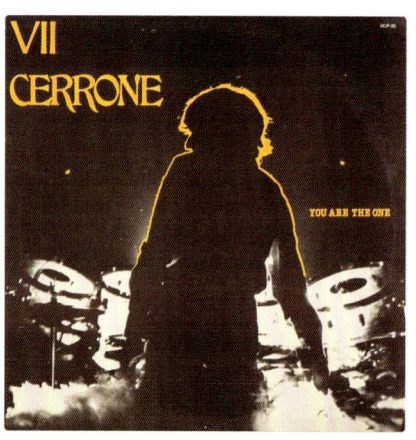

ZL 37.449 / 1980

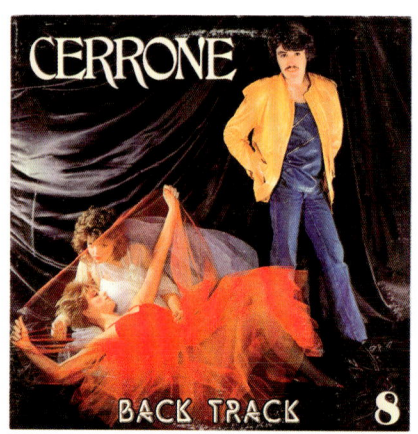

ZL 37 588 / 1982

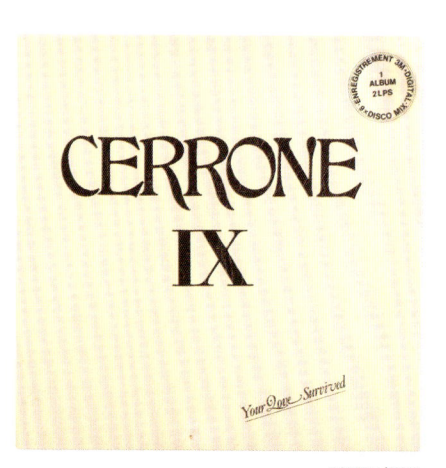

301-014 / 1982

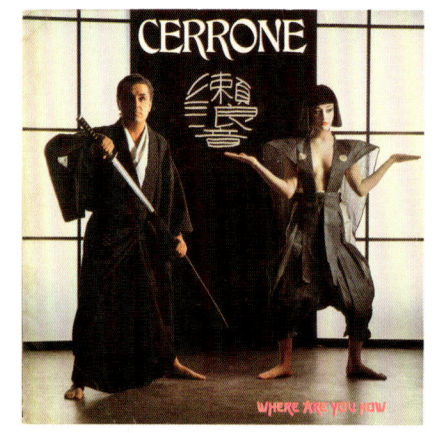

ZL 37825 / 1983

MAL-50216 / 2002

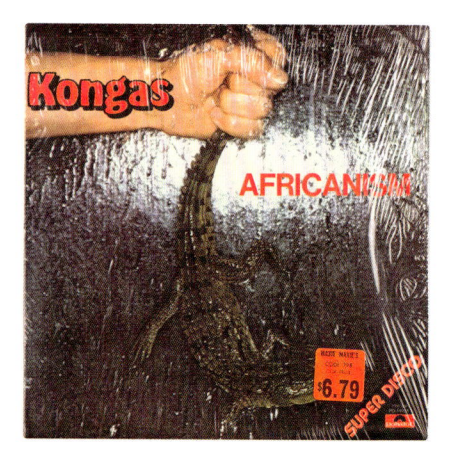

Crocos Records

337 701 / 1977

Matrix numbers

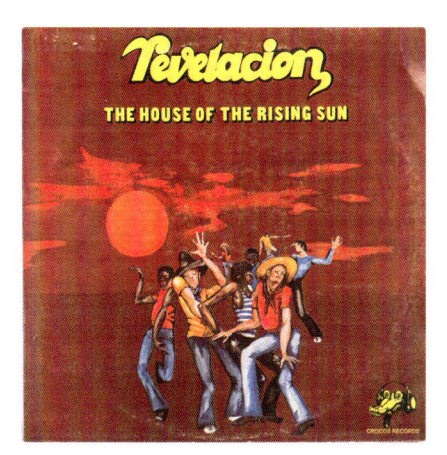

337 702 / 1977

337 703 / 1978

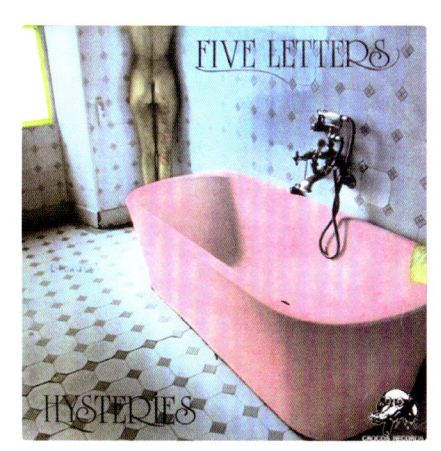

337 705 / 1978

MALLIGATOR

773 801	Cerrone	Love In C Minor	1976
773 802	Cerrone	Cerrone's Paradise	1977
773 803	Cerrone	Cerrone 3 - Supernature	1977
773 804	Don Ray	The Garden Of Love	1978
773 805	Cerrone	Brigade Mondaine	1978
773 807	Cerrone	Cerrone IV - The Golden Touch	1978
773 808	Various	Best Of Disco	1978
773 809	Cerrone	In Concert	1979
773 810	Cerrone	Cerrone V - Angelina	1979
773 811	Cerrone	Brigade Mondaine: La Secte De Marrakech	1979
FL 1611	Five Letters	Got Got Money...	1979
J 1611 161	Pado & Co	Pado & Co	1978
J 1611-182	Revelacion	Don't Give A Damn	1979
MRI 40-21000	Kongas	Kongas	1979
ZL 37.391	Cerrone	Cerrone VI	1980
ZL 37407	Cerrone	Vaudou Aux Caraïbes	1980
ZL 37.449	Cerrone	Cerrone VII - You Are The One	1980
ZL 37485	Cerrone	The Best Of Cerrone	1981
ZL 37 588	Cerrone	Back Track 8	1982
301-014	Cerrone	IX Your Love Survived	1982
ZL 37712	Cerrone	Cerrone Or	1983
ZL 37798	Cerrone	En Concert	1983
ZL 37825	Cerrone	Where Are You Now	1983
MAL-50216	Cerrone	Hysteria	2002

CROCOS

337 701	Kongas	Africanism	1977
337 702	Revelacion	The House Of The Rising Sun	1977
337 703	Leslie O'Hara	Gipsy Boy	1978
337 705	Five Letters	Hysteries	1978

Mother F

XXIV Minus (1)

Disco Labels & Albums

Chapter 10
Matra Records

CANADIAN DISCO LABEL WHOSE MAIN RELEASES WERE BY LIME, THE GROUP COMPOSED OF HUSBAND AND WIFE TEAM DENIS AND DENYSE LEPAGE.

Left: Mother F - XXIV Minus / Matra 1982

MLP-002 / 1982

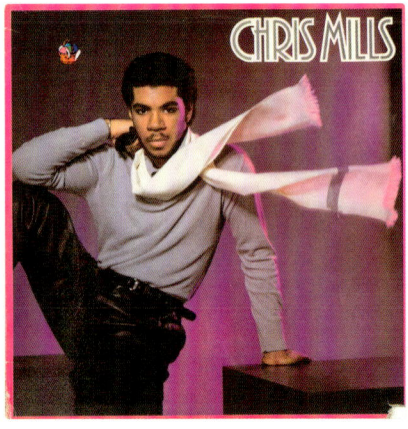

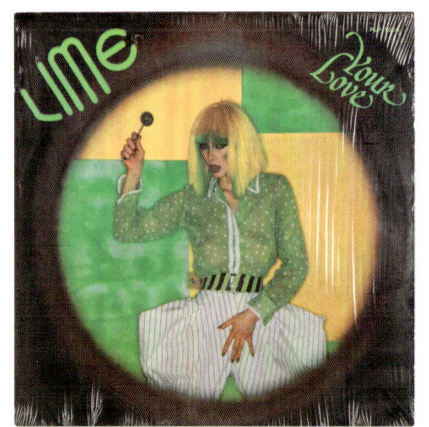

MLP-002 / 1982

MLP-1 / 1981

WLP-1026 / 1981

WLP-1030 / 1981

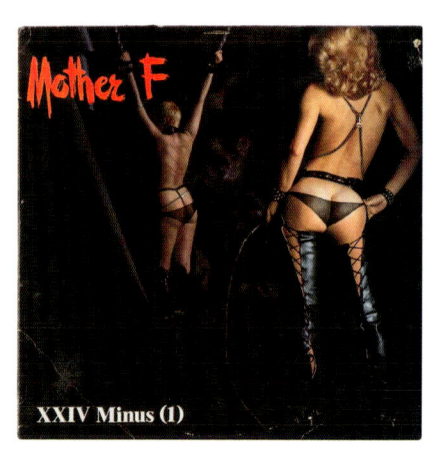

MLP-003 / 1982

MLP-004 / 1982

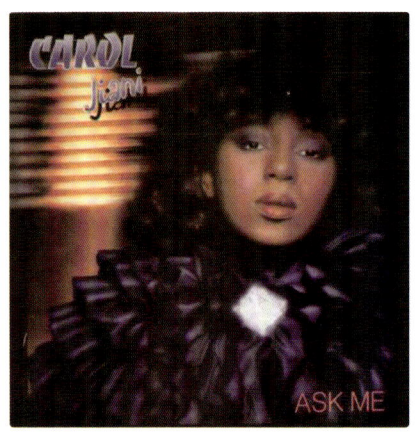

MLP-005 / 1982

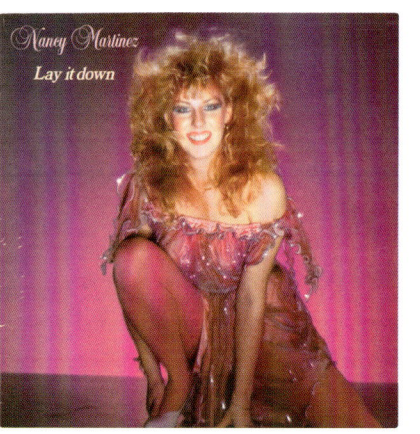

MLP-007 / 1983

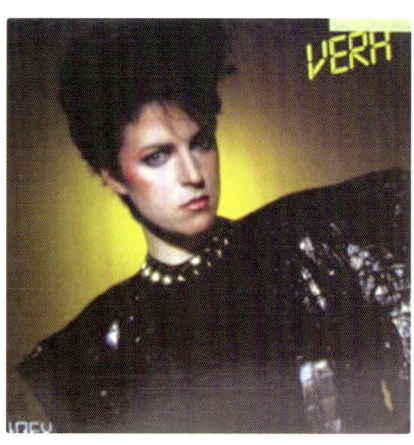

MLP-008 / 1983

Matrix numbers

MLP-010 / 1983

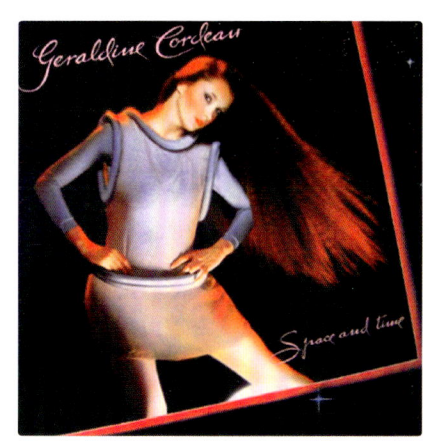

MLP-011 / 1984

MLP-012 / 1984

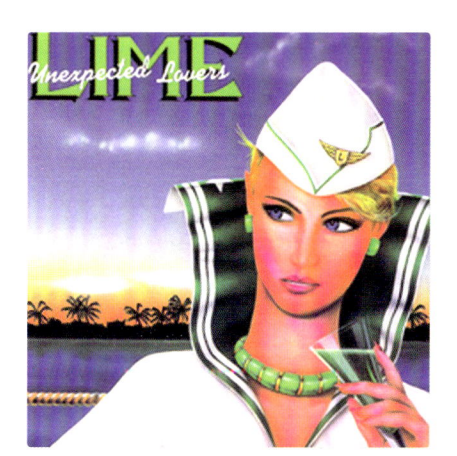

MLP-013 / 1985

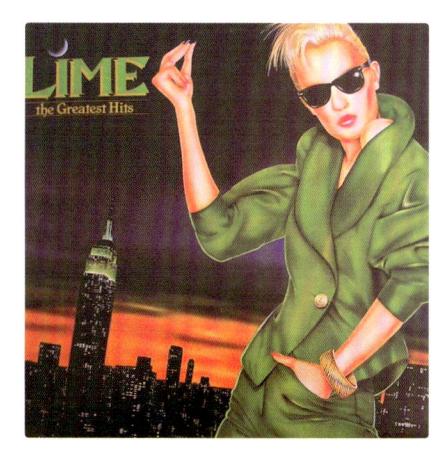

MLP-014 / 1985

MLP-015 / 1986

MANTRA

MLP-1	Chris Mills	Chris Mills	1981
WLP-1026	Lime	Your Love	1981
WLP-1030	Carol Jiani	Hit `N Run Lover	1981
MLP-002	Lime	Lime II	1982
MLP-003	Mother F	XXIV Minus	1982
MLP-004	Flower	Flower	1982
MLP-005	Carol Jiani	Ask Me	1982
MLP-006	Lime	Lime 3	1983
MLP-007	Nancy Martinez	Lay It Down	1983
MLP-008	Vera	Joey	1983
MLP-009	Voggue	Take 2	1983
MLP-010	Trans-X	Message On The Radio	1983
MLP-011	Geraldine Cordeau	Space And Time	1984
MLP-012	Lime	Sensual Sensation	1984
MLP-013	Lime	Unexpected Lovers	1985
MLP-014	Lime	The Greatest Hits	1985
MLP-015	Lime	Take The Love	1986
MLP-018	Lime	Caroline	1991

103

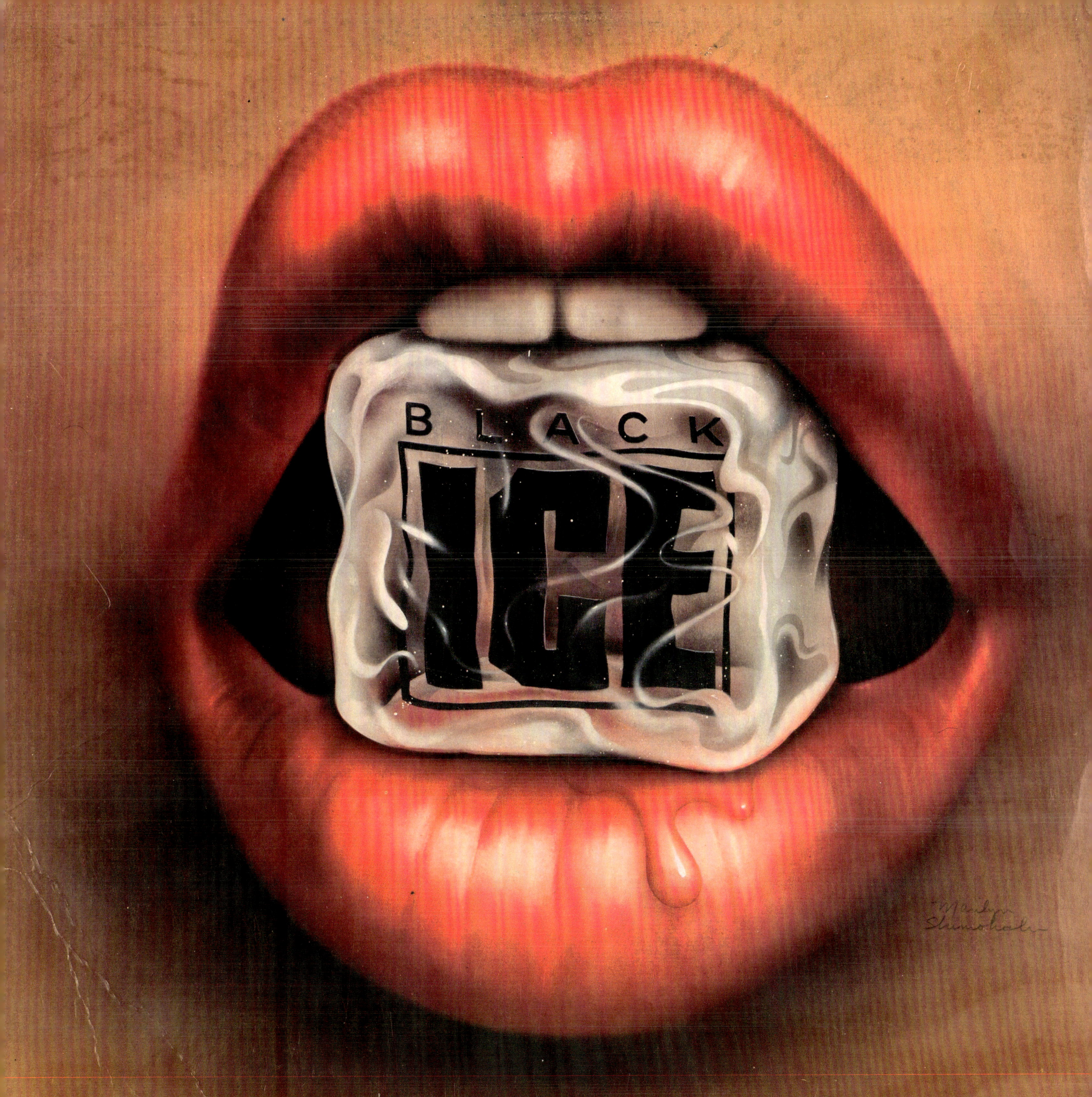
BLACK
ICE

Disco Labels & Albums

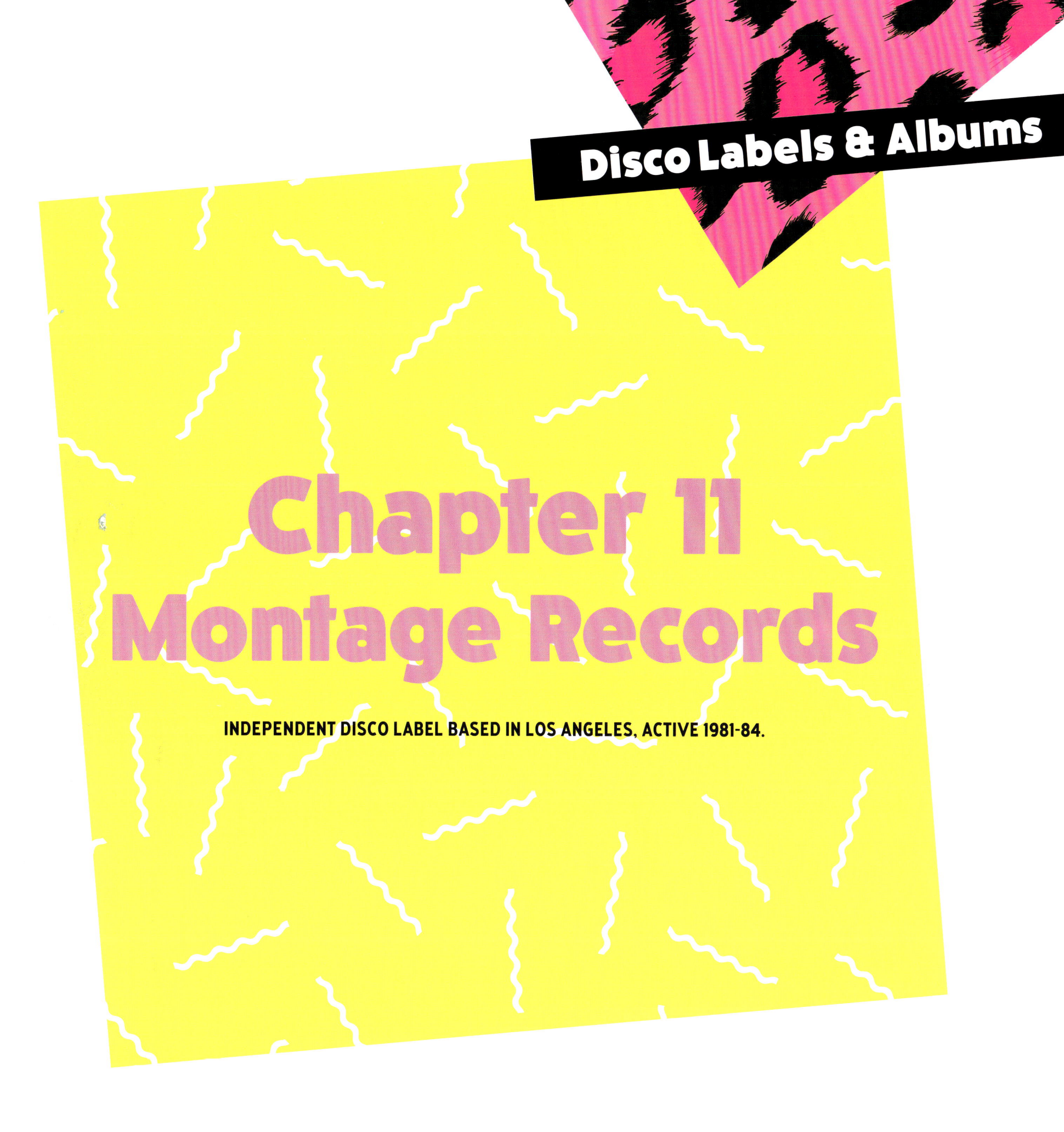

Chapter 11
Montage Records

INDEPENDENT DISCO LABEL BASED IN LOS ANGELES, ACTIVE 1981-84.

Left: Black Ice-Black Ice / Montage 1982
Design: Morillon

ST-72007 / 1982

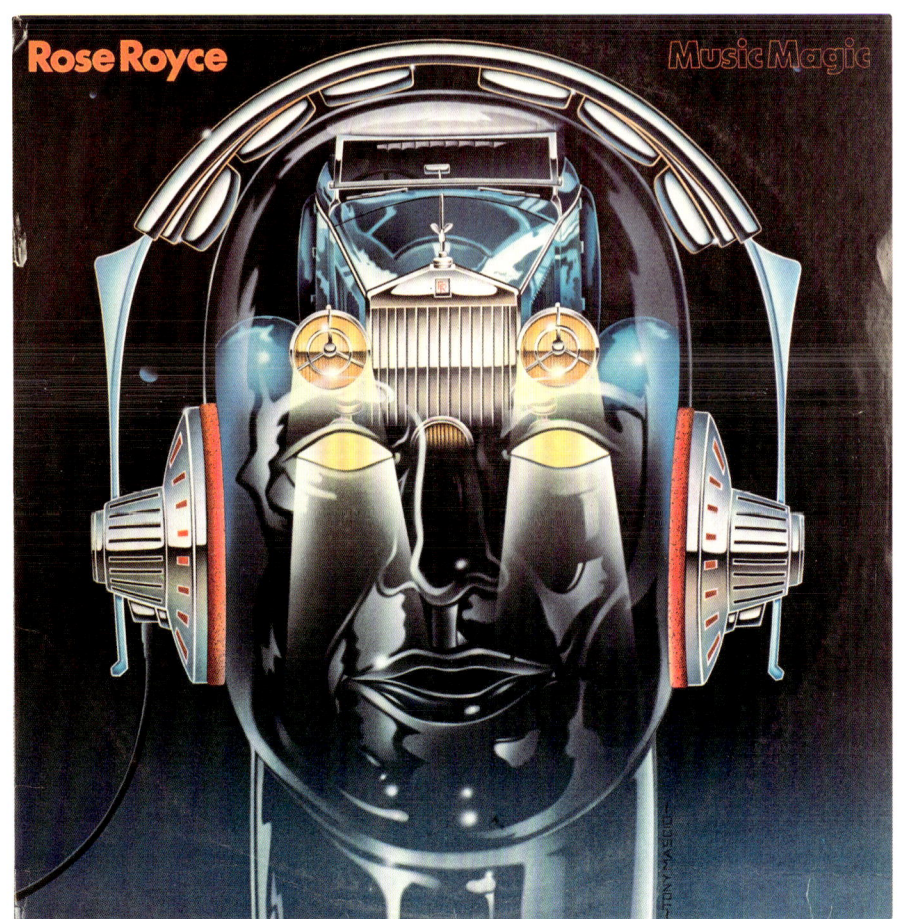

MA-106 / 1983

MA-105 / 1983

MA-110 / 1984

Matrix numbers

ST-72000 / 1981

ST-72001 / 1981

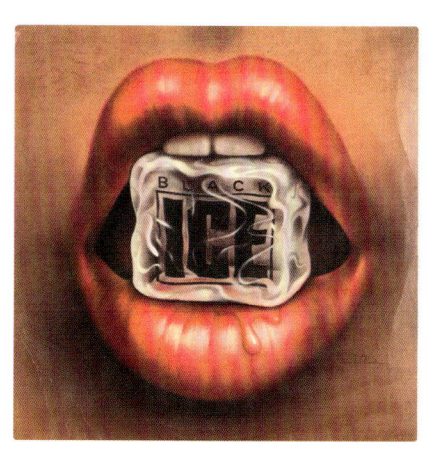

ST-72003 / 1982

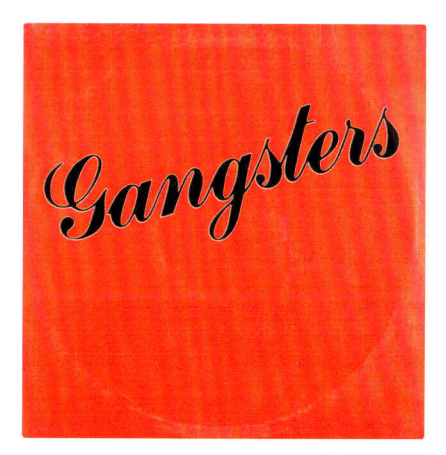

ST-72005 / 1982

ST-72006 / 1982

ST-72008 / 1982

ST-72009 / 1982

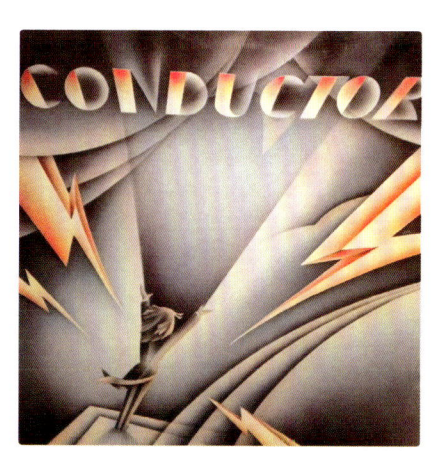

MLP-72500 / 1982

MONTAGE

ST-72000	Visitors	Visitors	1981
ST-72001	C. M. Lord	C. M. Lord	1981
ST-72003	Black Ice	Black Ice	1982
ST-72005	Chicago Gangsters	Gangsters	1982
ST-72006	Force 5	Force 5	1982
ST-72007	Shotgun	Ladies Choice	1982
ST-72008	Mandrill	Energize	1982
ST-72009	Flower	Flower	1982
MLP-72500	Conductor	Conductor	1982
MA-102	Flower	Flower	1983
MA-105	LTD	For You	1983
MA-106	Wilbur Niles	Thrust	1983
MA-110	Royce Royce	Music magic	1984

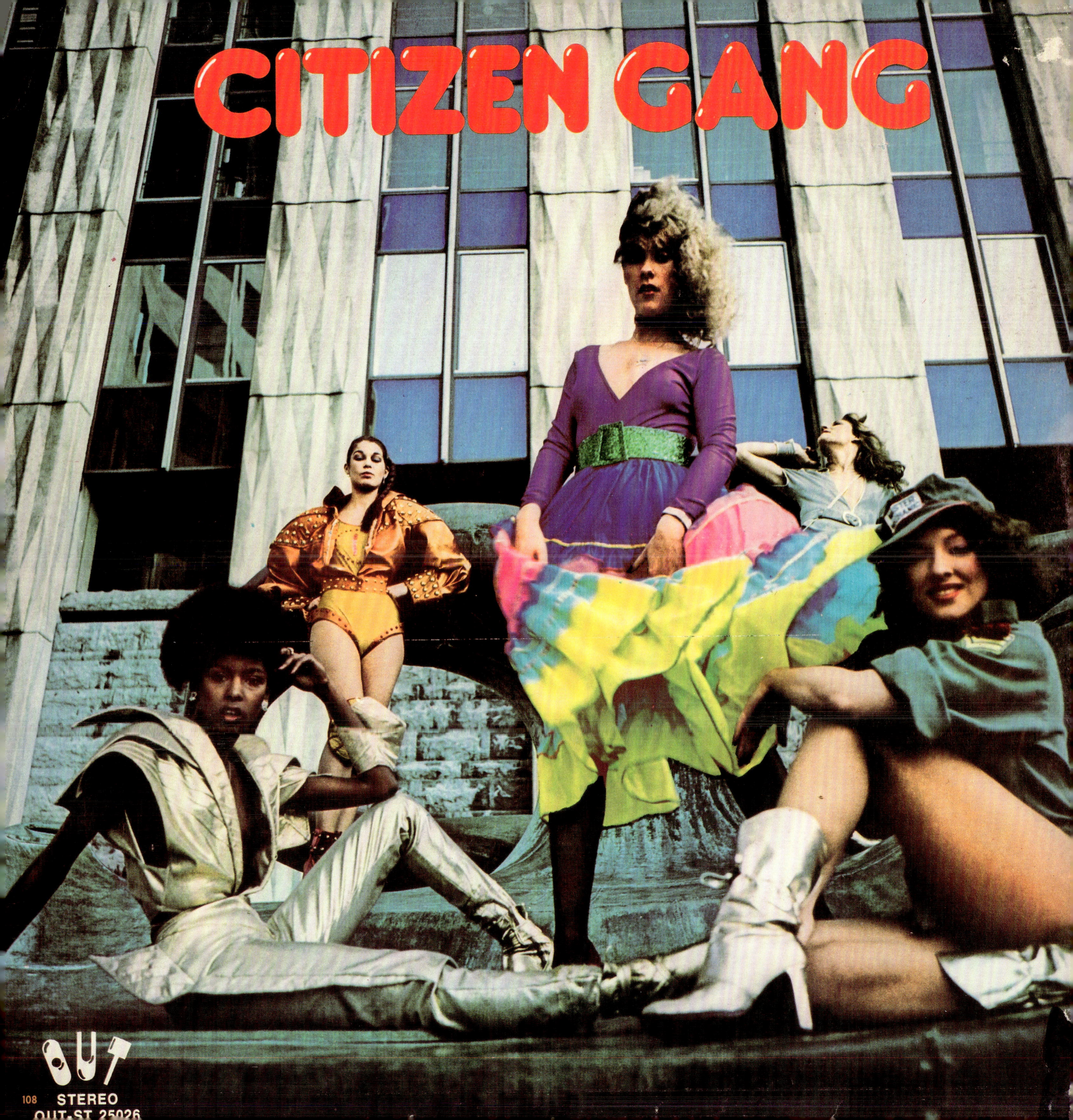
CITIZEN GANG
OUT
108
STEREO
OUT-ST 25026

Disco Labels & Albums

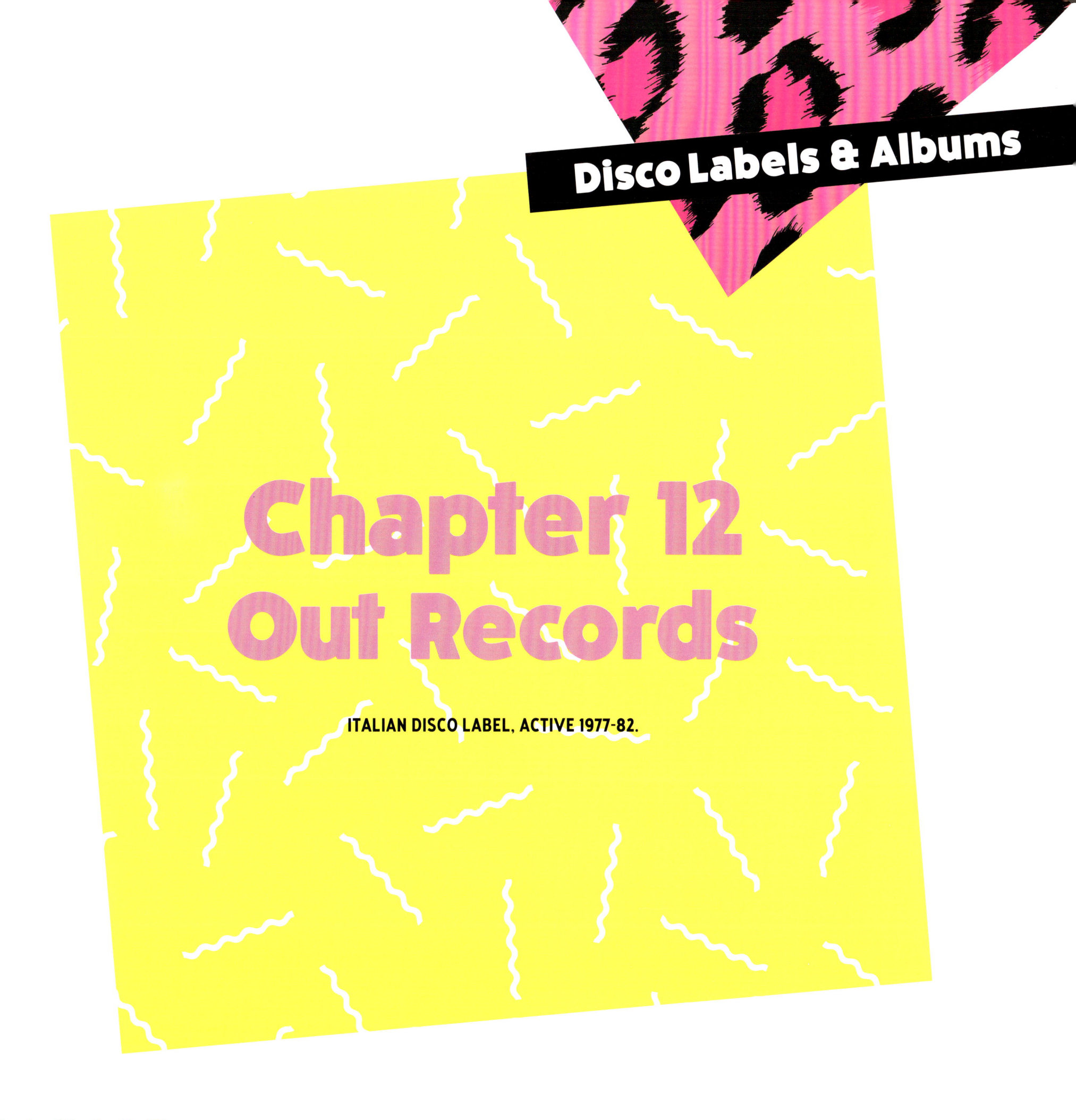

Chapter 12
Out Records

ITALIAN DISCO LABEL, ACTIVE 1977-82.

Left: Citizen Gang - Citizen Gang / Out 1979

OUT ST 25001 / 1977

OUT ST 25002 / 1977

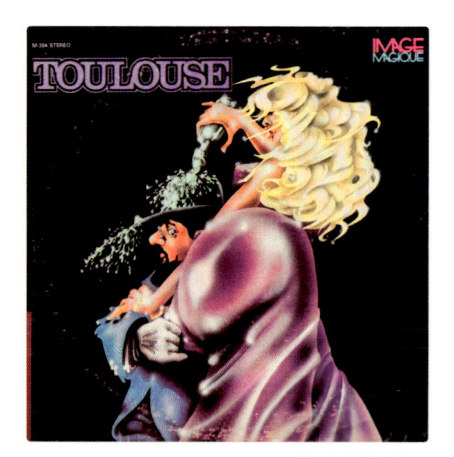

OUT ST 25004 / 1977

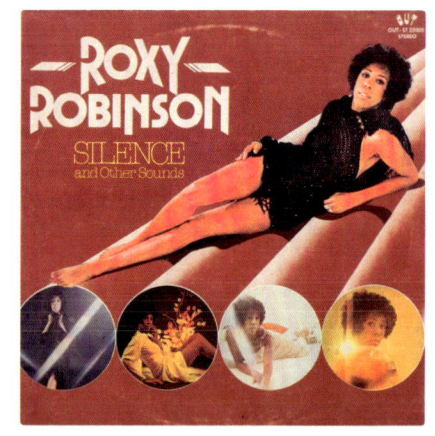

OUT ST 25005 / 1977

OUT ST 25006 / 1978

OUT ST 25007 / 1978

OUT ST 25008 / 1978

OUT ST 25010 / 1978

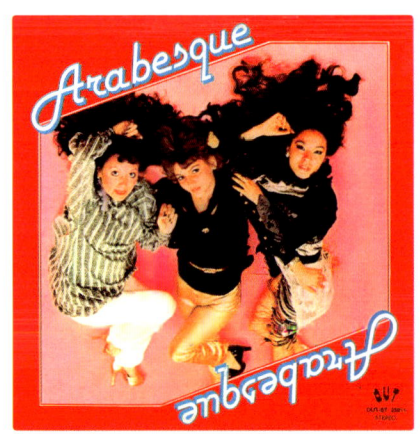

OUT ST 25011 / 1978

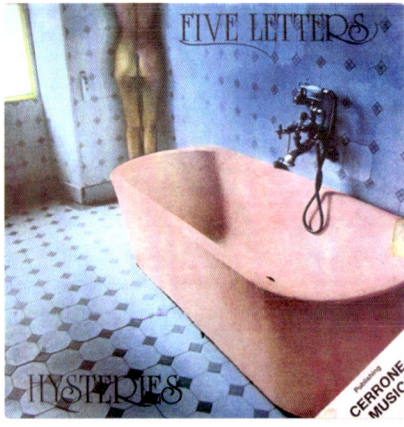

OUT ST 25012 / 1979

OUT ST 25013 / 1978

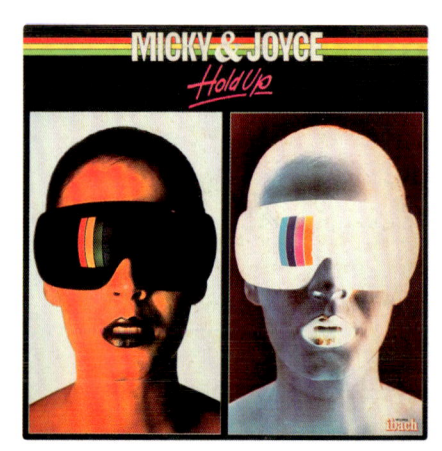

OUT ST 25016 / 1979

OUT ST 25019 / 1979

OUT ST 25022 / 1979

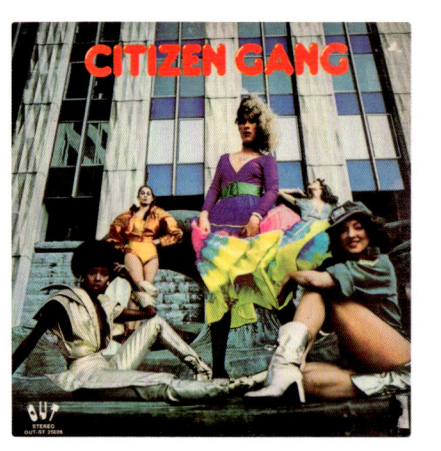

OUT ST 25026 / 1979

OUT ST 25027 / 1979

The Philarmonics-Four New Seasons / Out 1978

Black Devil - Black Devil / Out 1978
Cover Design: Patricia Fevre

Micky & Joyce - Hold Up / Out 1979
Photography: Michel Richard

Who's Who - Who's Who / Out 1980

Matrix numbers

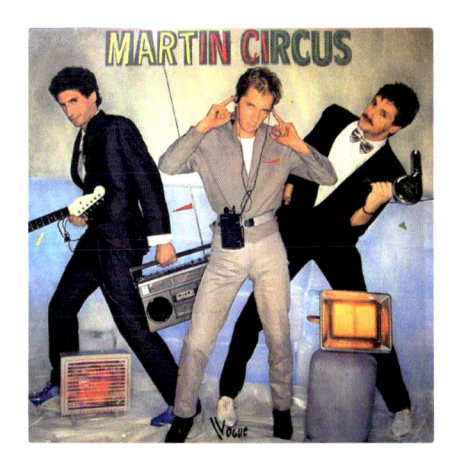

OUT ST 25028 / 1980

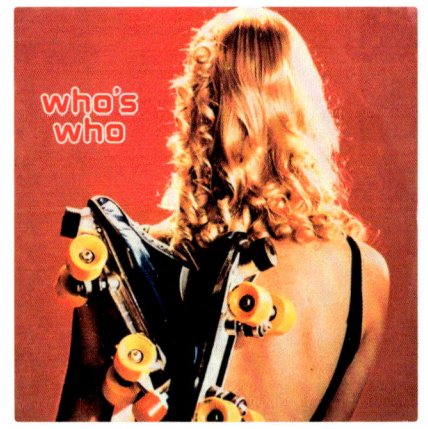

OUT ST 25029 / 1980

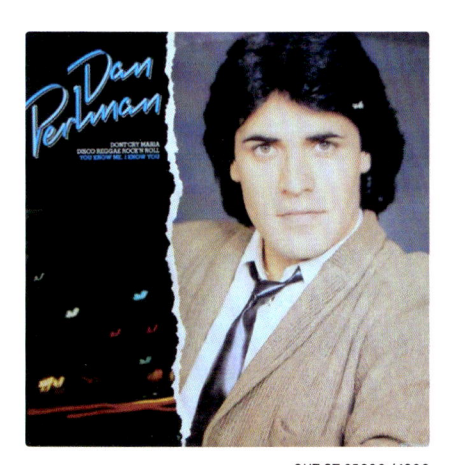

OUT ST 25030 / 1980

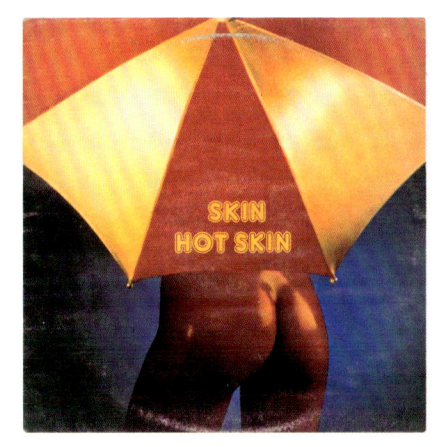

OUT ST 25038 / 1980

OUT ST 25039 / 1980

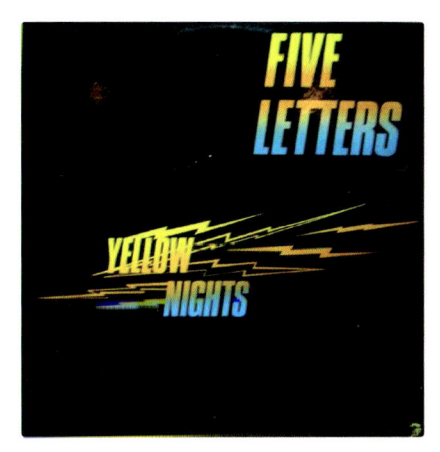

OUT ST 25040 / 1980

OUT ST 60503 / 1980

OUT

OUT ST 25001	Resonance	The Time Machine	1977
OUT ST 25002	Outbreak	Outbreak	1977
OUT ST 25004	Toulouse	Toulouse	1977
OUT-ST 25005	Roxy Robinson	Silence And Other Sounds	1977
OUT-ST 25006	Black Devil	Disco Club	1978
OUT-ST 25007	Queen Samantha	The Letter	1978
OUT-ST 25008	The Philarmonics	Four New Seasons	1978
OUT-ST 25010	Love Robot	Love Robot	1978
OUT-ST 25011	Arabesque	Arabesque	1978
OUT-ST 25012	Five Letters	Hysteries	1979
OUT-ST 25013	Queen Samantha	Queen Samantha II	1978
OUT-ST 25016	Micky And Joyce	Hold Up	1979
OUT-ST 25019	Five Letters	Got Got Money	1979
OUT-ST 25022	Ken Boothe	Who Gets Your Love ?	1979
OUT-ST 25026	Citizen Gang	Citizen Gang	1979
OUT-ST 25027	Queen Samantha	Queen Samantha	1979
OUT-ST 25028	Max Berlins	New Wave	1980
OUT ST 25029	Who's Who	Who's Who	1980
OUT ST 25030	Dan Perlman	Dan Perlman	1980
OUT ST 25038	Skin	Hot Skin	1980
OUT-ST 25039	Top Secret	Top Secret	1980
OUT-ST 25040	Five Letters	Yellow Nights	1980
OUT-ST 60503	Martin Circus	In Cold Blood	1980

We Got The Rhythm
People's Choice

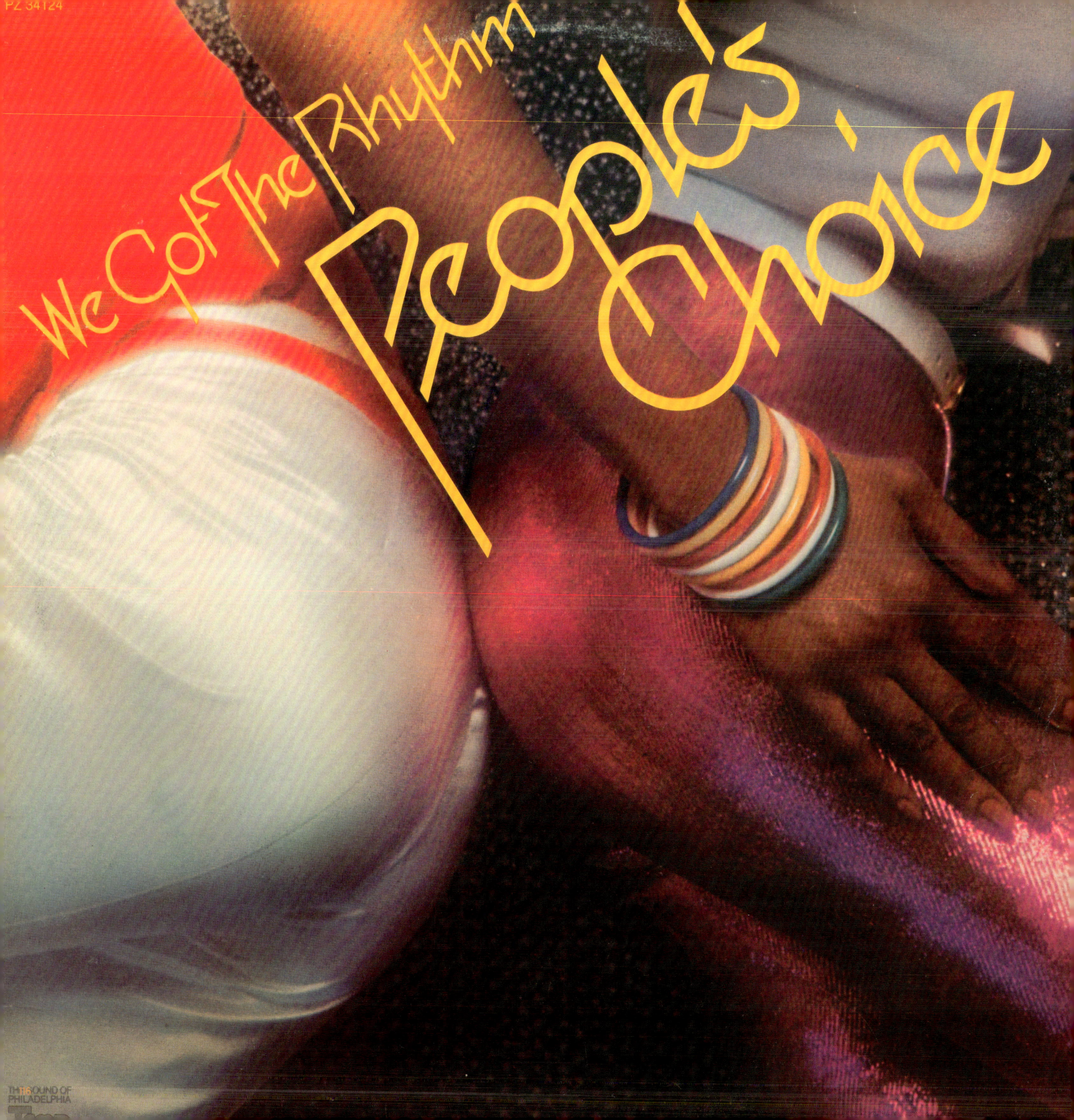

Disco Labels & Albums

Chapter 13
Philadelphia International Records

LEGENDARY RECORD LABEL FOUNDED BY KENNY GAMBLE AND LEON HUFF IN 1971.

Left: People's Choice - We Got The Rhythm / TSOP 1976
Design: Ed Lee, Marie De Oro / Photography: Frank Laffitte

KZ 30580 / 1971

KZ 31648 / 1972

KZ 31712 / 1972

KZ 31793 / 1972

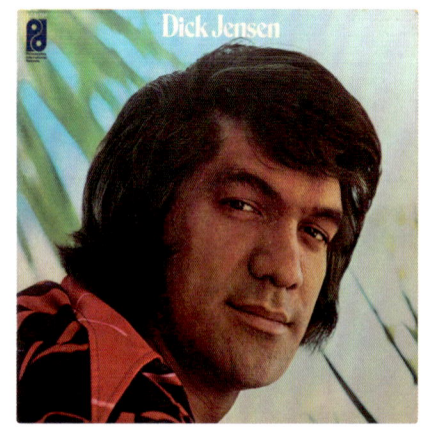

KZ 31794 / 1973

ZX 31991 / 1973

KZ 32046 / 1973

KZ 32118 / 1973

KZ 32119 / 1973

KZ 32120 / 1973

KZ 32404 / 1973

KZ 32406 / 1973

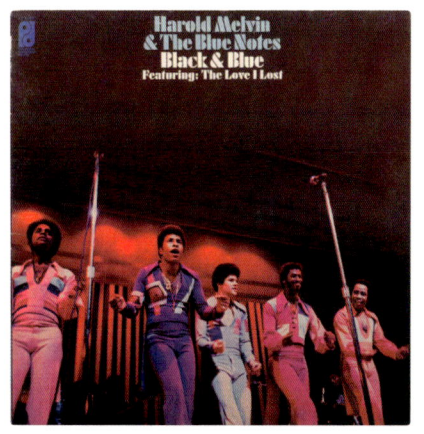

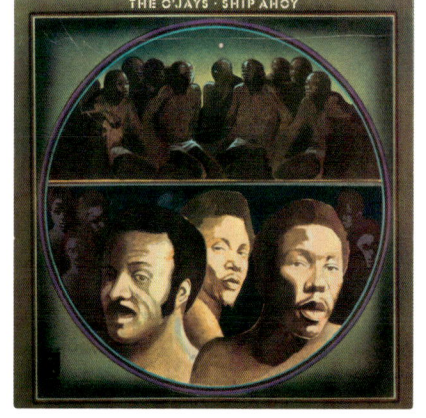

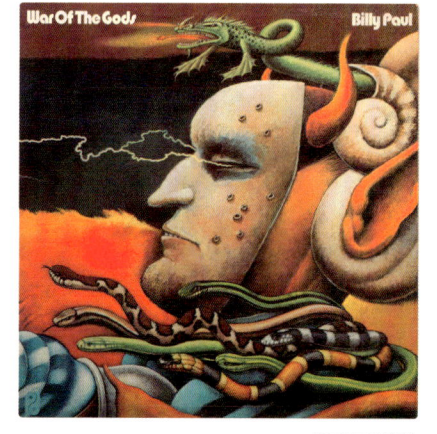

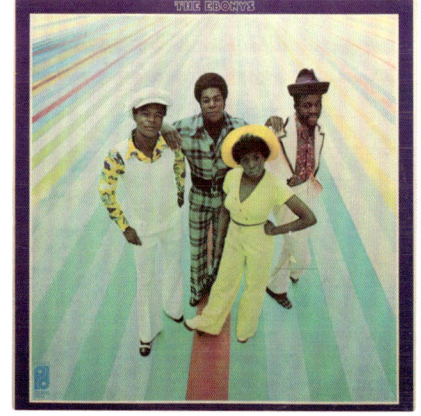

KZ/ZQ 32407 / 1973

KZ/PZ/PZQ 32408 / 1973

KZ 32409 / 1973

KZ 32419 / 1973

KZ/ZQ 32707 / 1973

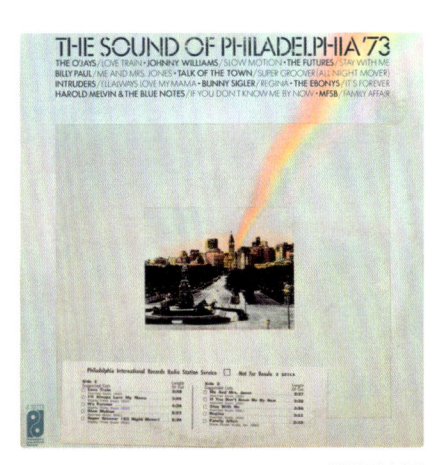

KZ 23713 / 1973

KZ 32859 / 1974

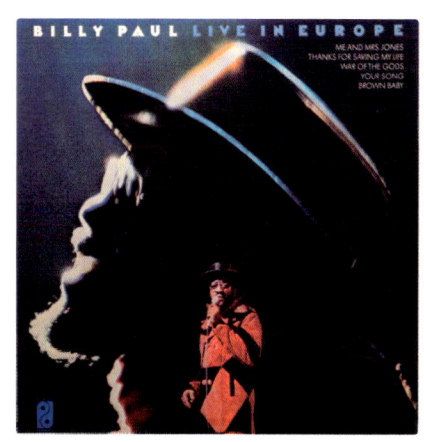

KZ 32952 / 1974

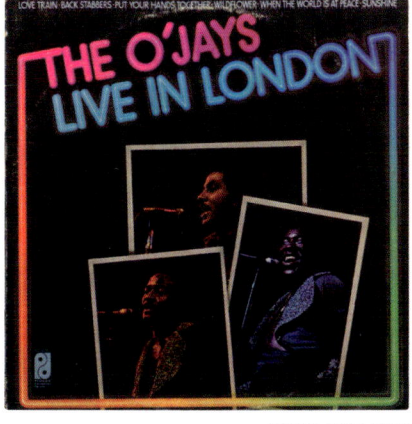

KZ/PZQ 32953 / 1974

KZ/PZ 33148 / 1975

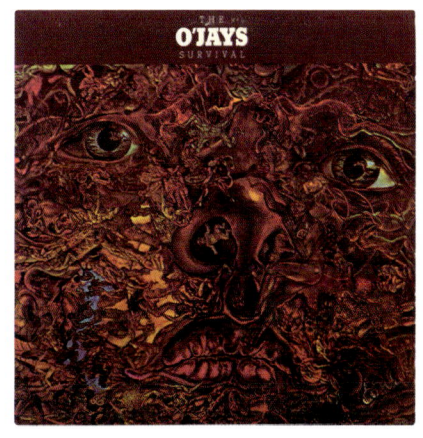

KZ 33150 / 1975

KZ 33152 / 1975

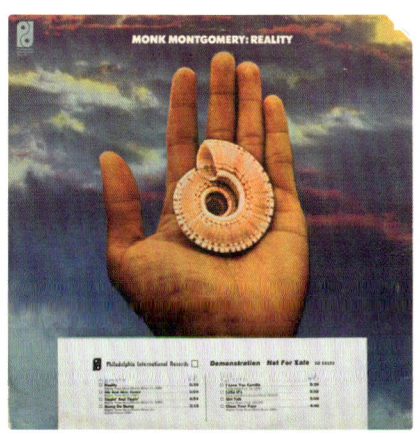

KZ 33153 / 1974

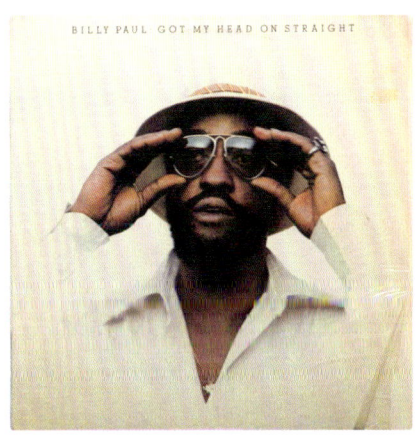

PZ 33157 / 1975

PZ 33158 / 1975

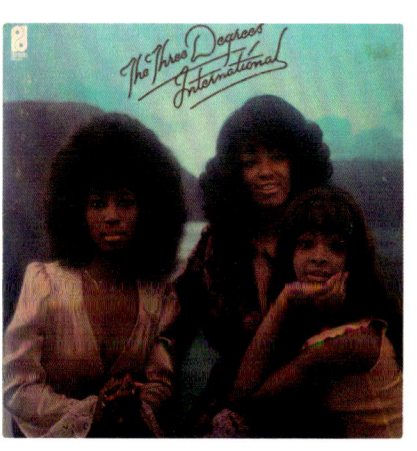

KZ 33162 / 1975

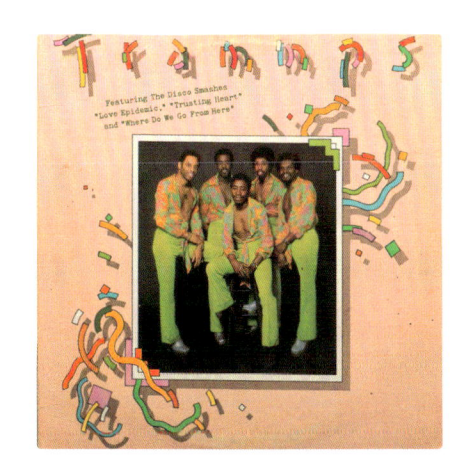

KZ 33163 / 1975

KZ 33249 / 1975

PZ/PZQ 33807 / 1975

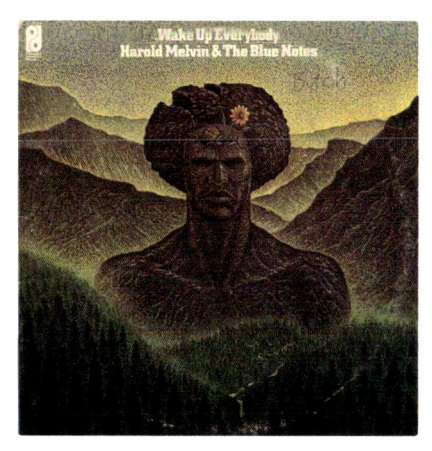

PZ/PZQ 33808 / 1975

SIDE A LOVE IS THE MESSAGE: MFSB TSOP (THE SOUND OF PHILADELPHIA): MFSB, FEATURING THE THREE DEGREES 3494
SIDE B DIRTY OL' MAN: THE THREE DEGREES I LOVE MUSIC: THE O'JAYS SIDE C DON'T LEAVE ME THIS WAY: HAROLD MELVIN & THE BLU
NOTES LOVE TRAIN: THE O'JAYS SIDE D I'LL ALWAYS LOVE MY MAMA: INTRUDERS BAD LUCK: HAROLD MELVIN & THE BLUE NOTE
ALL SONGS WRITTEN BY K. GAMBLE AND L. HUFF EXCEPT "DON'T LEAVE ME THIS WAY," BY K. GAMBLE, L. HUFF, AND C. GILBERT, "I'LL ALWAYS LOVE MY MAMA" BY K. GAMBLE, L. HUFF, J. WHITEHEAD AND G. McFADDEN; "BAD LUCK" BY J. WHITEHEAD, G. McFADDEN AND V. CARSTARPH

Album Art: Gerry Huerta / Art Direction: Ed Lee / © 1977 CBS Inc. / ℗ 1973, 1974, 1975, 1977 CBS Inc. / Distributed by CBS Records / CBS Inc. / 51 W. 52 St., New York City. Warning: All Rights Reserved. Unauthorized duplication is a violation of applicable law

0 7464-34940-1

Philadelphia International Records

Philadelphia Classics / PIR 1977
Album Art: Gerry Huerta / Art Direction: Ed Lee

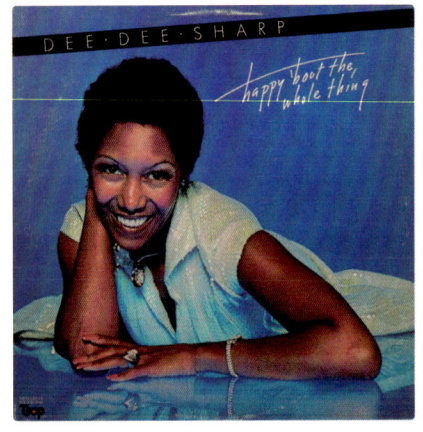

PZ 33839 / 1976 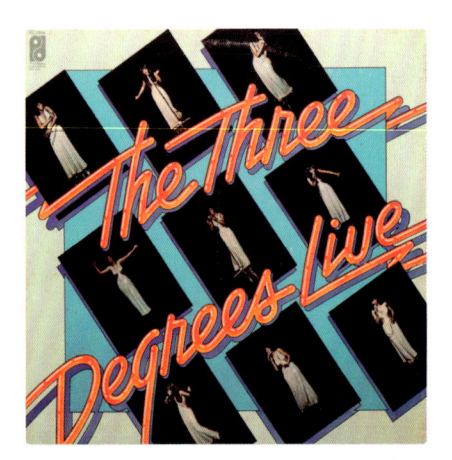
PZ 33840 / 1975 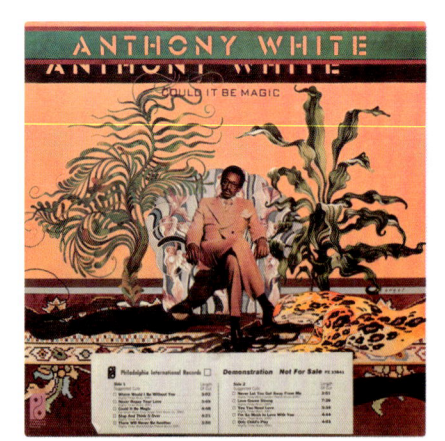
PZ 33841 / 1976 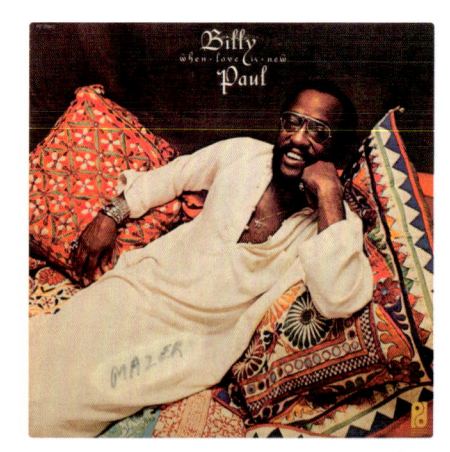
PZ 33843 / 1975

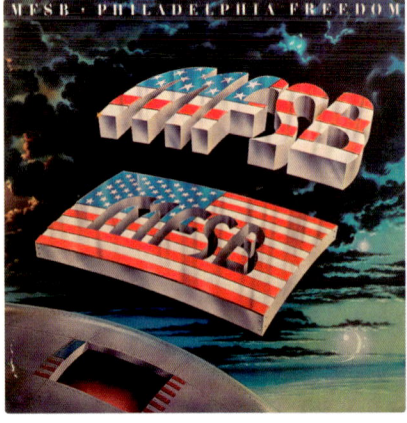

PZ/PZQ 33845 / 1975 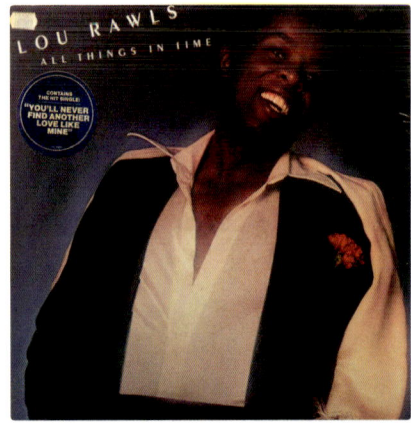
PZ 33957 / 1976 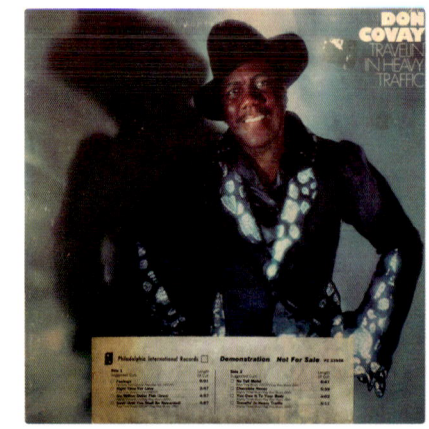
PZ 33958 / 1976 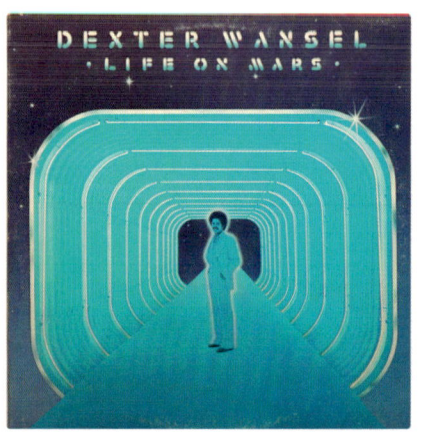
PZ 34079 / 1976

PZ 34122 / 1976 
PZ 34123 / 1976 
JE/PE 34229 / 1976 
PZ 34232 / 1976

PZ 34238 / 1976
PZ 43245 / 1976 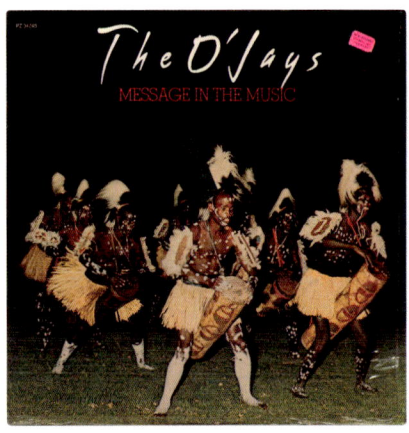
PZ 34267 / 1976 
PZ 34323 / 1976

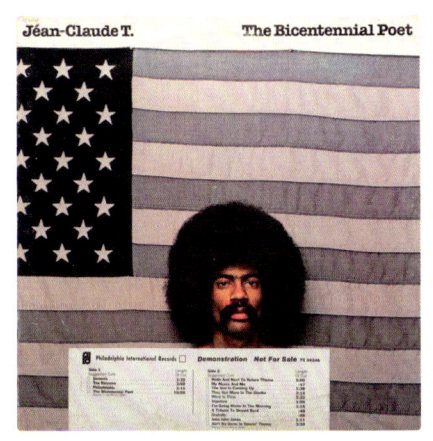

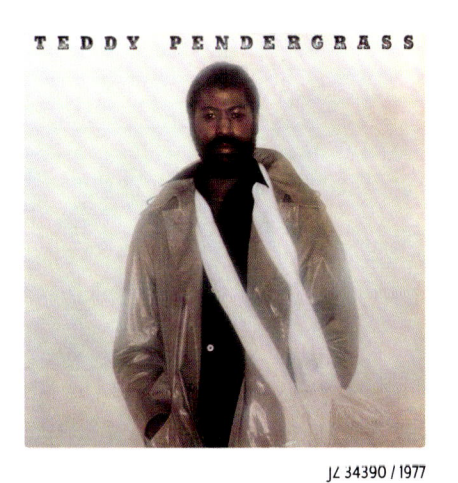

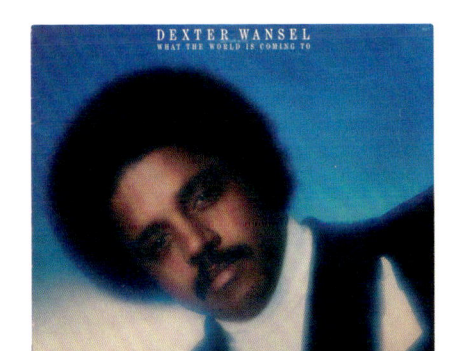

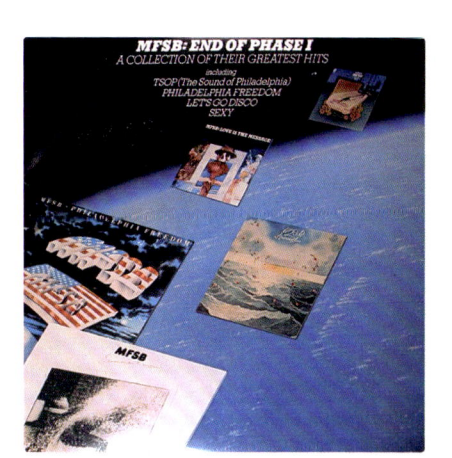

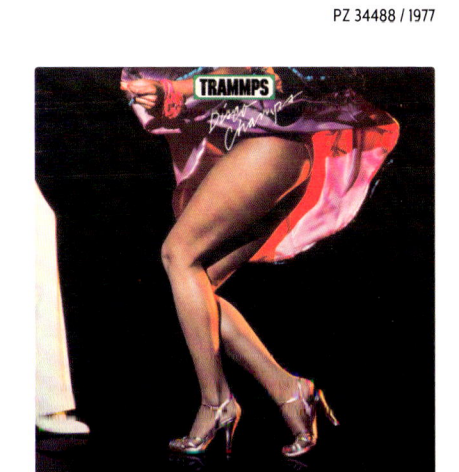

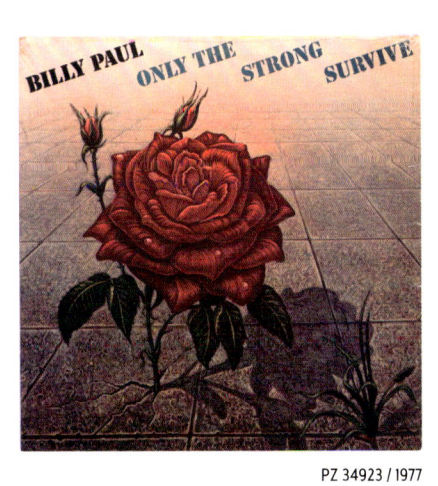

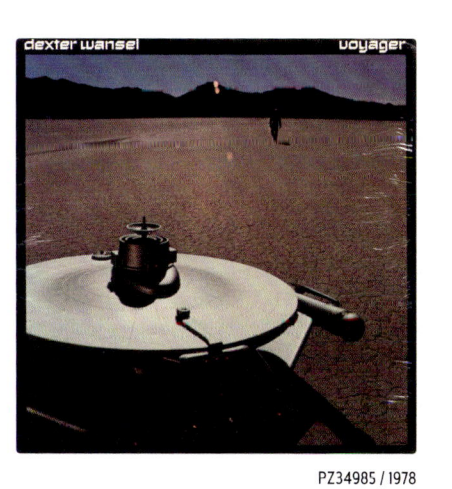

PZ 34346 / 1976	PZ 34389 / 1976	JZ 34390 / 1977	PZ 34394 / 1977
PZ 34437 / 1977	PZ 34487 / 1977	PZ 34488 / 1977	PZ 34658 / 1977
PZ 34659 / 1977	PZ 34684 / 1977	ZX 34728 / 1977	JE/PE 34835 / 1977
PZ 34855 / 1977	PZ 34923 / 1977	PZ 34940 / 1977	PZ 34985 / 1978

PZ 34986 / 1978

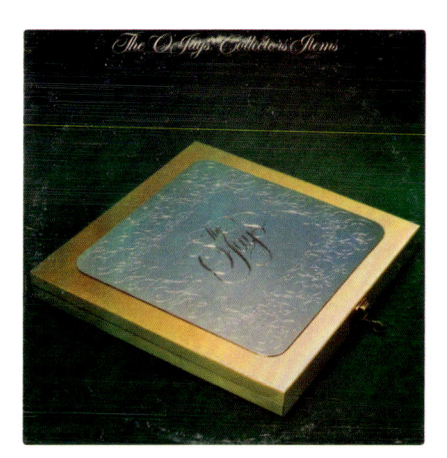

PGZ 35024/Z 235024 / 1977

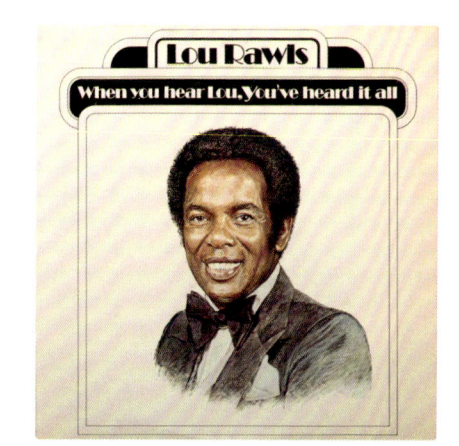

JZ 35036 / 1977

JZ 35095 / 1978

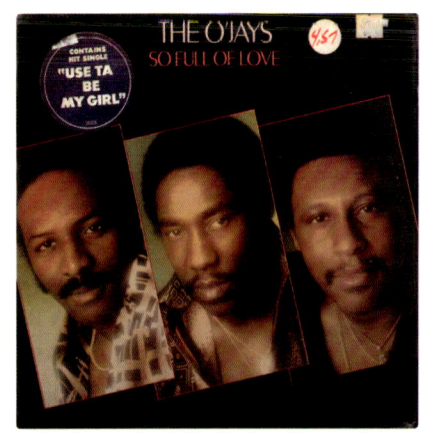

JZ/PZ 35355 / 1978

JZ 35363 / 1978

JZ 34458 / 1978

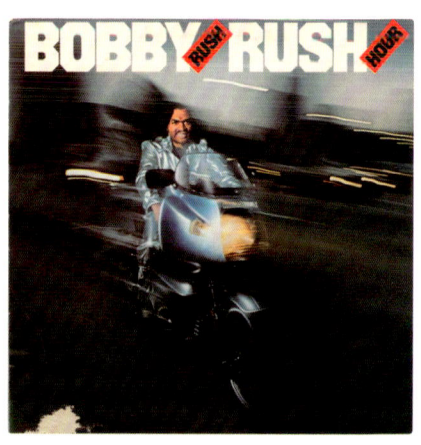

JZ 35509 / 1978

JZ 3515 / 1978

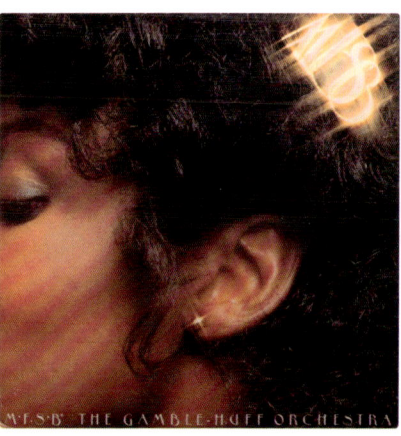

JZ 35516 / 1978

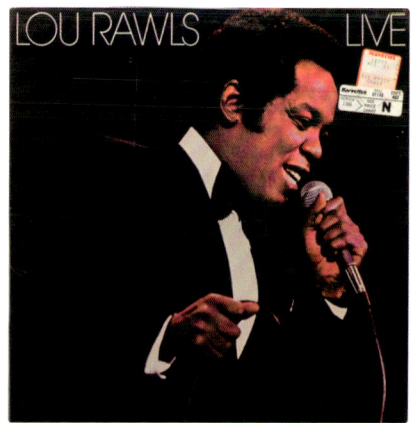

PZ 235517 / 1978

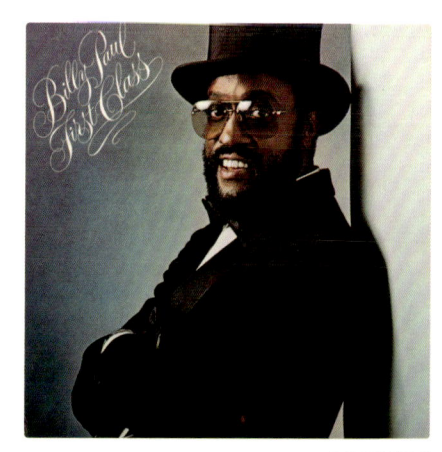

PZ 35756 / 1979

JZ 35757 / 1979

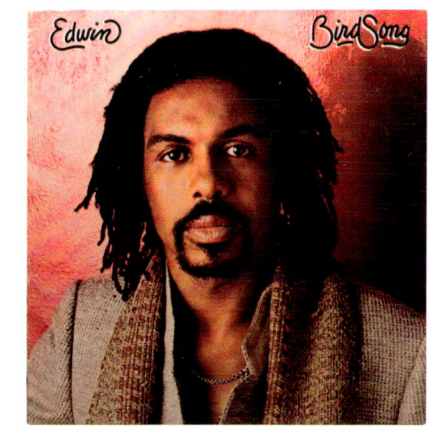

JZ 35758 / 1979

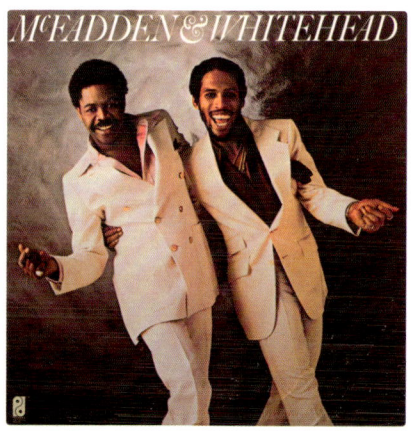

JZ 35800 / 1979

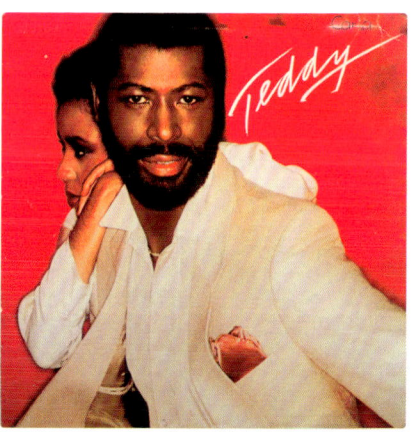

FZ 36003 / 1979

Instant Funk - Get Down With The Philly Jump / TSOP 1976
Art Director & Design: Ed Lee / Photography: Frank Laffitte

JZ/PZ 36006 / 1979	JZ 36007 / 1979	JZ 36024 / 1979	NJZ 36025 / 1979
FZ 36027 / 1979	JZ 36036 / 1979	JZ 36096 / 1979	JZ 36097 / 1979
JZ 36196 / 1979	JZ 36294 / 1979	JZ/PZ 36304 / 1979	JZ 36313 / 1980
Z 236314 / 1980	JZ 36370 / 1980	JZ 36413 / 1980	JZ 36414 / 1981

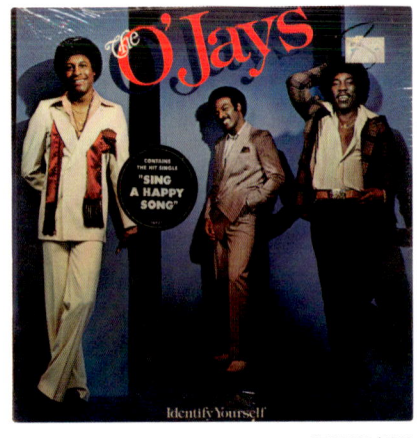

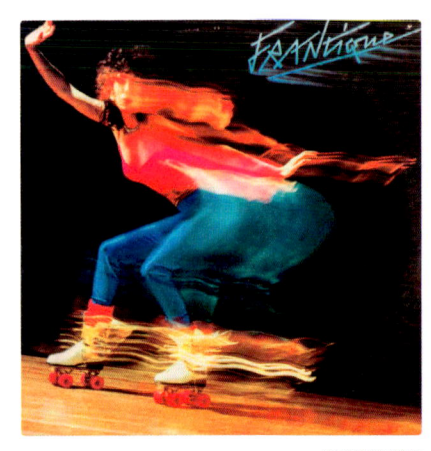

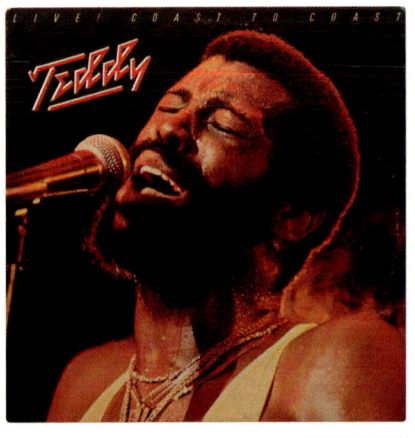

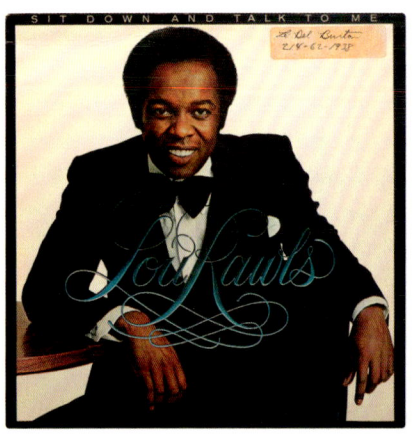

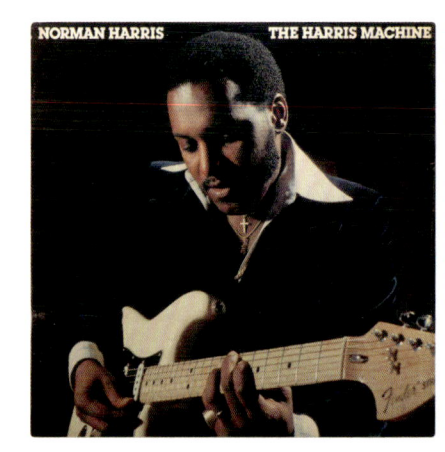

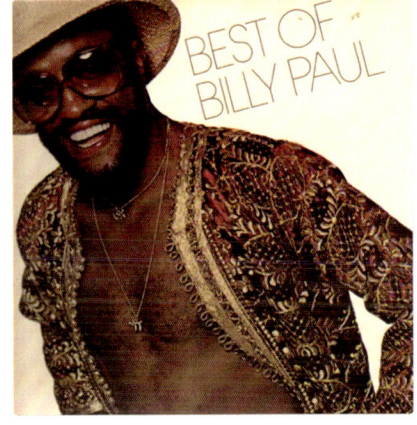

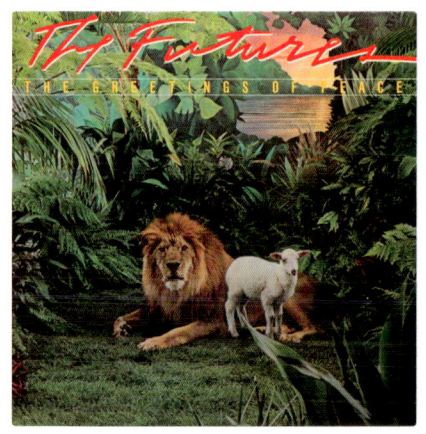

JZ 36745 / 1980	NJZ 36758 / 1980	JZ 36767 / 1980	JZ 36774 / 1980
FZ/PZ 37380 / 1981	FZ 37491 / 1981	FZ 37627 / 1981	FZ 37683 / 1982
FZ 37684 / 1982	FZ 37955 / 1982	FZ 37999 / 1982	FZ 38118 / 1982
FZ/PZ 38518 / 1983	FZ 38539 / 1983	FZ 38555 / 1984	FZ 38646 / 1983

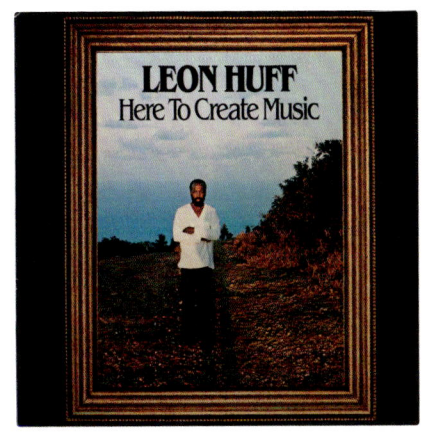

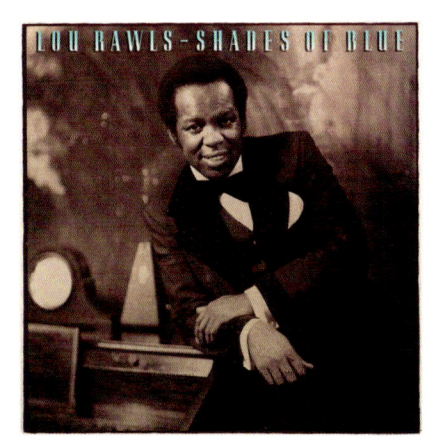

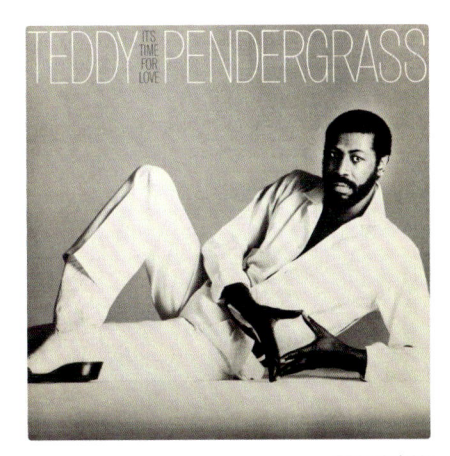

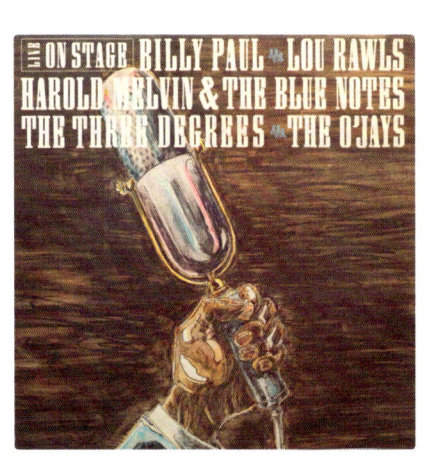

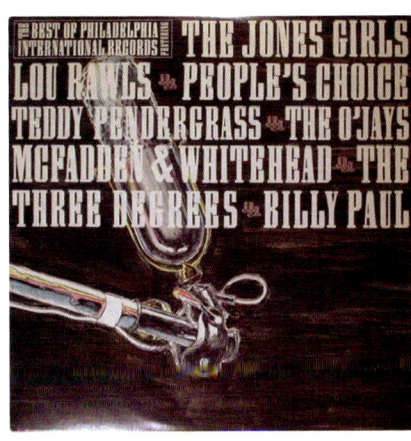

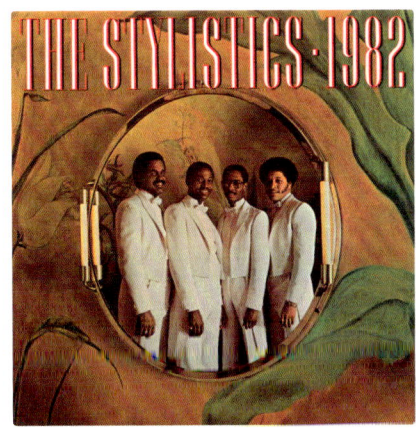

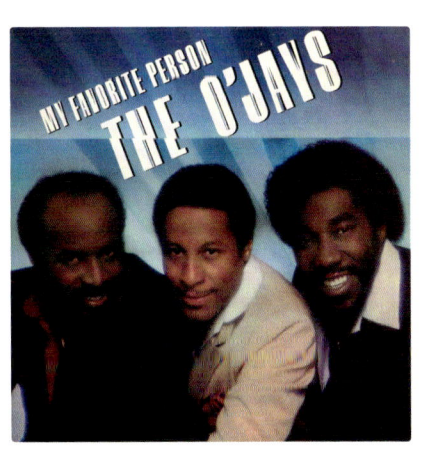

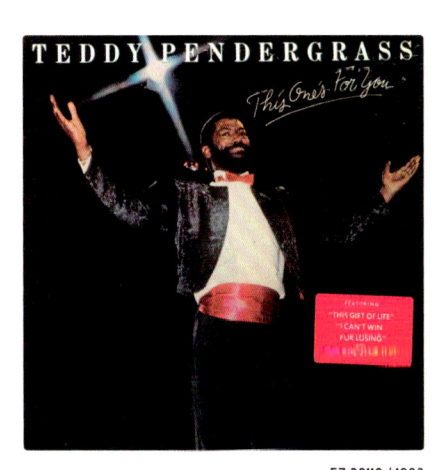

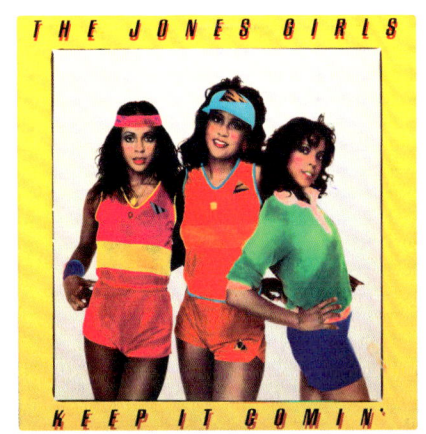

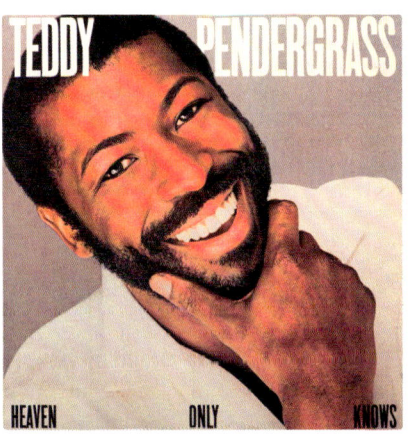

FZ 39252 / 1984

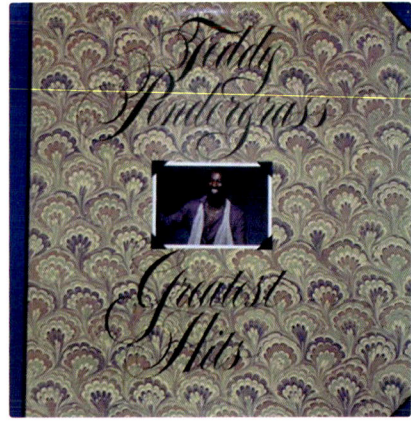

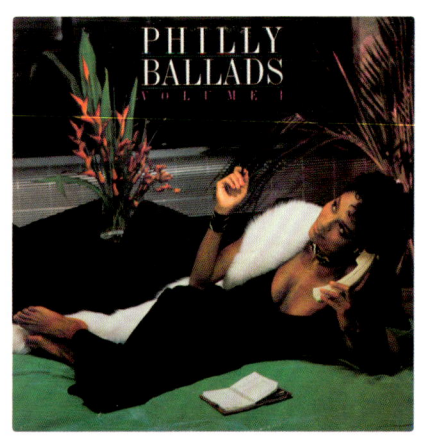

PZ 39255 / 1984

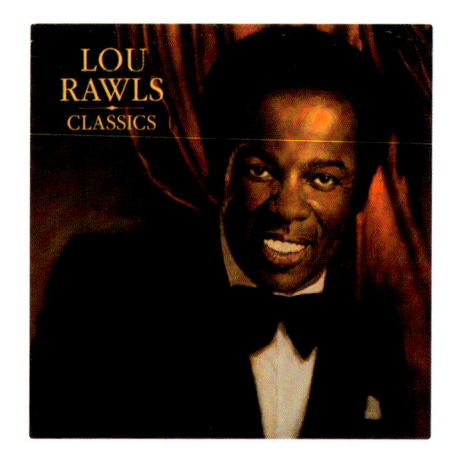

FZ 39285 / 1984

FZ 39367 / 1984

F7 40020 / 1985

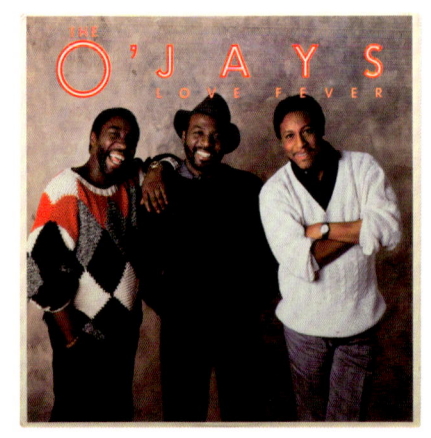

ST 53015 / 1985

ST 53028 / 1986

ST 53029 / 1985

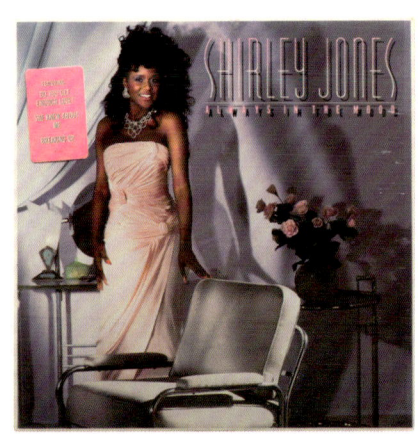

ST 53031 / 1986

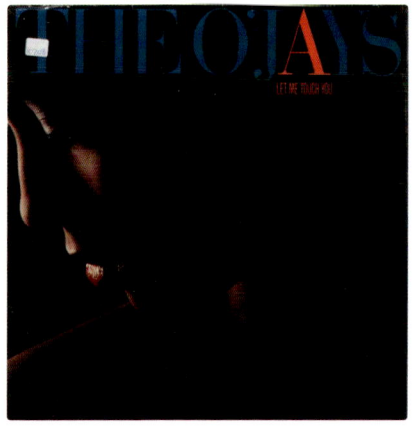

ST 53036 / 1987

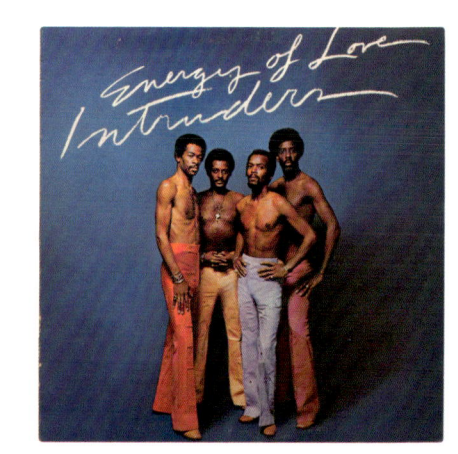

TSOP

KZ 33149 / 1974

KZ 33842 / 1975

KZ 33186 / 1975

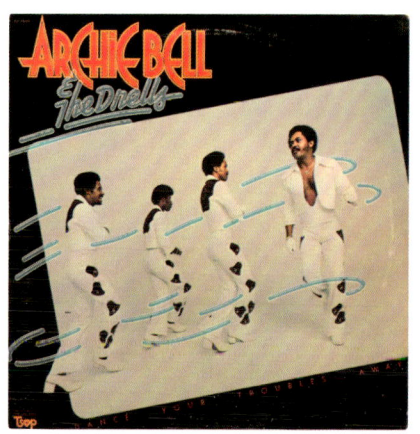

PZ 33844 / 1975

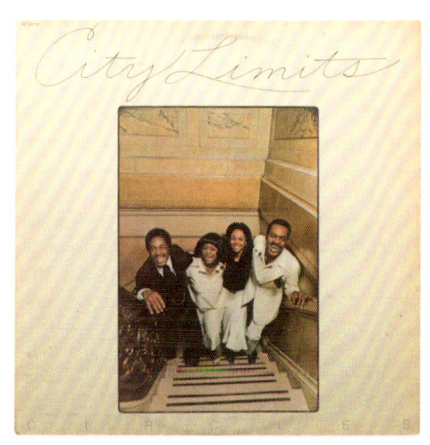

PZ 34110 / 1976

MFSB - Summertime / PIR 1976
Design: Ed Lee / Photography: Kenley A Gardner

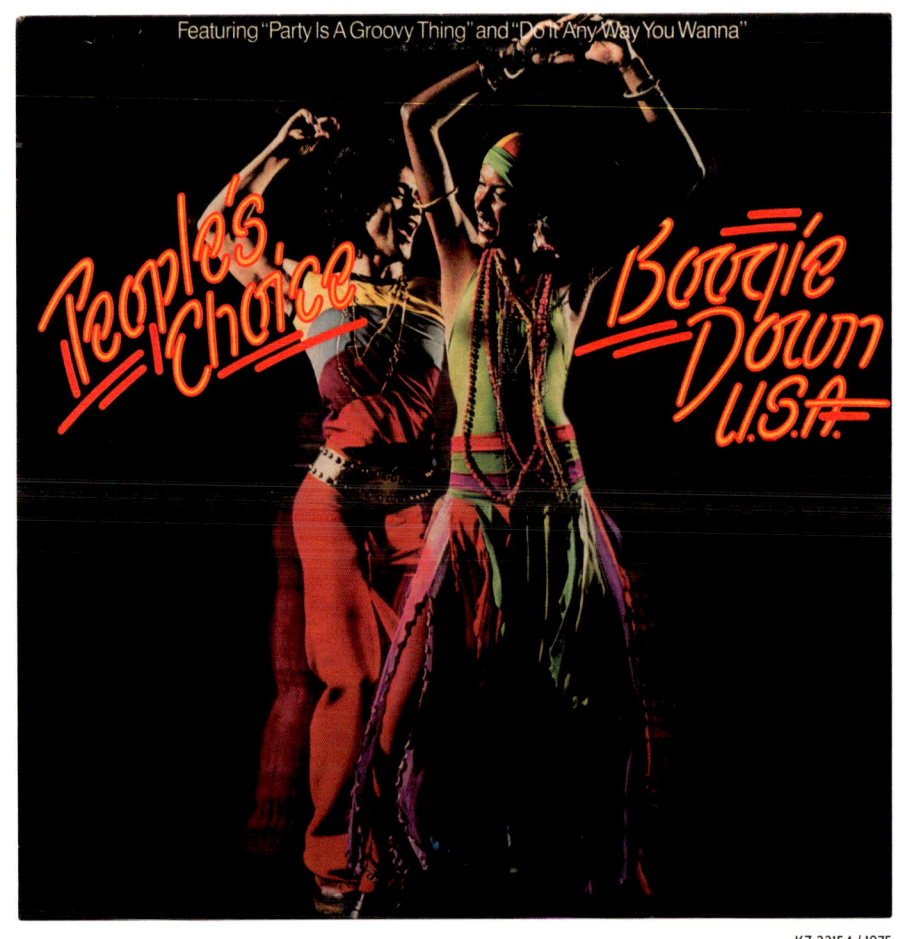

KZ 33154 / 1975

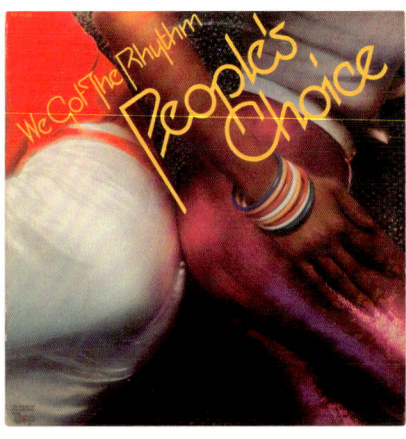

PZ 34124 / 1976

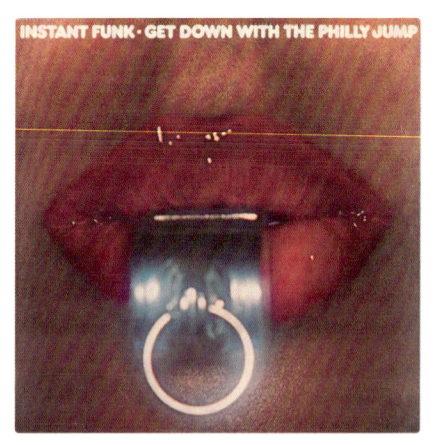

PZ 34358 / 1976

FZ 36416 / 1980

JZ 36470 / 1980

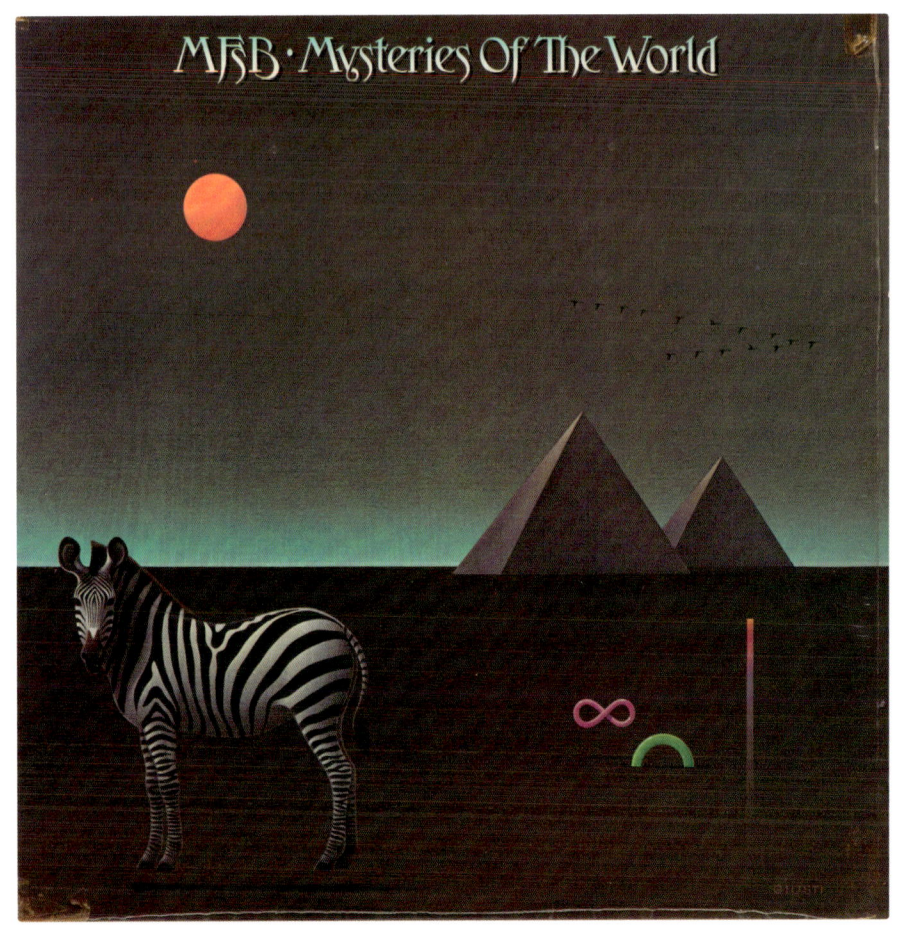

JZ 36405 / 1980

FZ 36773 / 1980

FZ 36775 / 1981

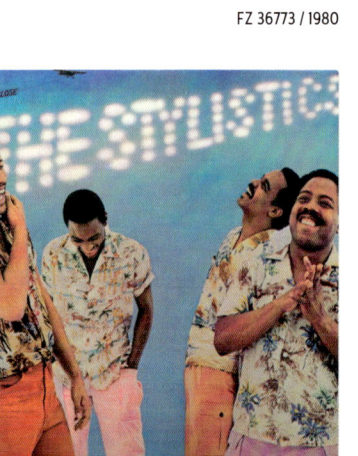

FZ 37458 / 1981

GAMBLE

SG 5007 / 1969

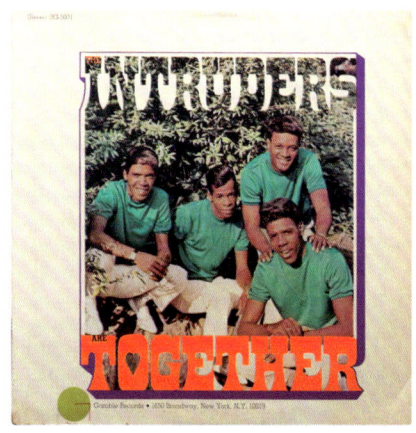

G/SG 5001 / 1967

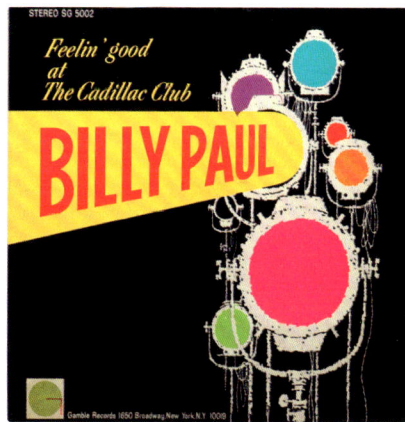

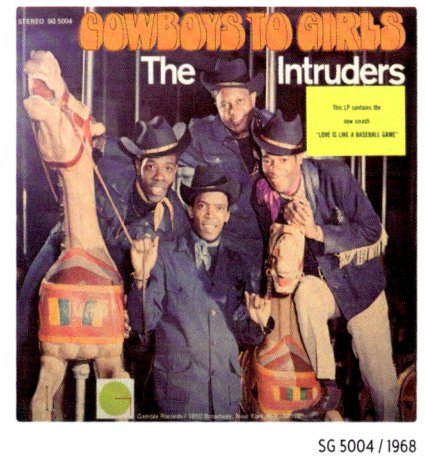

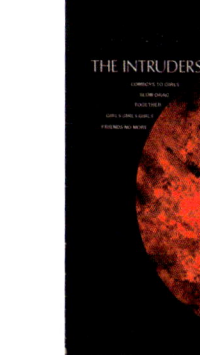

SG 5002 / 1968

SG 5004 / 1968

SG 5005 / 1969

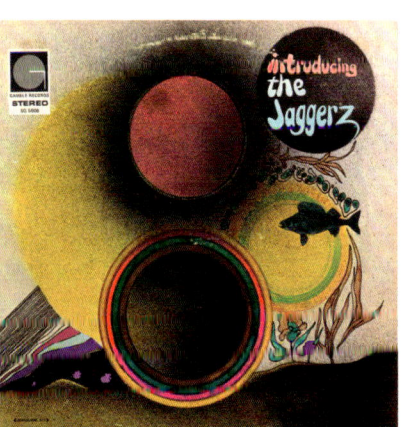

SG 5006 / 1969

SG 5008 / 1970

KZ 32405 / 1973

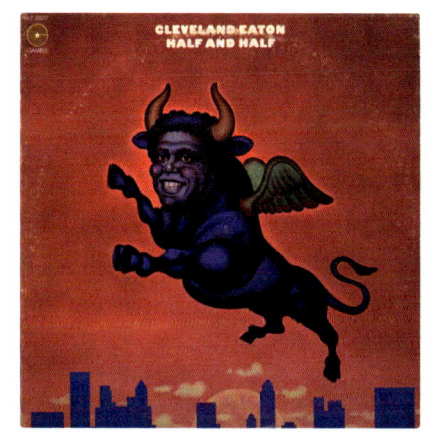

KZ 31991 / 1973

KZ 32077 / 1973

PIR

Cat#	Artist	Title	Year
KZ 30500	Billy Paul	Going East	1971
KZ 31648	Harold Melvin & Blue Notes	Harold Melvin & The Blue Notes	1972
KZ 31712	O'Jays	Back Stabbers	1972
KZ 31793	Billy Paul	360 Degrees Of Billy Paul	1972
KZ 31794	Dick Jensen	Penny For Your Thoughts	1973
ZX 31991	Intruders	Save The Children	1973
KZ 32046	MFSB	MFSB	1973
KZ 32118	Billy Paul	Ebony Woman	1973
KZ 32119	Billy Paul	Feelin' Good At The Cadillac Club	1973
KZ 32120	O'Jays	The O'Jays In Philadelphia	1973
KZ 32404	Spiritual Concept	Spiritual Concept	1973
KZ 32406	Three Degrees	The Three Degrees	1973
KZ/ZQ 32407	Harold Melvin & Blue Notes	Black And Blue	1973
KZ 32408	O'Jays	Ship Ahoy	1973
PZ 32408	O'Jays	Ship Ahoy	1973
PZQ 32408	O'Jays	Ship Ahoy	1973
KZ 32409	Billy Paul	War Of The Gods	1973
KZ 32419	Ebonys	The Ebonys	1973
KZ/ZQ 32707	MFSB	Love Is The Message	1973
KZ 32713	Various Artists	The Sound Of Philadelphia '73	1973
KZ 32859	Bunny Sigler	That's How I'll Be Loving You	1974
KZ 32952	Billy Paul	Live In Europe	1974
KZ/PZQ 32953	O'Jays	The O'Jays Live In London	1974
KZ/PZ 33148	Harold Melvin & Blue Notes feat. Theodore Pendergrass	To Be True	1975
KZ 33150	O'Jays	Survival	1975
KZ 33152	Thad Jones & Mel Lewis	Potpourri	1975
KZ 33153	Monk Montgomery	Reality	1974
PZ 33157	Billy Paul	Got My Head On Straight	1975
PZ 33158	MFSB	Universal Love	1975
KZ 33162	Three Degrees	International	1975
KZ 33163	Trammps	Trammps	1975
KZ 33249	Bunny Sigler	Keep Smilin'	1975
PZ/PZQ 33807	O'Jays	Family Reunion	1975
PZ/PZQ 33808	Harold Melvin & The Blue Notes Feat. Theodore Pendergrass	Wake Up Everybody	1975
PZ 33839	Dee Dee Sharp	Happy 'Bout The Whole Thing	1976
PZ 33840	Three Degrees	The Three Degrees Live	1975
PZ 33841	Anthony White	Could It Be Magic	1976
PZ 33843	Billy Paul	When Love Is New	1975
PZ/PZQ 33845	MFSB	Philadelphia Freedom	1975
PZ 33957	Lou Rawls	All Things In Time	1976
PZ 33958	Don Covay	Travelin' In Heavy Traffic	1976
PZ 34079	Dexter Wansel	Life On Mars	1976
PZ 34122	Dap Sugar Willy	From North Philly (Live)	1976
PZ 34123	Force Of Nature	Unemployment Blues	1976
JE/PE 34229	Jacksons	The Jacksons	1976
PZ 34232	Harold Melvin & Blue Notes	All Their Greatest Hits!	1976
PZ 34238	MFSB	Summertime	1976
PZ 34245	O'Jays	Message in the Music	1976
PZ 34267	Bunny Sigler	My Music	1976
PZ 34323	Archie Bell & Drells	Where Will You Go When The Party's Over	1976
PZ 34346	Jean	Bicentennial Poet	1976
PZ 34389	Billy Paul	Let 'Em In	1976
JZ 34390	Teddy Pendergrass	Teddy Pendergrass	1977
PZ 34394	Jean Carn	Jean Carn	1977
PZ 34437	Dee Dee Sharp	What Color Is Love	1977
PZ 34487	Dexter Wansel	What The World Is Coming To	1977
PZ 34488	Lou Rawls	Unmistakably Lou	1977
PZ 34658	MFSB	End Of Phase I	1977
PZ 34659	Various Artists	Let's Clean Up The Ghetto	1977
PZ 34684	O'Jays	Travelin' at the Speed of Thought	1977
ZX 34728	Trammps	Disco Champs	1977
JE/PE 34835	Jacksons	Goin' Places	1977
PZ 34855	Archie Bell & Drells	Hard Not To Like It	1977
PZ 34923	Billy Paul	Only The Strong Survive	1977
PZ 34940	Various Artists	Philadelphia Classics	1977
PZ 34985	Dexter Wansel	Voyager	1978
PZ 34986	Jean Carn	Happy To Be With You	1978
PGZ 35024	O'Jays	The O'Jays: Collectors' Items	1977
Z 235024	O'Jays	The O'Jays: Collectors' Items	1977
JZ 35036	Lou Rawls	When You Hear Lou, You've Heard It All	1977
JZ 35095	Teddy Pendergrass	Life Is A Song Worth Singing	1978
JZ/PZ 35355	O'Jays	So Full of Love	1978
JZ 35363	People's Choice	Turn Me Loose	1978
JZ 35458	Futures	Past, Present And The Futures	1978
JZ 35509	Bobby Rush	Rush Hour	1978
JZ 35510	Jerry Butler	Nothing Says I Love You Like I Love You	1978
JZ 35516	Huff Orchestra MFSB	The Gamble	1978
PZ 235517	Lou Rawls	Live	1978
JZ 35756	Billy Paul	First Class	1979
JZ 35757	Jones Girls	The Jones Girls	1979
JZ 35758	Edwin Birdsong	Edwin Birdsong	1979
JZ 35800	McFadden & Whitehead	McFadden & Whitehead	1979
FZ 36003	Teddy Pendergrass	Teddy	1979
JZ/PZ 36006	Lou Rawls	Let Me Be Good To You	1979

Matrix numbers

JZ 36007	Michael Pedicin Jr.	Michael Pedicin Jr.	1979
JZ 36024	Dexter Wansel	Time Is Slipping Away	1979
NJZ-36025	Silk	Midnight Dancer	1979
FZ 36027	O'Jays	Identify Yourself	1979
JZ 36036	Frantique	Frantique	1979
JZ 36096	Archie Bell & The Drells	Strategy	1979
JZ 36097	Force	The Force	1979
JZ 36196	Jean Carn	When I Find You Love	1979
JZ 36294	Teddy Pendergrass	Teddy Live! Coast To Coast	1979
JZ/PZ 36304	Lou Rawls	Sit Down And Talk To Me	1979
JZ 36313	Norman Harris	The Harris Machine	1980
Z 236314	Billy Paul	Best Of Billy Paul	1980
JZ 36370	Dee Dee Sharp Gamble	Dee Dee	1980
JZ 36413	Jerry Butler	The Best Love	1980
JZ 36414	Futures	Greetings Of Peace	1981
JZ 36745	Teddy Pendergrass	TP	1980
NJZ 36758	Leon Huff	Here to Create Music	1980
JZ 36767	Jones Girls	At Peace With Woman	1980
JZ 36774	Lou Rawls	Shades of Blue	1980
FZ/PZ 37380	Patti LaBelle	The Spirit's in It	1981
FZ 37491	Teddy Pendergrass	It's Time For Love	1981
FZ 37627	Jones Girls	Get As Much Love As You Can	1981
FZ 37683	Various Artists	Live On Stage	1982
FZ 37684	Various Artists	Best Of Philadelphia International	1982
FZ 37955	Stylistics	1982	1982
FZ 37999	O'Jays	My Favorite Person	1982
FZ 38118	Teddy Pendergrass	This One's For You	1982
FZ/PZ 38518	O'Jays	When Will I See You Again	1983
FZ 38539	Patti LaBelle	I'm In Love Again	1983
FZ 38555	Jones Girls	Keep It Comin'	1984
FZ 38646	Teddy Pendergrass	Heaven Only Knows	1983
FZ 39251	O'Jays	Greatest Hits	1984
FZ 39252	Teddy Pendergrass	Greatest Hits	1984
PZ 39254	Various Artists	Philadelphia International Dance Classics, Vol. I	1984
PZ 39255	Various Artists	Philly Ballads, Volume I	1984
FZ 39285	Lou Rawls	Classics	1984
FZ 39367	O'Jays	Love And More	1984
FZ 40020	Patti LaBelle	Patti	1985
ST 53015	O'Jays	Love Fever	1985
ST 53028	Whitehead Brothers	Kenny and Johnny	1986
ST 53029	Phyllis Hyman	Living All Alone	1985
ST 53031	Shirley Jones	Always In The Mood	1986
ST 53036	O'Jays	Let Me Touch You	1987
11006-1	Phyllis Hyman	Prime Of My Life	1991
11008-1	Universe	Universe	1991
11040-1	Phyllis Hyman	I Refuse To Be Lonely	1995
30902	Phyllis Hyman	Forever With You	1998

TSOP

KZ 33149	Intruders	Energy Of Love	1974
KZ 33154	People's Choice	Boogie Down U.S.A.	1975
KZ 33186	Soul Survivors	The Soul Survivors	1975
KZ 33842	Ted Wortham	I'm Going On A Journey	1975
PZ 33844	Archie Bell & Drells	Dance Your Troubles Away	1975
PZ 34110	City Limits	Circles	1976
PZ 34124	People's Choice	We Got The Rhythm	1976
PZ 34358	Instant Funk	Get Down With The Philly Jump	1976
JZ 36405	MFSB	Mysteries Of The World	1980
FZ 36416	O'Jays	The Year 2000	1980
JZ 36470	Stylistics	Hurry Up This Way Again	1980
FZ 36773	McFadden & Whitehead	I Heard It In A Love Song	1980
FZ 36775	Jean Carn	Sweet And Wonderful	1981
FZ 37458	Stylistics	Closer Than Close	1981

GAMBLE

G/SG 5001	Intruders	The Intruders Are Together	1967
SG 5002	Billy Paul	Feelin' Good At The Cadillac Club	1968
SG 5004	Intruders	Cowboys To Girls	1968
SG 5005	Intruders	The Intruders' Greatest Hits	1969
SG 5006	Jaggerz	Introducing The Jaggerz	1969
SG 5007	Various Artists	The Gamble Records All Stars	1969
SG 5008	Intruders	When We Get Married	1970
KZ 31991	Intruders	Save the Children	1973
KZ 32077	Cleveland Eaton	Half And Half	1973
KZ 32131	Intruders	Intruders Super Hits	1973
KZ 32405	Yellow Sunshine	Yellow Sunshine	1973

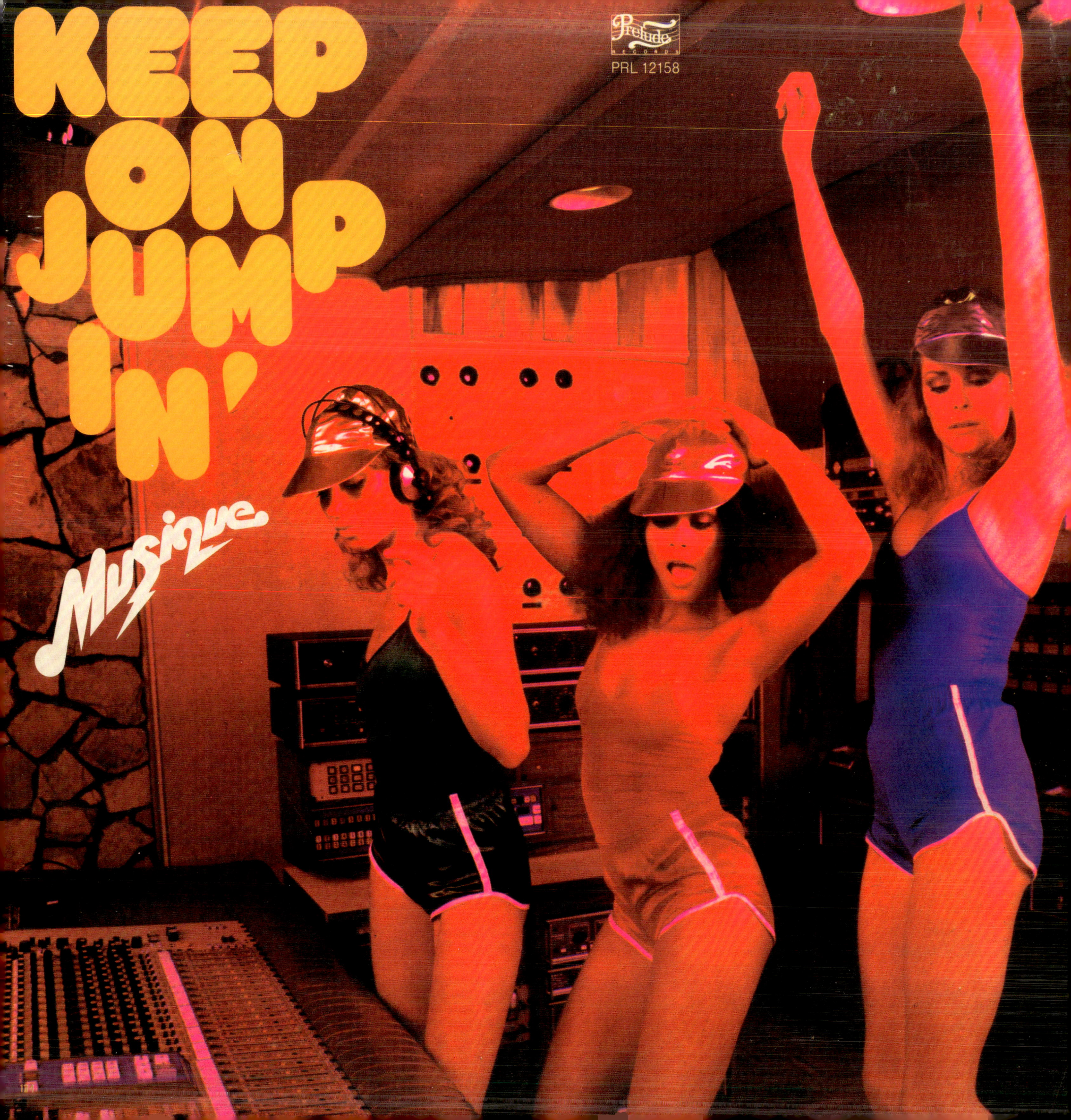

KEEP
ON
JUMP
IN'
Musique
Prelude RECORDS
PRL 12158

Disco Labels & Albums

Chapter 14
Prelude Records

PRELUDE RECORDS WAS A NEW YORK BASED INDEPENDENT DANCE LABEL THAT RAN FROM 1976 TO 1986 AND WAS OWNED BY MARVIN SCHLACHTER.

Schlachter had earlier been A&R/vice-president of Scepter/Wand Records and in 1975 had been brought in to run the new US division of a British label, Pye Records. When Pye decided to close this US operation, Schlachter (and his partner Stanley Hoffman) created Prelude Records.

The label was operated from an office on 57th Street and was a small company with a staff of less than ten. The company became one of the leading dance music labels during its ten year existence. For the first six years a young French DJ called François Kervorkian who had settled in New York quickly established himself as one of the finest remixers to emerge in the disco era with a series of stunning extended 12-inch releases for the label, which in the process established Prelude as one of the defining companies of New York's dance music scene. Some of Kervorkian's finest mixes include Musique's 'In The Bush' (produced by Patrick Adams), D Train's 'You're the One for Me', Unlimited Touch's 'I Hear Music in the Streets' and Sharon Redd's 'Beat the Street'.

Schlachter closed the label down in 1986 and the back catalogue of Prelude was sold to Unidisc.

Left: Musique-Keep On Jumpin' / Prelude 1978
Cover Concept: Ancona Design Atelier NY / Photography: Bob Lichtman & Trudy Schlachter

Marvin Schlachter Interview

Was starting Prelude something you dreamed of, or something that more of less just happened?

'No - it wasn't a dream and it didn't just happen. I had been in this business a long time. I had run another record company prior to that - Scepter/Wand - and I was president of Chess Records for several years. After that I was asked to take over Pye Records, a UK label who had started a label here in the States - I was asked to take it over after they had started it. It didn't last long because they refused to fund it. I had a contract with them and there were some artists that I had, or was in the process of signing and others I was about to purchase or license. So, when I left Pye Records I used that as a foundation to start Prelude Records.'

Do you remember which was the first act signed to the label?

'We had licensed a couple of things from Germany - I think it was a group called Jumbo or something like that — it's very difficult for me to remember those acts.'

Could you talk about some of the Prelude acts?

'Well, a lot of the artists that we signed were licensed from Europe, from various producers who were based in either Italy or France and a couple in Germany. I think for the most part, that kind of music was really the creation of the producer, much more so than the actual artists themselves. I think the producer was the creative talent there and in most of them, but not in every case, the artist was treated as an instrument. And quite frankly, there was no artist named Musique when Patrick Adams produced that for us. It was only after the record started to sell very well that we created a group. So again, these were just session singers that were hired to do vocals and then ultimately we turned around and created the group.

This young lady France Joli certainly was an interesting artist who was produced by a guy called Tony Green. She was very young when she first started, 16 or so. She was a very beautiful young lady and had a sort of magnetic appeal, which was appealing to everybody, but really it was the producer and the people behind her who directed her career.

When she felt that she wanted to rise above the disco market and left Prelude to sign with Columbia - her career disappeared. As I say, the talent was in the producers and the writers. Today the market is different, most artists are also writers - they write and produce their own music. In those days that wasn't the case, the producers were the artists, and the artists were just vehicles. Sad to say, but true.'

Patrick Adams wrote another of Prelude's best known hits - the 1979 disco song 'I'm Caught Up (In a One Night Love Affair)' by Inner Life. This tune he considered to be one of his best works as a writer. He used Jocelyn Brown as lead vocalist. One of the reasons why he likes it so much is because that record contained some fantastic background, insane string lines and tremendous energy from all involved - it rocked from beginning to end. The song was originally released as a 12-inch single by Greg Carmichael on TCT Records, but within a week of its release a bidding war broke out between Prelude and what was to become Profile Records. Prelude won by bidding $17,500 for the rights to the single. At the time this was an unheard of amount for a single - one year earlier, the album 'Keep On Jumpin' by Musique had cost just $16,000 to make.

What was Prelude's biggest hit?

'D Train sold an awful lot of records. France Joli sold a lot of records - but she also sold a lot more outside of this country and we did not have the rights to our music outside of North and South America. I would say the biggest sellers were both France Joli and D Train.'

What about Francois Kevorkian, is it correct he was the label's A&R man, besides being a remixer for the label?

'No, I was the A&R man. He did most of the remixing. He was a DJ and to some degree I can say that he did, in some instances, influence some of the signings that I made. For the most part they were acts and music that were sent to me and, based on my own personal tastes, signed by me. Francois in a couple of instances, I can't remember specifically which ones, did refer particular music to us. But the major artists and the major successes and major signings were done by me.'

Why were you focusing on 12-inch singles? Was it to get it to the discotheques, to the DJs?

'Well I think the 12-inch was a new vehicle, something that was part of this culture. And it enabled the record companies - the small independent companies - to put a lot more music on a format than they were able to with a seven-inch single. You could put out a single that was 10-12 minutes long. You couldn't do that with a seven-inch record. It offered a tremendous vehicle for producers to put out the kind of music that someone heard in a club. They wanted to buy the music that they heard in the clubs regardless of how long it was and so, this was a new format and we gave the people what they wanted. It's as simple as that!'

You also released double 12-inch promo albums. This was unique to Prelude. Why did you do this?

'We wanted the DJs who were playing the music to have the finest quality. We said, instead of losing quality (on an album), we'll put out another 12-inch record so that the DJs could still play it in the clubs. And obviously this was a marketing tool - if it sounded better in the clubs, and so we had a better chance of selling our music to the ultimate consumer.'

Do you remember when you closed the company down?

'We closed the company down in 1985 or 1986. That was about the time of the last release. We sold the catalog to Unidisc in Canada. We had also acquired another label, a gospel label called Savoy Records and we sold that as well to another company. And we literally closed the company down at that time.

Did you like disco music during the era, or was it just a job to you?

'Oh! I didn't like it - I loved it! I absolutely loved it! I loved the music. I spent a good deal of time at clubs, although not as much obviously as the producers, artists, DJs and so on, but I absolutely loved the music. So - aside from being the business venture which it certainly was - it was about being involved in a style of music that I really loved.'

Hi-Gloss - Hi Gloss / Prelude 1981
Cover Photo: Trudy Schlachter

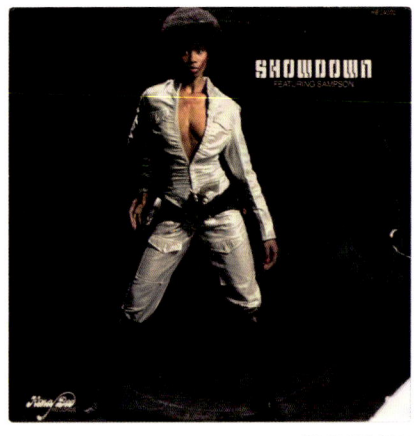

HB-24002 / 1977	PYE 12138 / 1975	PYE 12141 / 1976	PYE 12142 / 1976
PRL 12142 / 1976	PRL 12145 / 1977	PRL 1246 / 1977	PRL 12147 / 1977
PRL 12148 / 1977	PRL 12149 / 1977	PRL 12150 / 1977	PRL 12151 / 1977
PRL 12152 / 1977	PRL 12154 / 1977	PRL 12155 / 1978	PRL 12156 / 1978

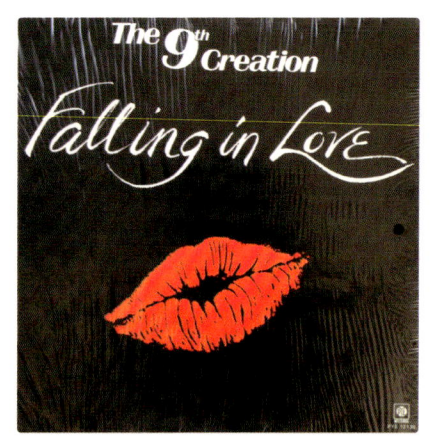

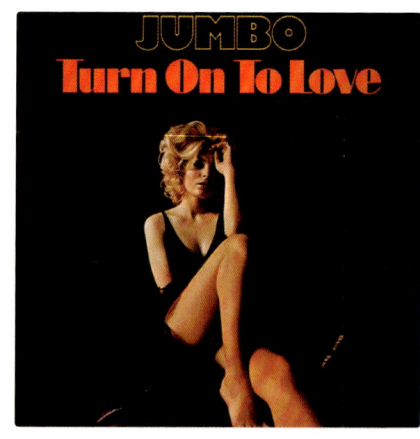

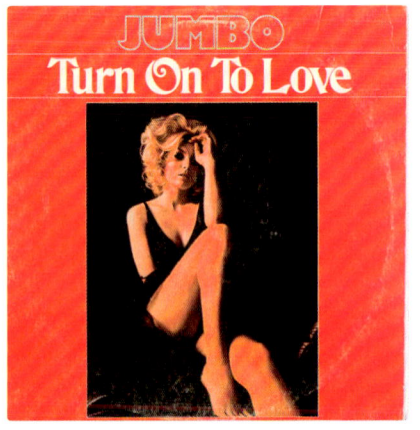

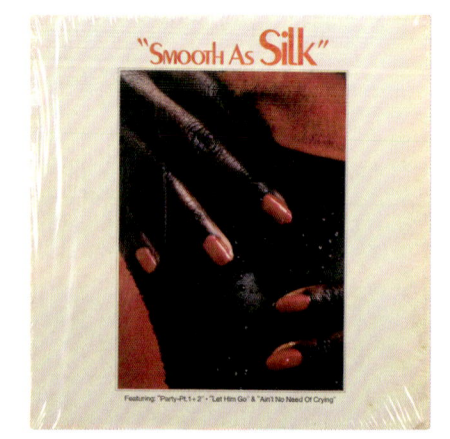

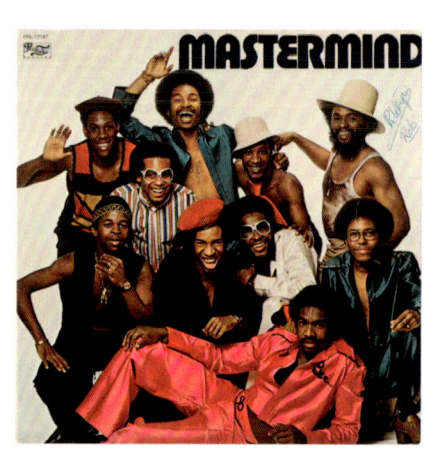

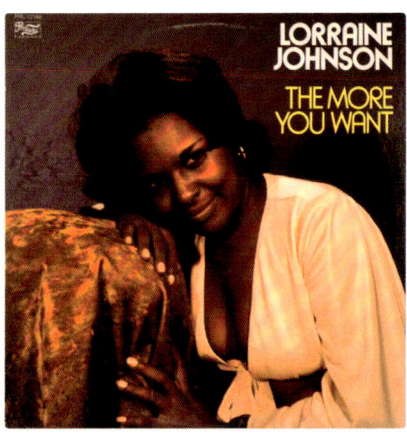

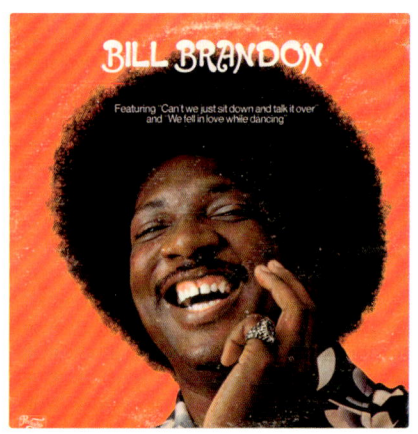

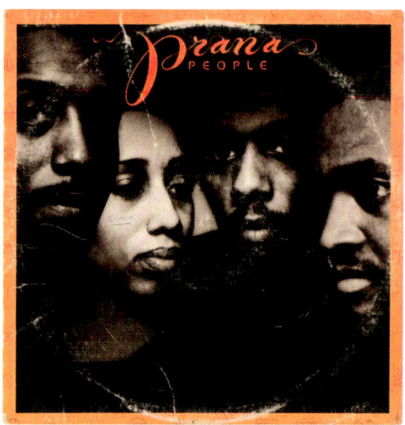

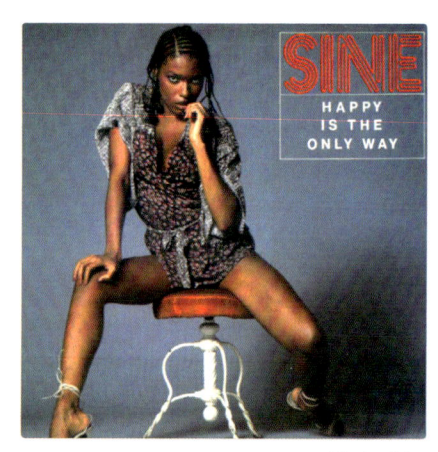

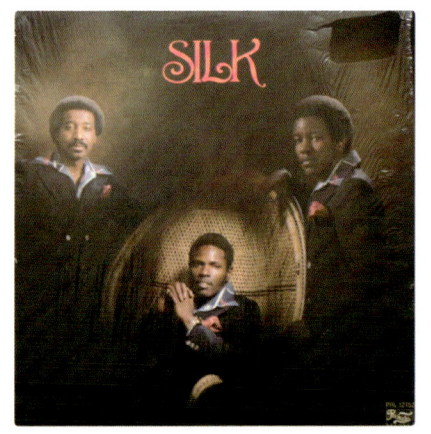

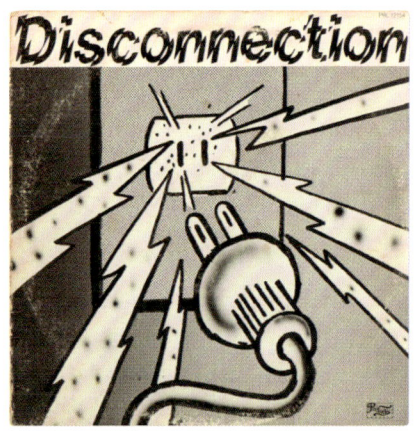

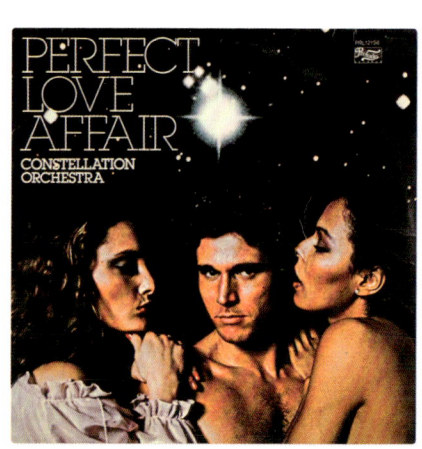

PRL 12157 / 1978	PRL 12158 / 1978	PRL 12159 / 1978	PRL 12160 / 1978
PRL 12161 / 1978	PRL 12162 / 1978	PRL 12162 / 1978	PRL 12163 / 1978
PRL 12164 / 1978	PRL 12165 / 1979	PRL 12166 / 1979	PRL 12167 / 1979
PRL 12168 / 1979	PRL 12169 / 1979	PRL 12170 / 1979	PRL 12171 / 1979

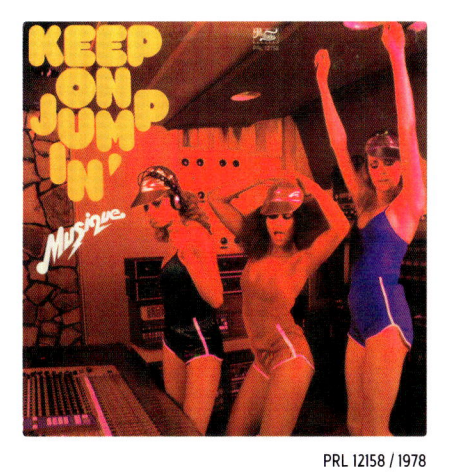

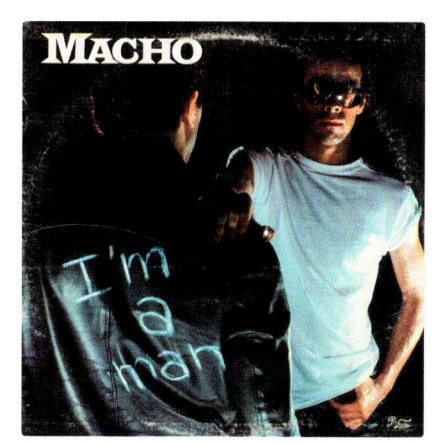

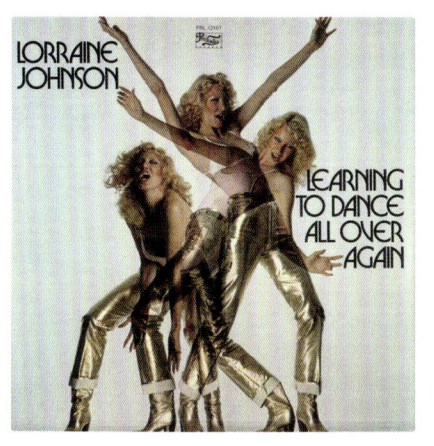

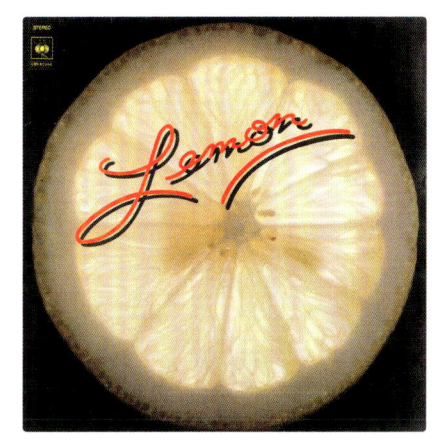

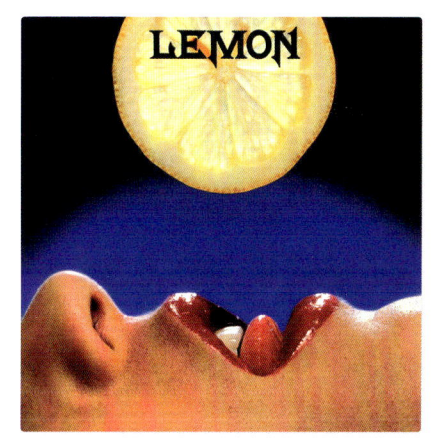

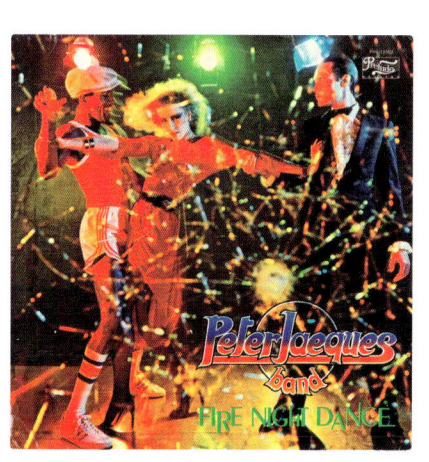

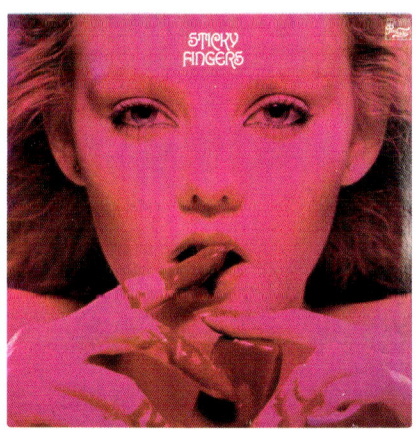

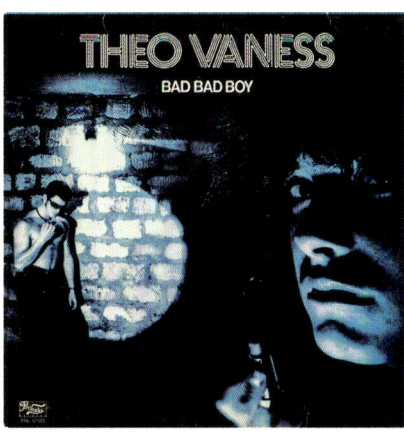

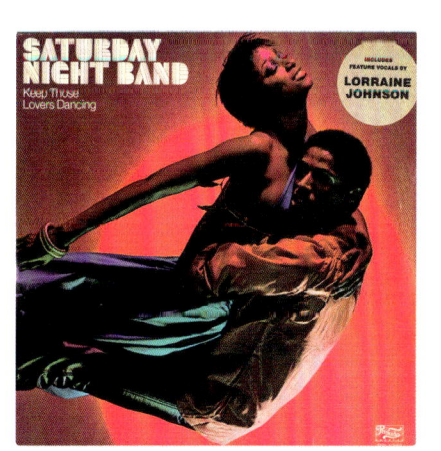

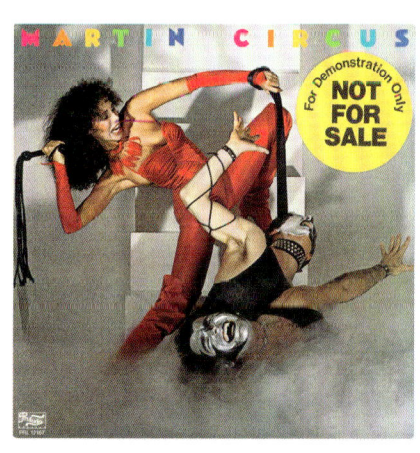

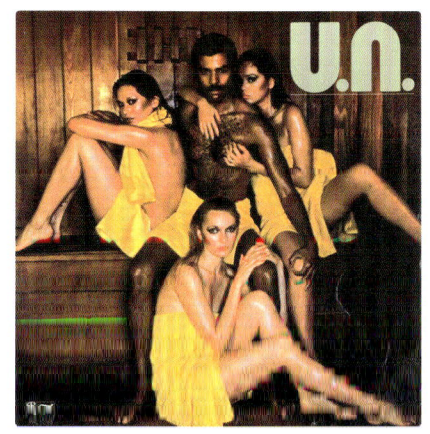

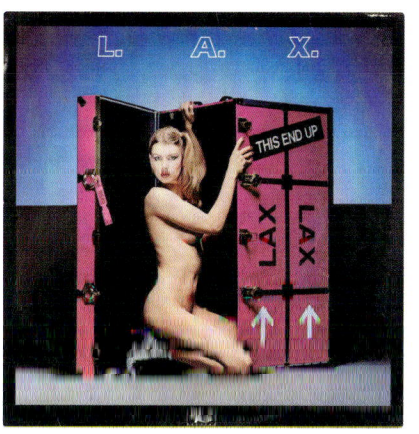

PRL 12172 / 1979 
PRL 12173 / 1977 
PRL 12174 / 1980 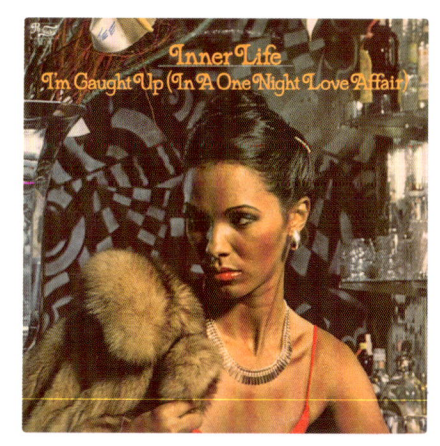
PRL 12175 / 1979

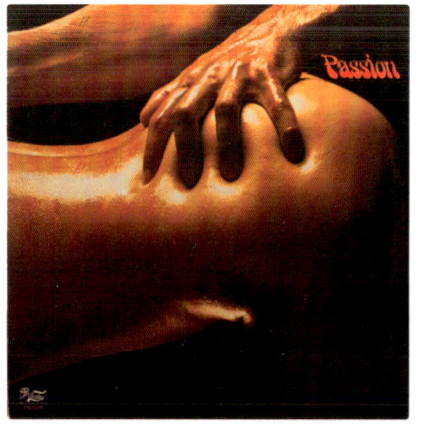

PRL 12176 / 1980 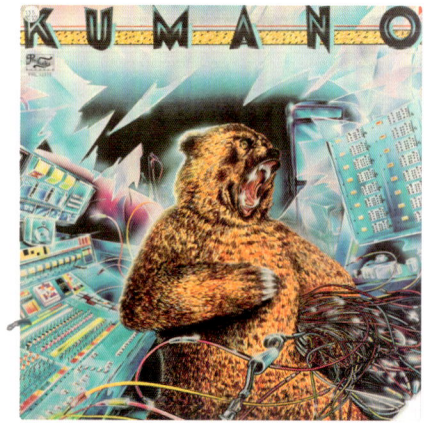
PRL 12177 / 1980 
PRL 12178 / 1980 
PRL 12179 / 1980

PRL 12180 / 1980 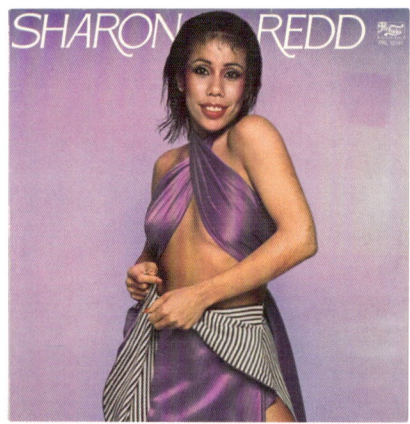
PRL 12181 / 1980 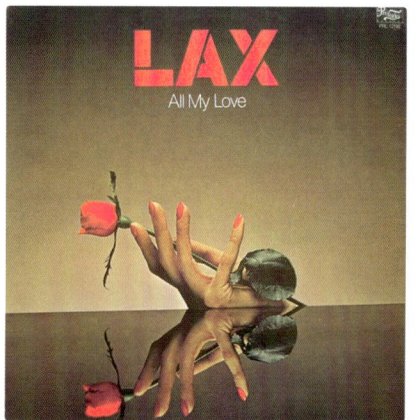
PRL 12182 / 1980 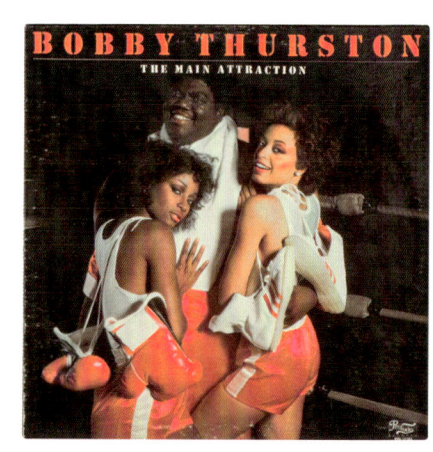
PRL 12183 / 1981

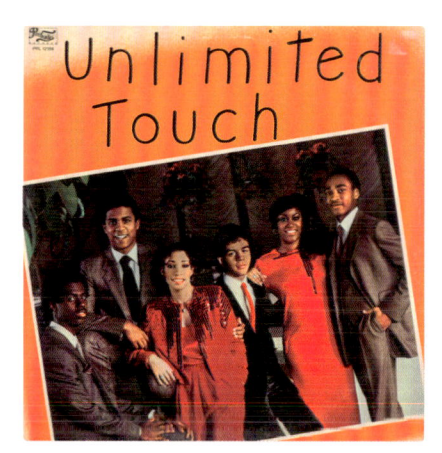

PRL 12184 / 1981
PRL 12185 / 1981 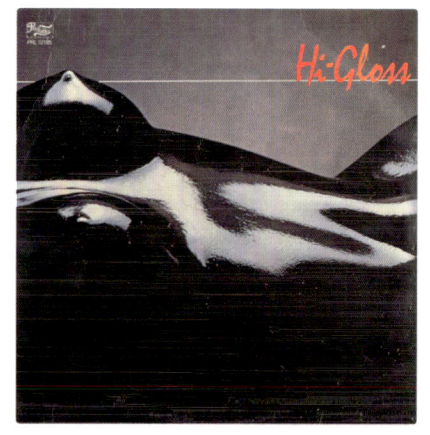
PRL 14100 / 1981 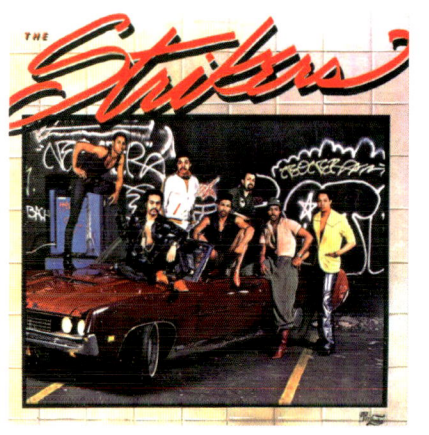
PRL 14101 / 1980

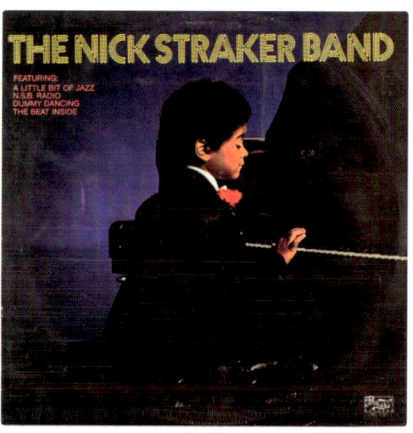

Passion - Passion / Prelude 1979
Design: Ancona Design Atelier / Photography: Trudy Schlachter

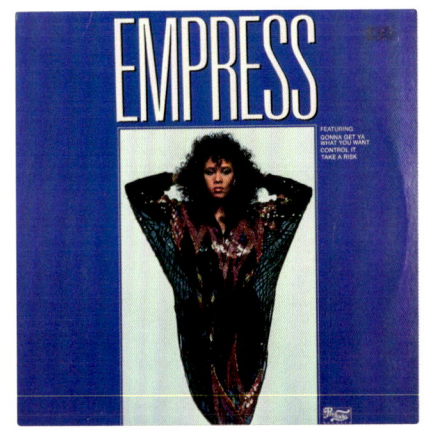

PRL 14102 / 1982 
PRL 14103 / 1982 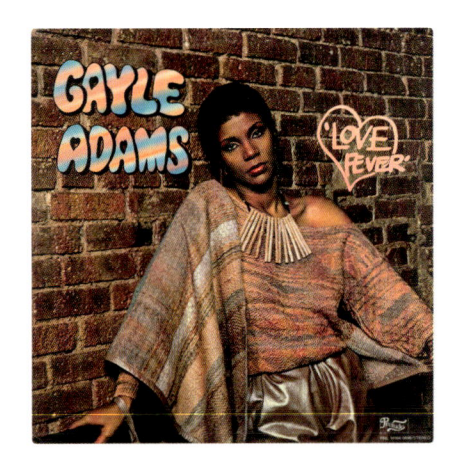
PRL 14104 / 1982 
PRL 14105 / 1982

PRL 14106 / 1982 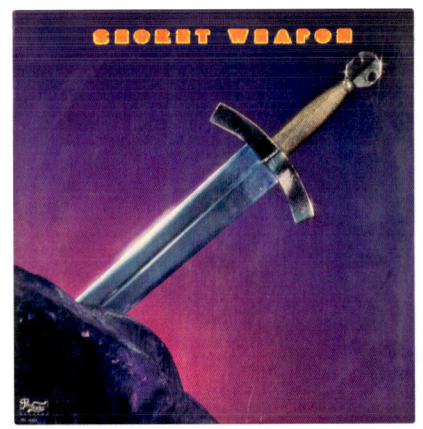
PRL 14107 / 1983 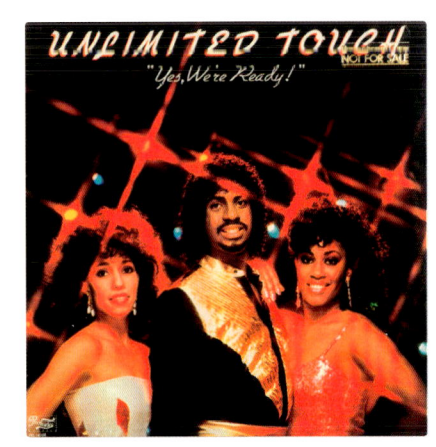
PRL 14108 / 1983 
PRL 14109 / 1983

PRL 14110 / 1983 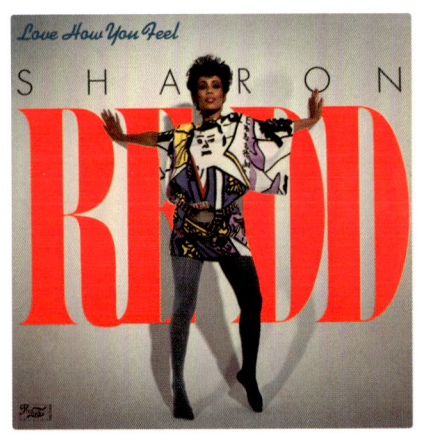
PRL 14111 / 1983 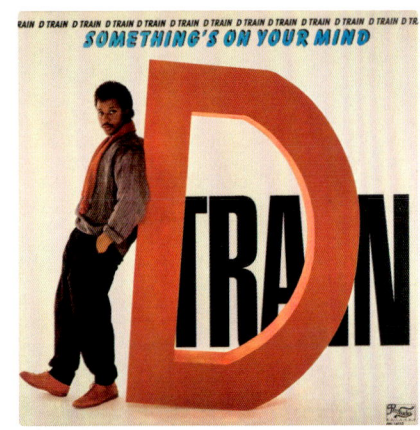
PRL 14112 / 1984 
PRL 14113 / 1985

PRL 14114 / 1983
PRL 14115 / 1985 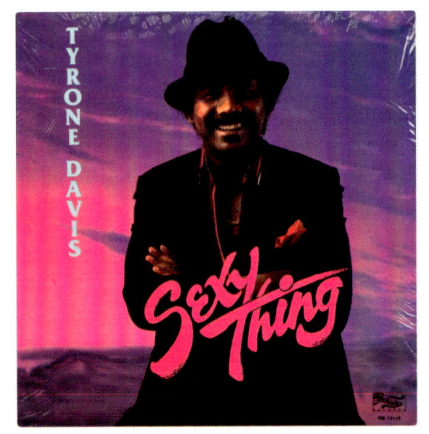
PRL 14116 / 1986 
PRL 19100 / 1982

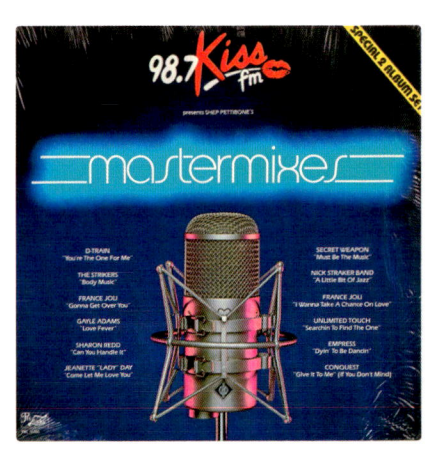

Kumano - Kumano / Prelude 1980
Cover Illustration: Michel "Zappy" DURR

Sticky Fingers-Stickey Fingers / Prelude 1978
Design: Ancona Design Atelier / Photography: Bernard Vidal

Matrix numbers

PRELUDE

PRL 12141	Lorraine Frisura	Be Happy	-
PRL 12142	Jumbo	Turn On To Love	1976
PRL 12145	Silk	Smooth As Silk	1977
PRL 12146	9th Creation	Reaching For The Top	1977
PRL 12147	Mastermind	Mastermind	1977
PRL 12148	Lorraine Johnson	The More You Want	1977
PRL 12149	Bill Brandon	Bill Brandon	1977
PRL 12150	Prana People	Prana People	1977
PRL 12151	Sine	Happy Is The Only Way	1977
PRL 12152	Silk	Silk	1977
PRL 12154	Disconnection	Disconnection	1977
PRL 12155	Saturday Night Band	Come On Dance, Dance	1978
PRL 12156	Constellation Orchestra	Perfect Love Affair	1978
PRL 12157	Theo Vaness	Back To Music	1978
PRL 12158	Musique	Keep On Jumpin'	1978
PRL 12159	Barbara Mason	I Am Your Woman, She Is Your Wife	1978
PRL 12160	Macho	I'm A Man	1978
PRL 12161	Lorraine Johnson	Learning To Dance All Over Again	1978
PRL 12162	Lemon	Lemon	1978
PRL 12163	Peter Jacques Band	Fire Night Dance	1978
PRL 12164	Sticky Fingers	Sticky Fingers	1978
PRL 12165	Theo Vaness	Bad Bad Boy	1979
PRL 12166	Saturday Night Band	Keep Those Lovers Dancing	1979
PRL 12167	Martin Circus	Disco Circus	1979
PRL 12168	U.N.	U.N.	1979
PRL 12169	Masquerade	Pinocchio	1979
PRL 12170	France Joli	France Joli	1979
PRL 12171	L.A.X.	L.A.X.	1979
PRL 12172	Musique	Musique II	1979
PRL 12173	Theo Vaness	Theo Vaness	1979
PRL 12174	Bobby Thurston	You Got What It Takes	1980
PRL 12175	Inner Life	I'm Caught Up (In A One Night Love Affair)	1979
PRL 12176	Passion	Passion	1980
PRL 12177	Kumano	Kumano	1980
PRL 12178	Gayle Adams	Gayle Adams	1980
PRL 12179	France Joli	Tonight	1980
PRL 12180	Rod	Shake It Up	1980
PRL 12181	Sharon Redd	Sharon Redd	1980
PRL 12182	L.A.X.	All My Love	1980
PRL 12183	Bobby Thurston	The Main Attraction	1981
PRL 12184	Unlimited Touch	Unlimited Touch	1981
PRL 12185	Hi Gloss	Hi Gloss	1981
PRL 14100	Strikers, The	The Strikers	1981
PRL 14101	The Nick Straker Band	The Nick Straker Band	1980
PRL 14102	Empress	Empress	1982
PRL 14103	France Joli	Now!	1982
PRL 14104	Gayle Adams	Love Fever	1982
PRL 14105	D Train	You're The One For Me	1982
PRL 14106	Sharon Redd	Redd Hott	1982
PRL 14107	Secret Weapon	Secret Weapon	1983
PRL 14108	Unlimited Touch	Yes, We're Ready	1983
PRL 14109	D Train	Music	1983
PRL 14110	One-Two-Three	One-Two-Three	1983
PRL 14111	Sharon Redd	Love How You Feel	1983
PRL 14112	D Train	Something's On Your Mind	1984
PRL 14113	New Jersey Mass Choir	I Want To Know What Love Is	1985
PRL 14114	Taka Boom	Boomerang	
PRL 14115	Tyrone Davis	Sexy Thing	1985
PRL 14116	D-Train	The Best Of "D" Train	1986
PRL 19100	Various	98.7 Kiss FM Presents Shep Pettibone's Mastermixes	1982
PRL 19101	Various	93 FM WZAK Mastermixes	1982
PRL 19102	Various	Mastermixes	1982
PRL 19103	Various	Prelude's Greatest Hits	1983
PRL 19104	Various	Kiss 98.7 FM Mastermixes Vol. II	1983
PRL 69800	Sharon Redd	The Classic Red	1985

HONEYBEE-PRELUDE

HB-24002	Showdown	Showdown Featuring Sampson	1977

Candido

CANDI'S FUNK

Disco Labels & Albums

Chapter 15
Salsoul Records and sub-labels

SALSOUL RECORDS WAS FOUNDED BY THREE BROTHERS, JOE, KEN AND STAN CAYRE IN 1974.

Their involvement in the music industry began with manufacturing and distributing Mexican material in North America on the then new 8-track tape format. In 1972 the brothers started the Mericana Record label, releasing latin music. One of these was the Joe Bataan album entitled 'Salsoul', a blend of salsa and soul. The success of this release in the R&B field led to the formation of the new Salsoul label. In the ten prime years of Salsoul's existence, the label put out hundreds of releases, many of which sold in considerable numbers.

Infei Candida — Candi's Funk / Salsoul 1980
Design: Lori L. Lambert / Photography: John Galluzzi

147

Ken Cayre Interview

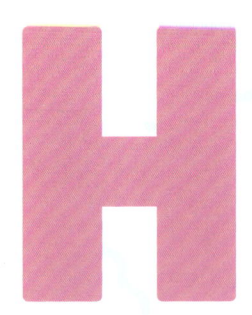

How does the Salsoul story start?

'We had been involved in the music business for quite a while when my brother Joe signed Joe Bataan and recorded his first album 'Salsoul' in 1973. They took it to the radio stations and it got mediocre play but to our pleasant surprise Frankie Crocker of WBLS - which at that time was one of the biggest stations in New York - started playing one song a lot. The song was 'Latin Strut', a cover of a Deodato tune. It became a big hit and we started taking it to other R&B stations.

Then CBS Records offered to buy it from us, wanting to take it into the pop market. They gave us a hundred thousand dollars - this was just what we asked for, because we thought that was how much we could make if we did it ourselves. We turned over the record to them and they had the rights to the album and an option on anything new in the next five years. They were not successful in taking it into the pop market but we got the money anyway.

So I told my brothers 'We have some money here, let's take a chance'. Joe Bataan's 'Latin Strut' had showed that you could be successful with an instrumental song - you didn't really need a singer. There were these new clubs opening up called 'discos', which were not big at the time but were just starting in New York. I knew about them because I was hanging out at these clubs with Joe Bataan. It was the first time that you had these big speakers and lights - really something you never heard or saw before. So I said to my brothers 'I think we should take a chance and try to do something in this market. It's something I know and I think there's an opportunity, there's not too many people doing it.' So they said 'OK!' and then I did three things:

First thing I did was go to Philadelphia. All the records that I liked I used to look on the back of the cover to see who the musicians were - and they were all from Philadelphia. The O'Jays, The Blue Notes, The Spinners. I found out that there was one set of musicians recording the rhythm section for all these groups and I tracked them down. They were Earl Young on drums, Ronnie Baker on bass, Norman Harris on guitar, Bobby Eli on guitar, Bunny Sigler on keyboard, Ron Kersey on keyboard, Vince Montana Jr. on vibes and Larry Washington on the congas.

This was the sound I was looking for to start the Salsoul label. So I went to Philadelphia and I met Vince Montana. I told him of my idea to do an instrumental record and call the group the Salsoul Orchestra, which I was also naming the label. We recorded three songs, one of them was 'Salsoul Hustle'.

Secondly I met Floyd Smith who came into my office in New York. He had an uncanny similarity to Barry White, so I recorded a couple of songs with him. And the third thing I did was record a couple of songs with Carol Williams. And there went my $100,000.

I finished the three songs with the Salsoul Orchestra, and at that time we had to take them to CBS, as they had the first right of refusal. CBS turned it down, they were busy with their other bigger artists like Barbra Streisand and Bob Dylan and they really didn't feel at that time that disco would be big.

So by turning us down they released us to shop it elsewhere or put it out ourselves. I shopped elsewhere, I went to Atlantic Records, I went to Polygram Records and I couldn't get anywhere. My brothers were upset at me that I spent the money they could have had and I said 'Look! Because they don't want it doesn't mean we can't get our money back from it. We have a distributorship set up here in New York, we're selling Spanish records, we know all the retailers, we have trucks going out to the area, let's take a chance and put it out ourselves, like we do on Mericana. We just make it on a different label - Salsoul. I think I can get it on some of the R&B stations, I think Frankie Crocker will play it. And Frankie played it and played it to death. From there we got it played around the country on all the R&B stations and we started selling a lot of the seven-inch singles of 'Salsoul Hustle' - some 400,000 copies. We then went into make up an album. We did seven or eight more songs, I was going out to Philadelphia twice a week. I did Tuesday and Thursday nights recording, starting at seven o'clock at night. After work I would drive down to record until three or four in the morning and then I'd get back in the car, drive back to my apartment, go to sleep for a couple of hours and then go to work again. It was exciting because the tracks were hot.

When the album came out I put all the musicians names on the back of the record. It was one of the first times that a company did that. Record companies never gave the musicians recognition and when I did that on the back of the first Salsoul Orchestra album all the R&B DJs around the country already knew these musicians from Philadelphia from their Gamble & Huff stuff and they loved them [they were essentially the group MFSB]. That really got us a lot of play just because they liked the musicians - Earl, Ronnie, Norman and Vince. So the first album we put out, The Salsoul Orchestra, sold about half a million copies. We didn't go 'gold' because we were not RIAA [Record Industry Association of America] certified, but it made a lot of noise.

Before we put out the 'Salsoul Hustle' album we did another with Joe Bataan and that was the first album on the Salsoul label. It was called Afrofilipino and I went into the studio with Joe to do a little more dance-oriented album. He did a remake of Gil Scott-Heron's 'The Bottle' and I'll never forget it. We were in the studio with Richard Tee on piano, Gordon Edwards on bass, James Madison on drums and it was the most amazing session I've ever been on.

At that time it was a 24-track session and luckily all our songs were recorded on 24-tracks. They still stand up today soundwise, because of that. Just a few years earlier some of the Beatles and the Rolling Stones albums were recorded on 8-track or 16-track so when you play them today they really don't match up to what's being played today. But we were fortunate, we were there at the right time when 24-track was invented.

We went into the studio with Joe in New York and did the session live with all the musicians. We had the Brecker Brothers, and they brought in a young saxophone player, David Sanborn, who did the tremendous sax solo on 'The Bottle'. What was most amazing to me was that this all happened on the first take, no overdubbing, no re-recording. The room was on fire. There was a magic in the air and everybody felt it as they were playing it - they knew we had a hit! You could just feel it in the air and it's a special moment that I was very honoured to be there and experience. The single went on Joe Bataan's album, the album did very well and the single was a hit. After that I went to Philadelphia to do the three songs with Vince Montana and then the ones with Floyd and Carol Williams. Through Floyd Smith I met Loleatta Holloway who was his common law wife and that started my relationship with Loleatta.'

What did the Cayre brothers do then?

'This was basically the beginning of Salsoul - as we had a hit with the Salsoul Orchestra, we began to get a lot of publicity and a lot of press. We also started licensing music overseas, other artists started coming to us hoping that what we did for Salsoul Orchestra in terms of promotion and air play we could do for them. That's basically how the label grew.

We also started promoting our records in the clubs. We had good relationships with all the clubs because we felt those were the people helping us break these records. At that time radio was really in tune to the clubs. Whatever was hot in the clubs would be added to the radio list. Because we went to the clubs we recognised the importance of the DJ. We respected them, they respected us and later on we got more involved with them.

We were the first company to let an outside person - someone not involved in the recording - come into the studio and sit down with the 24-tracks and mix the record. There was a lot of sensitivity at that time because the record producer or whoever was mixing the record on the creative side finds it offensive that you would bring someone from the outside. But once we explained to them what we were doing and trying to mix it from a different perspective they reluctantly agreed. We found that the producers involved in the recording were trying to put too much in the mix. They were not looking at it from a dance standpoint or from a club standpoint. So we were the first record company to let an outside mixer come in. His name was Walter Gibbons -Walter was the first disco DJ in history to come into the studio and to actually remix a record. The very first one he did was 'Hit and Run' by Loleatta Holloway. If you listen to both versions, the album and the 12-inch version, they're like day and night. Walter's mix is a legend. He did things that nobody would have thought of doing, in fact he even left Loleatta's voice out of the first two verses - but it worked! And there was a magic to it. It was a breakthrough at the time, nobody had ever done that. Then people realised that it worked and other people started doing it.'

Did you do the club promotions yourself? You didn't go through a promotions company like 'For the Record' or the other record pools that had just started?
'No, I had too much fun doing it myself. I mean, I came out of the studio with a mix and we would press up a test pressing, an acetate - I couldn't wait to go to the clubs that night or that weekend. I had a good relationship with all the clubs and the DJs and they would wait for me. You know, sometimes we tried something that didn't work, and sometimes we tried something that would work and I would get such a big kick out of it. I also enjoyed seeing the people dance and having a good sound system. And a lot of times we took a record to the club before it was finished and we saw the reactions to certain parts and it helped us, because we went back in and made changes. And you could only get that experience by doing it first hand.'

Were there any special clubs you geared your promotion towards?
'I used to go to the Paradise Garage, the Loft, Sanctuary, 12 West, Studio 54. I'm sure there's a few others that I've forgot. And remember, at the time that we first started Salsoul I was in my mid 20s, I loved good music and dancing, I was just at the right place at the right time.'

Who are your favourite remixers?
'My favourite remixers were Walter Gibbons, Larry Levan, Tom Moulton and Shep Pettibone. Walter was the first DJ that I took into the studio. You know, he really didn't care what was on the tracks, he just cared what would make them go crazy on the dancefloor. He just came with a completely different approach - knew what would work on the dance floor in his club. The other person who also did that and who I love was Larry Levan. With Instant Funk's 'I Got My Mind Made Up' he did a complete turn around on the song when he mixed it. I think his mix was something like twelve minutes long - still it didn't seem long enough!

Larry had a passion for music and seeing people having fun dancing. I used to go down to the Garage and Larry would be there in all his glory, the people dancing and he was doing his mixing. He really loved what he was doing, he loved the music, you could see it on his face, in his personality - he was an upbeat positive person and it was a thrill, an honour and a tremendous experience working with Larry. He had the Garage in uproar. People came from around the world just to hear the aura that he was creating for the whole club. It was just a feeling that you could get only by being there.

Even though he came on late, Shep Pettibone really developed into a great remixer. Salsoul brought in all the famous DJs and remixers to work on their tracks. One could also mention top names like Jim Burgess and Bobby DJ Guttadaro.'

Do you remember how many releases there were on Salsoul?
'There were approximately 100 albums released and approximately 200 12-inch singles during the ten year period we were active in the music business.'

There were a number of sub-labels connected to Salsoul — Gold Mind, Dream and others. What was the relationship with these sub-labels?
'Well some of them we gave to the producers and mixers who were really doing great work, to try to get them to have something that they had their name attached to, and that they would take some pride in their work. The first of these was Gold Mind with Norman Harris. He was my guitar player, arranger, producer and he was a member of B-H-Y [Baker-Harris-Young] that also played on all the Trammps hits and he also produced them.

Norman was quite a songwriter too. So, I thought by giving him his label it would inspire him to do greater work. When I signed First Choice, I put them on the Gold Mind label in the beginning.

With the Dream label - I think we just wanted to have some additional labels at the time, so that when our promotions men went out to the radio stations they would not be playing too many Salsoul records. Tom 'n' Jerry was a Tom Moulton label that I gave to him. Tom's brother's name is Jerry, and I think he did it as a take off of the cartoon. He also signed some artists and put them on his label.'

Which one of these sub-labels was the most successful?
'I would say the Gold Mind label with Norman Harris.'

How many employees did Salsoul have during its top years?
'At the peak I think Salsoul had, I don't know, maybe 20 employees.'

Who designed the trademark Salsoul logo and the clouds and rainbow sky disco 12-inch cover jacket?
'At the time when we started Salsoul I was friendly with a graphic artist named Johnny Crespo and I explained to Johnny what I wanted - a label for all the people, not just black, not just white, not just latinos - it was for everybody and we wanted to just have a good time in the music and that it would appeal to all kind of ethnic classes. Johnny came up with the rainbow and he came up with the clouds and he gets a 100% of the credit for that logo and the clouds.'

So, what happened in 1984?
'OK, we started around 1972-73, and Salsoul started a year or so after this. I got married in 1981 and at the time I got married I think Skyy had their big hit with us 'Call Me'. We were riding over a nice crest, but there were factors creeping in that were going to make it harder and harder for us. We had most of the field to ourselves in those eight or nine years, but I guess because we were doing so well - getting a lot of attention and making a lot of noise worldwide - the majors started beefing up their dollars towards dance music and they were putting on big staff roles, going for big artists. So we didn't have the same position that we had in the marketplace and another factor that was creeping in was the sound was changing a little bit. It was becoming more funk and more R&B. We kind of changed with that a little bit by signing Aurra, which I believe is one of the best funk groups around and Skyy. Then the eighties began, funk and rap started creeping in, not very popular but it was creeping in and I was getting married and I no longer had the desire to spend as many late hours that the record company needed every night.

The Salsoul Orchestra
Nice 'n' Naasty
Dance Your Ass Off

LEFT CHEEK

IT'S GOOD FOR THE SOUL
(Vincent Montana, Jr.; Little Jack Music/Anatom Music; BMI)

NICE 'N' NAASTY
(Vincent Montana, Jr.; Little Jack Music/Anatom Music; BMI)

IT DON'T HAVE TO BE FUNKY (To Be A Groove)
(Ron Baker; Little Jack Music/Burma East Publishing Co.; BMI)

NIGHTCRAWLER
(Vincent Montana, Jr.; Little Jack Music/Anatom Music; BMI)

DON'T BEAT AROUND THE BUSH
(Vincent Montana, Jr.; Little Jack Music/Anatom Music; BMI)

RIGHT CHEEK

STANDING AND WAITING ON LOVE
(Vincent Montana, Jr./ Floyd Smith; Little Jack Music/Anatom Music; ASCAP/BMI)

SALSOUL: 3001
(Adapted by Vincent Montana Jr. from Richard Strauss' Thus Spoke Zarathustra; Little Jack Music/Anatom Music; BMI)

WE'VE ONLY JUST BEGUN/FEELINGS
(Roger Nichols & Paul Williams; (Morris Albert ; Fermata International Melodies, Inc.; Irving Music, Inc.; BMI) ASCAP)

RITZY MAMBO
(Vincent Montana, Jr.; Little Jack Music/Anatom Music; BMI)

PRODUCED, ARRANGED AND CONDUCTED BY VINCENT MONTANA, JR.

EXECUTIVE PRODUCERS: JOE CAYRE, STAN CAYRE, KEN CAYRE

℗ & © 19 ·'s Salsoul Record Corporation • Manufactured and Distributed by Cayrtronics Corporation • A Cayre Industries Company • 240 Madison Avenue, New York, N.Y. 10016 • Printed in USA

The Salsoul Orchestra - Nice 'N Nasty / Salsoul 1976
Cover Photography: Joel Brodsky

KE 33471 / 1975

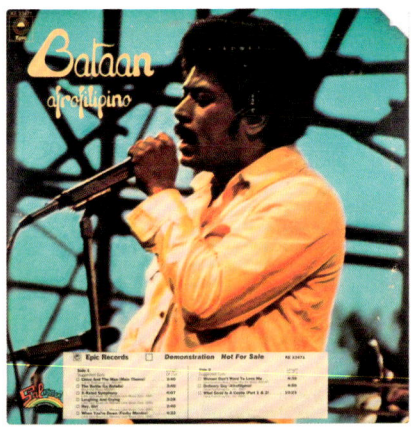

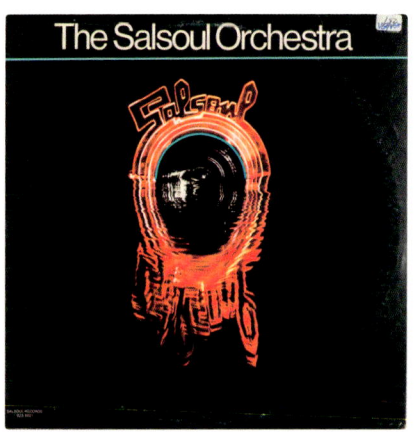

SZS 5500 / 1975

SZS 5501 / 1975

SZS 5502 / 1976

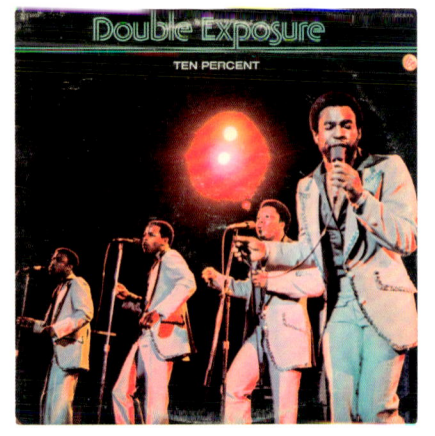

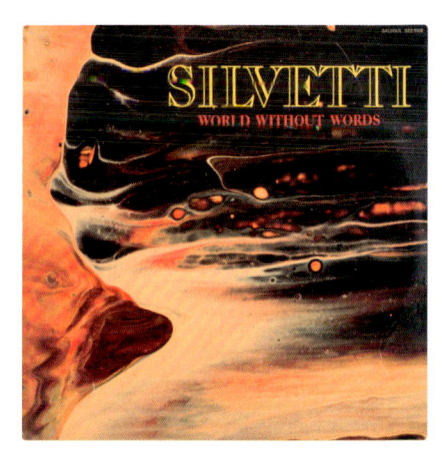

SZS 5503 / 1976

SZS 5506 / 1976

SZS 5507 / 1976

SZS 5508 / 1976

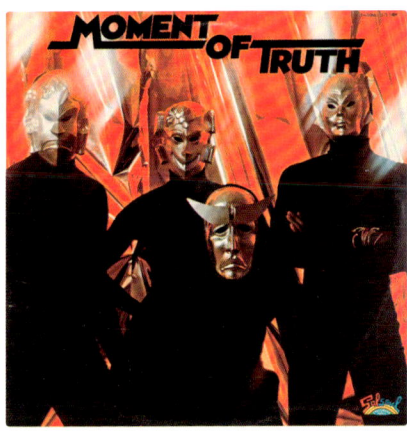

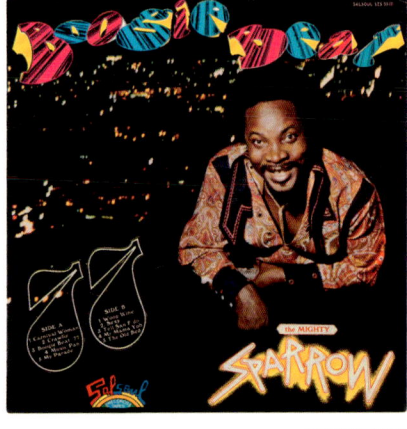

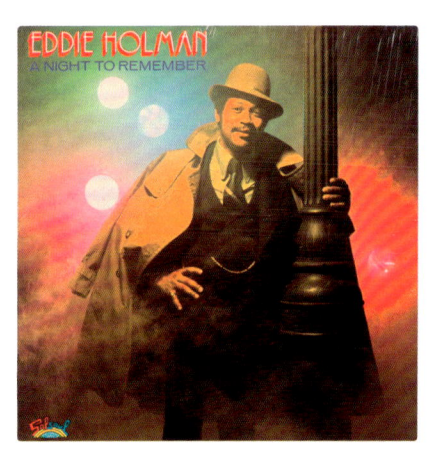

SZS 5509 / 1977

SZS 5510 / 1976

SZS 5511 / 1977

SZS 5512 / 1977

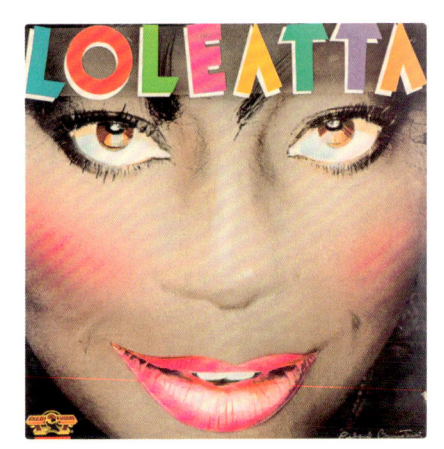

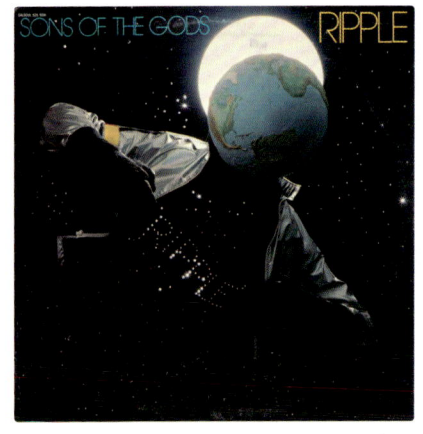

SZS 5513 / 1976

SZS 5514 / 1977

SZS 5515 / 1977

SZS 5516 / 1977

The Salsoul Orchestra – Up The Yellow Brick Road / Salsoul 1978
Design: Lori L. Lambert / Photography: Don Hunstein

SZS 5519 / 1977

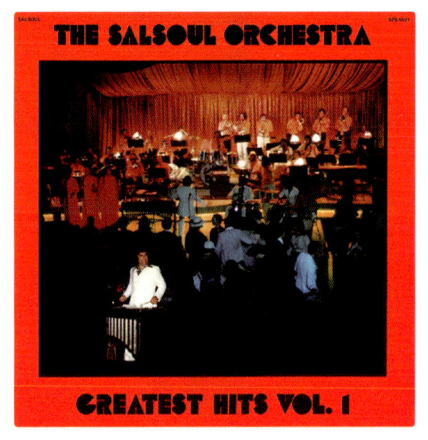

SZS 5521 / 1977

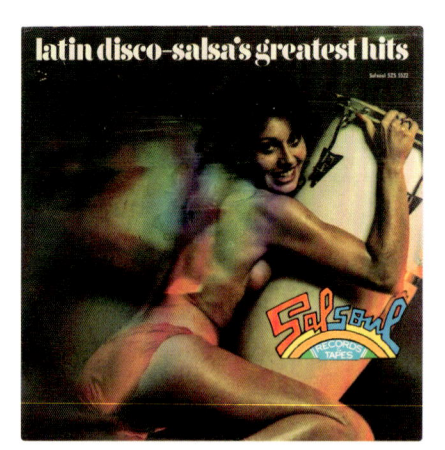

SZS 5522 / 1977

SA 5525 / 1977

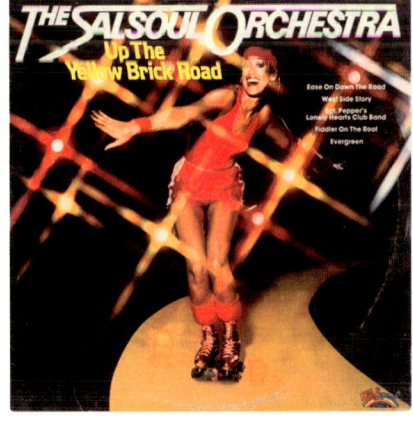

SA 8500 / 1978

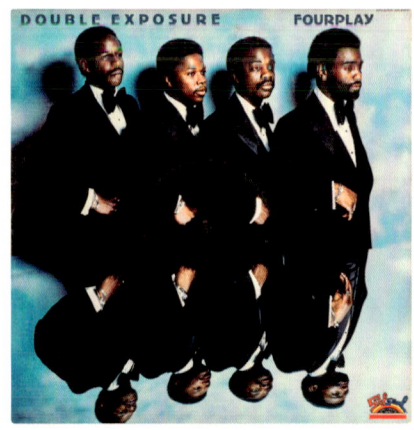

SA 8501 / 1978

SA 8502 / 1978

SA 8503 / 1978

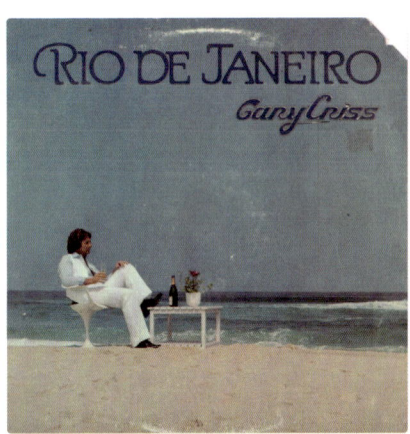

SA 8504 / 1978

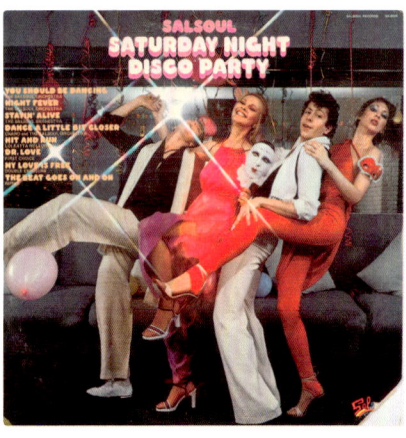

SA 8505 / 1978

SA 8506 / 1978

SA 8507 / 1978

SA 8508 / 1978

SA 8509 / 1978

SA 8509 (BACK) / 1978

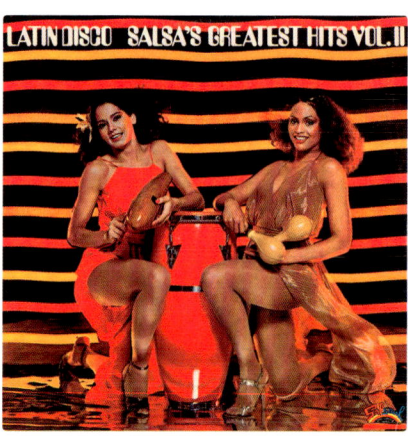

SA 8510 / 1978

154

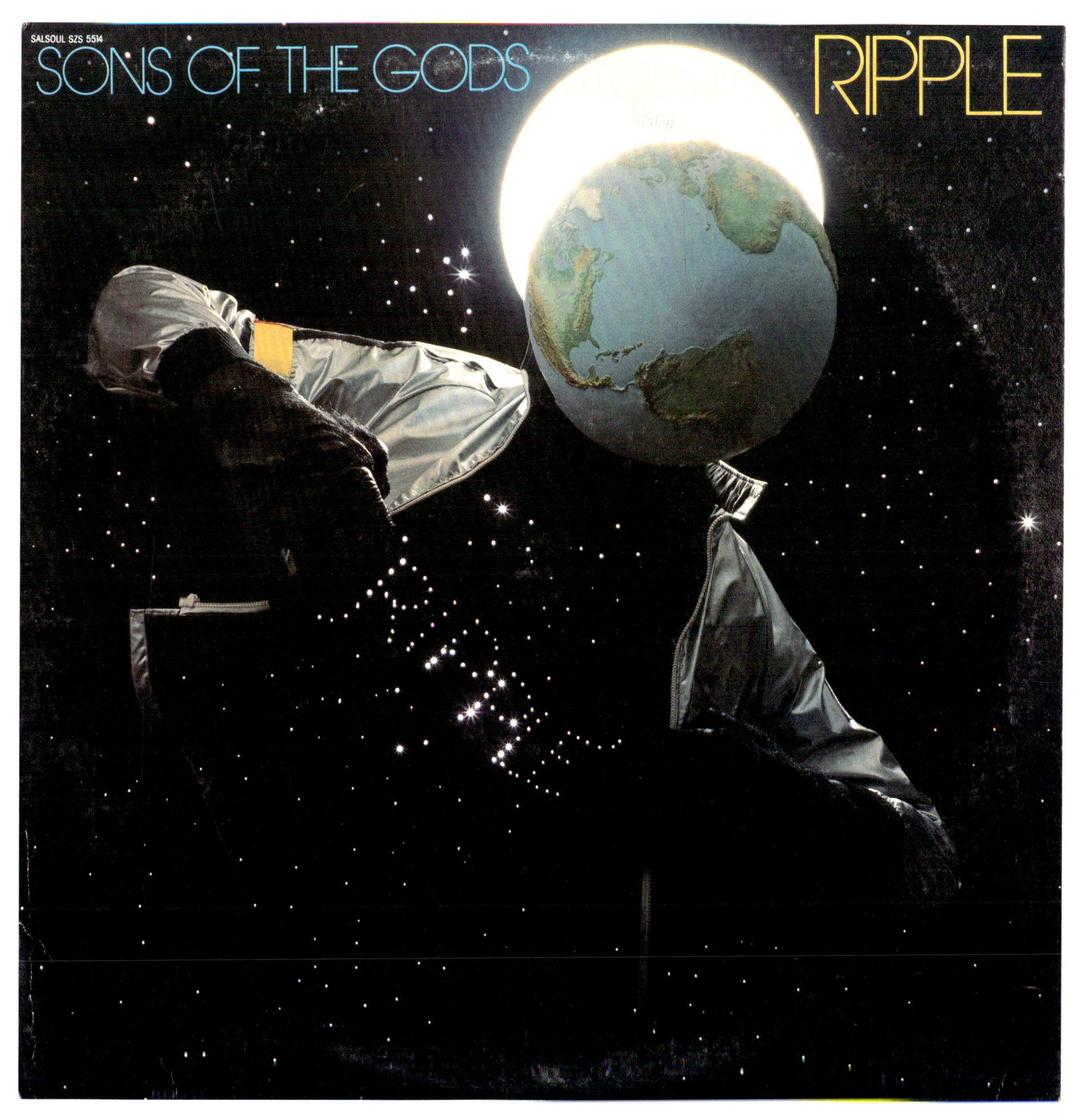

Ripple - Sons Of The Gods / Salsoul 1977
Cover Design: Mike Stromberg / Photography: Cosimo

SA 8510 (Back) / 1978    SA 8511 / 1978 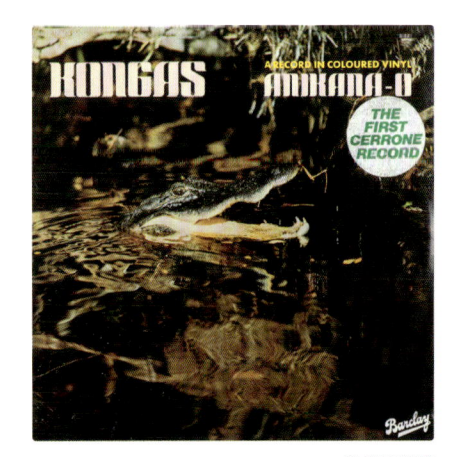   SA 8512 / 1978    SA 8513 / 1979

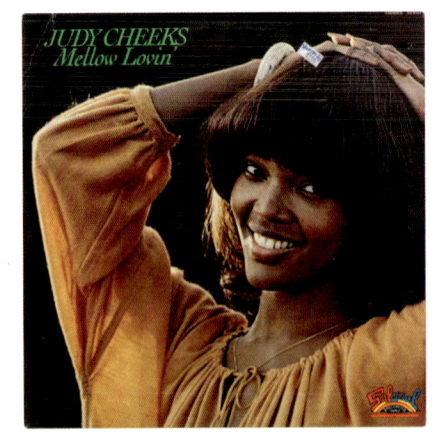

SA 8514 / 1978    SA 8515 / 1978    SA 8516 / 1979    SA 8522 / 1979

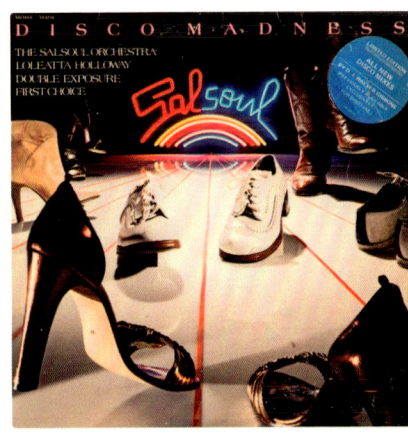

SA 8518 / 1979 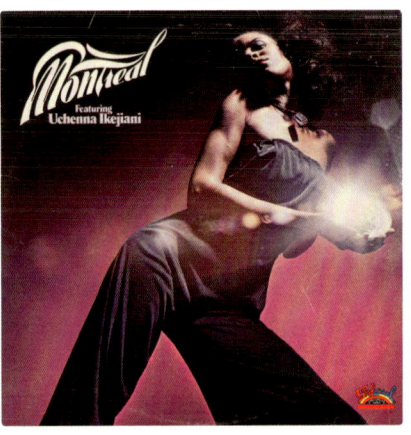   SA 8519 / 1979 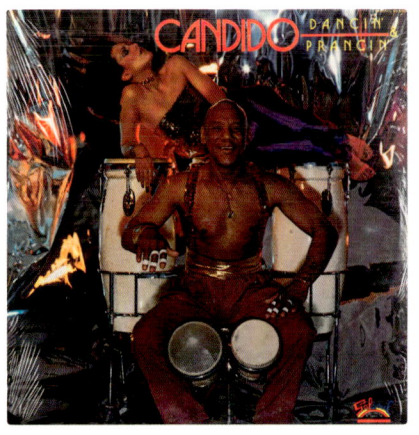   SA 8520 / 1979 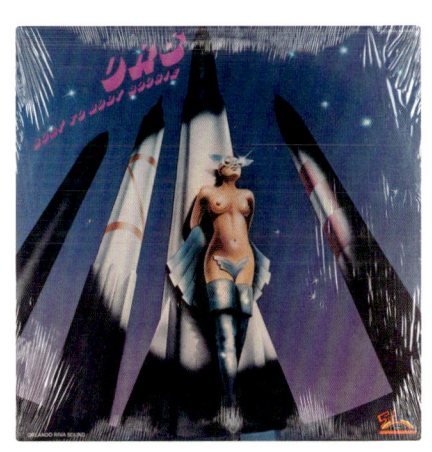   SA 8522 / 1979

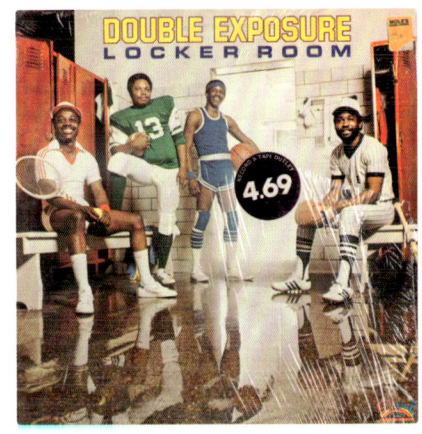

SA 8523 / 1979 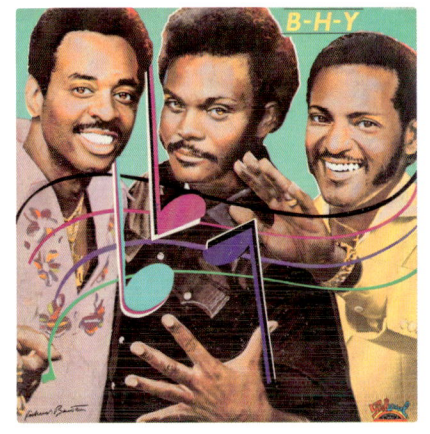   SA 8524 / 1979 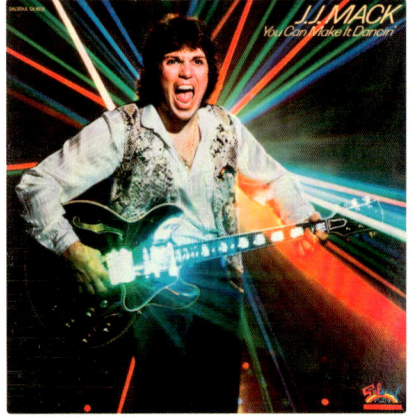   SA 8525 / 1979 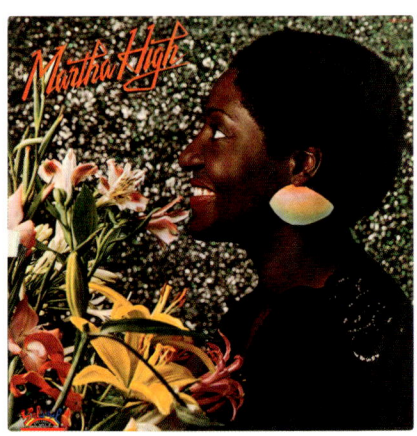   SA 8526 / 1979

Latin Disco • Salsa's Greatest Hits Vol. 1 / Salsoul 1978
Art Direction: Stan Hochstadt / Photography: Frank Kelleney / Design: Lori L. Lambert

SA 8527 / 1979

SA 8527 (Back) / 1979

SA 8528 / 1978

SA 8529 / 1979

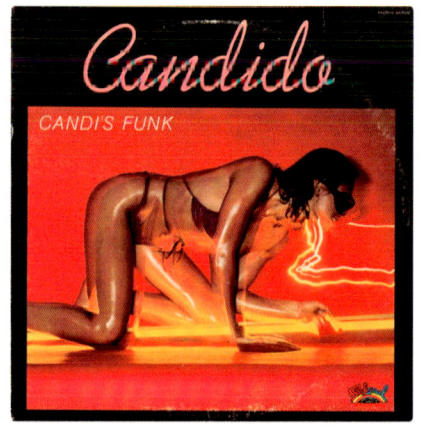

SA 8530 / 1979

SA 8531 / 1980

SA 8532 / 1980

SA 8533 / 1980

SA 8534 / 1980

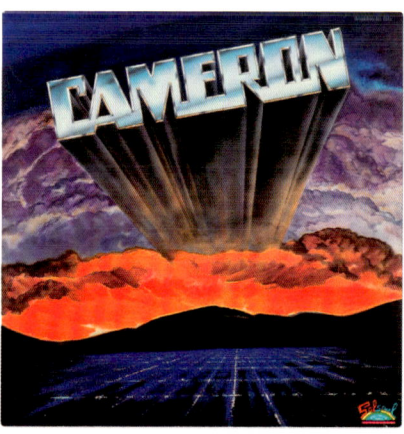

SA 8535 / 1980

SA 8536 / 1980

SA 8537 / 1980

SA 8538 / 1981

SA 8539 / 1981

SA 8540 / 1981

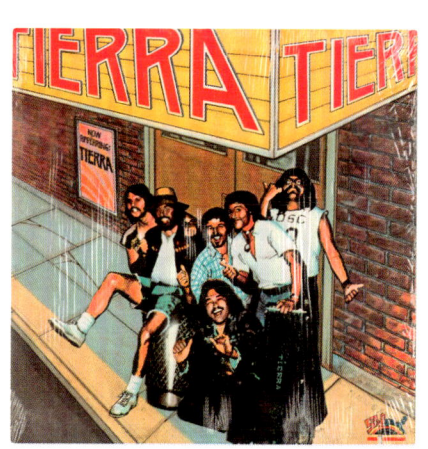

SA 8541 / 1981

Logg Logg / Salsoul 1981
Design: Roy Mendi / Photography: Len Kaltman

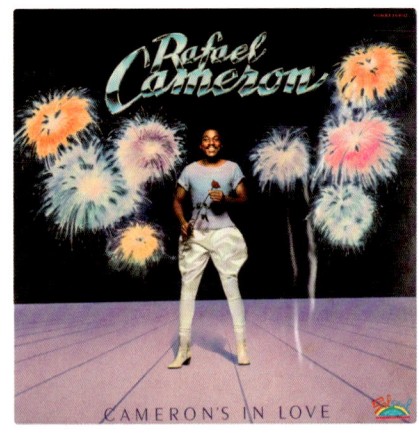

SA 8542 / 1981 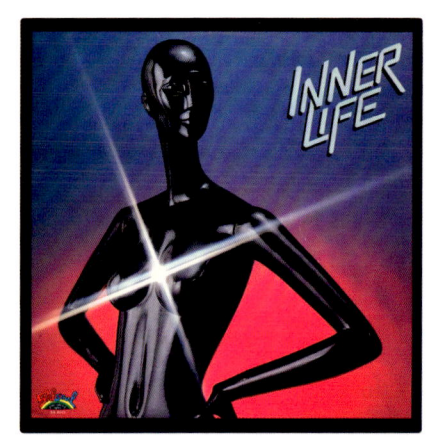
SA 8543 / 1981 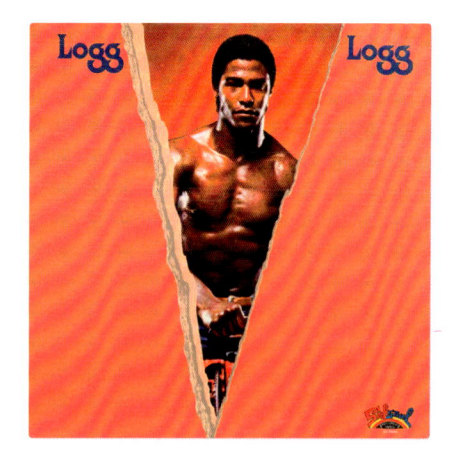
SA 8544 / 1981 
SA 8545 / 1982

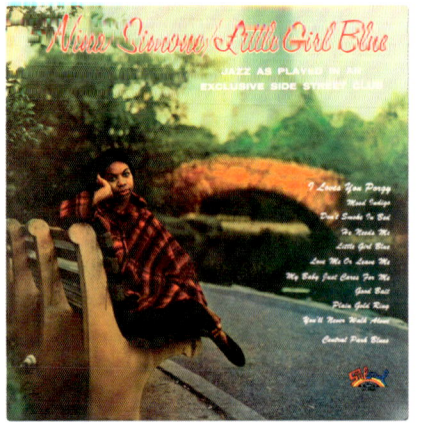

SA 8546 / 1981 
SA 8547 / 1981 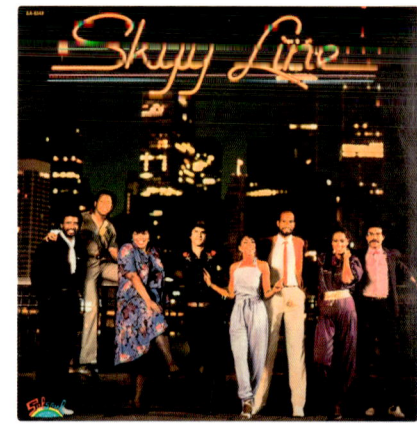
SA 8548 / 1981 
SA 8549 / 1981

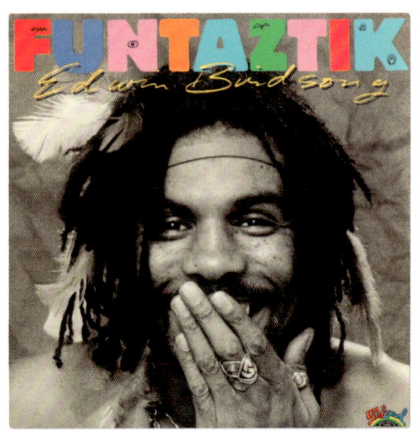

SA 8550 / 1981 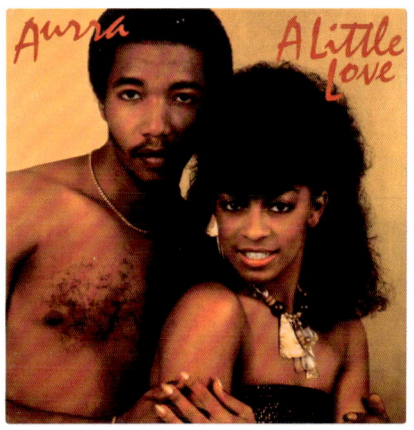
SA 8551 / 1982 
SA 8552 / 1982 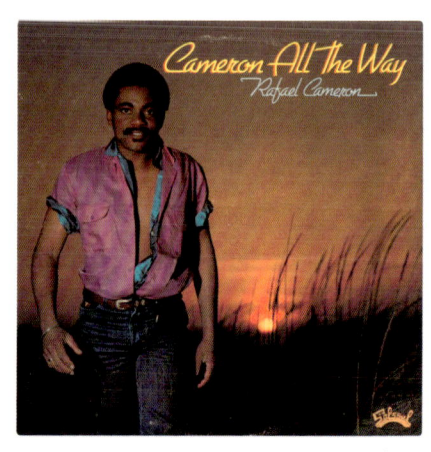
SA 8553 / 1982

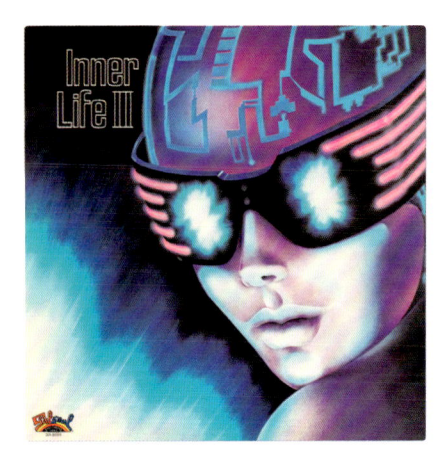

SA 8554 / 1982
SA 8555 / 1982 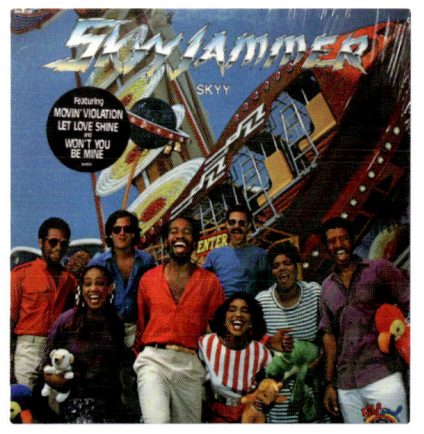
SA 8556 / 1982 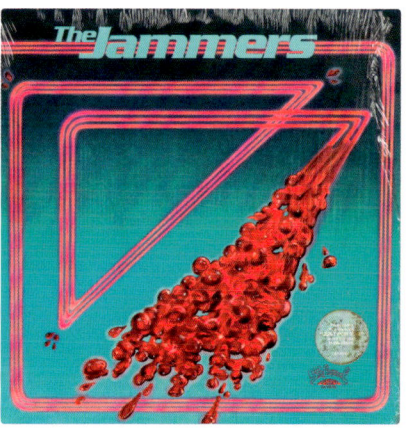
SA 8557 / 1983

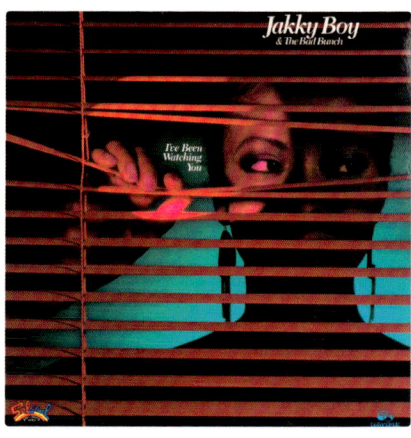

Cameron - Cameron / Salsoul 1980
Cover Art And Design: Jim O'Connell

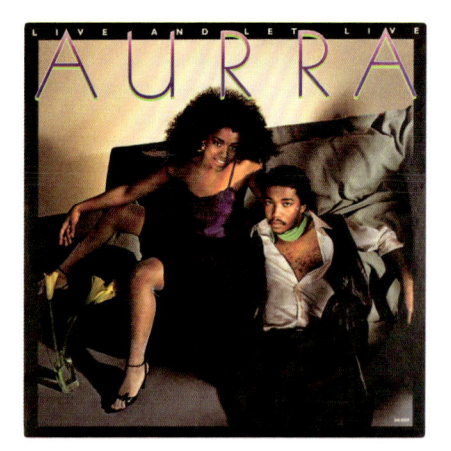

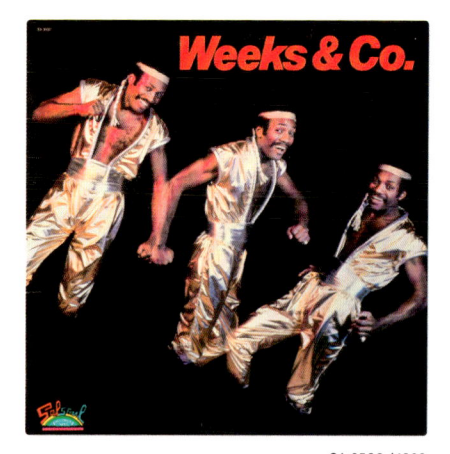

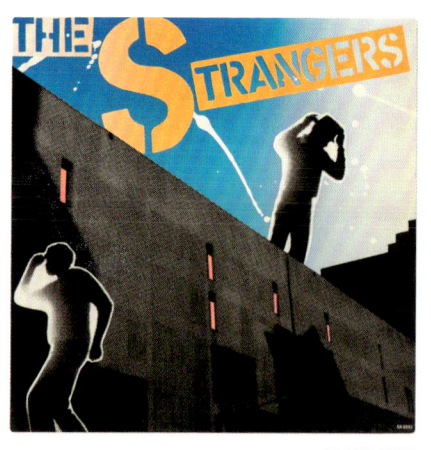

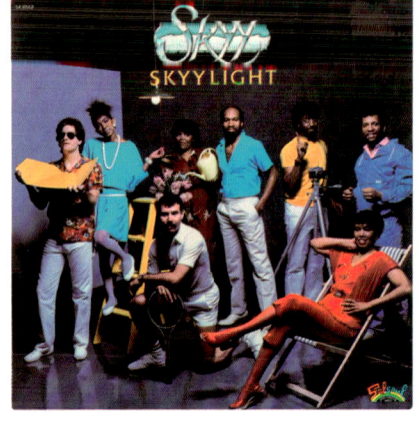

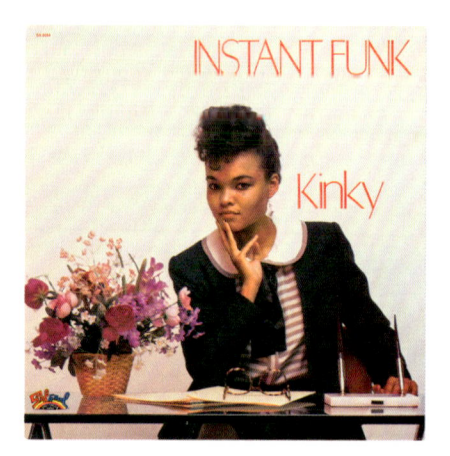

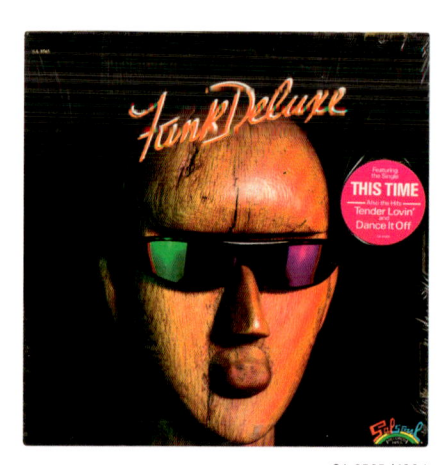

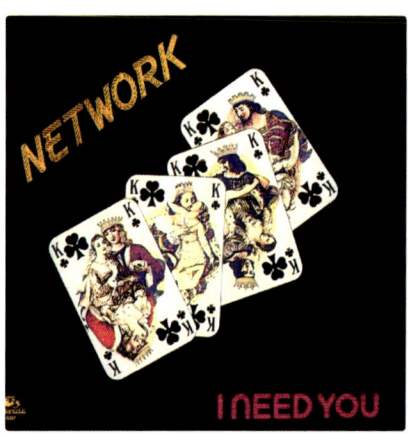

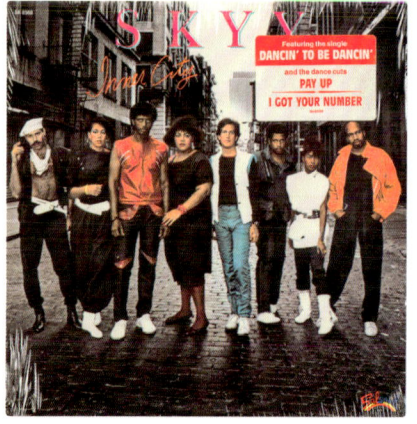

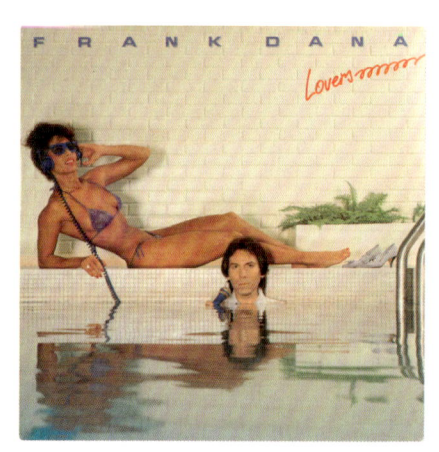

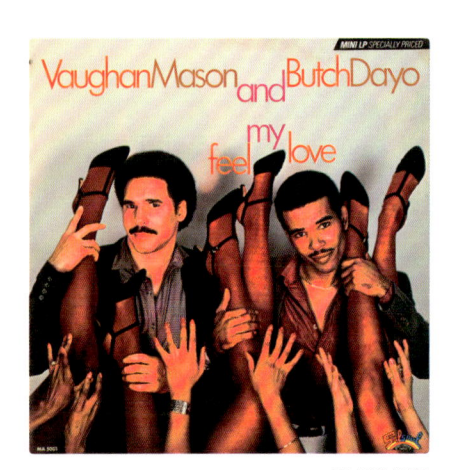

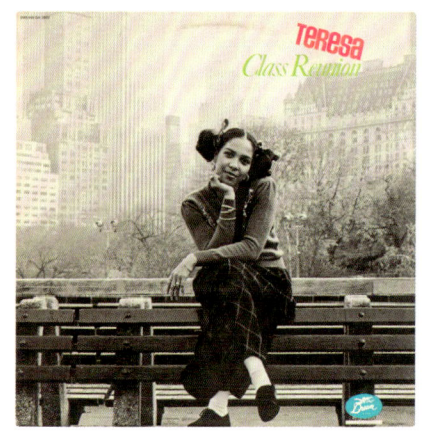

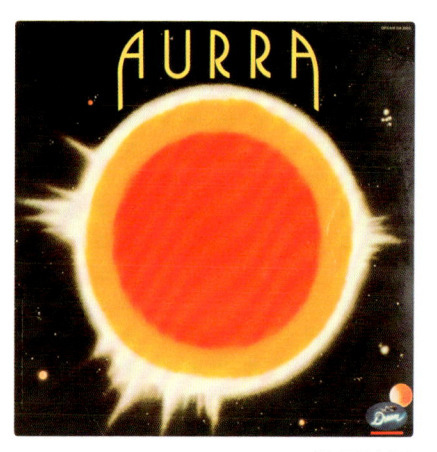

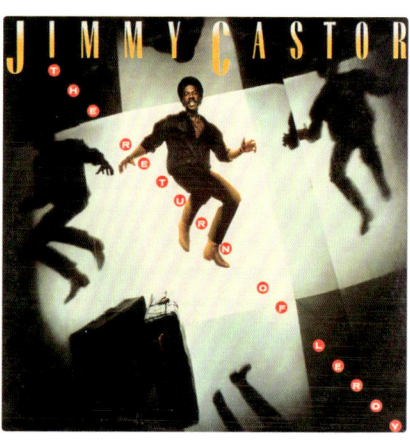

SA 8558 / 1983	SA 8559 / 1983	SA 8560 / 1983	SA 8561 / 1983
SA 8562 / 1983	SA 8563 / 1983	SA 8564 / 1983	SA 8565 / 1984
SA 8566 / 1984	SA 8567 / 1984	SA 8586 / 1984	150-150 / 1983
MA 5001 / 1983	DA 3502 / 1979	DA 3503 / 1980	DA 6001 / 1983

The Salsoul Orchestra - Heat It Up / Salsoul 1982
Design: Stan Hochstadt / Photography: Trudy Schlachter

163

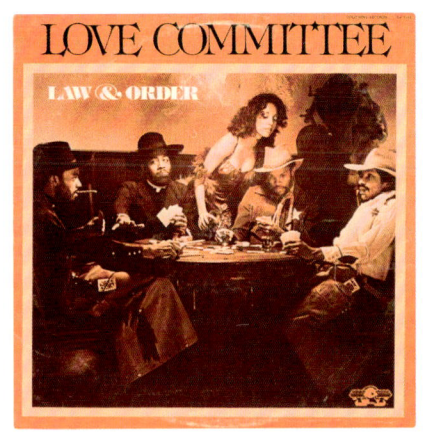

GA 9500 / 1978    GA 9501 / 1978    GA 9502 / 1979    GA 9503 / 1979

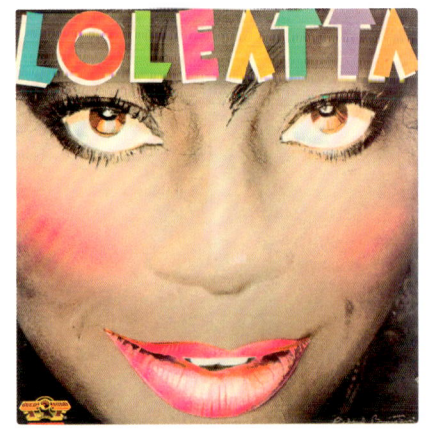

GA 9504 / 1979    GA 9505 / 1980 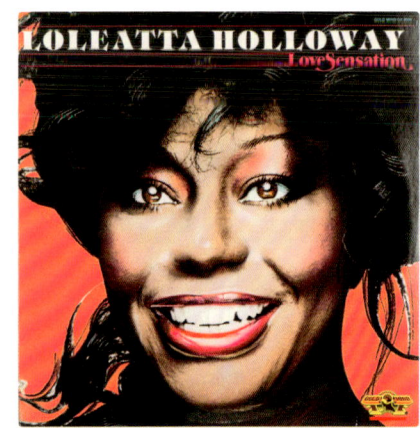   GA 9506    GZS 7500 / 1976

GZS 7501 / 1977 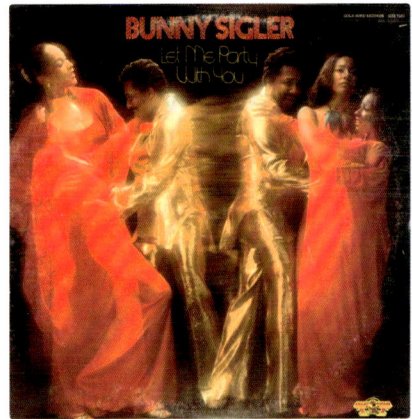   GZS 7502 / 1977 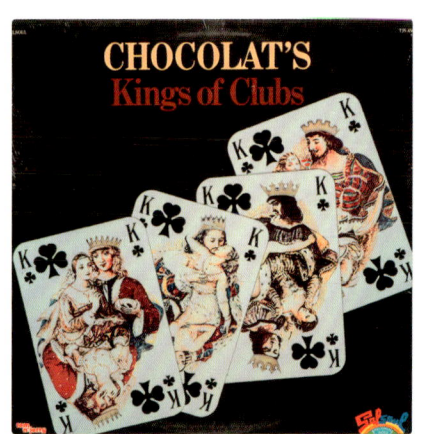   TJS 4500 / 1977 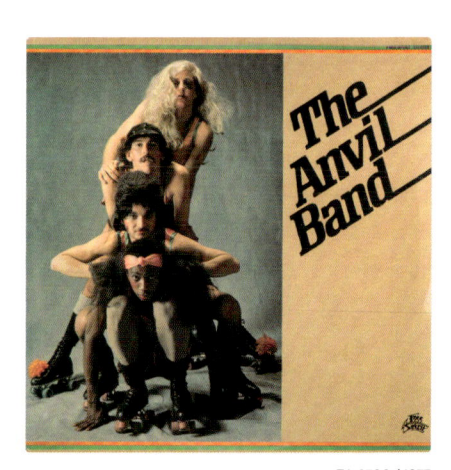   TA 6700 / 1977

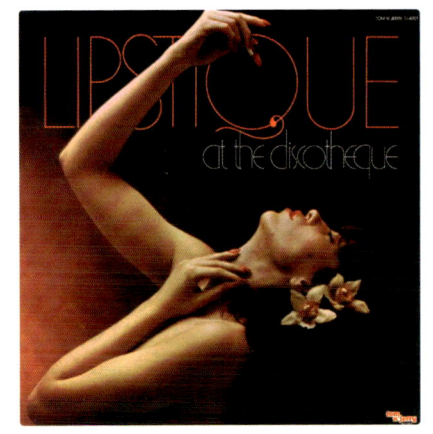

TA 4701 / 1978    TA 4702 / 1978    TA 4703 / 1978 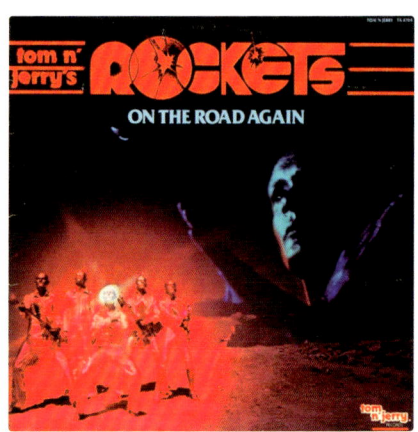   TA 4704 / 1978

Inner Life – II / Salsoul 1982
Design: Stan Hochstadt / Illustration: Jane Beaulieu

SALSOUL & SUBLABELS

Cat#	Artist	Title	Year
GA 9500	Love Committee	Law And Order	1978
GA 9501	Loleatta Holloway	Queen Of The Night	1978
GA 9502	First Choice	Hold Your Horses	1979
GA 9503	Bunny Sigler	I've Always Wanted To Sing… Not Just Write Songs	1979
GA 9504	Loleatta Holloway	Loleatta	1979
GA 9505	First Choice	Breakaway	1980
GA 9506	Loleatta Holloway	Love sensation	
GZS 7500	Loleatta Holloway	Loleatta	1976
GZS 7501	First Choice	Delusions	1977
GZS 7502	Bunny Sigler	Let Me Party With You	1977
KE 33471	Bataan	Afrofilipino	1975
SA 5525	Claudja Barry	Claudja	1977
SA 8500	Salsoul Orchestra, The	Up The Yellow Brick Road	1978
SA 8501	Double Exposure	Fourplay	1978
SA 8502	Kebekelektrik	Kebekelektrik	1978
SA 8503	Gaz	Gaz	1978
SA 8504	Gary Criss	Rio De Janeiro	1978
SA 8505	Various	Saturday Night Disco Party	1978
SA 8506	Salsoul Strings, The	How Deep Is Your Love	1978
SA 8507	Luv You Madly Orchestra	Luv You Madly Orchestra	1978
SA 8508	Salsoul Orchestra, The	Greatest Disco Hits - Music For Non-Stop Dancing	1978
SA 8509	Various	Latin Disco - Salsa's Greatest Hits Vol. 1	1978
SA 8510	Various	Latin Disco Salsa's Greatest Hits Vol. II	1978
SA 8511	Metropolis Feat. The Sweethearts	The Greatest Show On Earth	1978
SA 8512	Kongas	Anikana-O	1978
SA 8513	Instant Funk	Instant Funk	1979
SA 8514	Judy Cheeks	Mellow Lovin'	1978
SA 8515	Charo	Olé Olé	1978
SA 8516	Salsoul Orchestra, The	Street Sense	1979
SA 8517	Skyy	Skyy	1979
SA 8518	Various	Disco Madness	1979
SA 8519	Montreal Feat. Uchenna Ikejiani	Montreal Feat. Uchenna Ikejiani	1979
SA 8520	Candido	Dancin' & Prancin'	1979
SA 8522	O.R.S. (Orlando Riva Sound)	Body To Body Boogie	1979
SA 8523	Double Exposure	Locker Room	1979
SA 8524	B-H-Y	B-H-Y	1979
SA 8525	J.J. Mack	You Can Make It Dancin'	1979

Matrix numbers

Cat#	Artist	Title	Year
SA 8526	Martha High	Martha High	1979
SA-8527	Various	We Funk The Best	1979
SA 8528	Salsoul Orchestra, The	How High	1978
SA 8529	Instant Funk	Witch Doctor	1979
SA 8530	Candido	Candi's Funk	1979
SA 8531	Bunny Sigler	Let It Snow	1980
SA 8532	Skyy	Skyway	1980
SA 8533	Larry Levan	Larry Levan's Greatest Mixes Volume Two	1980
SA 8534	Joe Bataan And His Mestizo Band	Mestizo	1980
SA 8535	Cameron	Cameron	1980
SA 8536	Instant Funk	The Funk Is On	1980
SA 8537	Skyy	Skyyport	1980
SA 8538	Aurra	Send Your Love	1981
SA 8539	Hambone	Big Fat Juicy Fun	1981
SA 8540	Flakes	Flakes	1981
SA 8541	Tierra	Tierra	1981
SA 8542	Rafael Cameron	Cameron's In Love	1981
SA 8543	Inner Life	Inner Life	1981
SA 8544	Logg	Logg	1981
SA 8545	Instant Funk	Looks So Fine	1982
SA 8546	Nina Simone	Little Girl Blue	1981
SA 8547	The Salsoul Orchestra	Christmas Jollies 2	1981
SA 8548	Skyy	Skyy Line	1981
SA 8549	Joe Bataan	Joe Bataan II	1981
SA 8550	Edwin Birdsong	Funtaztik	1981
SA 8551	Aurra	A Little Love	1982
SA 8552	Salsoul Orchestra, The	Heat It Up	1982
SA 8553	Rafael Cameron	Cameron All The Way	1982
SA 8554	Inner Life	Inner Life II	1982
SA 8555	Skyy	Skyyjammer	1982
SA 8556	Jammers, The	The Jammers	1982
SA 8557	Jakky Boy & The Bad Bunch	I've Been Watching You	1983
SA 8558	Instant Funk	Instant Funk V	1983
SA 8559	Aurra	Live And Let Live	1983
SA 8560	Weeks & Co.	Weeks & Co.	1983
SA 8561	Strangers, The	The Strangers	1983
SA 8562	Skyy	Skyylight	1983
SA 8563	Civil Attack	Civil Attack	1983
SA 8564	Instant Funk	Kinky	1983
SA 8565	Funk Deluxe	Funk Deluxe	1984
SA 8566	Steve Washington	Like A Shot	1984
SA 8567	Network	I need you	1984
SA 8568	Skyy	Inner City	1984
150-150	Frank & Dana	Lovers	1983
MA5001	Vaughan Mason And Butch Dayo	Feel My Love	1983
SZS 5500	Tierra	Stranded	1975
SZS 5501	The Salsoul Orchestra	Salsoul Orchestra	1975
SZS-5502	The Salsoul Orchestra	Nice 'N' Naasty	1976
SZS 5503	Double Exposure	Ten Percent	1976
SZS 5505	Various	That's Salsoul	1976
SZS 5506	Carol Williams	Lectric Lady	1976
SZS 5507	The Salsoul Orchestra	Christmas Jollies	1976
SZS 5508	Silvetti	World Without Words	1976
SZS 5509	Moment Of Truth	Moment Of Truth	1977
SZS 5510	The Mighty Sparrow	Boogie Beat '77	1976
SZS 5511	Eddie Holman	A Night To Remember	1977
SZS 5512	Claudja Barry	Sweet Dynamite	1977
SZS 5513	Loleatta Holloway	Loleatta	1976
SZS 5514	Ripple	Sons of the gods	1977
SZS-5515	The Salsoul Orchestra	Magic Journey	1977
SZS 5516	Silvetti	Spring Rain	1977
SZS-5519	Charo And The Salsoul Orchestra	Cuchi-Cuchi	1977
SZS-5521	The Salsoul Orchestra	Greatest Hits Vol. 1	1977
SZS-5522	Latin Disco	Greatest Hits	1977
TA 4701	Lipstique	At The Discotheque	1978
TA 4702	Mc Lane Explosion	Pulstar	1978
TA 4703	Davis Christie	Back Fire	1978
TA 4704	Rockets	On the road	1978
TA 6700	The Anvil Band	The Anvil Band	1977
TJS 4500	Chocolat's	Kings Of Clubs	1977
2SS 0101	Various	Disco Boogie	1977
2SS 0102	Various	Disco Boogie Vol. 2	1978
DA 3501	Gotham	Gotham	1977
DA 3502	Teresa	Class Reunion	1979
DA 3503	Aurra	Aurra	1980
DA 6001	Jimmy Castor	It's just begun	1983

JOHN DAVIS AND THE MONSTER ORCHESTRA

UP JUMPED THE DEVIL

SAM 701

SAM RECORDS

Disco Labels & Albums

Chapter 16
SAM Records

SAM WEISS STARTED SAM RECORDS IN LONG ISLAND CITY, NEW YORK IN 1976.

No newcomer to the music business, he had been in the record industry since the 1940s together with his brother Hy Weiss (continues overleaf).

Left: John Davis And The Monster Orchestra - Up Jumped The Devil / SAM 1977
Photography: Rod Cook / Art Direction: Neil Terk / Design: Jeanette Adams

History of SAM Records

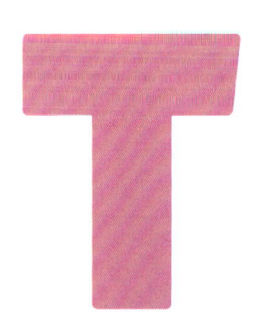

The Weiss brothers were born in Romania in the 1920s, but the family moved to the Bronx NYC when the boys were just a few years old. Hy, the older of the two brothers, first got into the record business and became a salesman for popular R&B labels like Apollo, Exclusive, Jubilee and Modern. He then brought in his brother Sam and together they began distributing mainly West coast labels on the East coast. Their new company Win Records became New York's first record distribution company.

The Weiss brothers launched their first record label in the late 1940s (Parody Records). In 1954 they started Old Town Records, which began as an R&B label and developed to include gospel, jazz and doo-wop through to pop, rock and soul. This label ran until the mid 1970s. Besides running Old Town, Hy Weiss also headed the promotional department of Stax Records in the late 1960s and early 1970s.

During the mid 1970s as disco was emerging Sam Weiss was quick to get on board and SAM Records was born in 1976. The first release, Doris Duke's 'Woman of the Ghetto', was followed by John Davis & the Monster Orchestra and their top five single 'Night and Day'. Davis would score several hits for SAM, and the label's first 12-inch release was the group's 'I Can't Stop' released in 1977.

In 1978 Lucy Hawkins had a minor hit for the label, but it was John Davis who was the most popular artist on the label. He recorded a disco version of the Kojak Theme from the TV series, followed by his biggest hit 'Ain't That Enough For You', which reached number four in the Billboard disco charts.

At this point Sam Weiss signed a licensing deal with Columbia Records and between late 1978 and 1980 precious few singles were released — a couple of Davis seven-inches and just one SAM 12-inch - Gary's Gang 'Keep On Dancin' which made number one in the disco charts and became an international success.

With the success of Gary's Gang Weiss went back into releasing his productions on SAM Records full time in 1980. One of the first releases was Rhyze's 'Just How Sweet Is Your Love' which got heavy rotation from Larry Levan at the Paradise Garage and from many other club DJs.

The label's next big club hit was the Leroy Burgess act Convertion's 'Let's Do It'. Producer Greg Carmichael brought out the best in Leroy's characteristic voice. Convertion was almost a family thing for Burgess - the group included his sister Renee J.J. Burgess on background vocals, his adopted brother James Calloway on bass and cousins Sonny T. Davenport and Willis Long who played drums and percussion. When the group left SAM and switched to Salsoul they were renamed Logg.

Other acts that brought success to the label were K.I.D, Vicky D, Komiko, Mike & Brenda Sutton and B.B.C.S. & A. But in 1983 the SAM Records saga came to an end, the last 12-inch single released being Klassique's 'Somebody's Loving You'. Over the years SAM had built a reputation of putting out quality dance music and many DJs noted 'If it's on SAM, just buy it, you won't be disappointed!'

SAM was revived in 1989. The label came back with a new logo and new music. Following current trends the repertoire included rap and dance music as well as updating earlier disco tracks. Their main act at this time was Richard Rogers, but there were also remixes of Gary's Gang and John Davis. Even Convertion's 'Let's Do It' got a ragga makeover with Jamal-Ski the Bead Master's 'Let's Do It in the Dancehall'.

In 1991 Sam's son Michael took over the Weiss family's legacy in the music business when he started his own Nervous Records. Sam became the vice-president of Nervous and the SAM Records catalog was brought into the new company.

Matrix numbers

SAM

SAM 700	John Davis & The Monster Orchestra	Night And Day	1976
SAM 701	John Davis & The Monster Orchestra	Up Jumped The Devil	1977
SAM 702	John Davis And The Monster Orchestra	Ain't That Enough For You	1978
JC 35793	Garry's Gang	Keep On Dancing'	1979
JC 36240	Garry's Gang	Gangbusters	1979
SAM 703	Rhyze	Just How Sweet Is Your Love	1980
SAM 704	Mike & Brenda Sutton	Don't Hold Back	1982

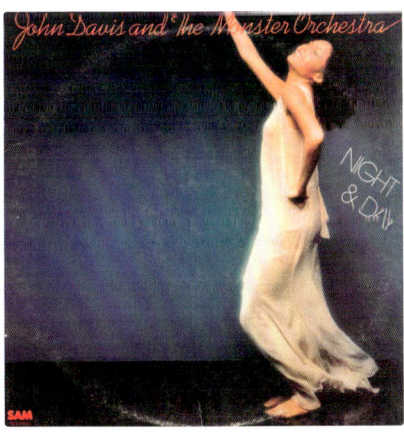

SAM 700 / 1976

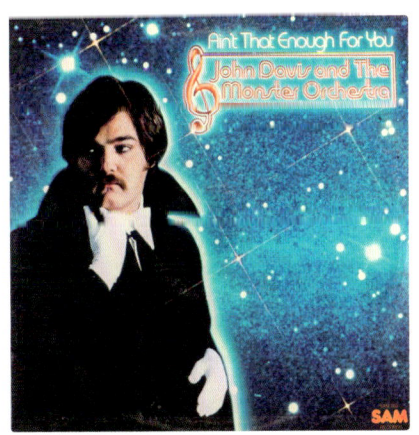

SAM 702 / 1978

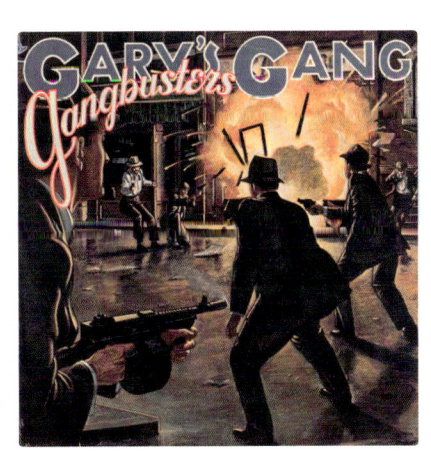

JC 36240 / 1979

SAM 704 / 1982

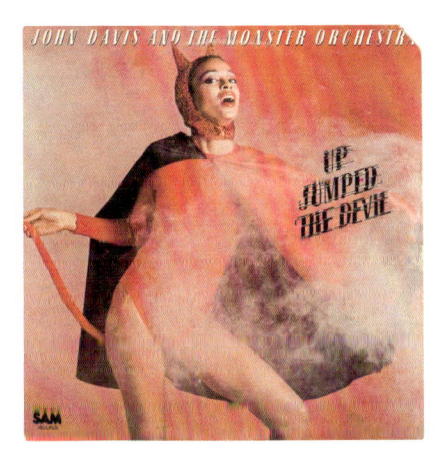

SAM 701 / 1977

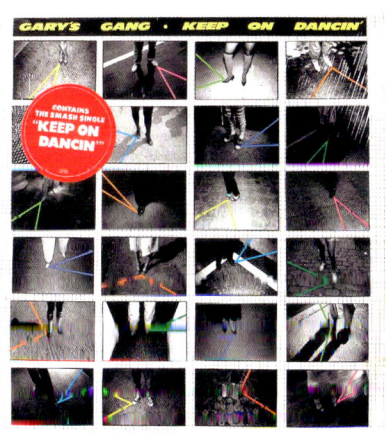

JC 35793 / 1979

SAM 703 / 1980

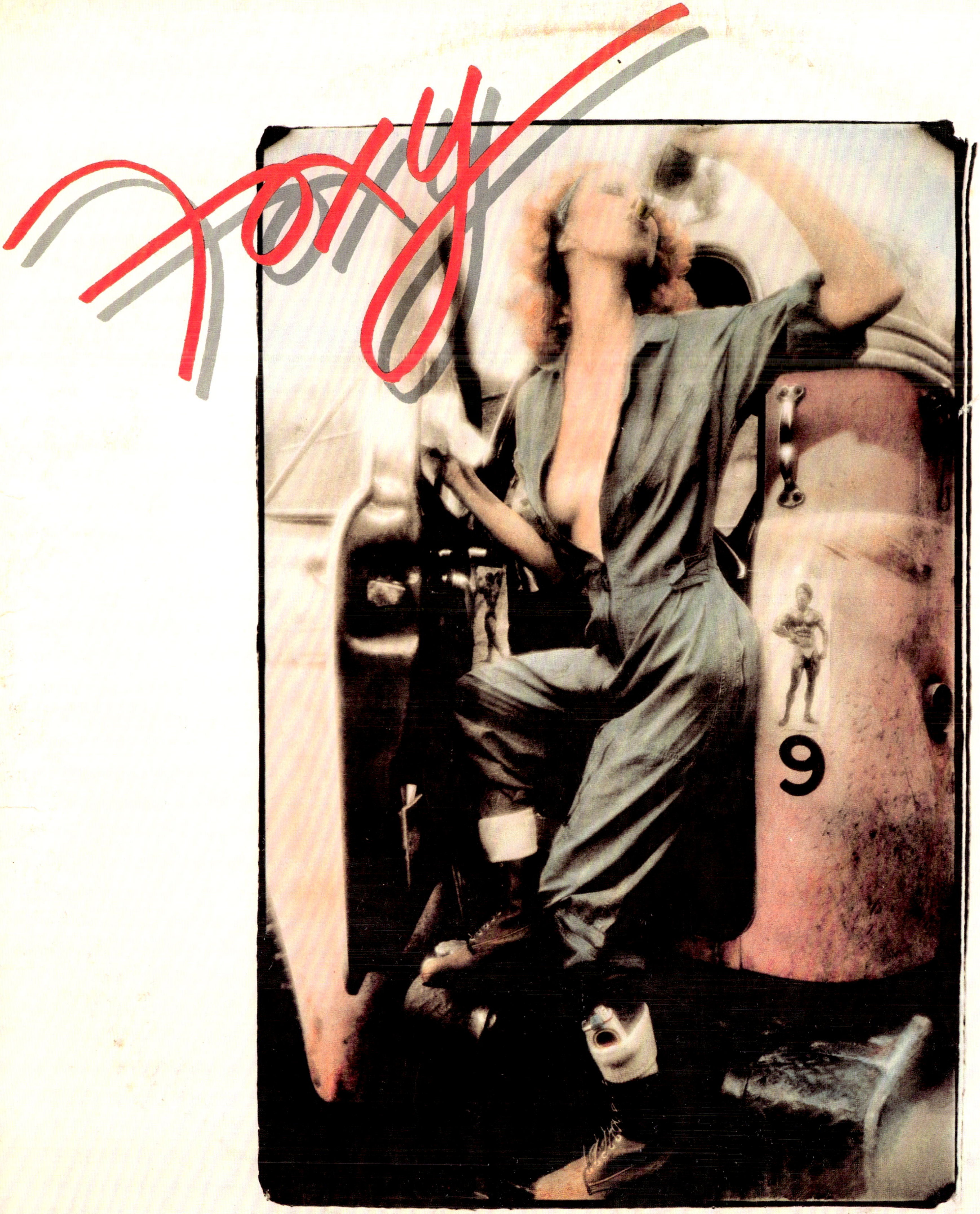
Foxy
9

Disco Labels & Albums

Chapter 17
TK and sub-labels

T.K. PRODUCTIONS WERE BASED IN MIAMI, FLORIDA AND THEY BEGAN RELEASING RECORDS IN THE EARLY 1970S.

The company was owned and run by Henry Stone up until it closed in 1981. T.K. Disco was actually not an official label - just the umbrella name to release 12-inch singles from products coming out on T.K. Records and the independent labels affiliated to T.K. Productions. Henry Stone was born in the Bronx, New York on June 3, 1921. His father died when he was six and Stone was sent to an orphanage in Pleasantville, New York. It was at the orphanage that his interest in music started when he began playing the trumpet, inspired by the famous jazz legend Louis Armstrong. In 1943 Henry joined a US army band, working with many black musicians who introduced him to black music — the music that would always be close to his heart (continues overleaf).

Left: Foxy - Foxy / Dash 1976
Art Direction & Design: Richard Roth, Howard Smiley / Photography: Richard Shaefer. With Permision Of Viva Magazine

Henry Stone Interview

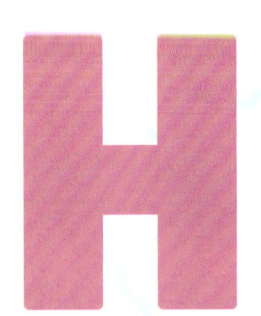

How did you get involved in the music business?
'Just to give you a glimpse into the story, I was born and raised in the tough borough of the Bronx, New York. I was always pulled to music from the early age of about 12, when I began playing the trumpet. Then I played in the first integrated army band during the second world war, which was based at Camp Kilmer, in New Jersey.

After the war I moved to California for a short time, maybe a year or so and there I found a niche selling records out of the trunk of my car to jukebox operators and I was also working as an A&R man for different record companies, like Jewel and Modern. But it was impossible to find a place to live while I was in California so I moved to Miami, Florida in late 1947 where I had some contacts.

Here I set up my first distribution company [Seminole] selling again mostly to jukebox operators, because at that time there was only one record store here in Miami. I also had a small recording studio called Crystal Recording Company, where in the early 1950s I recorded Ray Charles, Wilbert Harrison and other gospel and blues artists. James Brown and Hank Ballard came into my story in the middle of the 1950s, when I was aligned with King Records.'

In 1960 Stone established Tone Distribution and built the company into one of the largest independent distributors in the United States.

'My greatest success came during the 1970s with the arrival of the disco era, a genre I helped launch in its infancy via George McCrae's 'Rock Your Baby' and KC and the Sunshine Band.'

How and when did you come up with the idea of starting T.K.?
'I was the Miami record distributor for Atlantic, Warner Brothers and Electra Record Companies. They merged into one company called WEA and decided they would no longer use me as their independent distributor. At the time I was releasing my Alston label through Atlantic Records, and I had given them two records that sold over a million copies each, 'Clean Up Woman' by Betty Wright and 'Funky Nassau' by The Beginning Of The End. At this point I made my decision to start my own record label for distribution, which I named T.K. Records.

In 1970 Henry had his warehouse, distribution and recording companies located all together at 495 SE 10th Court in Hialeah, Florida and this is where the history of T.K. starts. The first record released under the T.K. banner was 'Why Can't We Live Together' by Timmy Thomas.

Thomas was a musician and lounge owner in Miami Beach, Florida. He first recorded the track on a small local label named Konduko but it was poorly distributed. When Stone heard the track in late 1972, he saw its potential and reissued it on his own Glades label, distributed by T.K. Records. It reached number one in the Billboard black music chart and was a great start for the new company.

What did the letters T.K. stand for?
'The letters T.K. stood for the name of the engineer who built my eight track recording studio. His name was Terry Kane. I already had a corporation set up with the T.K. initials and rather than file for a new corporate name, I decided to go ahead and use what I already had.'

What was the difference between T.K. Productions and T.K. Disco?
'T.K. Productions was the corporation that produced and distributed all my various different labels such as Alston, Drive, Glades, Dash, Marlin and so on.
T.K. Disco was basically any records I released on 12-inch singles that went to the clubs – T.K. Disco specialized in club and DJ mixes.'

T.K. Disco was like an umbrella for releasing 12-inch singles from the sub-labels?
'Yes, that is correct. Regardless of the sub-label all 12-inch releases were put out in the very special, now famous 12-inch T.K. jacket. The 12-inches were all club oriented disco music and that's what that jacket symbolised.'

Who painted the T.K. disco 12-inch sleeve and designed the bamboo logo?
'It was conceived by myself and one of my assistants, Howard Smiley and the artwork was done by Page Wood.'

What would you say T.K. Records/T.K. Disco stood for musically?
'It was one of the first record labels to hit the dance market worldwide that became known as 'disco'.'

You also owned the Marlin label, with disco acts like Amant and Voyage?
'Marlin was more of a soft disco sounding label where my other labels such as Dash, Drive and Alston, all had a little more funk to them.'

There were many sub-labels connected to T.K. Records. What was the relation to these sub-labels?
'We had so many releases that we had to set up different sub-labels to handle all of them. There wasn't one sub-label that was more successful than the rest and each one had its

own hits. Of course, the stand out label was T.K. itself which had six number one worldwide hit records with K.C. and the Sunshine Band and George McCrae.'

One other idea behind all the different labels was to let each of them have their own profile and, more importantly, get the records played on the radio. Stone had found out during his years as a distributor that radio stations had a hard time playing several hits from one label - even if they were huge hits. So the trick was to release hit singles under different labels - then all the hits could be played even in the same show.

**Is it correct that the company was going into bankruptcy in 1981?
And if so what caused this?**
'Yes, that is correct. I was going strong as a company, with hit after hit and then came the anti-disco movement in Chicago and that spread around the country. Then the CBS television news program 60 Minutes also picked up on it and said 'Disco Is Dead'. I had the number one record in the world at the time with KC's first ballad 'Please Don't Go', but the impact of all the bad media attention crippled my company financially. It was not long after that that T.K. shut down - all of it was shut down not just certain parts of it.'

When T.K. closed, Sunnyview Records and Hot Productions seemed to re-release the T.K. songs. What was their relation to T.K.?
'I formed a new company after T.K. called Sunnyview Records with Morris Levy of Roulette records. Sunnyview retained the rights to some of the T.K. masters, and thus was able to read T.K. material in the 1980s.

Today Stone still lives in Coconut Grove, Florida. He is married, spends his time with his children and grandchildren as well as traveling. He has now revived his T.K. label and at an age of 80-plus is still active in the dance music business.

Alarm Records

LP-1000 / 1976

Alstom Records

SD 33-260 / 1969

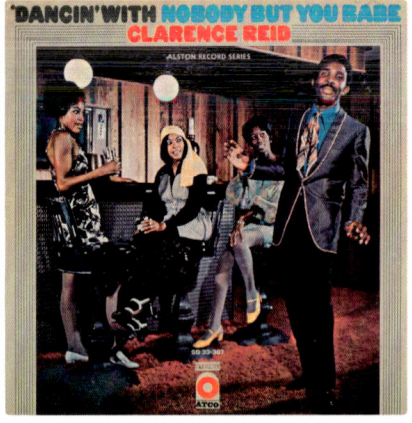

SD 33-307 / 1969

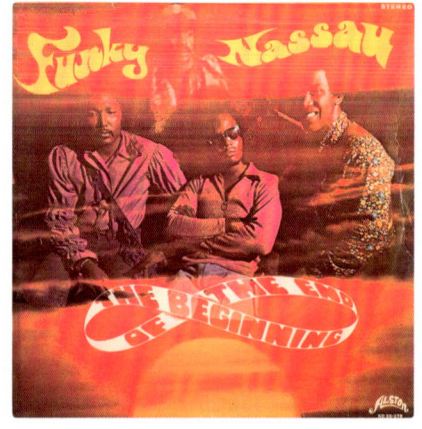

SD 33-379 / 1971

SD 33-388 / 1972

SD 7026 / 1973

SD 7026 / 1973

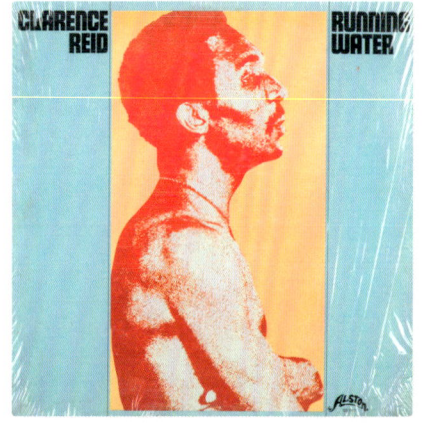

SD 7027 / 1973

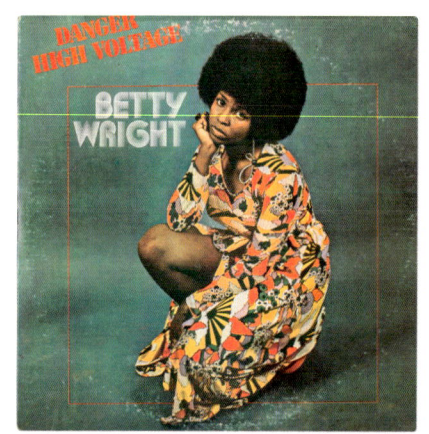

4400 / 1974

4401 / 1975

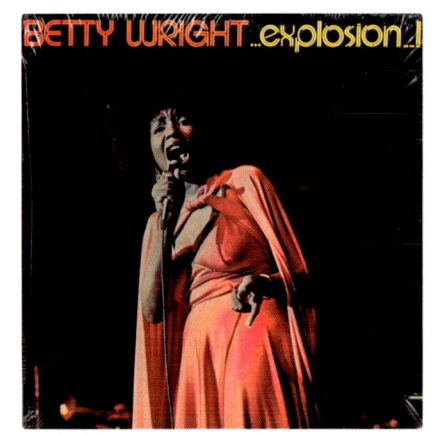

4402 / 1976

4403 / 1976

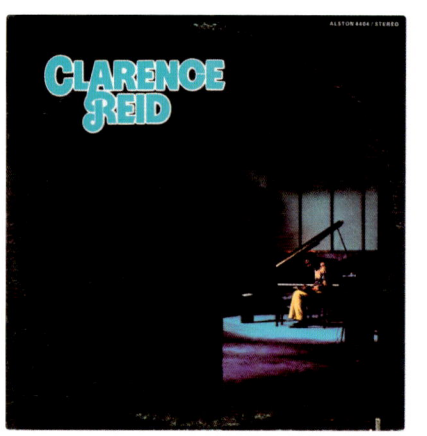

4404 / 1976

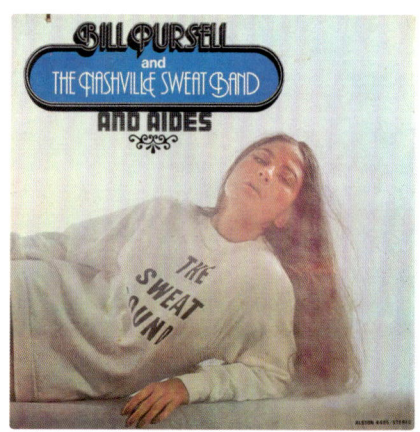

4405 / 1976

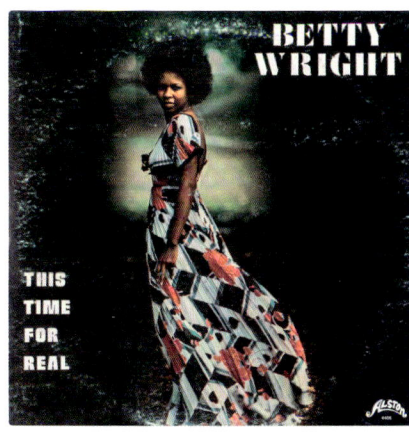

4406 / 1977

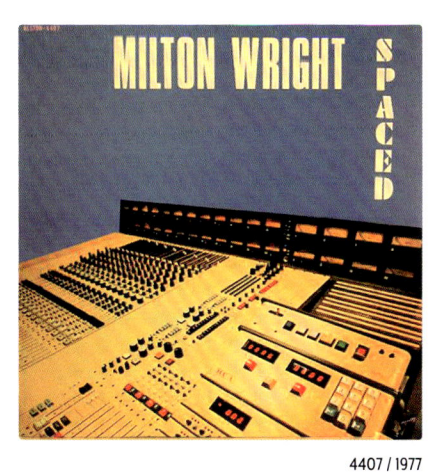

4407 / 1977

4408 / 1978

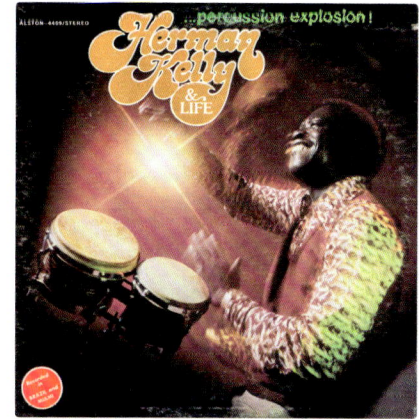

4409 / 1978

4410 / 1979

4411 / 1980

4412 / 1980

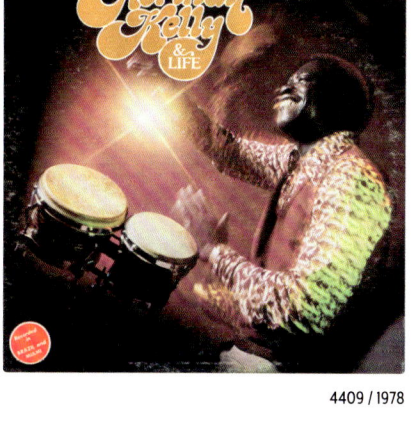

Amazon Records

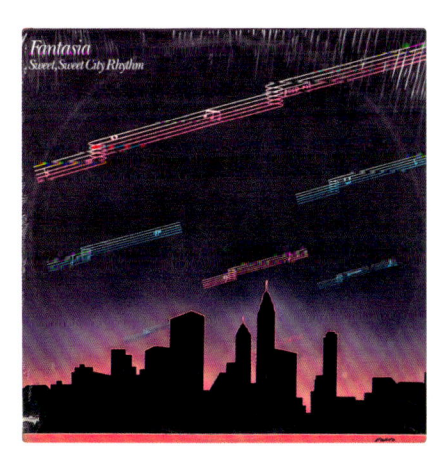

400 / 1978

Amour Records

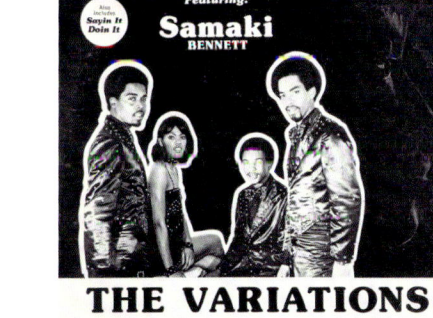

AMOUR-1001 / 1975

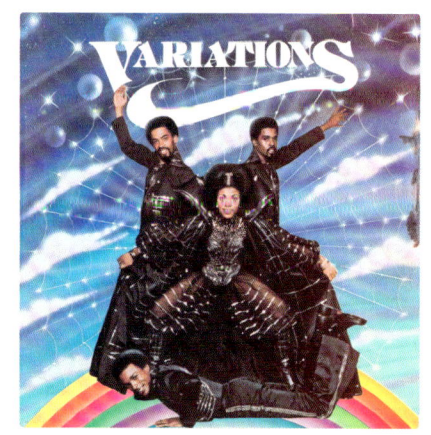

A-7777 / 1977

A-121675 / 1979

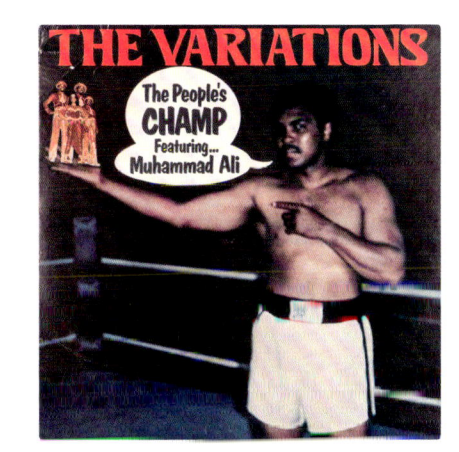

8900 / 1980

APA Records

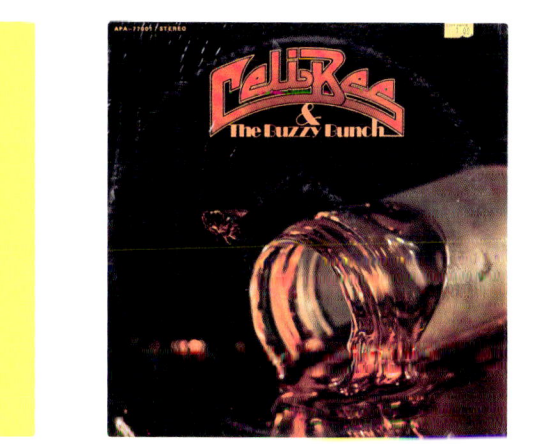

APA-77001 / 1977

177

The 13th Floor - Steppin Out / Blue Candle 1977
Cover Photo: Nelson Patterson / Album Design: Herbert Temple

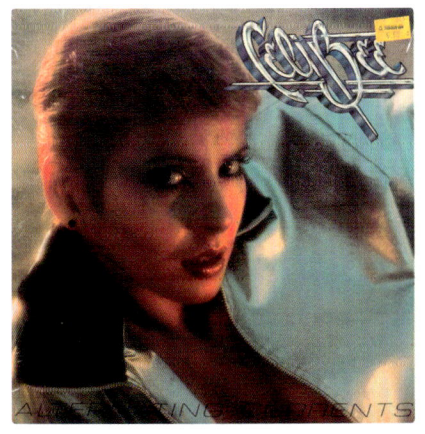

APA-77002 / 1978

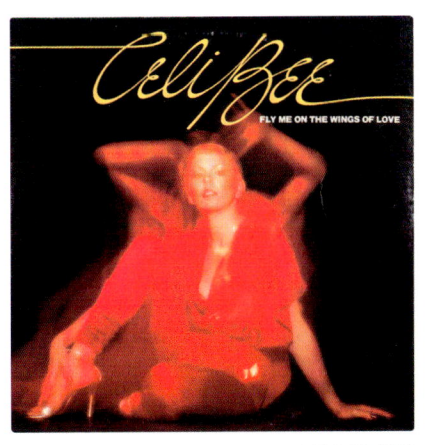

APA-77003 / 1978

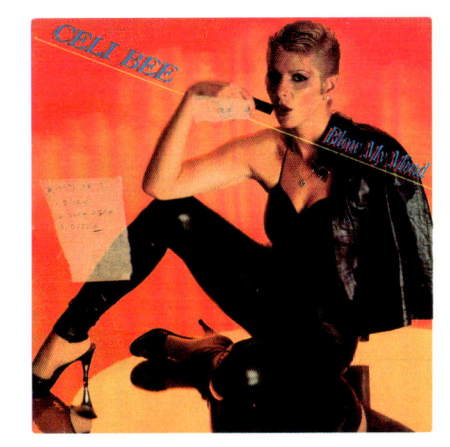

APA-77005 / 1979

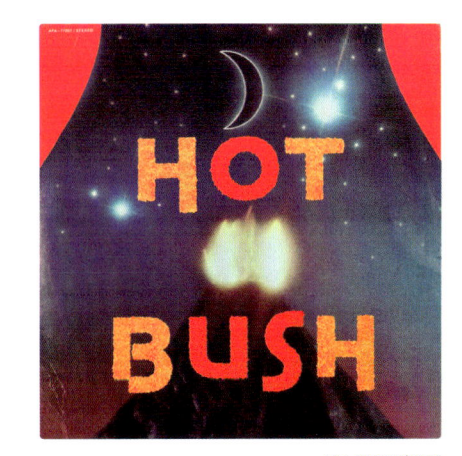

APA-770027 / 1980

Arth Records

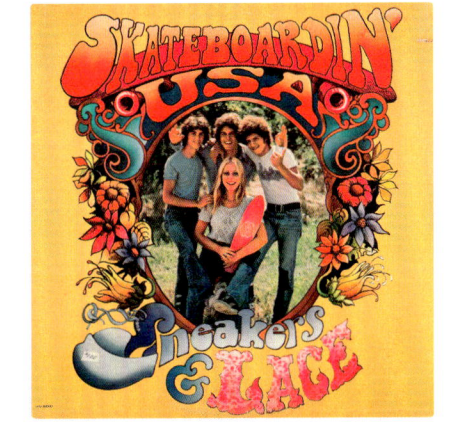

ARTH 40000 / 1978

Blue Candle Records

BL-55055 / 1976

BL-55056 / 1976

BL-55057

BL-55058 / 1977

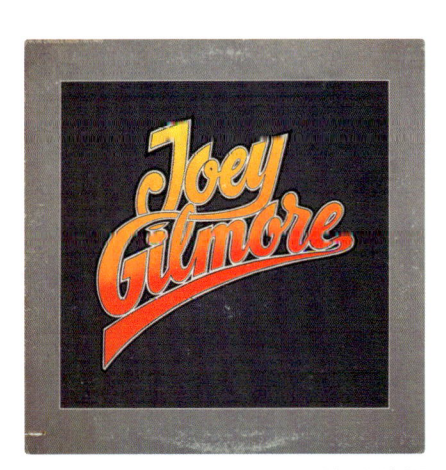

BL-55059 / 1977

Bold Records

301 (Rock Album) / 1977

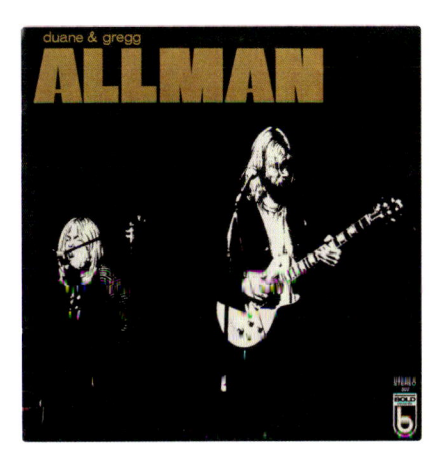

302 (Rock Album) / 1977

303 / 1977

179

T Connection - Magic / Dash 1977
Graphics Design: Cory Wade / Photography: Andy Lavalle

CAT Records

304 / 1977

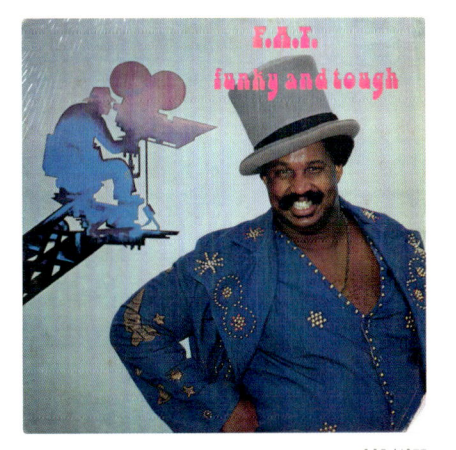

305 / 1977

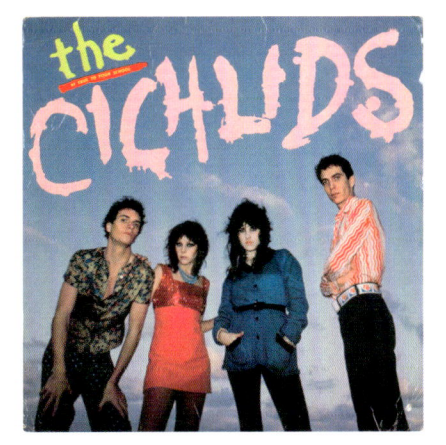

306 (Rock Album) / 1980

CAT-711

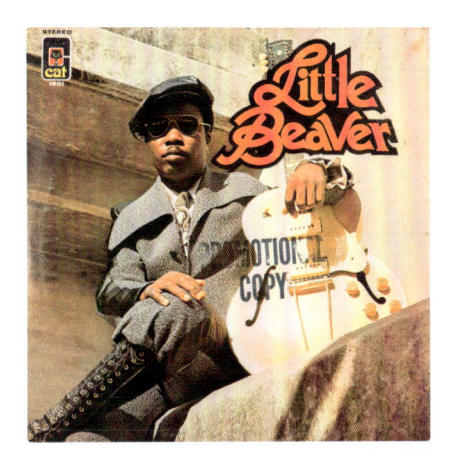

CAT-1601 / 1972

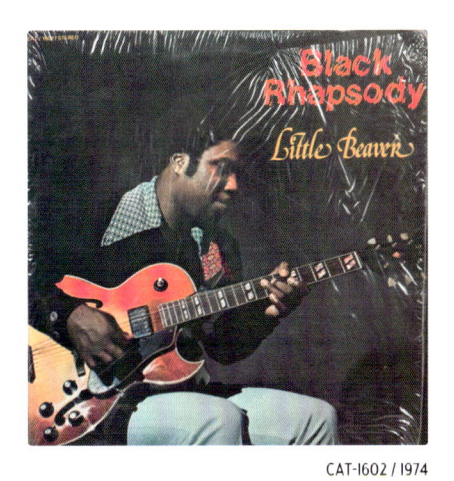

CAT-1602 / 1974

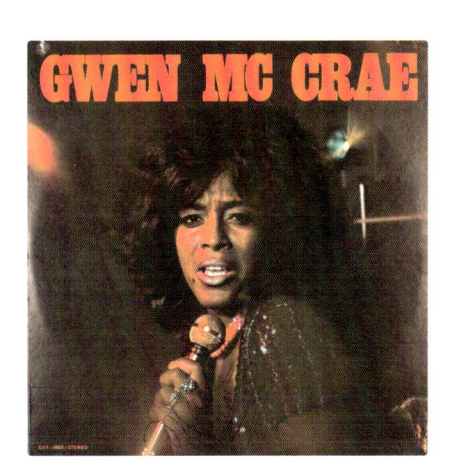

CAT-1603 / 1974

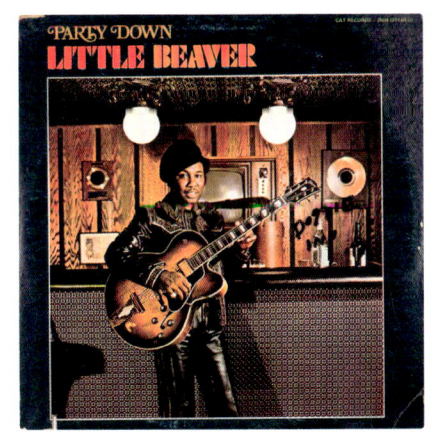

CAT-1604 / CAT-2604 / 1974

CAT-2605 / 1975

CAT-2606 / 1975

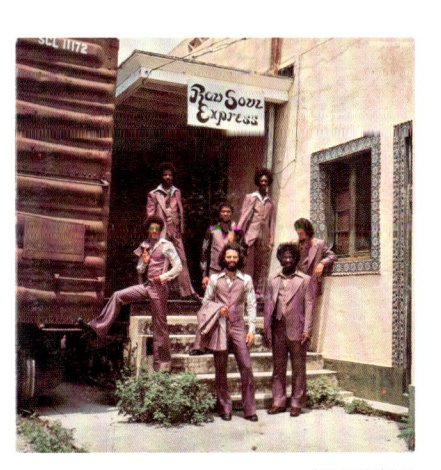

CAT-2607 / 1976

CAT-2608 / 1976

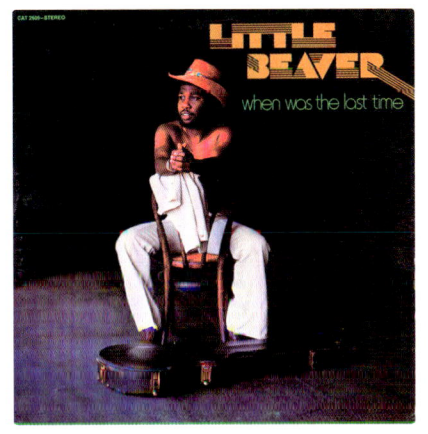

CAT-2609 / 1976

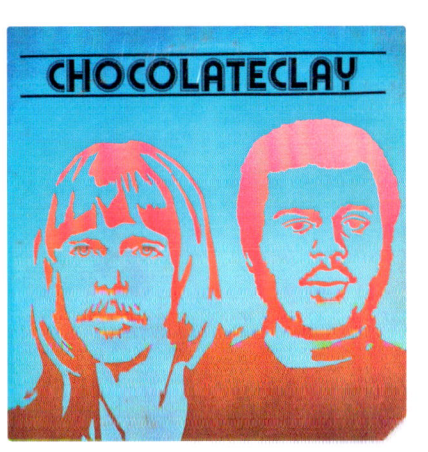

CAT-2610 / 1977

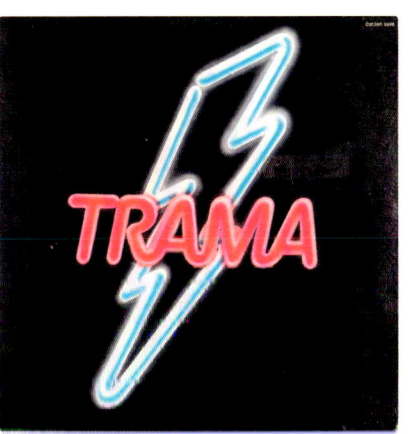

CAT-2611 / 1977

Bobby Caldwell - What You Won't Do For Love (10" Heart Shaped) / Clouds 1978

CAT-2613 / 1978    CAT-2614 / 1979 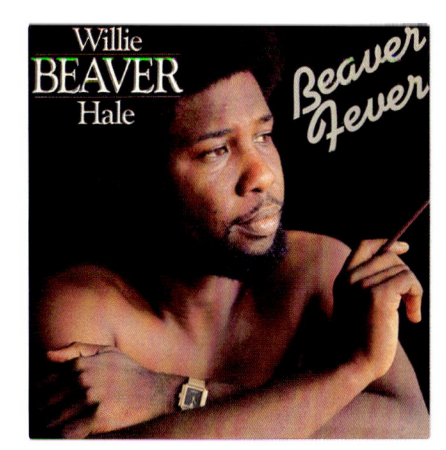   CAT-2615 / 1980

Chimneyville Records

201 / 1975 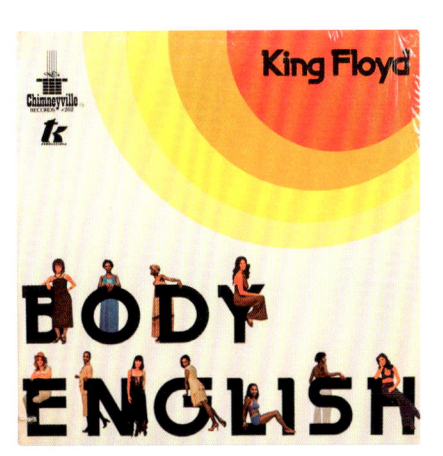   202 / 1977 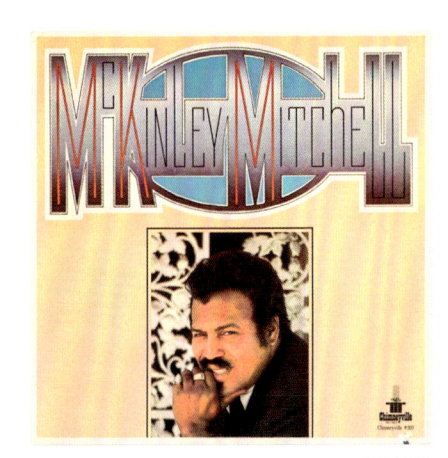   203 / 1978 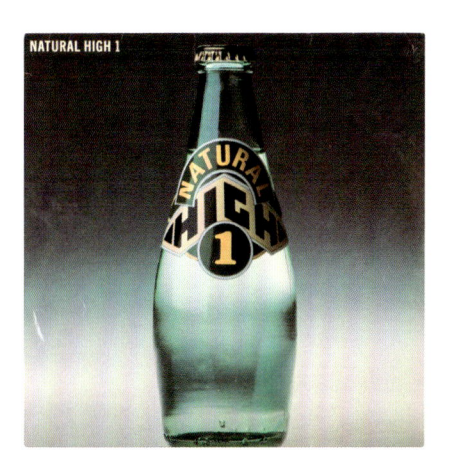   204 / 1979

Clouds Records

8801    8802 / 1977 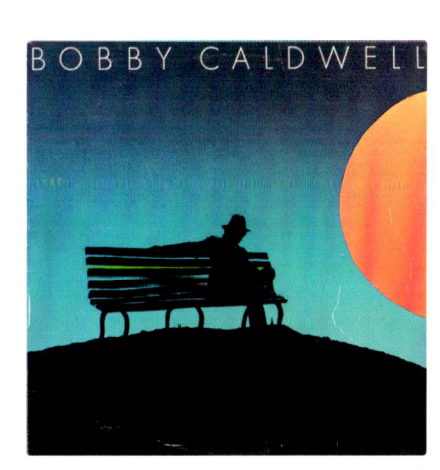   8804 / 1978

8805 / 1978 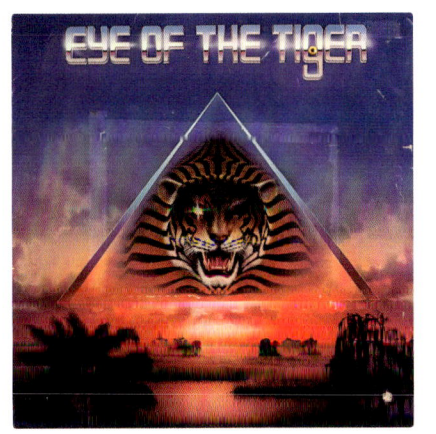   8806 / 1980    8807 / 1979 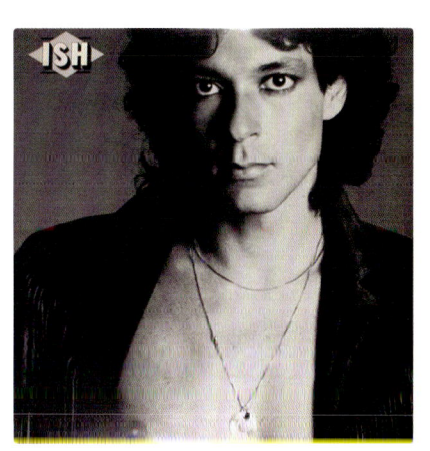   8808 / 1979

Miami - Party Freaks / Drive 1974
Design & Art: Drago / Photography: Larry G. Warmoth

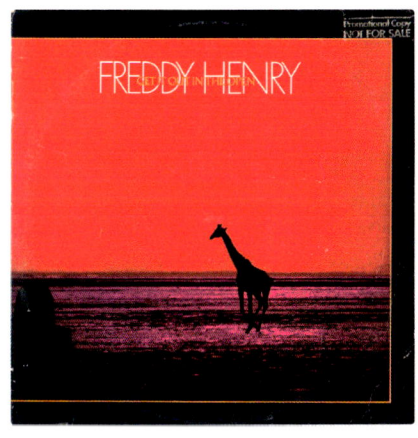

8809 / 1979	8810	**Contempo Records**	8001 / 1976
1101 / 1977	**Dash Records**	30001 / 1976	30002 / 1976
30003 / 1976	30004 / 1977	30005 / 1978	30006 / 1977
30007 / 1977	30008 / 1978	30009 / 1978	30010 / 1979

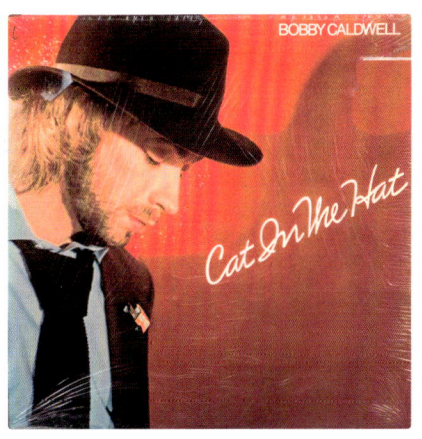

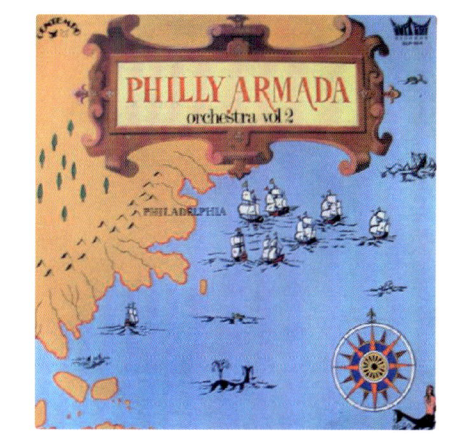

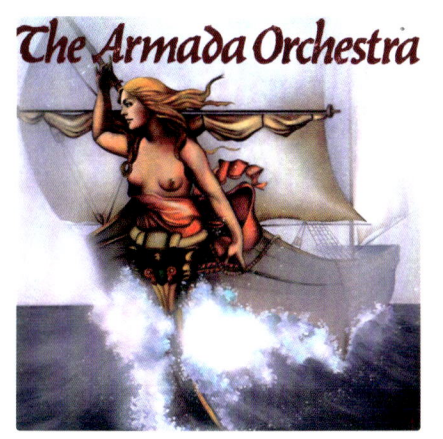

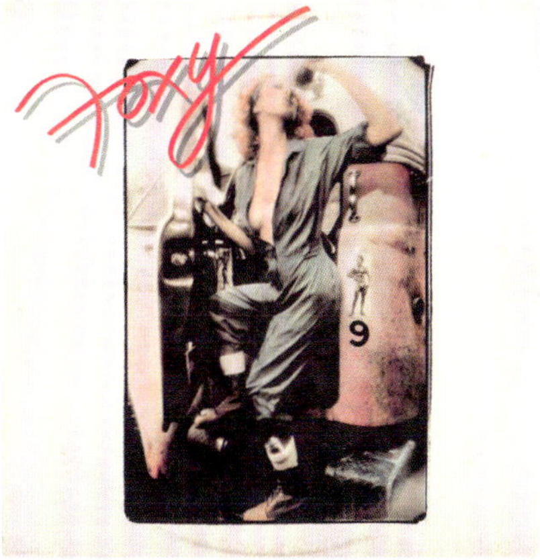

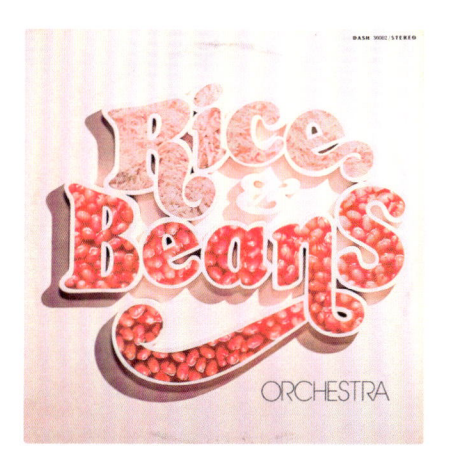

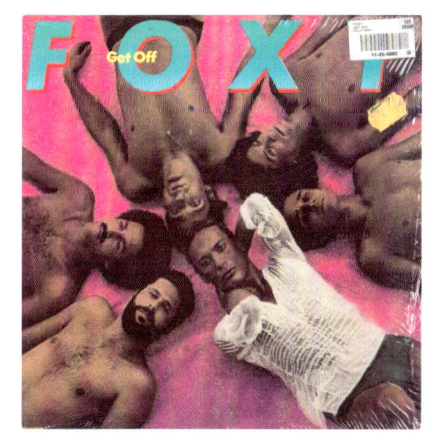

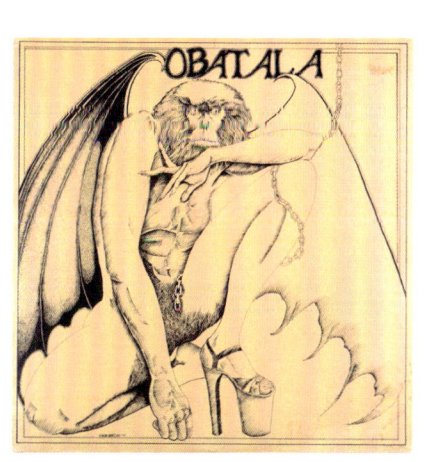

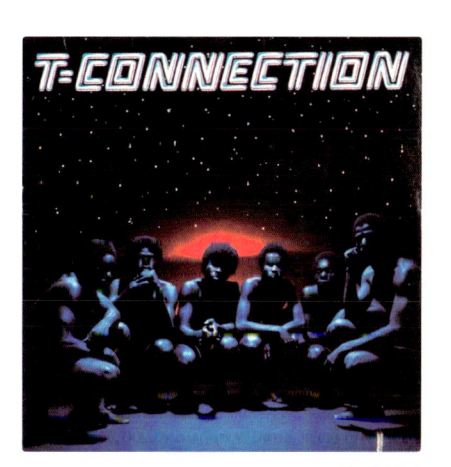

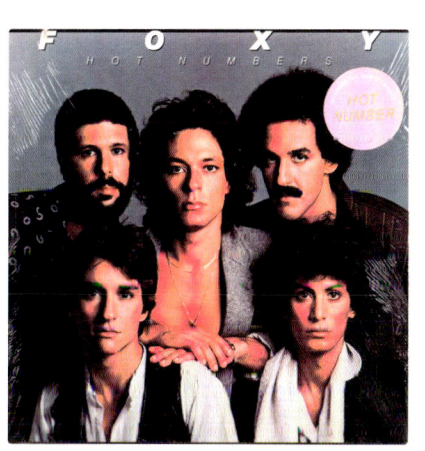

185

The JB's - Groove Machine / Drive 1979
Cover Art: Katheryn Holt / Design: Stephanie Zuras Agi / Art Direction: Bob Heimall Agi

30011 / 1979

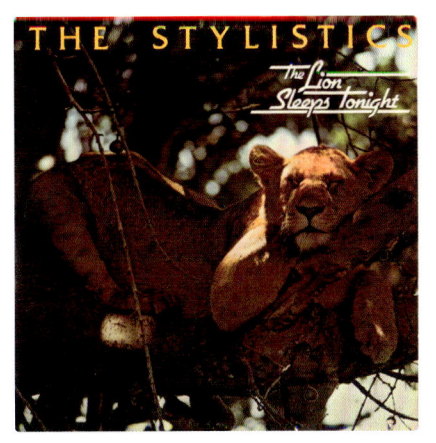

30013 / 1979

30014 / 1979

30015 / 1979

30016 / 1980

Dial Records

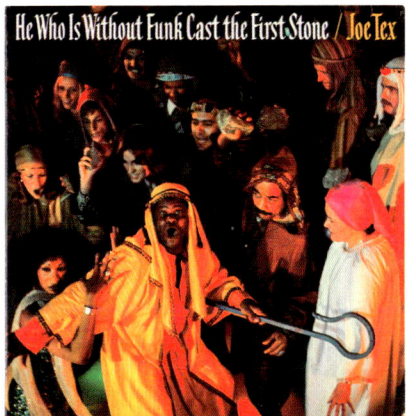

6100 / 1978

Drive Records

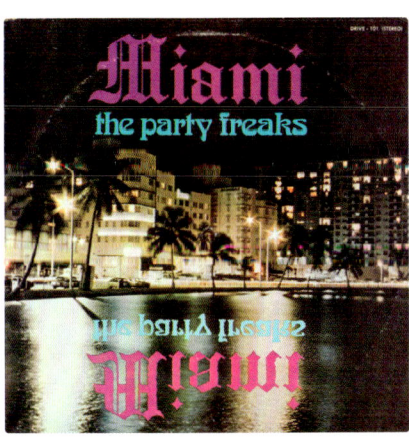

D-101 / 1974

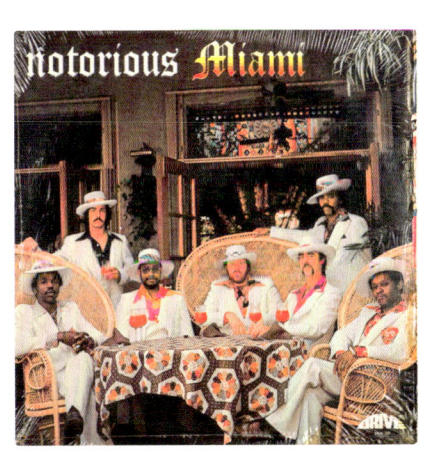

LP-102 / 1976

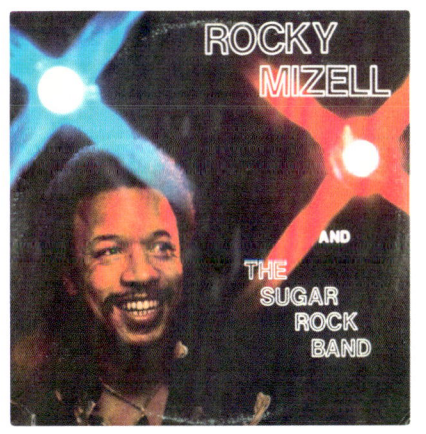

LP-103 / 1977

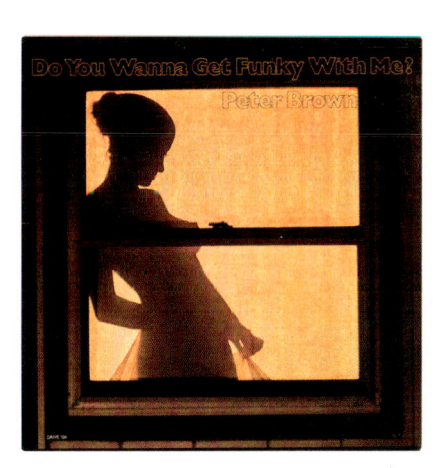

DR 104 / 1977

LP-105 / 1978

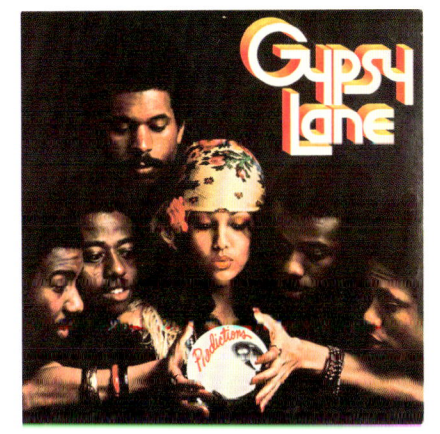

106 / 1978

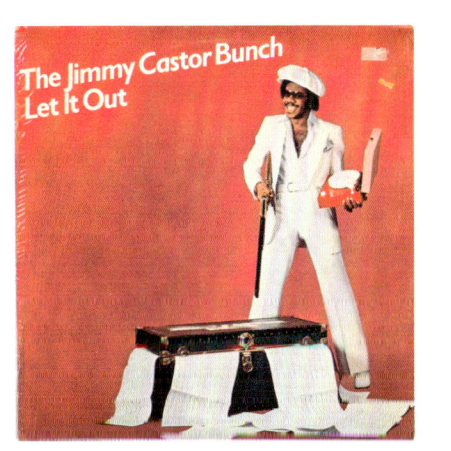

107 / 1978

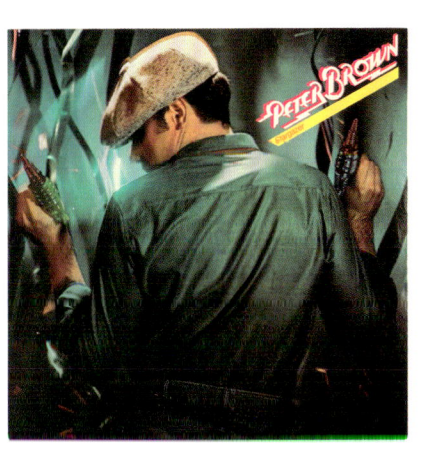

108 / 1979

187

109 / 1979

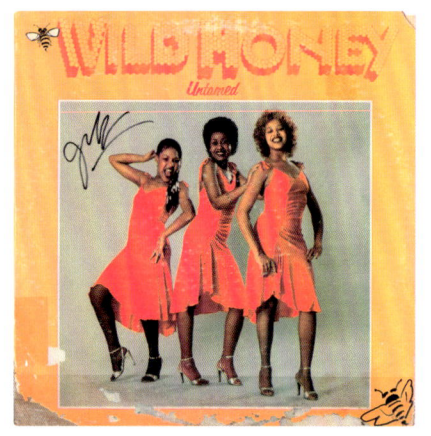

110 / 1979

111 / 1979

111 (Back) / 1979

Fabulous Records

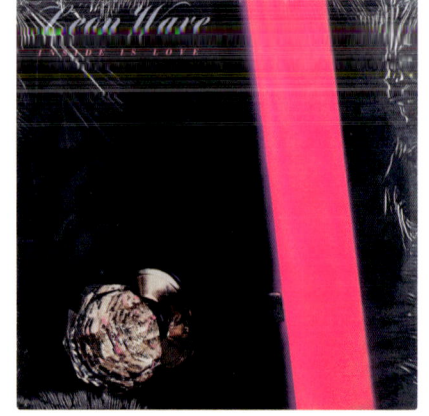

8500 / 1979

Funky Latin Records

1702 / 1972

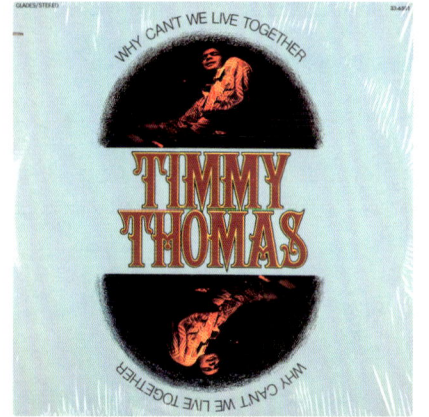

Glades Records

6501 / 1972

6502 / 1973

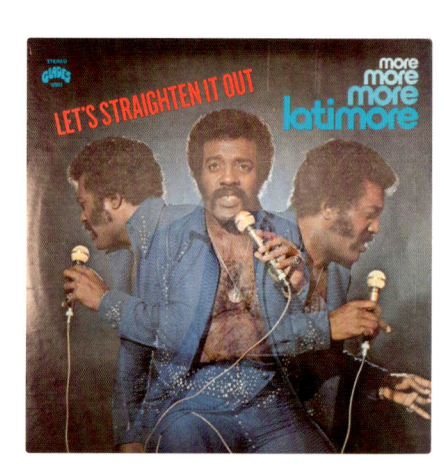

6503 / 1974

6504 / 1974

7505 / 1975

7506 / 1976

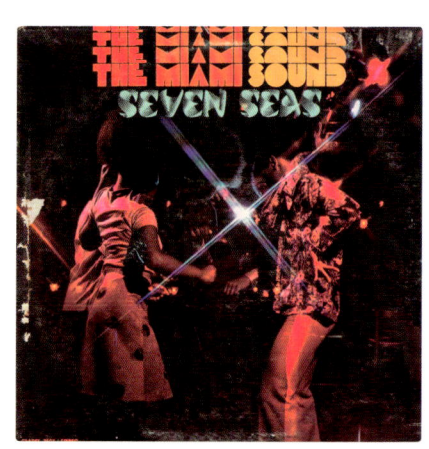

7507 / 1976

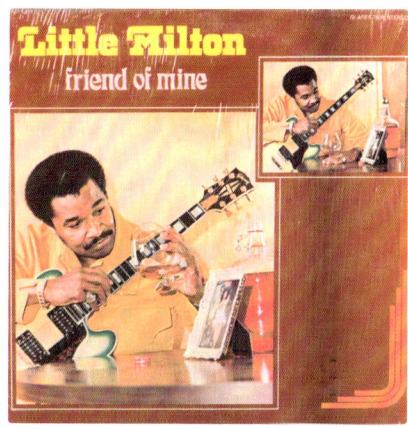

7508 / 1976 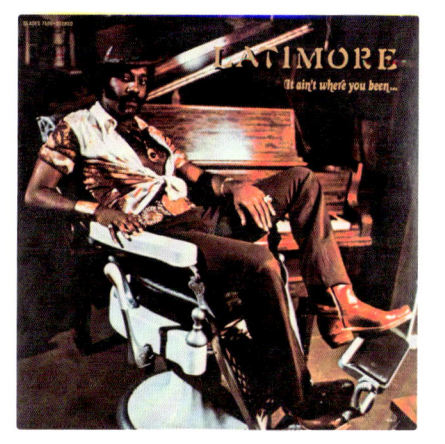
7509 / 1976 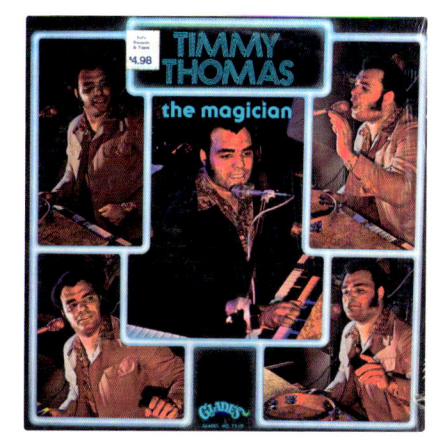
7510 / 1976 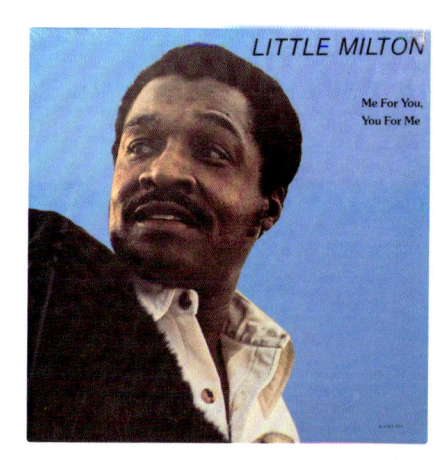
7511 / 1977

7512 / 1977 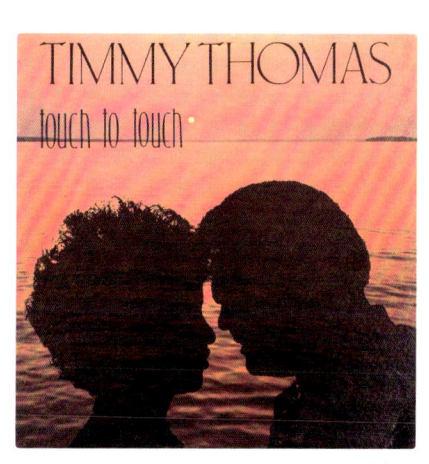
7513 / 1977 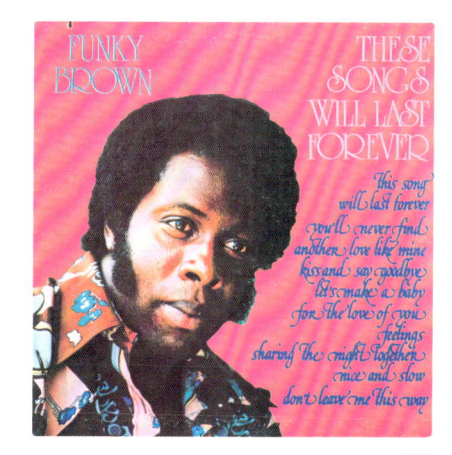
7514 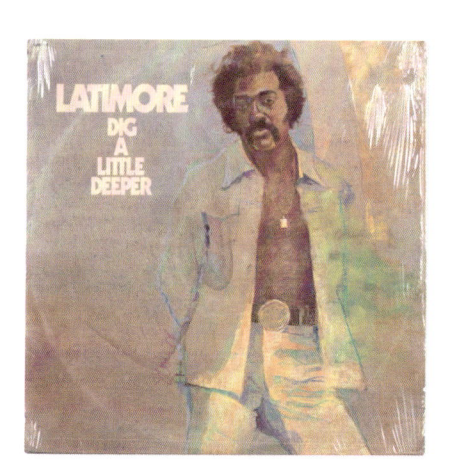
7515 / 1978

7516 / 1978
7517 / 1979 
7518 / 1980 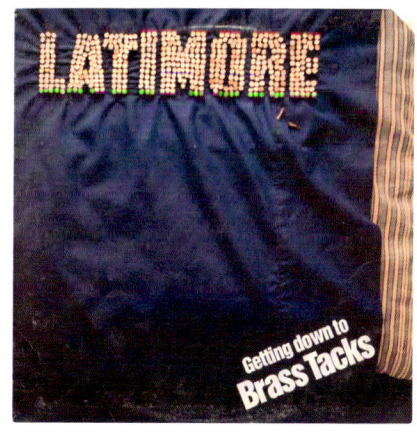

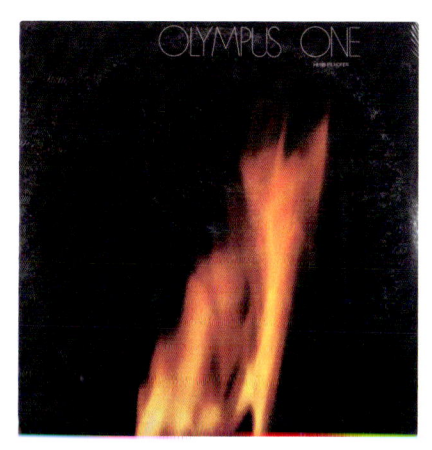

101 / 1976
102 / 1977
103 / 1977 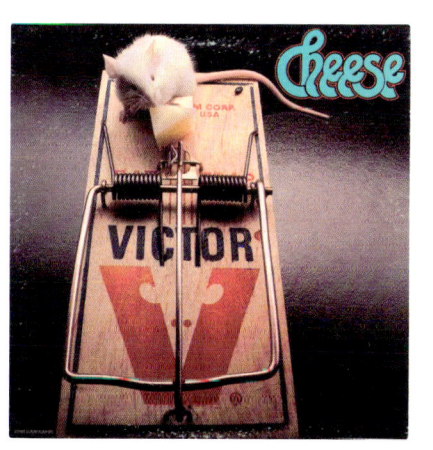
104 / 1978

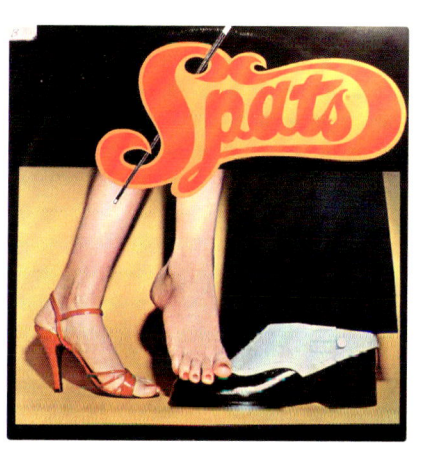

Greg Diamond's - Starcruiser / Marlin 1978
Artwork: Ernie Thormahlen / Photography: Mick Rock

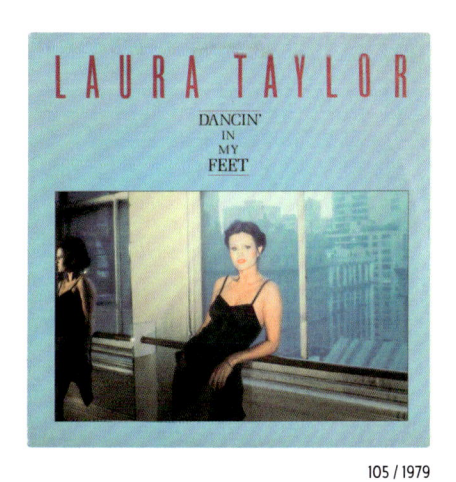

HDM Records

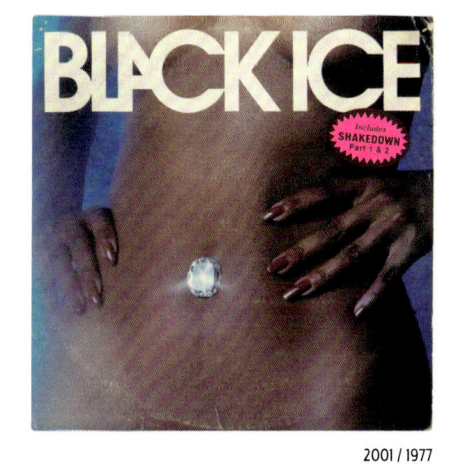

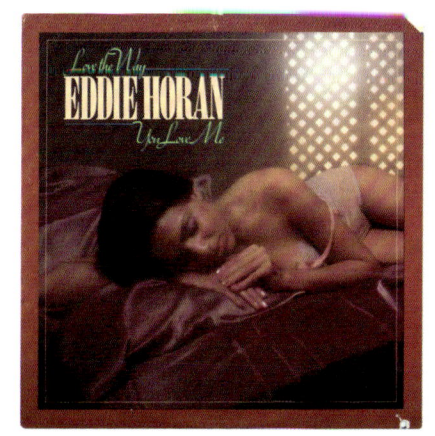

105 / 1979

2001 / 1977

2002 / 1979

Inphasion Records

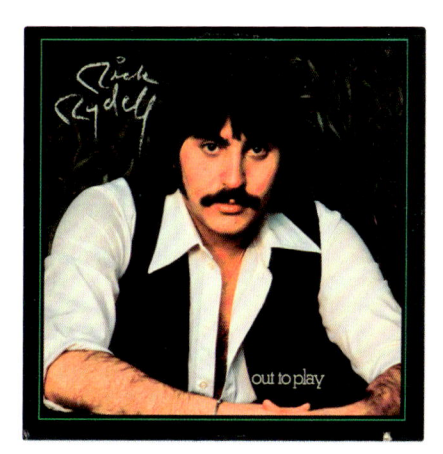

2003 / 1979

3900 / 1978

3901 / 1979

Juana Records

3902 / 1979

200000 / 1977

200001 / 1977

200002 / 1978

200003 / 1978

200004 / 1979

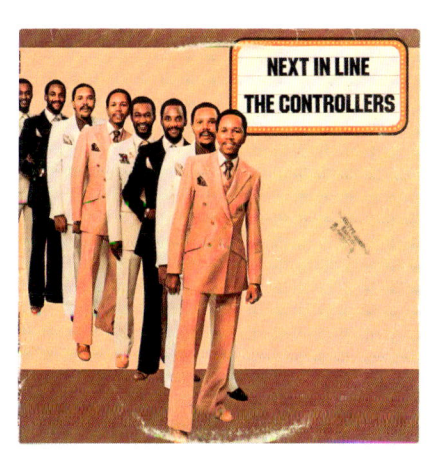

200005 / 1979

200006 / 1979

4000 / 1981

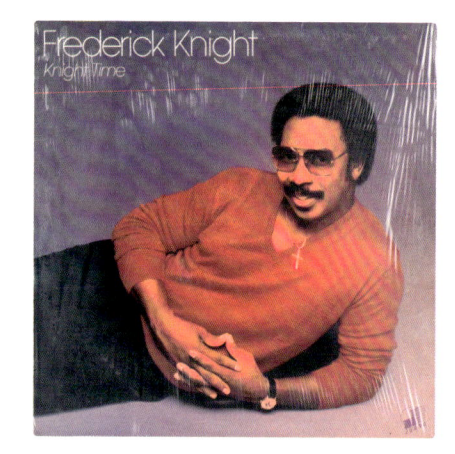

1003 / 1981

Kayvette Records

801 / 1975

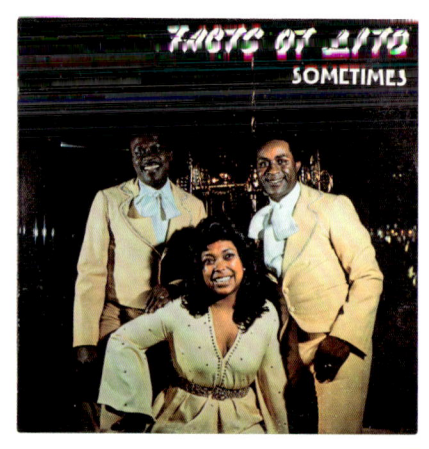

802 / 1977

803 / 1978

804 / 1978

Konduko Records

K-100000 / 1976

K-100001 / 1977

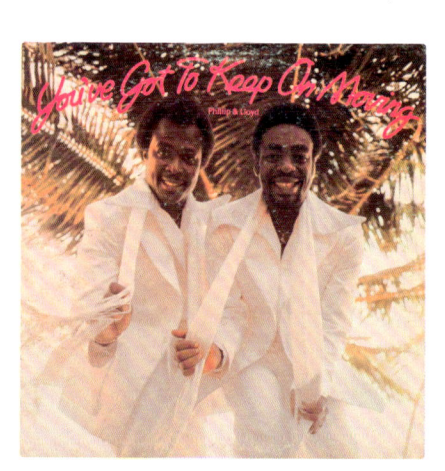

K-100002 / 1978

K-100003 / 1979

K-100004 . K-100005 / 1979

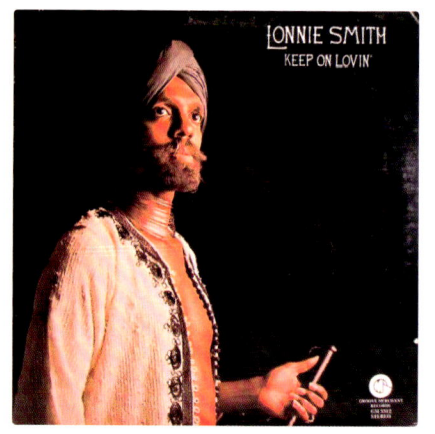

LRC Records

LRC-9312 / 1977

LRC-9313 / 1977

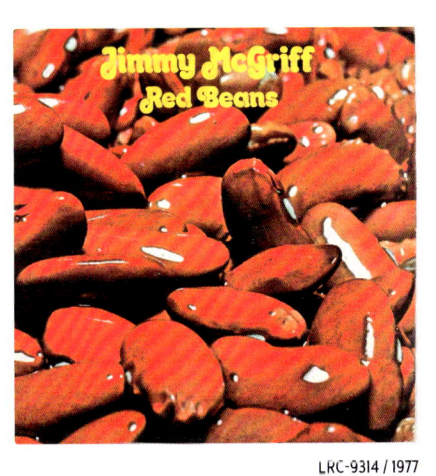

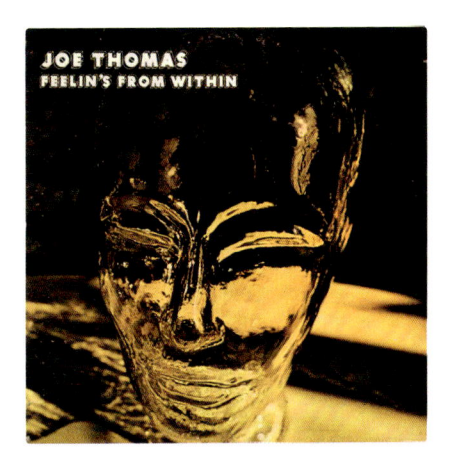

LRC-9314 / 1977

LRC-9315 / 1977

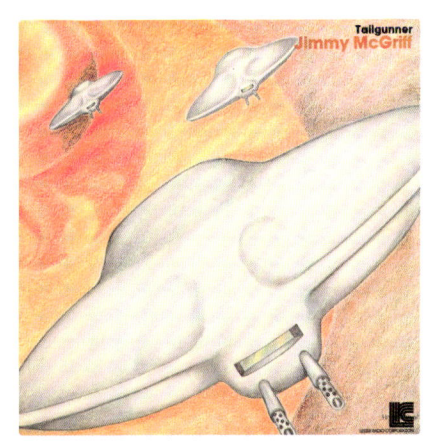

LRC-9316 / 1977

LRC-9317 / 1977

LRC-9318 / 1977

LRC-9319 / 1977

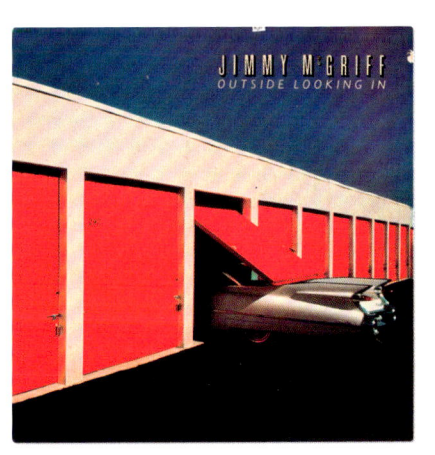

LRC-9320 / 1978

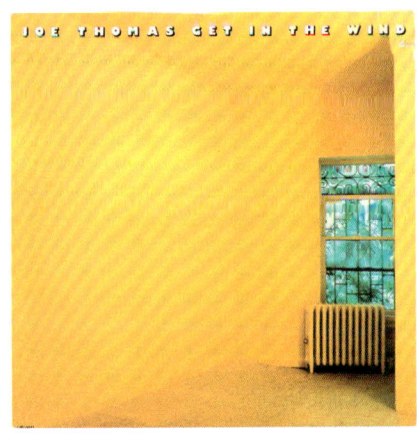

LRC-9321 / 1978

LRC-9322 / 1978

LRC-9323 / 1978

LRC-9325 / 1979

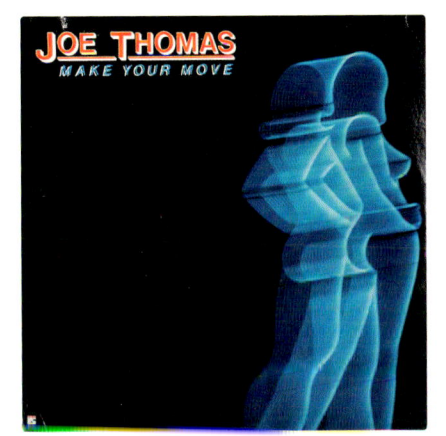

LRC-9327 / 1979

Malaco Records

6351 / 1976

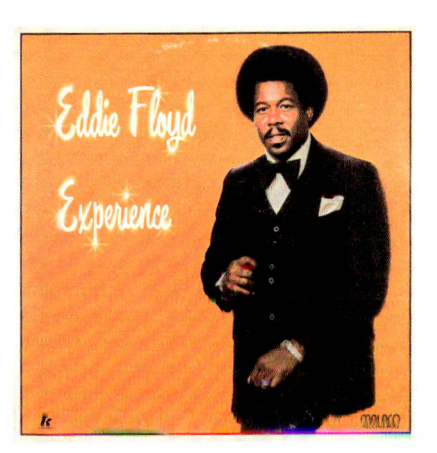

6352 / 1977

Tempest Trio -Tempest Trio / Marlin 1979
Design: Stephanie Zuras, Bob Heimall (AGI) / Photography: Benno Friedman

Marlin Records

6353 / 1977	6356 / 1978	6357 / 1978	6358 / 1979
6359 / 1979	6361 / 1979		MARLIN 2200 / 1975
MARLIN 2201 / 1976	MARLIN 2202 / 1976	MARLIN 2203 / 1977	MARLIN 2204 / 1977
MARLIN 2205 / 1977	MARLIN 2206 / 1977	MARLIN 2207 · MARLIN 2208 / 1977	MARLIN 2209 / 1978

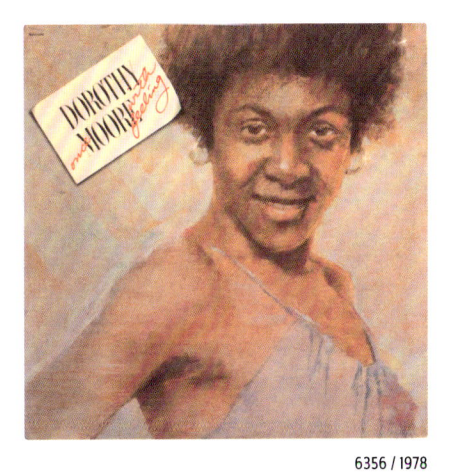

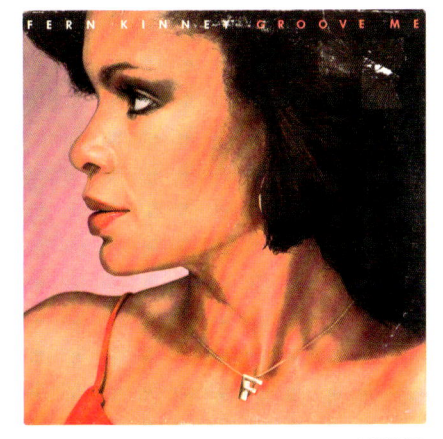

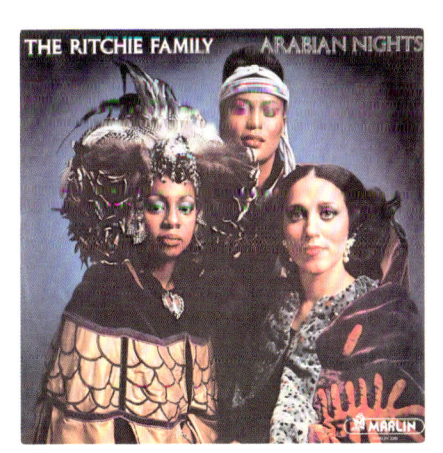

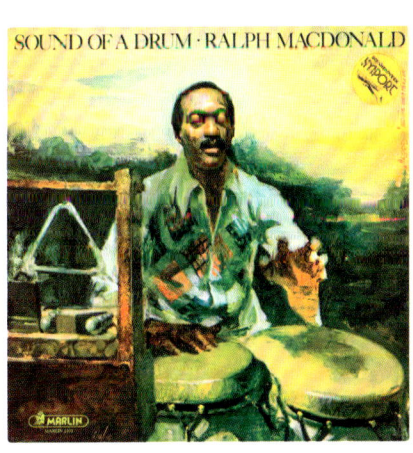

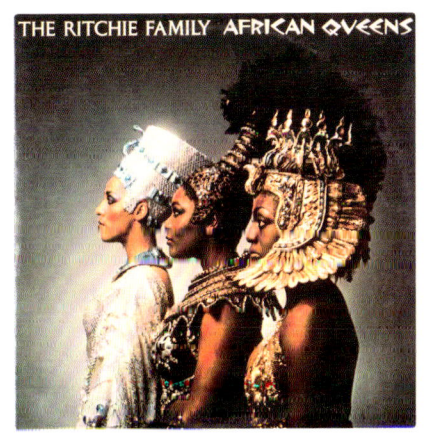

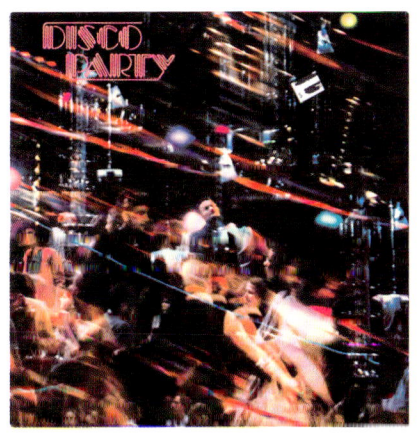

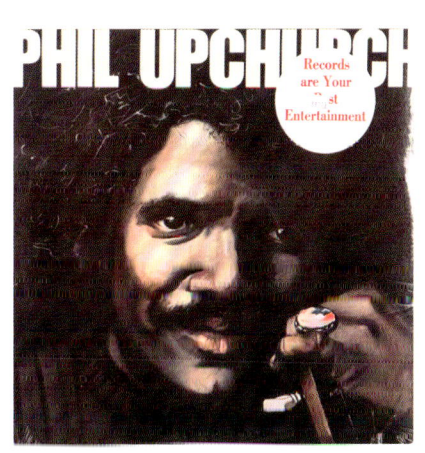

THE BREAK
(Denis Lepage)
DJAGA BOOGIE WOOGIE
(Serge Lamarche)
DON'T STOP, KEEP ON
(Peter Dowse, John Farley, Fritz Walton)
THERE'S ONLY BEEN A FEW
(Serge Lamarche)
MI CORAZÓN
(Serge Lamarche)

Produced by:
Joe La Greca and Joe Marandola for Dee Jay Productions Ltd.
Executive Producer:
Frank Dell'Accio for Dee Jay Productions Ltd.
Publishing:
All songs published by La Greca Publishing (Pro Canada) except for "The Break" published by Giacomo Publishing (Capac).
Arranged by:
Denis Lepage
Vocals:
Jimmy Ray
Background Vocals:
On "Djaga Boogie Woogie"
Cissy Houston
 (Courtesy of Columbia Records)
Jocelyn Shaw
Lorraine Moore

Album Coordination:
Dan Joseph
Illustration:
Michael Vernaglia
Recorded at Montreal Sound Studio MTL PQ.
Engineer: Bill Hill
Mixed by Steve Thompson and Michael Arato at Blank Tape Studios, New York City.
Engineer: Bob Blank
"The Break" and "Don't Stop, Keep On" Remixed by Steve Thompson and Michael Arato at Media Sound Studios, New York City.
Remix Engineer: Michael Barbiero.
Special Thanks to:
Peter Dowse, Graham Chambers, Denis Lepage, Dan Joseph and Laurie Ingber
and to all those who kept
on believing.

MARLIN
Marlin 2233
℗© 1979, T.K. Productions, Inc.
Tm Marlin Records
Distributed by TK Productions, Inc.
495 S.E. 10th Ct., Hialeah, Florida 33010

DJ production Inc.

Kat Mandu-Kat Mandu (Back) / Marlin 1979
Illustration: Michael Vernaglia

MARLIN 2210 / 1978	MARLIN 2211 / 1978	MARLIN 2212 / 1978	MARLIN 2213 / 1977
MARLIN 2214 / 1978	MARLIN 2215 / 1978	MARLIN 2216 / 1978	MARLIN 2217 / 1978
MARLIN 2218 / 1978	MARLIN 2219 / 1977	MARLIN 2220 / 1978	MARLIN 2221 / 1978
MARLIN 2222 / 1979	MARLIN 2223 / 1979	MARLIN 2225 / 1978	MARLIN 2226 / 1979

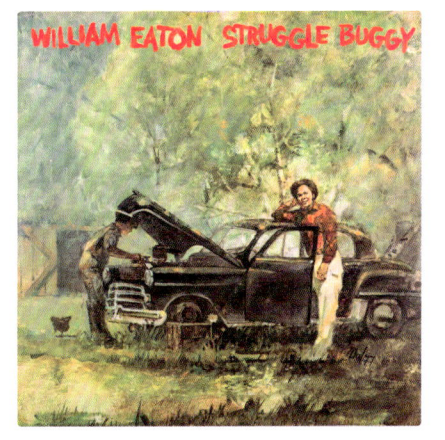

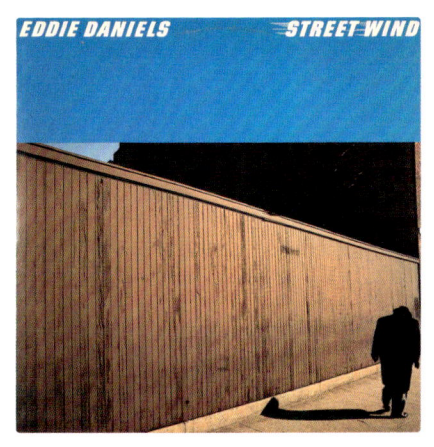

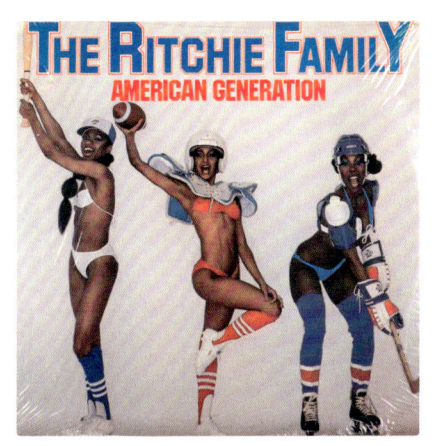

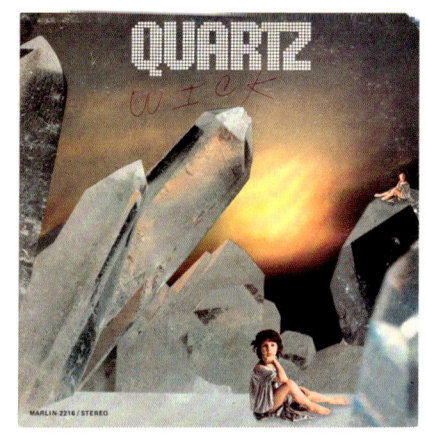

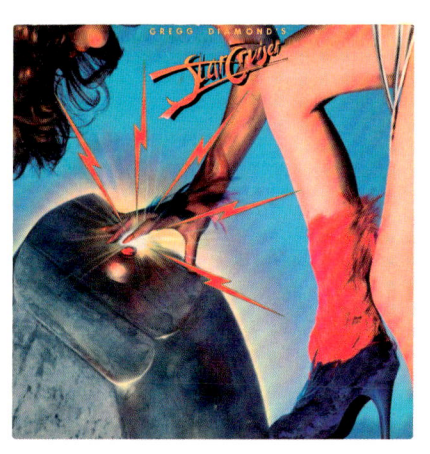

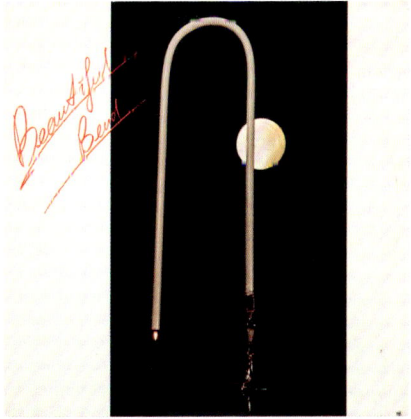

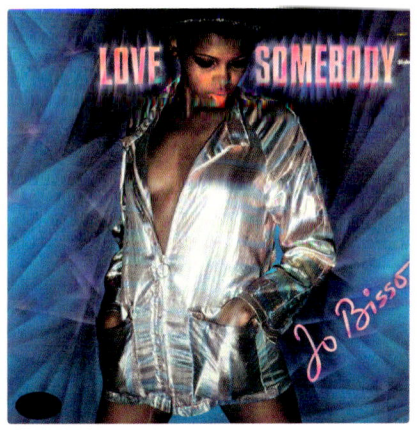

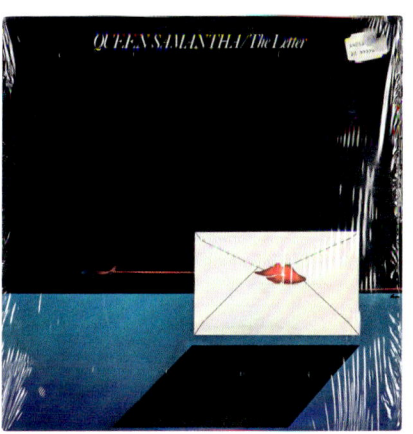

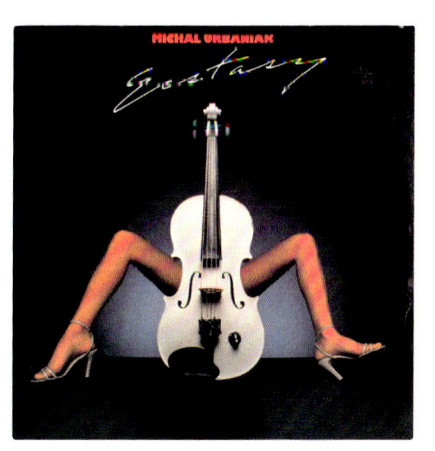

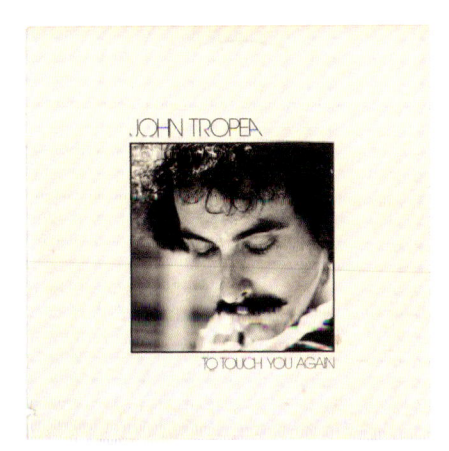

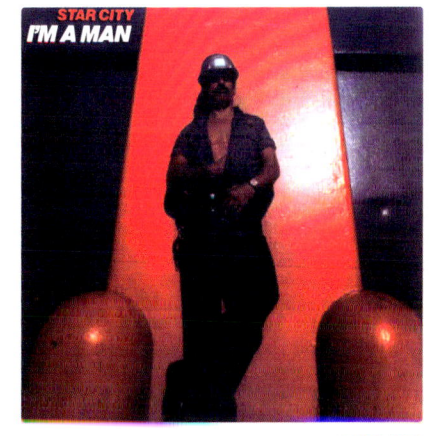

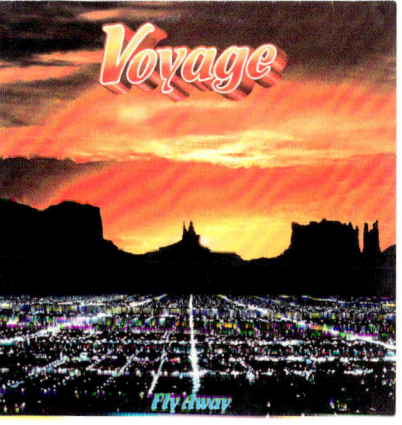

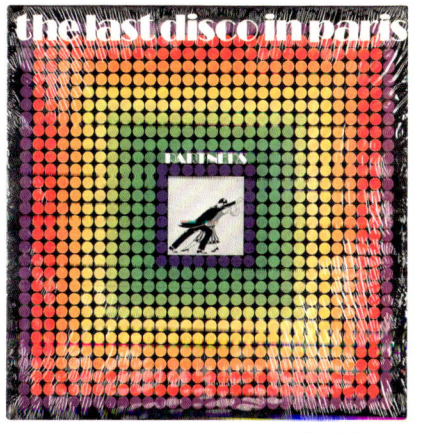

Regina James-Dancin' In The Flames Of Love / Reids World 1978
Design: Rob Vaughn / Photography: Howard Austin Feld

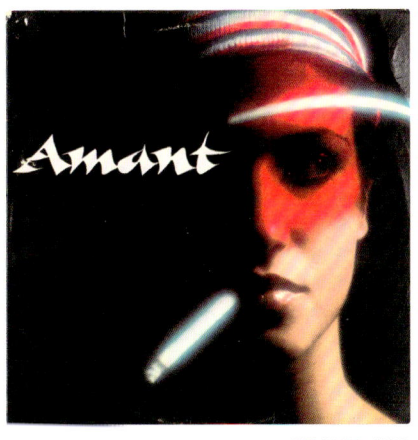

MARLIN 2227 / 1979	MARLIN 2228 / 1979	MARLIN 2229 / 1979	MARLIN 2230 / 1979
MARLIN 2231 / 1979	MARLIN 2232 / 1979	MARLIN 2233 / 1979	MARLIN 2234 / 1979
MARLIN 2235 / 1980	MARLIN 2236 / 1980	Innersleeve	**Pi Kappa Records**
PK-0000 / 1973	PKS-4000 / 1976	PKS-4001 / 1976	**Reids World Records**

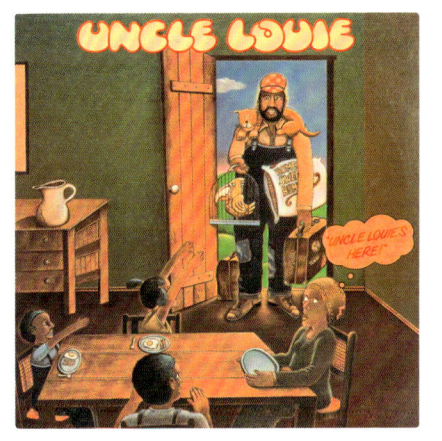

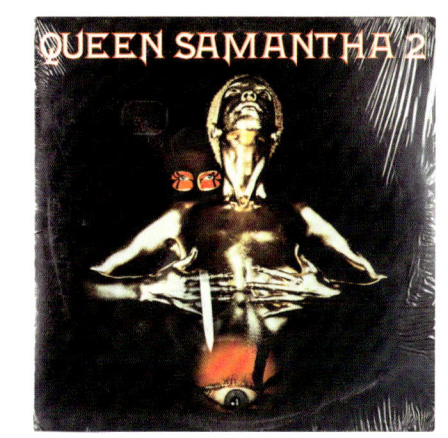

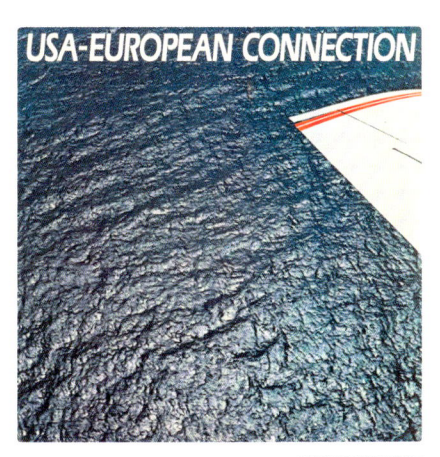

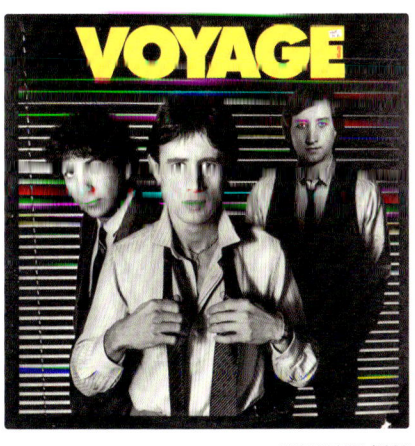

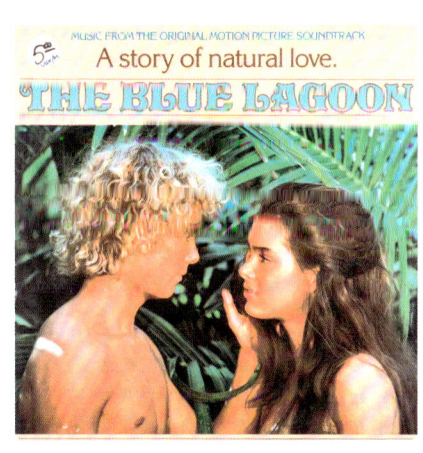

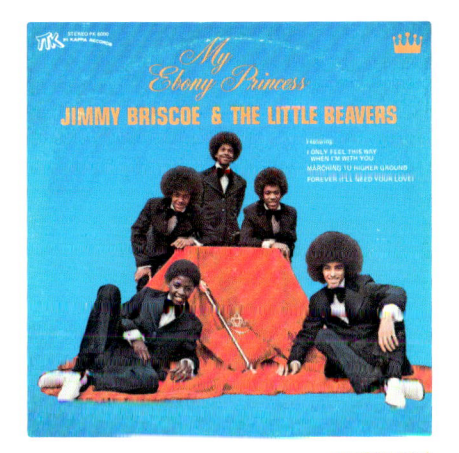

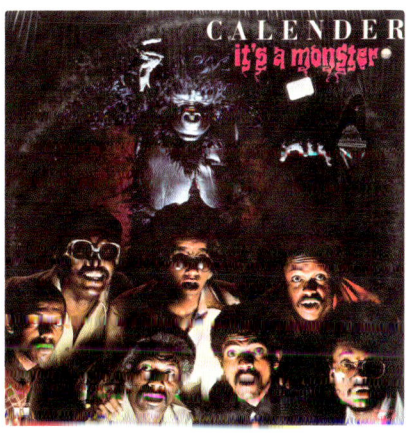

	Roots Records		
4001 / 1979		1001 / 1976	1002 / 1976
1003 / 1977	 1004 / 1977	**Royal Flush Records**	5500 / 1978
Shield Records	80000 / 1978	**Silver Blue Records**	50000 / 1977
Stone Dog Records	3001 / 1973	3002 / 1976	**Sunshine Records**

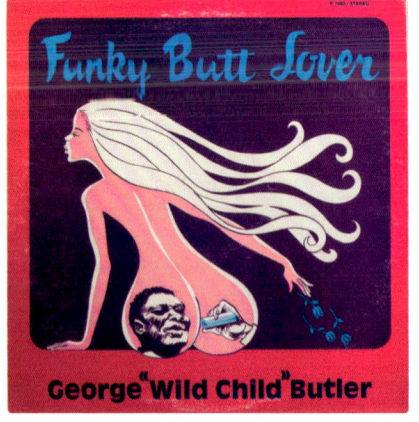

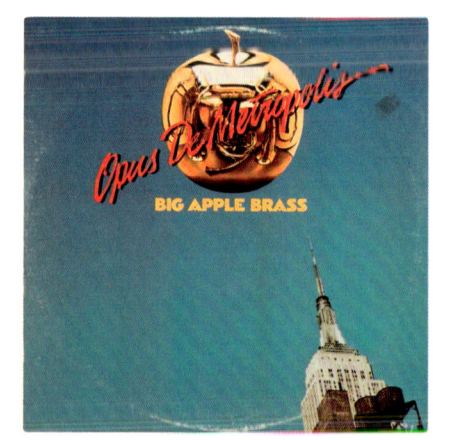

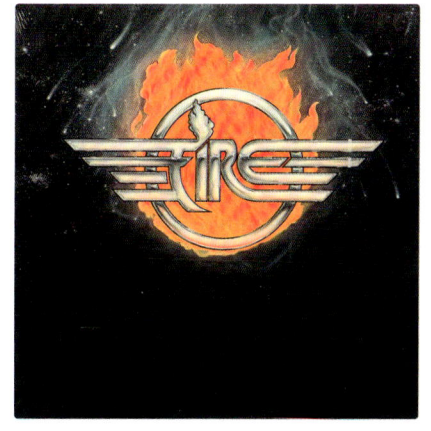

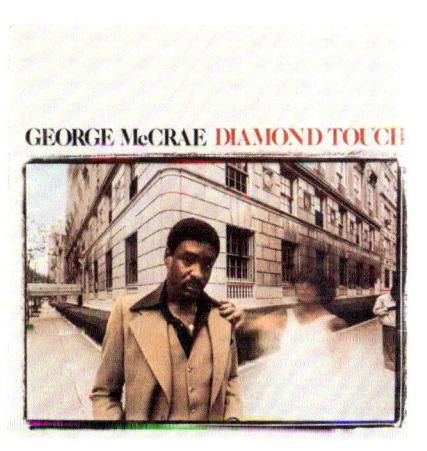

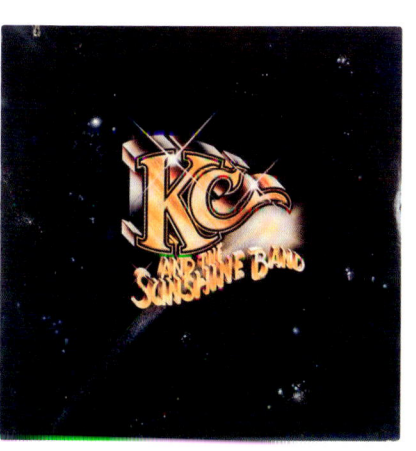

SSE-801 / 1978	SSE-802 / 1978	SSE-803 / 1978	SSE-804 / 1978
SSE-805 / 1979	**TK Records**	TK-1 / 1978	TK 500 / 1974
TK 501 / 1974	TK 600 / 1974	TK 602 / 1975	TK 603 / 1975
TK 604 / 1975	TK 605 / 1976	TK 606 / 1976	TK 607 / 1978

201

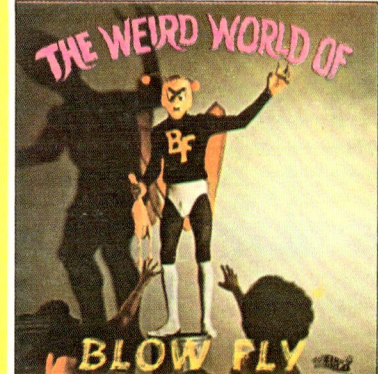

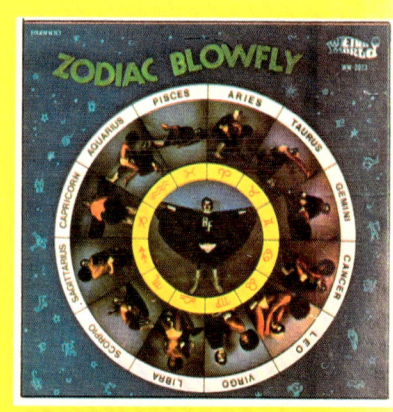

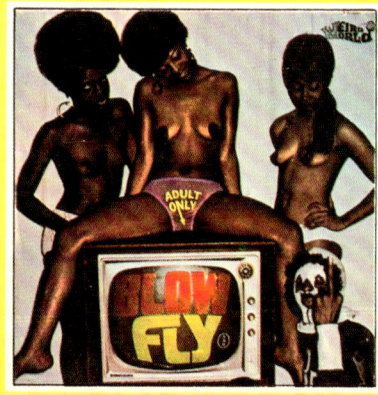

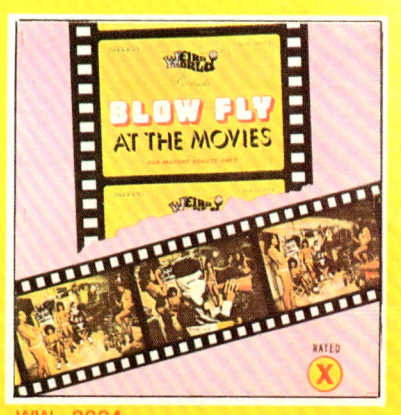

Blowfly - Butterfly / Weird World
Photography: Howard Smiley

TK 608 / 1978	TK 610 / 1978	TK 611 / 1979	TK 612 / 1979
TK 614 / 1980	TK 615 / 1980	**Wanderick Records**	66000 / 1977
Weird World Records	LP-2020	LP-2021	LP-2022
LP-2023	LP-2024	LP-2025	LP-2026

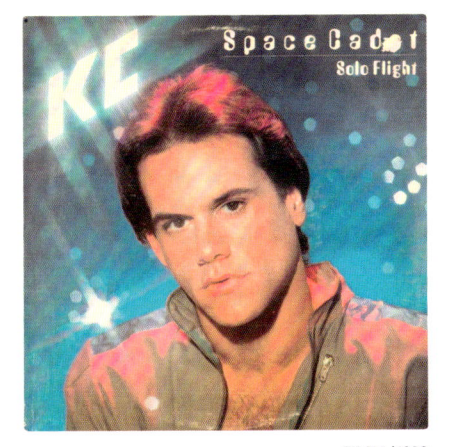

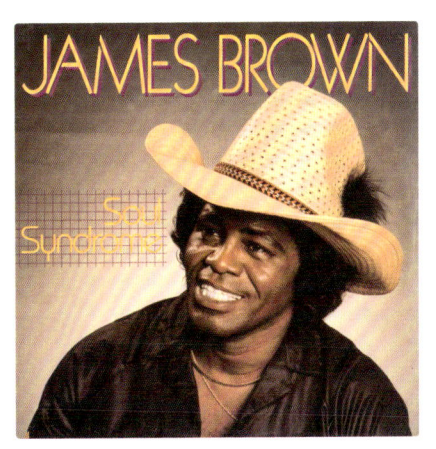

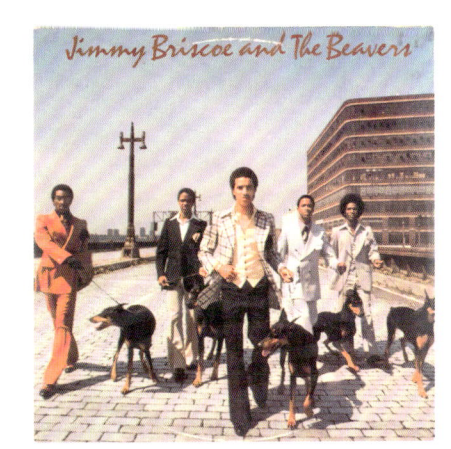

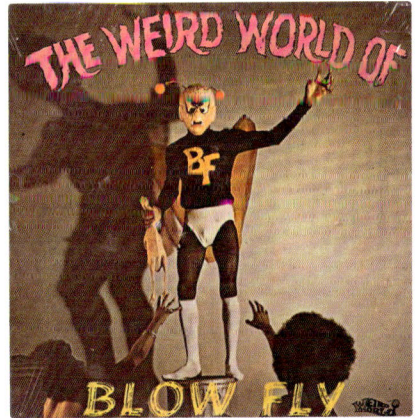

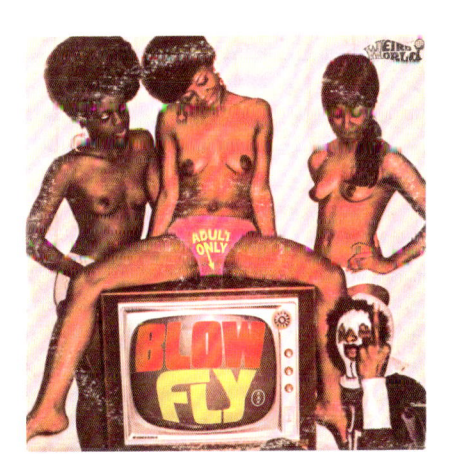

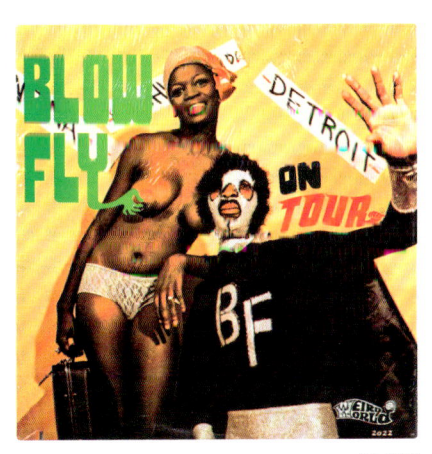

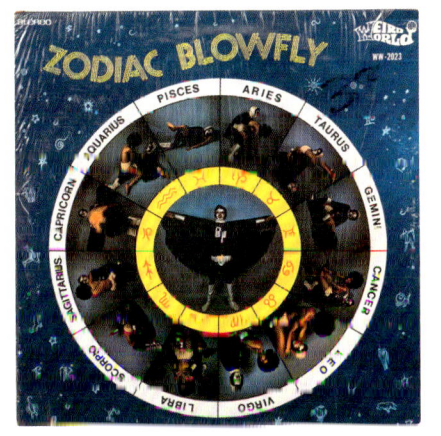

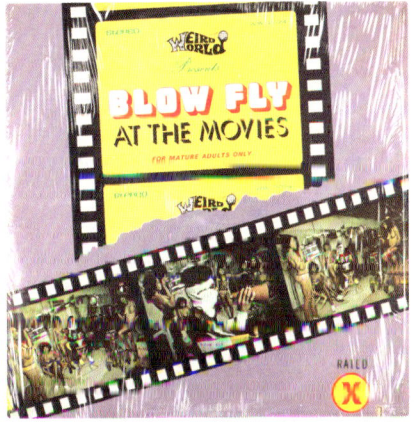

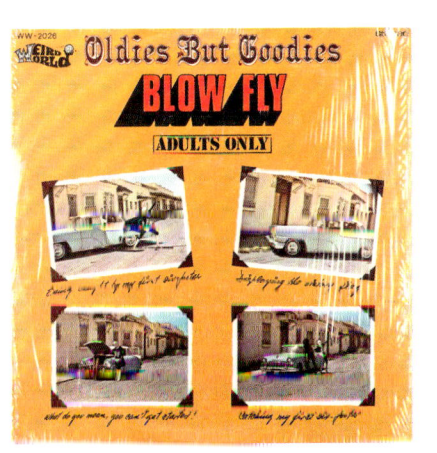

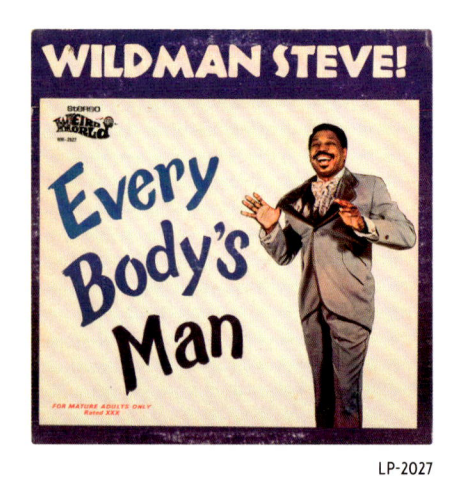

LP-2027	LP-2028	LP-2030	LP-2031
LP 2032	LP-2033	LP-2034	LP-2034
LP-2035	LP-2036	**Wicked Records**	9001 / 1976
Wolf Records	1201	1202	1203

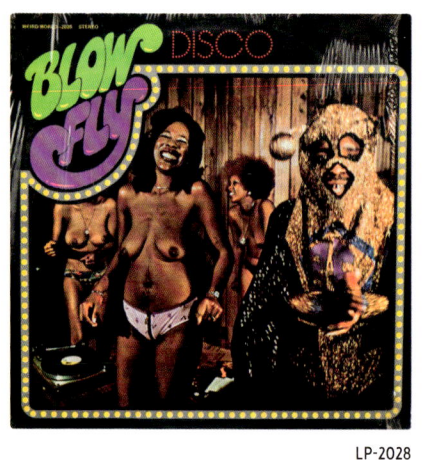

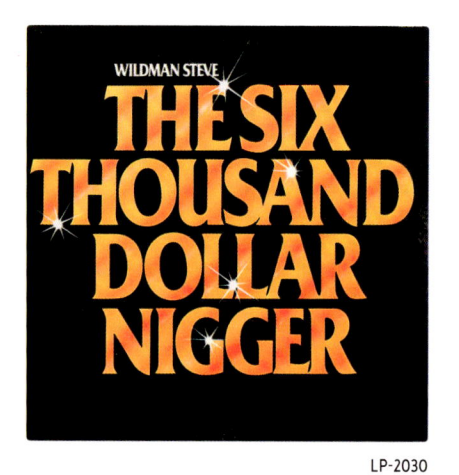

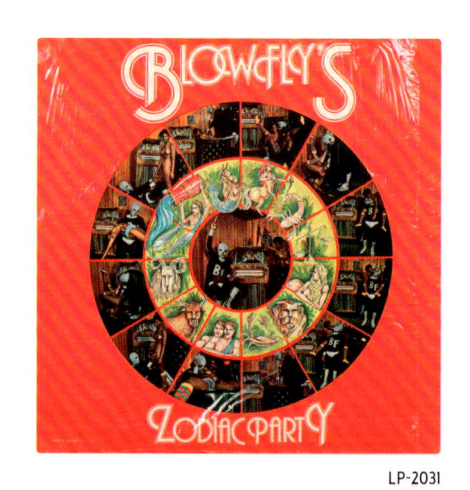

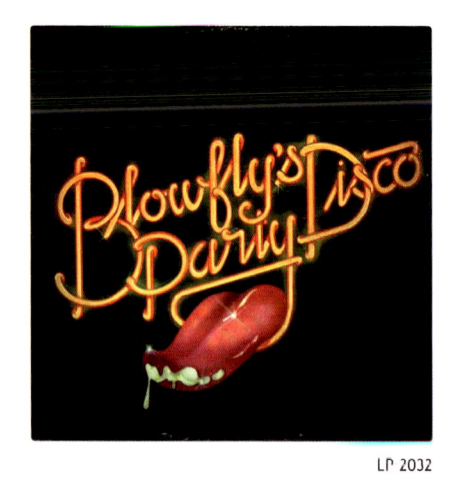

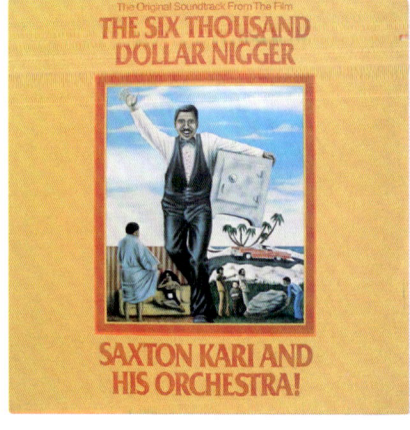

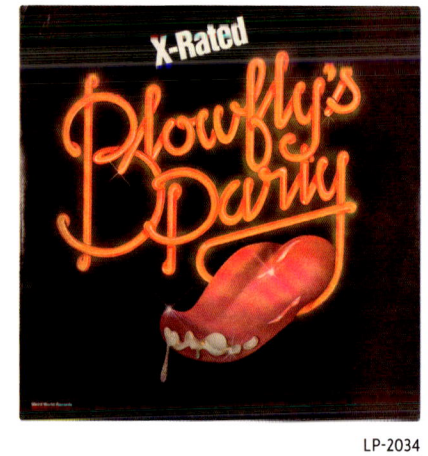

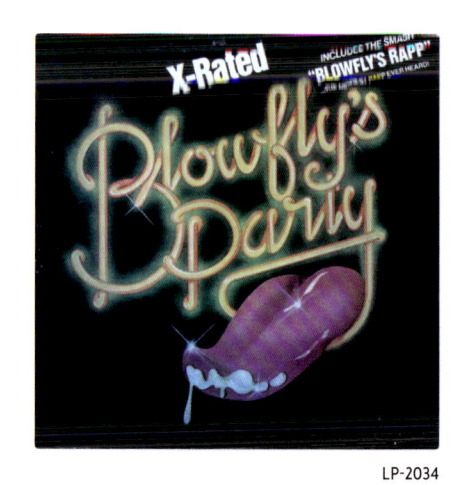

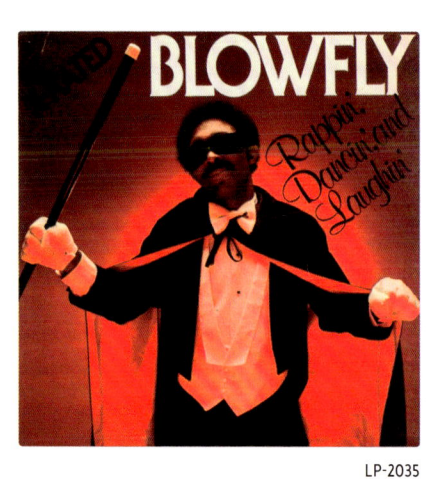

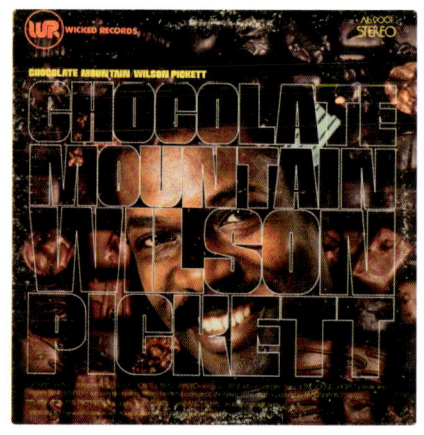

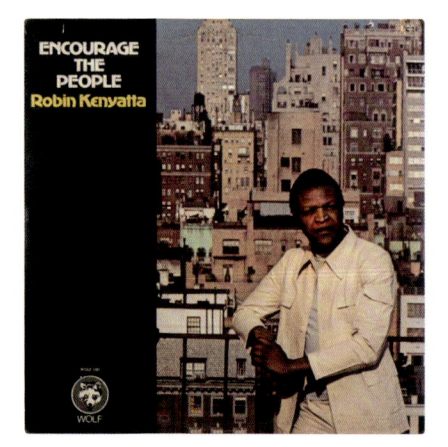

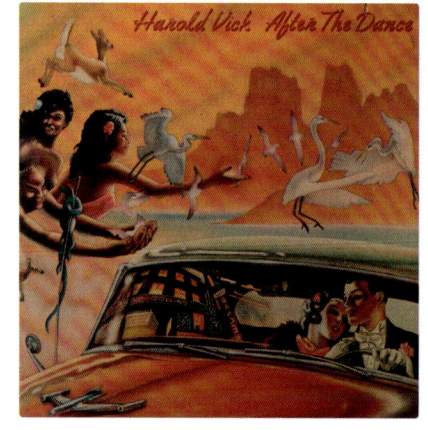

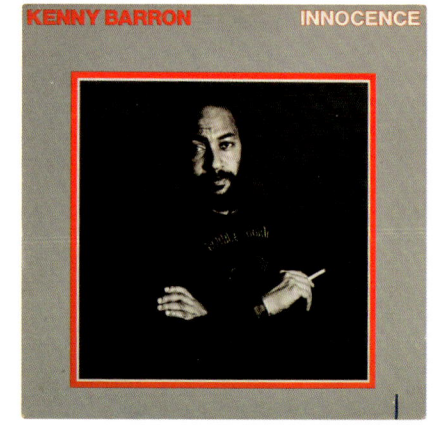

204

Matrix numbers

ALARM

LP-1000	Ted Taylor	Ted Taylor	1976

ALSTON

SD 33-260	Betty Wright	My First Time Around	1969
SD 33-307	Clarence Reid	Dancing With Nobody But You	1969
SD 33-379	Beginning Of The End	Funky Nassau	1971
SD 33-388	Betty Wright	I Love The Way You Love	1972
SD 7026	Betty Wright	Hard To Stop	1973
SD 7027	Clarence Reid	Running Water	1973
4400	Betty Wright	Danger High Voltage	1974
4401	Milton Wright	Friends & Buddies	1975
4402	Betty Wright	Explosion	1976
4403	Beginning Of The End	Beginning Of The End	1976
4404	Clarence Reid	On The Job	1976
4405	Bill Pursell & The Nashville Sweat Band	Bill Pursell & The Nashville Sweat Band	1976
4406	Betty Wright	This Time For Real	1977
4407	Milton Wright	Spaced	1977
4408	Betty Wright	Live	1978
4409	Herman Kelly & Life	Percussion Explosion	1978
4410	Betty Wright	Traveling In The Wright Circle	1979
4411	Lew Kirton	Just Arrived	1980
4412	David Hudson	To You Honey , Honey With Love	1980

AMOUR

AMOUR-1001	Variations	A Woman'S Blues	1975
A-7777	Variations	Variations	1977
A-121675	Variations	II	1979
8900	Variations	The Peoples Champ	1980

AMAZON

400	Fantasia Ft. Peggy Santiglia	Sweet Sweet City Rhythm	1978

APA

APA-77001	Celi Bee & The Buzzy Bunch	Celi Bee & The Buzzy Bunch	1977
APA-77002	Celi Bee & The Buzzy Bunch	Alternating Currents	1978
APA-77003	Celi Bee	Fly Me On The Wings Of Love	1979
APA-77005	Celi Bee	Blow My Mind	1979
APA-77007	Hot Bush	Hot Bush	1980

Arth

ARTH-40000	Sneakers & Lace	Skateboardin' Usa	1978

Blue Candle

BL-55055	Paulette Reaves	Secret Lover	1976
BL-55056	Thirteenth Floor	Steppin Out	1976
BL-55057	Snoopy Dean	Wiggle That Thing	
BL-55058	Paulette Reaves	All About Love	1977
BL-55059	Joey Gilmore	Joey Gilmore	1977

Bold

301	Duane & Gregg Allman	Duane & Gregg Allman (Rock Album)	1977
302	Duane & Gregg Allman	Duane & Gregg Allman (Rock Album)	1977
303	Leon Debouse	A Fine Instrument	1977
304	Reid Inc.	Reid Inc.	1977
305	Fat	Funky And Tough	1977
306	Cichlids	Be True To Your School (Rock Album)	

Chimneyville

201	King Floyd	Well Done	1975
202	King Floyd	Body English	1977
203	Mckinley Mitchel	Mckinley Mitchel	1978
204	Natural High	1	1979

CAT

CAT-711	Black Knight	Black Knight	
CAT-1601	Willie "Litlle Beaver" Hale	Joey	1972
CAT-1602	Willie "Litlle Beaver" Hale	Black Rhapsody	1974
CAT-1603	Gwen Mccrae	Gwen Mccrae	1974
CAT-1604	Willie "Litlle Beaver" Hale	Party Down	1974
CAT-2604	Willie "Litlle Beaver" Hale	Party Down	1974
CAT-2605	Gwen Mccrae	Rock'N Chair	1975
CAT-2606	Gwen Mccrae	George & Gwen	1975
CAT-2607	Raw Soul Expres	Raw Soul Express	1976
CAT-2608	Gwen Mccrae	Something So Right	1976
CAT-2609	Willie "Litlle Beaver" Hale	When Was The Last Time	1976
CAT-2610	Chocolate Clay	Chocolate Clay	1977
CAT-2611	Trama	Trama	1977
CAT-2613	Gwen Mccrae	Let's Straighten It Out	1978
CAT-2614	Gwen Mccrae	Melody Of Life	1979
CAT-2615	Willie "Litlle Beaver" Hale	Beaver Fever	1980

CLOUDS

8801	Chi Coltrane	Road To Tomorrow	
8802	Horrell Mcgann	April Fool	1977
8803	Wild Oats	Wild Oats	1977
8804	Bobby Caldwell	Bobby Caldwell	1978
8805	Michael Bloomfield	Count Talent And The Originals	1978
8806	Eye Of The Tiger	Tiger, Tiger	1980
8807	Steve Gibb	Let My Song	1979
8808	Ish	Ish	1979
8809	Freddy Henry	Get Out In The Open	1979
8810	Bobby Caldwell	Cat In The Hat	

CONTEMPO - SCEPTER

8001	Armada Orchestra	Same	1976
1101	Armada Orchestra	Philly Armada	1977

DASH

30001	Foxy	Foxy	1976
30002	Rice & Beans Orchestra	Rice & Beans Orchestra	1976
30003	Kracker	Hot	1976
30004	T-Connection	Magic	1977
30005	Foxy	Get Off	1978
30006	Obatala	Obatala	1977
30007	Rice & Beans Orchestra	Cross Over	1977
30008	T-Connection	On Fire	1978
30009	T-Connection	T-Connection	1978
30010	Foxy	Hot Numbers	1979
30011	Asha	L'Indiana	1979
30013	The Stylistics	The Lion Sleeps Tonight	1979
30014	T-Connection	Totaly Connected	1979
30015	Foxy	Party Boys	1979
30016	Foxy	Live	1980

DIAL

6100	Joe Tex	He Who Is Without Funk Cast The First Stone	1978

DRIVE

D-101	Miami	Party Freaks	1974
LP-102	Miami	Notorious	1976
LP-103	Rocky Mizell	Sugar Rock Band	1977
DR 104	Peter Brown	Do You Wanna Get Funky With Me	1977
LP-105	Miami	Miami	1978
106	Gipsy Lane	Predictions	1978
107	The Jimmy Castor Bunch	Let It Out	1978
108	Peter Brown	Stargazer	1979
109	Brenda&Herb	In Heat Again	1979
110	Wild Honey	Untamed	1979
111	Jb's	Groove Machine	1979

FABULOUS

8500	Leon Ware	Inside Is Love	1979

FUNKY LATIN

1702	Paul Roman	La Chaperona	1972

GLADES

ST-6501	Timmy Thomas	Why Can'T We Live Together	1972

Matrix numbers

ST-6502	Latimore	Latimore	1973
ST-6503	Latimore	More, More, More	1974
ST-6504	Timmy Thomas	You're The Song I Alway's Wanted To Sing	1974
ST-7505	Latimore	III	1975
ST-7506	Irene Reid	The Two Of Us	1976
ST-7507	Miami Sound	Seven Seas	1976
ST-7508	Litlle Milton	Friend Of Mine	1976
ST-7509	Latimore	It Aint Where You Been	1976
ST-7510	Timmy Thomas	The Magician	1976
ST-7511	Litlle Milton	Me For You , You For Me	1977
ST-7512	Blue Notes	Thruth Has Come To Light	1977
ST-7513	Timmy Thomas	Touch To Touch	1977
ST-7514	Funky Brown	These Songs Will Last Forever	
ST-7515	Latimore	Dig A Little Deeper	1978
ST-7516	Soundtrack	Stony Island	1978
ST-7517	Timmy Thomas	Live	1979
ST-7518	Latimore	Getting Down To Brass Tracks	1980

GOOD SOUNDS

101	Herb Pilhofer	Olympus One	1976
102	Billion Dollar Band	Billion Dollar Band	1977
103	Cheese	Cheese	1977
104	Spats	Spats	1978
105	Laura Taylor	Dancing In My Feet	1979
5001	Rcr	Scandal	1980

HDM

2001	Black Ice	Black Ice	1977
2002	Eddie Horan	Love The Way You Love Me	1979
2003	Black Ice	I Judge The Funk	1979

INPHASION

3900	Lu Janis	Or Durvs	1978
3901	Rick Rydell	Out To Play	1979
3902	Daddy Dewdrop	Meet The Beat	1979

JUANA

200000	Frederick Knight	Knight Kap	1977
200001	Controllers	In Control	1977
200002	Controllers	Fill Your Life With Love	1978
200003	Frederick Knight	Let The Sun Shine In	1978
200004	Anita Ward	Songs Of Love	1979
200005	Controllers	Next In Line	1979
200006	Anita Ward	Sweet Surrender	1979
4000	Frederick Knight	Knight Time	1981
4001	Controllers	Controllers	1981
1003	Tommy Tate	Tommy Tate	1981

KAYVETTE

801	Jackie Moore	Make Me Feel Like A Woman	1975
802	Facts Of Life	Sometimes	1977
803	Facts Of Life	A Matter Of Fact	1978
804	Brandye	Cross Over To Brandye	1978

KONDUKO

K-100000	King Sporty & Root Rockers	Deep Reggea Roots	1976
K-100001	King Sporty & Root Rockers	Mr Rhythm	1977
K-100002	Phillip & Lloyd	You've Got To Keep On Moving	1978
K-100003	King Sporty & Root Rockers	Fire Keep On Burning	1979
K-100004	Various	Konduko Six Pack	1979
K-100005	Various	Konduko Six Pack	1980

LRC

LRC-9312	Lonnie Smith	Keep On Lovin'	1977
LRC-9313	O'Donel Levy	Windows	1977
LRC-9314	Jimmy McGriff	Red Beans	1977
LRC-9315	Joe Thomas	Feelings From Within	1977
LRC-9316	Jimmy Mcgriff	Tailgunner	1977
LRC-9317	Lonnie Smith	Funk Reaction	1977
LRC-9318	Joe Thomas	Here I Come	1977
LRC-9319	O'Donel Levy	Times Have Changed	1977
LRC-9320	Jimmy Mcgriff	Outside Looking In	1978
LRC-9321	Joe Thomas	Get In The Wind	1978
LRC-9322	Jimmy Ponder	All Things Beautiful	1978
LRC-9323	Lonnie Smith	Gotcha	1978
LRC-9325	B. Baker & Chocolate Company	B. Baker & Chocolate Company	1979
LRC-9327	Joe Thomas	Make Your Move	1979

MALACO

6351	Dorothy Moore	Misty Blue	1976
6352	Eddie Floyd	Experience	1977
6353	Dorothy Moore	Dorothy Moore	1977
6356	Dorothy Moore	Once More With Feeling	1978
6357	Freedom	Farther Than Imagination	1978
6358	James Bradley	James Bradley	1979
6359	Dorothy Moore	Defenitely Dorothy	1979
6361	Fern Kinney	Groove Me	1979

MARLIN

MARLIN 2200	John Tropea	Tropea	1975
MARLIN 2201	Ritchie Family	Arabian Nights	1976
MARLIN 2202	Ralph Mcdonald	Sound Of A Drum	1976
MARLIN 2203	Ritchie Family	Life Is Music	1977
MARLIN 2204	John Tropea	Short Trip To Space	1977
MARLIN 2205	W.M. Saltner	It's So Beautiful To Be	1977
MARLIN 2206	Ritchie Family	African Queens	1977
MARLIN 2207	Various	Disco Party	1977
MARLIN 2208	Various	Disco Party 2	1977
MARLIN 2209	Phill Upchurch	Phill Upchurch	1978
MARLIN 2210	Ralph Mcdonald	The Path	1978
MARLIN 2211	William Eaton	Struggle Buggy	1978
MARLIN 2212	Usa European Connection	Come Into My Heart	1978
MARLIN 2213	Voyage	Voyage	1977
MARLIN 2214	Eddie Daniels	Streetwind	1978
MARLIN 2215	Ritchie Family	American Generation	1978
MARLIN 2216	Quartz	Quartz	1978
MARLIN 2217	Gregg Daimond	Starcruiser	1978
MARLIN 2218	Beautiful Bend	Make That Feeling Come Again	1978
MARLIN 2219	Jo Bisso	Love Somebody	1977
MARLIN 2220	Queen Samantha	The Letter	1978
MARLIN 2221	Michael Urbaniak	Ecstasy	1978
MARLIN 2222	John Tropea	To Touch You Again	1979
MARLIN 2223	Starcity	I Am A Man	1978
MARLIN 2224	USA European Connection	USA European Connection	
MARLIN 2225	Voyage	Fly Away	1978
MARLIN 2226	Partners	Last Disco In Paris	1979
MARLIN 2227	Amant	Amant	1979
MARLIN 2228	Uncle Louie	Uncle Louie's Here	1979
MARLIN 2229	Ralph Mcdonald	Counterpoint	1979
MARLIN 2230	Queen Samantha	II	1979
MARLIN 2231	USA European Connection	USA European Connection	1979
MARLIN 2232	Tempest Trio	Tempest Trio	1979
MARLIN 2233	Kat Mandu	Kat Mandu	1979
MARLIN 2234	Osiris	O-Zone	1979
MARLIN 2235	Voyage	3	1980
MARLIN 2236	Basil Poledouris	Blue Lagoon	1980

PI-KAPPA

PK-6000	Jimmy Briscoe & The Beavers	My Ebony Princess	1973
PKS-4000	Super Disco Band	Super Disco Band	1976
PKS-4001	Calendar	It'S A Monster	1976

REID'S WORLD

4001	Regina James	Dancin' In The Flames Of Love	1979

ROOTS

1001	Jimmy Reed	Is Back	1976
1002	Gene Ammons	Swinging The Jugg	1976
1003	George "Wild Child" Butler	Funky Butt Lover	1977
1004	Lee "Shot" Williams	Country Disco	1977

ROYAL FLUSH

5500	Big Apple Brass	Opus De Metropolis	1978

SHIELD

80000	Special Delivery	Special Delivery	1978

Matrix numbers

SILVER BLUE

| 50000 | Eli's Second Coming | Eli's Second Coming | 1977 |

STONE DOG

| 3001 | Swamp Dogg | Gag A Maggot | 1973 |
| 3002 | Swamp Dogg | Greatest Hits ????? | 1976 |

SUNSHINE SOUND

SSE-801	Jimmy "Bo" Horne	Dance Across The Floor	1978
SSE-802	Fire	Fire	1978
SSE-803	Ron Louis Smith	Party Freaks	1978
SSE-804	Michelle White	Sweet Innosence	1978
SSE-805	Jimmy "Bo" Horne	Going Home For Love	1979

TK

TK 1	The TK Jazz Smapler	Various	1970
TK 500	Kc & The Sunshine Band	Do It Good	1974
TK 501	George Mccrea	Rock Your Baby	1974
TK 600	Kc & The Sunshine Band	Do It Good	1974
TK 602	George Mccrea	George Mccrea	1975
TK 603	Kc & The Sunshine Band	Kc & The Sunshine Band	1975
TK 604	Sunshine Band	The Sound Of Sunshine	1975
TK 605	Kc & The Sunshine Band	Part 3	1976
TK 606	George Mccrea	Daimond Touch	1976
TK 607	Kc & The Sunshine Band	Who Do Ya (Love)	1978
TK 608	George Mccrea	George Mccrea	1978
TK 610	George Mccrea	We Did It	1978
TK 611	Kc & The Sunshine Band	Do You Wanna Party	1979
TK 612	Kc & The Sunshine Band	Greatest Hits	1979
TK 614	Kc	Space Cadet (Solo Flight)	1980
TK 615	James Brown	Soul Syndrome	1980

WANDERICK

| 66000 | Jimmy Briscoe & The Beavers | Jimmy Briscoe & The Beavers | 1977 |

WICKED

| 9001 | Wilson Picket | Chocolate Mountain | 1976 |

WEIRD WORLD

LP-2020	Blowfly	The Weird World Of Blowfly
LP-2021	Blowfly	On Tv
LP-2022	Blowfly	On Tour
LP-2023	Blowfly	Zodiac Blowfly
LP-2024	Blowfly	At The Movies
LP-2025	Blowfly	Butterfly
LP-2026	Blowfly	Oldies But Goodies
LP-2027	Wild Man Steve	Everybody's Man
LP-2028	Blowfly	Disco
LP-2030	Wild Man Steve	S6000 Nigger
LP-2031	Blowfly	Zodiac Party
LP-2032	Blowfly	Disco Party
LP-2033	Saxton Kari & Orch.	The Six Thousand Dollar Nigger
LP-2034	Blowfly	Blowflys Party
LP-2035	Blowfly	Rappin' Dancin' Laughin'
LP-2036	Blowfly	Porno Freak

WOLF

1201	Robin Kenyata	Encourage The People
1202	Harold Vick	After The Dance
1203	Kenny Barron	Innosence

Tangerue

Disco Labels & Albums

Chapter 18
Unidisc Records

UNIDISC IS A CANADIAN DISCO AND DANCE MUSIC LABEL FOUNDED IN 1977 BY GEORGE CUCUZZELLA.

Cucuzzella began his career as a DJ in Montreal in the 1970s and formed a Canadian record pool, supplying mixes to DJs across Quebec. This was then followed by opening a record store, Downstairs Records. Through this he launched the Unidisc Music Inc record label.

Artists released on the label included Lime, Erotic Drum Band, Gino Soccio, Nightlife Unlimited, Trans X, Freddie James and Geraldine Hunt. Unidisc initially released music by Canadian groups but also began successfully licensing American and European disco for the Canadian market. Later on the label bought the rights to the New York-based Prelude Records catalogue. After this Unidisc began to acquire many other dance labels including Megatone, Emergency, Midland International, De-Lite, Network, Pickwick and Sound of New York.

In 2010 the company merged with Universal Music Canada and today Unidisc Music Inc is one of Canada's largest independent record labels.

Left: Tangerue - Tangerue / Unidisc 1979
Design: Studio Grafiti / Photography: Michael Perez

Erotic Drum Band - Action 78 / Unidisc 1978
Photography: Michael Perez / Design: Moez Shabudin

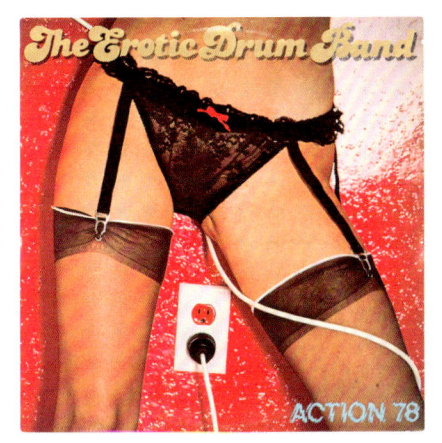

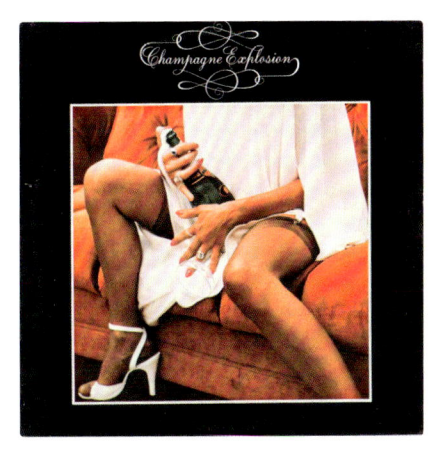

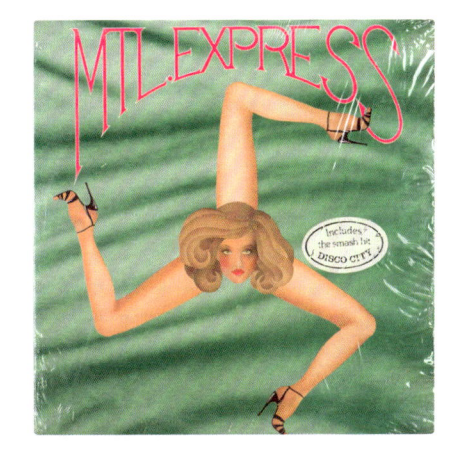

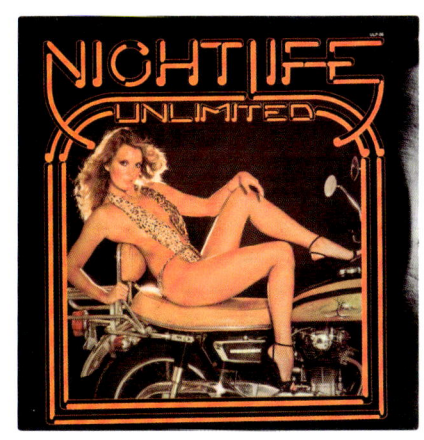

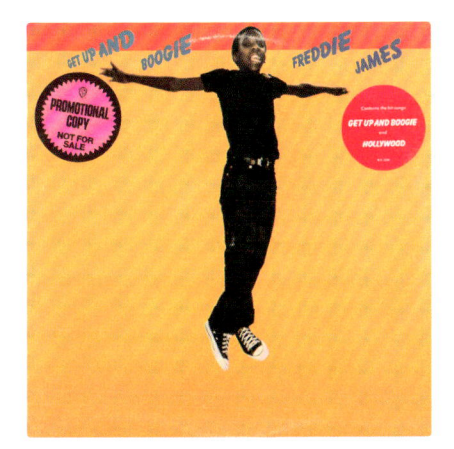

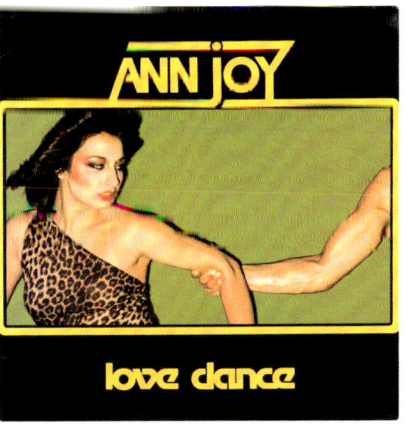

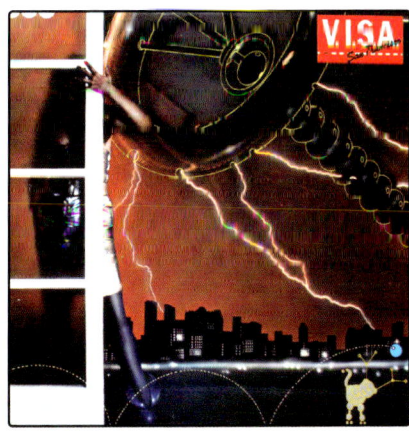

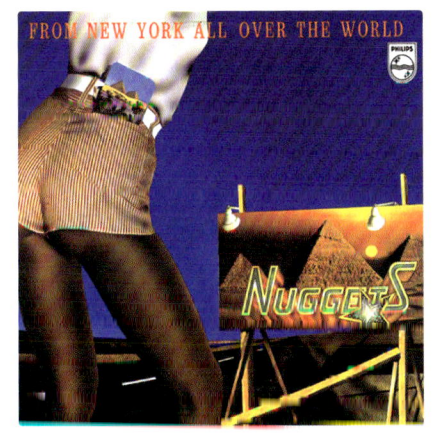

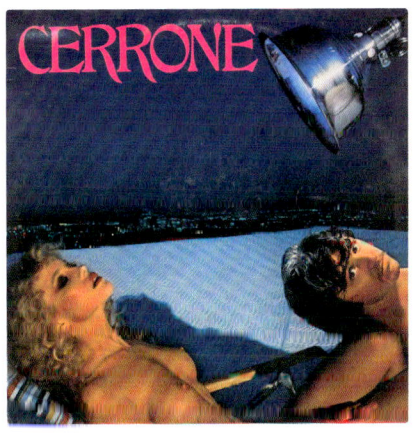

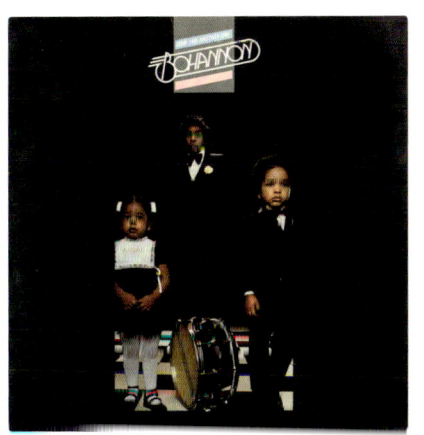

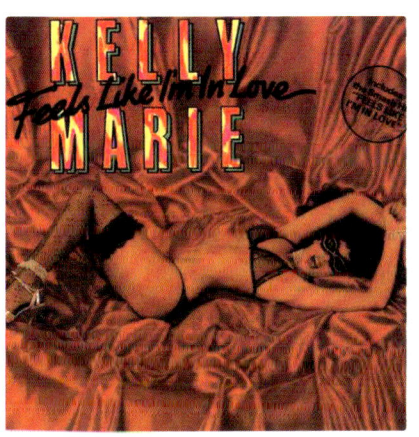

ULP-01 / 1978
ULP-02 / 1978
ULP-03 / 1978
ULP-06 / 1979
ULP-007 / 1979
ULP-08 / 1979
ULP-09 / 1979
ULP-10 / 1979
ULP-12 / 1980
ULP-13 / 1980
ULP-14 / 1980
ULP-15 / 1981
ULP-16 / 1980
ULP-19 / 1980
ULP-21 / 1981
ULP-23 / 1981

Plastic Surprise - Bang Bang / Unidisc 1980

Inner Life-Inner Life / Unidisc 1981
Design: Stan Hochstadt / Photography: Len Kaltman

Hydro - Hydro featuring Lorna / Unidisc 1979
Illustration: Moez Shabudin, Sam Montesano / Album Design: Studio Graffiti

Matrix numbers

ULP-25 / 1981

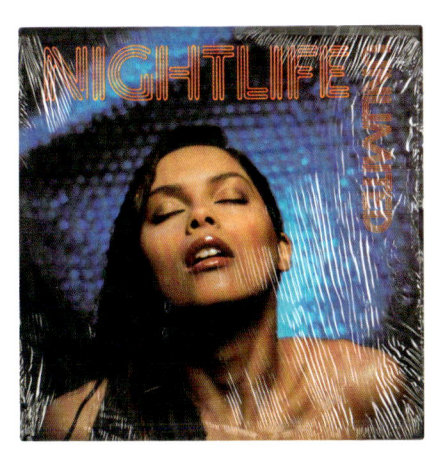

ULP-26 / 1981

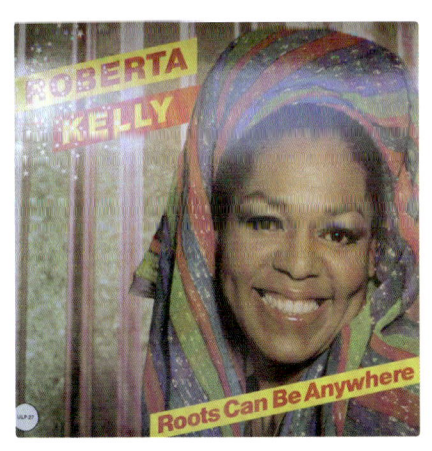

ULP-27 / 1981

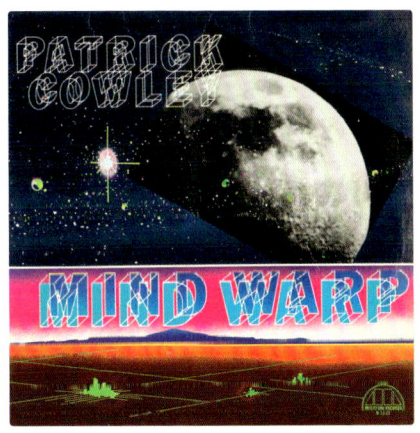

ULP-38 / 1981

UNIDISC

ULP-01	Erotic Drum Band	Action 78	1978
ULP-02	Champagne Explosion	Champagne Explosion	1978
ULP-03	MTL Express	MTL Express	1978
ULP-04	David Boydell	City Music	1978
ULP-05	Elvin Shaad	Live For Love	1979
ULP-06	Nightlife Unlimited	Nightlife Unlimited	1979
ULP-007	Freddie James	Get Up And Boogie	1979
ULP-08	Hydro Featuring Lorna	Hydro	1979
ULP-09	Kat Mandu	Kat Mandu	1979
ULP-10	Tangerue	Tangerue	1979
ULP-12	Easy Going	Fear	1980
ULP-13	Plastic Surprise	Bang Bang	1980
ULP-14	Ann Joy	Love Dance	1980
ULP-15	V.I.S.A.	San Francisco	1981
ULP-16	Nuggets	From New York All Over The World	1980
ULP-17	Tantra	Mother Africa	1981
ULP-18	Tantra	Hills Of Katmandu	1981
ULP-19	Cerrone	Cerrone VI	1980
ULP-21	Bohannon	Goin' For Another One	1981
ULP-22	Originals, The	Yesterday And Today	1981
ULP-23	Kelly Marie	Feels Like I'm In Love	1981
ULP-25	Jesse Green	Jesse Green	1981
ULP-26	Nightlife Unlimited	Nightlife Unlimited	1981
ULP-27	Roberta Kelly	Roots Can Be Anywhere	1981
ULP-28	Caroline Bernier	Caroline Bernier	1981
ULP-29	Inner Life	Inner Life	1981
ULP-30	Patrick Cowley	Menergy	1981
ULP-31	Tommy Nilsson	No Way No How	1981
ULP-32	Saint Tropez	Hot And Nasty	1982
ULP-33	Eloise Whitaker	Eloise Whitaker	1982
ULP-34	Flirts, The	Calling All Boys	1982
ULP-36	Saint Tropez	Belle De Jour	1982
ULP-37	Various	Superstars On Donna	1982
ULP-38	Patrick Cowley	Mind Warp	1982
ULP-40	Flirts, The	Born To Flirt	1984
ULP-41	Doris D And The Pins	Starting At The End	1984
ULP-43	Jolley & Swain	Back Trackin'	1984

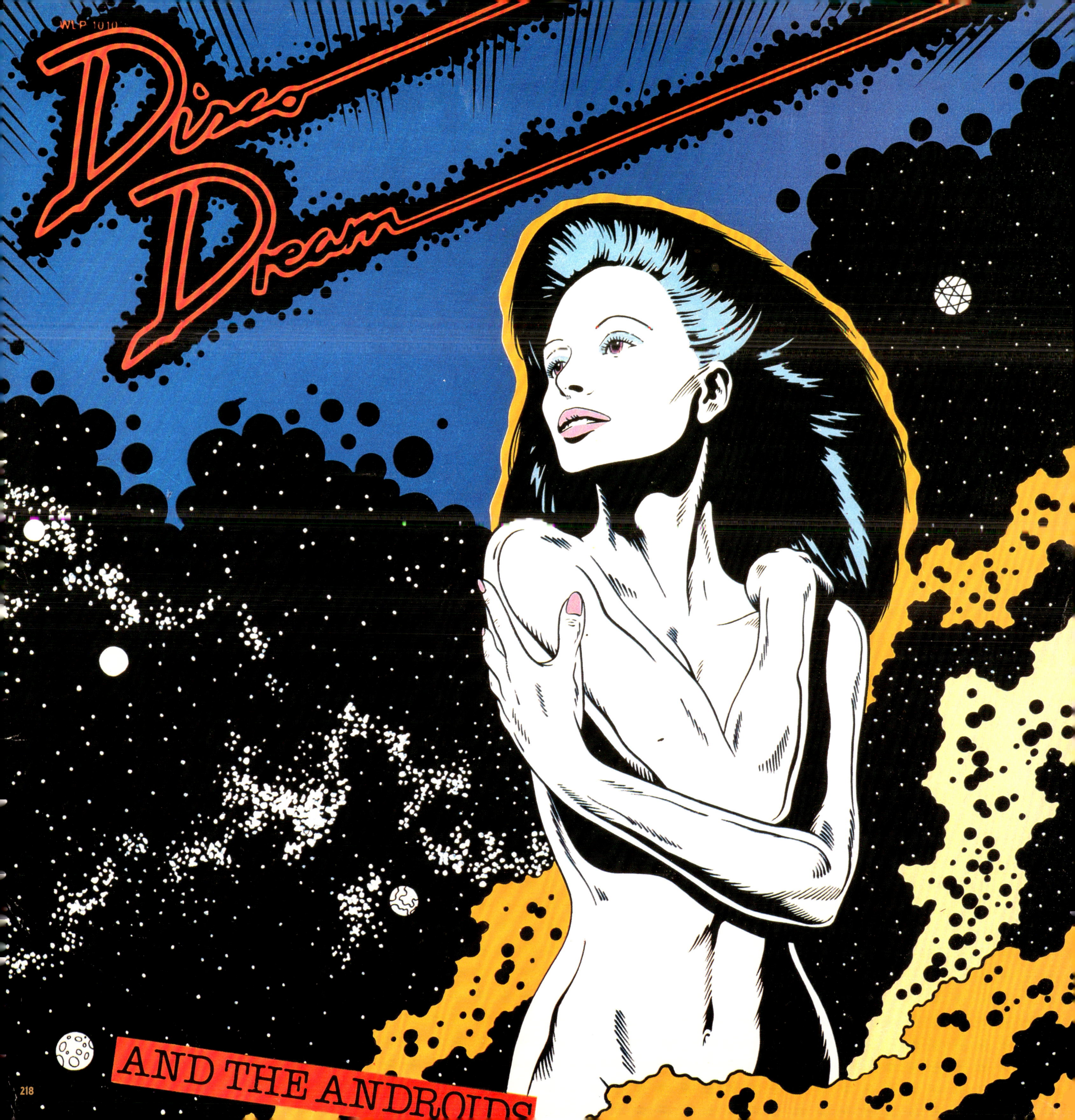
WLP 1010
Disco Dream
AND THE ANDROIDS

Disco Labels & Albums

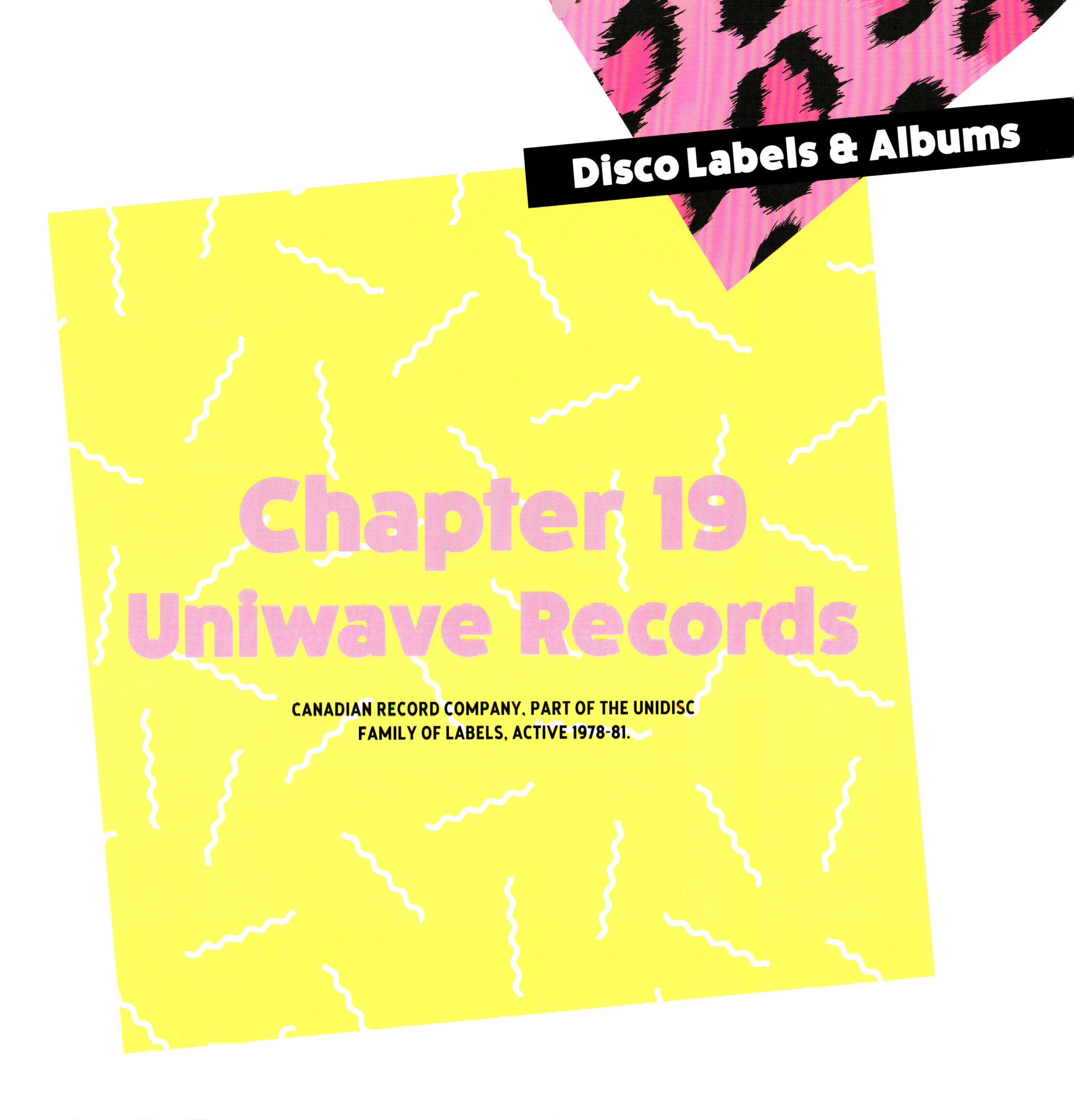

Chapter 19
Uniwave Records

CANADIAN RECORD COMPANY, PART OF THE UNIDISC FAMILY OF LABELS, ACTIVE 1978-81.

Left: Disco Dream And The Androids / Uniwave 1980
Design: Rod Vass

HARRY THUMANN – American Express WLP-1007 / 1980	extensive care – Sexy Thrills WLP-1004 / 1980
BODY to BODY – GEPY & GEPY WLP-1005 / 1979	KAT MANDU VOL. 2 WLP-1017 / 1980

WLP-1002 / 1980
WLP-1003 / 1979 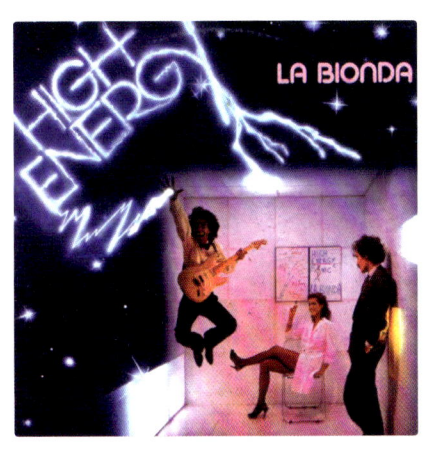
WLP-1006 / 1980 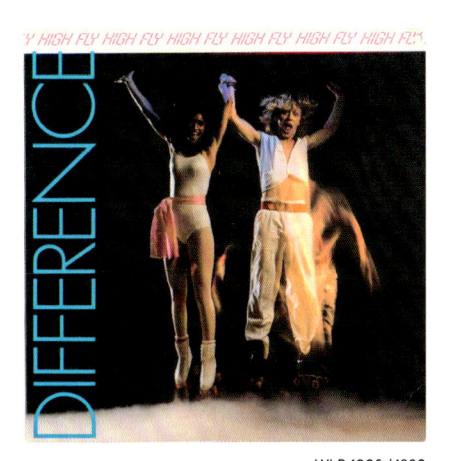
WLP-1009 / 1980 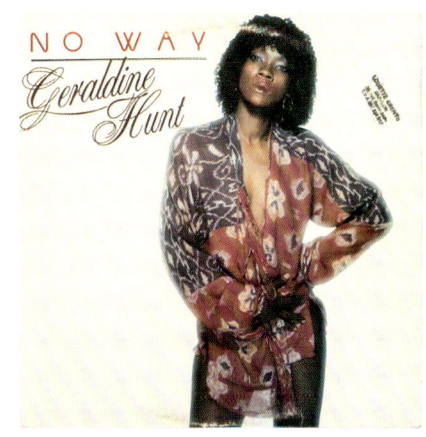
WLP-1010 / 1980 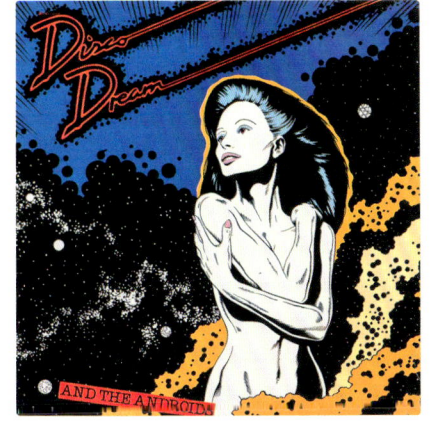
WLP-1010 (Back) / 1980 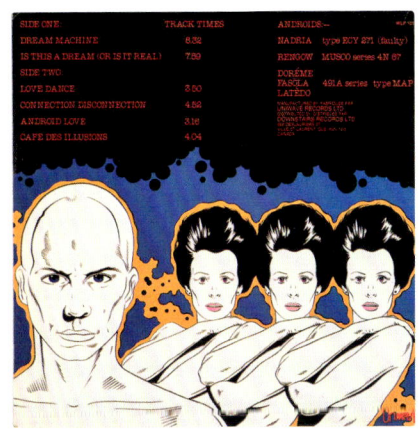
WLP-1012 / 1980 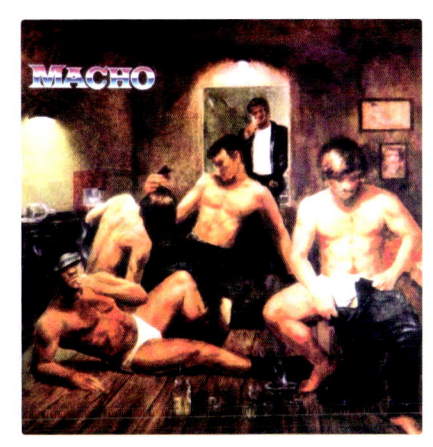
WLP-1013 / 1980 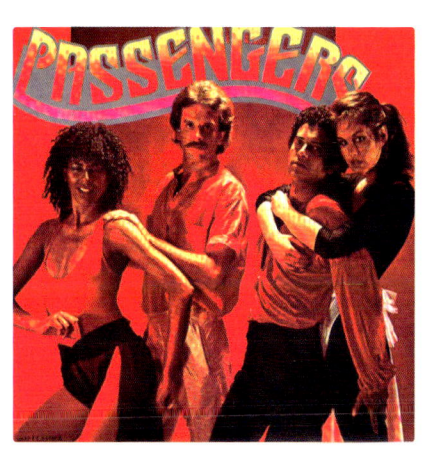
WLP-1014 / 1980 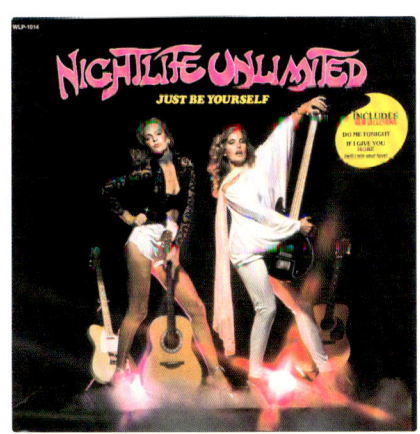
WLP-1016 / 1980 
WLP-1019 / 1980 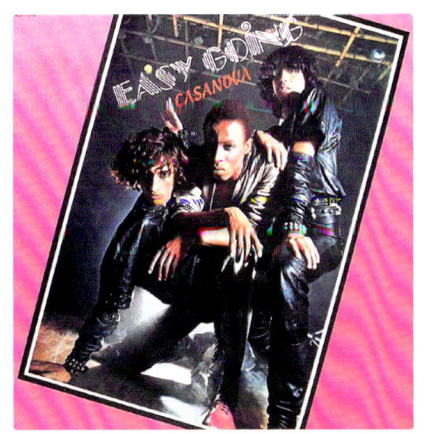
WLP-1021 / 1980 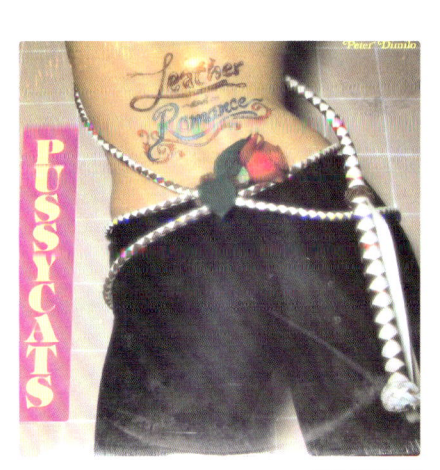
WLP-1025 / 1980 
WLP-1028 / 1981 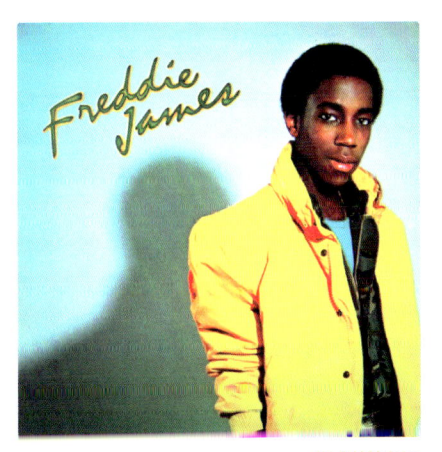
WLP-1029 / 1981 
WLP-1032 / 1981 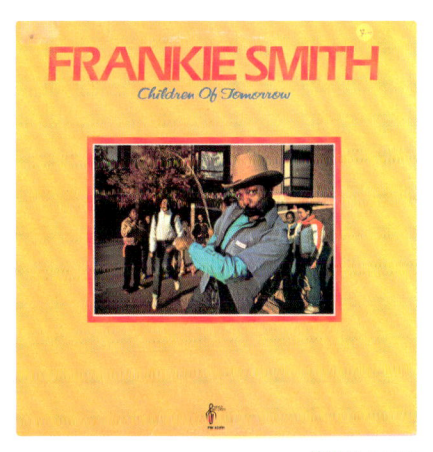

221

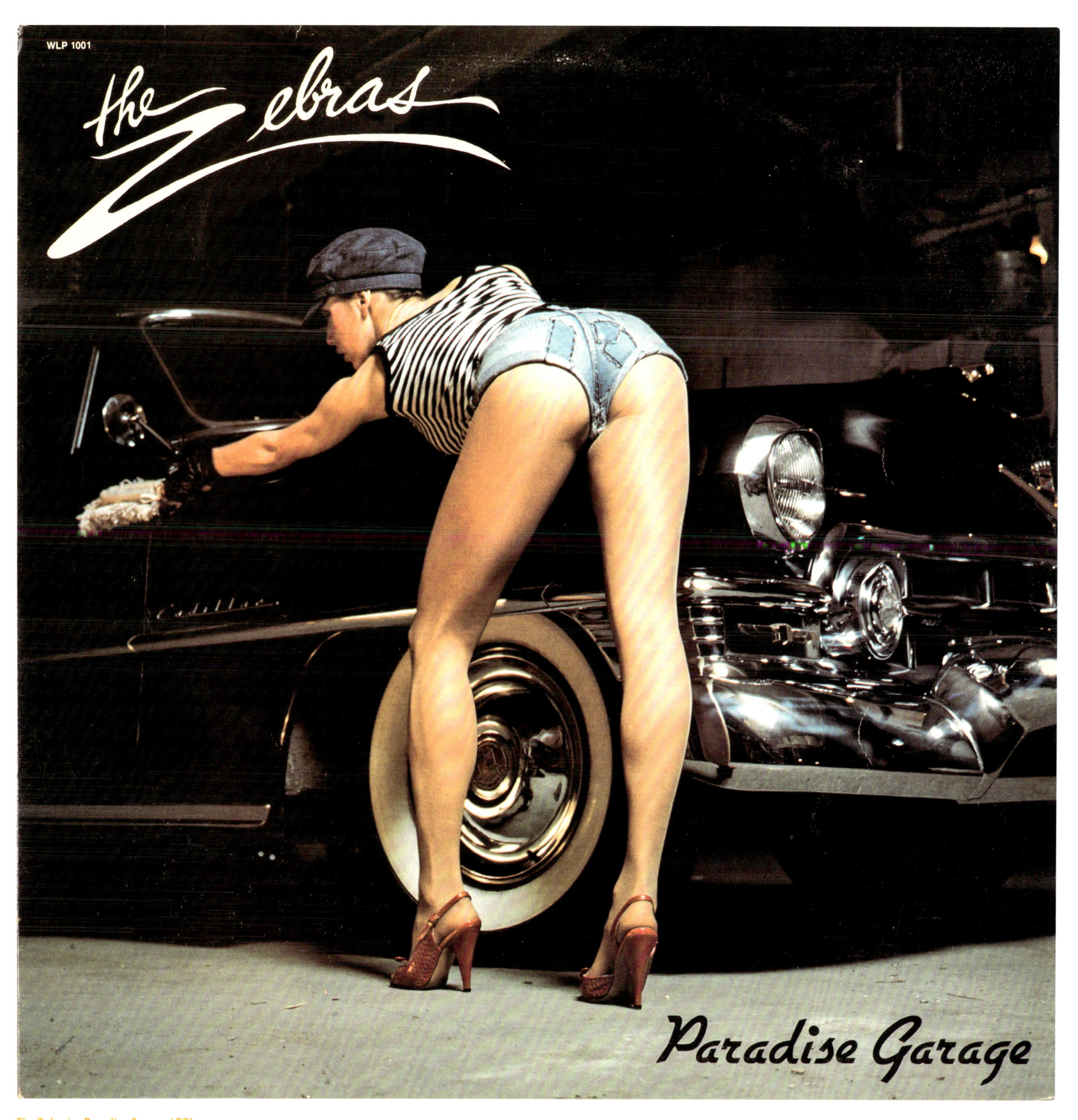

The Zebra's - Paradise Garage / PBI
Design: Illusions Too P'tit / Photography: Gilles Bernier

Matrix numbers

UNIWAVE

WLP-1001	The Zebras	Paradise Garage	
WLP-1002	Five Letters	Got Got Money	1980
WLP-1003	La Bionda	High Energy	1979
WLP-1004	Extensive Care	Sexy Thrills	1980
WLP-1005	Gepy & Gepy	Body To Body	1979
WLP-1006	Difference	High Fly	1980
WLP-1007	Harry Thumann	American Express	1980
WLP-1008	Pete Richards	I Had A Dream	1980
WLP-1009	Geraldine Hunt	No Way	1980
WLP-1010	Disco Dream And The Androids	The Androids	1980
WLP-1012	Macho	Roll	1980
WLP-1013	Passengers	Passengers	1980
WLP-1014	Nightlife Unlimited	Just Be Yourself	1980
WLP-1015	Madleen Kane	Sounds Of Love	1980
WLP-1016	Wonder	Up & Down	1980
WLP-1017	Kat Mandu	Get Crackin	1980
WLP-1019	Easy Going	Casanova	1980
WLP-1020	Kano	Kano	1980
WLP-1021	Pussycats	Leather And Romance	1980
WLP-1025	Passengers	Passengers	1980
WLP-1028	Freddie James	Freddie James	1981
WLP-1029	The Zebras	The Zebras	1981
WLP-1032	Frankie Smith	Children Of Tommorow	1981

THE PLAYERS ASSOCIATION
Turn The Music Up!

VSD • 79421
STEREO

VANGUARD
RECORDINGS FOR THE CONNOISSEUR

Disco Labels & Albums

Chapter 20
Vanguard Records

VANGUARD RECORDS WAS FOUNDED BY SEYMOUR AND MAYNARD SOLOMON IN NEW YORK IN 1949.

Starting with a $10,000 loan from their father and renting a tiny one room office at 80 East 11th Street the company grew to become one of America's leading independent labels. In the early days the brothers concentrated on the music they knew best - classical, jazz and folk. At the beginning of 1977 the disco scene had started to grow rapidly and in April of that year Mark Berry started working for the company as an assistant engineer. Berry together with Danny Weiss, who was the company's main jazz producer, became responsible for bringing disco music into the company. The pair became Vanguard's in-house remixing team and their names are mentioned on most of the label's disco releases.

Mark and Danny were later joined by Ray 'Pinky' Velazquez, a famous New York DJ and remixer and together they made magic with many Vanguard 12-inch singles releases.

Left: The Players Association-Turn The Music Up / Vanguard 1978
Photography: Frank Kolleogy / Design: Jules Halfant

Ray "Pinky" Velazquez Interview

Danny Weiss was working as an in-house jazz producer and A&R man at Vanguard. He was given the task to come up with some disco records to release. The Players Association was his first release. He studied what Gamble & Huff were doing at Columbia Records with their jazzy R&B style of records.

'Mark Berry could edit tape – he could edit complicated issues like a magician. He had a great ear for strong melodies and pop basslines. He liked pop, he liked the synthesizer material that was coming out of Europe that was creating the disco craze and rocking dancefloors across the country. He was young and talented and visited many clubs to support this European vision. He loved disco! So his comfort zone was euro-disco - this was his cup of tea. He was also assisting Bobby Orlando with 'O' Records, which was part of the Vanguard family. Bobby 'O' had a very European sound and this is where they both connected. Mark was just a great person to have in the Vanguard days, when it came to disco. And he really helped Danny Weiss expand his vision of what he would consider disco. So the two of them had different backgrounds. Eventually I came into the picture and tried to bridge both of their sounds - I like R&B and I also like the disco stuff. So the three of us kind of gave Vanguard our initial vision of the Vanguard Disco label.'

What do you think made Vanguard one of the hottest labels on the disco scene?
'The acts that Danny Weiss and I were signing. Acts like Poussez, Rainbow Brown (with vocals by Fonda Rae) and Alisha. We were also engineering a lot for Arthur Baker and we mixed everything at Vanguard Studios.'

Have you got any special memories from your days at Vanguard?
'Definitely the Alisha success. From the street to a worldwide hit with 'Baby Talk'. Alisha was incredibly talented along with Patrick Adams who I worked with a lot. Patrick is a great songwriter and Alisha was a tremendous vocalist for her young age of 15.'

What was the first song Vanguard released on 12-inch single?
'Love Hangover' by The Players Association. The Players Association were a studio act put together by the writer Chris Hills and producer Danny Weiss. This band was more or less the Vanguard 'house band', similar to Salsoul Records' Salsoul Orchestra. For the Players Association tunes, Chris and Danny hired professional session musicians - usually the best around.

Which of your remixes are among your favourites?
'I would say 'Over Like A Fat Rat' by Fonda Rae. It was a great record on the dancefloor and for the R&B market and R&B radio. That record was great. And Carol Williams' 'Can't Get Away From Your Love'. The original dance mix and then a special 10-inch version that I did were both favourites of mine. I also remember the excitement of getting involved with Frisky's 'You Got Me Dancing In My Sleep', plus another cut from the album, 'Tutty Frutty Booty'.'

'In the late 1970s a young ex-boxer called Bobby Orlando started writing and producing records for Vanguard. For the label he produced Lyn Todd, he also wrote and produced Free Expression's 'Chill-Out!' and he brought Roni Griffith to the label. The young two even became a couple for a while and in 1980 'Mondo Man' was released, but the year after the big break came for both of them when Bobby wrote and produced the song 'Desire' which became a huge hit, especially in Europe, but also in US club land. At Vanguard he worked a lot with Danny Weiss. Together they worked on several Vanguard recordings and Bobby kept working with Danny even after leaving the label to start his own labels, which is why you can find Danny's name on many Bobby Orlando productions.'

Vanguard was sold to the Lawrence Welk Group in 1986.

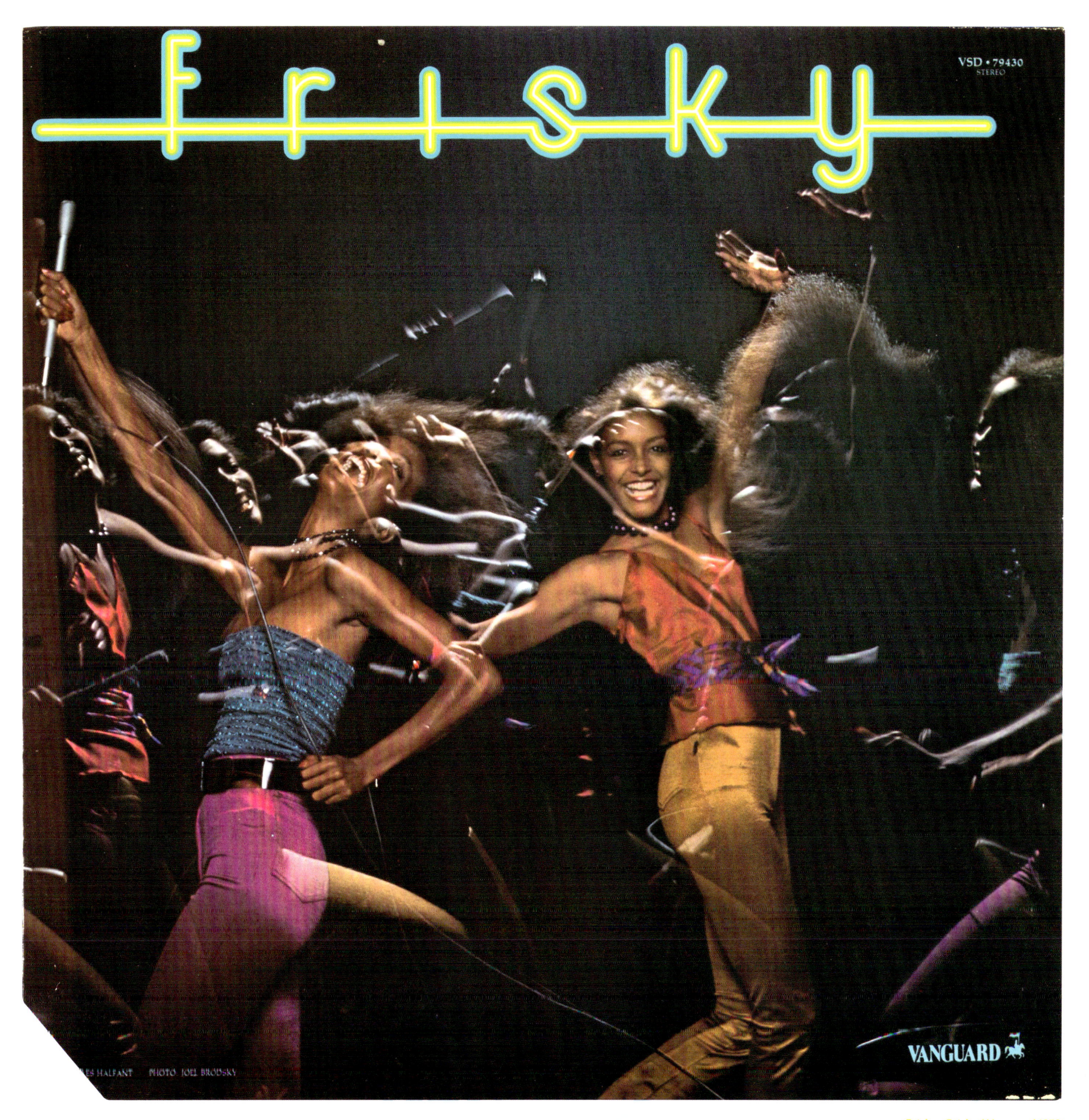

Frisky - Frisky / Vanguard 1979
Photography: Joel Brodsky / Design: Jules Halfant

Poussez! - Poussez! / Vanguard 1979
Photography: Frank Kolleogy / Design: Jules Halfant

VSD 79364 / 1975

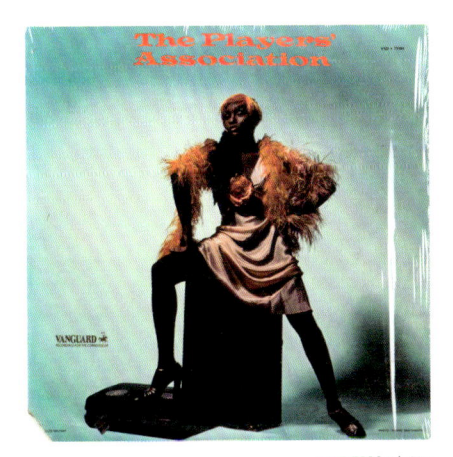

VSD 79384 / 1977

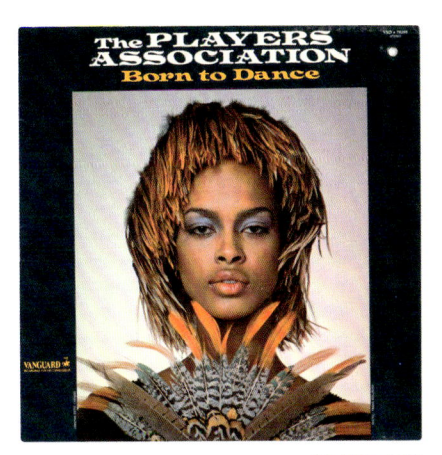

VSD 79398 / 1977

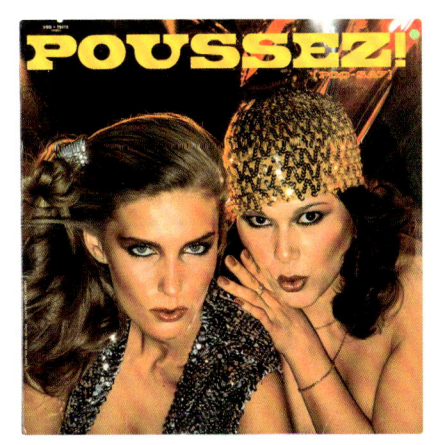

VSD 79412 / 1978

VSD 79421 / 1979

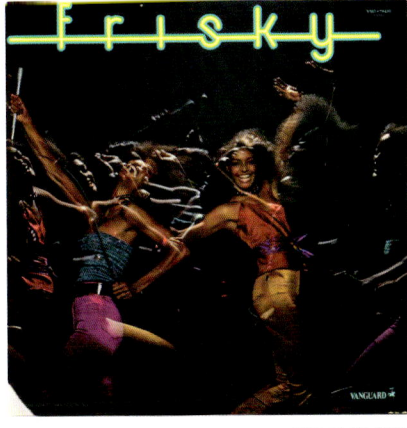

VSD 79430 / 1979

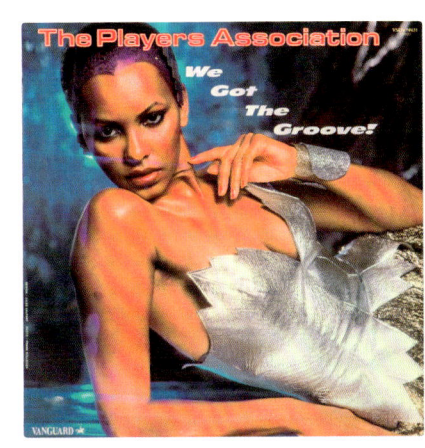

VSD 79431 / 1980

VSD 79433 / 1980

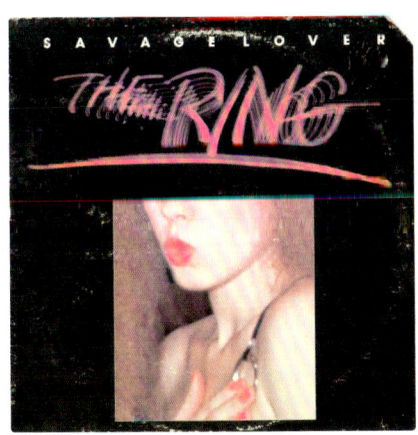

VSD 79435 / 1981

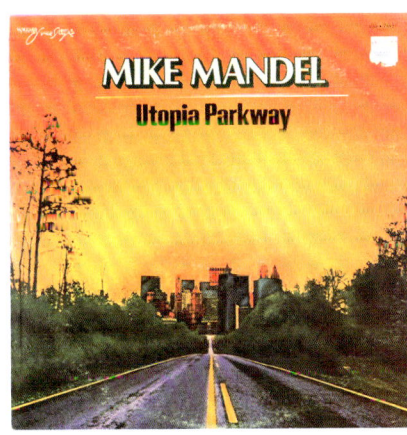

VSD 79437 / 1980

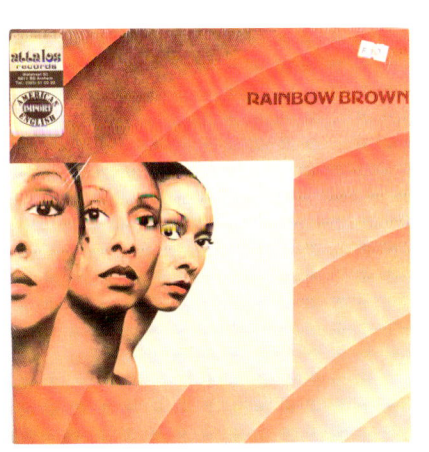

VSD 79439 / 1981

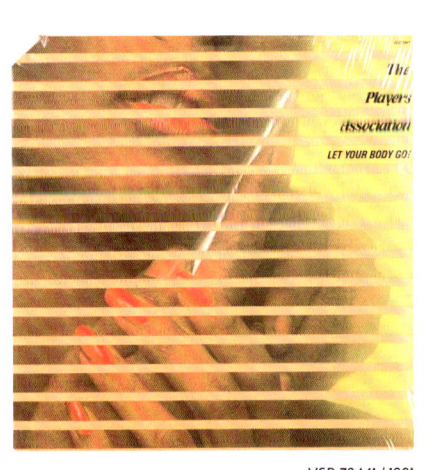

VSD 79441 / 1981

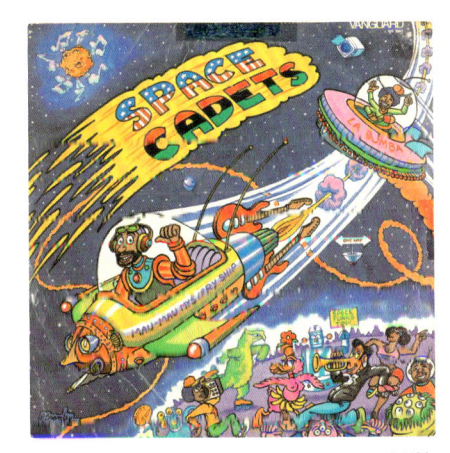

VSD 79442 / 1981

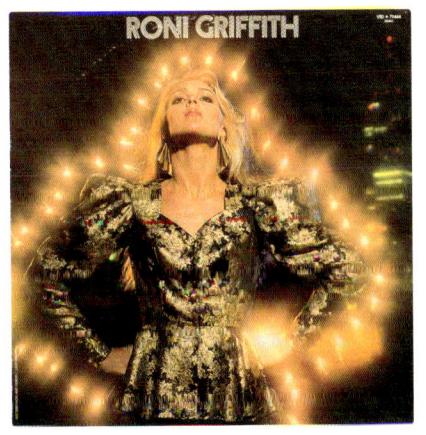

VSD 79444 / 1982

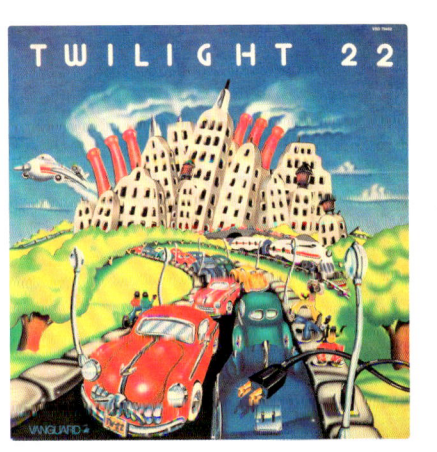

VSD 79452 / 1984

VSD 79456 / 1985

The Players Association - We Got The Groove / Vanguard 1978
Photography: Frank Kolleogy / Design: Jules Halfant

Matrix numbers

VANGUARD

VSD 79364	The Pazant Bros.	Loose And Juicy	1975
VSD 79384	The Players Association	The Players' Association	1977
VSD 79398	The Players Association	Born To Dance	1977
VSD 79404	James Moody	Beyond This World	1978
VSD 79409	Mike Mandel	Sky Music	1978
VSD 79412	Poussez!	Poussez!	1979
VSD 79421	The Players Association	Turn The Music Up!	1979
VSD-79423	Karl Ratzer	Street Talk	1979
VSD 79430	Frisky	Frisky	1979
VSD 79431	The Players Association	We Got The Groove!	1980
VSD 79433	Poussez!	Leave That Boy Alone!	1980
VSD 79434	The Players Association	Let Your Body Go! (UK)	1981
VSD 79435	Ring, The	Savage Lover	1981
VSD 79437	Mike Mandel	Utopia Parkway	1980
VSD 79439	Rainbow Brown	Rainbow Brown	1981
VSD 79441	The Players Association	Let Your Body Go! (US)	1981
VSD 79442	Space Cadets	Space Cadets	1981
VSD 79444	Roni Griffith	Roni Griffith	1982
VSD 79452	Twilight 22	Twilight 22	1984
VSD 79454	Evelyn Thomas	High Energy	1984
VSD 79456	Alisha	Alisha	1985

Symba • BODY BAIT

Disco Labels & Albums

Chapter 21
Venture Records

LOS ANGELES DISCO LABEL STARTED BY SUCCESSFUL SOUL PRODUCER/ARRANGER TONY CAMILLO AND CECILE BARKER, ACTIVE 1978-83.

Left: Symba – Body Bait / Venture 1980
Art Direction And Design: John Georgopoulos / Photgraphy: Tom Keller

VL-1001 / 1979

VL-1002 / 1979

VL-1004 / 1979

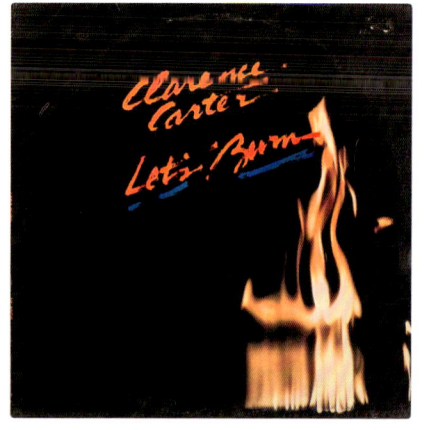

VL-1005 / 1980

VL-1007 / 1980

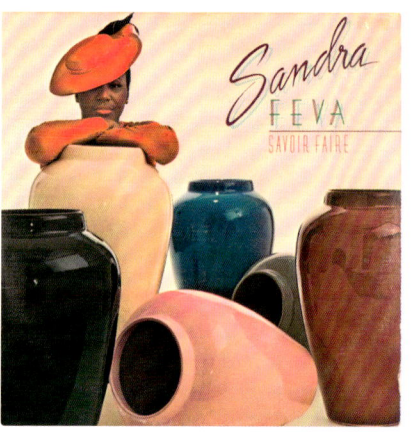

VL-1008 / 1981

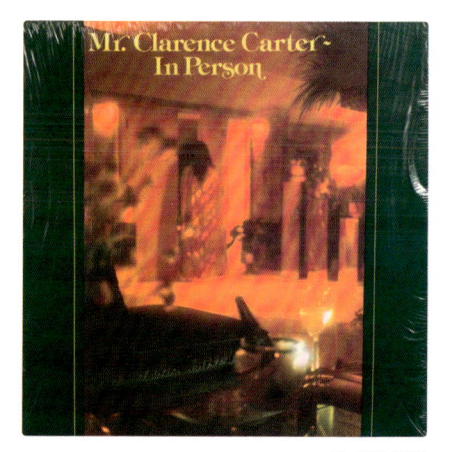

VL-1009 / 1981

VL-1003 / 1979

VL-1010 / 1982

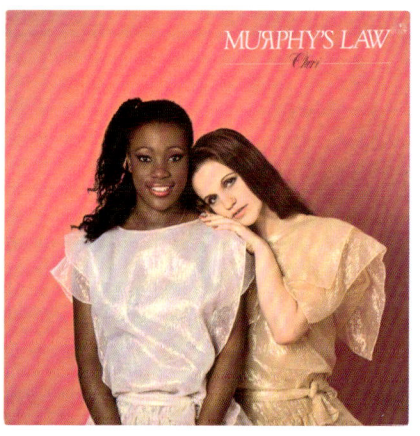

VL-1011 / 1982

Matrix numbers

VENTURE

VL-1001	Creme D'Cocoa	Funked Up	1978
VL-1002	Sandra Feva	The Need To Be	1979
VL-1003	Sir John Roberts	And The Sophisticated Funk Orchestra	1979
VL-1004	Creme D' Cocoa	Nasty Street	1979
VL-1005	Clarence Carter	Let's Burn	1980
VL-1007	Symba	Body Bait	1980
VL-1008	Sandra Feva	Savoir Faire	1981
VL-1009	Clarence Carter	In Person	1981
VG-1001	Reverend Larry Laster	Just To Be There	1981
VL-1010	Redd Hott	#1	1982
VL-1011	Cheri	Murphy's Law	1982

Taana Gardner
DOUBLE YOUR PLEASURE
2
RECORD SET
All Extended
Length Versions
Including the Hits
Paradise Express
When You Touch Me
Work That Body
WE-107
236

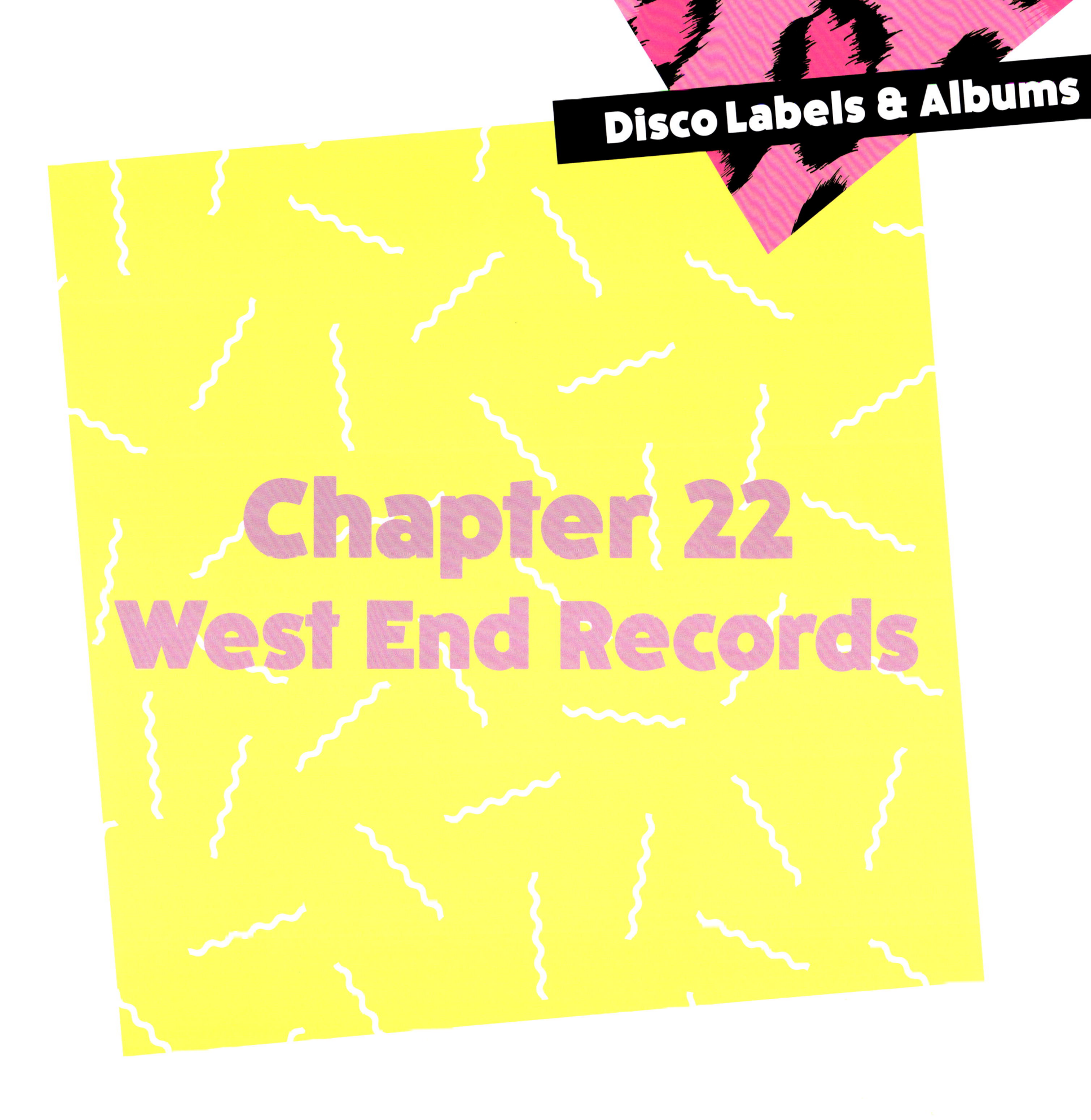

Disco Labels & Albums

Chapter 22
West End Records

Left: Taana Gardner - Taana Gardner / West End 1979
Cover Concept And Styling: Diane Strafaci / Art Direction, Design: Queen Grapics

The History Of West End Records

West End Records was formed in 1976 by Mel Cheren and Ed Kushins and the label went on to define the sound of New York City in the heyday of disco. Cheren and Kushins were colleagues at Scepter Records so when Scepter closed down in 1975 the pair decided to form West End Records. They got the name from the location of their office, which was located close to Broadway in Manhattan's theatre district – the West End. Their address was 254 W 54th Street, an address that soon would be known to the rich and famous, the fashion crowd and disco lovers all over as the home of Studio 54. Actually, it was just coincidence that both these legendary disco institutions were located in the same building. Later the company moved to another West End address, at 250 W. 57th Street.

Cheren had been head of production for Scepter Records and was one of the main figureheads to help launch the disco era. He also came up with the idea of putting an instrumental version of a song on the B-side of Scepter singles; and for this new idea Scepter won Billboard's Trend Setter Of The Year Award. Besides this, and even more important – he helped create the first 12-inch single! This was whilst still at Scepter: 'The idea came from Tom Moulton, because he suggested that if we put the record on 12-inch we could spread the grooves and make it hotter [louder] for the club DJs. We were the first company to put it out for DJs. Salsoul put their first 12-inch record out at about the same time commercially – 'Ten percent' by Double Exposure. That's how it came about, due to the fact that you could spread the grooves and make it hotter than on 45 [seven-inch] records.'

Their first release and hit for West End was an album called – Sessomatto, which was actually a soundtrack to an Italian movie. This record was, according to Grandmaster Flash, one of the first records early hip hop DJs used to play and scratch with. Mel knew from the first time he heard rap that this would become a whole musical style of its own.

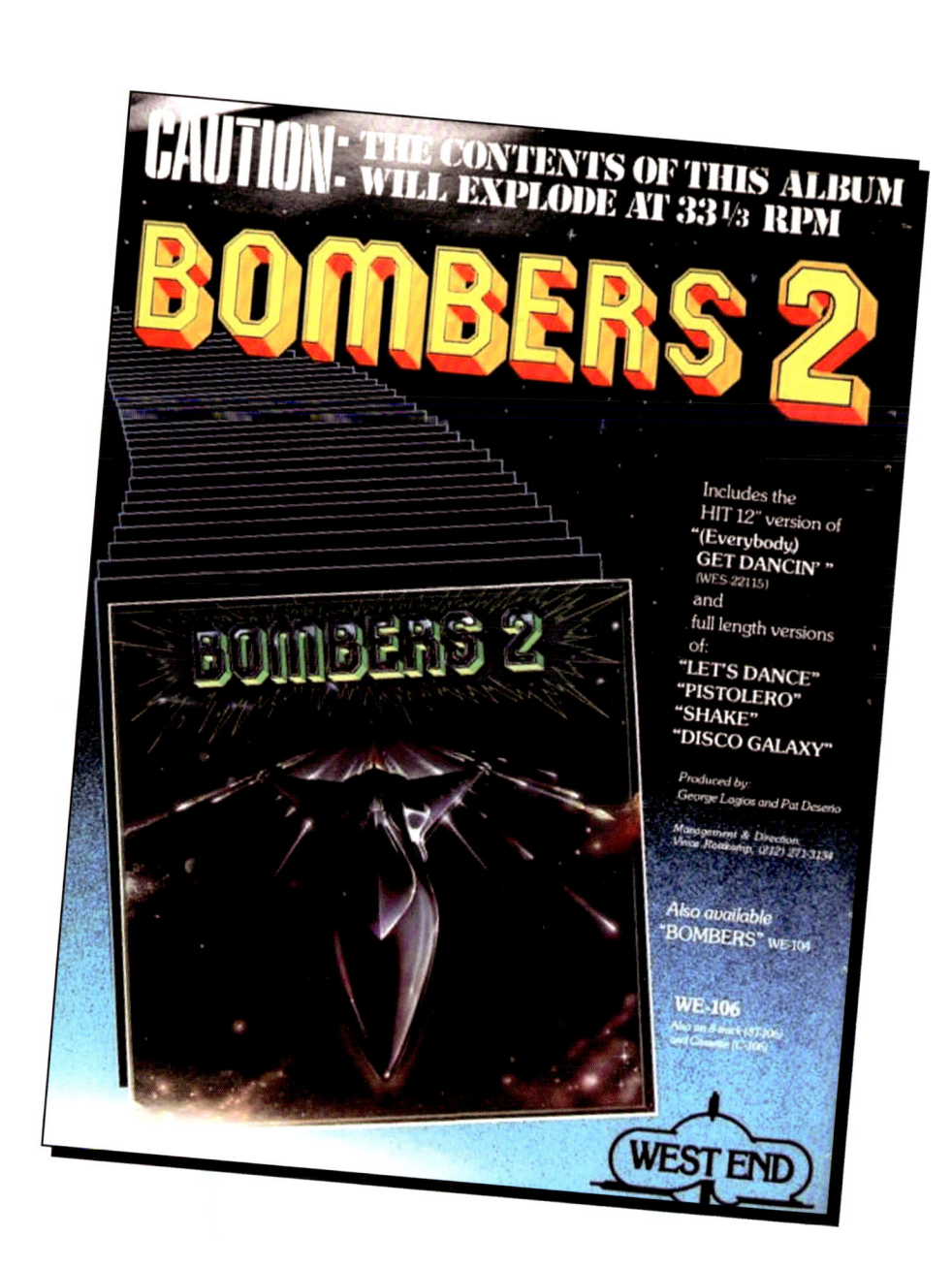

Mel Cheren 2004 Interview

West End was one of the hottest disco labels. What was it that made it so hot? Is there anything special you can think of?
'I think you have to be into the music and I have always had this love for music. I have always loved black music, R&B tunes with a good melody and lyrics and I have always loved to dance. I've always heard we had a special sound, but until today I still don't know what that was. If I liked a song we would put it out!'

We know you as one of the driving forces behind the disco genre, but did you really like disco or just consider it as a job?
'Did I like it!! That was the only reason I did it. I kept on putting it out because I used to go dancing. And 'til this day I still do.'

The reason I ask is because it seems that many people were in the business just to make money!
'Oh, that's what separates the men from the boys. I mean I did it because of a love for the music. I was very fortunate to get into the music business and I loved it. You can not do a good job if you don't have passion for what you do.'

West End had the same address as Studio 54, but the label was closer spiritually to another of the worlds most famous and legendary clubs - the Paradise Garage.
'Michael Brody [owner of the Garage] was my life partner, so the connection to the Garage was natural. I've got lots of memories of Larry Levan and the Garage that are very important to me. I really hope someone would like to make a movie and that for the movie would restore the Garage to its original condition. And then open it again with a diner in the bottom floor, which was never used before - like the Hard Rock Café or Planet Hollywood. And I really wish the profit should go to charity. Also, I've got the ashes of the late Larry Levan and I would like to have the urn with the ashes in the entrance of the Garage so the fans from all over would be able to see it.'

Which was West End's biggest hit?
'Hot Shot' by Karen Young. It sold over 800 000 copies and that's one of the biggest selling 12-inch singles in the history of disco. But these days Taana Gardner's 'Heartbeat' is even bigger since it has been sampled several times and most recently Ini Kamoze used it in 'Here Comes the Hot Stepper', which became a number one hit in many countries all over the world.'

But 'Heartbeat' was not an instant hit. Besides being a great song, it became a hit because of Larry Levan's love for this record. When he first played 'Heartbeat' at the Garage, this song's slow tempo was too slow for the audience in the club and the dancefloor was left empty. But Levan did not give up, playing the song several times a night and within a few weeks everyone was running to the floor instead of off the floor when it was played. This song also became the biggest selling record ever in the little record store just around the corner from the club - Vinyl Mania - which sold over 5000 (!) copies of the 12-inch single.

Other hits West End released include - just to mention a few — Loose Joints' 'Is It All Over My Face', NYC Peech Boys' 'Don't Make Me Wait', Mahogany's 'Ride On the Rhythm', Bombers' '(Everybody) Get Dancin' and Ednah Holt's 'Serious, Sirius Space Party'.

Both West End and Prelude Records were New York labels. Have you got any idea why New York labels released so many songs that are considered disco classics today? I mean many of the other bigger labels didn't release that many classics.
'Well, just because of that reason - we were small independent labels. The same way it is today. The small labels are the ones that are on the cutting edge, you know. When you're on the street and you know what's going on. And the major labels always copy the small labels.

And why in New York! Because that's where all excitement started. It wasn't in California - it was here in New York. All the excitement with the Garage, the Loft, the Gallery, Studio 54 and the Saint. Those were the clubs. Then things happened on in California, but at that period most record companies' offices were in New York. It wasn't until years later that lots of them moved to California.'

WE 103 / 1977

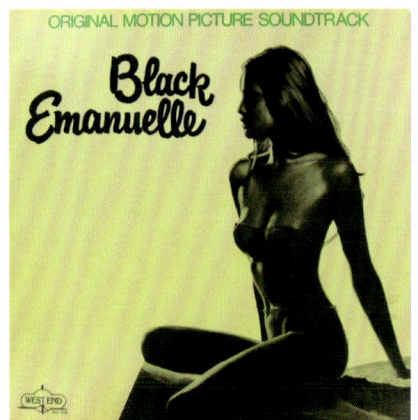

WE 100 / 1976

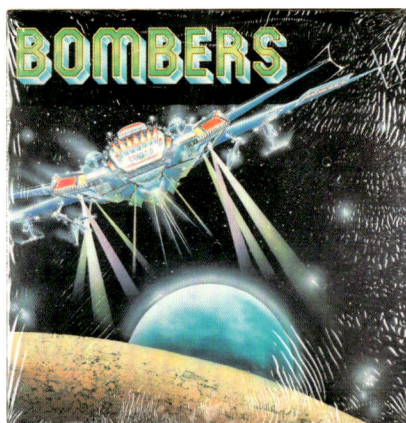

WE 104 / 1978

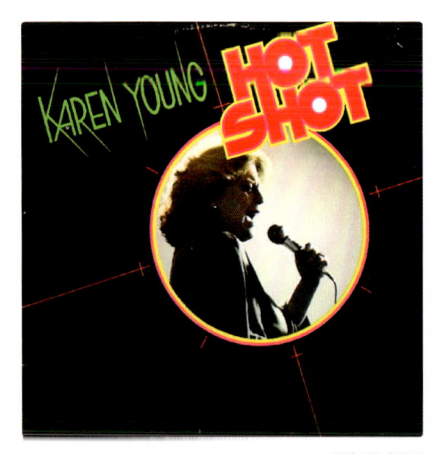

WE 105 / 1976

WE 107 / 1979

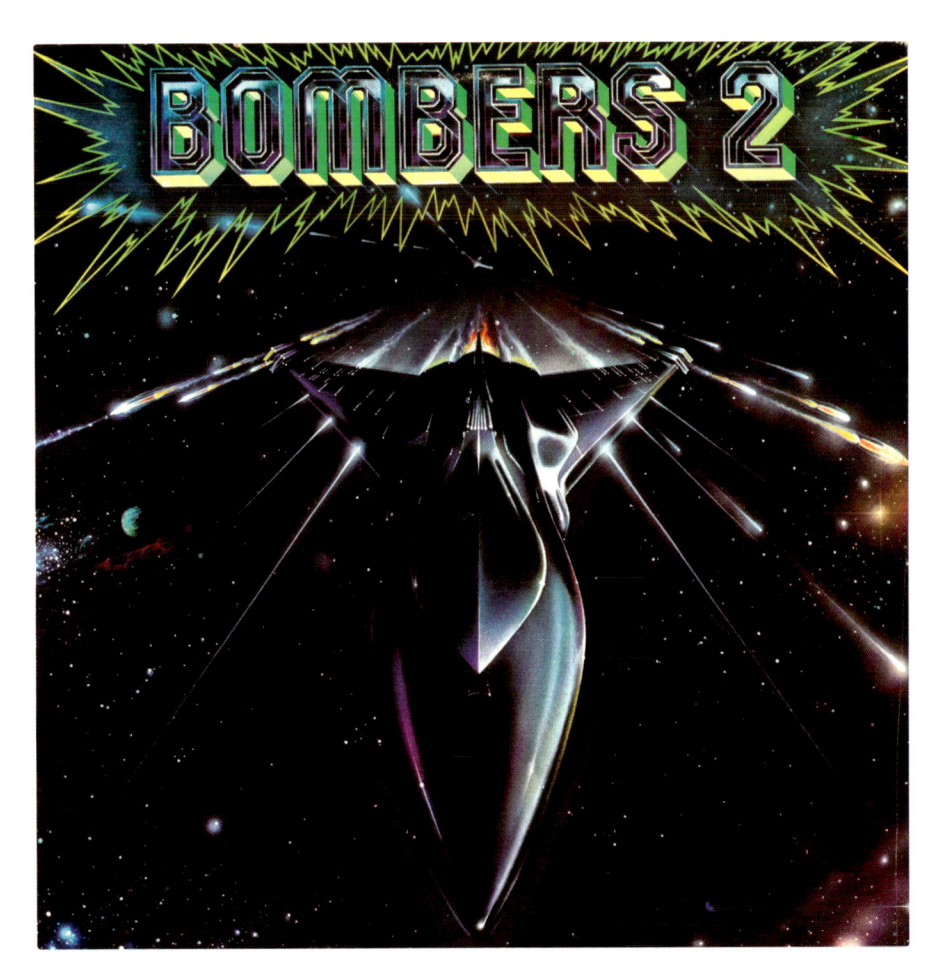

WE 106 / 1979

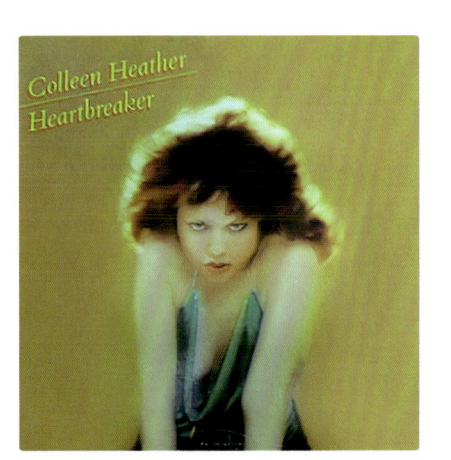

WE 108 / 1979

WE 109 / 1979

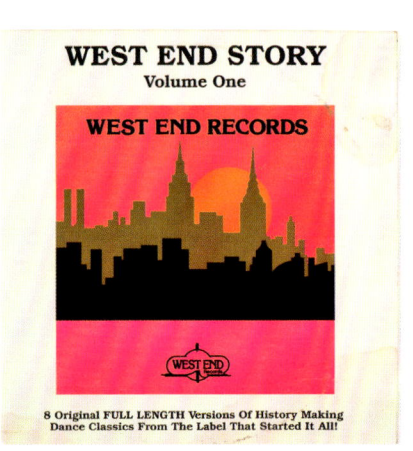

WES 110

240

Matrix numbers

WEST END

WE 100	Nico Fidenco	Original Motion Picture Soundtrack "Black Emanuelle"	1976
WE 101	Armando Trovaioli	Original Motion Picture Soundtrack "How Funny Can Sex Be?"	1976
WE 103	Michelle	Magic Love	1977
WE 104	Bombers	Bombers	1978
WE 105	Karen Young	Hot Shot	1978
WE 106	Bombers	Bombers 2	1979
WE 107	Taana Gardner	Taana Gardner	1979
WE 108	Colleen Heather	Heartbreaker	1979
WE 109	Various	Master Mix Medley By Tony Humphries	1979
WES 110	West end Story	Volume 1	

BOUNCE, ROCK, SKATE, ROLL

BL 754221

VAUGHAN MASON AND CREW

Brunswick RECORDS

Other Albums & 12 inches

Chapter 23
Roller Disco

Left: Vaughan Mason And Crew - Bounce, Rock, Skate, Roll / Brunswick 1980
Design: N R Ward Assoc. / Art Director: Carl Napoletano

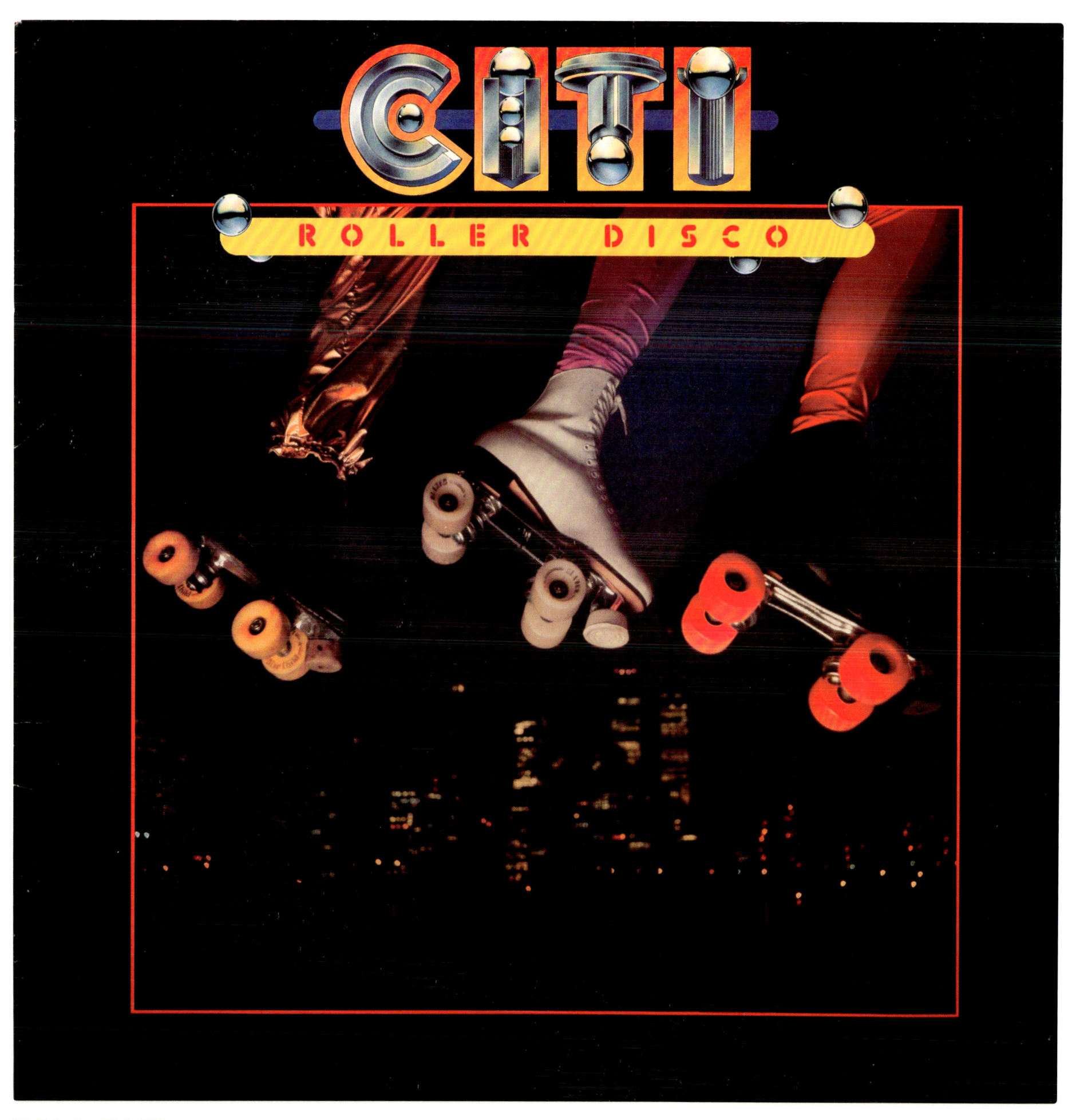

Citi - Roller Disco / Delite 1979
Design: Joe Kotleba / Photography: Greg Heisler

Lightning - Lightning / Casablanca 1979
Design: Murry Whiteman And Michael Kevin Lee, Gribbitt / Photography: Scott Hensel

Next page: Roller Dancing For Fun & Fitness / Gateway R7609, 1980

Roller Dancing for fun and fitness

Bonus instruction book inside with over 100 photos. If you can walk, you can skate—and roller dancing is simply moving on wheels to the musical beat. The illustrated instruction book teaches you the fundamentals, and the record provides the ideal music to develop your roller dancing style. The album-size instructions can be propped up for easy viewing, and you can practice indoors or outdoors on any smooth surface. The music selections begin with simple disco beats, then progress to more complex rhythms that will have you whirling on wheels in no time! And for the grand finale, there's a choreographed routine. Skating works wonders for your body. While you're having fun, you're burning 600 calories per hour, and as an aerobic exercise, skating ranks with running and swimming. According to Olympic team medical advisor Dr. Max Novich, "No other sport provides the agility with the fun element...you will be rewarded with a sound heart for a lifetime."

A product of Gemcom Inc.
P.O. Box 5087
F.D.R. Station
New York, NY 10022

© 1980 Gemcom Inc.

This product will work equally

Roller Dancing
for fun and fitness

GSLP 7609

GATEWAY RECORDS

Record and Book

DOLLARS and Sense

CO-ED'S GUIDE TO GETTING YOUR MONEY'S WORTH

BEST DEALS ON WHEELS

WHEELS
Hard, soft, or combination. Many are made of urethane. Note: Softer wheels are for outdoor skating; harder wheels for indoors. You can use outdoor urethane wheels indoors, but not the reverse.

BEARINGS
Small metal balls inside core of wheel. Loose ball bearings need constant cleaning and mean a noisier ride. Precision bearings rarely need cleaning and mean a quieter and smoother trip.

TOE STOPS
Protect toe of boot and rink floor from scratches. Not absolutely necessary.

TRUCK
Available in single, double, or triple action. More "action" means more maneuverability and shock absorption.

A skate-buying guide that's sure to get you rolling!

If you're into roller skating ask yourself a few questions be-

PREASSEMBLED OUTDOOR/INDOOR OUTFITS UP TO $25
Boot skates: vinyl uppers • composition rubber sole • steel plate • loose ball bearings • single action trucks • urethane wheels • toe stops (available sizes may be only up to 8).

$75 TO $150
Boot skates: top-grain leather or suede uppers • leather lining • firmer ankle support • com-

double action trucks • urethane wheel • toe stops.
Sneaker skates: low-cut suede and leather or nylon uppers • other features same as above.
Clamp-on skates: adjustable steel frame • precision bearings • high rebound urethane wheels • leather ankle straps.

$20 to $170 • Bearings: $10 to $50 • Wheels (set of eight): $10 to $100 • Toe stops: $3 to $10.

OTHER TIPS FOR A GOOD FIT
• Buy your regular shoe size and width • Wear thin cotton socks • Make sure your heel fits firmly in the boot. When laced, they should feel snug but not too tight. • Talk to other skaters about skate features and your skating needs. Before you buy, visit skates a few times to see what you like

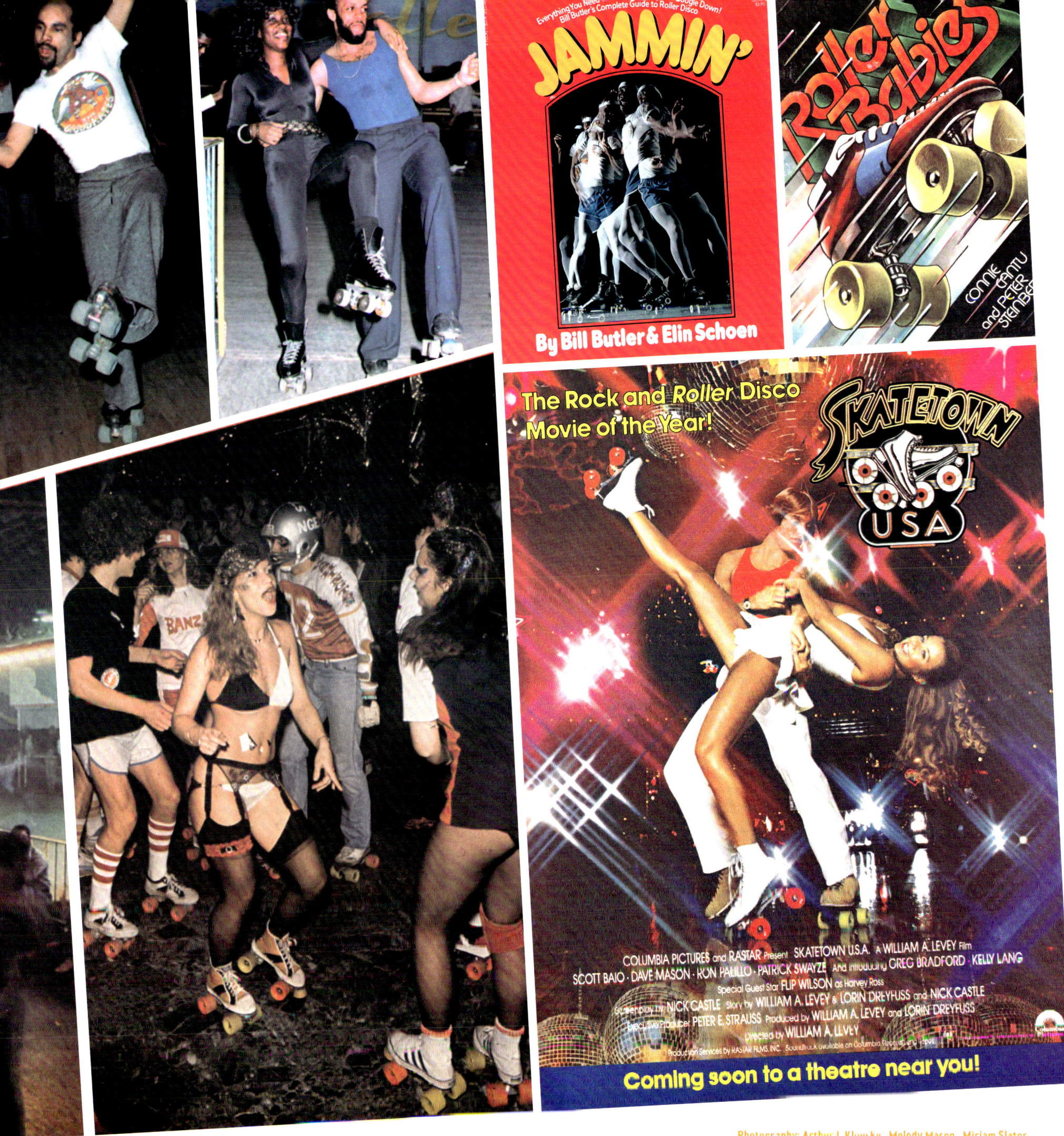

Photography: Arthur J. Klonsky, Melody Mason, Miriam Slater.

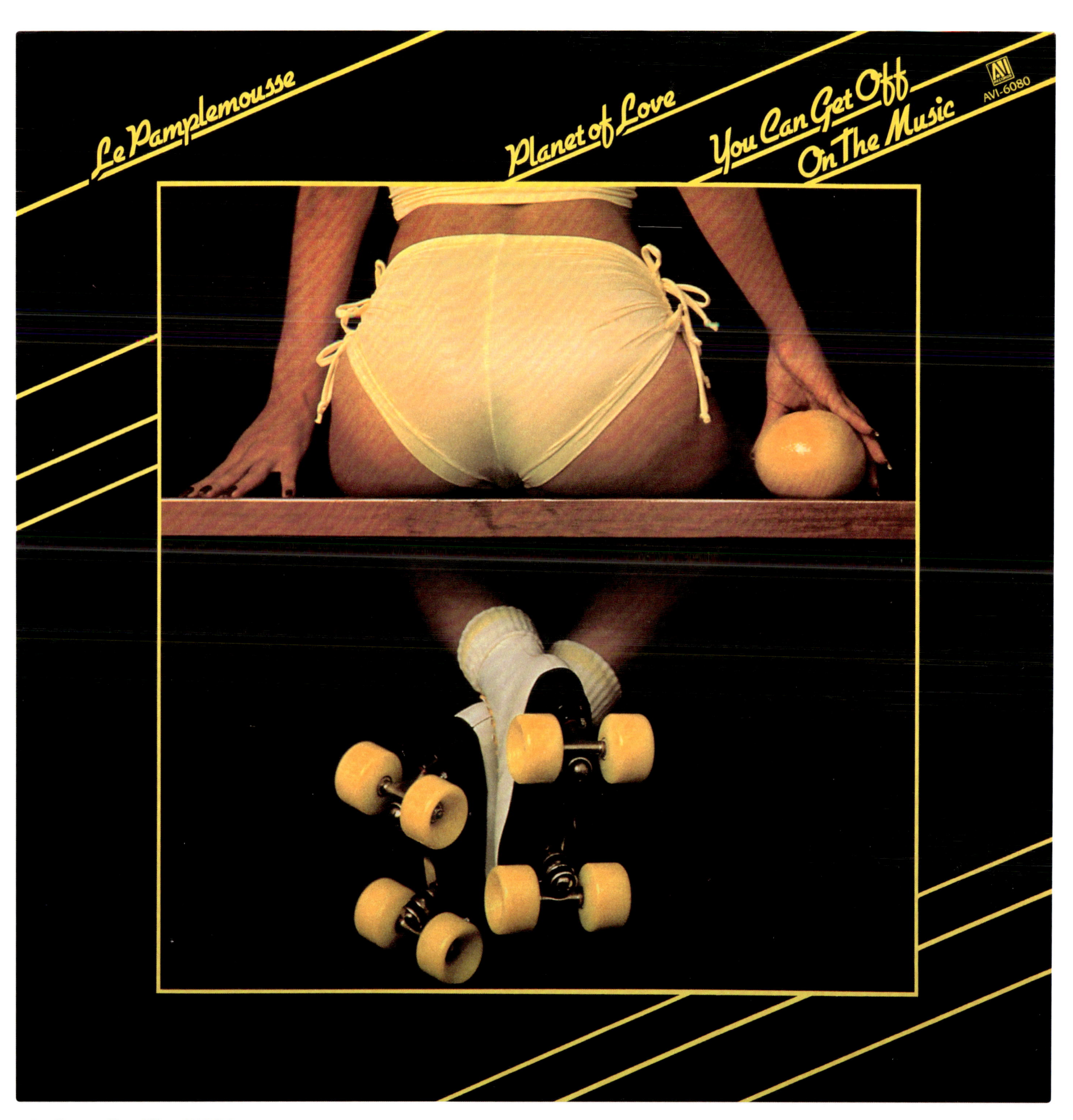

Le Pamplemousse Planet Of Love / AVI 1979
Design: The Committee / Photography: James Mares

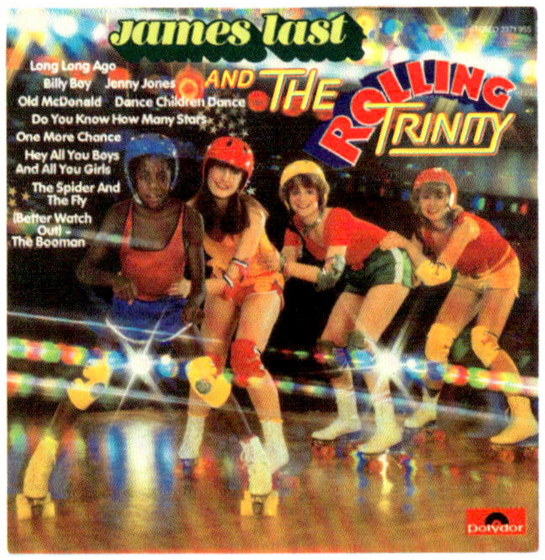

James Last and The Rolling Trinity Polydor / 1979	Chailo-Let's Roller Skate Chailo Records	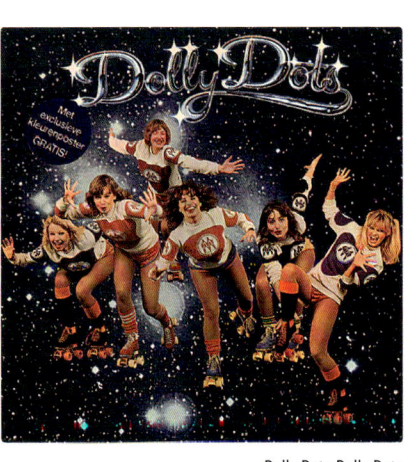 Dolly Dots-Dolly Dots WEA / 1979	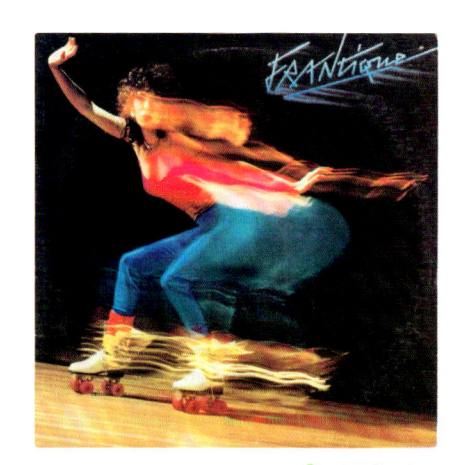 Frantique-Frantique PIR / 1979
Rock 'N Roller Disco-Sampler Ronco / 1979	 Roller Boogie Polydor / 1979	Carte Blance-Get Up Your Feet PYE / 1979	Grand Circuit-Roller Skate Symphony Disques Yona / 1979
King's Row-Rock +Roller Skates PPL / 1980	Difference-High Fly Emergency / 1979	 Let's Roller-Sampler Som Livre / 1981	Roundtree-Roller Disco Island / 1979
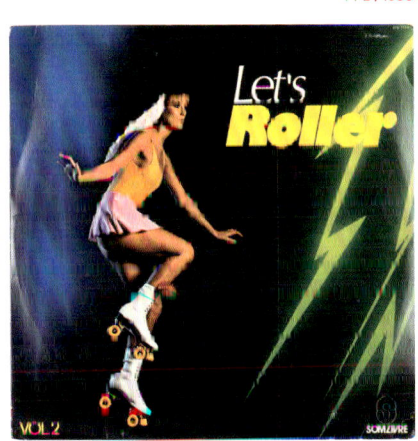 Let's Roller-Vol 2 Som Livre / 1981	Vin Zee-Funky Be Bop Full Time / 1979	Who's Who-Roll Jacky Roll Philips / 1980	Martin Ford-Smoovin Mountain / 1976

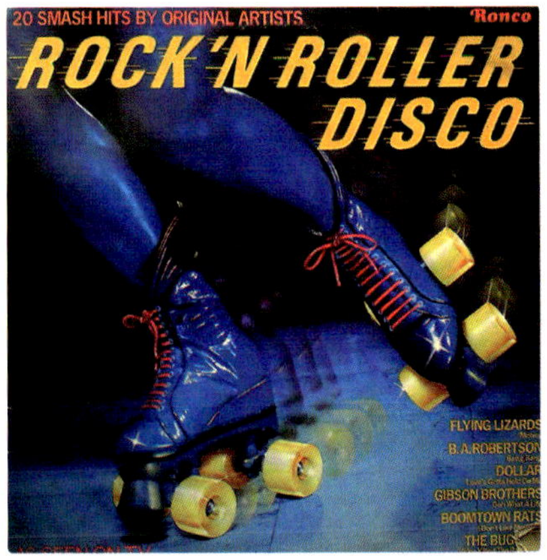

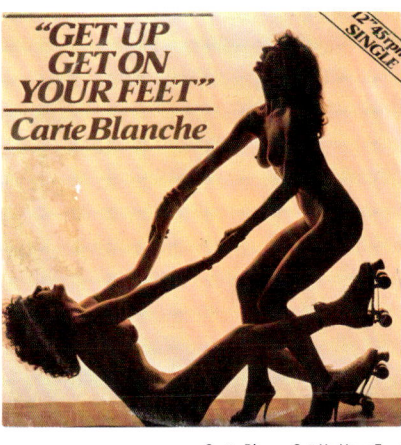

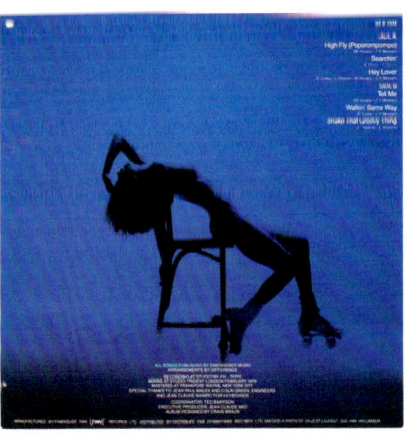

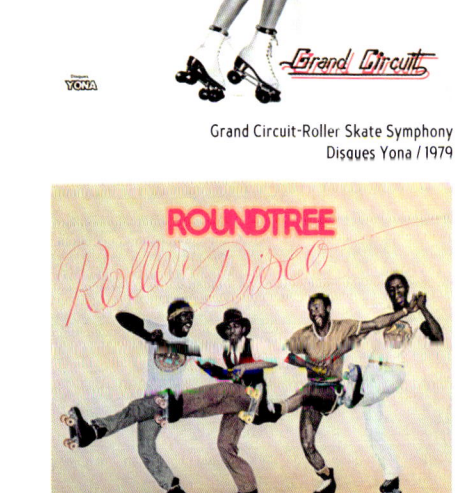

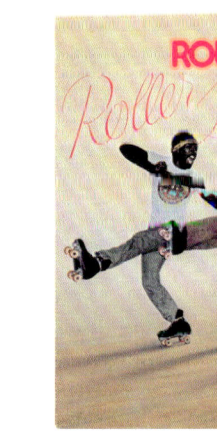

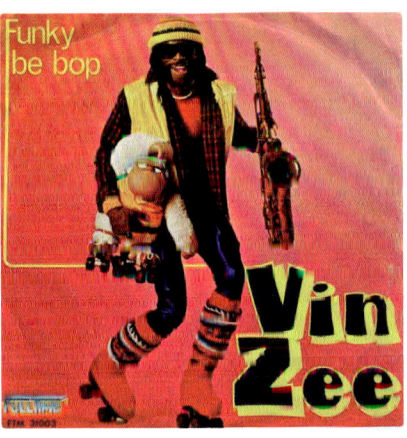

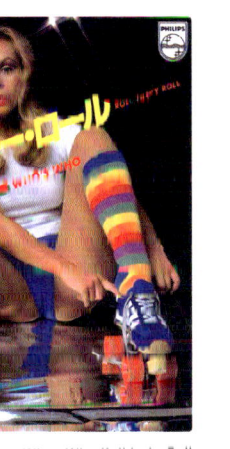

251

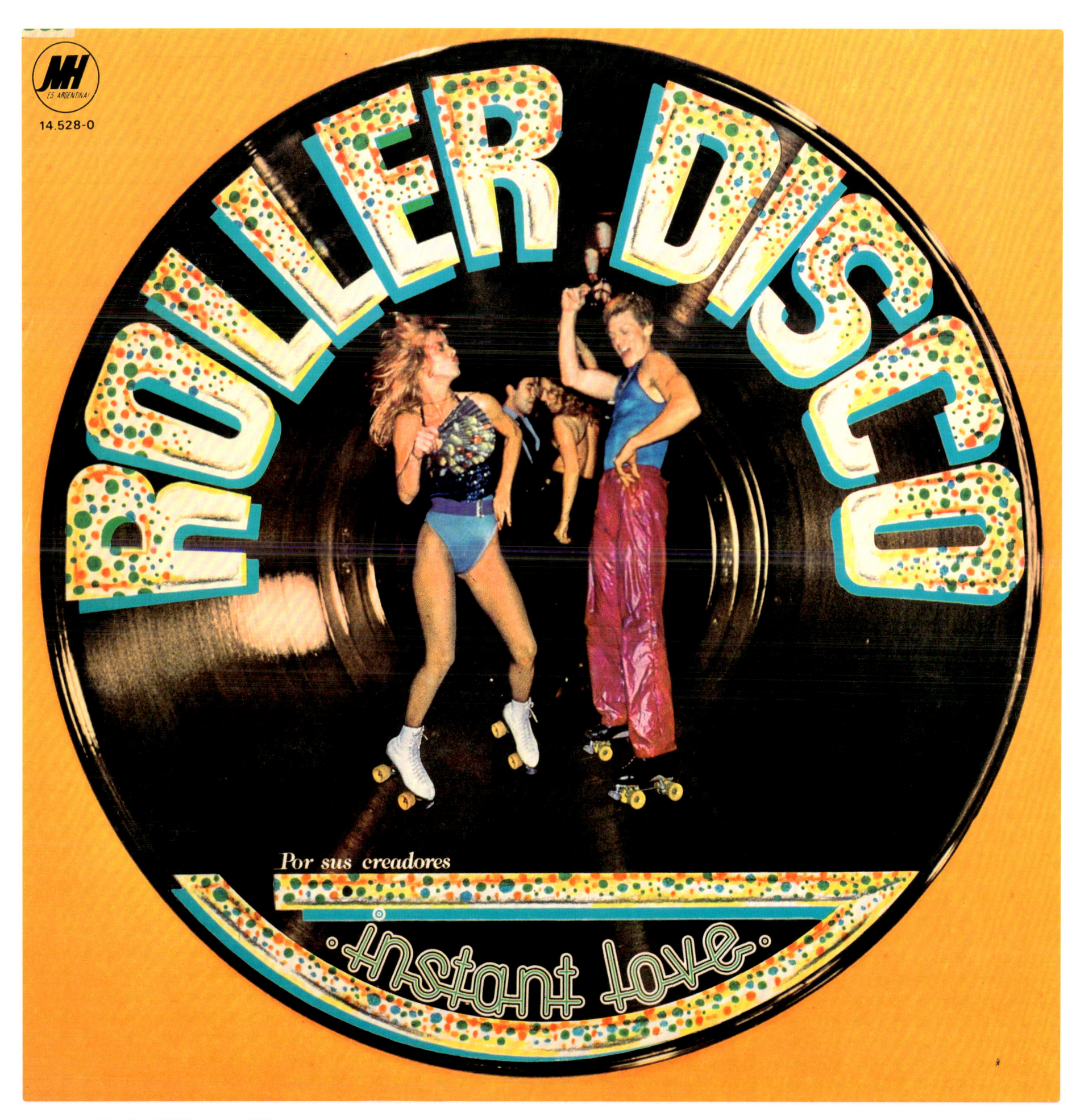

Instant Love - Roller Disco / MH ES Argentina 1980

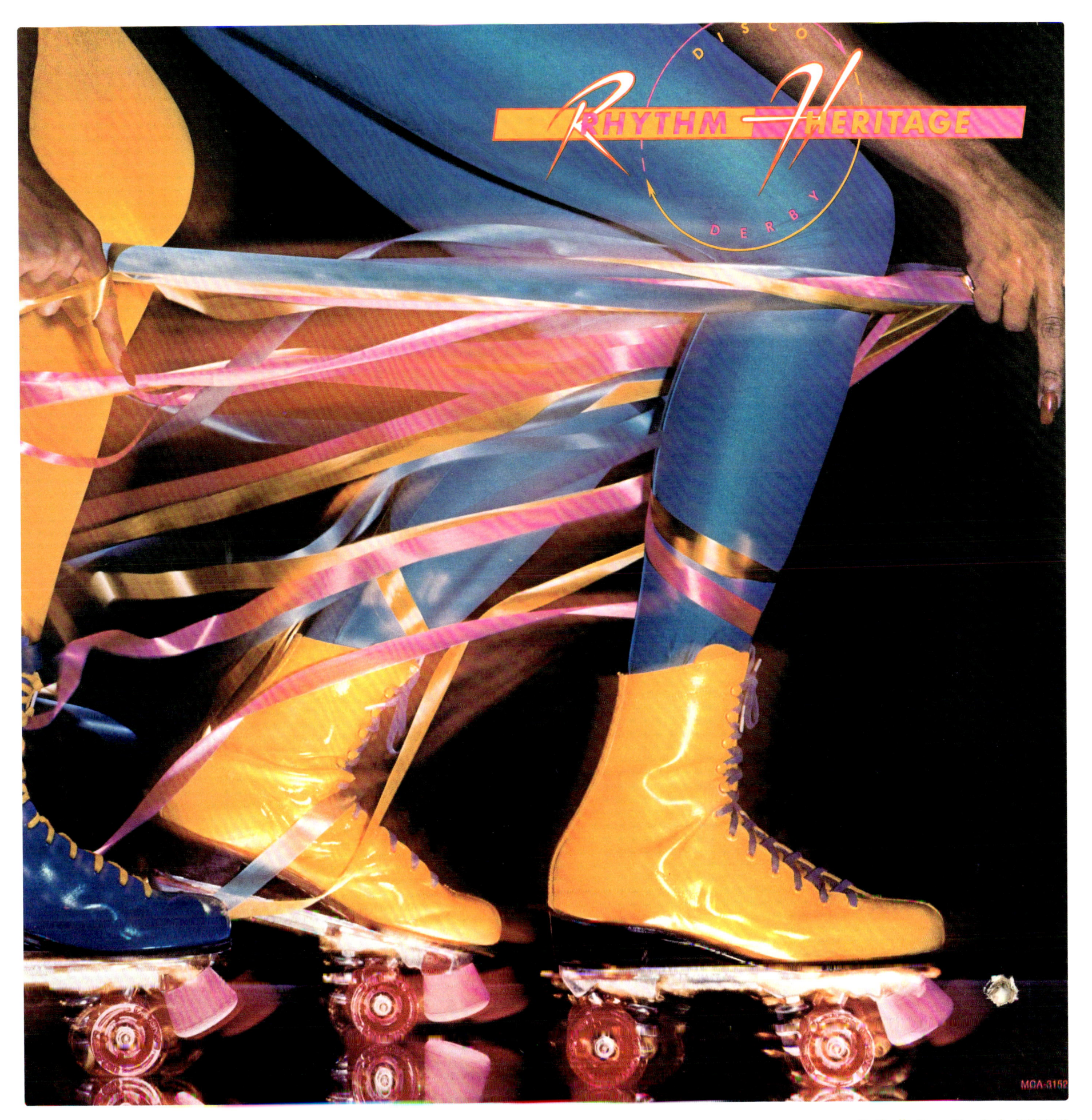

Rhythm Heritage – Disco Derby / MCA 1979

AR 569

DISCO and SOUL DANCES

FROM "THE HUSTLE" ON

- The Hustle
- Bus Stop
- Bump
- Wiggle
- Spanish Hustle
- B.T./Jaws
- Old Man/Bus Stop Shuffle
- Roller Coaster

for upper elementary through adult

by Rosemary "Red" Hallum

EDUCATIONAL ACTIVITIES, INC.
Freeport, N.Y. 11520

Other Albums & 12 inches

Chapter 24
Disco Dance Instructions

Left: Rosemary Hallum - Disco And Soul Dances / Educational Activities 1976
Design: Carol Squicci / Photography: Chuck Willis, Photo Craft Studios

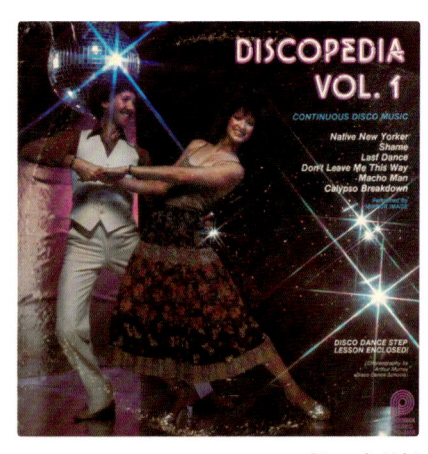

Discopedia Vol. 1
Pickwick / 1979

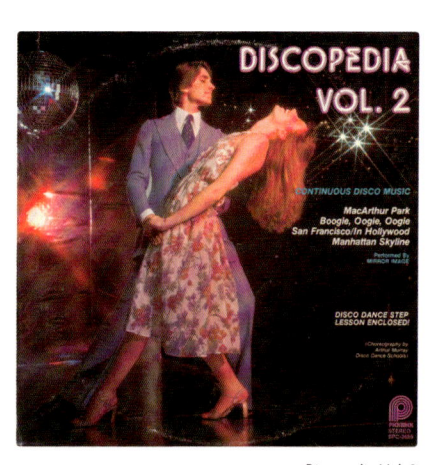

Discopedia Vol. 2
Pickwick / 1979

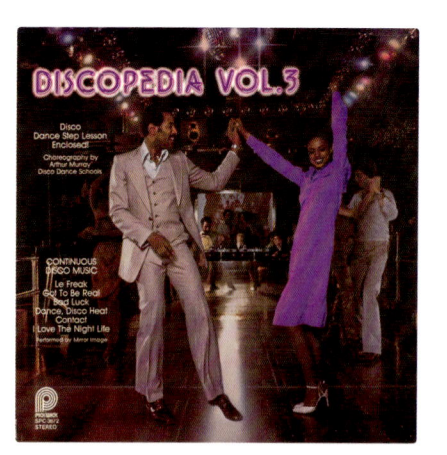

JDiscopedia Vol. 3
Pickwick / 1979

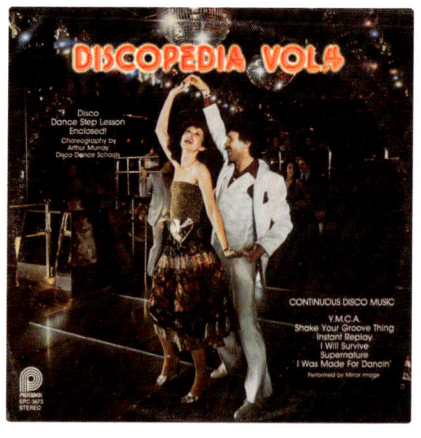

JDiscopedia Vol. 4
Pickwick / 1979

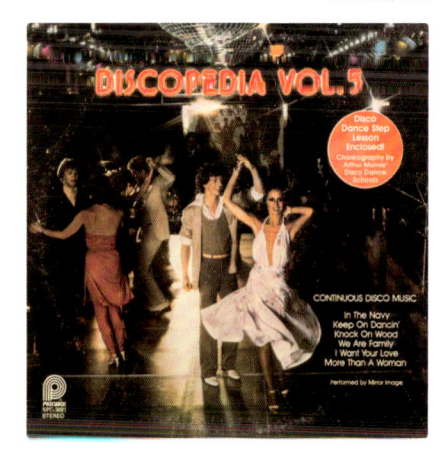

Discopedia Vol. 5
Pickwick / 1979

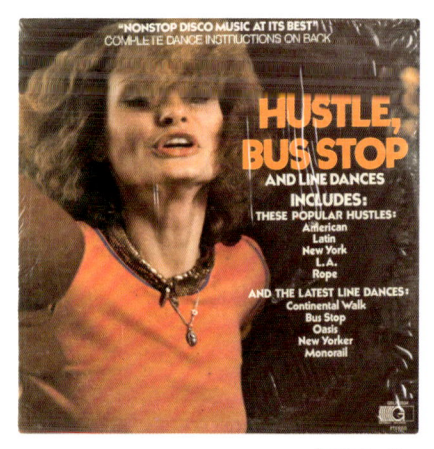

Hustle Bus Stop
Gateway Records

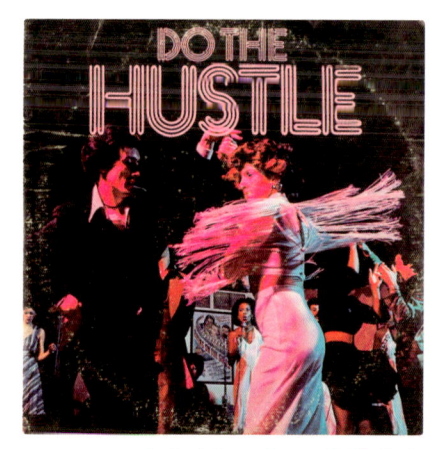

The Hustle Factory Presents: Do The Hustle
Realm Records / 1976

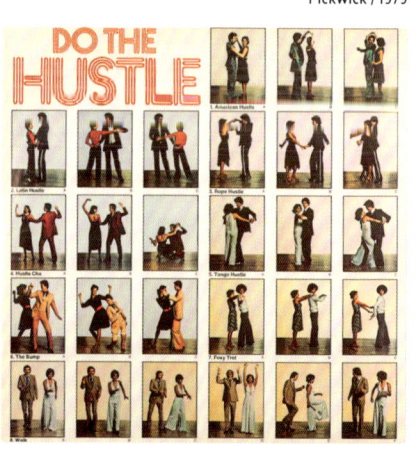

The Hustle Factory Presents: Do The Hustle
Realm Records / 1976

New York-Latin-Rope-Hustle Lessons
Karosel / 1978

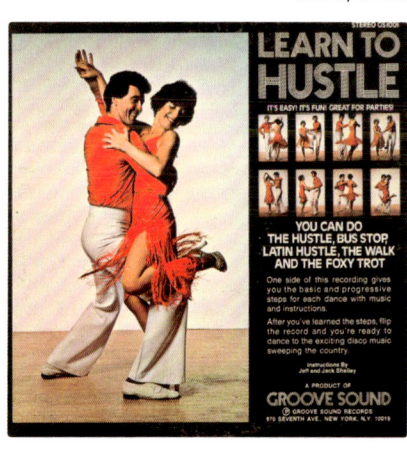

Learn To Hustle
Groove Sound / 1976

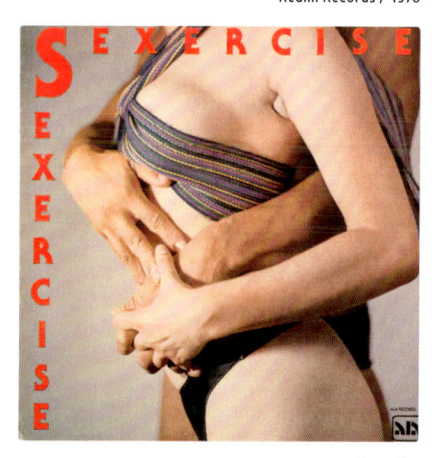

Sexersise
Ala / 1982

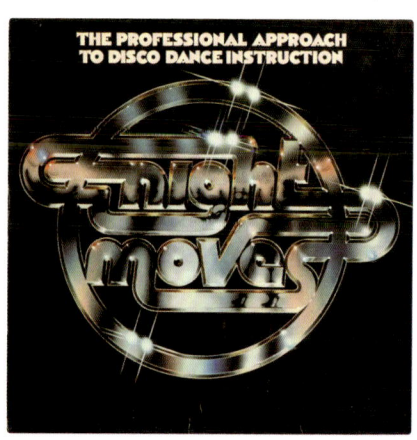

Night Moves-The Professional Approach To Disco Dance
K-Tell / 1979

Steppin' Out
Golden Egg Records

Popmobility-Sampler
Bond Clarkson Russel / 1977

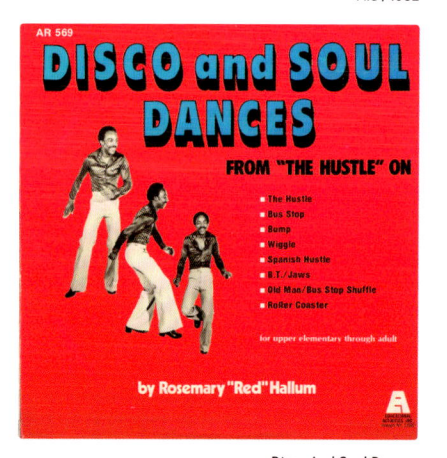

Disco And Soul Dances
Activitiy Records / 1976

Disco Dancin
Activitiy Records / 1978

256

Shiva - 20 Minute Workout (A Ron Harris Presentation) / Ronco 1983

DO THE HUSTLE

1. American Hustle — A, B, C
2. Latin Hustle — A, B, C
3. Rope Hustle — A, B, C
4. Hustle Cha — A, B, C
5. Tango Hustle — A, B, C
6. The Bump — A, B, C
7. Foxy Trot — A, B, C
8. Walk — A, B, C, D, E, F

Do The Hustle / Design: Harry W. Fass / Photography: Al Freni / Realm 1979

STEREO GS 1001

LEARN TO HUSTLE

IT'S EASY! IT'S FUN! GREAT FOR PARTIES!

YOU CAN DO THE HUSTLE, BUS STOP, LATIN HUSTLE, THE WALK AND THE FOXY TROT

One side of this recording gives you the basic and progressive steps for each dance with music and instructions.

After you've learned the steps, flip the record and you're ready to dance to the exciting disco music sweeping the country.

Instructions By Jeff and Jack Shelley

A PRODUCT OF

GROOVE SOUND

Ⓟ GROOVE SOUND RECORDS
870 SEVENTH AVE., NEW YORK, N.Y. 10019

Learn To Hustle / Groove Sound 1976
Photography: Dick Kranzler

SUPER DISCO D'OR
VOL 2

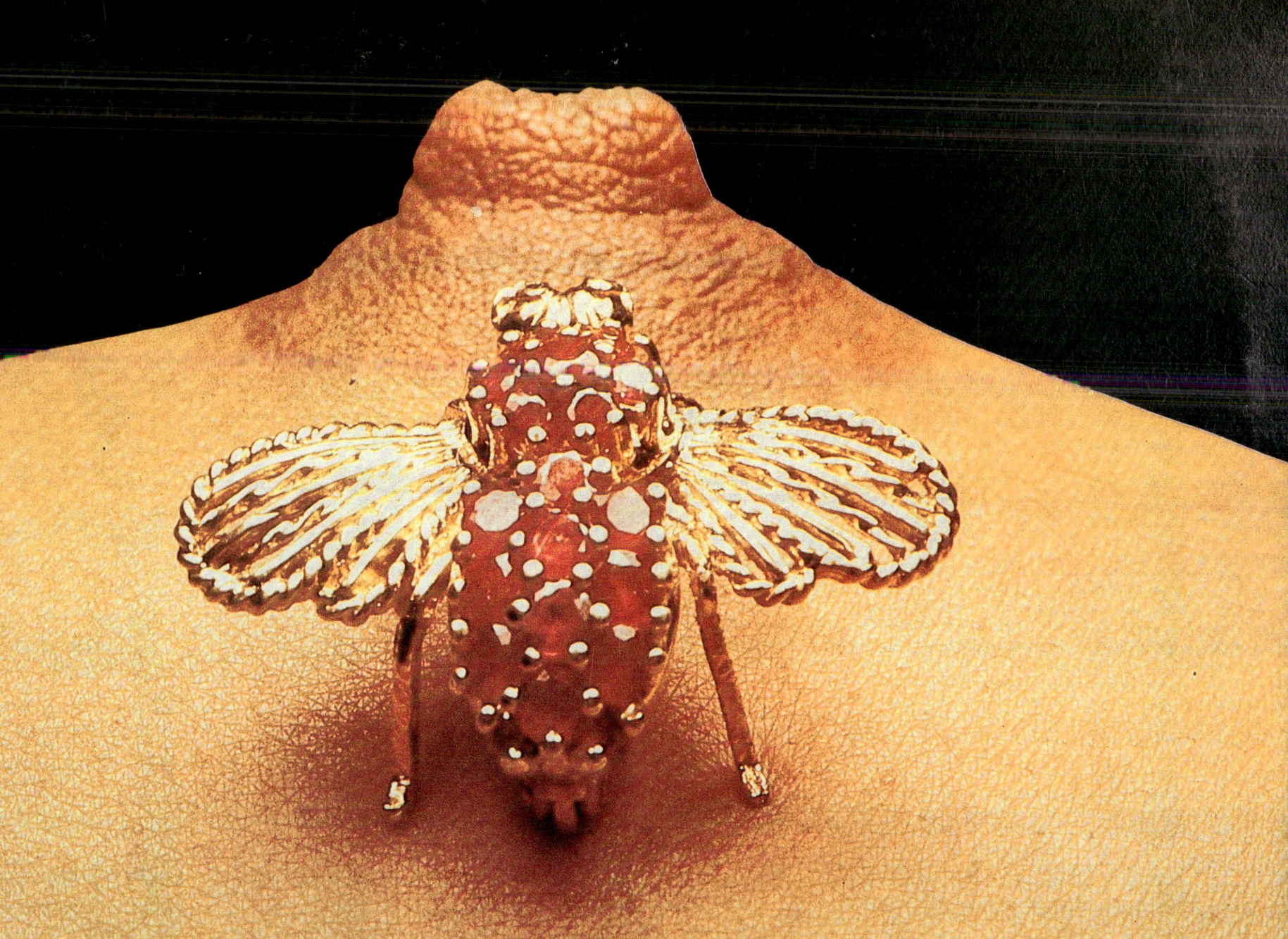

ibach RECORDS

Chapter 25
Disco Samplers

Other Albums & 12 inches

Left: Various - Super Disco D'or Vol. 2 / Ibach 1979
Photo: Image Bank

Bumper 2 Bumper Calibre / 1982	Bumper 2 Bumper-Volume 2 Calibre / 1983	Danceteria SPQR / 1983	Skate Dance SMI / 1979
Disco Party-Four Record Set Motown / 1979	Non Stop Disco Den Production	Philadelphia Classics Philadelphia International / 1977	Steppin' Out-Disco's Greatest Hits Polydor / 1978
Extasy Lotus records / 1979	Super Disco D'or-Vol.1 Ibach	Super Disco D'or-Vol.2 Ibach	Direct Disco-Featuring Gino Dentie And The Family Crystal Clear Records / 1976
Disco Gold-Special Disco Mixes Scepter / 1975	The Salsoul Invention-Salsoul Explosion Musidisc	Dance Paarrrty Contempo / 1977	James Last and The Rolling Trinity Polydor / 1979

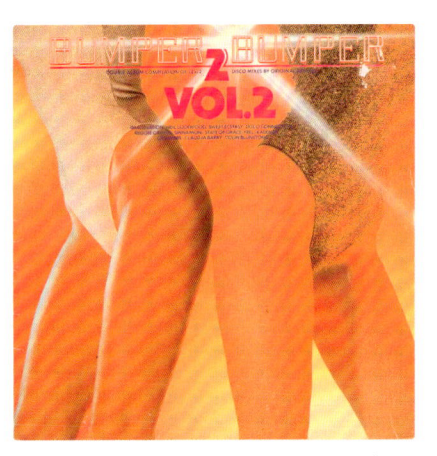

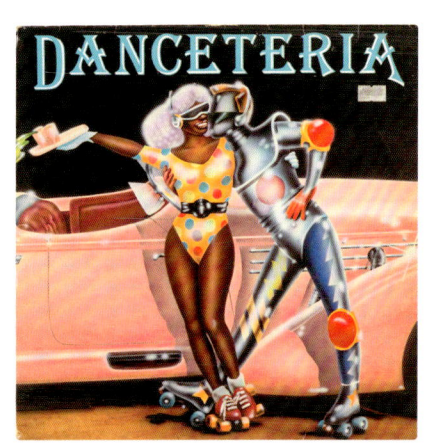

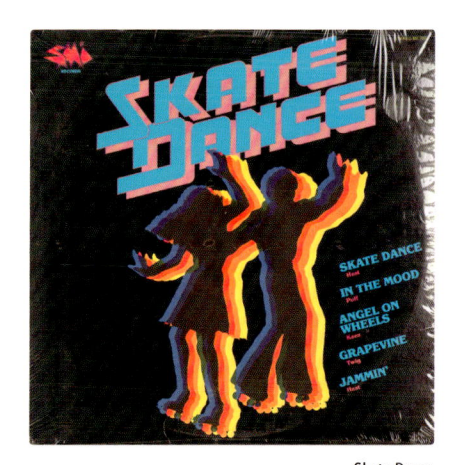

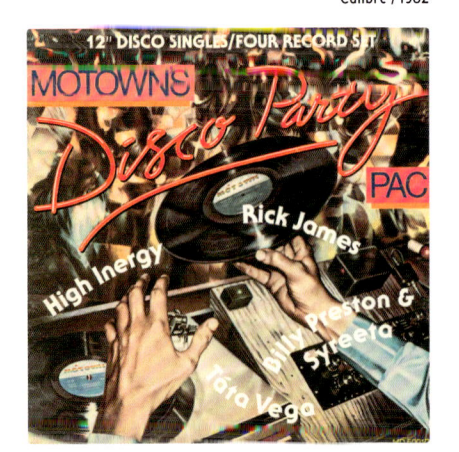

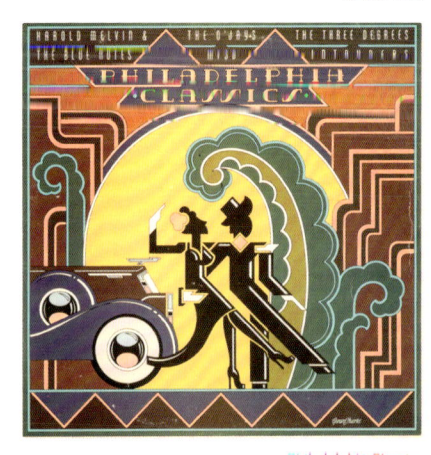

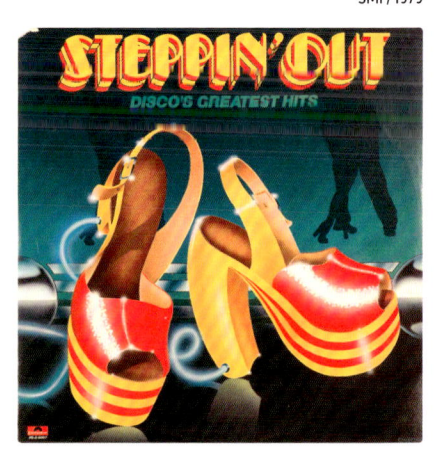

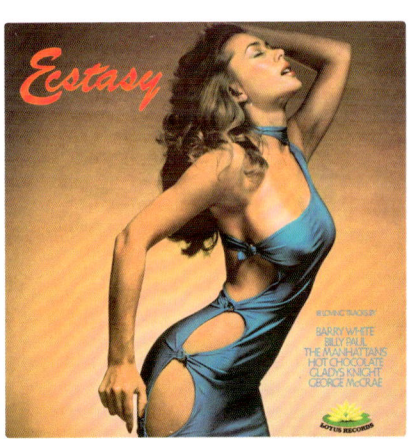

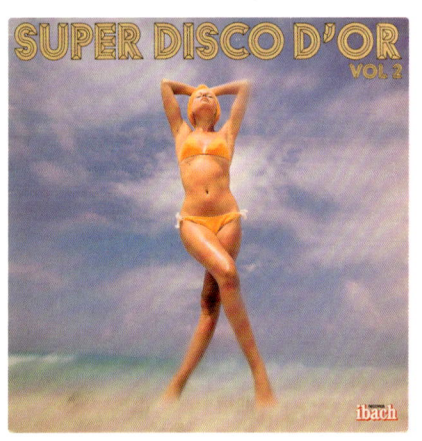

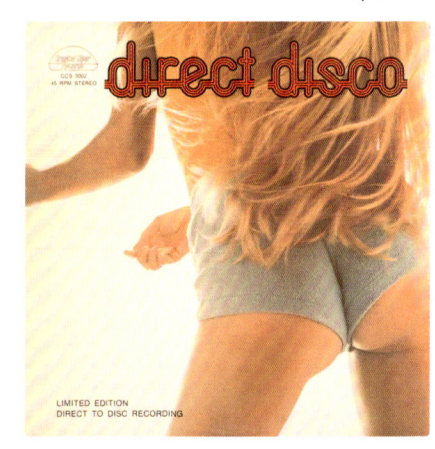

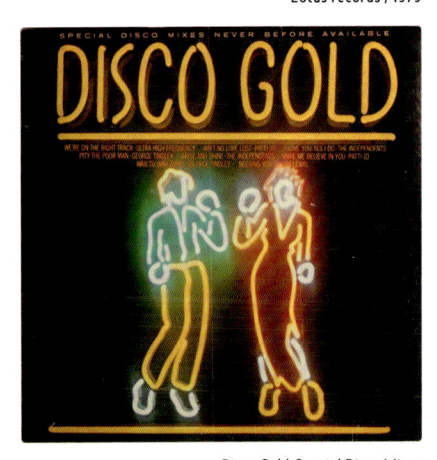

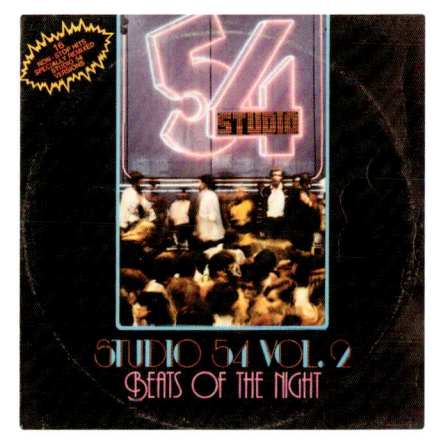

262

Various - Disco Express Vol. 2 / RCA 1976

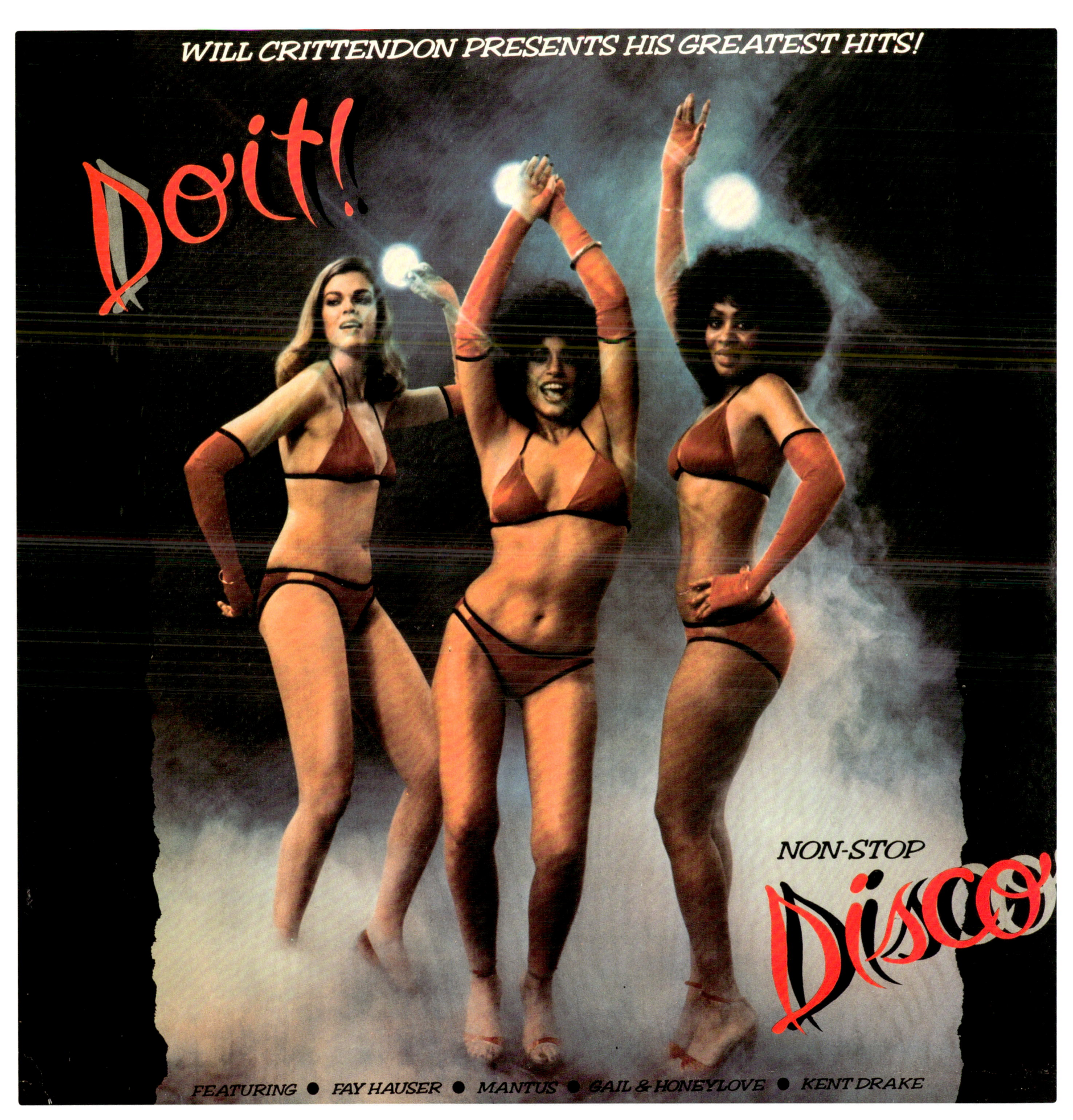

Will Crittendon Presents: Do It Non Stop Disco / SMI 1979
Photography: Hugh Bell / Album Design, Lettering, Art Director: Ron Warwell / Cover Concept: Will Crittendon & Ron Warwell

Down Right Disco - Hot Stuff And The Bandits / Splash 1979

FULLTIME *Spring*

SIDE ONE

Show You my Love	GOLDIE ALEXANDER
Rock your World	WEEKS AND CO.
I Wanna Dance	KAT MANDU
Make your Body Move	J.R. FUNK

SIDE TWO

Stay (I need your Love)	MATRIX
I'm so Glad	SELECTION
Spirit at the End	SELECTION
Bite the Apple	RAINBOW TEAM
Take me Up	MATRIX
Good Lovin'	J.R. FUNK

Mixed by Jonathan (Jan Edouard Philippe) - Studio Jonathan 67 (MILANO)
Photo by Lionel Pasquon - Art Direction: Novella Massaro - Cover Concept & Artwork: Michelangelo Farina
Fulltime Bunny: Miss Gwen Audrey Antti

Fulltime - Spring / Full Time 1982
Art Direction: Novella Massaro / Photography: Lionel Pasquon / Cover Concept & Artwork: Michelangelo Farina

CKLM 1570-Disco Mix
LM

Discoh '82
CBS / 1982

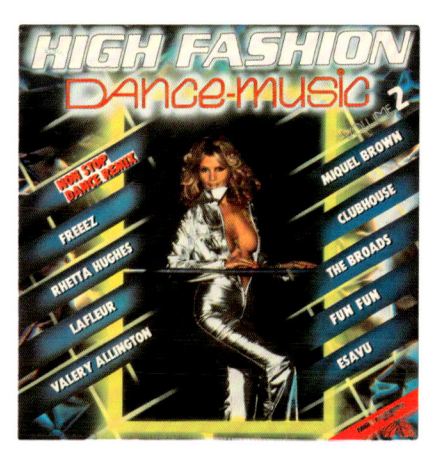

High Fashion Dance Music Volume 2
Dureco / 1983

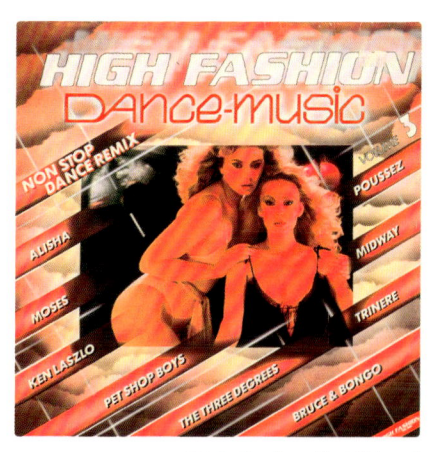

High Fashion Dance Music Volume 3
Dureco / 1986

Disco Cross
F1 Team / 1981

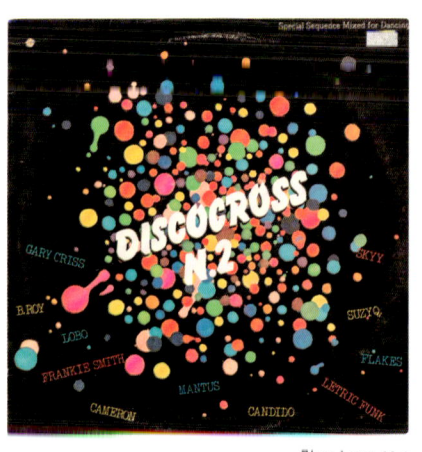

Disco Cross-no.2
F1 Team / 1981

Disco Cross-no.3
F1 Team / 1982

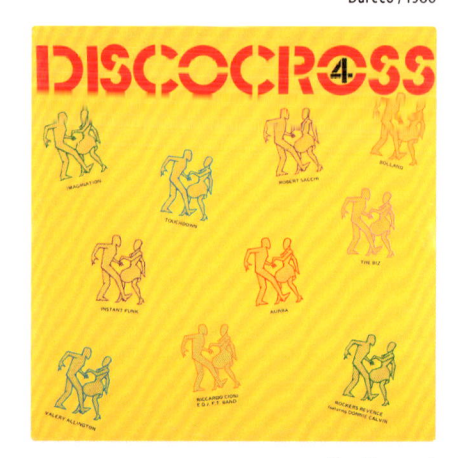

Disco Cross-no.4
F1 Team / 1982

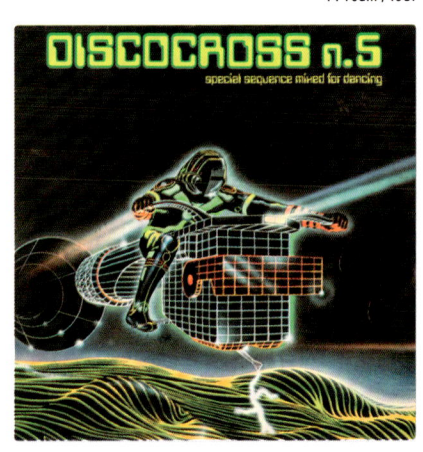

Disco Cross-no.5
F1 Team / 1983

Wrap 'Em Up -Sounds That Spread The Joy Around
Arista / 1984

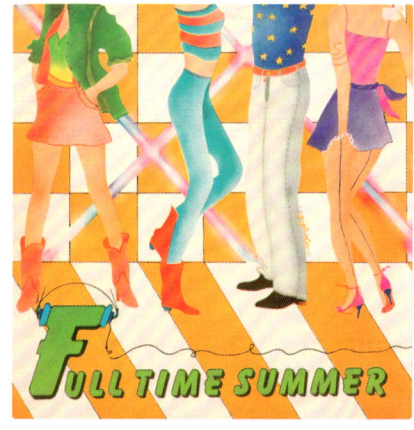

Full Time Summer
Full Time / 1981

Discotheque Aquarius

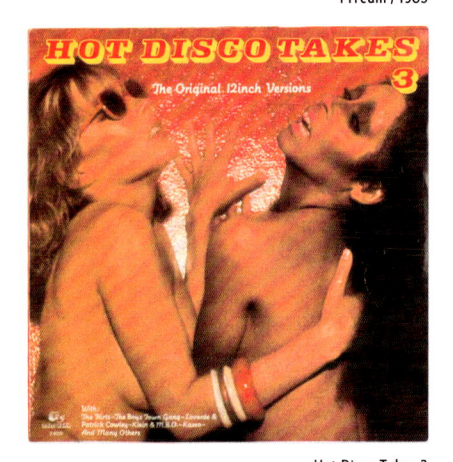

Hot Disco Takes 3
Ramshorn / 1983

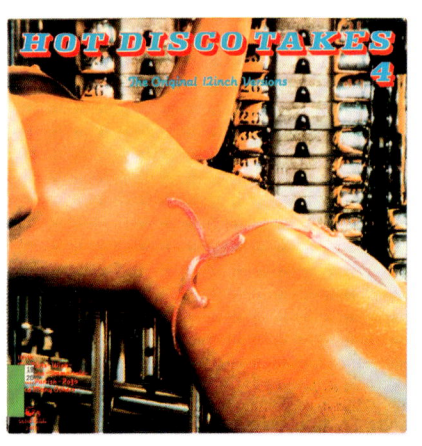

Hot Disco Takes 4
Ramshorn / 1983

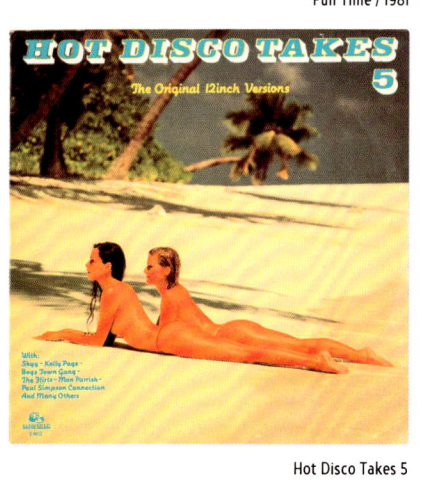

Hot Disco Takes 5
Ramshorn / 1983

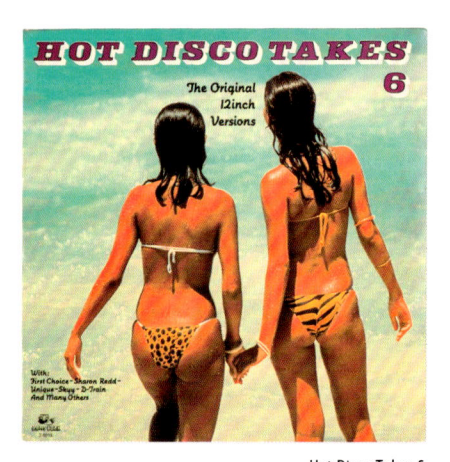

Hot Disco Takes 6
Ramshorn / 1984

Various - High Fashion Dance Music (Non Stop Dance Remix) / Dureco 1983
Cover design: Bart Falkman / Photography: Monno Rienks

Various – Disco Explosion Vol.2 / RCA 1977
Photography: Keystone Nemes

The Disco Express - Funky Stuff (Get Down Tonight) / Sunset 1976

Boogie People

Other Albums

Chapter 26
Atlantic, Motown and other labels

Nearly all of the record labels which feature at the start of this book came into existence in the disco era (an exception is Vanguard Records which was originally a folk label). Like any new emerging style of music, disco was rarely at first understood by the established record companies and in some ways the genre was a reaction against everything that preceded it.

Of the major record companies Atlantic Records and Motown, both powerhouse labels of black music in the 1960s, were able to understand the transition of funk and soul music into disco, a link that many, many people failed to understand at the time, and thus maintain their position through the 1970s and into the 1980s. Atlantic Records particularly had huge commercial successes with acts like Chic, The Trammps and Sister Sledge. Columbia Records was another major label that was able to ride on the disco train through its association with Philadelphia International Records (see the first section of this book).

In the main though disco music launched a multitude of independent labels, from like-minded individuals and entrepeneurs with enough passion and intelligence to understand this new art form.

Left: Boogie People - Boogie People / Magnum 1979
Design: Heather Brown / Photography: Ari Giverts

The Vast Majority - Move It! / D & M SOUND 1976
Design: Mick Wells

The Vast Majority - Mindblowers! / D & M Sound 1976
Design: Mick Wells / Photography: Ted Ward-Hart

The Trammps - Disco Inferno / Atlantic 1976
Art Direction: Abie Sussman, Bob Defrin / Illustration: Charles White III

ATLANTIC

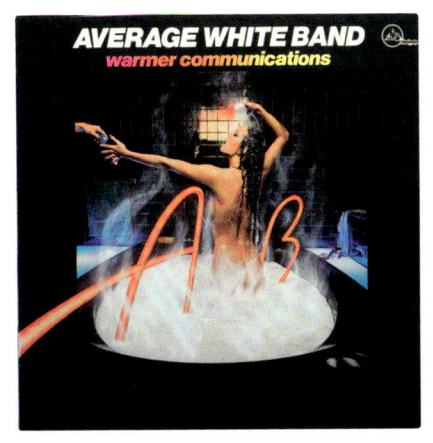

Average White Band-Warmer Communications
Atlantic / 1978

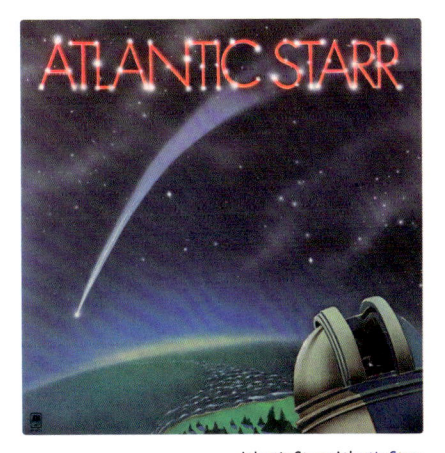

Atlantic Starr-Atlantic Starr
Atlantic / 1978

Blue Magic-Mystic Dragons
Atlantic / 1976

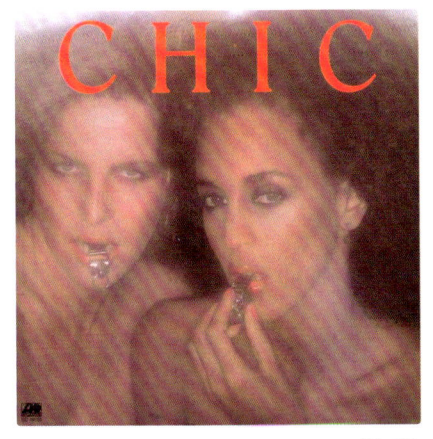

Chic-Chic
Atlantic / 1977

Chic-C'est Chic
Atlantic / 1978

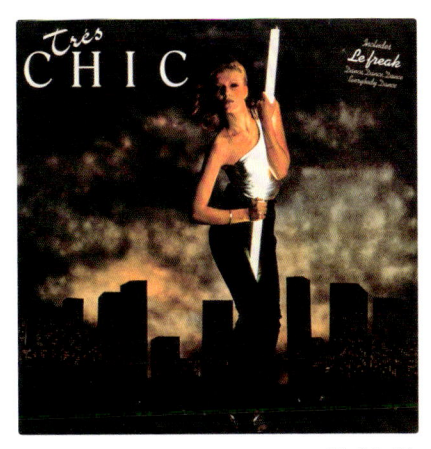

Chic-Trés Chic
Atlantic / 1979

Chic-Risqué
Atlantic / 1979

Chic-Greatest Hits
Atlantic / 1979

Chic-Real People
Atlantic / 1980

Chic-Take It Off
Atlantic / 1981

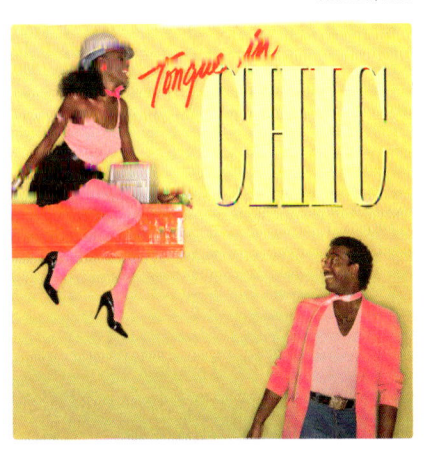

Chic-Tongue In
Atlantic / 1982

Chic-Believer
Atlantic / 1983

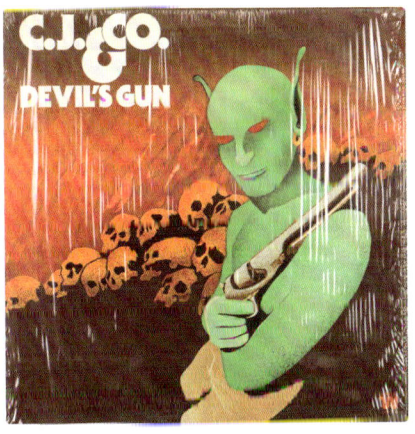

C.J.& Co-Devil's Gun
Westbound / 1977

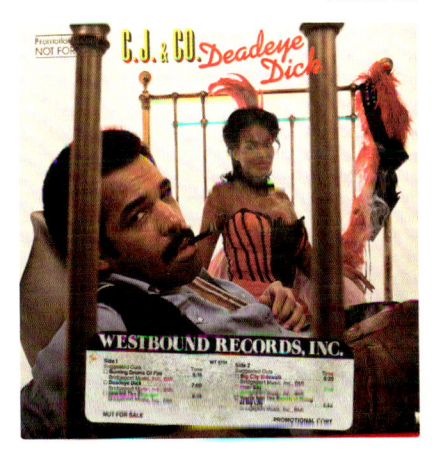

C.J.& Co-Deadeye Dick
Westbound / 1978

Change-The Glow Of Love
Atlantic / 1980

The Jimmy Castor Bunch-Butt Of Course Atlantic / 1975	Dennis Coffey-Finger Licking Good Westbound / 1975	Dennis Coffey-Back Home Westbound / 1977	The Dennis Coffey Band-A Sweet Taste Of Sun Westbound / 1978
Detroit Emeralds-Feel The Need Westbound / 1977	Detroit Emeralds-Let's Get Together Westbound / 1978	King Errisson L.A. Bound Westbound / 1977	Fantastic Four Got To Have Your Love Westbound / 1977
Fantastic Four-B.Y.O.F. Westbound / 1978	Kleeer-I Love To Dance Atlantic / 1979	Kleeer-Winners Atlantic / 1979	Manhattan Transfer-Extensions Atlantic / 1979
Herbie Mann-Discotheque Atlantic / 1975	Herbie Mann-Super Mann Atlantic / 1978	Montana-A Dance Fantasy Atlantic / 1977	Montana-I Love Music Atlantic / 1978

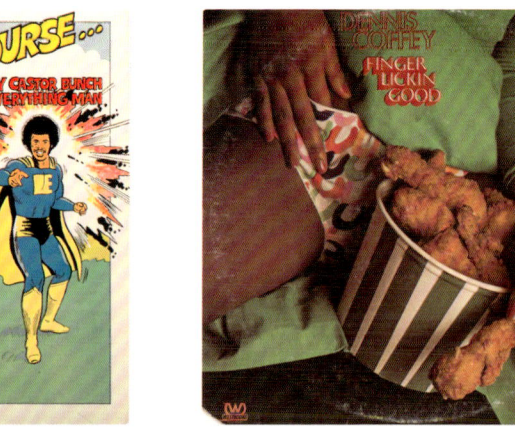

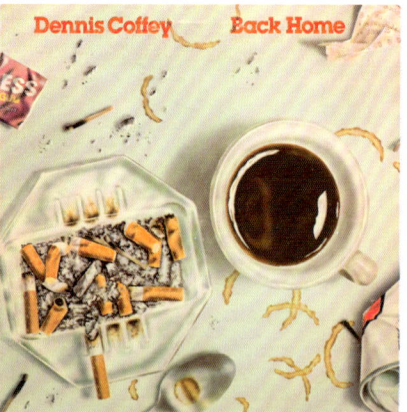

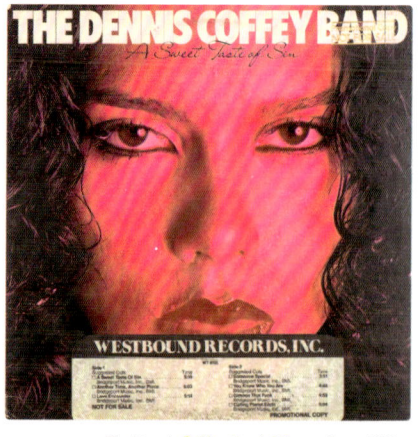

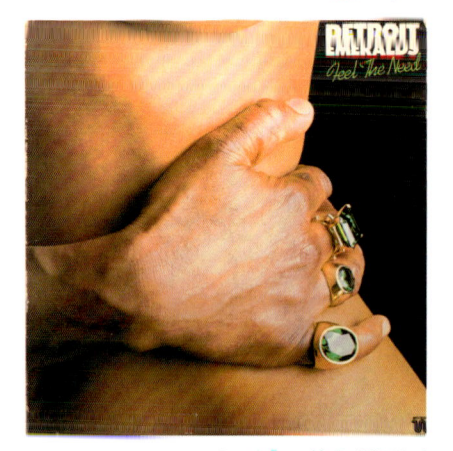

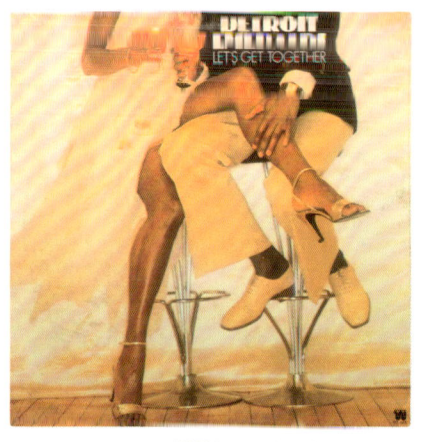

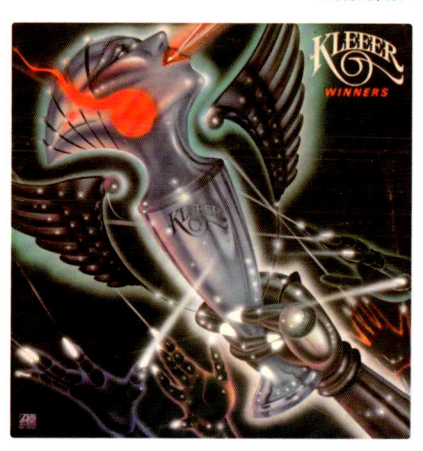

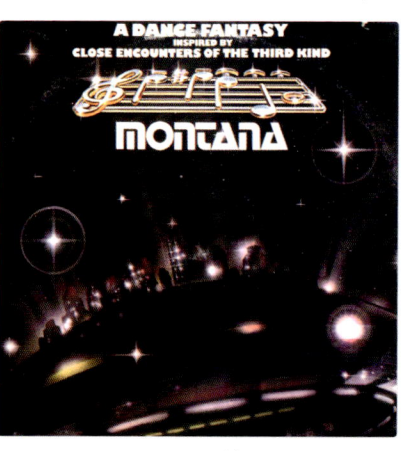

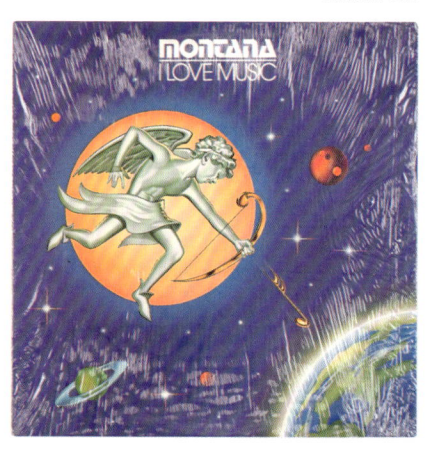

ADC Band-Talk That Stuff
Cotillion / 1979

Mass Production-Believe
Atlantic / 1977

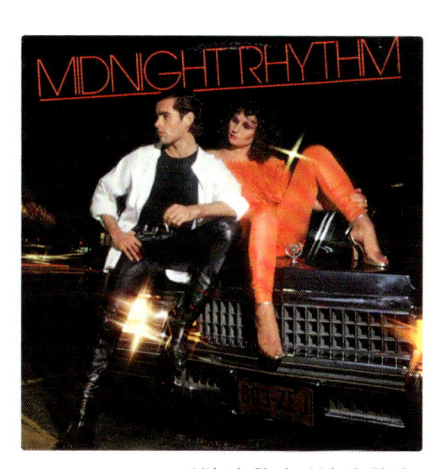

Midnight Rhythm-Midnight Rhythm
Atlantic / 1978

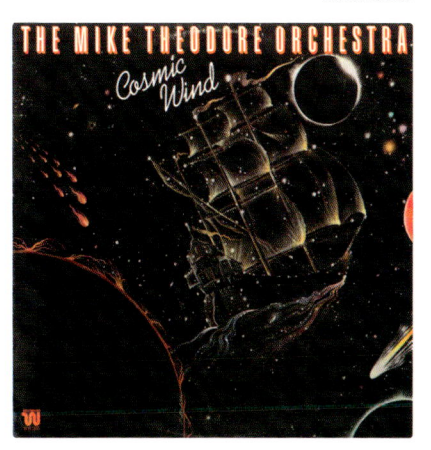

The Mike Theodore Orchestra-Cosmic Wind
Westbound / 1977

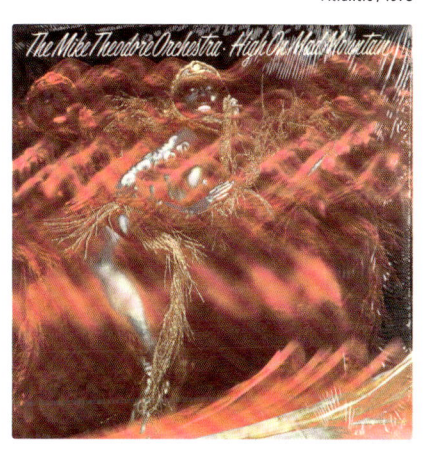

The Mike Theodore Orchestra-High On Mad Mountain
Westbound / 1979

The Jimmy Castor Bunch-Supersound
Atlantic / 1975

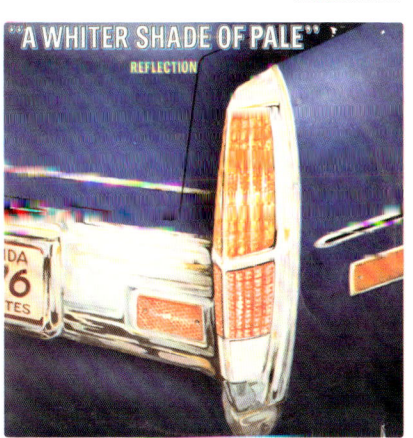

Reflection-A Whiter Shade Of Pale
Atlantic / 1978

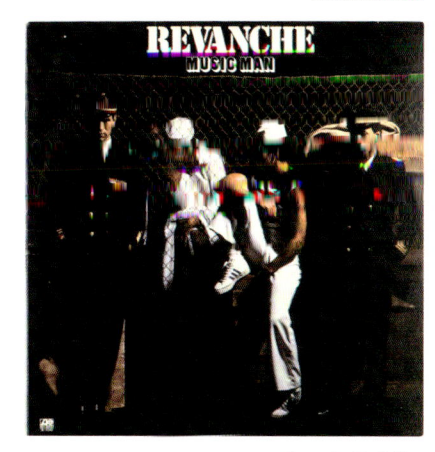

Revanche-Music Man
Atlantic / 1979

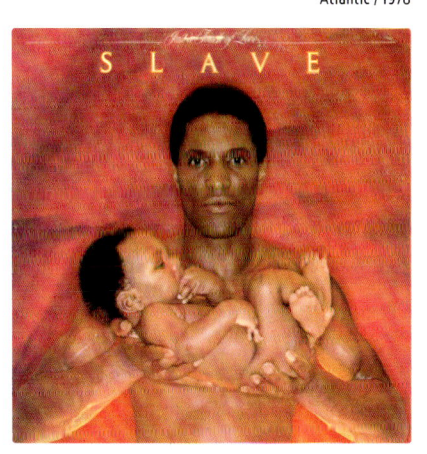

Slave-Just A Touch Of Love
Cotillion / 1979

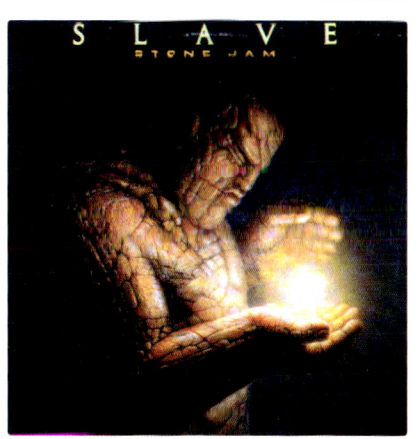

Slave-Stone Jam
Cotillion / 1979

The George Bussey Experience-Disco Extravaganza Phase I
Atlantic / 1979

Sister Sledge-We Are Family
Cotillion / 1979

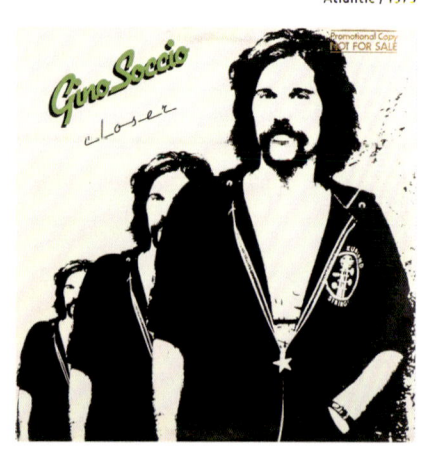

Sister Sledge-Love Somebody Today
Cotillion / 1980

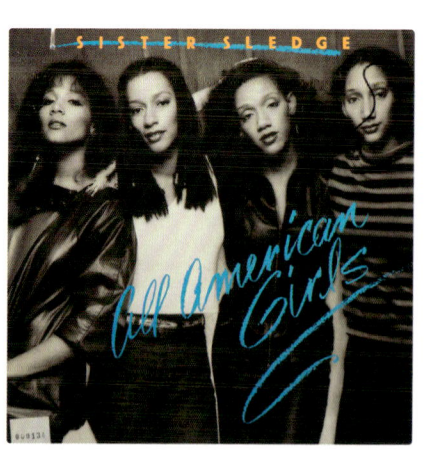

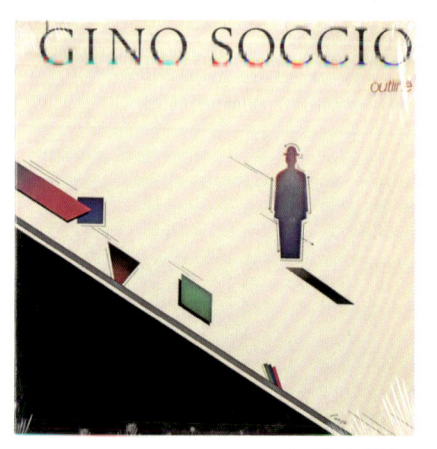

Gino Soccio-Outline
Atlantic / 1979

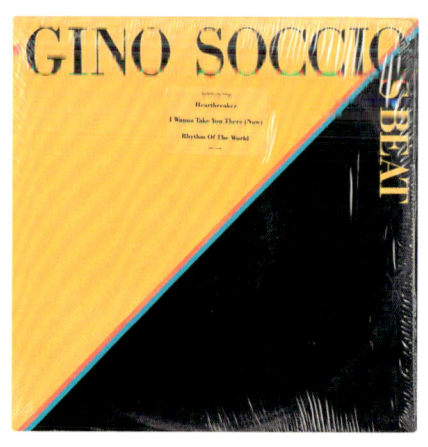

Gino Soccio-Closer
Atlantic / 1981

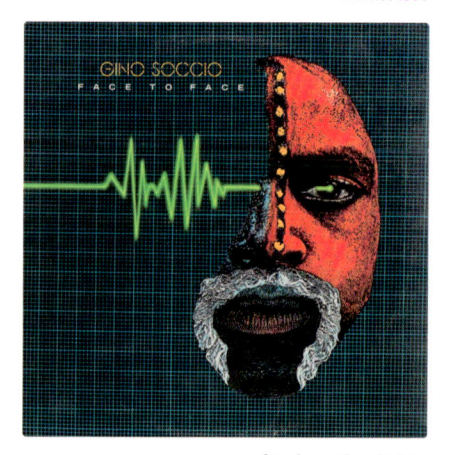

Supermax-World Of Today
Atlantic / 1977

Sister Sledge-All American Girls
Cotillion / 1981

Gino Soccio-S-Beat
Atlantic / 1980

Gino Soccio-Face To Face
Atlantic / 1982

Spinners-Dancin' and Lovin'
Atlantic / 1979

Spinners-Labor Of Love
Atlantic / 1981

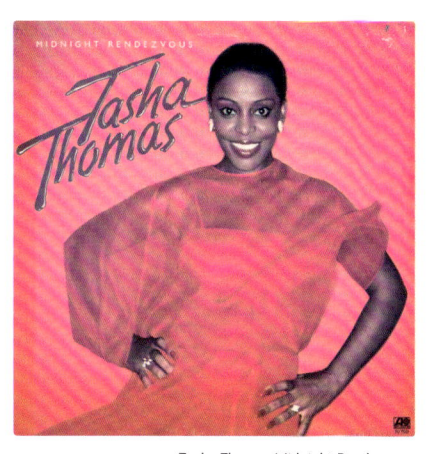

Tasha Thomas-Midnight Rendezvous
Atlantic / 1979

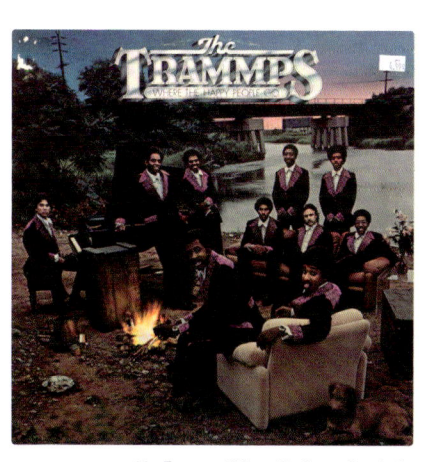

The Trammps-Where The Happy People Go
Atlantic / 1976

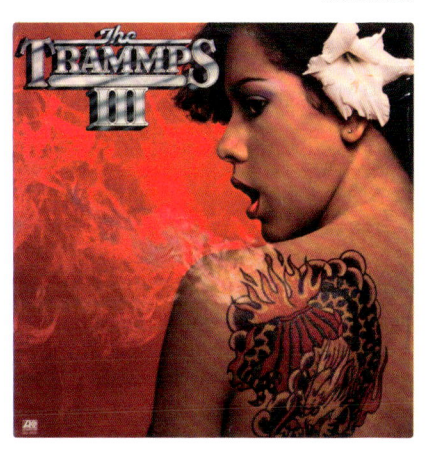

The Trammps-III
Atlantic / 1977

The Trammps-The Best Of
Atlantic / 1977

THP-Good To Me
Atlantic / 1979

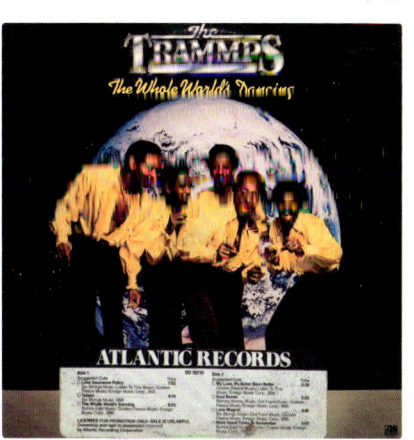

The Trammps-The Whole World's Dancing
Atlantic / 1979

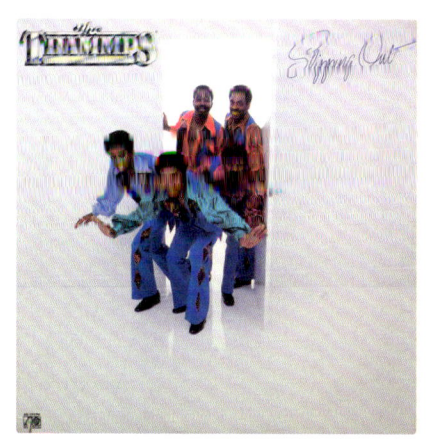

The Trammps-Slipping Out
Atlantic / 1980

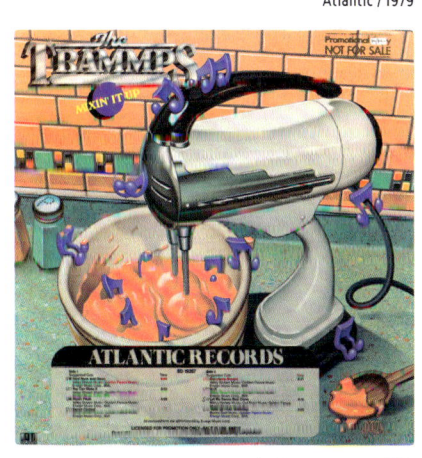

The Trammps-Mixin It Up
Atlantic / 1980

Narada Michael Walden-The Dance Of Life
Atlantic / 1979

Finished Touch - Need To Know You Better / Motown 1978
Design: Norm Ung, Denise Minobe / Photography: Gary Heery

MOTOWN

Apollo-Apollo
Gordy / 1979

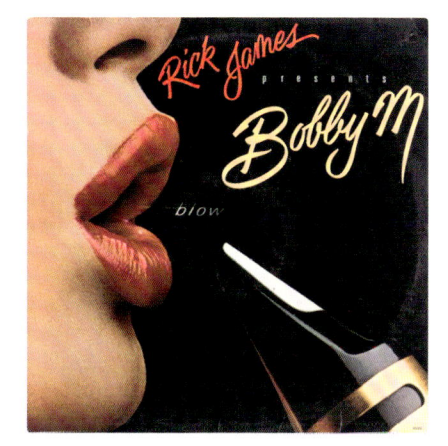

Bobby M-Blow
Gordy / 1982

Commodores-Machine Gun
Motown / 1974

Commodores-Caught In The Act
Motown / 1975

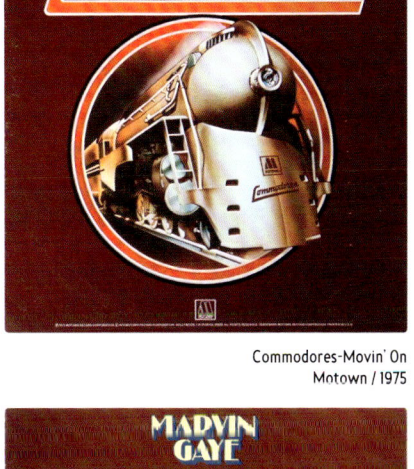

Commodores-Movin' On
Motown / 1975

Commodores-Hot On The Tracks
Motown / 1976

Commodores Live
Motown / 1977

DeBarge-Rhythm Of The Night
Gordy / 1985

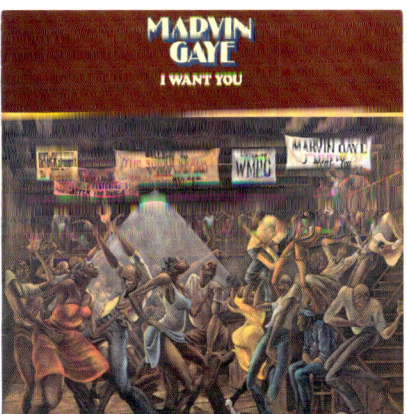

Marvin Gaye-I Want You
Tamla / 1976

High Energy-Steppin' Out
Gordy / 1978

Jermaine Jackson-Let's Get Serious
Motown / 1980

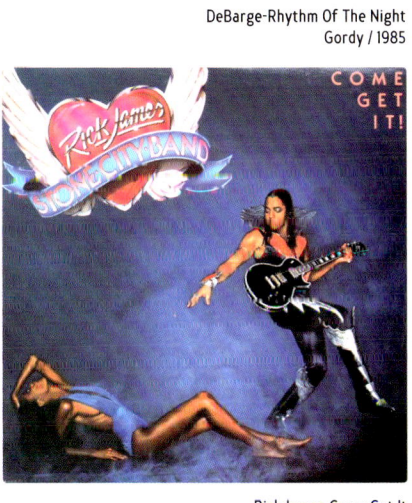

Rick James-Come Get It
Gordy / 1978

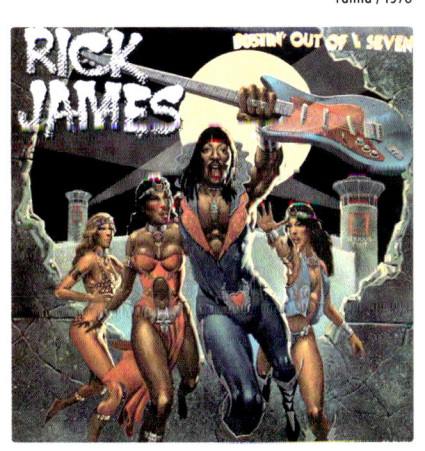

Rick James-Bustin' Out Of L Seven
Gordy / 1979

Rick James-Fire It Up
Gordy / 1979

Rick James-Street Sounds
Gordy / 1981

283

The Magic Disco Machine-Disc O Tech
Motown / 1975

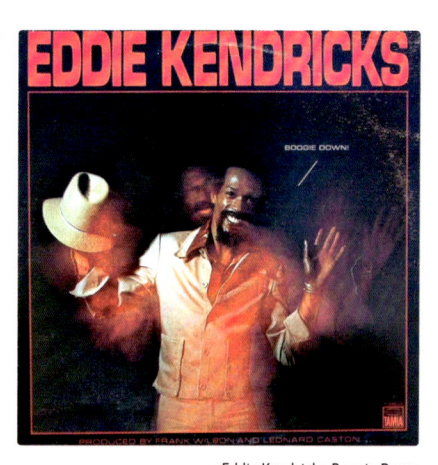

Eddie Kendricks-Boogie Down
Tamla / 1974

Bonnie Pointer-Bonnie Pointer
Motown / 1978

Bonnie Pointer-Bonnie Pointer
Motown / 1979

Diana Ross-The Boss
Motown / 1979

Syreeta-Syreeta
Tamla / 1980

The Temptations-Reunion
Gordy / 1982

Jackson Five-Moving Violation
Motown / 1979

Ta Ta Vega-Try My Love
Tamla / 1978

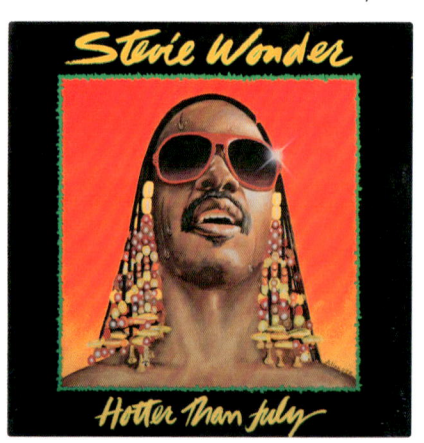

Stevie Wonder-Hotter Than July
Tamla / 1980

The Originals-Down To Love Town (Front)
Soul / 1976

The Originals-Down To Love Town (Back)
Soul / 1976

Leon Ware-Musical Massage (Back)
Gordy / 1976

Leon Ware-Musical Massage (Front)
Gordy / 1976

OTHER LABELS

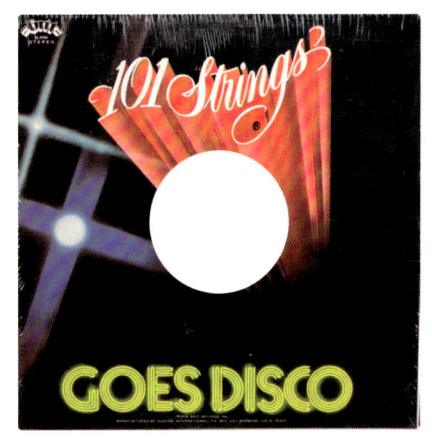

101 Strings-Goes Disco
Grit / 1978

5000 Volts-5000 Volts
Philips / 1976

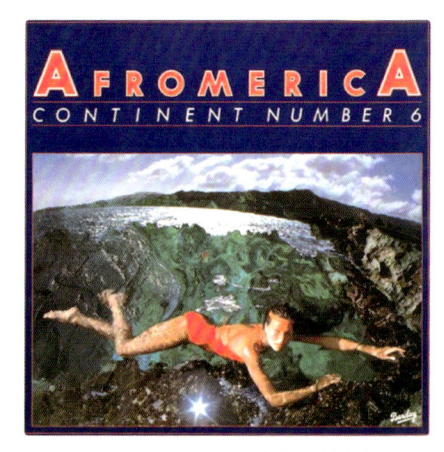

Afromerica-Continent No.6
Barclay / 1976

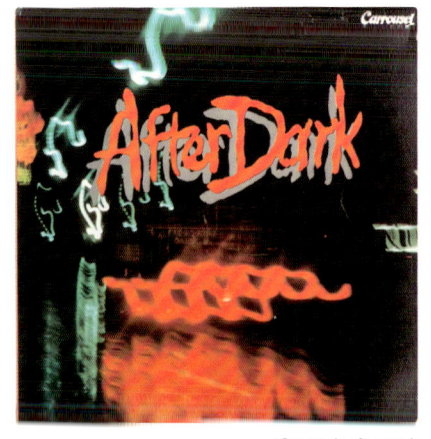

After Dark-After Dark
Carrousel / 1980

AKB Rhythmic Feet
RSO / 1979

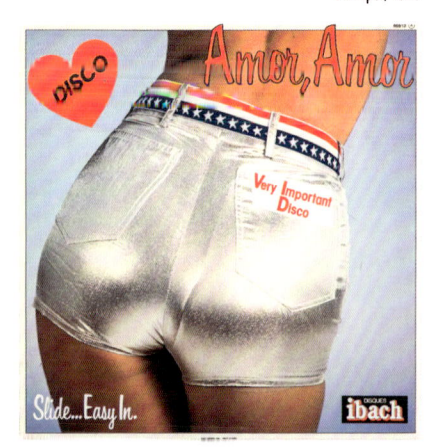

Amor, Amor Rod Mc Kuen
ibach / 1977

The Andrea True Connection-White Witch
Buddah / 1977

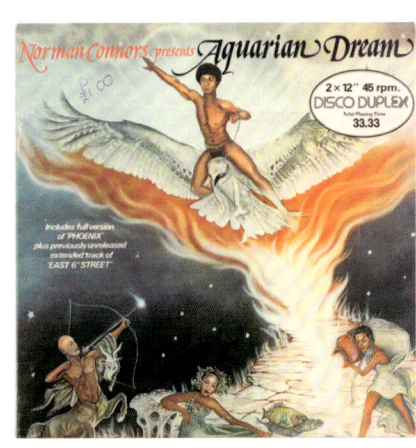

Aquarian Dream-Norman Conners Presents Aquarian Dream
Buddah / 1976

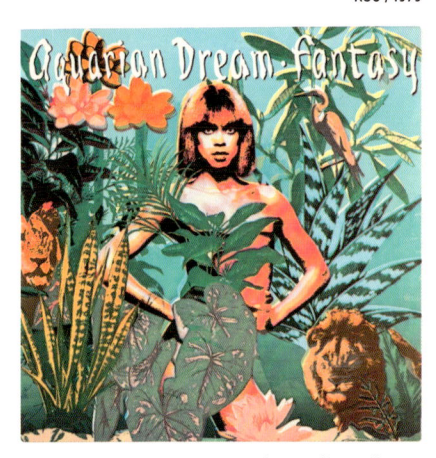

Aquarian Dream-Fantasy
Elektra / 1978

Aquarian Dream-Chance To Dance
Elektra / 1979

Aural Exiters-Spooks In Space
ZE / 1979

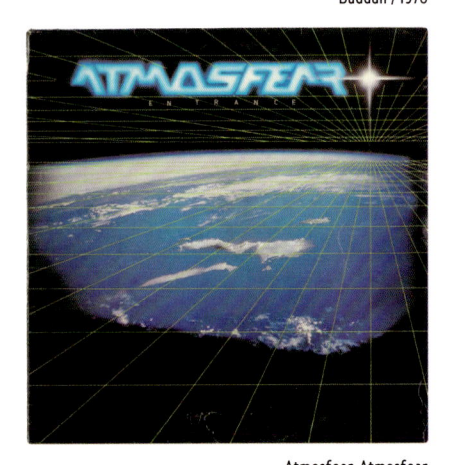

Atmosfear-Atmosfear
Elite / 1981

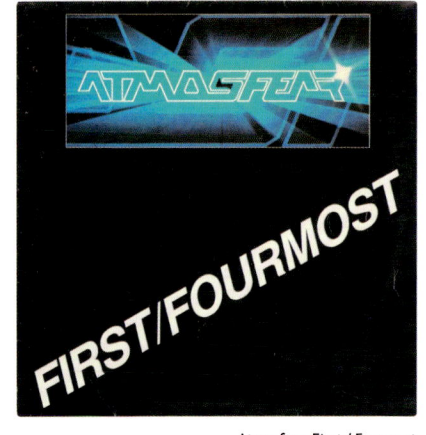

Atmosfear-First / Fourmost
Elite

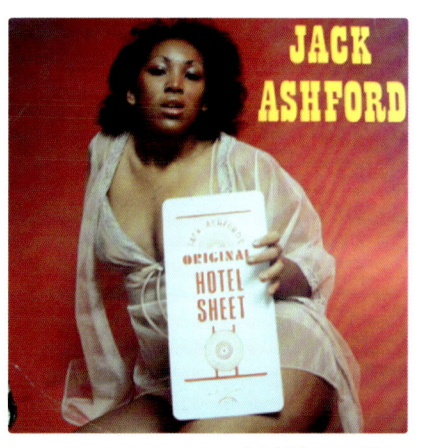

Jack Ashford-Hotel Sheet
Magic Disc / 1977

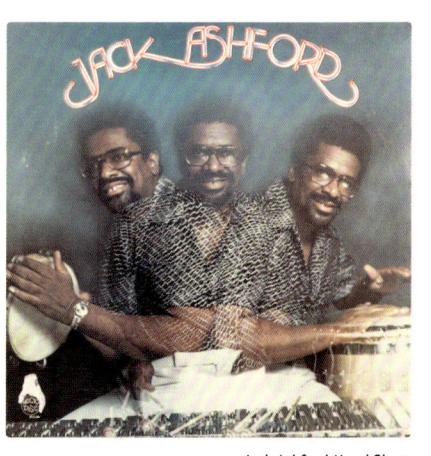

Jack Ashford-Hotel Sheet
Magic Disc / 1977

Hot Sause - Hot Sauce / Altophone
Photography. J.Janlsson

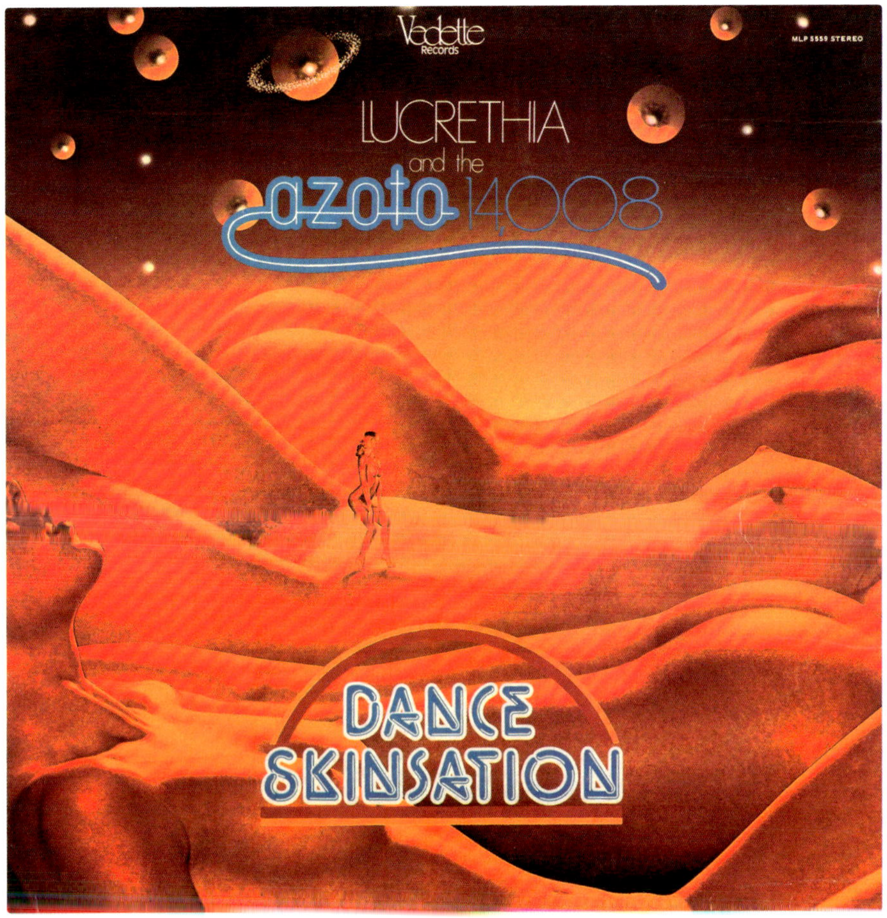

Lucrethia and the Azoto 14,008-Dance Skinsation
Vedette / 1978

Azoto Music Makers Ltd.
Vedette / 1978

Azoto-Disco Fizz
Vedette / 1979

Bob-a-Rela-Bob-A-Rela
Channel / 1979

B&B-Boogaloo CBS / 1978	Baby O-You've Got It Baby O / 1980	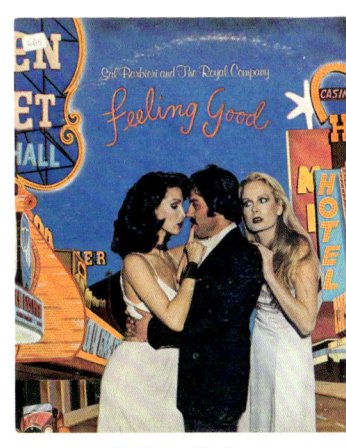 Sal Barbieri and The Royal Company-Feeling Good BSO / 1980	Claudja Barry-I Wanna Be Loved By You Lollypop Records / 1978
Bay Ridge Band-Saturday Night Fever Musicor / 1978	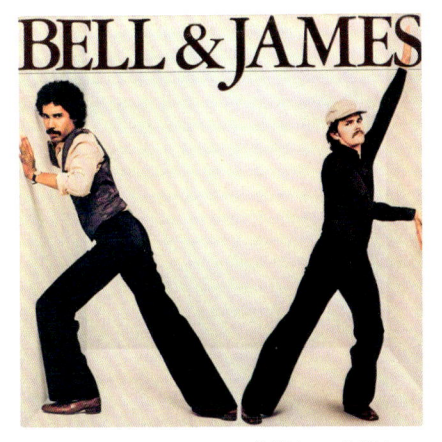 Bell & James -Bell & James A&M / 1978	Bell &James-Only Make Believe A&M / 1979	Bell &James-In Black And White A&M / 1981
 Travis Biggs-Solar Funk Source / 1979	 Black Ivory-Hangin' Heavy Buddah / 1979	Carolyne Bernier-Carolyne Bernier Private Stock / 1978	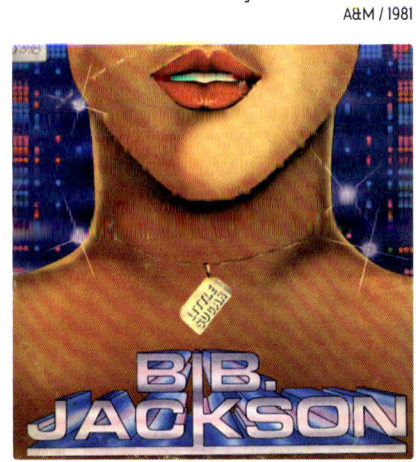 BIB Jackson-BIB Jackson
Jo Bisso-Mademoiselle Jobiss / 1978	Jo Bisso-The best Disco In Town Jobiss / 1978	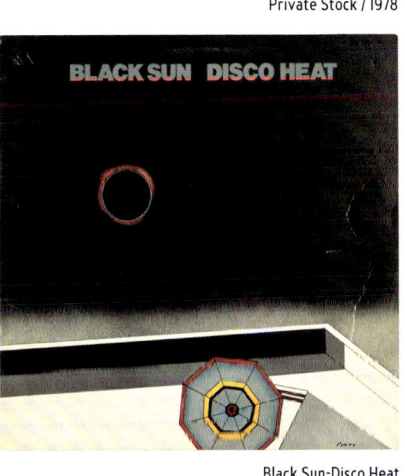 Black Sun-Disco Heat Buddha / 1978	 Jurgen Pluta-Blanche Rocktopus / 1980

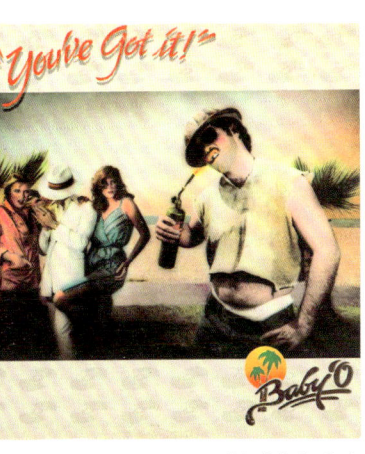

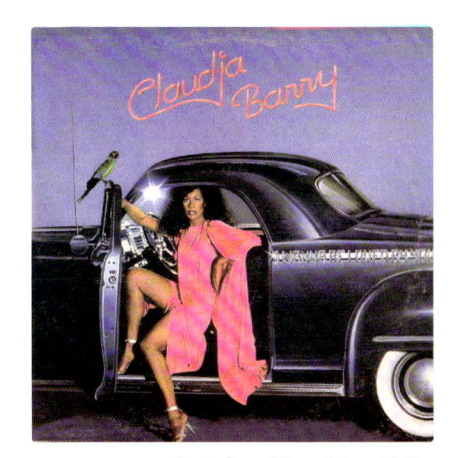

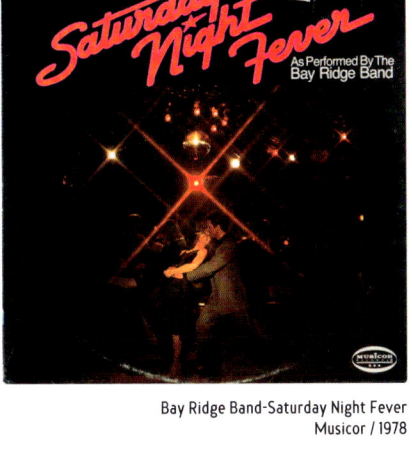

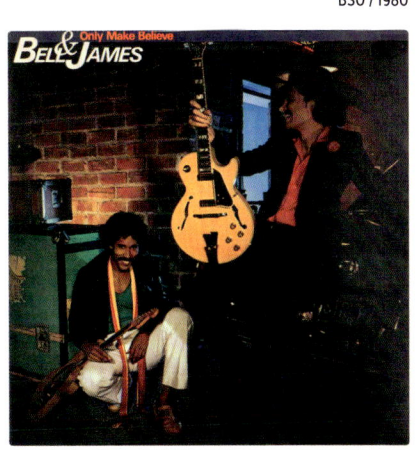

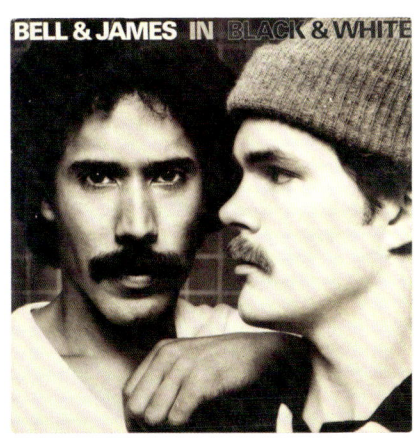

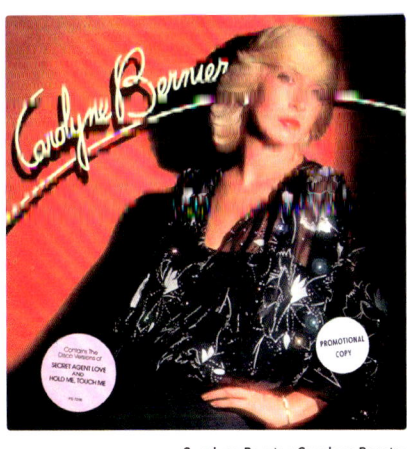

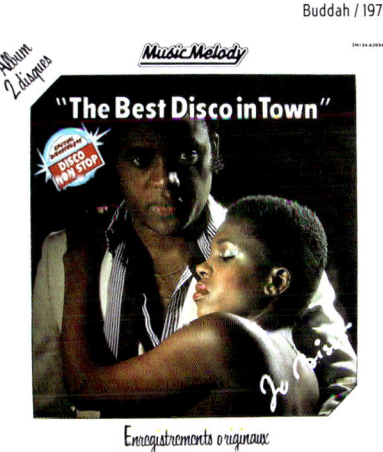

289

Black White And Co.-Stop JPLL / 1982	The Bob Crewe Generation-Street Talk Elektra / 1978	 Jocelyn Brown-Somebody's Else's Guy Vinyl Dreams / 1984	Bohannon-Stop And Go Dakar / 1972
Bohannon-Dance Your Ass Off Brunswick / 1976	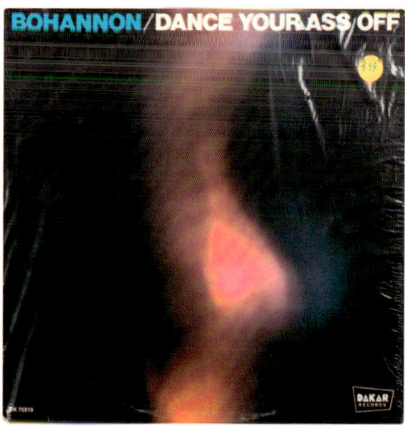 Bohannon-Dance Your Ass Off Dakar / 1976	Bohannon-Cut Loose Mercury / 1979	 Bohannon-Summertime Groove Mercury / 1978
Gregg Diamond Bionic Boogie-Hot Butterfly Polydor / 1978	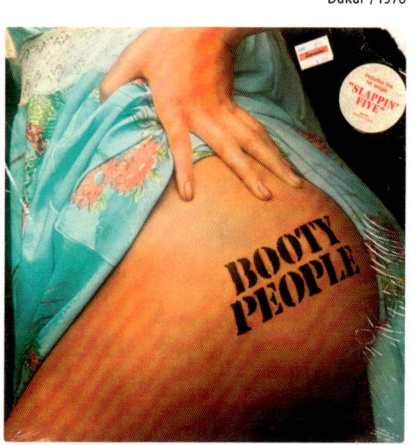 Booty People-Booty People ABC / 1977	Bonnie Boyer-Give In To Love Columbia / 1979	 Brass And Congas-Brass And Congas CBS / 1979
Brainstorm-Stormin Tabu / 1977	Brainstorm-Journey To The Light Tabu / 1978	 Brainstorm-Funky Entertainment Tabu / 1979	 Dee Dee Bridgewater-Bad For Me Elektra / 1979

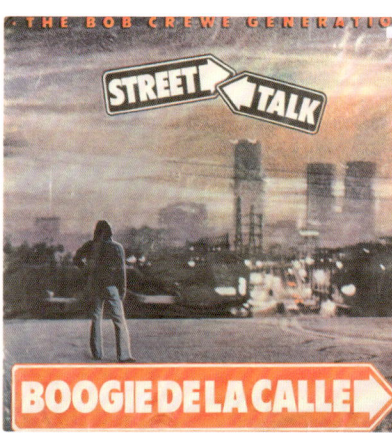

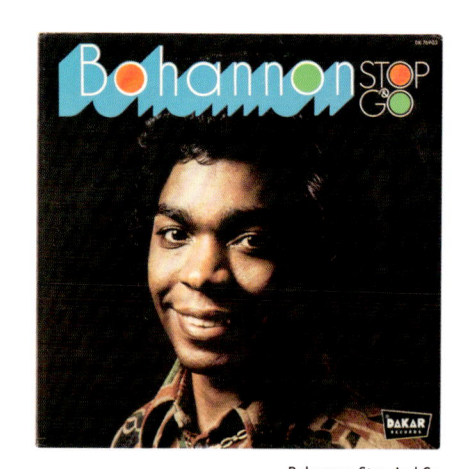

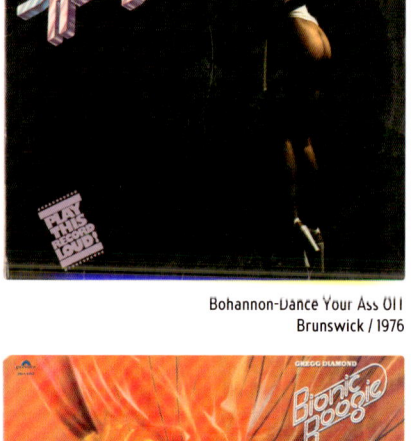

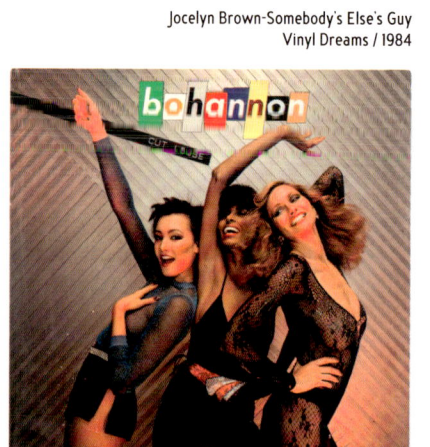

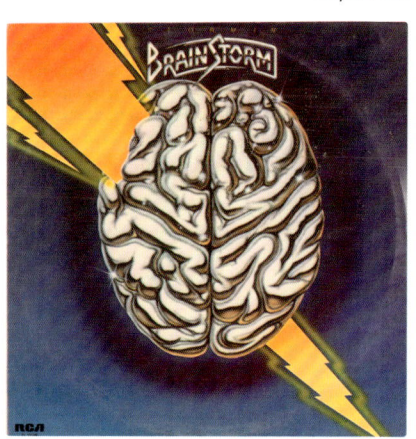

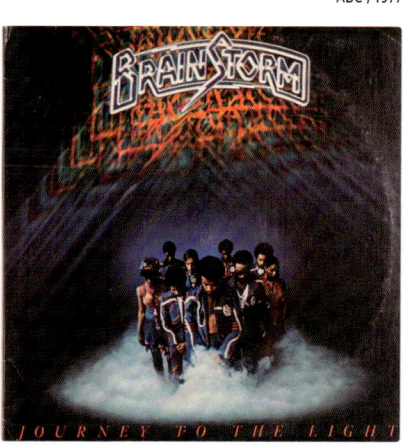

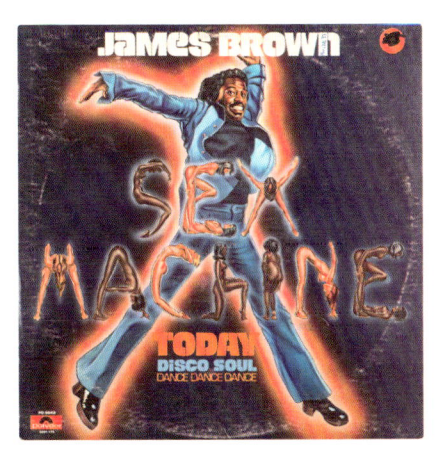

James Brown-Sex Machine Today Polydor / 1975	James Brown-The Original Disco Man Polydor / 1979	Bumblebee Unlimited-Sting Like A Bee RCA / 1978	Buari-Disco Soccer Makossa International / 1979
Chatelaine-Chatelaine Musicon / 1980	Camouflage-A Disco Symphony State / 1977	Camouflage-A Disco Symphony Dureco / 1977	Camp Galore-Deco Disco DAM / 1976
Caress-Caress RFC / 1977	Cosa Nostra Disco Band-Tarantella Disco Building / 1978	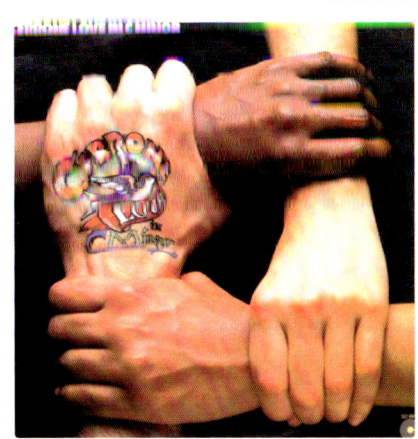 cerrone-Love In C Minor Cotillion / 1976	Iris Chacon-Disco AAD / 1979
Gene Chandler-Get Dwon 20 th. Century / 1978	Charisma-Out Of Time Barclay / 1978	Chilly-For Your Love Polydor / 1979	Chilly-For Your Love Polydor / 1979

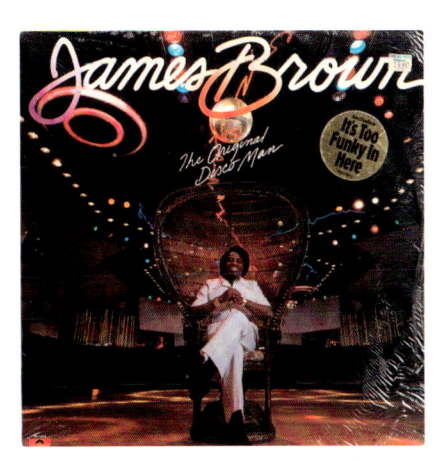

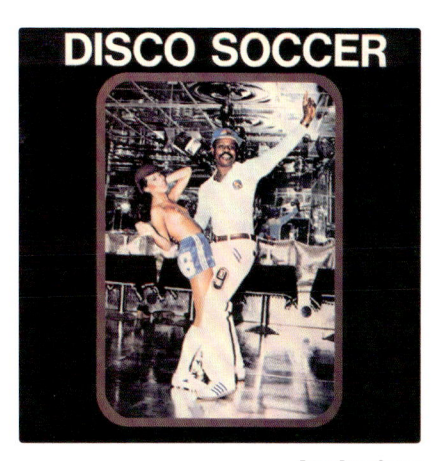

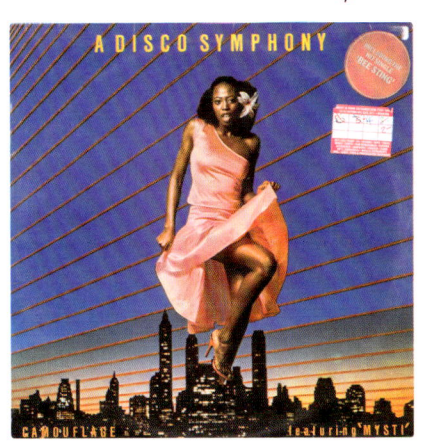

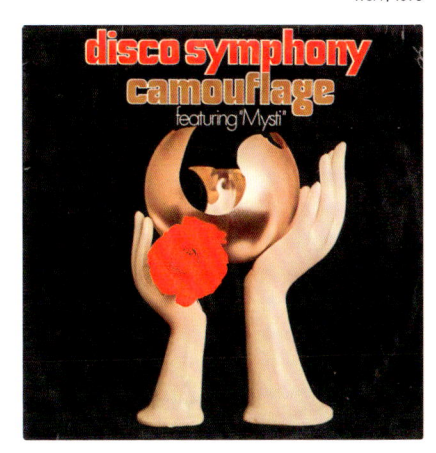

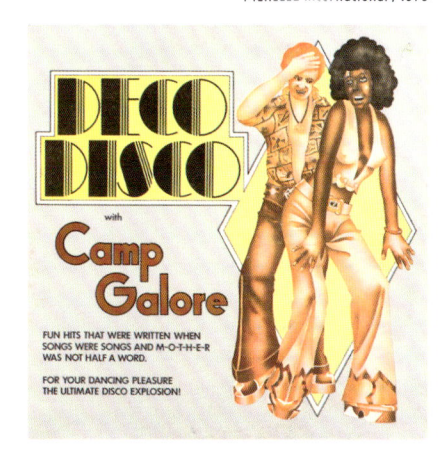

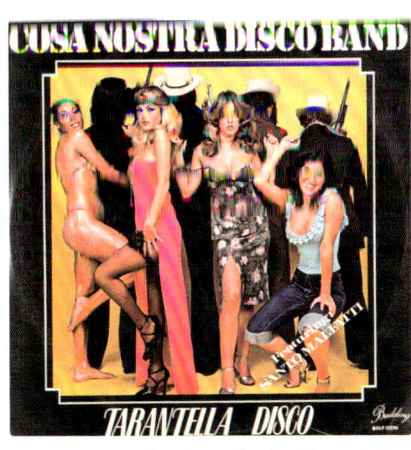

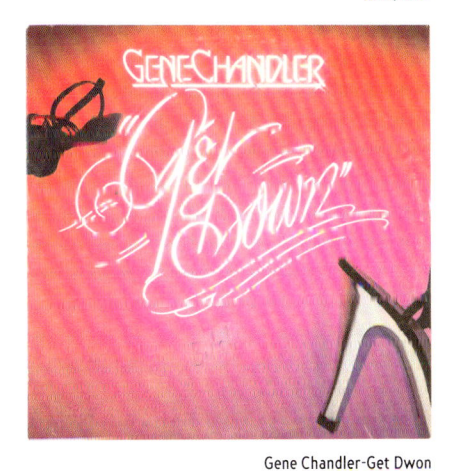

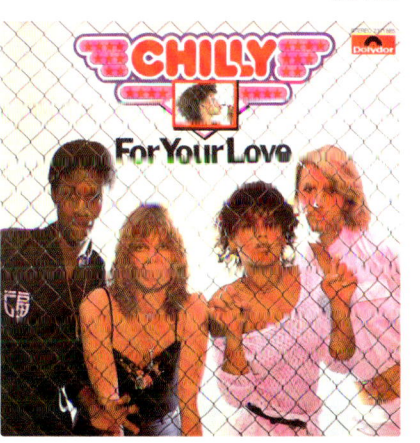

**IN A GADDA DA VIDA/
GARDEN OF EDEN
DIG IT*
SOUL SISTER***

**OVER AND OVER
GET UP AND DANCE***
THE MEXICAN

An Original Lollipop
Recording conceived
and produced by Jurgen
S. Korduletsch
Recorded at Arco
Studios,
MusicLand
Studios and
Union Studios,
Munich by Jurgen
Koppers, Peter
Lundemann, Mack
and Dave Siddle
Mixed at Arco
Studios by Dave Siddle and
Jurgen S. Korduletsch
Arranged by Mats Bjoerklund
except (*) arranged by
Jorg Evers
All brass and strings
arranged by Jorg Evers
Illustration: Robert
Grossman
Design: Paula Scher

0 7464-36049-

Disco Circus - Disco Circus / Lollipop 1979
Design: Paula Scher / Illustration: Robert Grossman

Chromium-Star To Star
Infinity / 1979

The Counts-Funk Pump
Aware / 1974

Cloud One-Atmosphere Strut
P&P / 1976

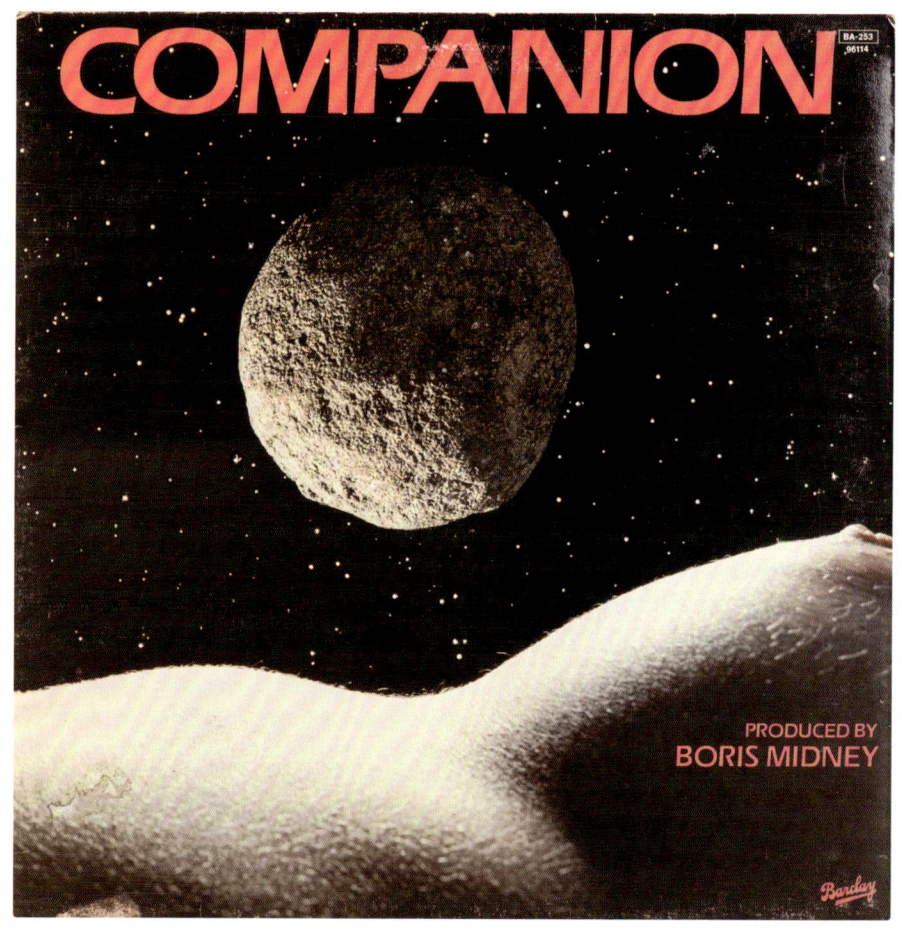

Companion-Companion
Barclay / 1981

Bohannon - Dance Your Ass Off / Brunswick 1976
Photography: David Wedgbury

Chime-Keep It Up
Toledo / 1980

Chime-Disco
Supraphon / 1982

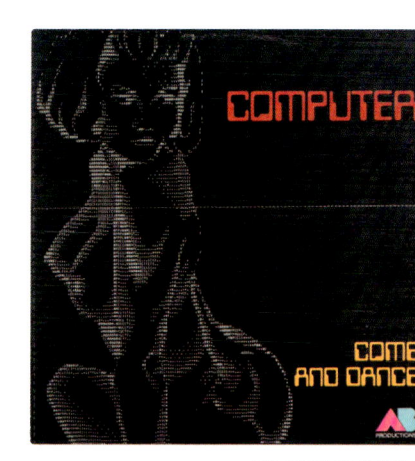

Computer-Come And Dance
AB / 1977

Norman Conners-Invitation
Buddah / 1979

Patrick Cowley-Megatron Man
Megatone / 1981

C.P.Salt-C.P.Salt
Surrend / 1982

Cream & Sugar-Cream And Sugar
Celsius / 1979

Cosmic Gal-Keep On Moving
Overseas / 1979

Chantal Curtis-Get Another Love
Buddah / 1979

D.D.Sound-Gimme Some
Baby / 1977

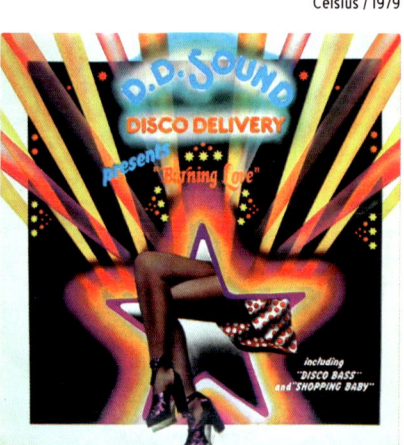

D.D.Sound-Disco Delivery
Baby / 1977

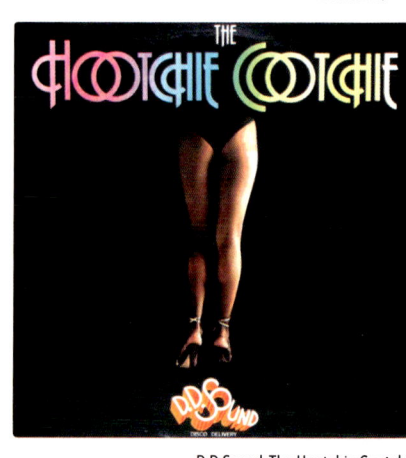

D.D.Sound-The Hootchie Cootchie
Baby / 1980

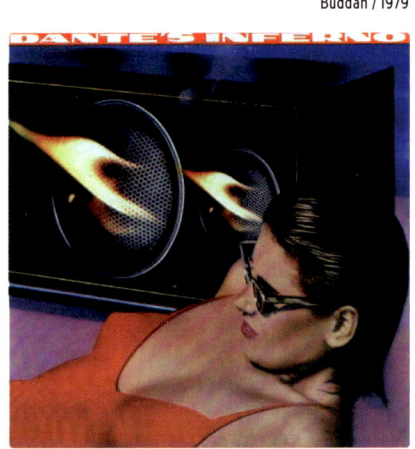

Dante's Inferno-Dante's Inferno
Infinity / 1979

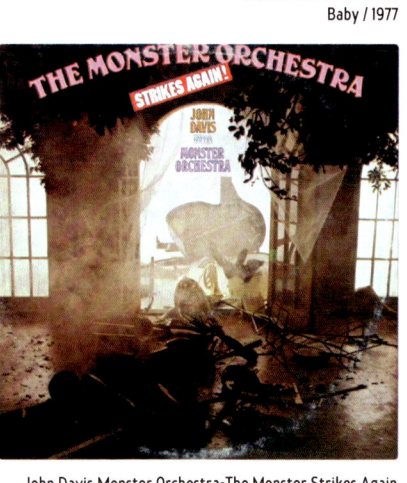

John Davis Monster Orchestra-The Monster Strikes Again
Columbia / 1979

Debra Dejean-Debra Dejean
Handshake / 1981

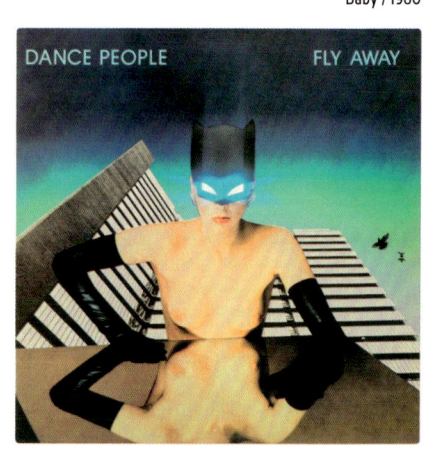

Dance People-Fly Away
Satril / 1979

296

Gregg Diamond-Hardware
Mercury / 1979

Direct Current-Direct Current
TEC / 1979

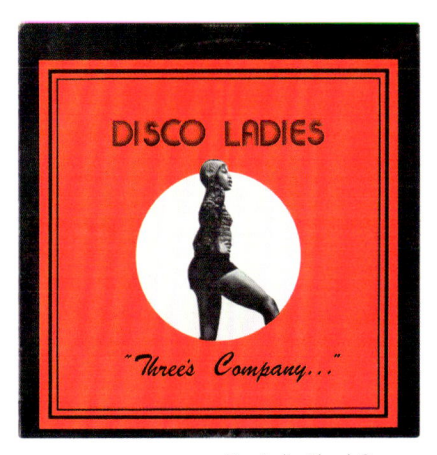

Disco Ladies-Three's Company
Baby Grand / 1977

Disco Rock Machine-Time To Love
Lotus / 1978

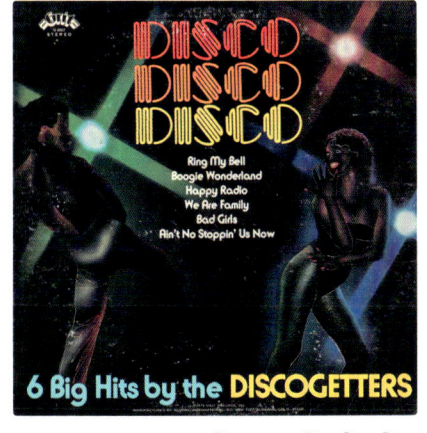

Discogetters-Disco,Disco,Disco
Grit / 1979

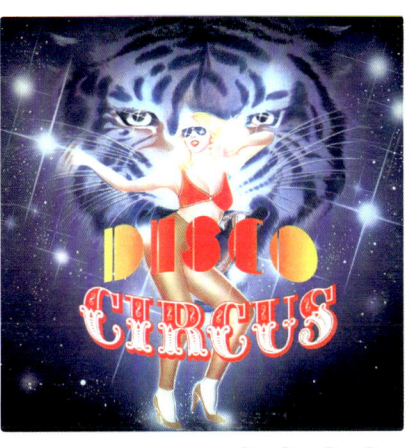

Disco Circus-Disco Circus
Lollipop / 1978

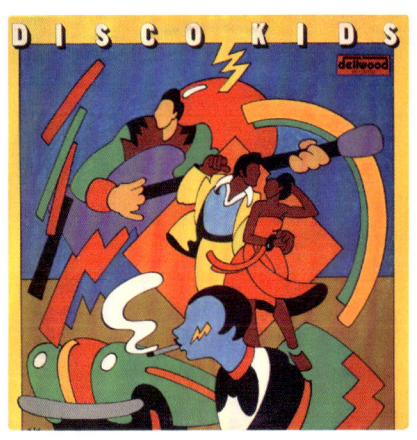

Disco Kids-Disco Kids
Dellwood / 1979

The Echoes-Disco Mix

Venus Dodson-Night Rider
RFC / 1979

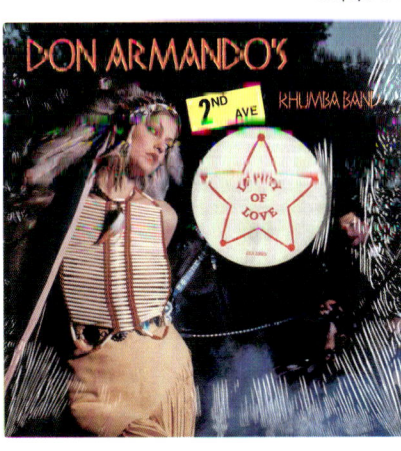

Don Amandos 2nd AVE Rhumba Band-Deputy Of Love
ZE / 1979

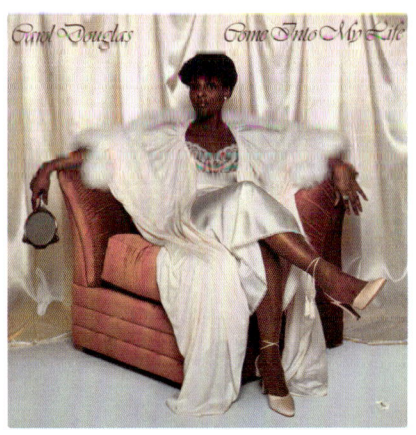

Carol Douglas-Come Into My Life
Midsong / 1979

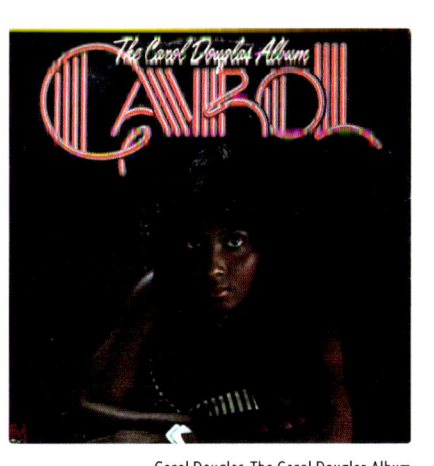

Carol Douglas-The Carol Douglas Album
Midland / 1975

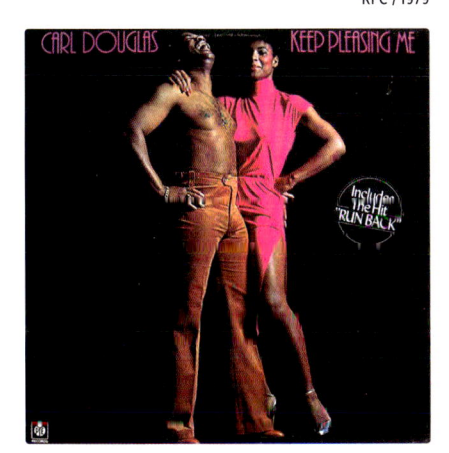

Carl Douglas-Keep Pleasing Me
Pye / 1978

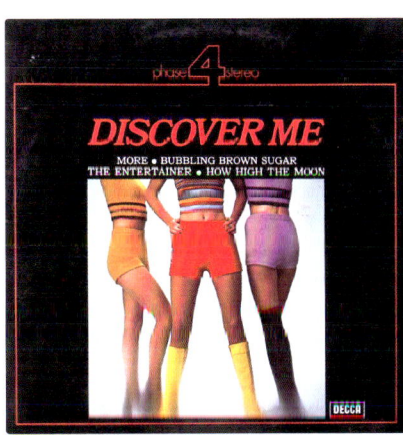

Discover Me
Decca

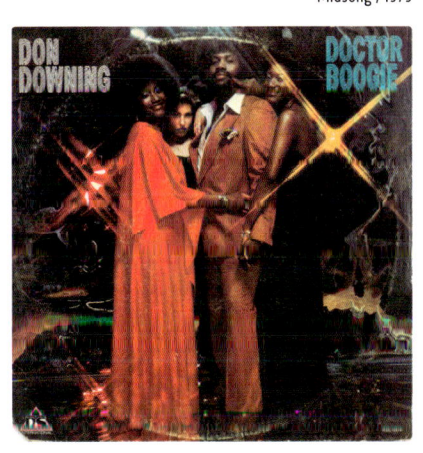

Don Downing-Doctor Boogie
Roadshow / 1978

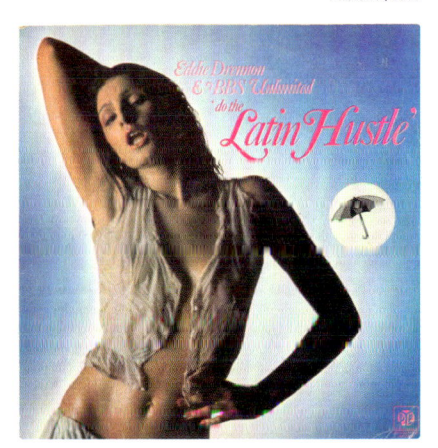

Eddie Drennon & BBS Unlimited Do The Latin Hustle
Pye / 1976

Droids-Star Peace
Barclay / 1978

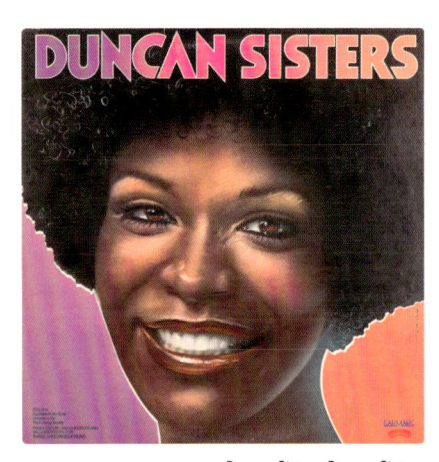

Duncan Sisters-Duncan Sisters
Earmarc / 1979

The Duncans-Gonna Stay In Love
Malaco / 1981

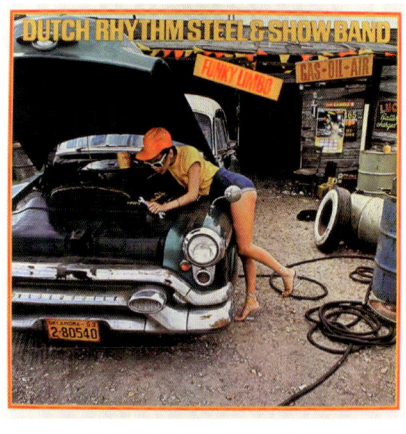

Dutch Rhythm Steel & Show Band-Funky Limbo
Bovema / 1978

East Coast-East Coast
RSO / 1979

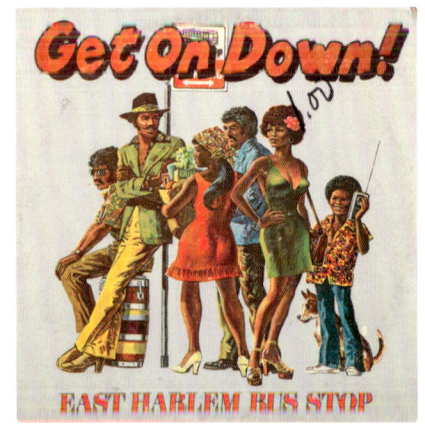

East Harlem Bus Stop-Get On Down
D&M / 1976

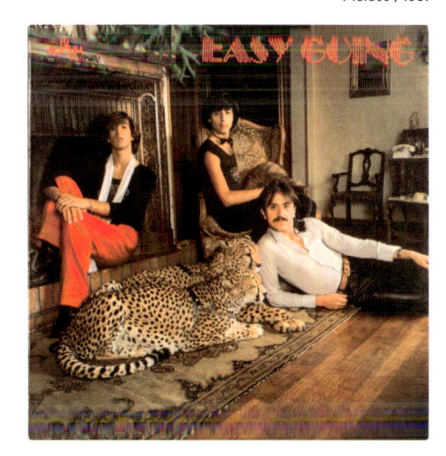

Easy Going-Easy Going
Podium

Easy Going-The Best Of
Delirium / 1983

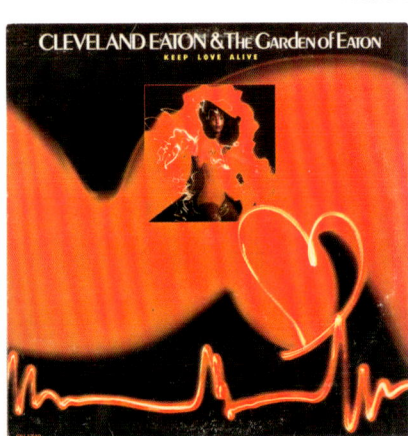

Cleveland Eaton & The Garden Of Eaton-Keep Love Alive
Ovation / 1979

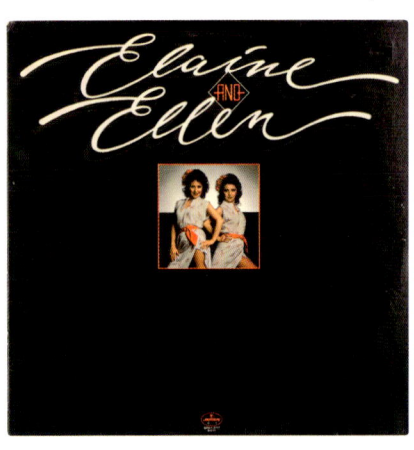

Elaine And Ellen-Elaine And Ellen
Mercury / 1979

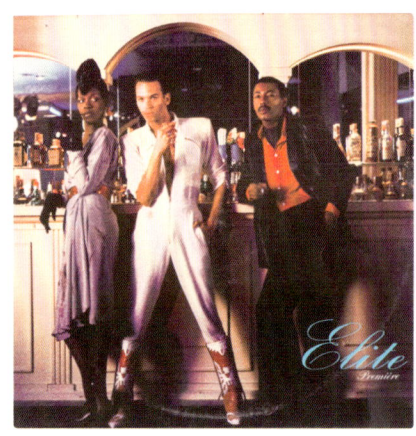

Elite-Premiere
Derby / 1980

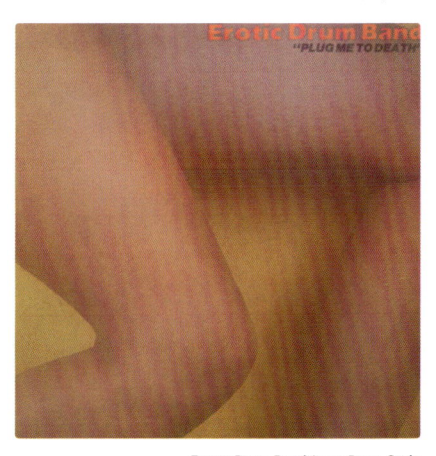

Erotic Drum Band-Love Disco Style
Prism / 1978

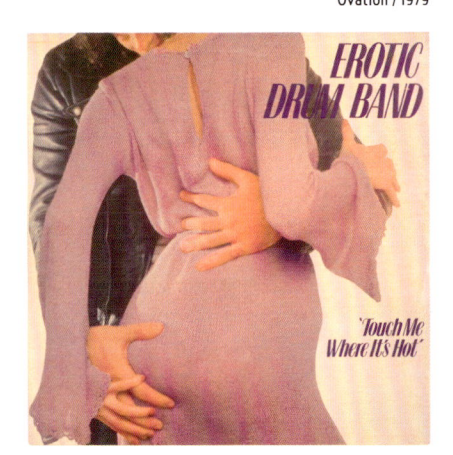

Erotic Drum Band-Touch Me Where It's Hot
Prism / 1980

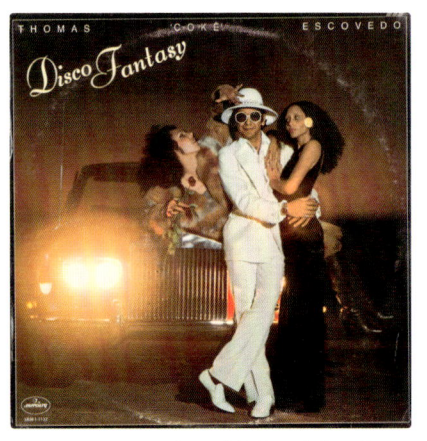

Thomas Coke Escovido-Disco Fantasy
Mercury / 1977

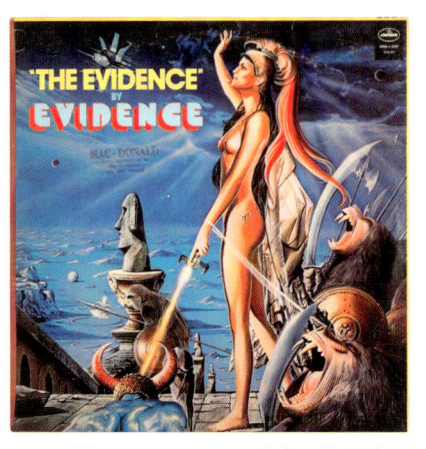

Evidence-The Evidence
Mercury / 1979

Joe Farrell-Night Dancing
Warner Bros. / 1978

298

Cleveland Eaton – Instant Hip / Ovation 1976
Cover Design: Herb Bruce / Photography: Judson / Graphic Production: Bob Dorobiala

La Flavor-Mandolay
Sweet City / 1978

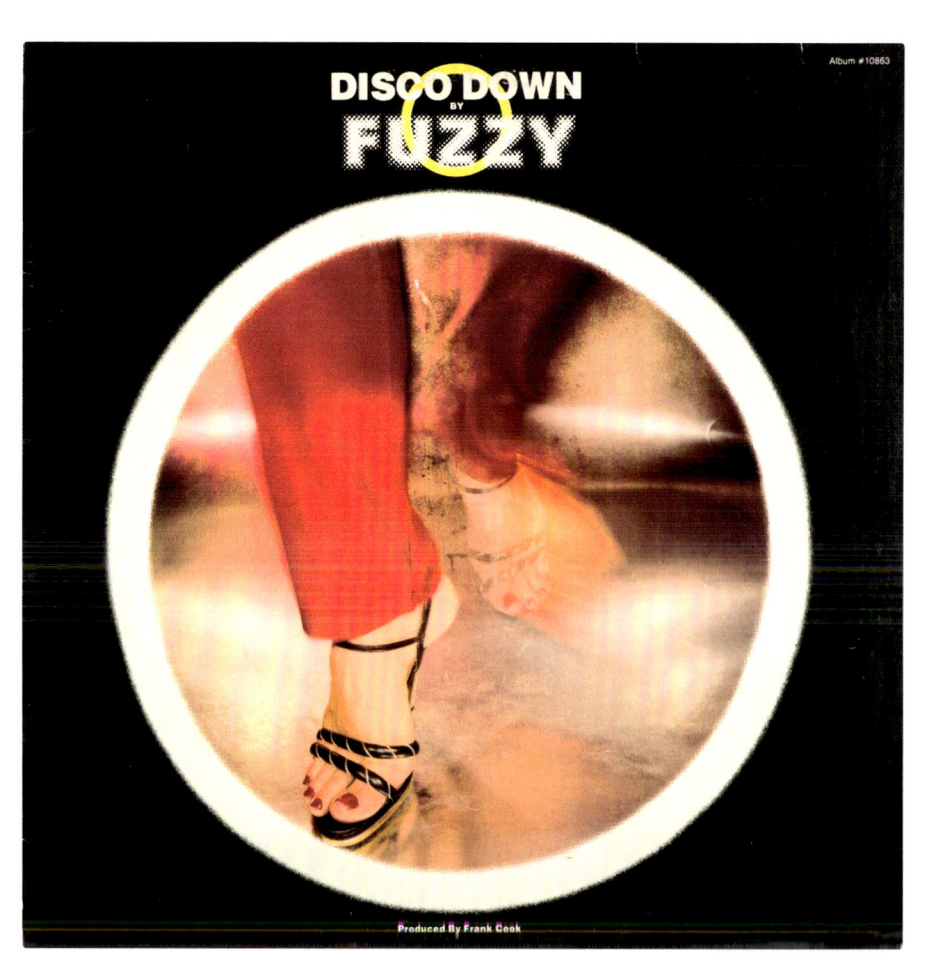

Fuzzy-Disco Down
Nervie / 1977

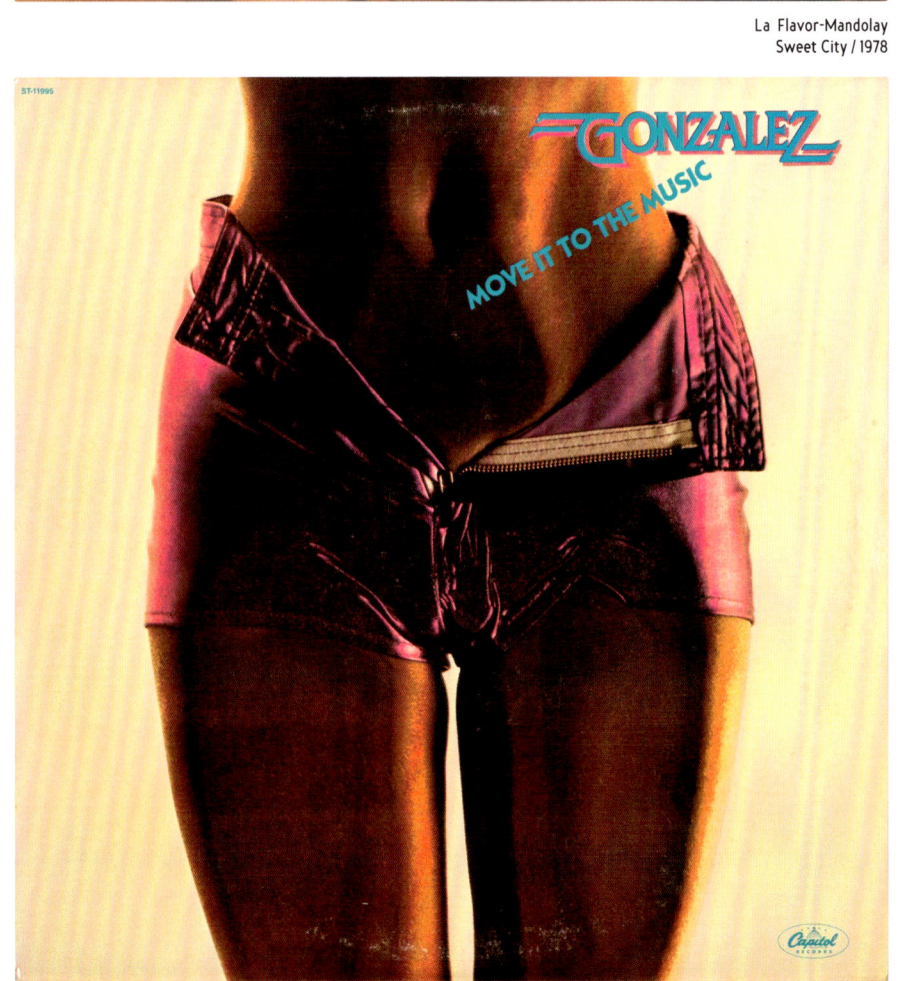

Gonzalez-Move It To The Music
Capitol / 1979

Goody Goody-Goody Goody
Atlantic / 1978

The Fatback Band-Yum Yum Event / 1975	The Fatback Band-Night Fever Event / 1976	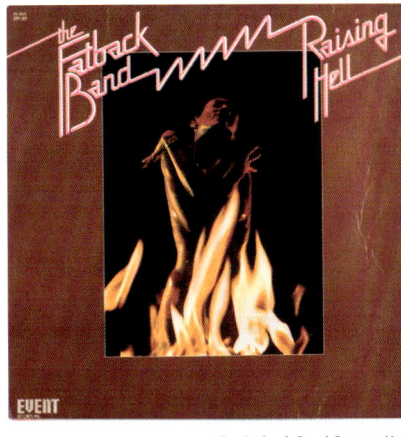 The Fatback Band-Raising Hell Event / 1975	Fatback -Man With The Band Spring / 1977
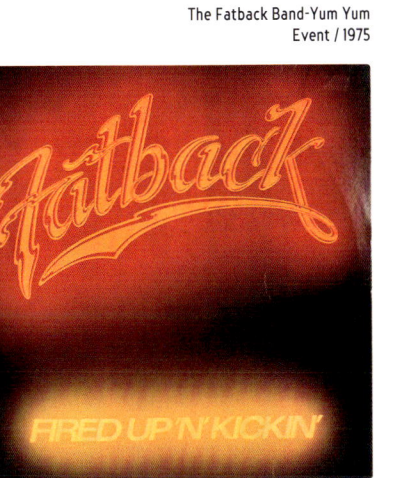 Fatback -Fired Up 'N' Kickin' Spring / 1978	Fatback -Brite Lites Big City Spring / 1979	 Alma Faye-Doin' It RCA / 1979	Festival-Evita RSO / 1979
Ferrara-Wuthering Heights Midsong / 1979	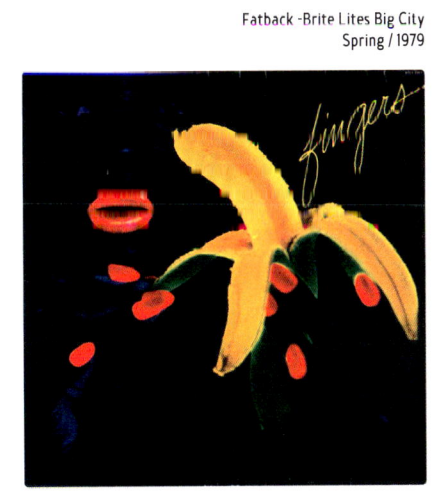 Fingers-Fingers RCA / 1979	Flakes-1980 Magic Disc / 1980	 Flower-Heat MCA / 1979
Free Life-Free Life Epic / 1978	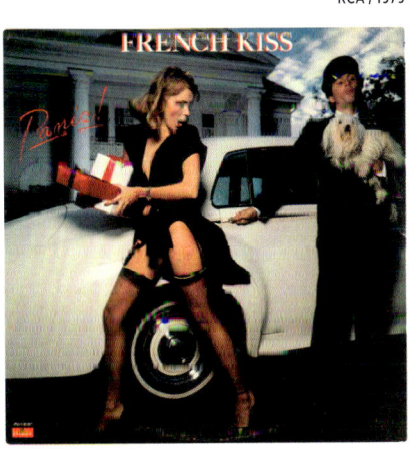 French Kiss-Panic Polydor / 1979	Fun Fun-Have Fun Energy / 1904	Friends-Trans Am Dancing Vitamin / 1979

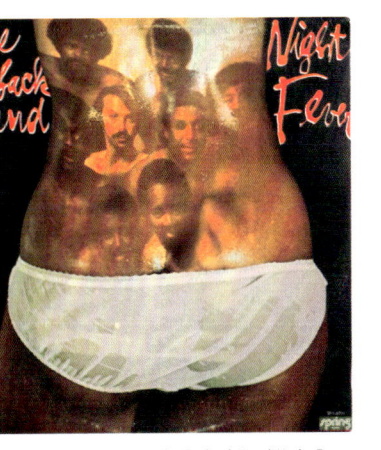

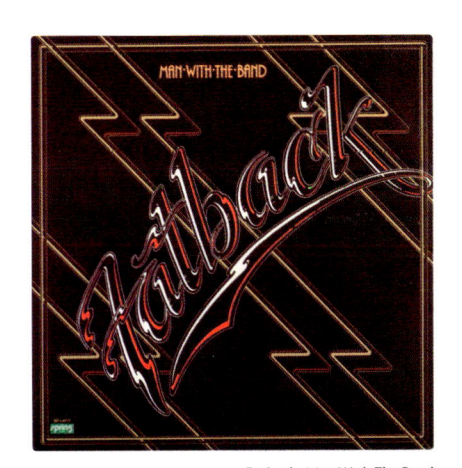

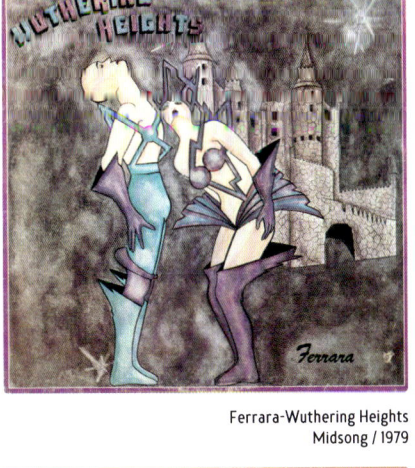

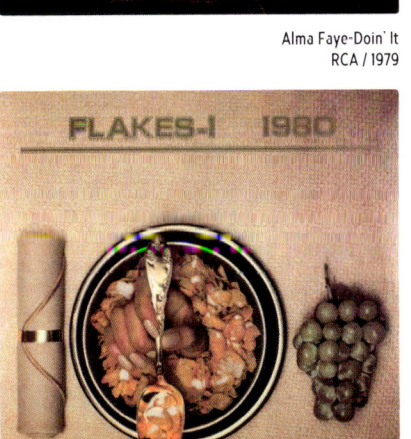

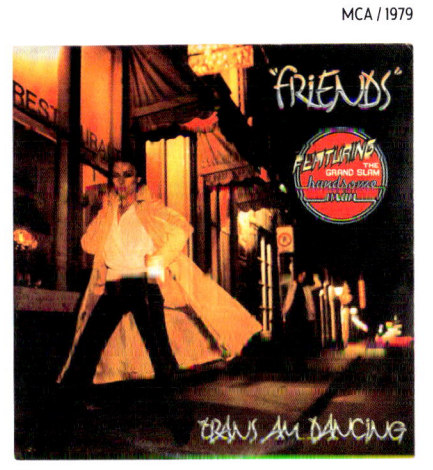

Galaxy-Hot Wet And Sticky Arista / 1978	Ganymed-Takes You Higher Bellaphone / 1978	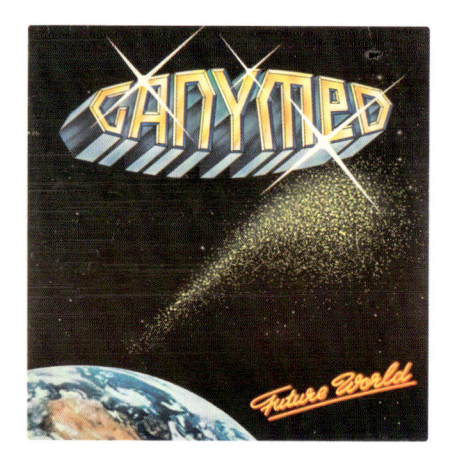 Ganymed-Future World Bellaphone / 1979	Gotham-Flasher Keylock / 1979
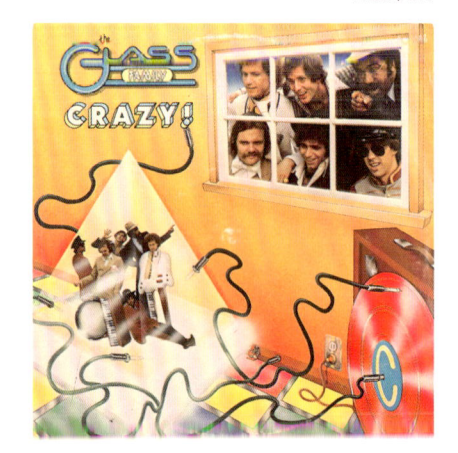 Glass Family-Crazy JDC / 1978	Glass Family-Mr DJ You Know How To Make Me Dance JDC / 1978	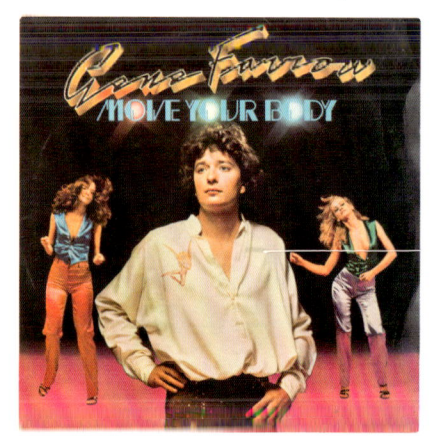 Gene Farrow-Move Your Body Magnet / 1978	 Giants-Giants Polydor / 1979
Gotham-Void Aurum / 1979	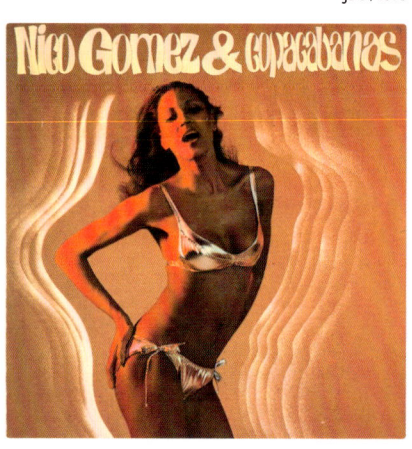 Nico Gomez & Copacabanas -Same GIP / 1979	Gloria Gaynor-Experience MGM / 1975	Gloria Gaynor-Never Can Say Goodbye MGM / 1975
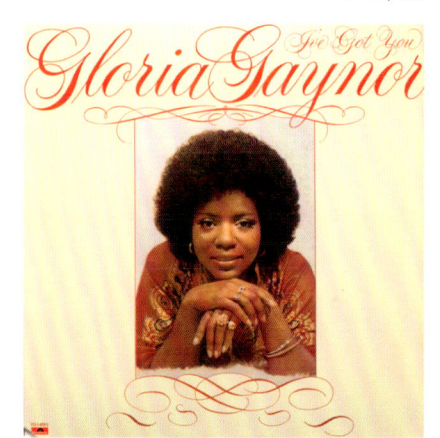 Gloria Gaynor-I've Got You Polydor / 1976	Gloria Gaynor-Glorious Polydor / 1977	Gloria Gaynor-I Have A Right Polydor / 1979	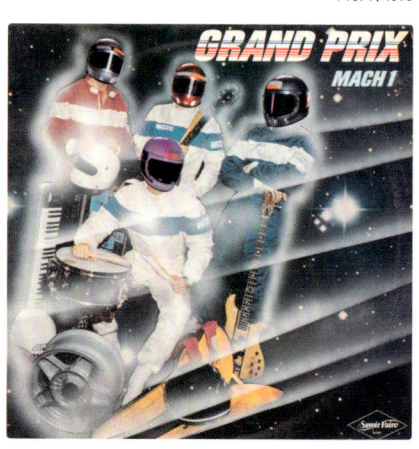 Grand Prix-Mach 1 Savoir Faire / 1983

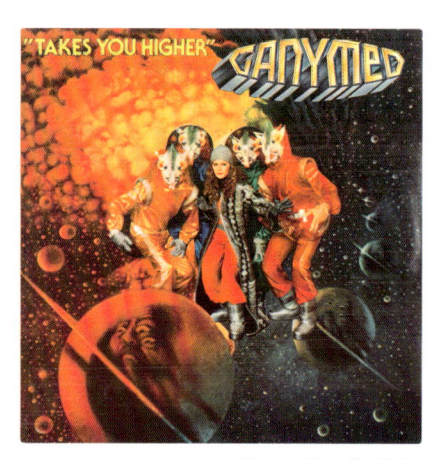

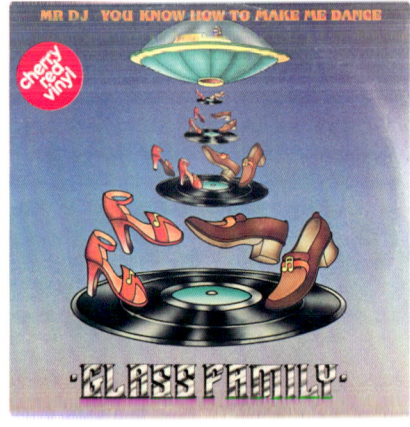

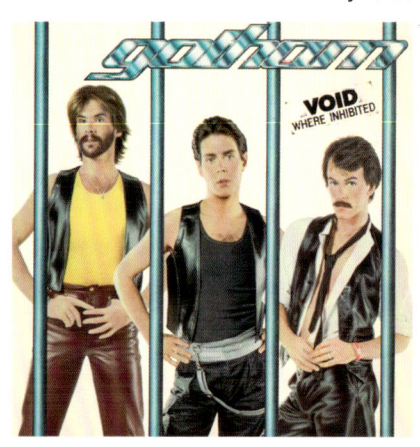

Grey And Hanks-You Fooled Me RCA / 1978	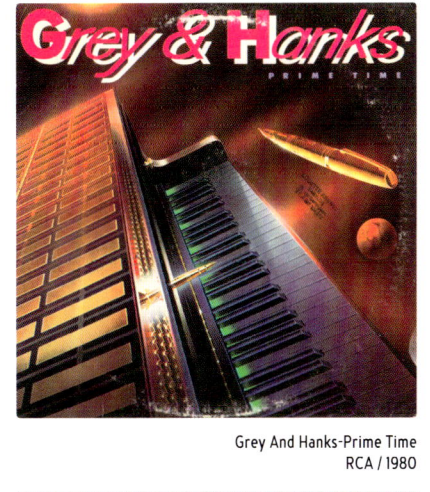 Grey And Hanks-Prime Time RCA / 1980	Gennaro Mambelli-Neopolitan Sound Harmony / 1977	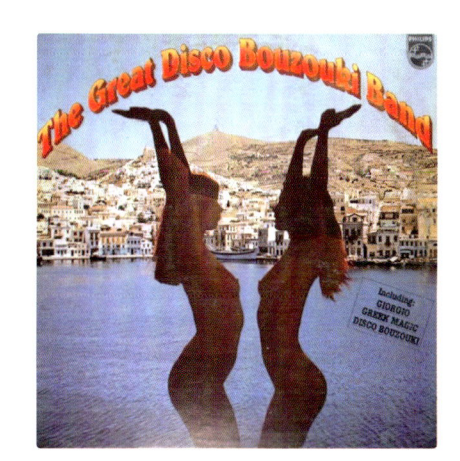 The Great Disco Bouzouki Band Decca / 1978
GQ-Disco Nights Arista / 1979	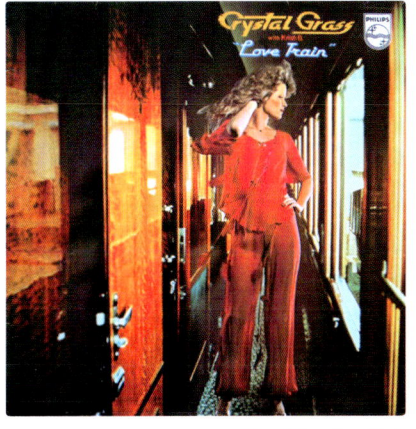 Crystal Grass-Love Train Philips / 1978	Harlow-Take Off Celsius / 1980	Hair-Disco Spectacular RCA / 1979
 Patrick Hernandez-Born To Be Alive Aquarius / 1979	Hot Ice-Pall Mall Groove polydor / 1977	Hot Ice-Hot Ice No.1 Rage / 1976	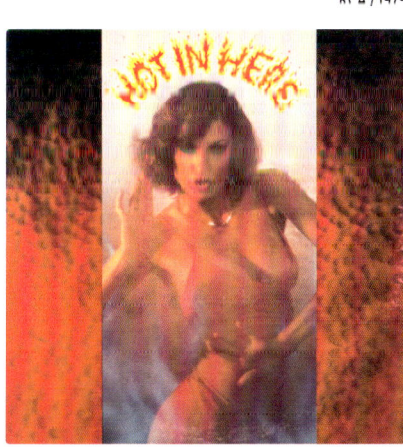 Hot In Here-Hot In Here Baby Grand / 1977
Dan Hartman-Instant Replay Blue Sky / 1978	 Black jack-Hot Passion Pinball / 1979	Halloween-Come See What It's All About Mercury / 1979	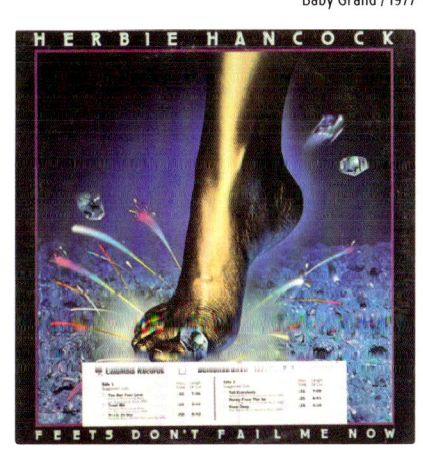 Herbie Hancock-Feets Don't Fail Me Now Columbia / 1979

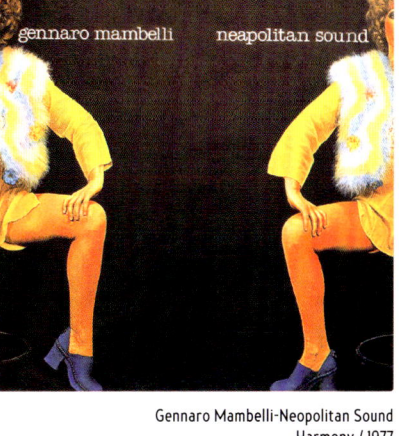

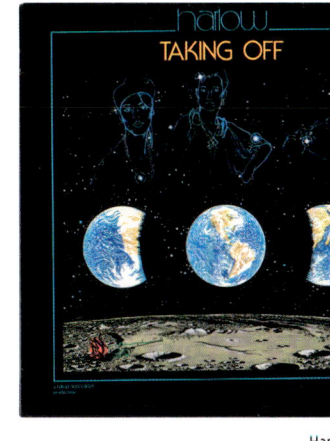

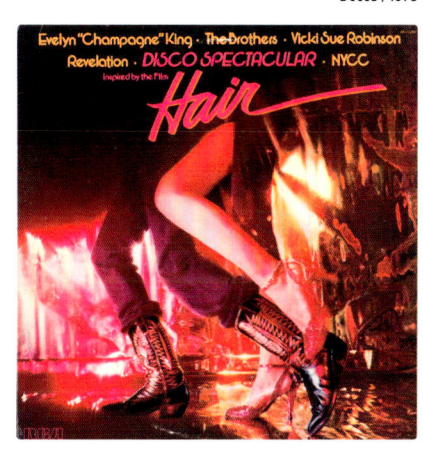

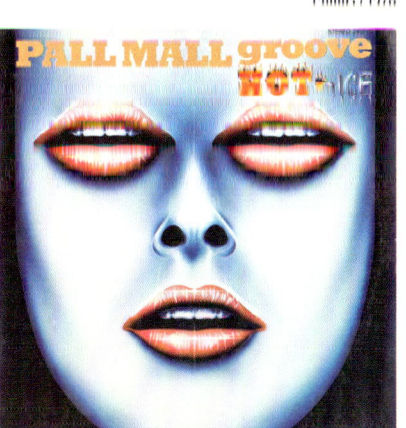

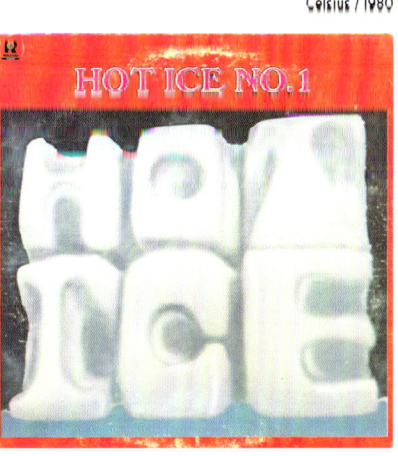

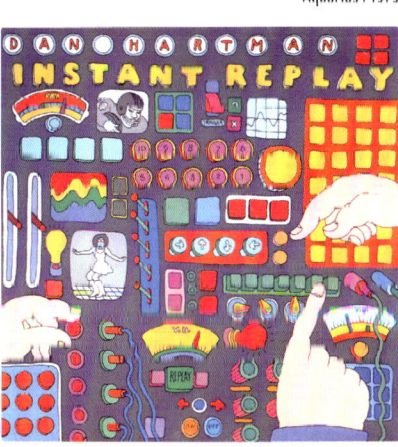

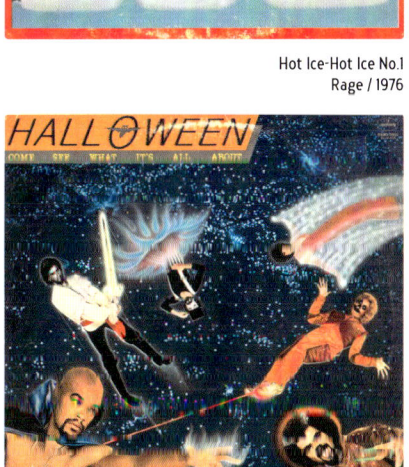

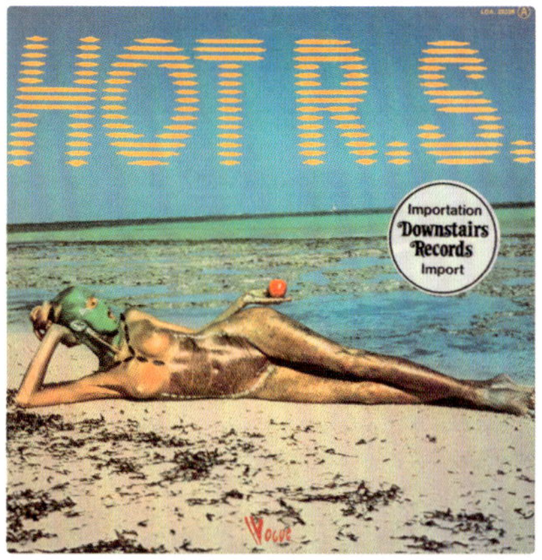

Hot R.S.-House Of The Rising Sun Vogue / 1977	Hot R.S.-Heads Or Tails RPM / 1980	 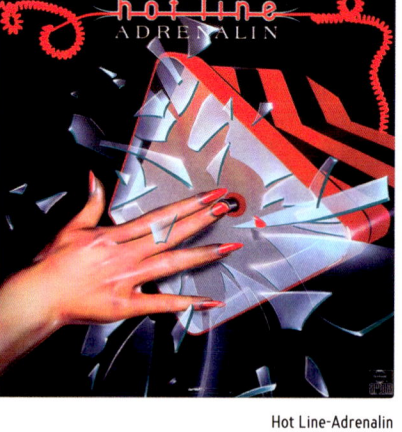  Hot Line-Adrenalin Ariola	Cissy Houston-Warning Danger Columbia / 1978
Hot Blood-Disco Dracula Dynamo / 1977	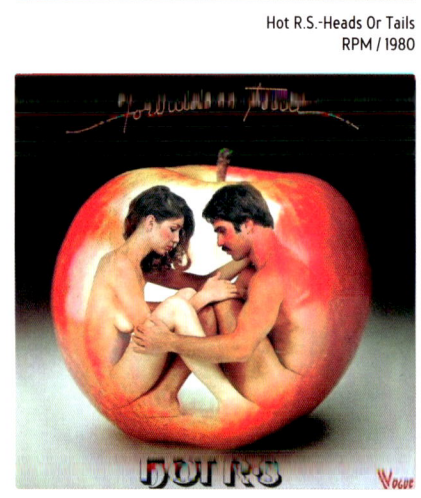 Hot R.S.-Forbidden Fruit Vogue / 1978	Isaac Hayes Movement-Disco Connection ABC / 1975	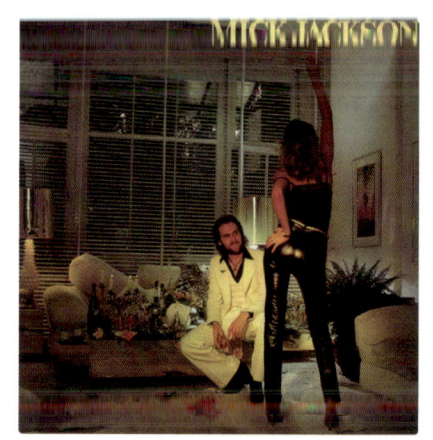 Mick Jackson -Mick Jackson Atlantic / 1979
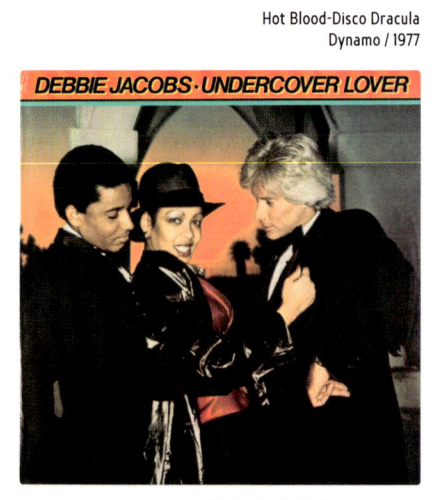 Debbie Jacobs-Undercover Lover MCA / 1979	Debbie jacobs-High On Your Love MCA / 1980	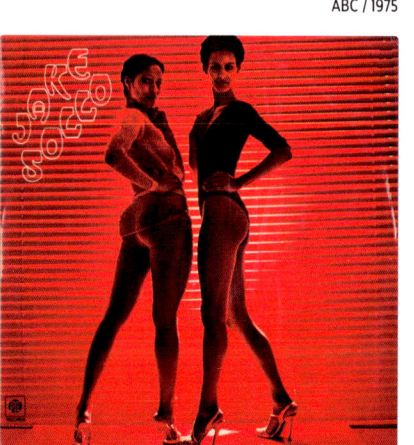 Jake Solo-Jake Solo Pye / 1979	J.B's Internationals-Jam II Disco Fever Polydor / 1978
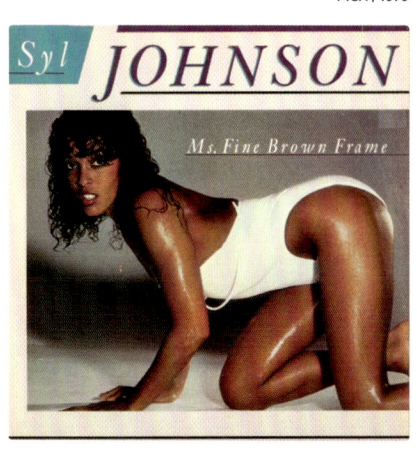 Syl Johnson-Ms. Fine Brown Frame Boardwalk / 1982	T.C James-Get Up On Your Feet Quality / 1978	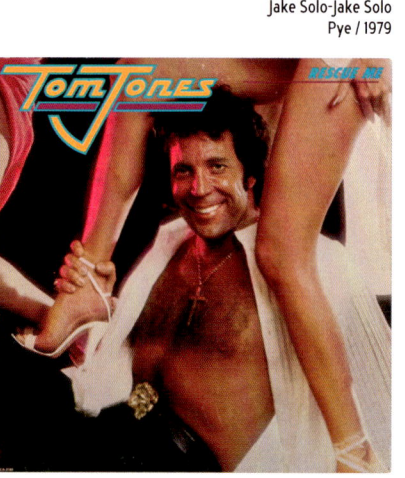 Tom Jones-Rescue Me MCA / 1979	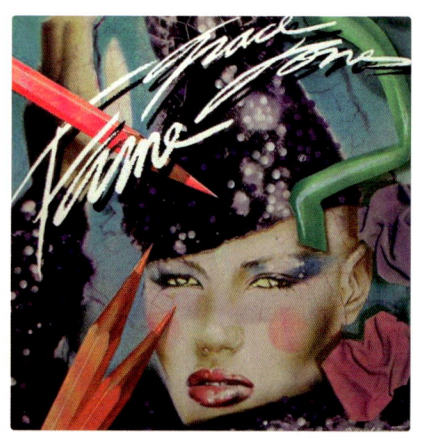 Grace jones-Fame Island / 1978

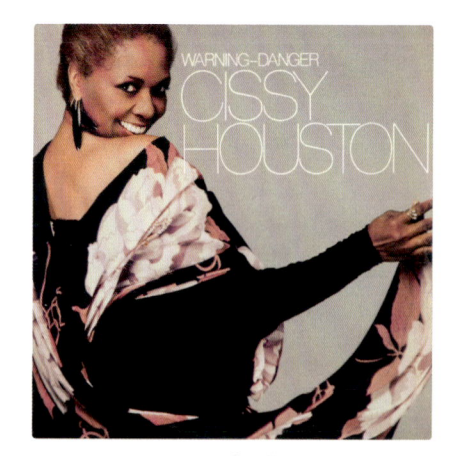

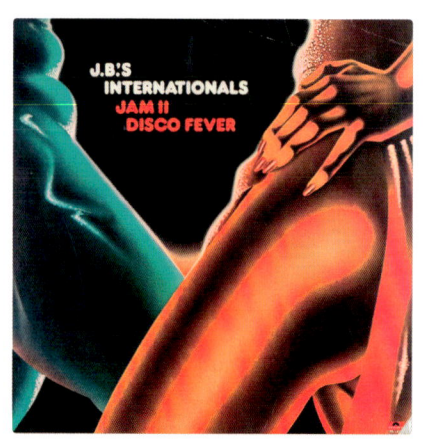

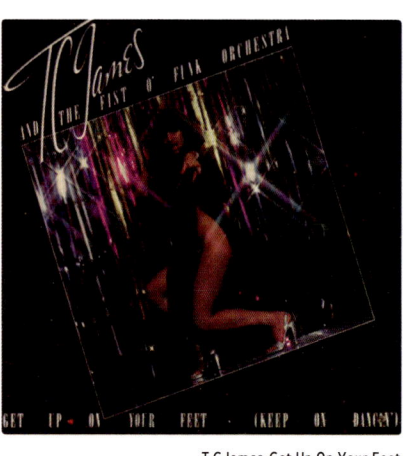

Love De-Luxe - Again and Again / Atlantic 1979

Grace Jones-Do Or Die Island / 1978	Grace Jones-Portofolio Island / 1977	Grace Jones-Muse island / 1979	Jupiter Sunset Band-Disco Rhapsody Ariston / 1977
Madleen Kane-Cheri Pye / 1979	Madleen Kane-Cheri Pye / 1979	Madleen Kane-Sounds Of Love Chalet / 1980	Kasso-Kasso F1-Team / 1981
Kat Mandu-The kat Is Back Manhattan-Formula / 1982	kikrokos-Jungle DJ Polydor / 1978	Kassav-Love And Ka Dance FM Productions / 1979	kébekélektrik-Same Unidisc / 1977
Suzi Lane-Oh La La Elektra / 1979	DC La Rue-The Tea Dance Pyramid / 1976	Laser-Laser Decca / 1979	La Barbichette-Soundtrack Barclay / 1979

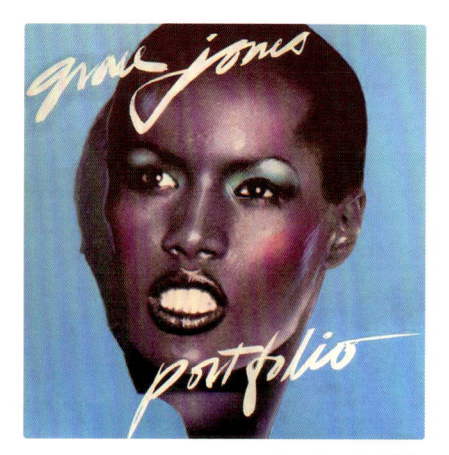

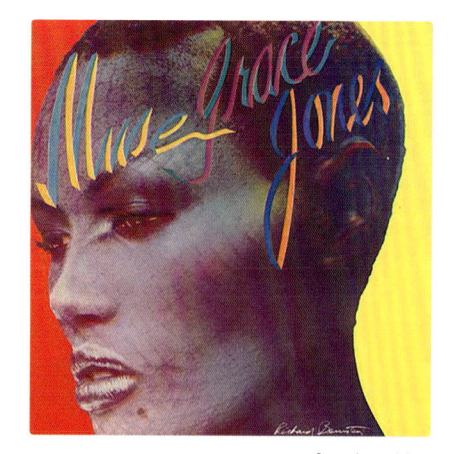

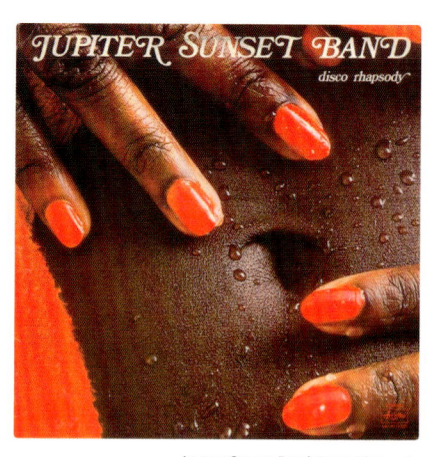

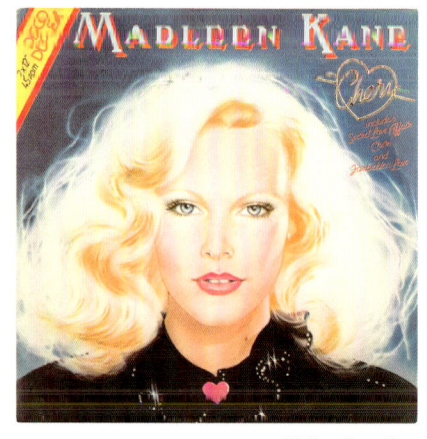

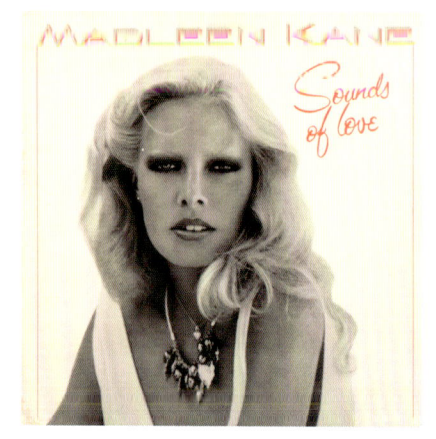

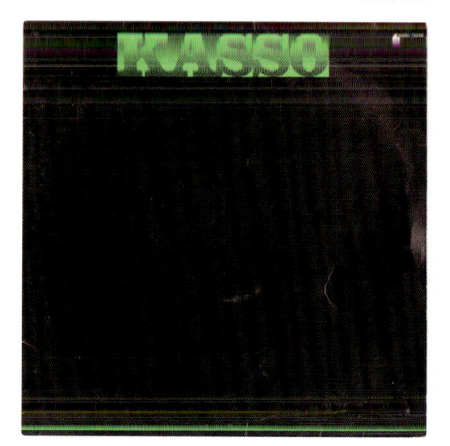

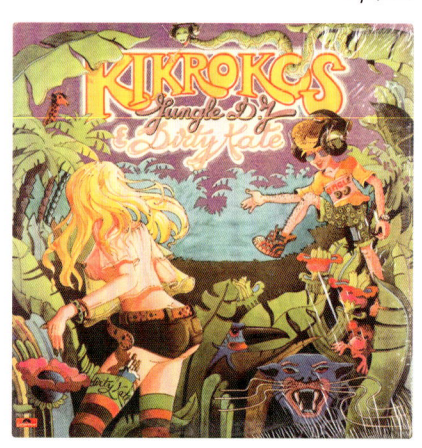

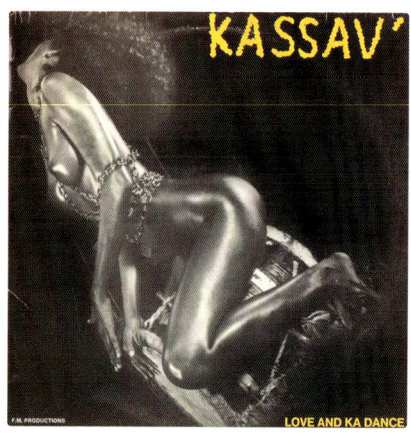

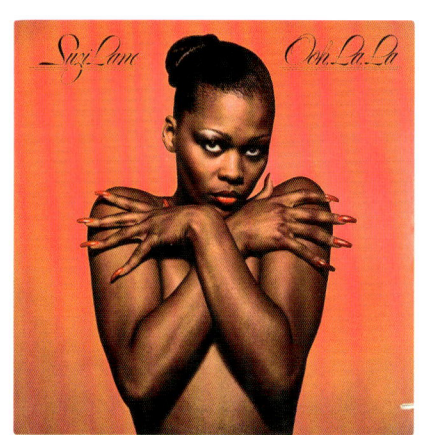

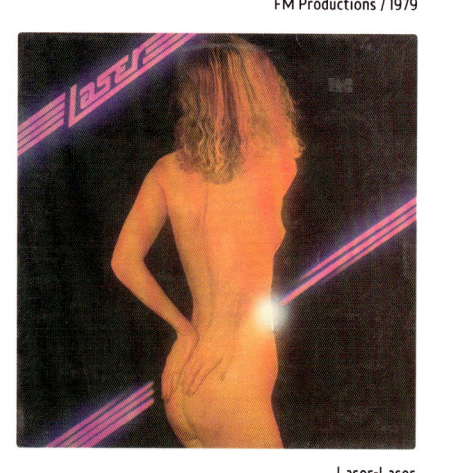

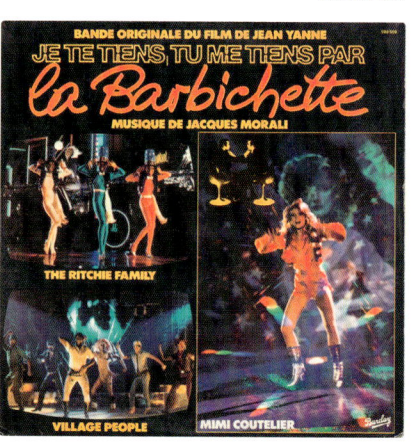

L.E.B. Harmony-Disco Boogie
Chic / 1979

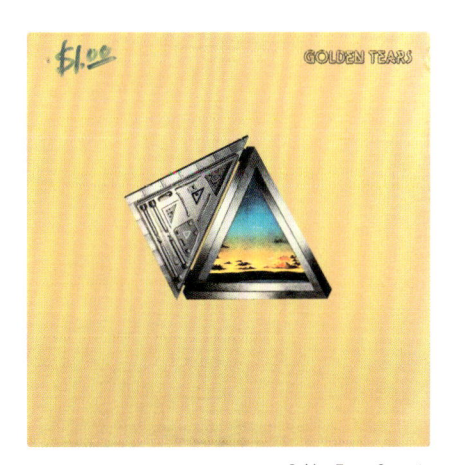

Golden Tears-Sumeria
Polydor / 1977

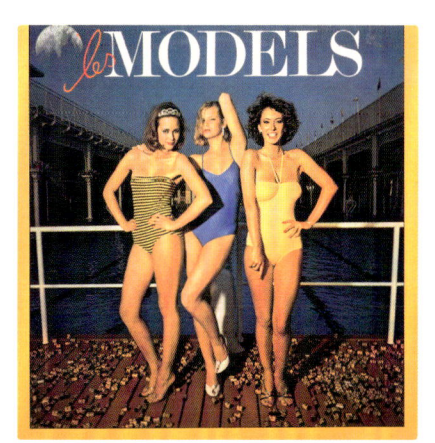

Les Models-Les Models
Dryfus / 1979

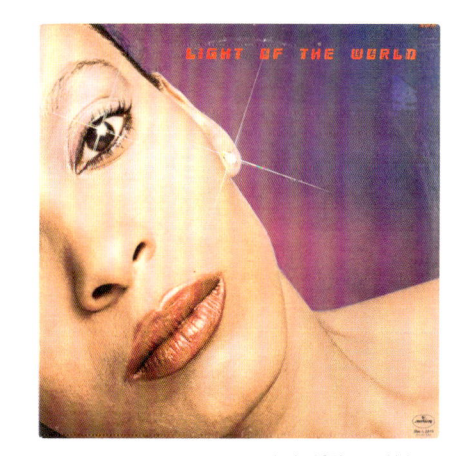

Light Of The World-Same
Mercury / 1979

Love Committee-Same
Elektric / 1980

Love Deluxe-Here Comes That Sound
Warner Bros. / 1977

The Love Machine-Feel The Love
Charmdale / 1977

Lovequake-Lovequake
Ibach / 1977

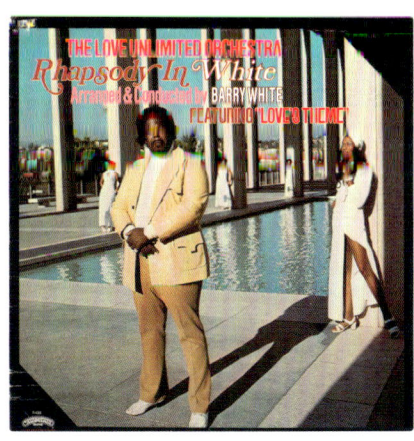

The Love Unlimited Orchestra-Rhapsody In White
20 Century Records / 1973

Love Unlimited-Love Is Back
Unlimited Gold / 1979

The Love Unlimited Orchestra-Latin Dance
Unlimited Gold / 1981

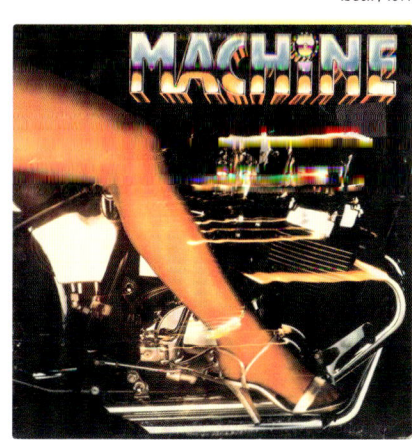

Machine-Machine
RCA / 1979

Machine-Moving On
RCA / 1980

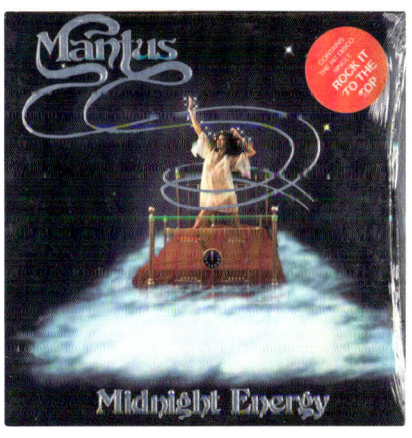

Mantus-Midnight Energy
SMI / 1979

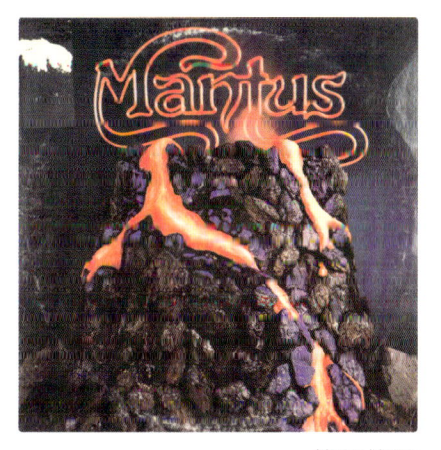

Mantus-Mantus
SMI / 1980

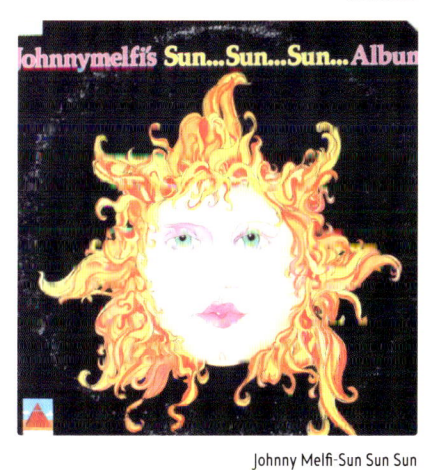

Johnny Melfi-Sun Sun Sun
Pyramid / 1977

307

The Meters-Trick Bag
Reprise / 1976

Donna Mcghee-Make it Last Forever
Red Greg / 1978

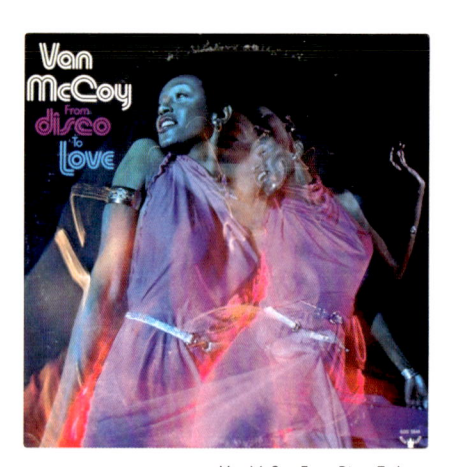

Van McCoy-From Disco To Love
Buddhah / 1975

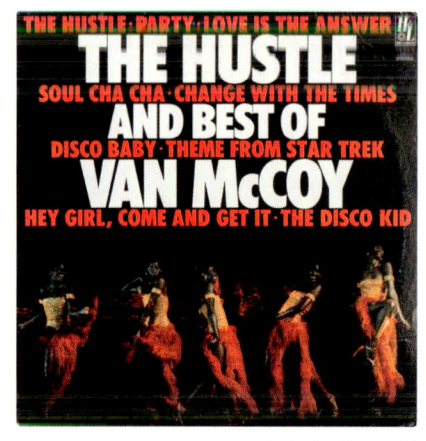

Van McCoy-The Best Of
H&L / 1976

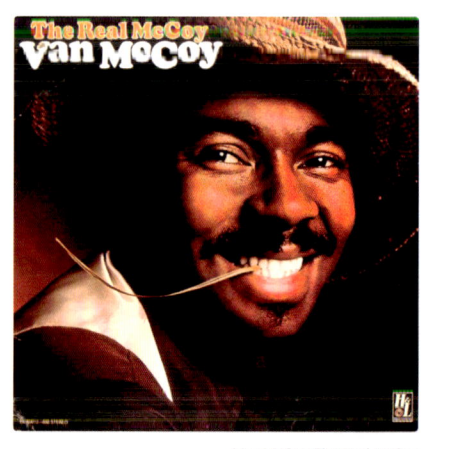

Van McCoy-The Real McCoy
H&L / 1976

Jackie Moore-I'm On My Way
Columbia / 1979

Mighty Pope-Sway
RFC / 1979

Mouzon's Electric Band-Baby Come back
Metronome / 1979

Montana Orchestra-Heavy Vibes
Philly Sound Works / 1983

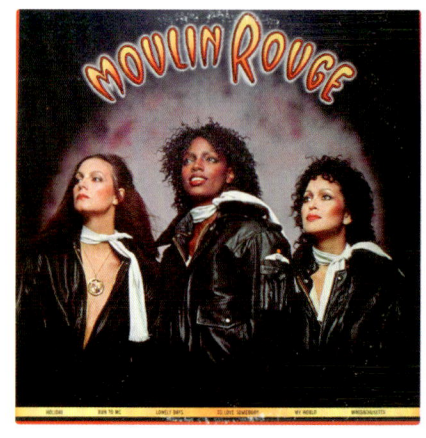

Moulin Rouge-Moulin Rouge
ABC / 1979

Mascara - See You In L.A. / Ensign 1979
Design: Hothouse / Photography: Hanchew

Montreal Sound-One More Time
Totem / 1979

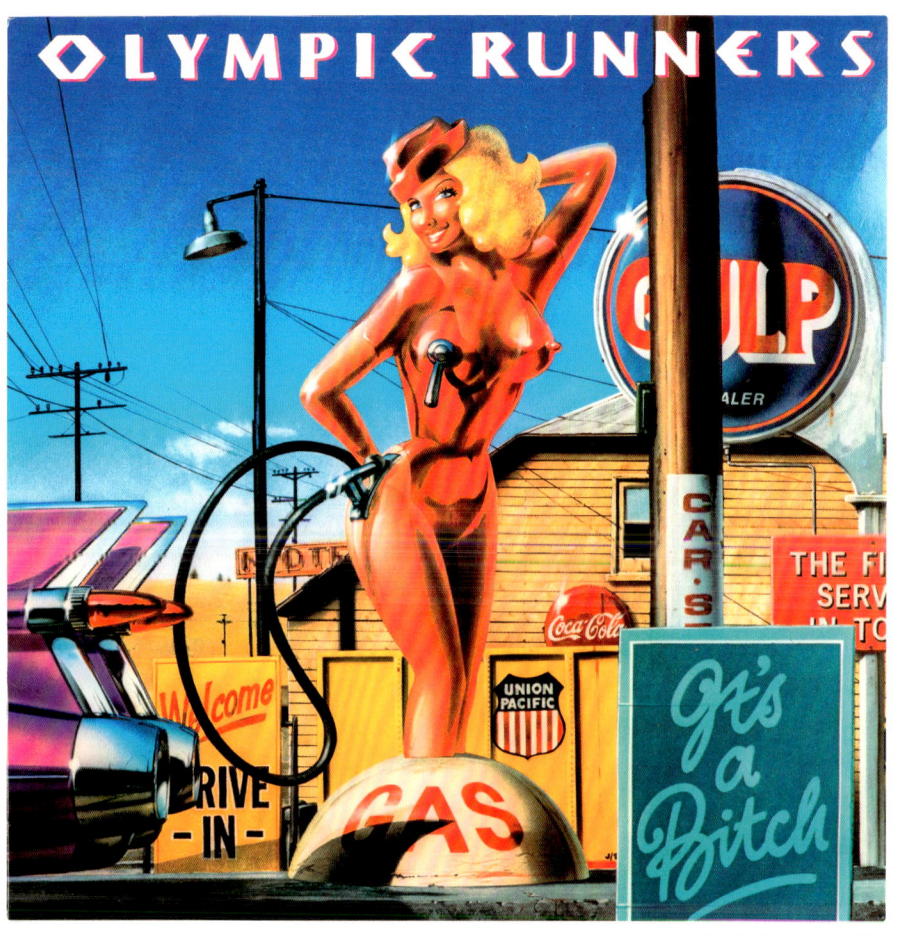

Olympic Runners-It's A Bitch
Polydor / 1979

Patrick Adams Presnts Phreek
Atlantic / 1978

Satin-Satin
Solo / 1979

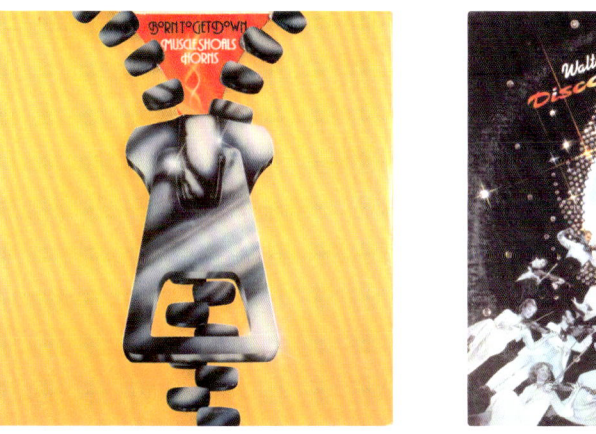

Muscle Shoals Horns-Born To Get Down Bang / 1976	Walter Murphy-Discosymphony New York Int. / 1979	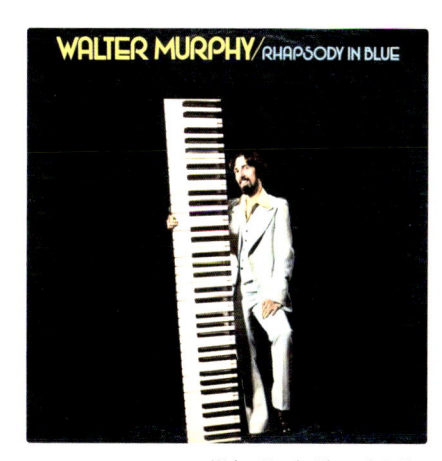 Walter Murphy-Rhapsody In Blue Private Stock / 1977	Nino Tempo & 5 th. Ave Sax-Come See Me Round Midnight A&M / 1974
 Nightlife Unlimited-I Love The Night In New York City Tojo / 1983	Nowy-Nowy 2 Atlantic / 1975	Nuggets N.Y Mercury / 1979	 New Paradise-New Paradise F1-team / 1981
Number One Ensemble-Gipsylon Radio / 1980	Olympic Runners-Puttin' It On Ya Polydor / 1978	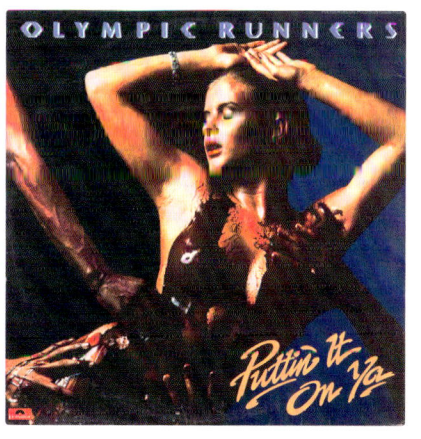 Olympic Runners-Puttin' It On Ya (Back) Polydor / 1978	Olympic Runners-Out In Front London / 1975
Olympic Runners Don't Let Up London / 1976	 Leonore O' Malley-First Be A Woman Polydor / 1979	Orchestra Julian-Latin Fire TPI	 Orient Express-A Desert Fantasy Polydor / 1978

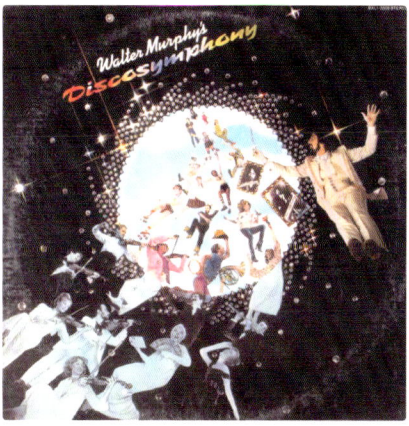

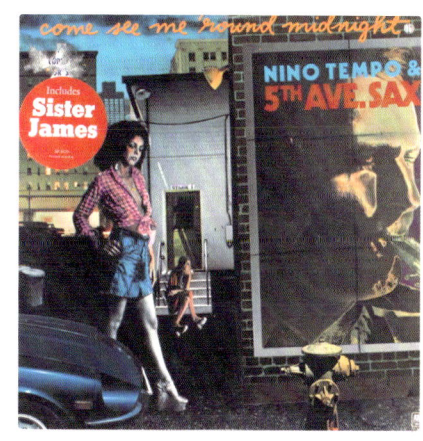

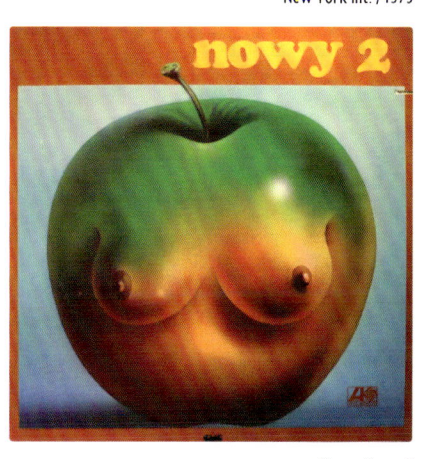

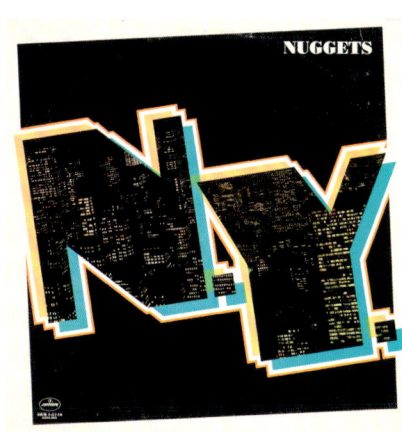

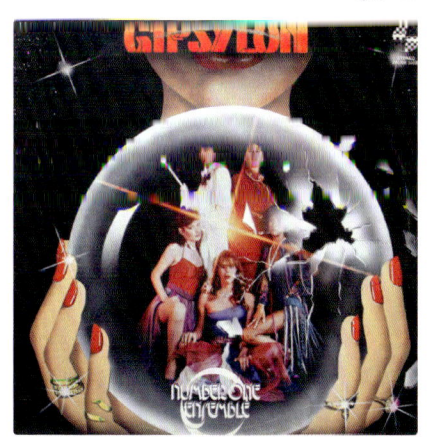

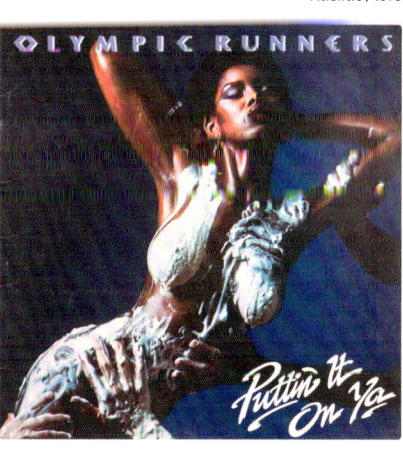

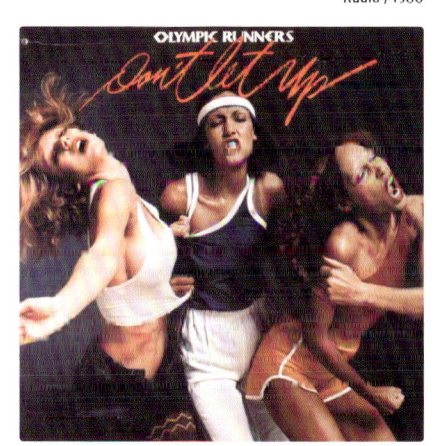

Bruni Pagan-Just Bruni
Elektra / 1979

Panache-This Is Panache
Roche / 1979

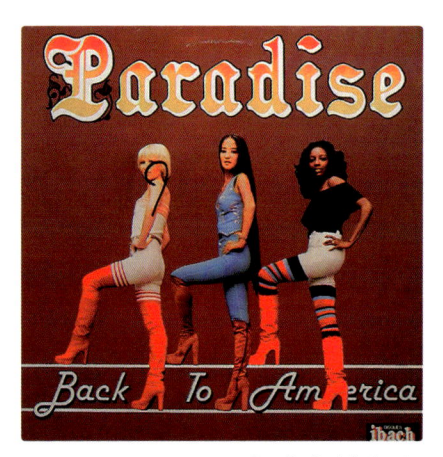

Paradise-Back To America
Ibach / 1979

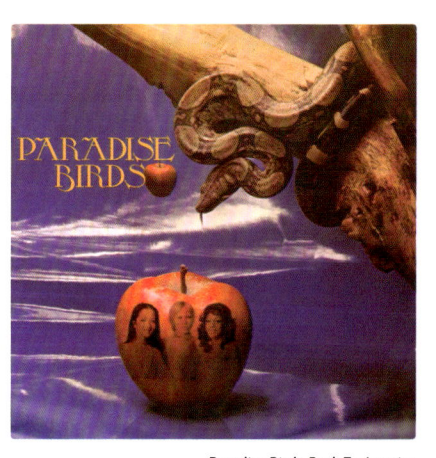

Paradise Birds-Back To America
CBS / 1979

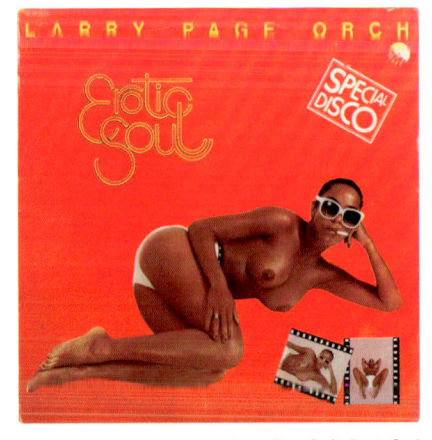

Larry Page Orch.-Erotic Soul
EMI / 1977

Larry Page Orch.-Skin Heat
Rampage / 1978

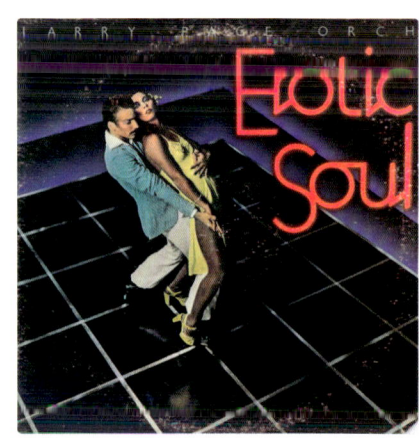

Larry Page Orch.-Erotic Soul
London / 1977

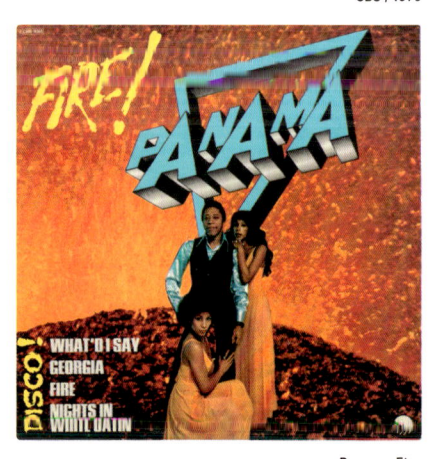

Panama-Fire
EMI / 1978

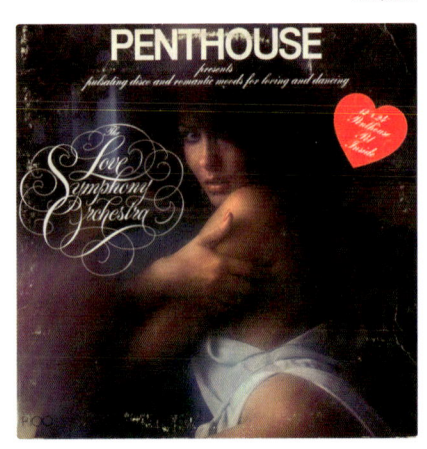

Penthouse-Love Symphony Orchestra
Quality / 1978

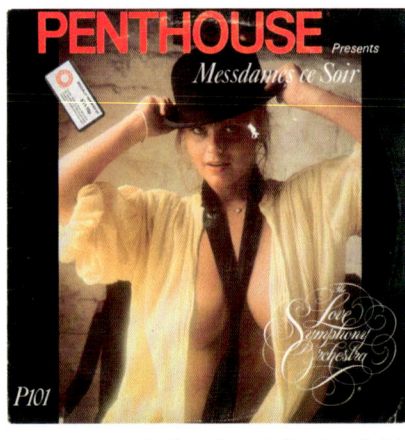

Penthouse-Presents Messdames Ce Soir
Talpro / 1979

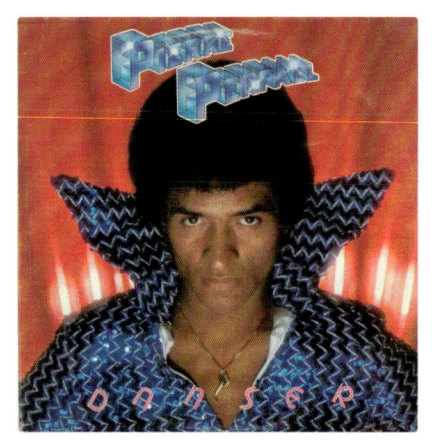

Pierre Perpall-Danser
Solo

Kellee Patterson-All The Things You Are
Shadybrook/ 1979

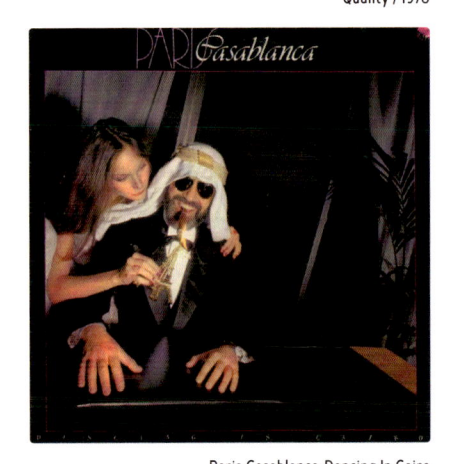

Paris Casablanca-Dancing In Cairo
Pathé / 1979

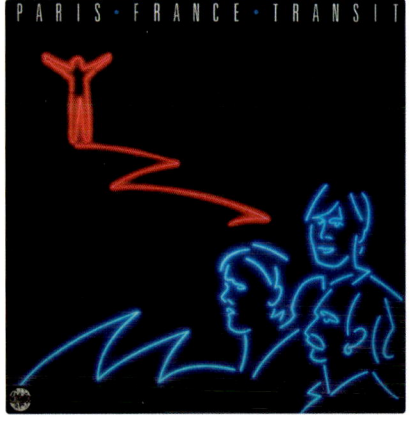

Paris-France-Transit
Celcius / 1982

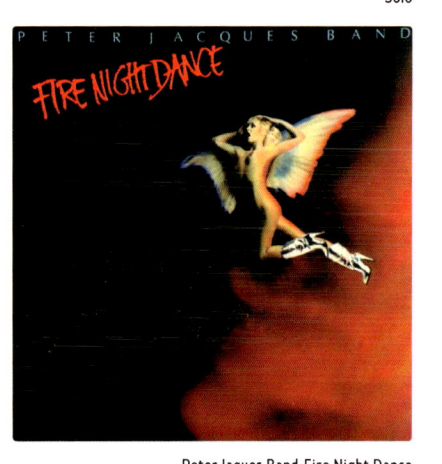

Peter Jaques Band-Fire Night Dance
Goody / 1979

Panama-Panama
EMI / 1979

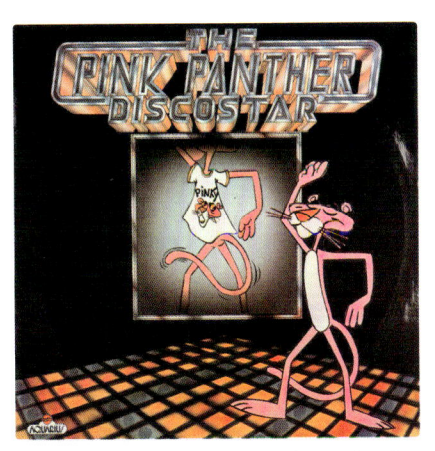

The Pink Panter Disco Star
Aquarius / 1978

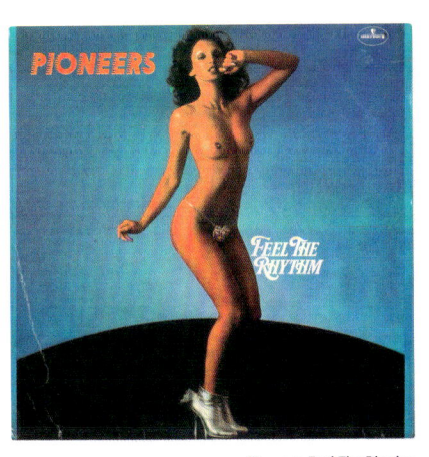

Pioneers-Feel The Rhythm
Mercury / 1976

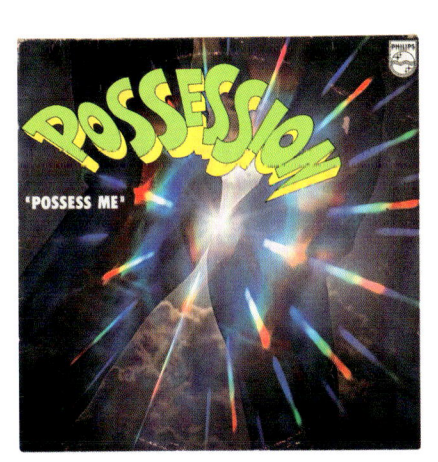

Possession-Possess Me
Philips / 1978

Plaza-Plaza
EMI / 1979

The Raes-Dancing Up A Storm
A&M / 1979

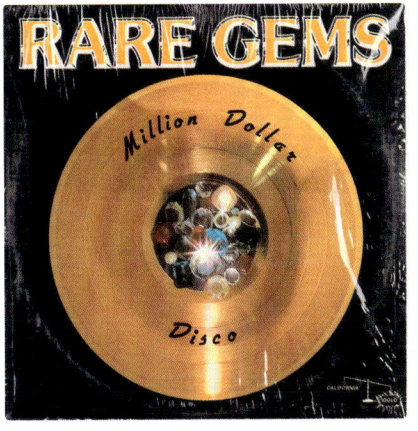

Rare Gems-Million Dollar Disco
California Gold / 1978

Real Thing-Can You Feel The Force
Pye / 1978

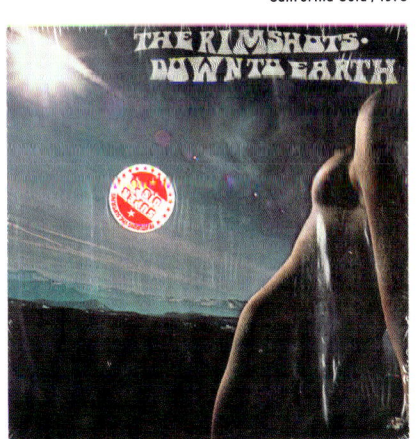

Pole Position-Starter
Zip / 1979

The Rimshots-Down To Earth
Stang / 1976

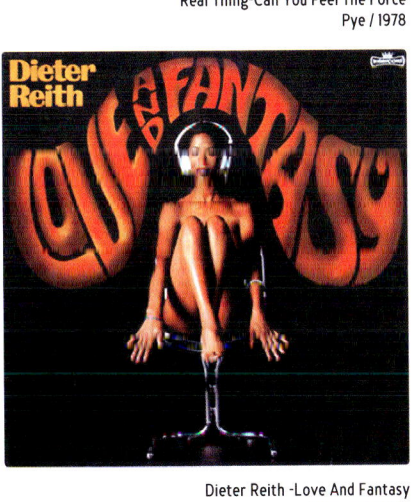

Dieter Reith -Love And Fantasy
Intercord / 1978

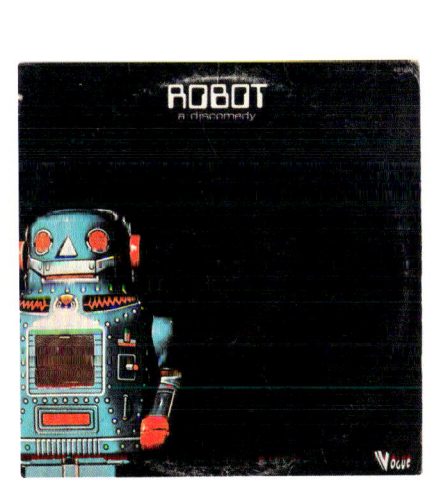

Robot-A Discomedy
Vogue / 1978

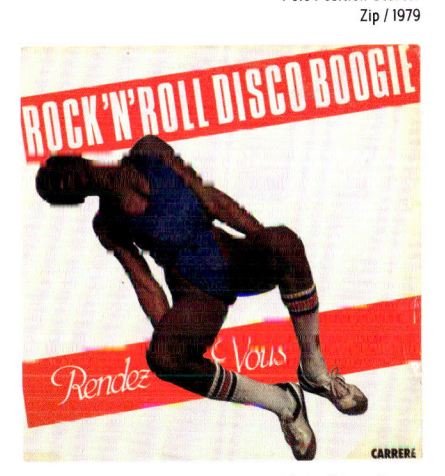

Rendez Vous-Rock 'N' Roll Disco Boogie
Carrere / 1979

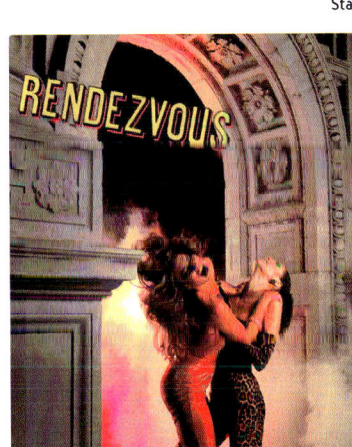

Rendez Vous-Rock 'N' Roll Disco Boogie
ATTIC / 1979

313

Rockets-Galaxy
Carrere / 1980

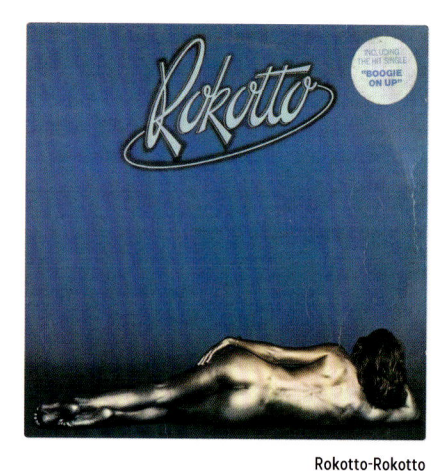

Rokotto-Rokotto
State / 1978

Roots-Roots
Derby / 1979

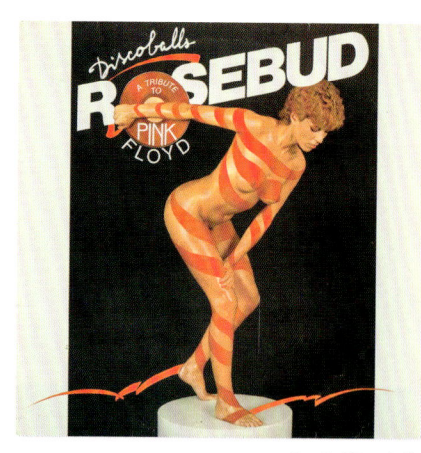

Rosebud-Discoballs
WEA / 1977

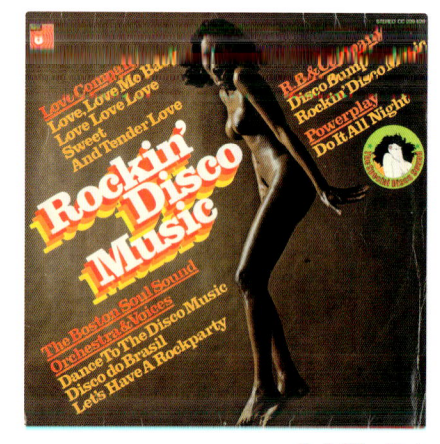

Rockin' Disco Music
BASF / 1976

Saint Tropez-Hot And Nasty
Destiny / 1982

Sanctuary-Sanctuary
Sanctuary / 1980

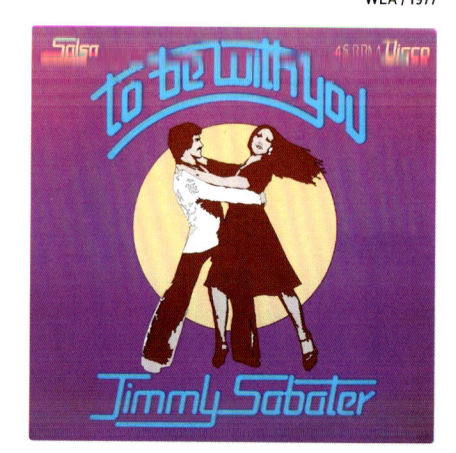

Jimmy Sabater-To Be With You
Salsa / 1976

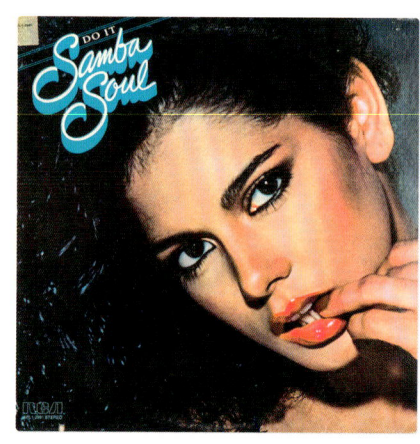

Samba Soul -Do It
RCA / 1978

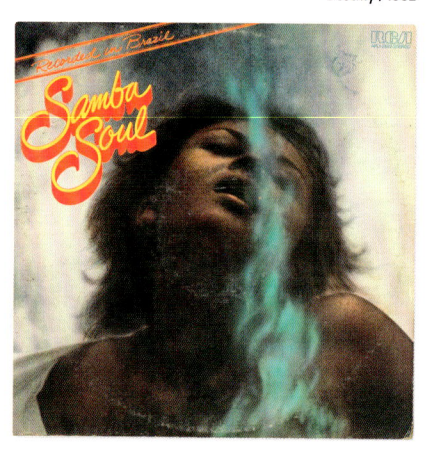

Samba Soul-Samba Soul
RCA / 1976

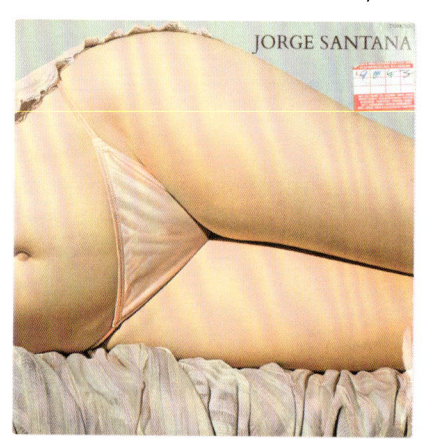

Jorge Santana
Tomato / 1978

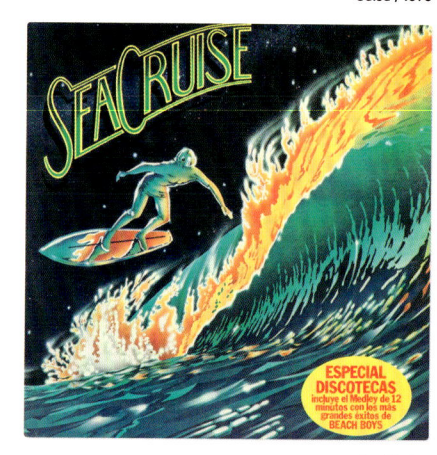

Sea Cruise
Celcius / 1978

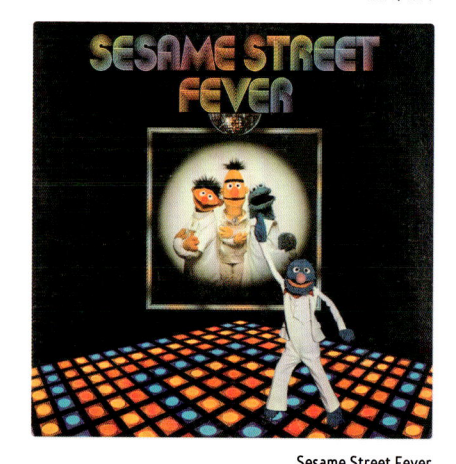

Sesame Street Fever
Sesame Street / 1978

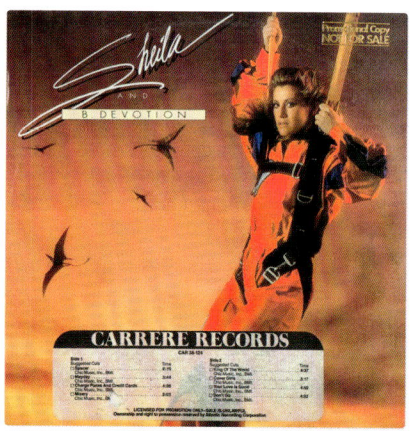

Sheila And B. Devotion-Sheila And B. Devotion
Carrere / 1980

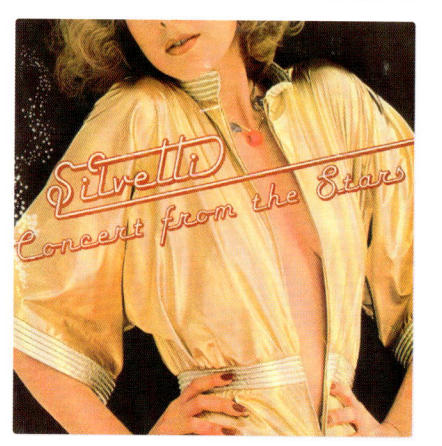

Silvetti-Concert From The Stars
Sire / 1978

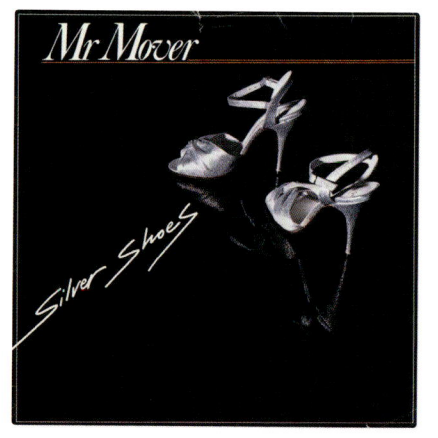

Silver Shoes-Mr. Mover
Carrere / 1979

Wood, Brass & Steel - Wood, Brass & Steel / Turbo 1976
Illustration: Nick Caruso

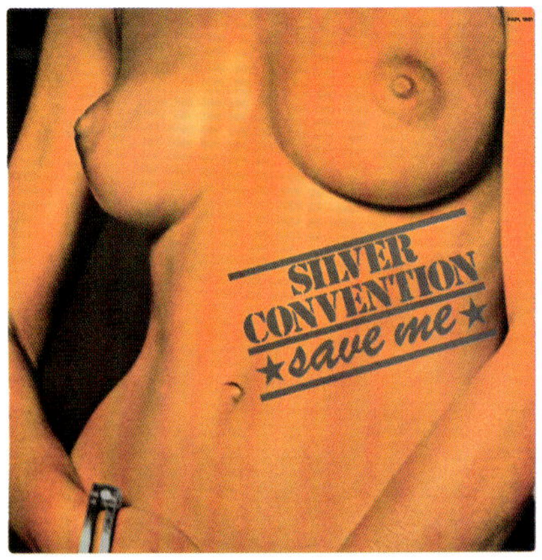

Silver Convention-Save Me
Jupiter / 1975

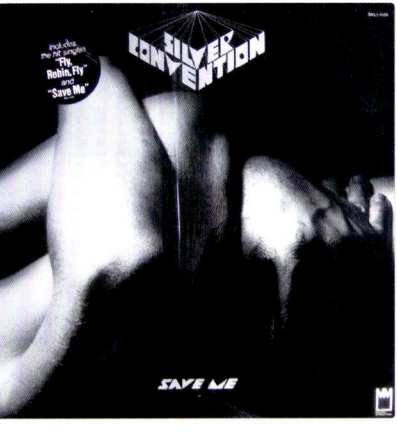

Silver Convention-Save Me
Midsong / 1975

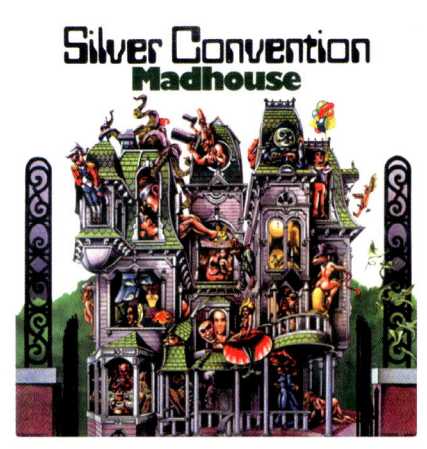

Silver Convention-Madhouse
Jupiter / 1976

Silver Convention-Summernights
Durium / 1977

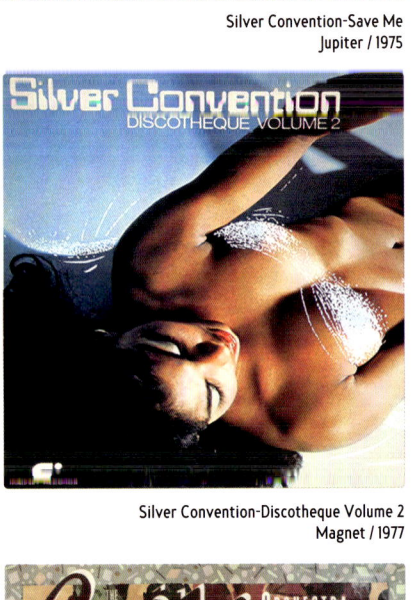

Silver Convention-Discotheque Volume 2
Magnet / 1977

Silver Convention-Love In A Sleeper
Jupiter / 1978

The Simon Orchestra-Mr. Big Shot
Polydor / 1979

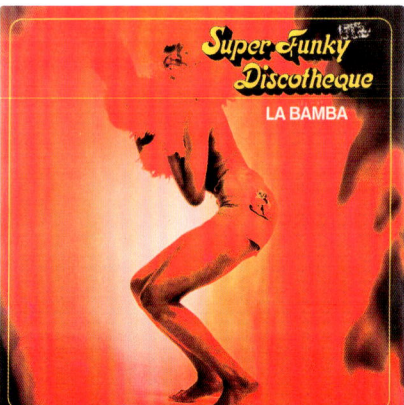

Supercharge-Body Rhythm
Virgin / 1979

Super Funky Discotheque-La Bamba
Blue Elephant / 1975

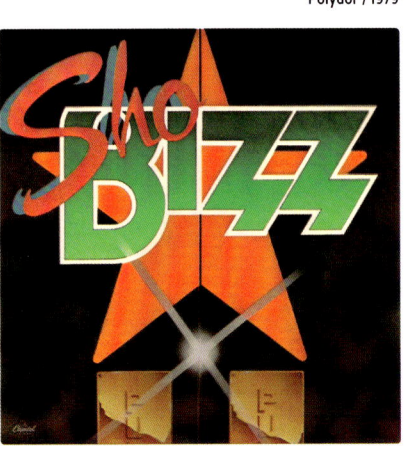

Sho Bizz-Sho Bizz
Capitol / 1979

Slang-Slang
Vedette / 1978

Soirée-Soirée
Roadshow / 1979

Soirée-Soirée
Unison / 1979

Southern Cookin'-Southern Cookin'
Polydor / 1979

Southern Exposure-Headin' South
RCA / 1979

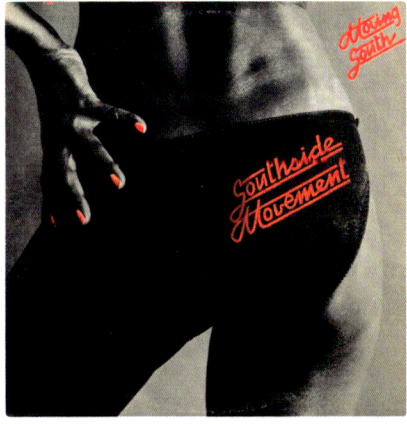

Southside Movement-Moving South
20th Century / 1975

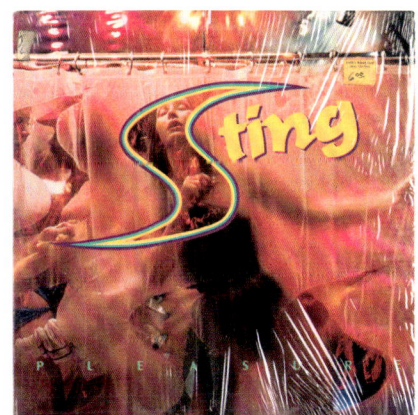

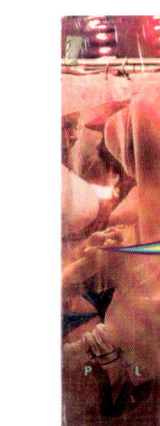

Sting-Pleasure
ABC / 1978

Street Corner Symphony-Little Funk Machine
ABC / 1976

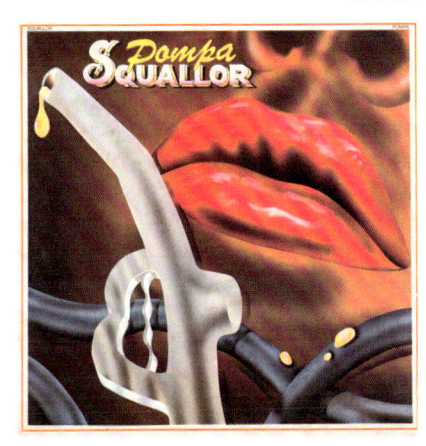

Squallor-Pompa
CGD / 1977

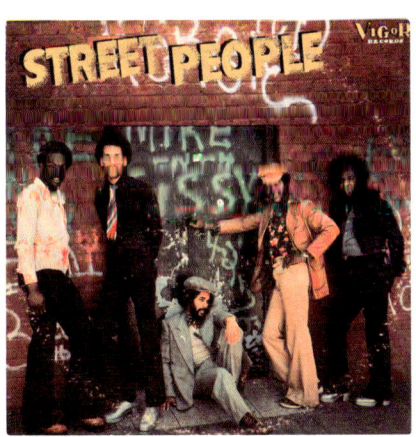

Street People-Street People
Vigor / 1976

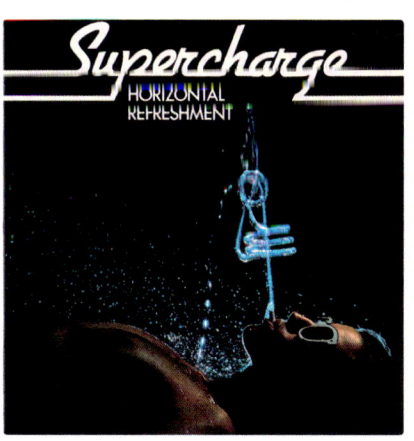

Street Feet-Street Feet
Baby Grand / 1977

Supercharge-Horizontal Refreshment
Virgin / 1976

Supercharge-I Think I'm Gonna Fall In Love
Virgin / 1978

Sparkle-Sparkle
Jam Sessions / 1979

Gino Soccio-Dance Exercise Music
Celebration / 1982

Supermax-Supermax
Voyage / 1978

317

OHIO PLAYERS
EVERYBODY UP

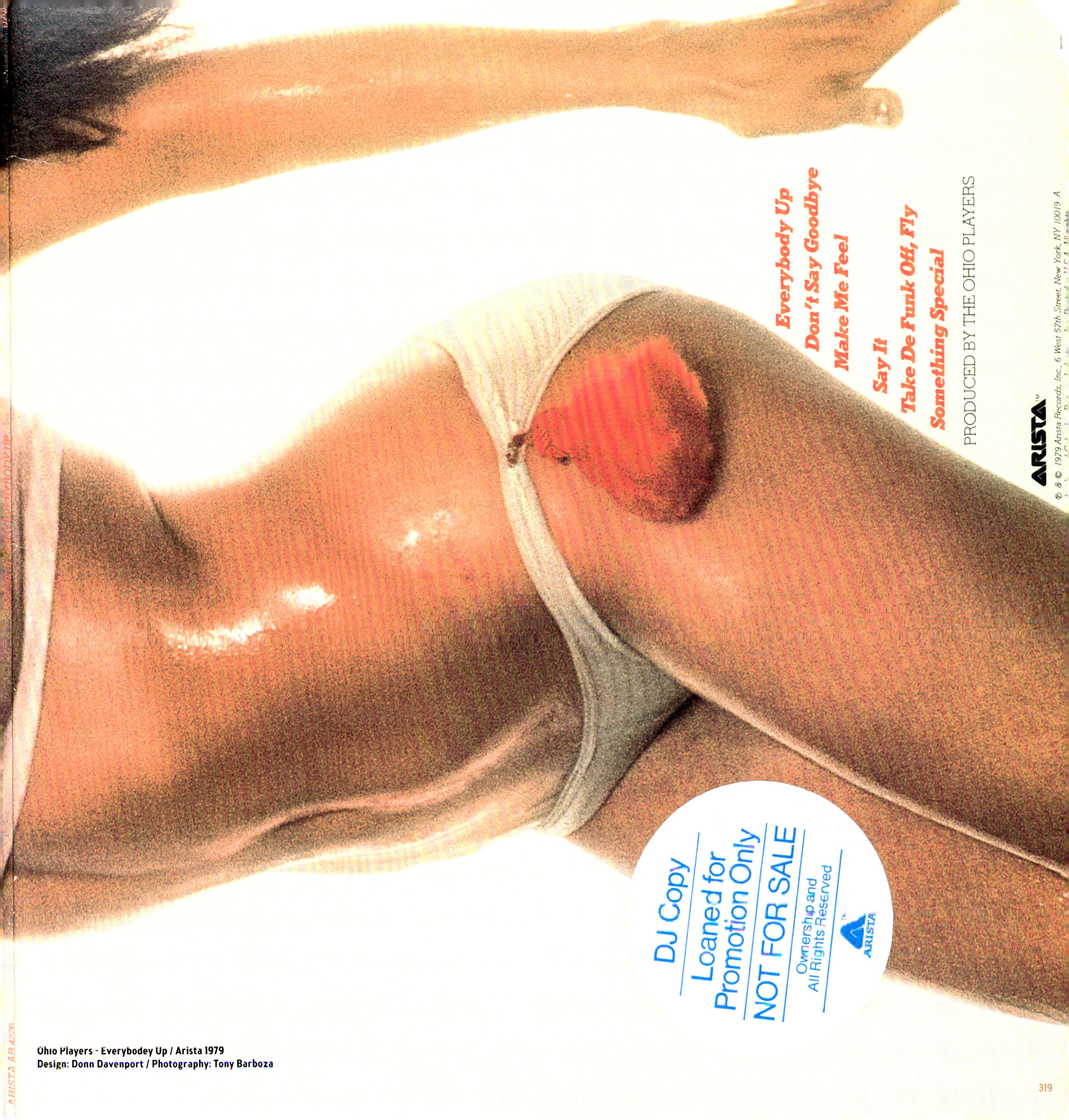

Everybody Up
Don't Say Goodbye
Make Me Feel
Say It
Take De Funk Off, Fly
Something Special

PRODUCED BY THE OHIO PLAYERS

ARISTA™

℗ & © 1979 Arista Records, Inc. 6 West 57th Street, New York, NY 10019.

DJ Copy
Loaned for Promotion Only
NOT FOR SALE
Ownership and All Rights Reserved
ARISTA

Ohio Players - Everybodey Up / Arista 1979
Design: Donn Davenport / Photography: Tony Barboza

Sho Nuff-From The Gut To The Butt
Stax / 1978

Silver Blue-Silver Blue
Epic / 1978

Smash-Smash
Source / 1979

Soccer-Soccer
Roy B / 1980

Supermax-Supermax
Epic / 1978

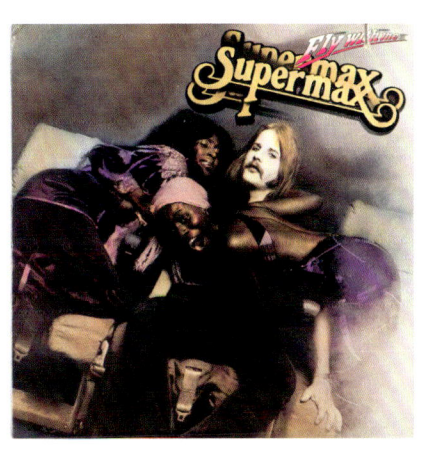

Supermax-Fly With Me
Elektra / 1979

Supermax-Types Of Skin
Elektra / 1980

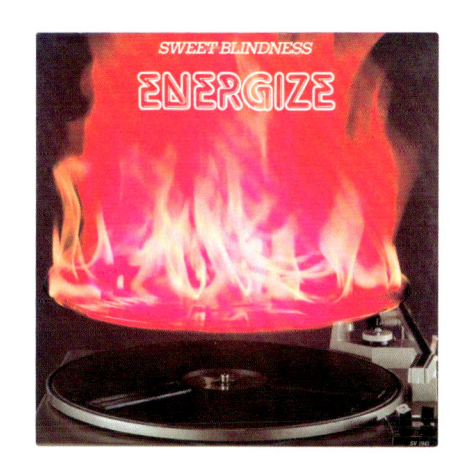

Sweet Blindness-Energize
Quality / 1977

Sweet Talks-Sweet Talks
Mercury / 1979

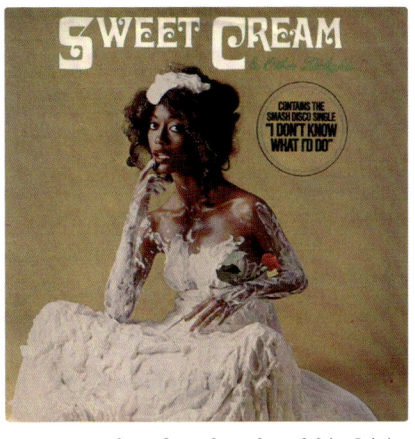

Sweet Cream-Sweet Cream & Other Delights
Shadybrook / 1978

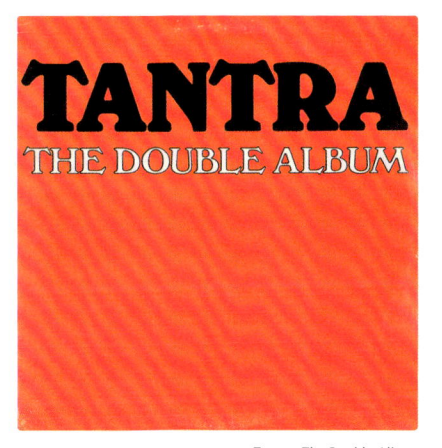

Tantra-The Double Album
Importe / 1980

Texico-Texico
Gamma / 1977

The Armada Orch.-NY Bus Stop
Contempo / 1975

The Bendeth Band-The Bendeth Band
Ensign / 1981

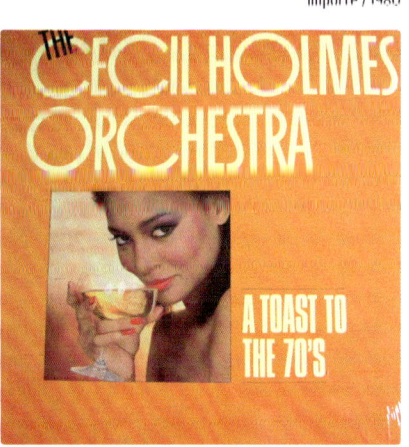

The Cecil Holmes Orchestra-A toast to The 70's
Accord / 1981

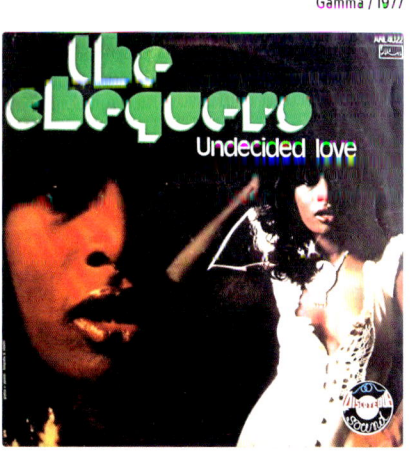

The Chequers-Undecided love
Aris / 1979

The Force-The Force
Philadelphia Int. / 1979

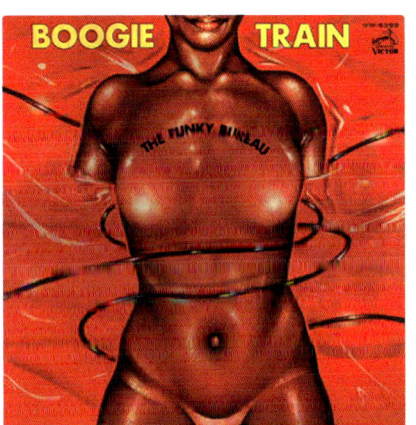

The Funky Bureau-Boogie Train
Victor / 1977

The Galactic Force Band-Spaced Out Disco
Springboard / 1978

The Trammps-The Legendary ZING Album
Buddah / 1975

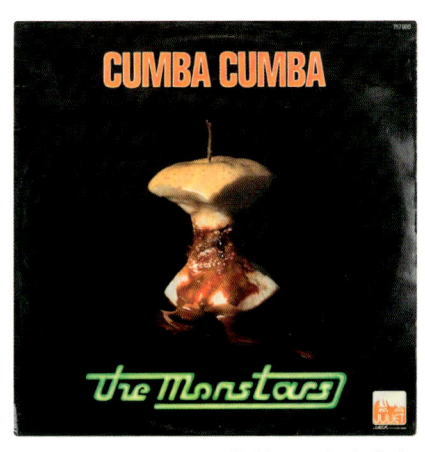

The Monstars-Cumba Cumba
Juliet / 1976

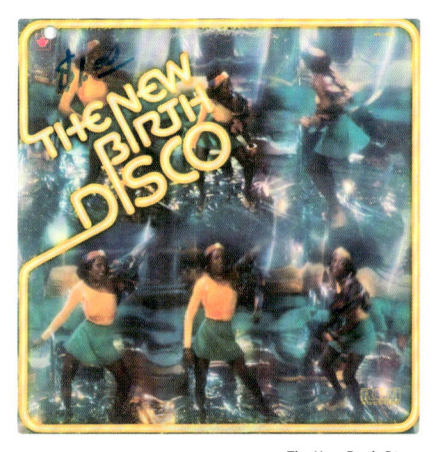

The New Birth-Disco
RCA / 1976

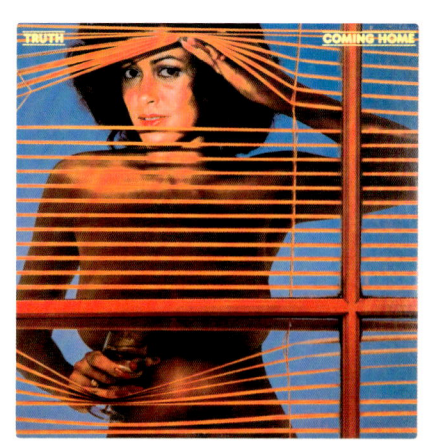

Truth-Coming Home
Devaki / 1980

The Ritchie Family-Brazil
20 century / 1975

THP #2-Tender Is The Night
RCA / 1978

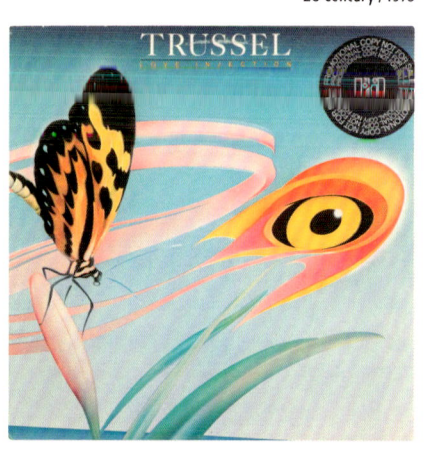

Trussel-Love Injection
Elektra / 1980

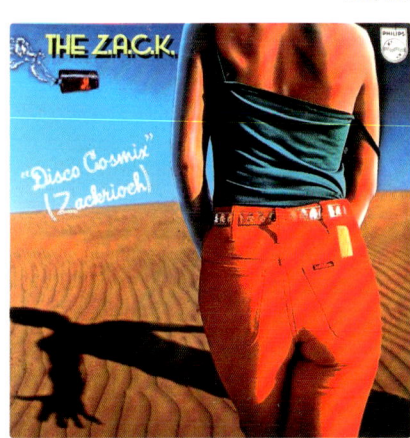

The Z.A.C.K.-Disco Cosmix
Philips / 1979

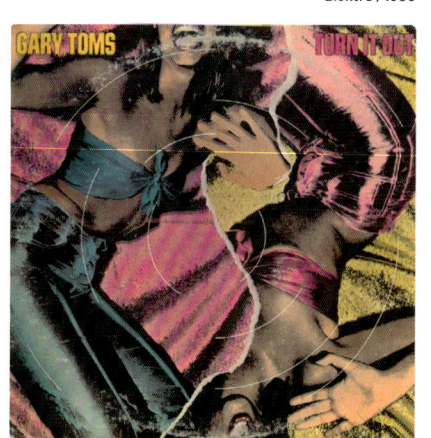

The New Ventures-Rocky Road
United Artists / 1976

Gary Thoms-Turn it Out
MCA / 1977

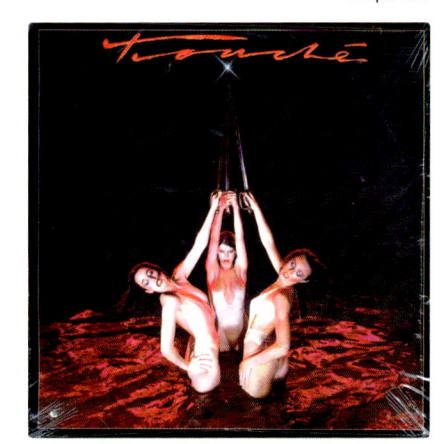

Touché-Touché
Magnum / 1979

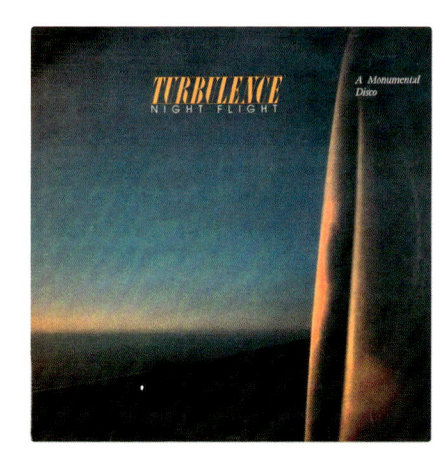

Turbulence-Night Flight
Intersound / 1979

Pam Todd-Together
Channel / 1979

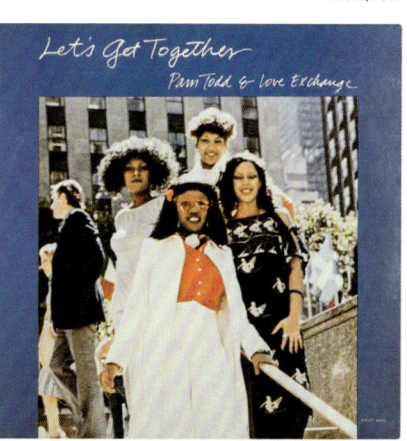

Pam Todd & Love Exchange-Let's Get Together
Shyrlden / 1977

Wild Cherry - Electrified Funk / Epic, Sweet City 1977
Photography: Frank Laffitte / Artwork: Ed Lee, Bob Rath, Myron Polenberg

Strange Affair-Strange Affair
Targa / 1980

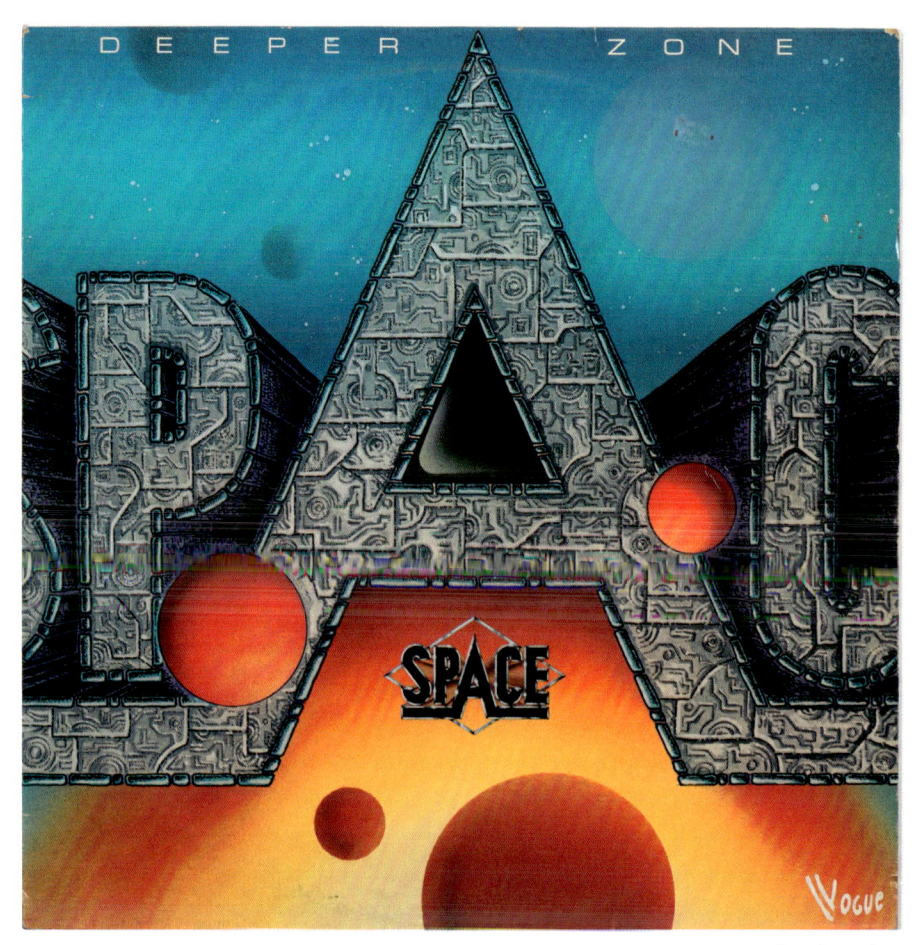

Space-Deeper Zone
Vogue / 1980

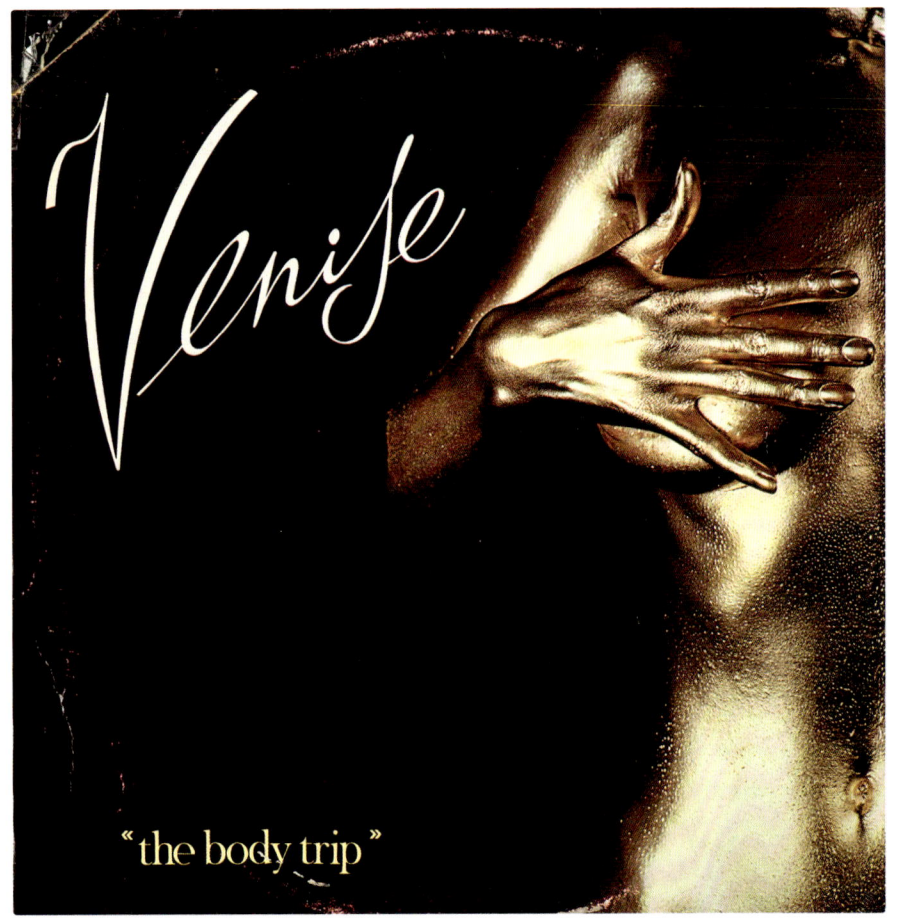

Venise-The Body Trip
Mercury / 1979

Venise-The Best Disco In Town
Jobiss / 1978

Universal Energy-Universal Energy
EMI / 1977

Universe City-Universe City
Midland / 1976

Ultrafunk-Ultrafunk
Contempo / 1975

Ultrafunk-Meat Heat
Contempo / 1977

Universal Robot Band-Dance And Shake Your Tambourine
Red Greg / 1977

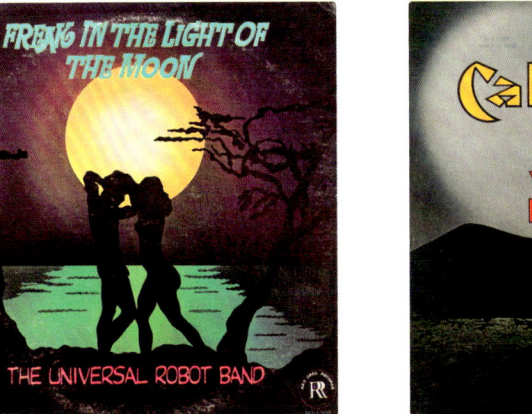

Universal Robot Band-Freak In The Light Of The Moon
Red Greg / 1978

Velvet Hammer-Call Me
Soozy / 1977

Venus Gang-Galactic Soul
Derby / 1978

Venus Gang-Galactic Soul
Epic / 1978

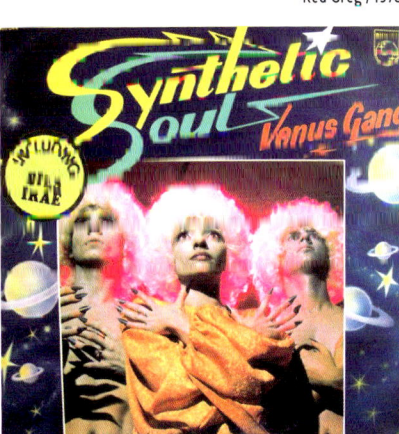

Venus Gang-Synthetic Soul
Philips / 1978

Tony Valor Sounds Orchestra-Gotta Get It
Brunswick / 1975

Tony Valor Sounds Orchestra-Gotta Get It
Brunswick / 1975

Tony Valor Sounds Orchestra-Love Has Come My Way
Paula / 1978

Vivien Vee-With Vivien Vee
Banana / 1983

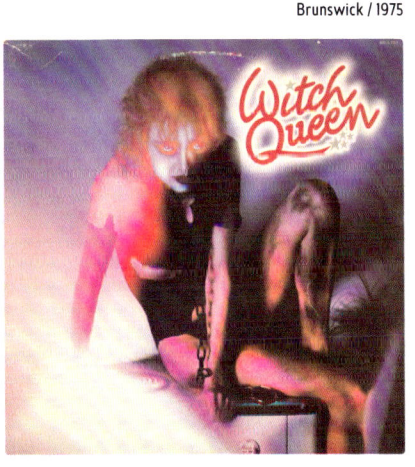

Witch Queen-Witch Queen
Roadshow / 1979

Wonder-Up And Down
Baby / 1980

Rudy-Just Take My Body
Polydor / 1979

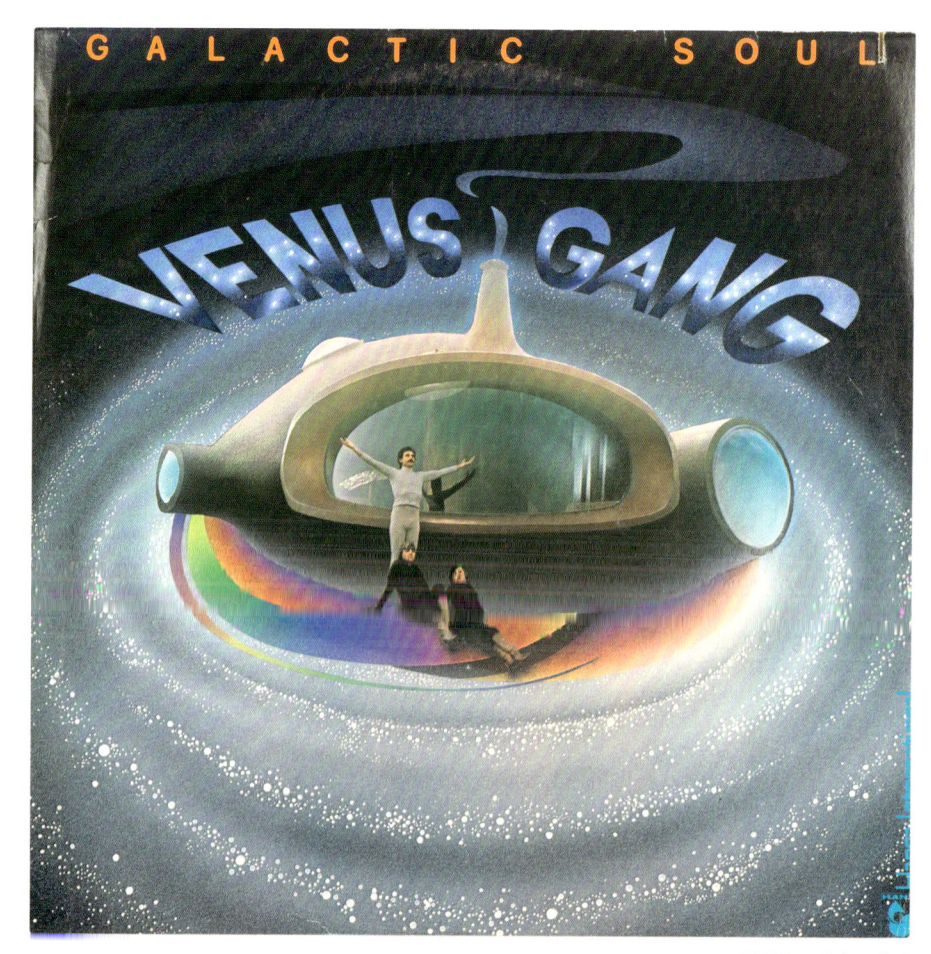

Venus Gang-Galactic Soul
Hansa / 1978

Wham-Wham
GRT / 1978

Zebra-Zebra
Polydor / 1979

Spargo-Go
I-Scream Music / 1981

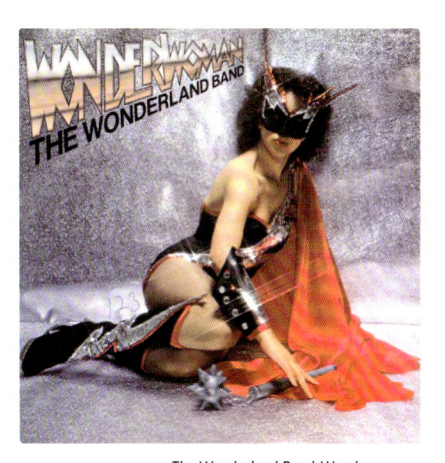

The Wonderland Band-Wonderwoman
Quality / 1979

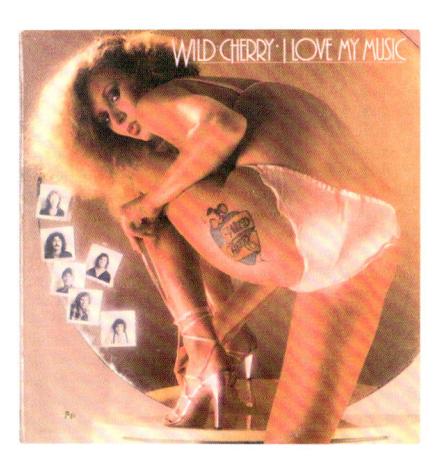

Wild Cherry-I Love My Music
Epic / 1978

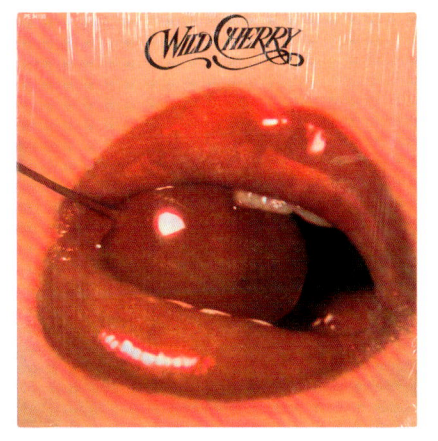

Wild Cherry-Wild Cherry
Epic / 1976

Wild Cherry-Only The Wild Survive
Epic / 1979

Watsonian Institute-Extra Disco Perception
DJM / 1979

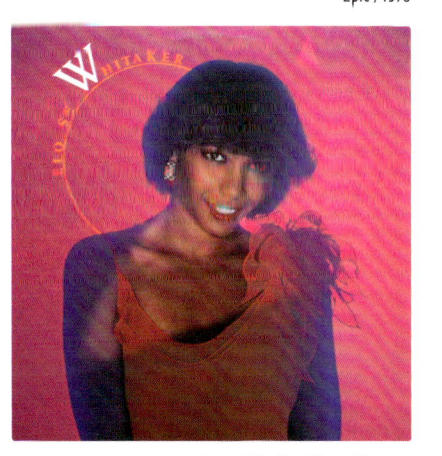

Eloise Whitaker-Eloise Whitaker
Destiny / 1981

Barry White-Sheet Music
Unlimited Gold / 1980

The Michael Zager Band-Let's All Chant
Private Stock / 1978

Zeus B. Held-Zeus' Amusement
Metronome / 1978

Venus Rising - Live On Venus / Derby 1977
Cover: Studio Tallarini's Group

Hot In Here - Hot In Here / Baby Grand 1977
Photography: Enrique / Art Direction, Liner Photograph: Paul Ross

Yvon Rioland & Jean-Marie Hauser - Discoritmo / Crea Sound Ltd. 1979
Photo: The Image Bank. Jan Cobb

M. Chantereau/P.A. Dahan/S. Pezin - Disco & Co Vol. 2 / Tele Music 1979
Photo: Image Bank

Disco & Co
Tele Music / 1979

Disco & Co-Vol.2
Tele Music / 1979

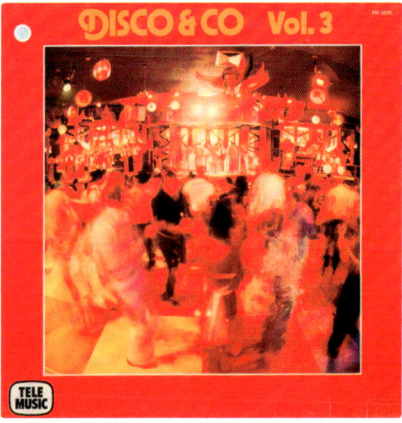

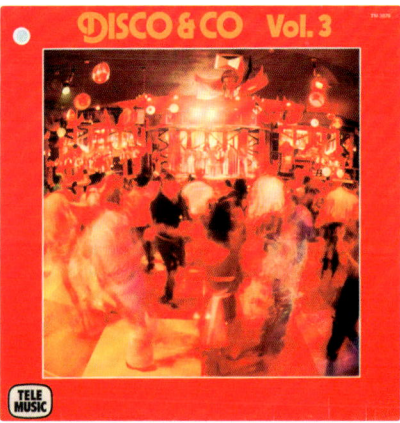

Disco & Co-Vol.3
Tele Music / 1979

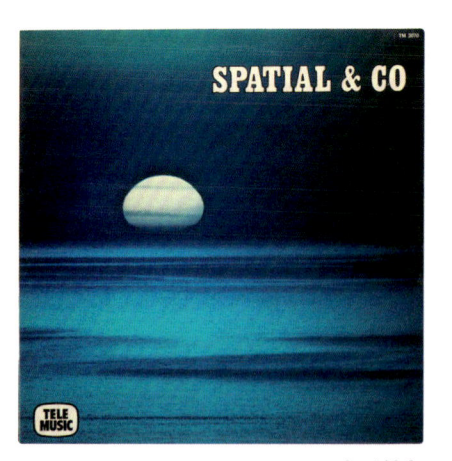

Spatial & Co
Tele Music / 1979

Spatial & Co-vol.2
Tele Music / 1979

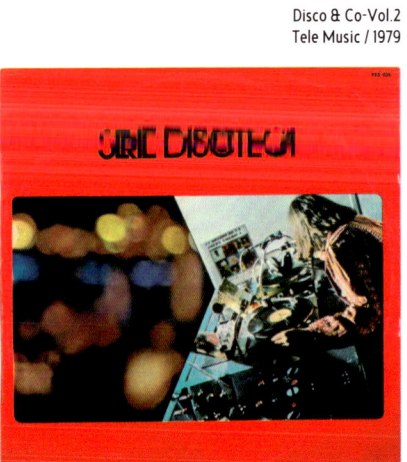

Serie Discoteca
RCA / 1977

KPM-Disco Fever
KPM / 1979

Bruton Music-Disco Happening
Bruton / 1970

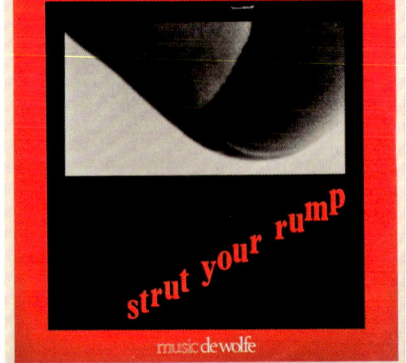

Music De Wolfe-Strut Your Rump
De Wolfe Music / 1980

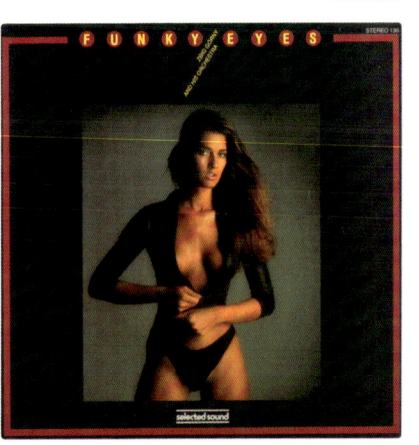

Zbig Gorny And His Orchestra-Funky Eyes
Selected Sound / 1982

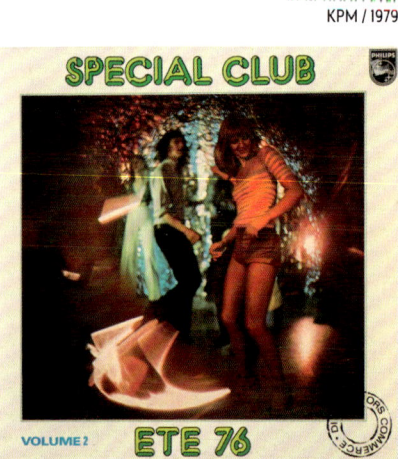

Special Club-Ete 76
Philips / 1976

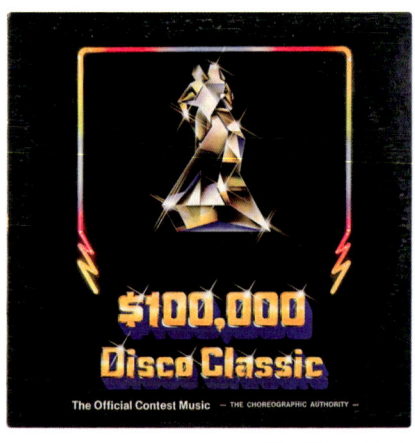

$100.000 Disco Classic
Pacific Beach Records / 1979

Superman And Other Disco Hits-The Doctor Exx Band
Pickwick / 1979

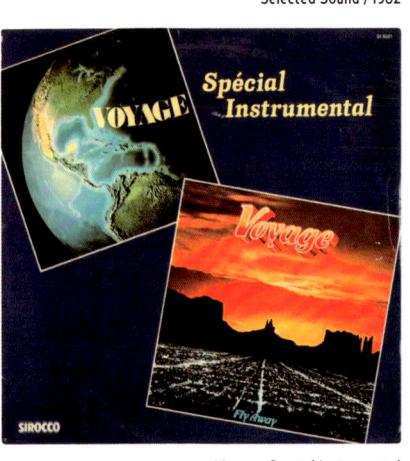

Voyage-Special Instrumental
Sirocco / 1978

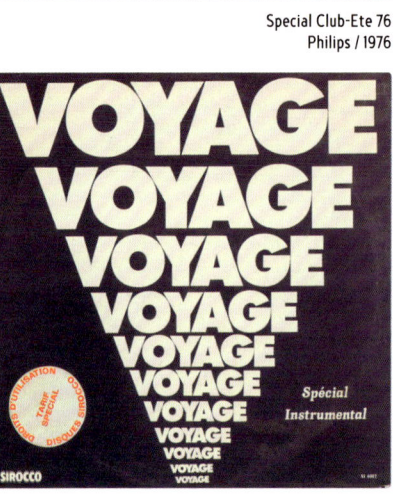

Voyage-Special Instrumental-Vol.2
Sirocco / 1979

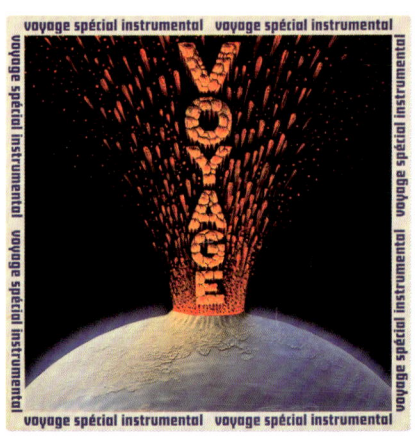

Voyage-Special Instrumental-Vol.3
Sirocco / 1982

Vine Street Disco Band - Disco Delight / Gateway 1977
Art Director: Cyd Kilbey / Cover Illustration: Bruce Emmett

© CALLIOPE RECORDS, INC. DISTRIBUTED BY FESTIVAL DISTRIBUTION, INC., 15300 VENTURA BLVD., SHERMAN OAKS, CA. 91403

12-Inch Covers

Chapter 27
12-Inch Covers

Arista Records

History of the 12-Inch

The 12-inch single record came into existence with the advent of disco music in the 1970s and the man directly responsible for its success is Tom Moulton.

The first 12-inch (30 cm) single was actually a 10-inch (25 cm) acetate used by a mix engineer (José Rodríguez) in need of a Friday-night test copy for famed disco mixer Tom Moulton. As no seven-inch (18 cm) acetates could be found, a 10-inch blank was used instead. Moulton, feeling silly with a large disc which only had a couple of inches of groove on it, asked Rodríguez to re-cut it so that the grooves looked more spread out. The first actual 12-inch cut as a Tom Moulton Mix was So In Love by Moment of Truth. Because of the wider spacing of the grooves, a broader overall dynamic range (distinction between loud and soft) was made possible. This was immediately noticed to give a more favourable sound for discothèque play.

Moulton's position as the premiere mixer and 'fix-it man' for pop singles ensured that this fortunate accident would instantly become industry practice. This would perhaps have been a natural evolution: As songs became much longer than had been the average for a pop song, and as DJs in the clubs wanted sufficient dynamic range, the format would have surely had to be changed from the seven-inch single eventually.

Also worth noting is that the visual spacing of the grooves on the 12-inch assisted the DJ in locating the approximate area of the 'breaks' on the disc's surface (without having to listen as they dropped and re-dropped the stylus to find the right point). A quick study of any DJs favourite discs will reveal mild wear in these 'break points' on the discs' surfaces that can clearly be seen by the naked eye, which further eases the 'cueing' task.

Many DJ-only remix services, such as Disconet and Hot Tracks, issued sets with deliberately visualised groove separations (ie the record was cut with wide spacings, marking the mix points on the often multi-song discs).

The very first 12-inch single was released in 1973 by the soul/R&B artist Jerry Williams Jr, known as Swamp Dogg. 12-inch promotional copies of 'Straight From My Heart' were released on his own Swamp Dogg Presents label (Swamp Dogg Presents #501/SDP-SD01, 33rpm), distributed by Jamie/Guyden Distribution Corporation. The B-side of the record is blank.

The first official promotional 12-inch single was Southshore Commission's 'Free Man'. At first, these special versions were only available as promotional copies to DJs.

The first commercial track sold to the general public on a 12-inch single is 'Ten Percent' by Double Exposure on Salsoul Records. The 12-inch single trend also spread to Jamaica, where hundreds of reggae 12 inch singles were pressed and commercially issued as 'discomix' to catch on the disco hype.

Many record companies began producing 12-inch singles at 33rpm, as the slower speed enhanced the bass on the record. By the same token, however, 45rpm gave better treble response and was also used on many 12-inch singles, especially in the UK.

Increasingly in the 1980s, many pop and even rock artists released 12-inch singles that included longer, extended, or remixed versions of the actual track being promoted. These versions were frequently labeled with the parenthetical designation '12-inch version', '12 Inch mix', 'extended remix', 'dance mix', or 'club mix'.

337

Smash Records

Brookville Records

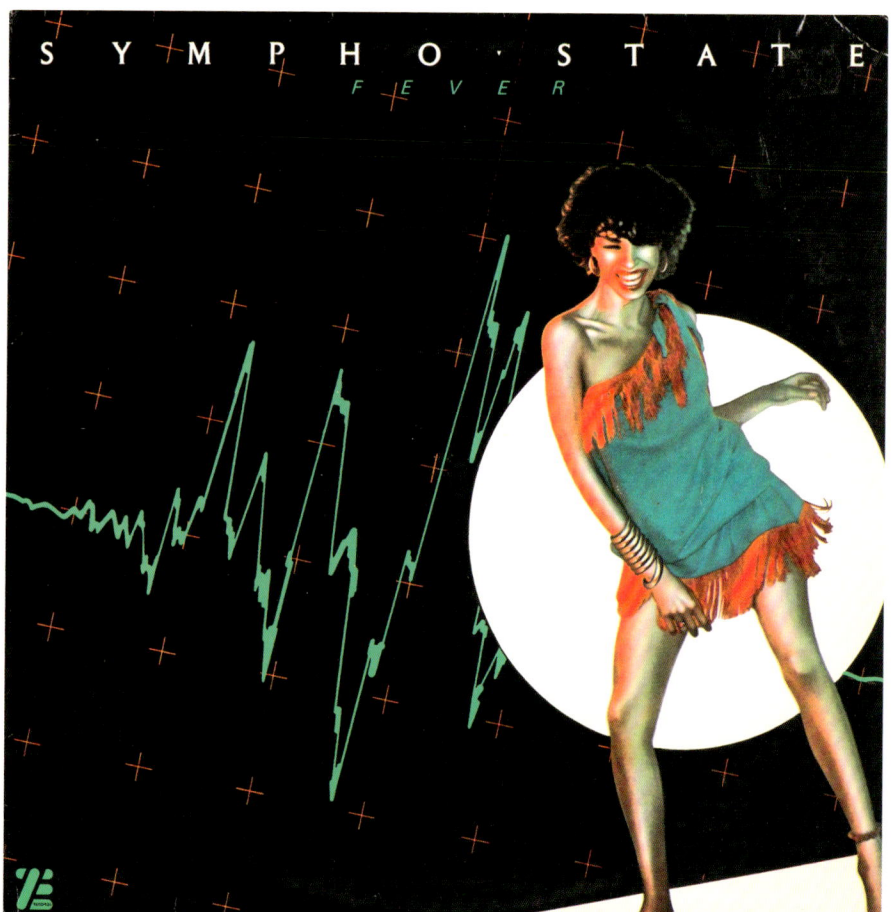

ZE Records

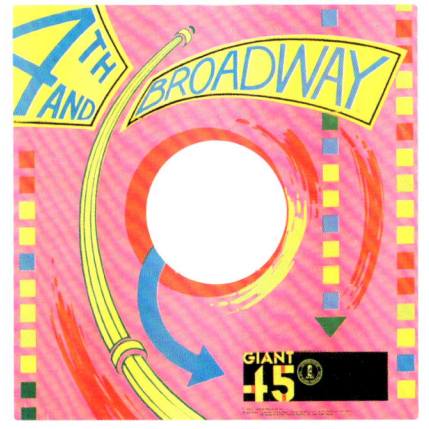

4 Th Broadway Records	20th Century Records	A&m Records	A&m Records
A&m Records	A&m Records	A&m Records	A&m Records
ABC Records	Ala Records	All American Records	Apexton Records
Ariola Records	Ariola Records	Amherst Records	Arista Records

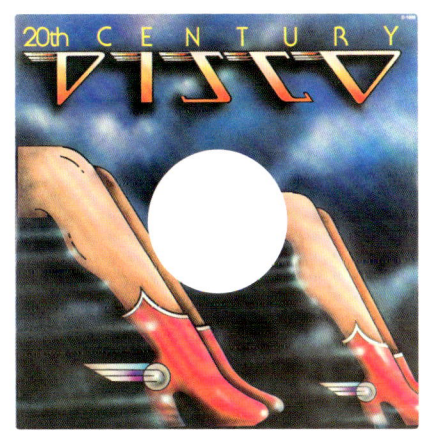

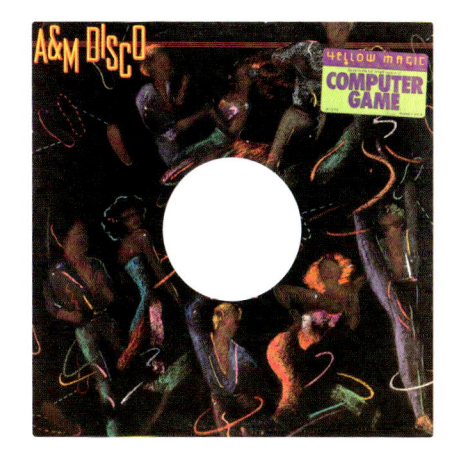

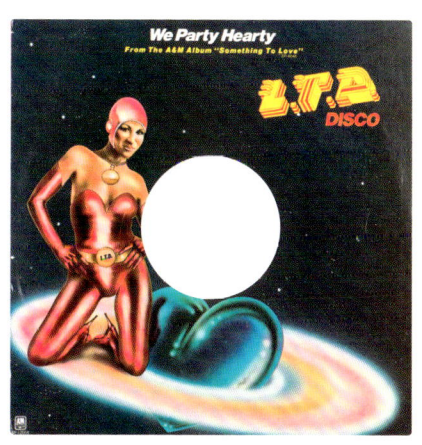

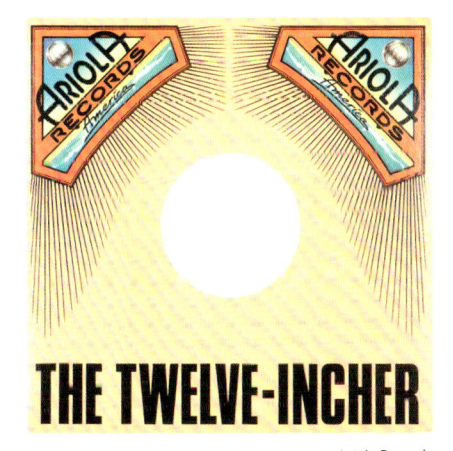

339

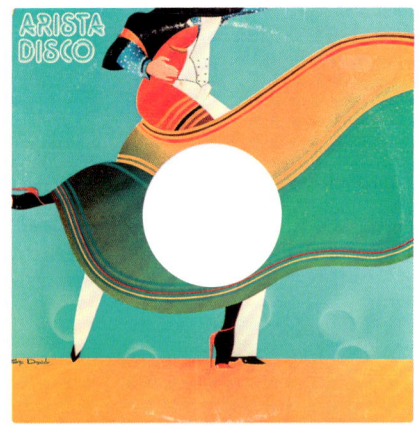

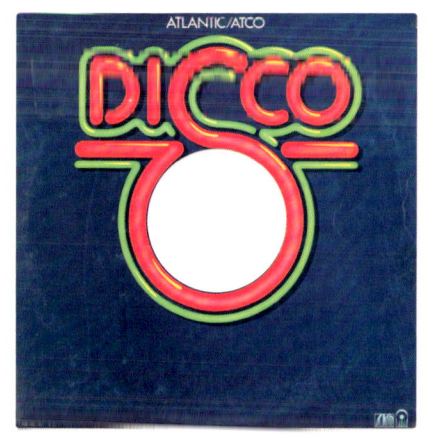

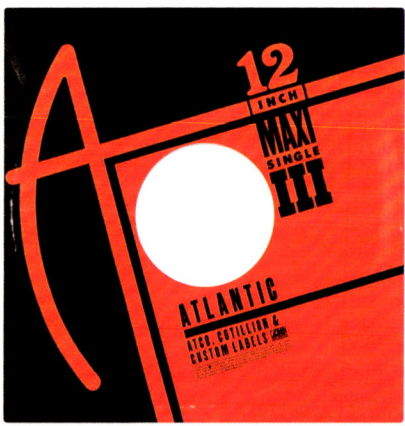

Arista Records	Arista Records	Arista Records	Arista Records
Arista Records	Atlantic Records	Atlantic Records	Atlantic Records
Atlantic Records	Atlantic Records	Atlantic Records	Atlantic Records
Atlantic Records	Atlantic Records	AVI Records	AVI Records

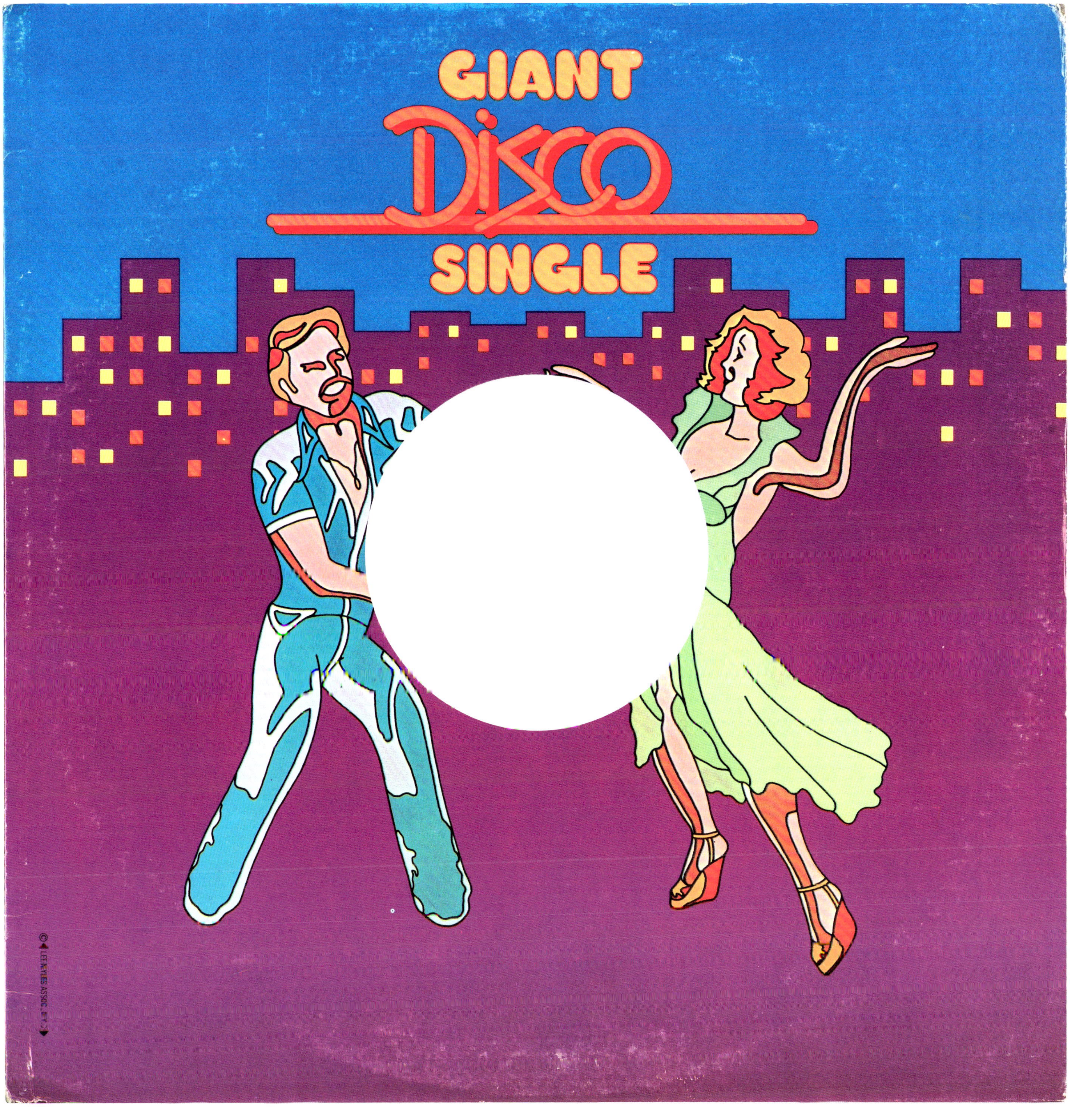
GIANT
DISCO
SINGLE

AVI Records	Bang Records	BC Records	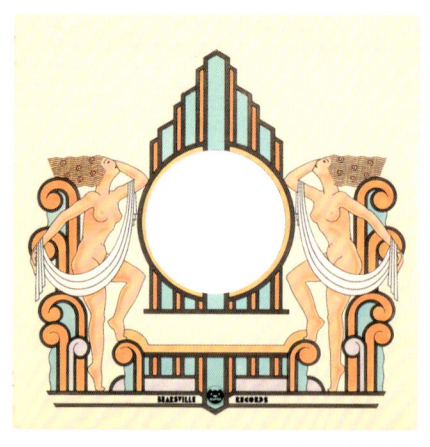 Bearsville Records
Becket Records	Blue Parrot	Buddah Records	Buddah Records
Brass records	Calla Records	Capitol Records	Capitol Records
Capitol Records	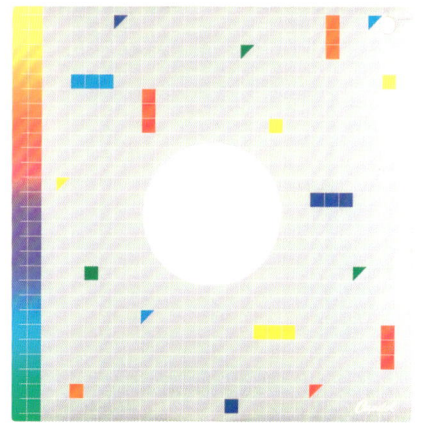 Capitol Records	Casablanca Records	Casablanca Records

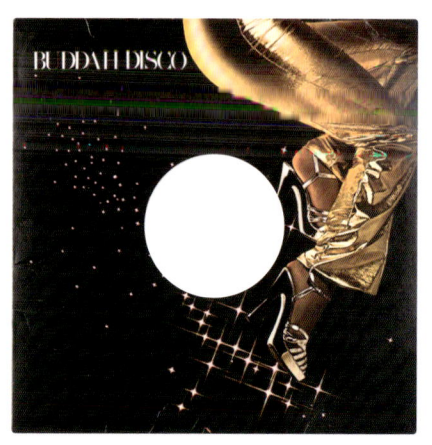

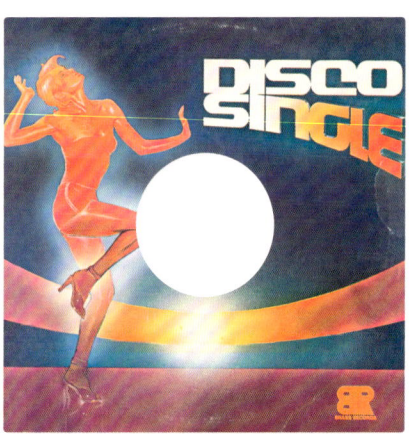

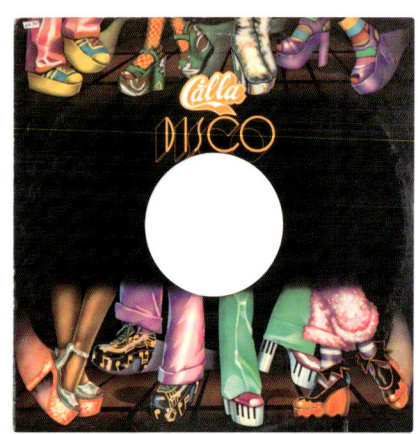

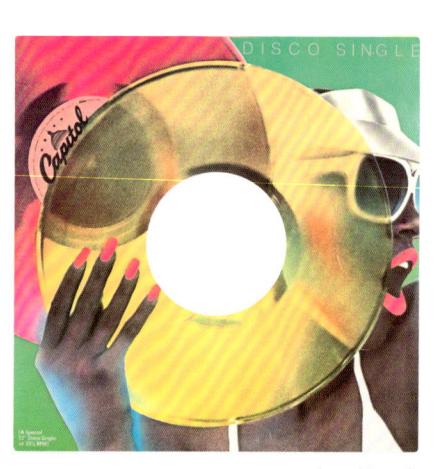

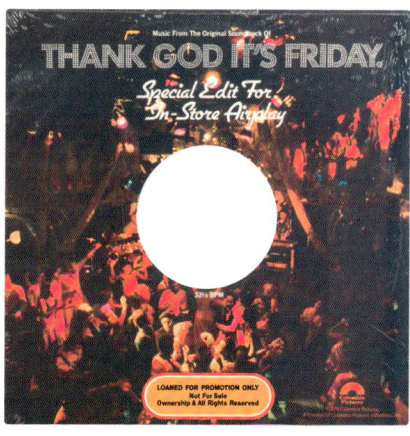

THE DISCO SINGLE

MANUFACTURED AND DISTRIBUTED IN THE U.S.A. BY RED GREG ENTERPRISES, INC.

Red Greg Records

Casablanca Records	CBS Records	Celcius Records	Century Records
 Claridge Records	 Champagne Records	Chocolate Cholly's Records	Chrysalis Records
Cloudborn Records	 Columbia Records	Columbia Records	Columbia Records
Columbia Records	CRC Records	Cresendo Records	CTI Records

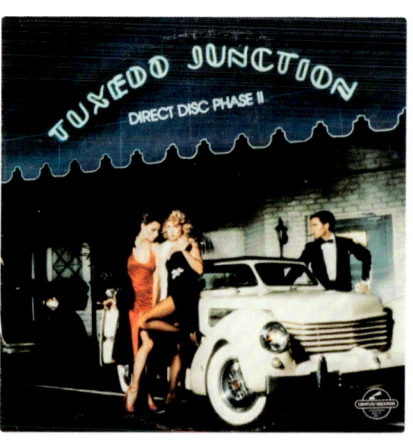

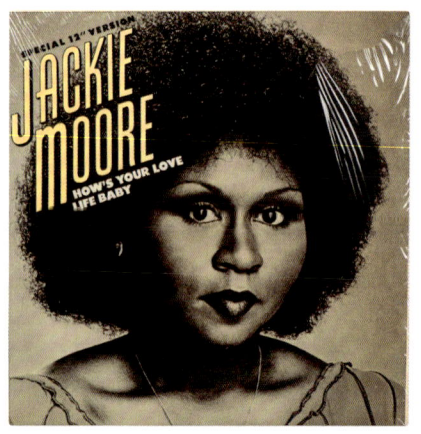

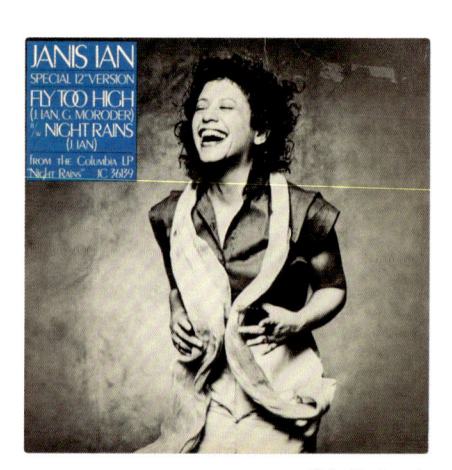

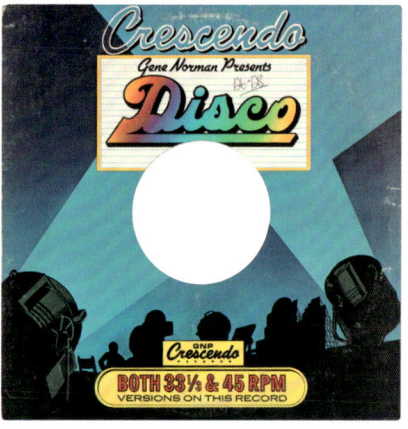

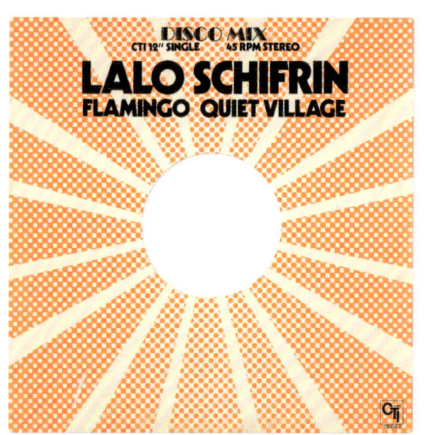

Aristo-Camille Records

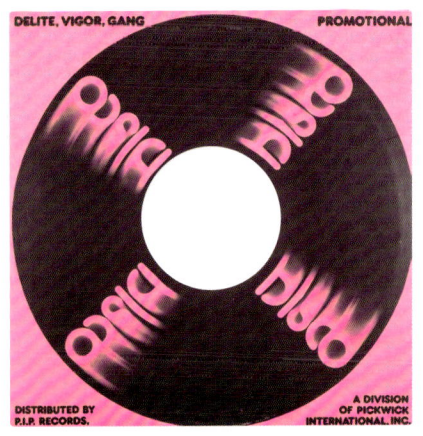

PIP Records	Destiny Records	Dice Records	Direction Records
Disco International Records	Disco	Disk o Mania Records	DJ Records
DK Records	DK Records	Easy Street Records	Elektra Records
Elektra Records	Elektra Records	Elektra Records	Emergency Records

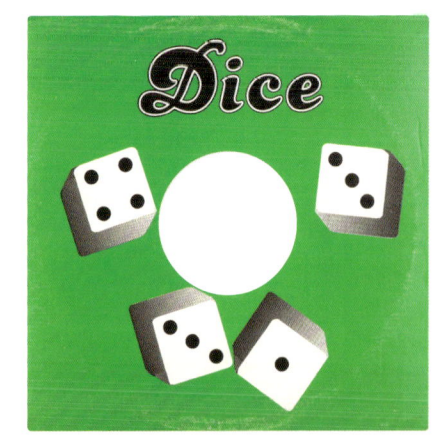

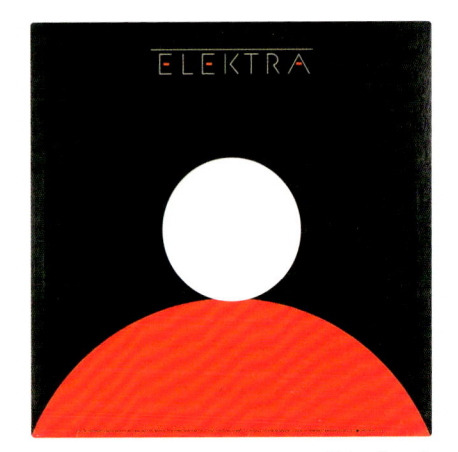

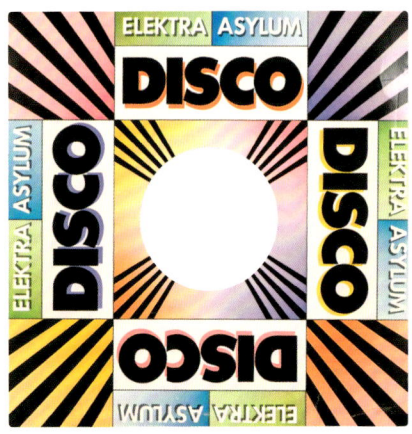

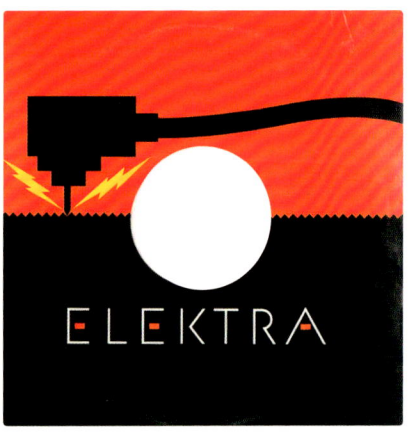

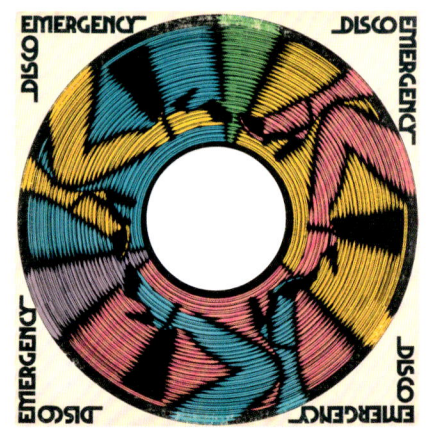

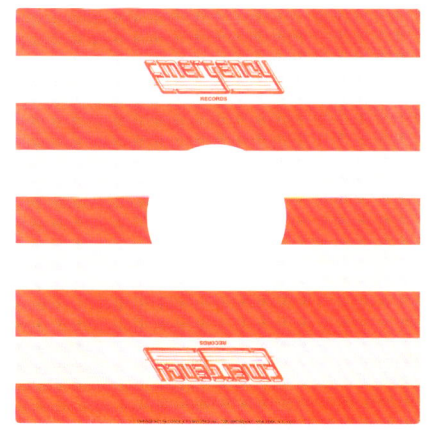

Emergency Records	Epic Records	Epic Records	Epic Records
Erect Records	Fantasy Records	Fantasy Records	Fantasy Records
Fantasy Records	Fantasy Records	Fantasy Records	Fantasy Records
Fantasy Records	Fantasy Records	First Take Records	Formula Records

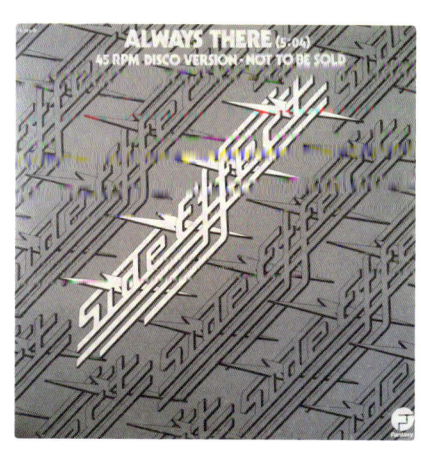

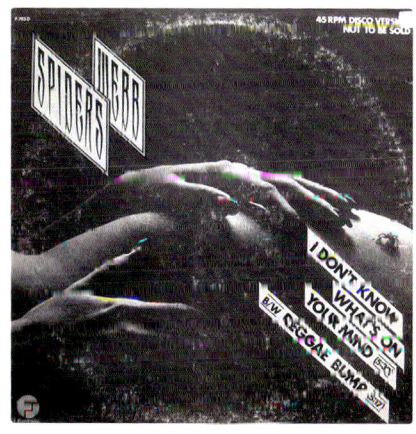

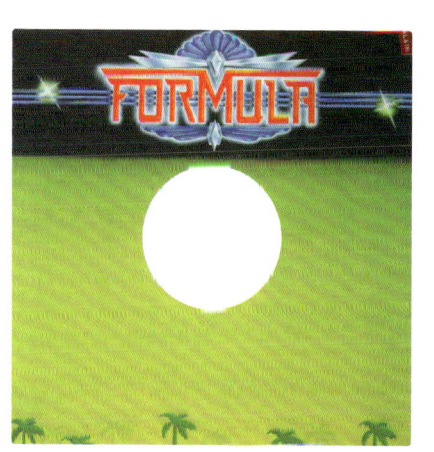

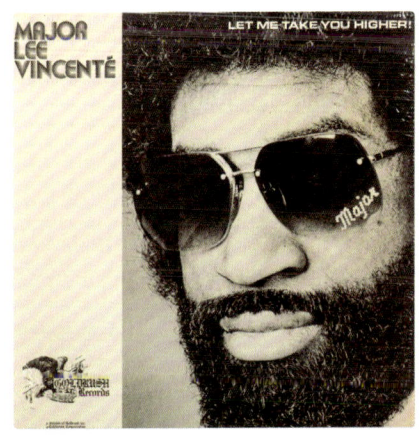

Goldrush Records	Greedy Records	GRT Records	Gold Mind Records
H&L Records	Handshake Records	Hi Smoke Records	Direction Records
II Disc Records	Importe Records	Island Records	Island Records
Island Records	Island Records	Island Records	Island Records

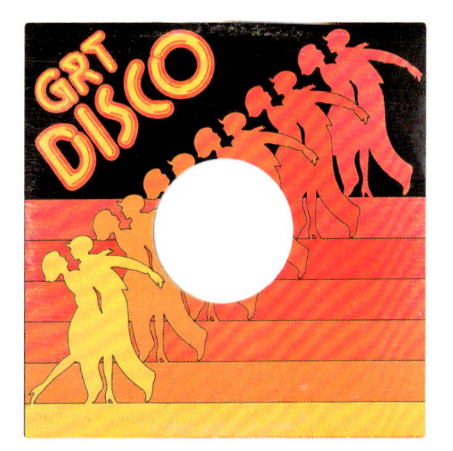

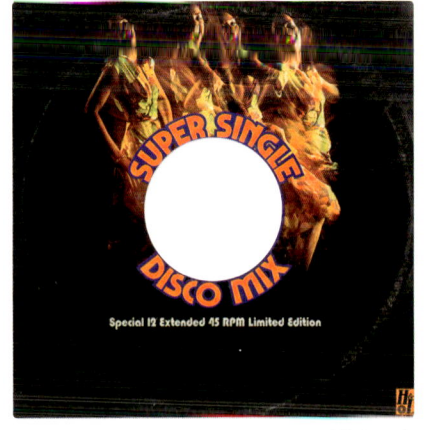

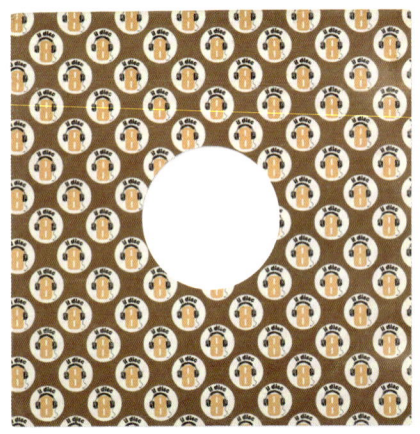

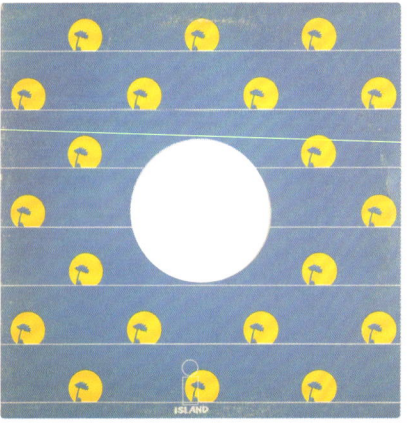

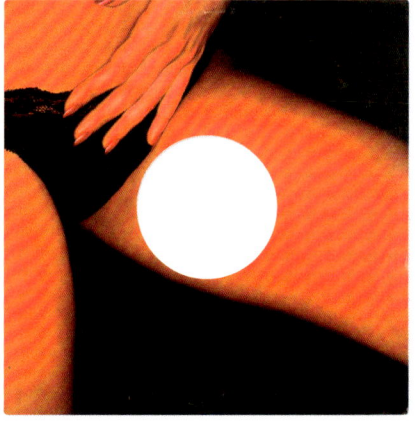

348

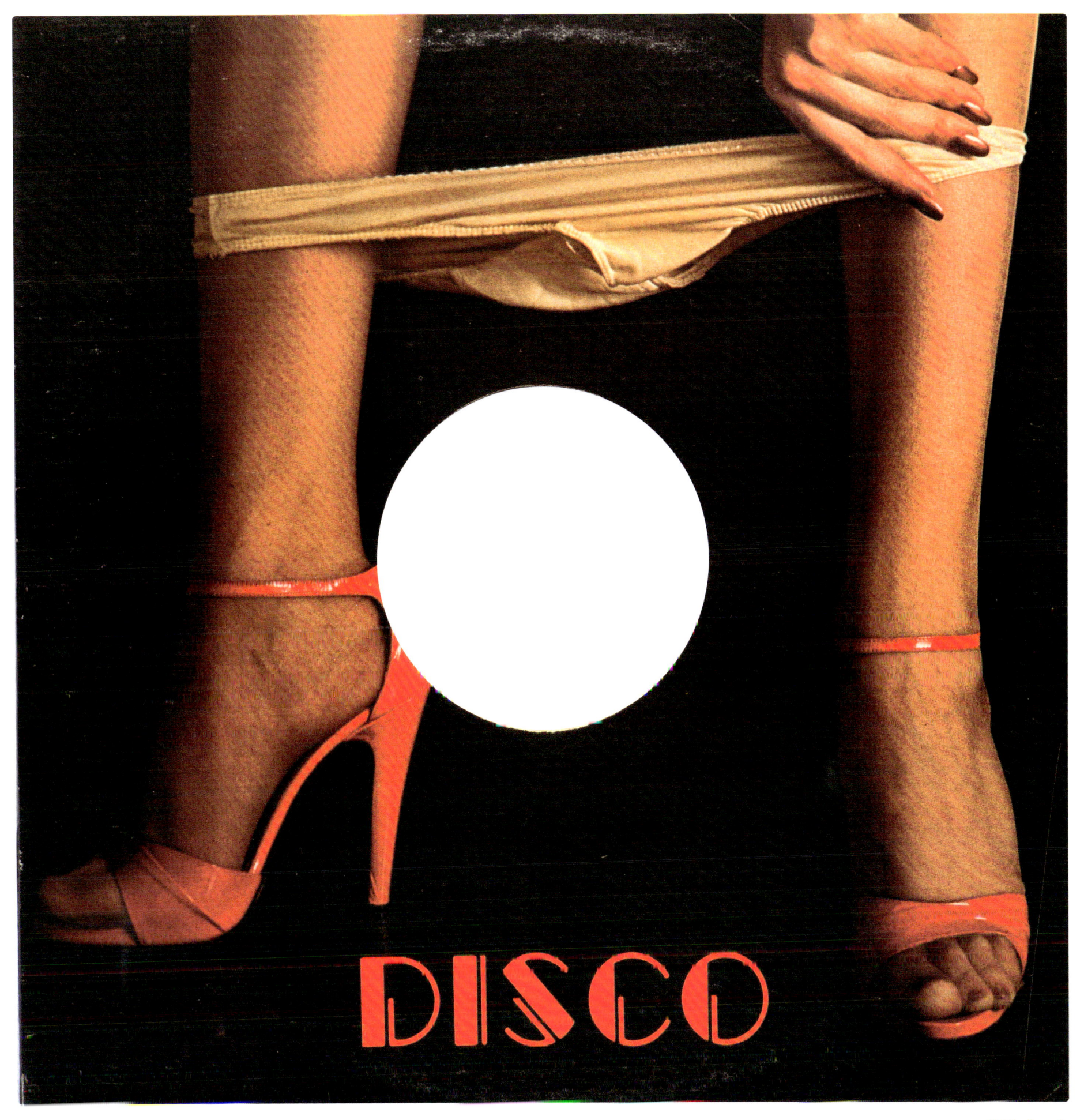

Unidisc Records

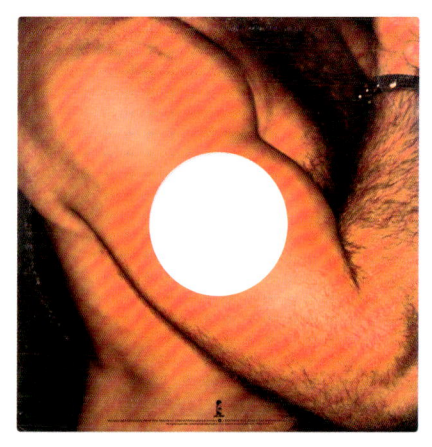

Island Records

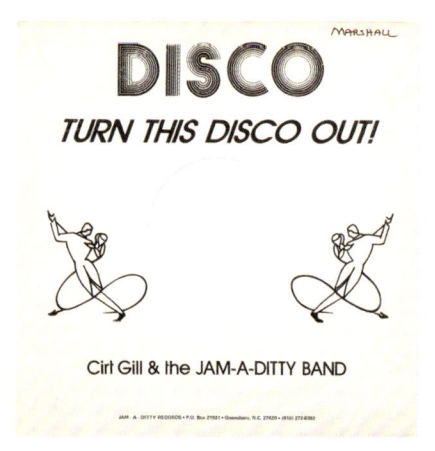

Jam-A-Ditty Records

Jam Sesions Records

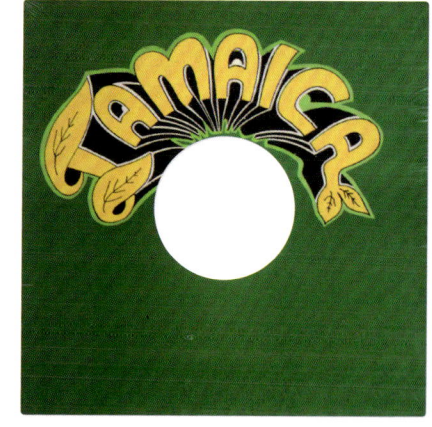

Jamaica Records

Joe Gibbs Records

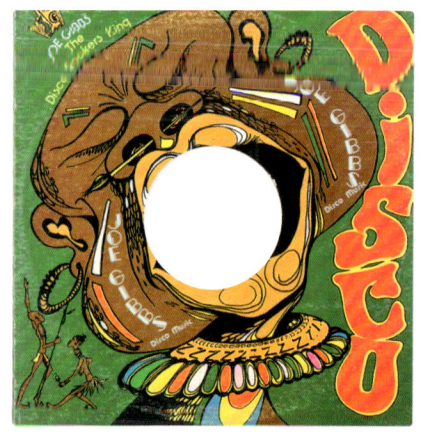

Joe Gibbs Records

Jumbo Caribbean Records

JDC Records

Libra Records

Key Records

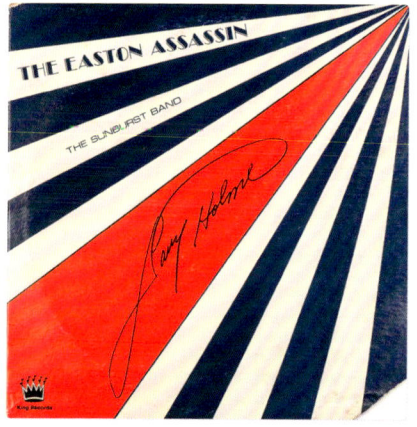

King Records

London Records

London Records

London Records

Mercury Records

Magic Disc Records

350

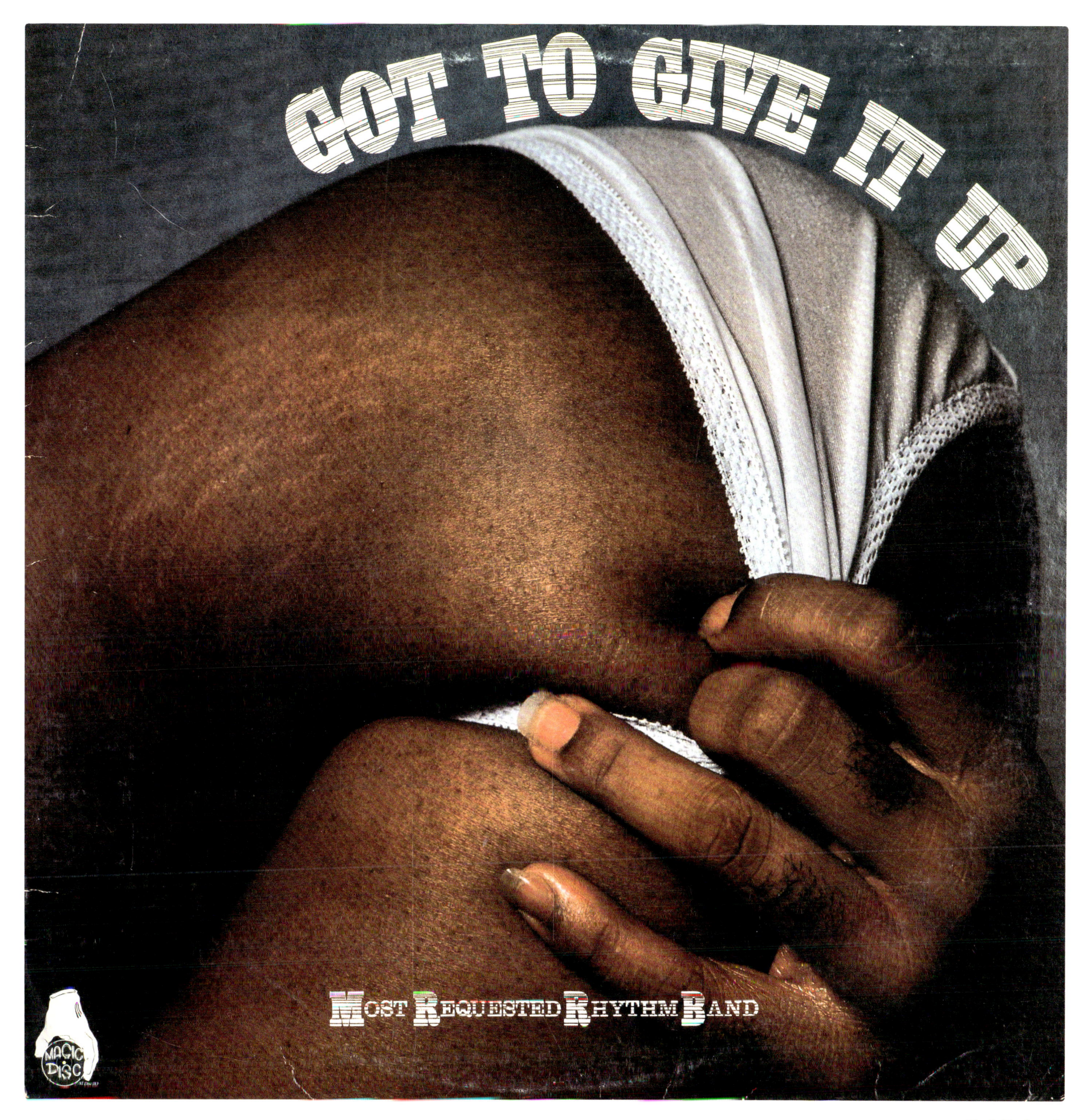

Magic Disc Records

000066 FOR PROMOTIONAL USE OF SUBSCRIBER — NOT FOR SALE **DISCONET/VOLUME 1** NUMBER 2	000543 FOR PROMOTIONAL USE OF SUBSCRIBER — NOT FOR SALE **DISCONET/VOLUME 2** SPECIAL BONUS PROGRAM
Disconet	Disconet
 FOR PROMOTIONAL USE OF SUBSCRIBER — NOT FOR SALE **VOLUME 3**	**NEW YORK STRUT** Fist O Funk Orchestra
Disconet	Fist-O-Funk Records

Mango Records

Mango Records

Manhattan Formula Records

Maycon Records

Manhattan Records

Matra Records

MCA Records

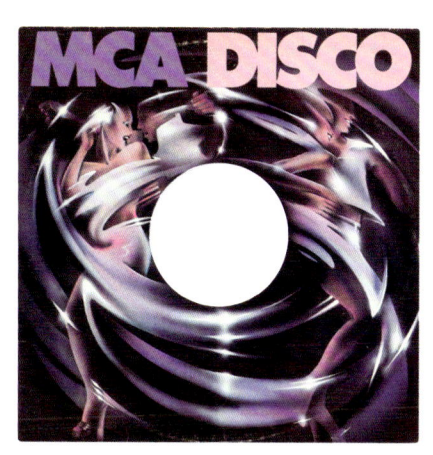

MCA Records

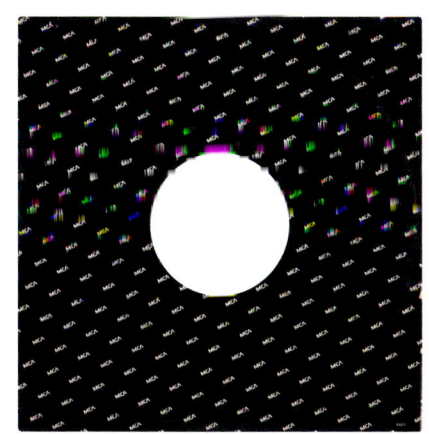

MCA Records

MCA Records

Mercury Records

Mercury Records

Mercury Records

Mercury Records

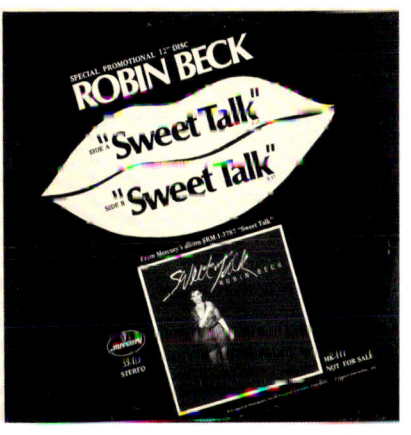

Mercury Records

Mercury Records

353

Megatone Records	Megatone Records	Mercury Records	Mercury Records
Mercury Records	 Mercury Records	Mercury Records	Midsong Records
Millennium Records	Mini Records	Moby Dick Records	 Montage Records
Mopres Records	Motown Records	Motown Records	Motown Records

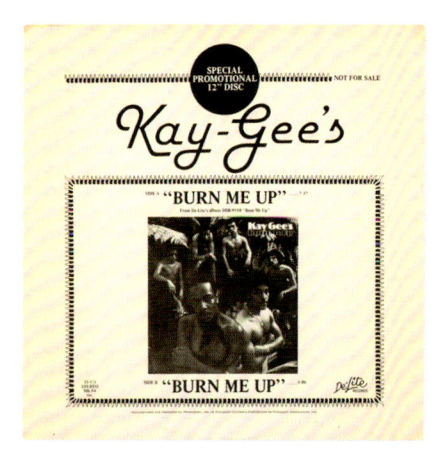

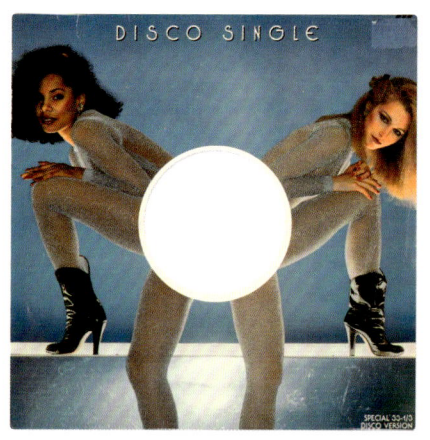

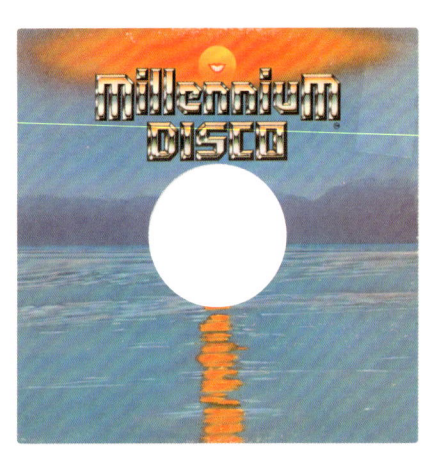

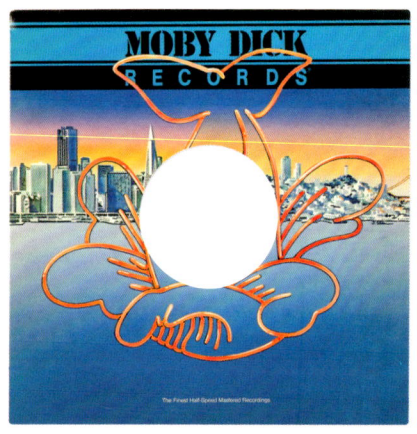

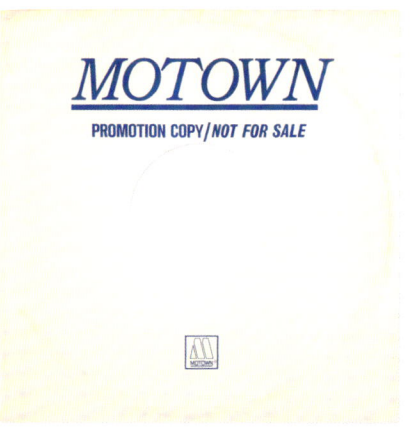

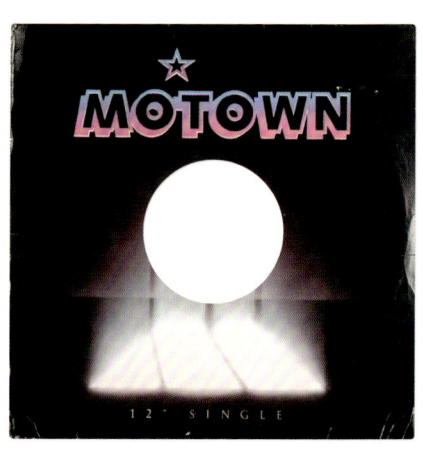

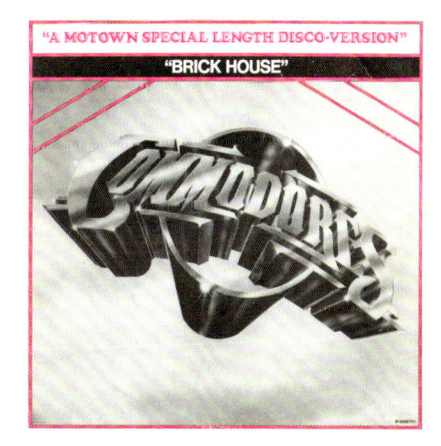

Motown Records	Motown Records	Motown Records	Motown Records
MSB Records	Nelwin Records	Olympus Records	Orbit Records
Ovation Records	Panorama Records	Parachute Records	Park Place Records
Partytime Records	Partytime Records	Passion Records	Personal Records

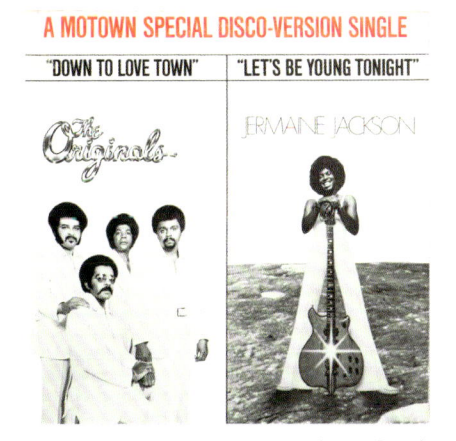

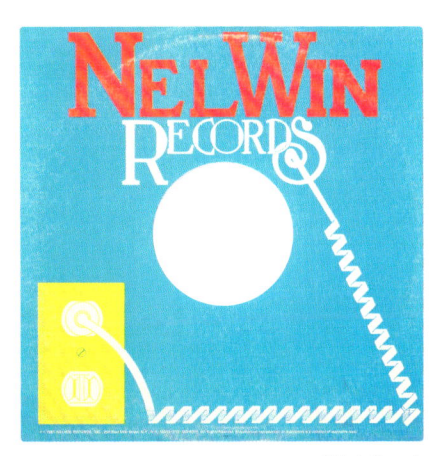

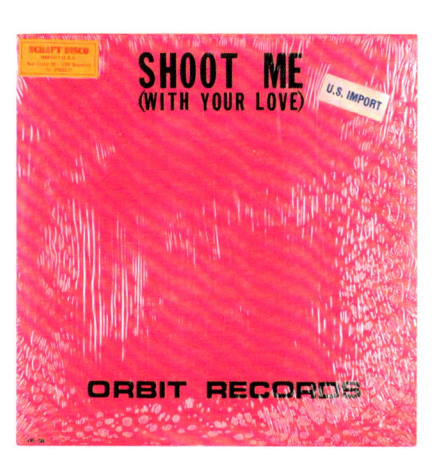

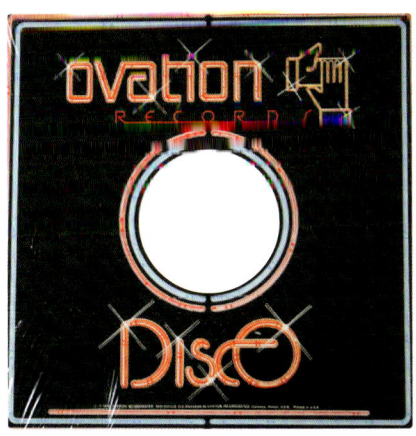

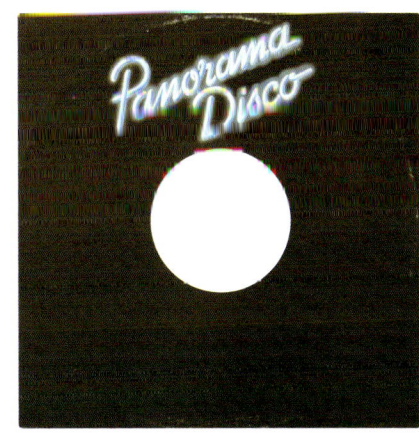

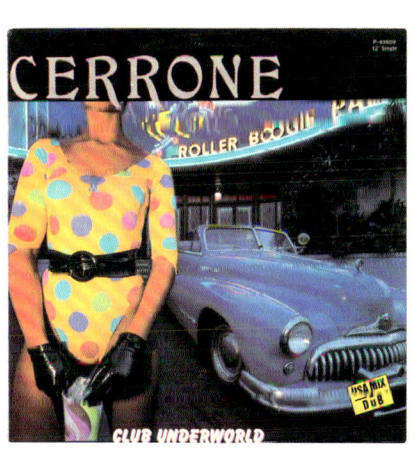

Perspective records

Philadelphia International Records

Philly World Records

Phonodisc Records

P.I.P Records

Planet Records

Platinum Records

Polydor Records

Polydor Records

Polydor Records

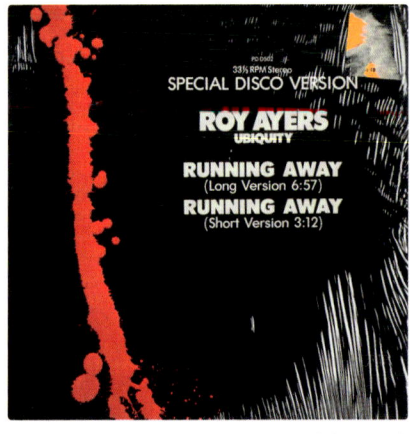

Polydor Records

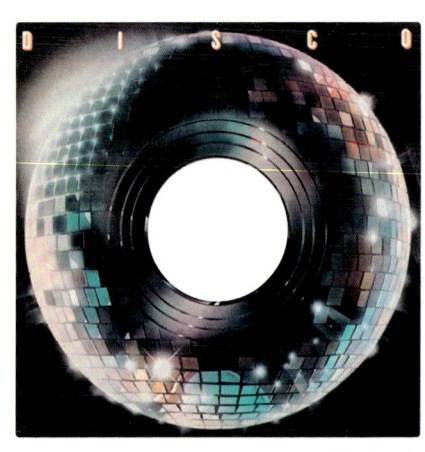

Polydor Records

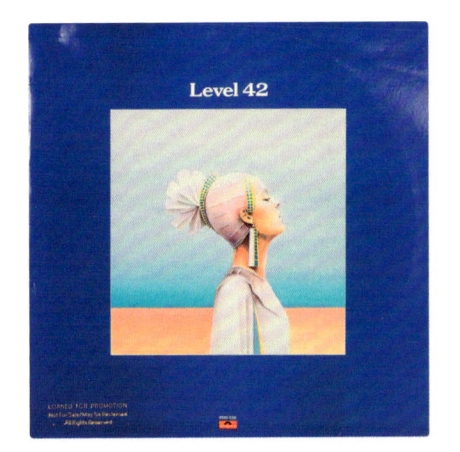

Polydor Records

Prelude Records

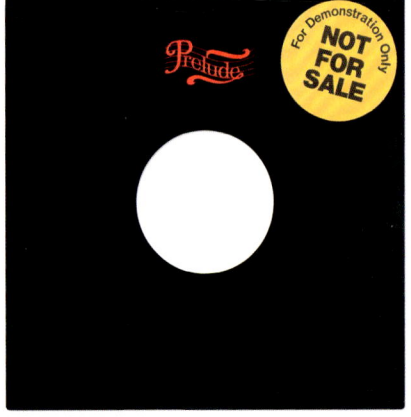

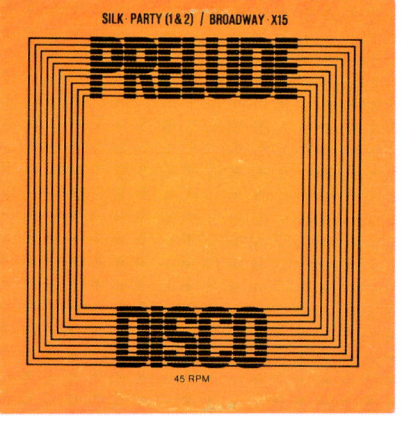

Prelude Records

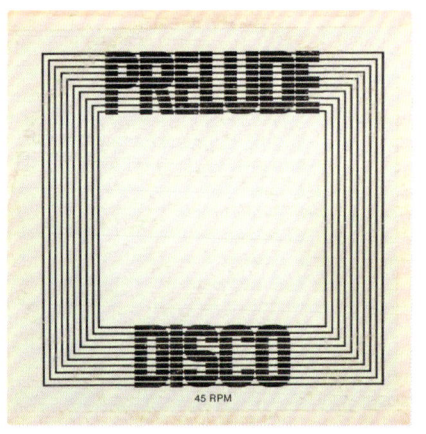

Prelude Records

STRATUS

(1) STRATUSHIP

WINDALL · **JEFF**

LOUIE · **STEPHEN**

PAUL · **TYRONE** · **ROGER**

DISCO SINGLE

STEREO M-0001

"PUDDIN"
Belle Farms Estates

Mayail Records

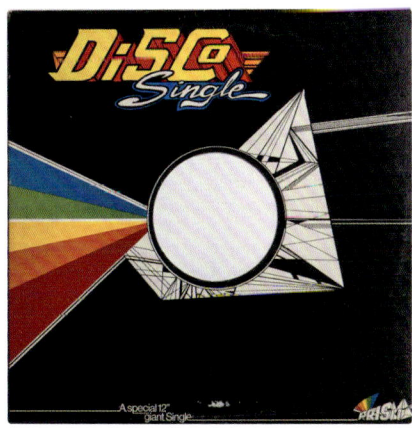

Prism Records	Prism Records	Profile Records	PYE Records
Pyramid Records	Private Stock Records	Quality Records	Quality Records
Quality Records	Q West Records	Radar Records	Radar Records
RCA Records	 RCA Records	RCA Records	RCA Records

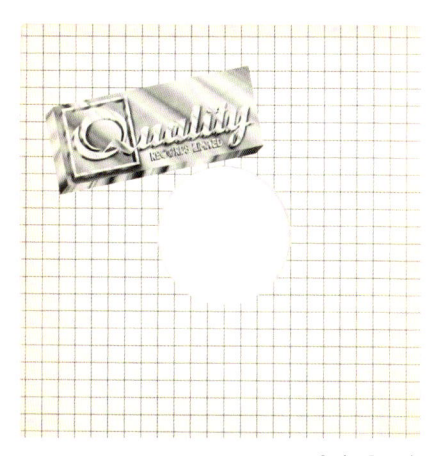

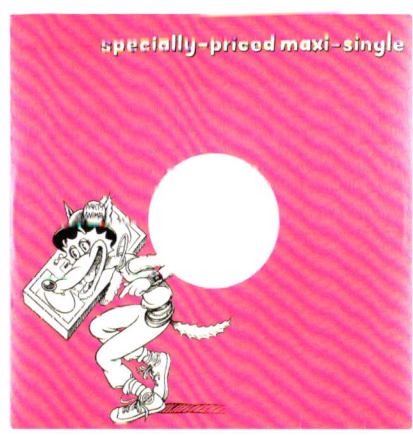

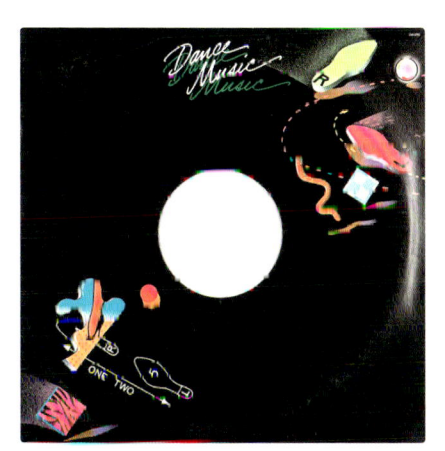

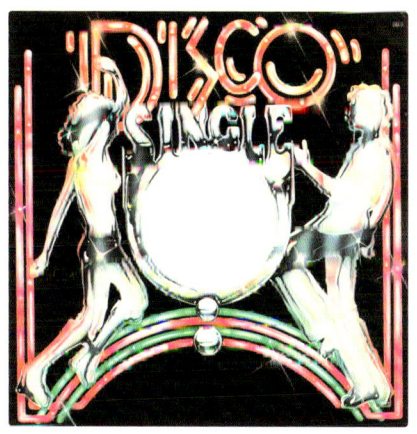

SMI Records

Eargasm Records

Eargasm Records

Eargasm Records

Eargasm Records

361

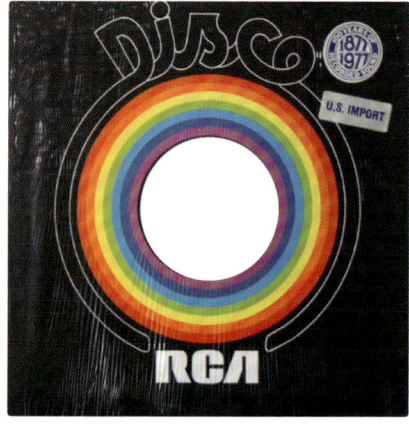

RCA Records	Red Greg Records	Red Greg Records	Reflection Records
Reflection Records	Rissa-Chrissa Records	Nashe Records	Rota Records
RS Records	RS Records	RSO Records	ROYB Records
Salsoul Records	Salsoul Records	Salsoul Records	Salsoul Records

RSO Records

Source Records

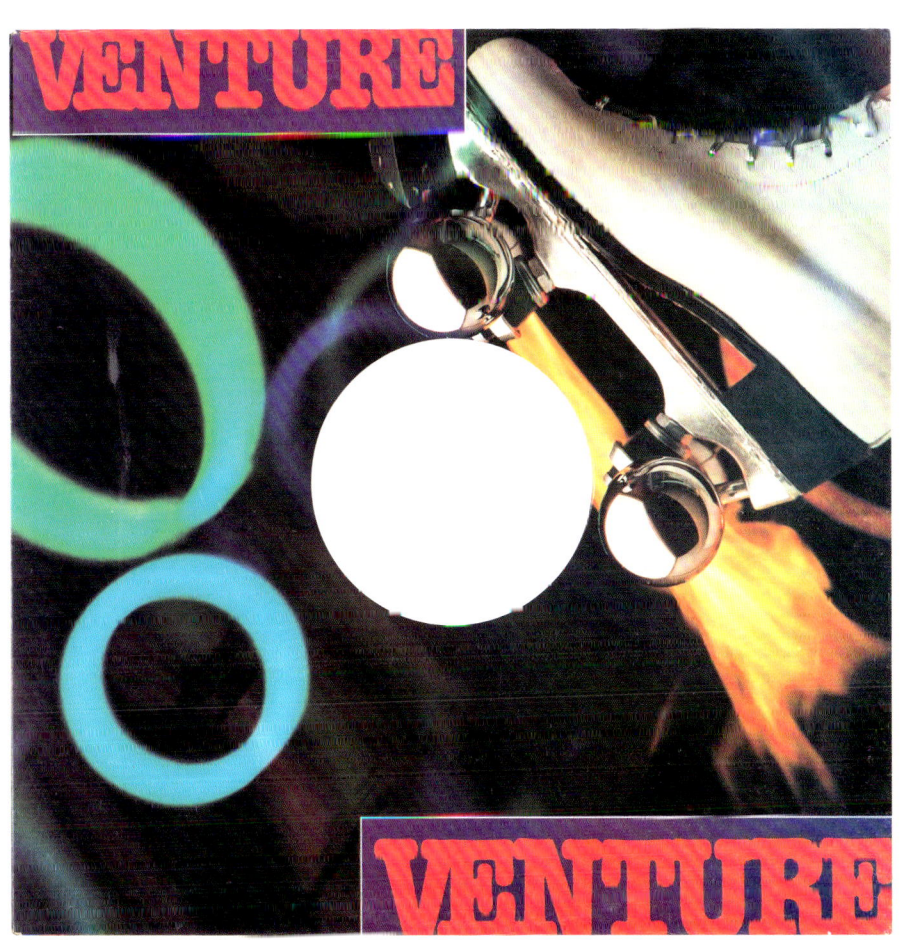

Venture Records

Warner Bross. Records

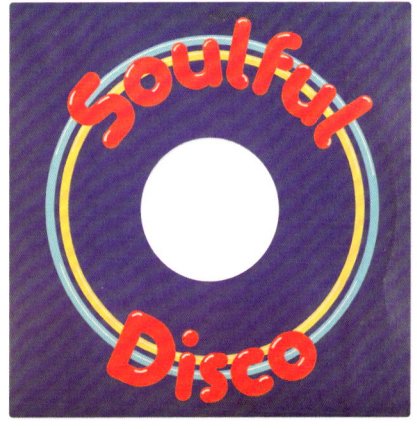

SAM Records	SAM Records	SAM Records	SAM Records
Select Records	Select Records	Silver Cloud Records	Sire Records
 Sleeping Bag Records	SMI Records	 SMI Records	 SMI Records
SMI Records	SMI Records	SMI Records	Sizzle Records

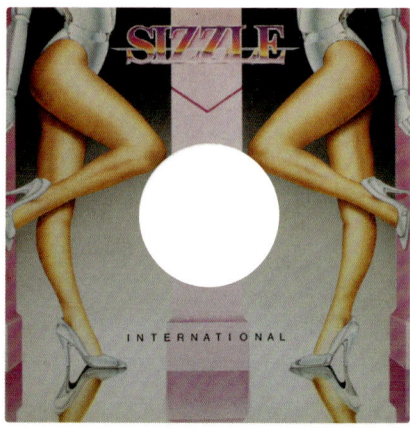

364

Smooth Tracks Records	Solar Records	Solar Records	Sound Of New York Records
Source Records	 Source Records	Spring records	Spring Records
Spring Records	Streetwise Records	Sugar Hill Records	Sugar Hill Records
Sugarscoop Records	Sunnyview Records	Sunshine Sound Records	Superfunk Records

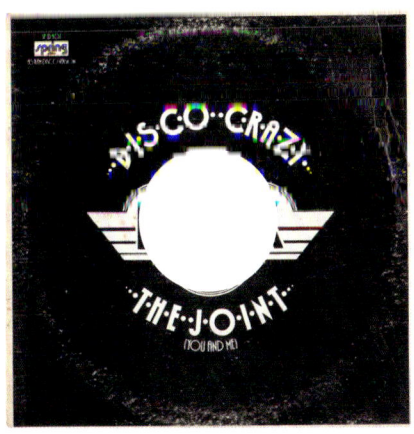

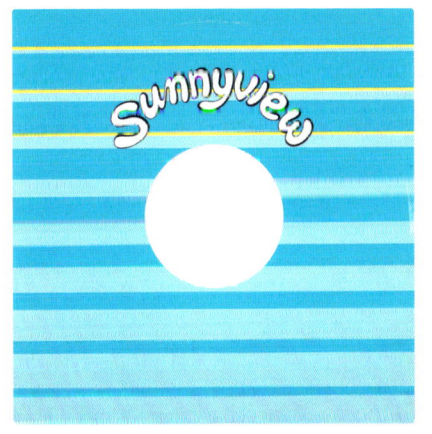

365

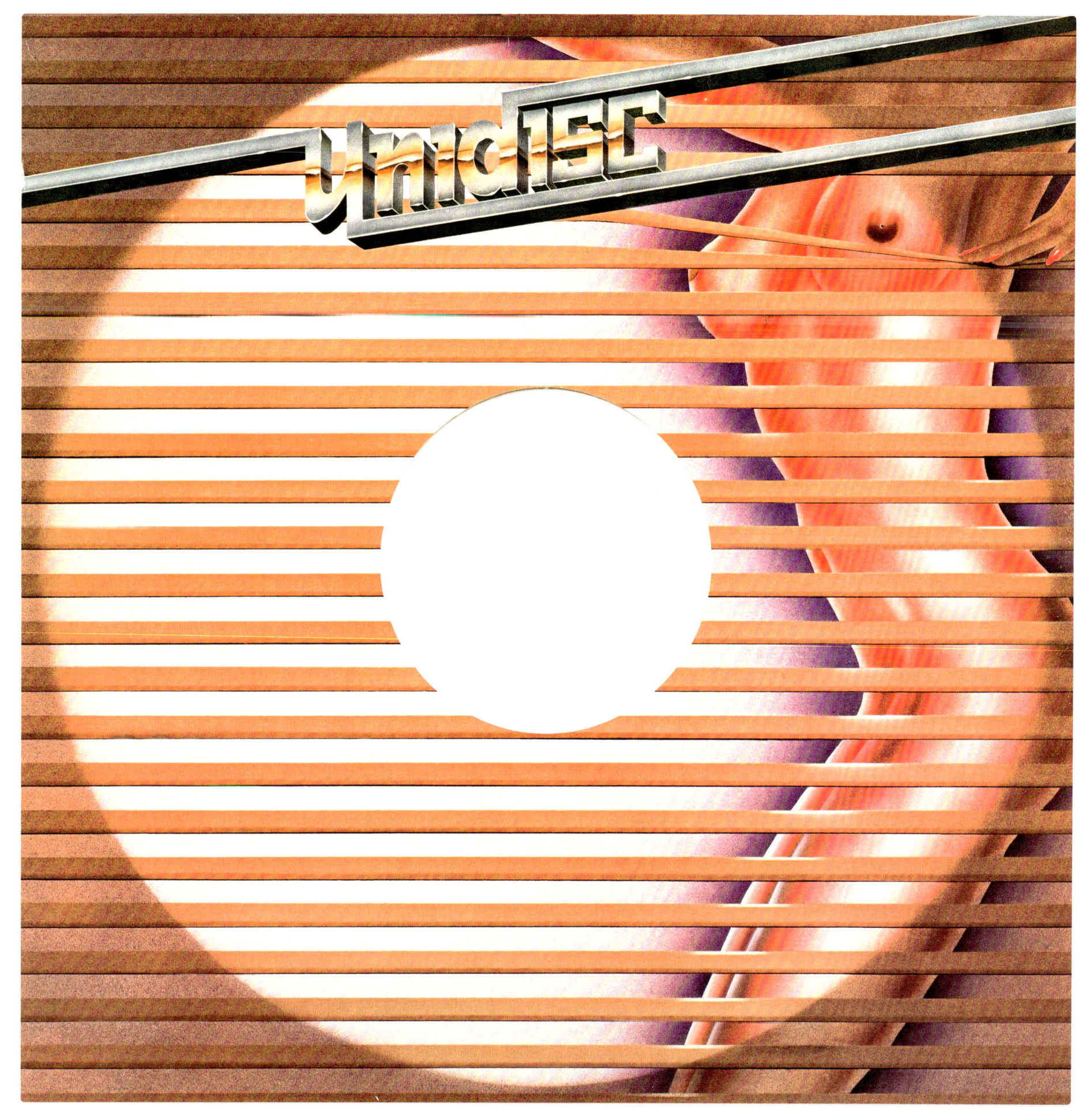

Unidisc Records

Sutra Records	Sweet Mountain Records	Sweet City Records	TEC Records
TEC Records	TK Disco Records	TK Disco Records	TK Disco Records
To-Key Records	Total Experience Records	Total Experience Records	TR Records
 Tryon Park Records	TSOB Records	 Unidisc Records	Unidisc Records

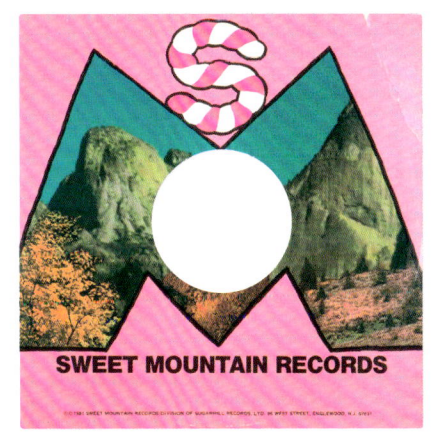

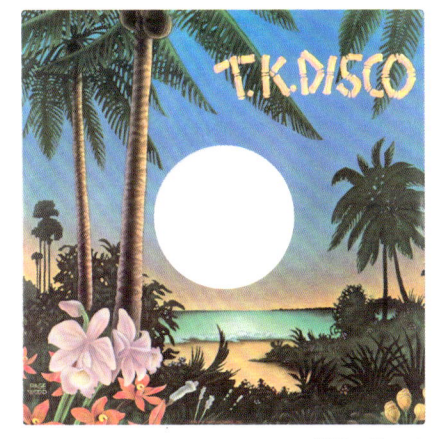

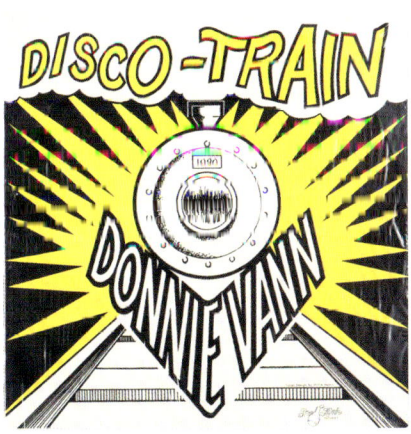

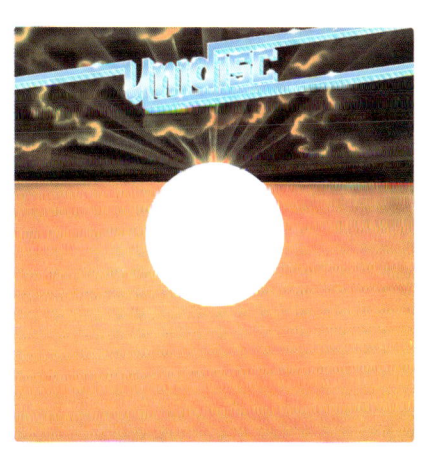

IS THIS A DREAM
(OR IS IT REAL)
THE ANDROIDS

Uniwave Records

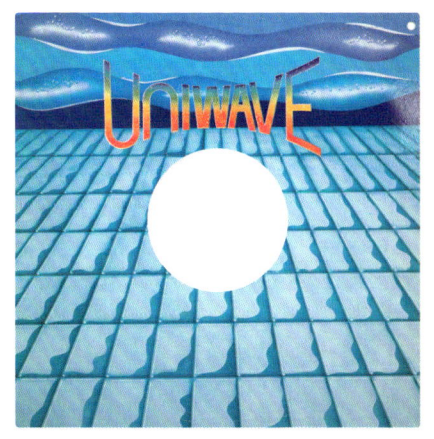

Uniwave Records	Unidisc Records	Unidisc Records	Unidisc Records
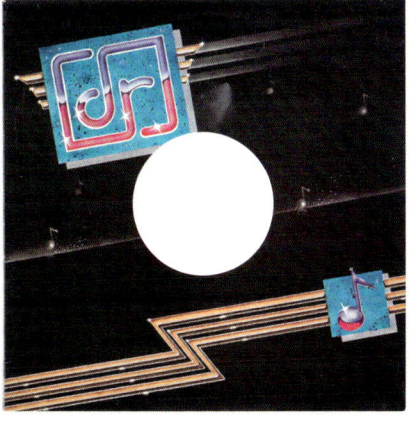 Downstairs Records	United Artists Records	Urban Rock Records	Uptown Records
Voyage Records	Vanguard Records	World Enterprise Records	Warner Bross. Records
Warner Bross. Records	West End Records	Womar Records	Zebra Records

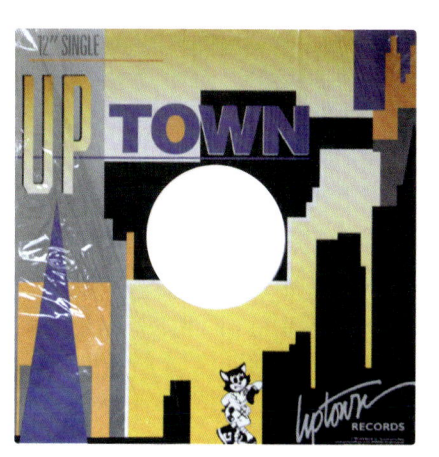

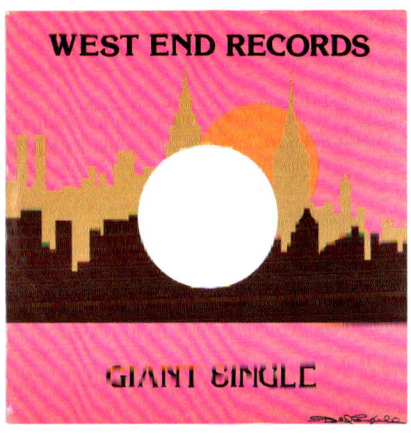

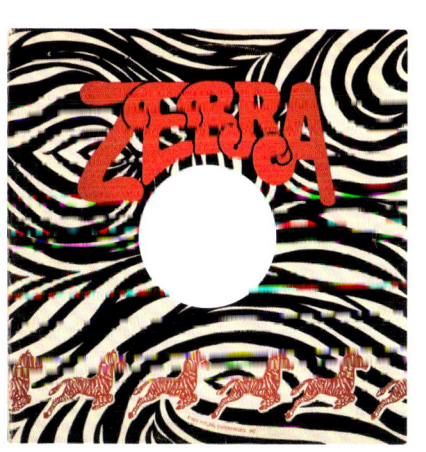

369

Salsoul Records

European 12 inches

	Lark Records	Festival Records	Epic Records
Pinnacle Records	A&M Records	CNR	Able Records
Vedette Records	Vedette Records	New Look	Chrysalis
Ariola	Polydor	Vanguard	TSR

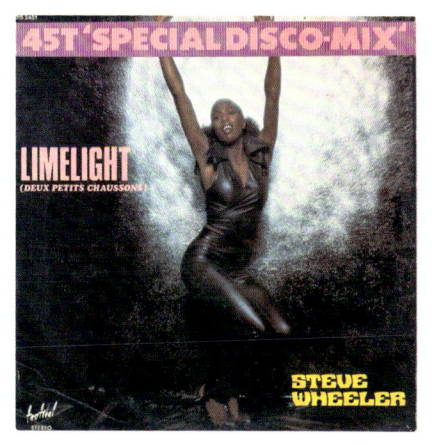

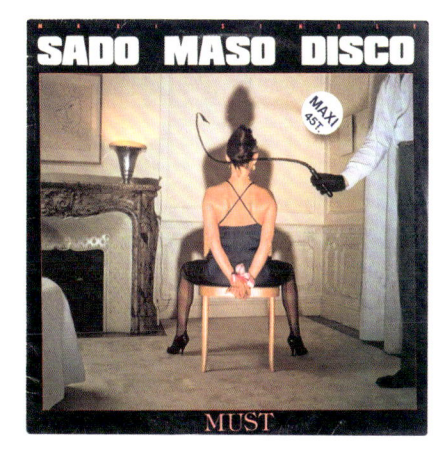

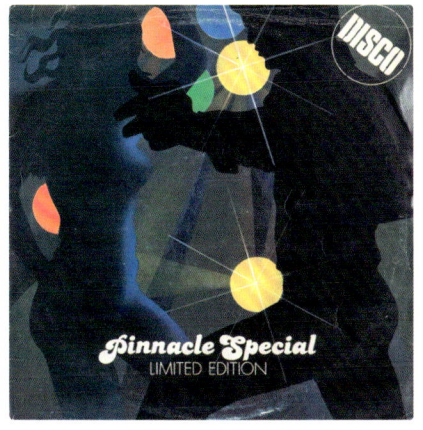

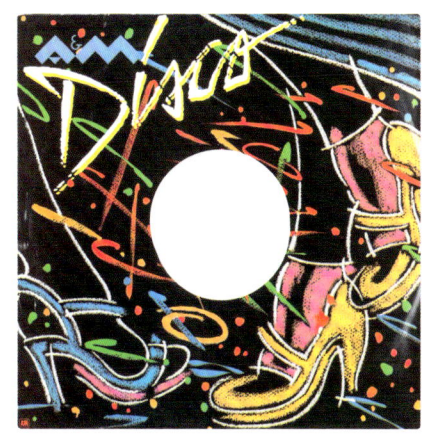

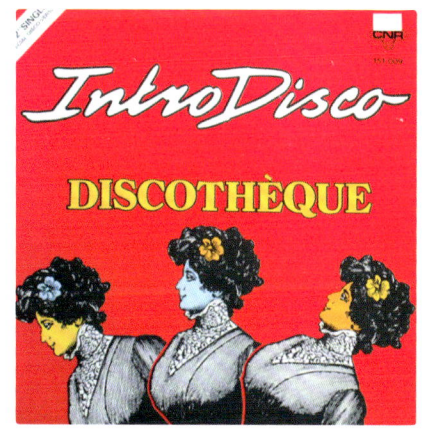

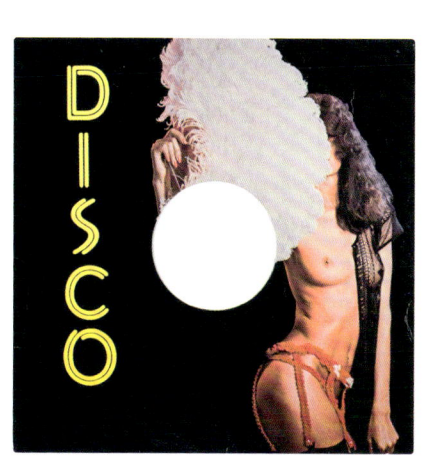

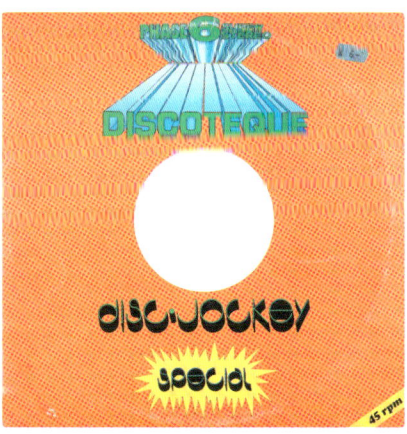

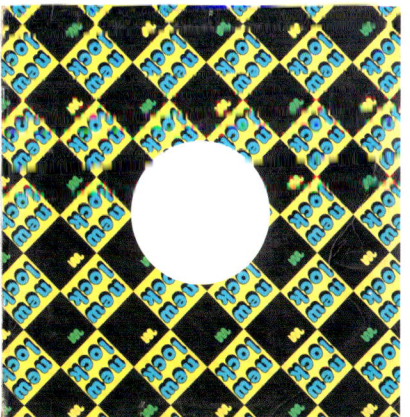

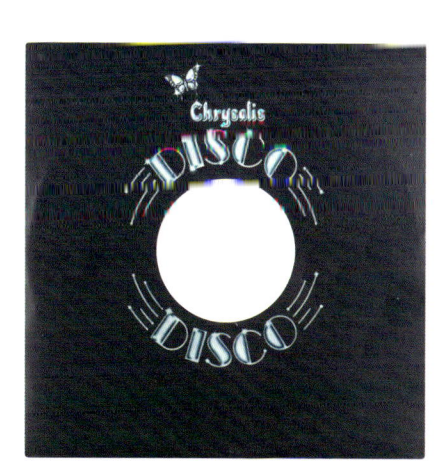

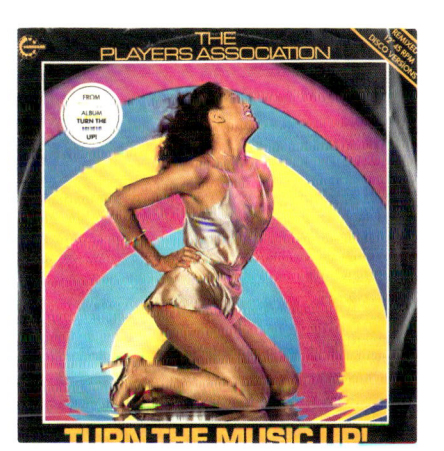

United Artists Records

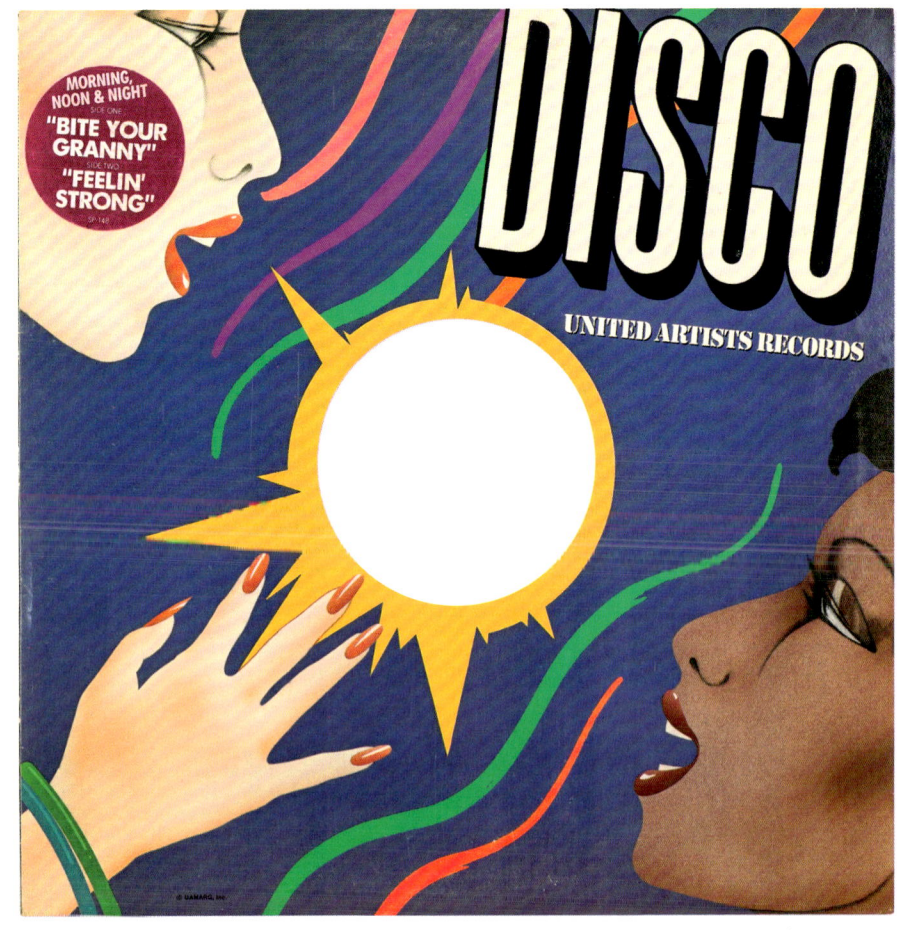

Unison Records

VAP Records

Warner Bross. Records

Bovema Records

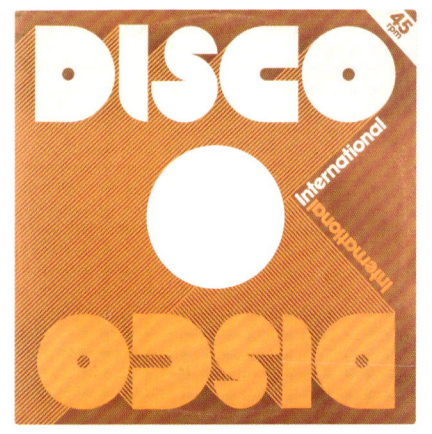

International Records

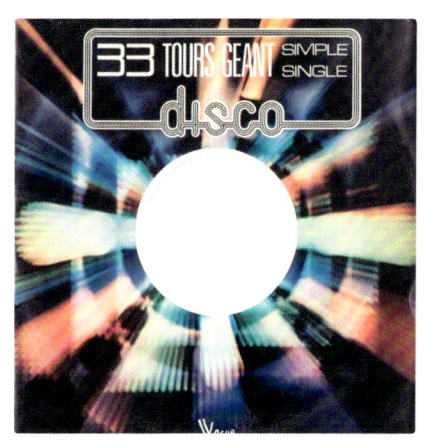

Vogue Records

WEA Records

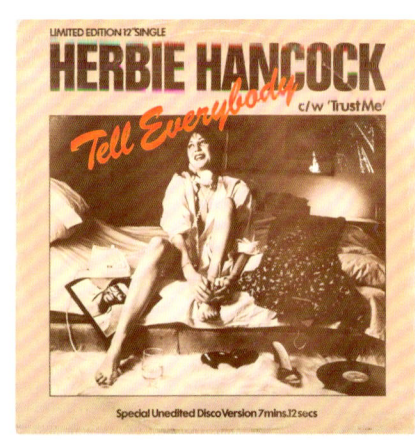

CBS Records

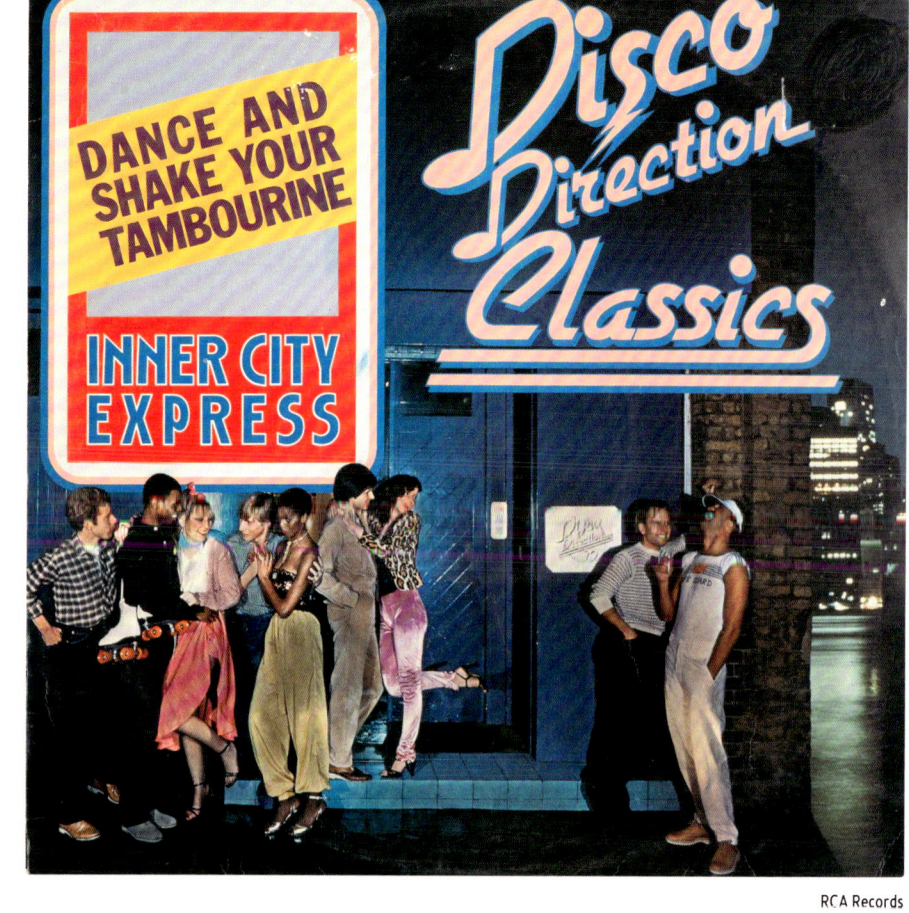

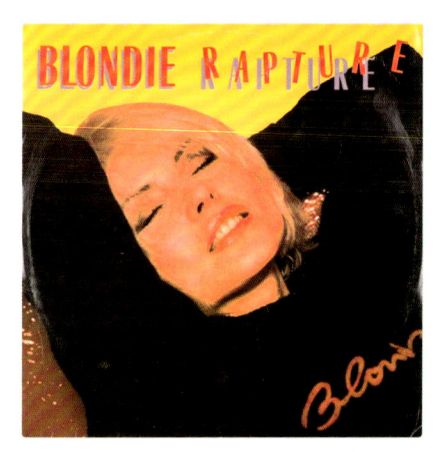

RCA Records

Chrysalis Records

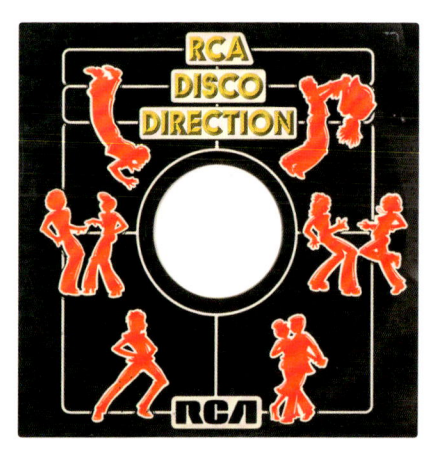

RCA records

CNR Records

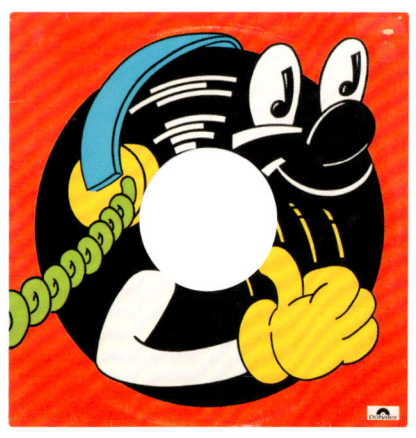

Polydor Records

Pierrot Records

374

BIMBO JET
Love To Love

LR Records

Fantasy Records

MAXI

FAT LARRY'S BAND

LOOKIN' FOR LOVE

WMOT Records

MUSIQUE 'KEEP ON JUMPIN'

Musique's 'Keep On Jumpin'' must be the hottest album on the disco scene right now. 'Keep On Jumpin'' features the smash hit single 'In The Bush', and plenty more to keep you jumpin' right through winter.

'KEEP ON JUMPIN'' the new album featuring 'In The Bush'. Produced by Patrick Adams.

HEATWAVE'S 'HOT PROPERTY'. YOU'LL HAVE A BURNING DESIRE TO GET IT.

'HOT PROPERTY' HEATWAVE'S NEW ALBUM ABSOLUTELY GUARANTEED TO FIRE YOU UP ON EPIC RECORDS AND TAPES.

Produced by Phil Ramone
Management Budd Carr
The Carr Company

Scrapbook

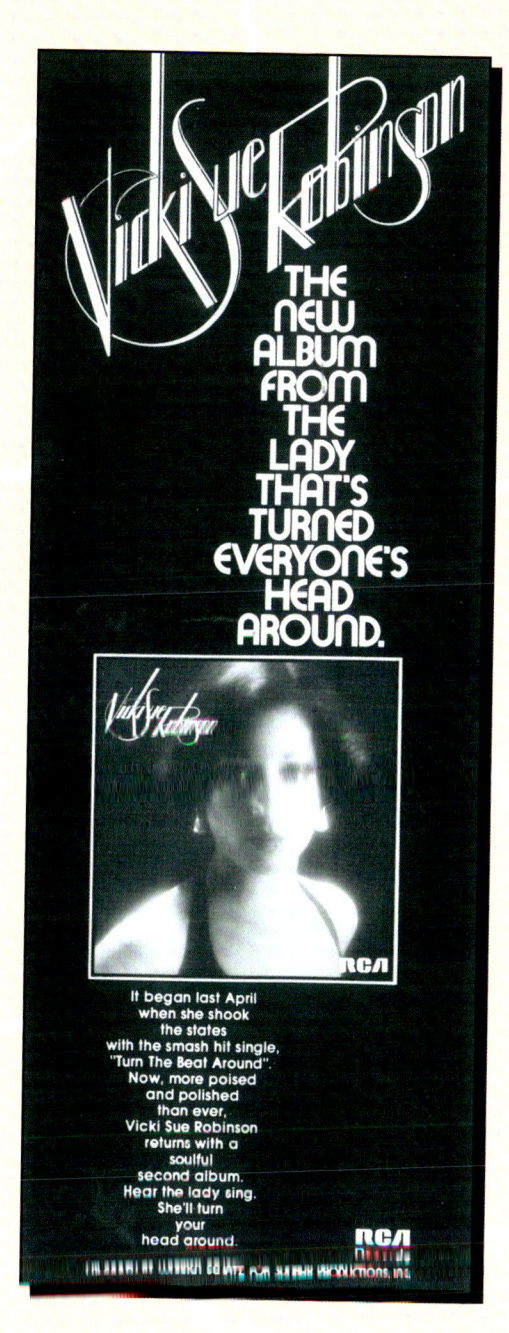

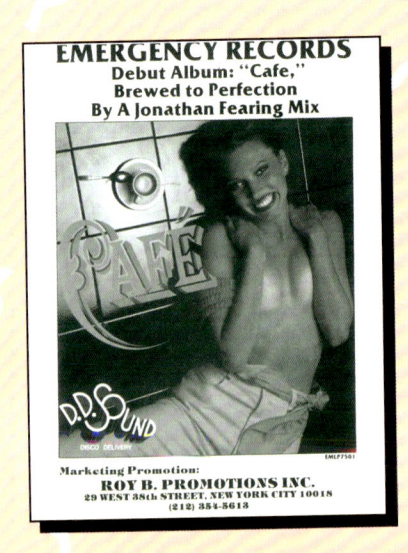

EMERGENCY RECORDS
Debut Album: "Cafe,"
Brewed to Perfection
By A Jonathan Fearing Mix

Marketing Promotion:
ROY B. PROMOTIONS INC.
29 WEST 38TH STREET, NEW YORK CITY 10018
(212) 354-5613

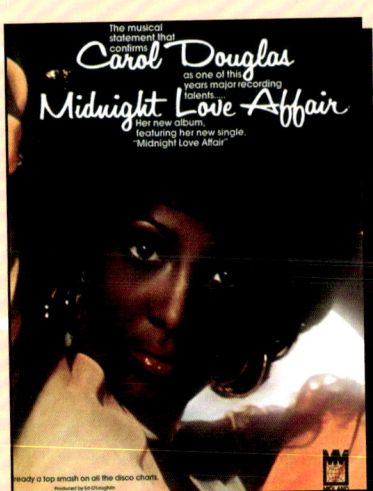

7 world/US premieres (and 2 more hot songs) from Bobby DJ.

Valapucci's "Contact" Medley featuring Edwin Starr (the remix of remixes!)

This is not VALAPUCCI.
This is not BOBBY DJ GUTTADARO.
DISCO BIBLE

VOLUME 2, PROGRAM 7 (Superhottttttttt!)
It Hurts So Good/Rhonda Heath
After Midnight/Valverde Brothers
Disco Boogie/L.E.B. Harmony
(You've Got) My Love, My Life, My Soul/ George McRae
Island In The Sun/Dark Tan
Nanu, Nanu (I Want To Get Funky With You)/ Daddy Dewdrop
I Got My Mind Made Up/Instant Funk
Always There/Willie Bobo
"Contact" Medley (17:30!) featuring Edwin Starr

(Use the coupon below, or see your Pool director.)

DISCONET
600 Third Avenue
New York, New York 10016 U.S.A.
212/687-2313

We are a ☐ Roller Rink ☐ Disco DJ ☐ Disco ☐ Mobile Disco. Please send us a DISCONET subscription for:
☐ One year. 26 regular programs + Special Bonus Programs. Up to 350 new disco releases. $500.
☐ Six months. 13 regular programs + Special Bonus Programs. Up to 175 new disco releases. $300.
☐ Trial subscription. Two programs. $50.
We agree to complete and return the "Standard Subscription Agreement" you will send us.

NAME
CARD #
EXPIRATION DATE
Send programs to this
NAME
DISCO
ADDRESS
CITY
Signed

MANDRÉ
A HEAD OF HIS TIME
ON MOTOWN RECORDS AND TAPES

©1979 MOTOWN RECORDS CORPORATION. PRINTED IN U.S.A. CLOTHES: BON TON CLOTHING COMPANY

The musical statement that confirms **Carol Douglas** as one of this years major recording talents.

Midnight Love Affair
Her new album, featuring her new single, "Midnight Love Affair"

already a top smash on all the disco charts.

Produced by Ed O'Loughlin

Disco To Go!
"Down To Love Town" by **The Originals**

Includes
"Six Million Dollar Man",
"Hurry Up And Wait",
"Down To Love Town"
and many more!

THE ORIGINALS
Down To Love Town

©1977 Motown Record Corporation
Available now on Motown Records & Tapes.

Chico Super Starr plays hot new stuff and mixes!

Simon, Brad and A.J. give you French Kiss.

Captain Mike meets Brian and "Here Comes The Night" Medley.

CHICO SUPER STARR
The Anvil, NYC

VOLUME 2, PROGRAM 10 (Hothothothothothot!)
Panic/Right Combination/FRENCH KISS
Get Another Love/CHANTEL CURTIS
Dancing In The Moonlight/KEANE BROTHERS
Music Is My Way of Life/PATTI LA BELLE
Get On Back/JOE THOMAS
Lollipop/EDWIN BIRDSONG
Sweet San Francisco/QUEEN SAMANTHA
A Nice Feeling/CAROLINE CRAWFORD
Hold On To Love/SEAWIND
What A Fool Believes/THE DOOBIE BROTHERS
Here Comes The Night/California Girls/Wouldn't It Be Nice/Do It Again/You're So Good To Me/ I Can Hear Music/Wendy/Help Me Rhonda/ THE BEACH BOYS

DISCONET
600 Third Avenue
New York, New York 10016 U.S.A.
212/687-2313

We are a ☐ Roller Rink ☐ Disco DJ ☐ Disco ☐ Mobile Disco. Please send us a DISCONET subscription for:
☐ One year. 26 regular programs + Special Bonus Programs. Up to 350 new disco releases. $500.
☐ Six months. 13 regular programs + Special Bonus Programs. Up to 175 new disco releases. $300.
☐ Trial subscription. Two programs. $50.
We agree to complete and return the "Standard Subscription Agreement" you will send us.

NAME
CARD #
EXPIRATION DATE   INTERBANK # (MC)
Send programs to this UPS-deliverable address:
NAME
DISCO
ADDRESS
CITY   STATE   ZIP
Signed   Date

Original Motion Picture Soundtrack
CAR WASH
Music composed and produced by Norman Whitfield.
Grammy award winner.
40 gold records.
Over 60 million records sold.
Songs performed by Rose Royce and featuring the Pointer Sisters and Richard Pryor.
19 compositions, including the single "Put Your Money Where Your Mouth Is" "Zig Zag."
Available on MCA records and tapes.
2 Record Set
Special price only
£4.99
Single no. MCA 259
Album no. MCSP 278
MCA RECORDS

AL HUDSON
ONE WAY
NEW ALBUM
ONE WAY
INCLUDES FULL LENGTH VERSIONS OF THE SINGLES.
YOU CAN DO IT
AND
MUSIC
ON TOUR
Tue 11th Dec WHITEHAVEN, White House Hotel
Wed 12th Dec LEEDS, Warehouse
Thurs 13th Dec HOUNSLOW, Red Lion Hotel
Fri 14th Dec SOUTHGATE, Royalty Ballroom
Sat 15th Dec LEYSDOWN, Isle of Sheppey, Island Hotel
Sun 16th Dec BLACKPOOL, Tiffanys
Mon 17th Dec MAIDSTONE, Greenways
Tue 18th Dec SOUTHEND, Talk of the South
MCA RECORDS

"JUST LET IT LAY"
SENSATIONAL NEW DISCO SINGLE FROM
GONZALEZ
LIMITED EDITION
available as 12" single in full-colour bag
12 EMI 2868

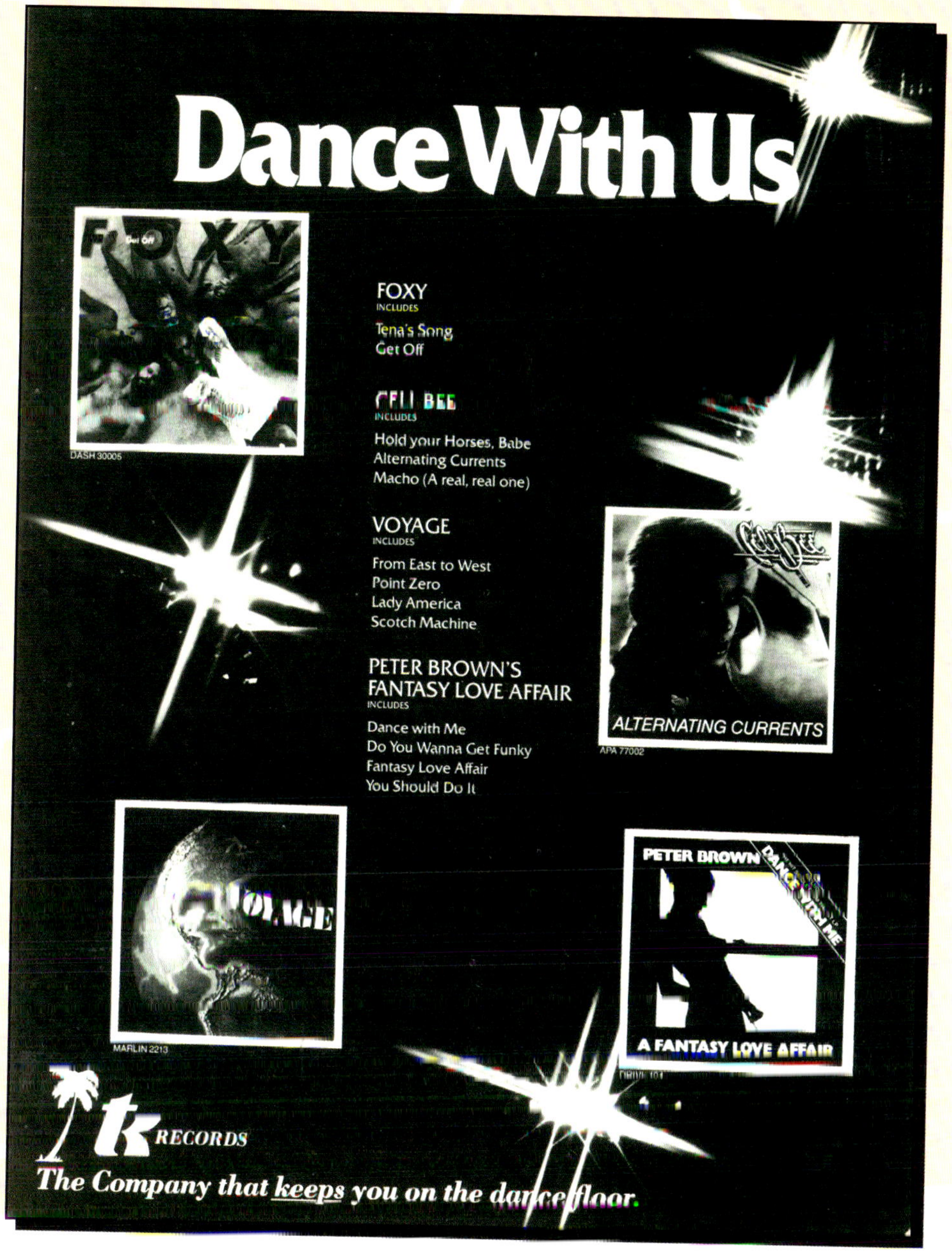
Dance With Us
FOXY
DASH 30005
FOXY
INCLUDES
Tena's Song
Get Off
CELI BEE
INCLUDES
Hold your Horses, Babe
Alternating Currents
Macho (A real, real one)
VOYAGE
INCLUDES
From East to West
Point Zero
Lady America
Scotch Machine
PETER BROWN'S FANTASY LOVE AFFAIR
INCLUDES
Dance with Me
Do You Wanna Get Funky
Fantasy Love Affair
You Should Do It
ALTERNATING CURRENTS
APA 77002
VOYAGE
MARLIN 2213
PETER BROWN
A FANTASY LOVE AFFAIR
TK RECORDS
The Company that keeps you on the dancefloor.

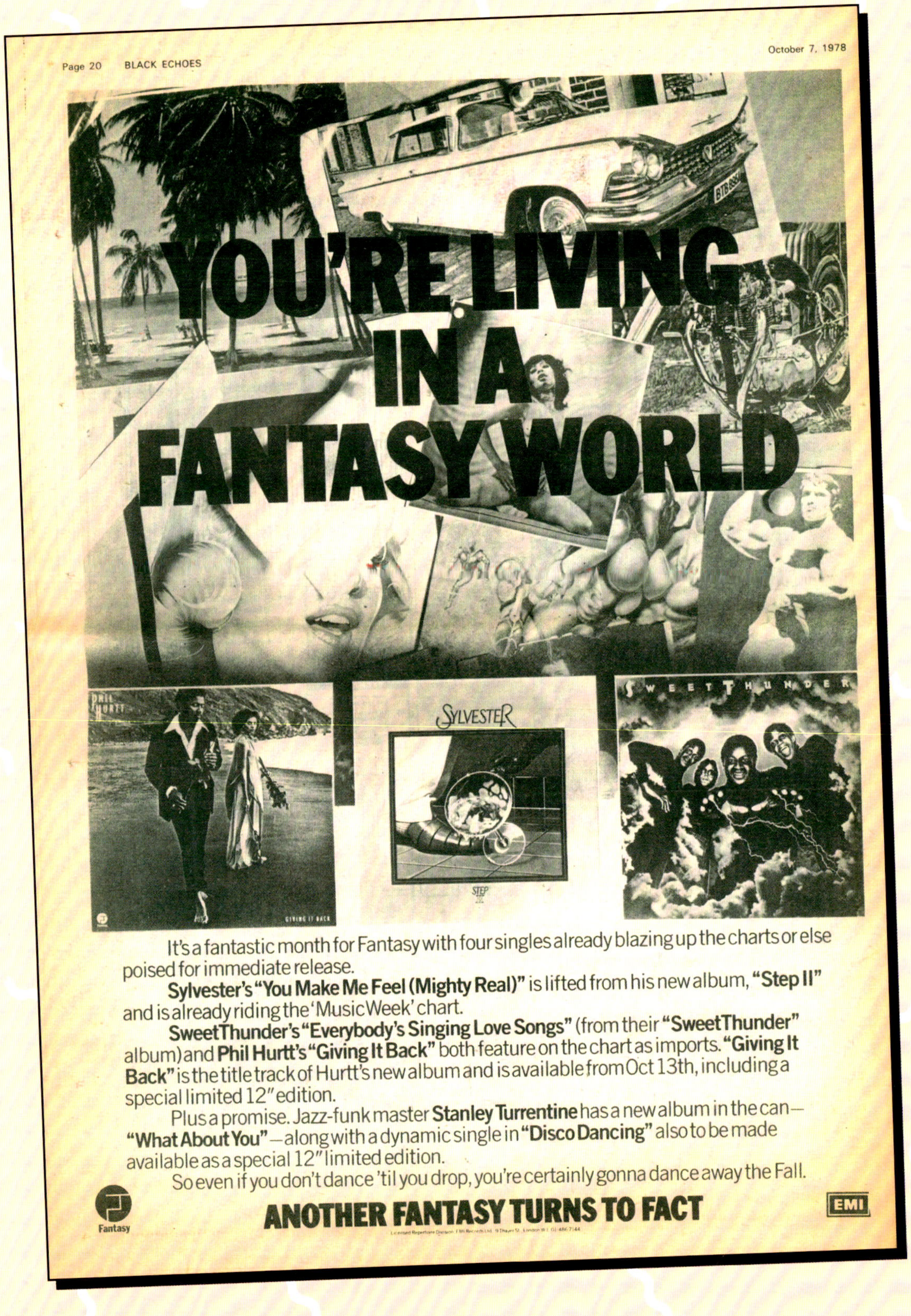

Page 20 BLACK ECHOES
October 7, 1978
YOU'RE LIVING IN A FANTASY WORLD
SYLVESTER
STEP
SWEET THUNDER
It's a fantastic month for Fantasy with four singles already blazing up the charts or else poised for immediate release.
Sylvester's "You Make Me Feel (Mighty Real)" is lifted from his new album, "Step II" and is already riding the 'Music Week' chart.
Sweet Thunder's "Everybody's Singing Love Songs" (from their "Sweet Thunder" album) and Phil Hurtt's "Giving It Back" both feature on the chart as imports. "Giving It Back" is the title track of Hurtt's new album and is available from Oct 13th, including a special limited 12" edition.
Plus a promise. Jazz-funk master Stanley Turrentine has a new album in the can—"What About You"—along with a dynamic single in "Disco Dancing" also to be made available as a special 12" limited edition.
So even if you don't dance 'til you drop, you're certainly gonna dance away the Fall.
Fantasy
ANOTHER FANTASY TURNS TO FACT
EMI

THE CROWN HEIGHTS AFFAIR TAKES DISCO A STEP FURTHER.
DREAM WORLD
Crown Heights Affair
There's never been a disco album quite like the Crown Heights Affair's "Dream World." Sure, it's got all the essentials. But it's also got something no other disco album can touch—perfectly crafted CHA arrangements.
So, when you want to take a step beyond ordinary disco, "Dream World" will get you there.
The Crown Heights Affair's "Dream World."
On De-Lite Records & Tapes.
Produced by Freida Nerangis and Britt Britton
De-Lite RECORDS
Marketed by Phonogram, Inc.

Two great 12" disco singles~
FROM CERRONE & HERBIE HANCOCK
'You Bet Your Love' by Herbie Hancock and 'Je Suis Music' by Cerrone—two sounds that are bound to brew up a storm on the dance floors this month.
They're both from undisputed disco masters, they're both 12 inch full-tilt full-length versions and they both come hot on the heels of chart success for both artists.
SPECIAL LIMITED EDITION 12" SINGLE
HERBIE HANCOCK
'YOU BET YOUR LOVE'
b/w KNEE DEEP
LIMITED EDITION 12" SINGLE
CERRONE
JE SUIS MUSIC
HERBIE HANCOCK
'YOU BET YOUR LOVE'
8 min. 11 sec.
CBS 12-7010
CERRONE
'JE SUIS MUSIC'
7 min. 48 sec.
CBS 12-6918
CBS Records
FROM CBS—the company that keeps you dancing.

"THESE ARE TWO OF THE BADDEST CATS I HAVE EVER HEARD."
—Quincy Jones

That's how overwhelmed Quincy was upon first hearing George and Louis Johnson. And he didn't stop there: "When they walked into the studio and started to play I could not believe my ears. Louis, the younger of the two is 20. He picked up the bass and started playing and in a matter of ten seconds the entire studio was silent with all eyes on him. Then George, 22, picked up his guitar and fell in, rocking the walls of The Record Plant with intensity. They told me they also had some songs for me to hear."

Four of those songs are on Quincy's latest album, "Mellow Madness." Their latest brand of "futuristic funk" is on their own very first album, "Look Out For #1." And from the way it sounds, look out for The Brothers Johnson.

THE BROTHERS JOHNSON "LOOK OUT FOR #1" ON A&M RECORDS & TAPES

Produced by Quincy Jones

LORRAINE JOHNSON — PRL 12161
PETER JACQUES — PRL 12163
LEMON — PRL 12162
STICKY FINGERS — PRL 12164

Super Albums Bring Super Thanks To All Who Helped Bring Prelude Records To The Top!

Special Thanks from: Roy B., Starr, Francois, Marvin, Stan & Staff

---

I'M A MAN
the 12" single by **MACHO**
12 EMI 2882

taken from the album 'I'm A Man'
EMC 3290